DeWitt
on
THE GENERAL EPISTLES

HEBREWS, JAMES, FIRST AND SECOND PETER,
FIRST, SECOND AND THIRD JOHN, & JUDE

By
E. E. DeWitt

> **Disclaimer**
> The author of this work has quoted the writers of many articles and books. This does not mean that the author endorses or recommends the works of others. If the author quotes someone, it does not mean that he agrees with all of the author's tenets, statements, concepts, or words, whether in the work quoted or any other work of the author. There has been no attempt to alter the

Copyright © February, 2018 by Dr. Ed DeWitt
All Rights Reserved
Printed in the United States of America

REL067030: Religion: Christian Theology – Apologetics.

ISBN: 978-0-9993545-3-7

All Scripture quotes are from the King James Bible except those verses compared and then the source is identified.

No part of this work may be reproduced without the expressed consent of the publisher, except for brief quotes, whether by electronic, photocopying, recording, or information storage and retrieval systems.

Address All Inquiries To:
THE OLD PATHS PUBLICATIONS, Inc.
142 Gold Flume Way
Cleveland, Georgia, U.S.A. 30528

Web: www.theoldpathspublications.com
E-mail: TOP@theoldpathspublications.com

1.0

DEDICATION

This book is dedicated to Rev. Jon Carlson who is still tirelessly serving the Lord as a pastor at Bethany Baptist Church of Galesburg, IL – where he and this writer attended as children back during the time of the dinosaurs.

FOREWORD

Several years ago, I took the time to type the entire text of the Bible into my computer. I could have found such already done for me. But, I wanted the experience of taking that care of my daily reading. I could not simply hurry past a place because it was necessary to copy each word to complete my task. While doing this I found my attention drawn more fully to the Words of Life.

It was with shock that I found I had somehow overlooked the fact that my name was in Joshua 22:34. I wondered what else I had missed by inattention. As I began to pay more attention to the Scripture, I began to make notes in the places that leaped off the page. During my time as pastor at my last church, I began to write commentary on those passages used in the worship services to be passed out to the people at each service.

Now that I am retired from the active pastorate, I have begun to expand those early efforts. What you now hold in your hands is an example of that work. I invite you expand on my work as the Spirit leads you into His inspired and preserved Words. The Bible is a closed Book only to those who refuse to open its pages in prayerful attention to the Spirit

Dr. Ed DeWitt
February, 2018

TABLE OF CONTENTS

- DEDICATION 3
- FOREWORD 5
- TABLE OF CONTENTS 7
- HEBREWS 9
  - HEBREWS - CHAPTER ONE 9
  - HEBREWS - CHAPTER TWO 22
  - HEBREWS - CHAPTER THREE 37
  - HEBREWS - CHAPTER FOUR 54
  - HEBREWS - CHAPTER FIVE 66
  - HEBREWS - CHAPTER SIX 80
  - HEBREWS - CHAPTER SEVEN 97
  - HEBREWS - CHAPTER EIGHT 116
  - HEBREWS - CHAPTER NINE 130
  - HEBREWS - CHAPTER TEN 155
  - HEBREWS - CHAPTER ELEVEN 196
  - HEBREWS - CHAPTER TWELVE 237
  - HEBREWS - CHAPTER THIRTEEN 267
- JAMES 283
  - JAMES - CHAPTER ONE 283
  - JAMES - CHAPTER TWO 305
  - JAMES - CHAPTER THREE 327
  - JAMES - CHAPTER FOUR 345
  - JAMES - CHAPTER FIVE 361
- FIRST PETER 387
  - FIRST PETER - CHAPTER ONE 387
  - FIRST PETER - CHAPTER TWO 415
  - FIRST PETER - CHAPTER THREE 439
  - FIRST PETER - CHAPTER FOUR 457
  - FIRST PETER - CHAPTER FIVE 471
  - ADDENDA 483
  - LUKE 16:19 483
- SECOND PETER 485
  - SECOND PETER - CHAPTER ONE 485
  - SECOND PETER - CHAPTER TWO 502
  - SECOND PETER - CHAPTER THREE 520
- FIRST JOHN 531
  - FIRST JOHN - CHAPTER ONE 531
  - FIRST JOHN - CHAPTER TWO 539
  - FIRST JOHN - CHAPTER THREE 559
  - FIRST JOHN - CHAPTER FOUR 579
  - FIRST JOHN - CHAPTER FIVE 595
- SECOND JOHN 613
- THIRD JOHN 623
- JUDE 633

DeWitt on the GENERAL EPISTLES

ADDENDA 649
    Genesis 3:15 649
    Genesis 17:2 652
    Genesis 26:3 653
    Isaiah 28:13 653
    Luke 16:19 654
    First Corinthians 10:4 655
BIBLIOGRAPHY OF CONSULTED BOOKS 657
ABOUT THE AUTHOR 659

HEBREWS

HEBREWS - CHAPTER ONE

1.1 *God, who at sundry times and in divers manners spoke in time past unto the fathers by the prophets,*

[It was the custom of letter writers of this period to start the letter with their name. We put our name at the end of our letters. The letters of this era let people know at the beginning who was speaking to them.

I am somewhat convinced that Paul was the human penman of this letter. The reason is quite simple. The letters which had the stamp of authority upon them were letters penned by the apostles.

Paul claimed to be an apostle; he claimed so under the "moving of the Spirit," via inspiration. (see I Corinthians 15:7-9)

Paul was met on the Damascus Road by Jesus. Paul received training from the Lord. (see the 12th chapter of II Corinthians) Therefore, Paul was an apostle. Thus, I believe that Paul, also on the argumentation made in the Book, was the human penman of this Book.

The fact that the Book begins with "God" is a beautiful illustration of just Who was the True Author of Scripture. The words may have come from the pen of humans, but the Words came from the very breath of God.

The verse says that God spoke at various times, at His prerogative and in His time, and through several methods - poetry, didactic prose, narrative, etc. This is saying, quite effectively, that the words of Scripture are the Words of God.

As such they are eternal, as is He, and not subject to decay or dilution by time. Time is a subsidiary created from the primary reality of eternity. Time cannot overcome eternity. To argue, as did Tischendorf, Hort, Westcott, et. al., that the Words of God were decayed and needed to be restored is not consistent with any real view of time and eternity.

This verse says that God "spake" in the writings of the prophets. In II Timothy 3:16 we find that the Scripture is "inspired" of God. The word "inspire," of course, means to "breathe out." Since this is an illustration of speech in that our speech is the action of our breath upon our vocal cords, this verse in Hebrews is further clarification that the Scripture, while written down by men, is in actuality the very Words of God.

This means that the idea of a "concept" inspiration and preservation is a false view. God inspired His very Words. It is these Words, from the eternal realms, which are still inspired. To argue for only a concept preservation is to argue against God's stated method of inspiration.

Therefore, this verse clearly states that we have a Bible which is as secure in its preservation as is God. Logically, to argue for a decay in one is to argue for decay in Both. This would limit the power and purposes of God.

God's Words are God's Words, forever preserved because they are of eternity. To argue otherwise is to argue against the initial inspiration of even the "original manuscripts."]

1.2 *Hath in these last days spoken unto us by his Son, whom he hath appointed heir of all things, by whom also he made the worlds,*

II Timothy 3:1; II Peter 3:3

[Since Paul described his time as the "last days" how much more are we living in the last days in this time! Since the "last days" began during the times of the apostles we know that there can be no further revelation added to the Scriptural library in our own time. The closing of the canon of Scripture ended with the Revelation to John. New, or further, or expanded Revelation comes at the beginning of a dispensation. Indeed, it is this which distinguishes a new dispensation. There is only new light and teaching from God into a new dispensation as the principles of the former dispensations are further explained and the shadow gives way to substance.

Just to be precise: The "new" light given at the beginning of a dispensation does not negate the light already given. It merely amplifies that light so it can be more fully understood what it was that God wished to convey. The teaching manner of God is described in Isaiah 28:10. Line and precept build upon already revealed line and precept. It is much like a child learning math. The child may believe he has all knowledge of math because he has learned his numbers; why, he can now write "his numbers" and count to one hundred. Then the child finds the concepts of addition and subtraction. Surely he knows all about arithmetic now. Then he finds multiplication and division. ...and on and on. Those earlier precepts of simply writing the numbers and counting are not dismissed; they are enhanced at each stage of instruction.

So it is with the teachings of the dispensations of God. The most obvious example would concern the teaching of the animal sacrifice as fulfilled in the Ultimate Sacrifice of Jesus Christ on the Cross of Calvary. Further on in this Book of Hebrews we will find that very sequence of teaching explained and illustrated.

This verse is speaking of the office of Jesus as Savior of the World. He is positionally appointed heir of all things in His Office of Redemptive Agent. In this office He is representative of humanity. This concept of "heir" is a legalistic concept meaning that He is worthy, as the representative of humanity, to assume this right.

This is a matter of God teaching spiritual realities to people in a picture that we humans are able to understand. It is not a picture of a subservient Jesus. It is a picture of the great glory and honor which is due Him.

We also need to consider, from this verse, that Jesus created more than this one little planet. There is a vast universe which was also created by Him. Our view of the majesty of Jesus does not begin to reach past the very superficial. He is Almighty God. Almighty beyond even our wildest dreams and considerations!]

1.3 *Who being the brightness of his glory, and the express image of his person, and upholding all things by the word of his power, when he had by himself purged our sins, sat down on the right hand of the Majesty on high;*

[vv. 1 – 3. There are a couple things I'd like you to notice about these verses. First, Jesus is called the "express image of his person." Jesus is not a copy of God. Jesus is the express image of God. That quite simply means that Jesus is God.

Second, Jesus is the One Who upholds "all things by the word of his power." Since only God could do this, Jesus is God.

HEBREWS: Chapter 1

Finally, it was Jesus who "by himself purged our sins." We know the truth of what Jesus did at Calvary. We thus understand that this verse is speaking of Jesus. Jesus is God.

Jesus reflected the picture to mankind of just Who is God. Jesus came as a man into the world of men. He gave us a physical picture of the Spiritual God. We could never have begun to understand the fullness of the Godhead had not Jesus come to show us those truths in a form which we could understand.

This verse speaks of the Glory that shines from the Person of Jesus Christ. One of the proofs of His Glory is that His Glory shines from His Person. His Glory is What and Who He is. You will notice that the term "...being the brightness of his glory..." does not speak of a reflection, or of a binary Glory. The Glory which is Jesus is the Glory of God.

When the term "...express image of his person..." is used the meaning is that Jesus is of the very same essence as is the Father. The phrase was not "image like His Person." (Capital letters added. I just don't feel comfortable not capitalizing terms in reference to God!) The phrase is "...express image of his person..."

When one looks at a picture of me, why I do not know!, he will see a picture of me. When I look at a mirror I see an image of myself. But when someone else looks at me, they see me rather than a duplication. That is the meaning of the phrase used here. Looking at Jesus is the same, because He is of the same essence, as looking at God. The image is not a reflection, not a picture, not any duplication. The image of Jesus is of God's very Person.

One proof of His glory shines through His sinless life and resurrection. None other has ever lived a sinless life. No one. Although there are Biblical examples of others who have risen from the dead, none of these did so on their own volition as did Jesus. He was raised from the dead in His Own power. He defeated death and walked in His Own life at His Own discretion.

Another proof of this glory shines through the lives He touches yet today. I have great respect for the work done by Alcoholics Anonymous. But Jesus only needs one step to change a person's life from sinner to saint. His salvation can give a new meaning to an old life. His salvation can give a lifetime of purpose to a young life. His salvation can raise a person from the sickbed of sin and whisk them through the stars to a Home in Heaven. His salvation can give meaning and contentment in the direst of circumstance.

In an age of superstition and a myriad of religious observance, it was men and women who had an experience with the Master who "turned the world upside down" (see Acts 17:6) in the Name of Jesus. Even the great empire that persecuted them had to eventually come to an accommodation with those who claimed His Name. Time, be it BC/AD which acknowledges Him or the BCE/CE which does not, is dated from an approximation of His birth.

Even those who would deny and defame our Savior pay Him homage each time they write out checks for their monthly bills.

We see several things in this verse about Jesus. The first is that the glory is "his glory." To suggest that Jesus had any "glory" would be a problem were He not God. For a devout, monotheistic Jew, who had centuries of cultural baggage pointing to the religious view of but "One God," to have suggested that a mere mortal had a glory about him would be preposterous unless he were convinced that Jesus was, indeed, God.

The "express image of his person" takes us back to verse two where the conversation is about God. Therefore, Jesus is said to be the exact image of God. He is not said to "look" like God, or to be a "duplicate" of God. Jesus is said to be the certain image of that God.

Even the power of God is assigned to Jesus as He is seen "upholding all things by the word of his power." The power of the Father is not referenced. As Jesus sits "on the right hand of the Majesty on high," we must not suppose that this means that He and the Father are separate entities. The picture is of a position of power rather than a spatial situation.

In verse two, just previous to this verse, Jesus is again, as in John 1:3, described as the Creative Agent Who made the universe and all that is therein. Now, in verse three, this same Jesus is described as the One Who "sustains" that very creation. It is He Who upholds "all things."

Since all means all; there just ain't nothing left over, Jesus is the Ultimate Power of the universe. This means that He is God.

Again, the picture of Jesus sitting "on the right hand of the Majesty on high," is not ascribing an inferior position to Him. This is an anthropomorphism which gives to us a picture of Him sitting in the place of power. This is actually a picture of Jesus as the Lord of Glory.

The word "brightness" is "apaugasma," number 541 in Strong's. It is a compound word used only here in the New Testament. The first part of the word is "apo," number 575 in Strong's. Strong defines this word as: "a primary particle, 'off,' i.e. away (from something) near, in various senses (of place, time, or relation, literal or figurative)...(X here-)after, ago, at, because of, before, by (the space of), from, in, (out) of, off, (up-)on)-ce), with. In composition (as a prefix) it usually denotes separation, departure, cessation, completion, reversal, etc."

The word 'apo" is commonly used in the New Testament. It means to be "from" some thing. The great slaughter of the innocents by Herod in the second chapter of Matthew (2:16) uses this word when it speaks of the children from two years old and under being killed.

In the third chapter of Matthew (verse four) the word is used to describe raiment made of camel's hair. This, quite obviously, is hair from a camel

The second part of the compound word is "augazo," number 826 in Strong's. Strong defines the word as "to beam forth (figuratively)—shine." The word appears only here and in Acts 20:11 where it refers to the "break of day."

Putting the two words together we do not get a picture of a glory either reflected or bestowed upon Christ. What we see is the brightness of the glory of God as emanating from Jesus, Himself. This, of course, means that the human penman of Hebrews wrote that Jesus is God in that the Glory of God emanates from Him.

The Pulpit Commentary weighs in on the verse. "The rays which stream from the sun reveal the sun itself; so Christ is the ever-visible radiance of the unapproachable light."

The popular view that God just created the universe and then sat back to see what would happen is a false view. With the deconstruction of this view the theories of "theistic evolution" fall by the wayside. Jesus not only created the universe, He also continues to take an active and controlling interest in the affairs and applications of the workings of that universe.

So active and interested is Jesus in the affairs of this world that He, Personally,

HEBREWS: Chapter 1

came to offer Himself as The Atonement for the sins of those who would believe.]

1.4 *Being made so much better than the angels, as he hath by inheritance obtained a more excellent name than they.*

[In Hebrews 2:9 we read that Jesus was made "a little lower than the angels." "But we see Jesus, who was made a little lower than the angels for the suffering of death, crowned with glory and honour; that he by the grace of God should taste death for every man."

This is the Kenosis whereby He emptied Himself of the outward glory of His rightful Divinity. He became a man so that He might die as a completely righteous man and thereby purchase salvation for us.

Note well the obvious. Jesus was "made." This cannot be considered as a time of creation of Jesus. That He was "made" into a human – a little lower than the angels – gives and obvious indication that He enjoyed a previous existence before this. This previous existence was a full equality with the Father as God. Philippians 2:6-8 speak of His emptying Himself of the outward glories of His rightful Divinity. In Acts we see Him returned to His rightful glory in Heaven. His standing at the right hand of God, the Father, at the stoning of Stephen displays Jesus at the position of power in Heaven. Paul, the penman of Hebrews in my opinion, follows through with this thought as he describes Jesus as above the angels in His glorification at the retrieval of that glory He had previously laid aside.

The Targum, which of course does not accept the concept of the Triune God, sees the angels to be the "Privy Council" of God. This work argues that it is among the angles that God seeks council in the phrase "Let us make man in our image," in the first chapter of Genesis.

The New Testament Christian sees an early indication of the Trinity of the God as speaking among Himself in this passage. From the Scriptural accounts we realize that each of the "Persons" of the Trinity are individuals who are joined in a way we can never understand this side of Glory into the Eternal Essence of One God.

It is even argued within the Targum that angels may be worshipped for the sake of God's dignity. The angels are never said to be worthy of worship in their own essence.

The "inheritance" of Jesus is an anthropomorphical phrase used to explain the unknowable spiritual fact that Jesus is God. "The inheritance" is the fact that Jesus is of the essence of God – as is also the Holy Spirit. The "inheritance" is a thing that is owned by Jesus simply by His right as the Person of God, The Son.]

1.5 *For unto which of the angels said he at any time, Thou art my Son, this day have I begotten thee: and again, I will be to him a Father, and he shall be to me a Son?*

Psalm 2:7; II Samuel 7:14

[Starting with the previous verse the penman is drawing a conclusion that the majesty of The Son is such that He stands above the angels. As above in verse four, the pious Jew of the day would have given great reverence to the angels. He saw the angels as far above man in that they were the designated messengers of God. In John 14:26 Jesus points out that it is the Holy Spirit Who guides the apostles into all truth even unto the penning of the New Testament Canon. This would put the Spirit on the same level as is Jesus, as above the angels. Therefore, this passage also points to the Godhood of the Spirit as the "Third Person" of the Trinity.

A note must be made here in regard to the designation of the Spirit as the "Third Person" of the Trinity. There is no hierarchy among the three "Persons" of the Trinity. Each is equally God. The designation refers only to the introduction of that "Person" into the Scriptural narrative.

Paul, I believe him to be the human penman of the Book of Hebrews, asks a very simple question in regard to Jesus and the angels: "For unto which of the angels said he at any time, Thou art my Son, this day have I begotten thee?" This is quoted from Psalm 2:7; it is considered by most to be a Messianic Psalm.

This is a rhetorical question. No answer is expected because Scripture never makes this claim about angels. The answer from this Scriptural silence is that Jesus must be higher than the angels because this was never said of them.

There are three instances in Job (1:6; 2:1; 38:7) where angels are called "sons of God." Notice that this is a plural designation. The meaning is not a personal qualification of any angel but a recognition of the entire class of angel as beings who are subservient to God.

There is also a quotation from II Samuel 7:14: "I will be to him a Father, and he shall be to me a Son."]

1.6 *And again, when he bringeth in the firstbegotten into the world, he saith, And let all the angels of God worship him.*

[There are cultists who use verses such as this to contend that Jesus is a created being rather than God, Incarnate. Do not misunderstand this term, "first begotten." It is a positional term rather than a chronological term. A simple look back to John 3:16 will show that Jesus is the "only begotten" of God.

My son, Ethan, is my only son. If I were to call him my first begotten son it would indicate that there was another son. Since there is not another, such a statement would confuse rather than illuminate.

The very term "begotten" is a Biblical term which relates the truth of Christ to the ears of physical people. Compare Isaiah 9:6; the first part of this verse says, "For unto us a child is born, unto us a son is given..." When we consider the necessity that the Savior of humanity be human, therefore able to be sacrificed in our place, and sinless, we are struck with the truth that no mere mortal human could be both.

Therefore, Jesus, the Second Person of the Trinity, came to inhabit human flesh via the Virgin Birth. He was, thus, fully human while retaining His complete Deity. The verse from Isaiah makes this clear. "A child is born" speaks of the humanity of Jesus. "A son is given" speaks of His eternal existence as God.

Consequently, to refer to Jesus as the "firstborn," while grammatically and literally true, in no way detracts from His eternal existence as God. This concept, further, makes it impossible that any other could be "Christ" or a Savior to mankind.

In the culture of the day in which the Bible was written, the "first begotten" was a term which designated a position of power and privilege within the family. Since there is no distinction of position among the "Persons" of the Triune Godhead, this concept of understanding would be faulty on our part.

But, as we read the term, and understand the term, in the Scripture we must understand just to whom that Scripture was written. It was written to us. It is, to us, the Name of Jesus which is powerful unto salvation. God, the Father, may forgive us. The Spirit may call us into salvation through His convicting work. But, it is Jesus Christ, and His Work on Calvary which has purchased that salvation for us.

Again, speaking to humanity, God's Word says of Jesus, "Wherefore God also hath highly exalted him, and given him a name which is above every name: That at the name of Jesus every knee should bow, of things in heaven, and things in earth, and things under the earth." (Philippians 2:9-10)

Notice that this last mentioned verse also spoke of Heavenly entities, as well as human, and sinful entities as well ("Under the earth" seems to indicate that even the demons of Hell must ultimately admit that worship rightly belongs to Him.) are to give Him worship. The last two denote His power and position. The first, "in heaven," denotes the angels of God as did also Hebrews 1:6. These angels understand to Whom worship is to be given. They would not make the "mistake: of offering worship to any but God.

The angels were called to worship Jesus. Only God is rightfully allowed to accept Worship in the universe. Others may, as Satan, accept worship from others. But, they are doing this illegally. Since this is Scripture, and the Father is speaking, the call to worship is a clear reference to the Deity of the Son.

The ancient Jews had the highest regard for the angels. They considered them the highest council of God. The angels could even be worshiped as God's representatives, although not for themselves. None but God was thought to be entitled to the worship of angels. The writer of Hebrews, in saying that Jesus is above the angels, and that the angels are instructed to worship Jesus, is claiming Deity for Jesus.

This passage is speaking of relationships. In relationship, the Son and the Father are distinct. This passage does not suggest that Jesus began at Bethlehem. Such a construct would be foreign to the rest of Scripture. The Father said these things. Through the medium of the Virgin Birth Jesus was "brought into the world." But, it is equally true that Jesus existed in Glory and as Deity, before these events.

If Jesus were not God, to suggest that the angels must worship Him would be considered the highest of blasphemy. Since Jesus is God, this is simply His right by virtue of Who He is. The worship of the angels, which belongs only to the Creator (Remember, the basic sin of Satan was to seek the honor which belongs only to God.) is to be given to Jesus.]

1.7 *And of the angels he saith, Who maketh his angels spirits, and his ministers a flame of fire.*

[The first thing I notice in this verse is that the angels are spirit beings. They are not eternal but created. They have only the authority of their commission for a certain task. Beyond that they have no power. It is God Who gives the orders which set the angels in motion.

Several commentators argued that the phrase "Who maketh his angels spirits," should have been "winds" instead of "spirit." Such a construct might possibly be argued from the meaning of the word. I would think it a losing argument. This would make the angels described as simply forces of nature in this world. The fact that the angels can assume the form of a person when this is needed for their tasks would discount this argument on the face of it! The argument to change the word seems to be more an attempt to "downgrade" the miraculous. This is a common error in our time. God is The God of miracle. He created the entire universe and can do that which He pleases. This includes creating a class of spirit, angel, which will do His will.

It is good to keep in mind that angels are heavenly beings. Jesus assumed the actual robes of humanity. Thus, He can do much more than angels in this world for this is not simply a world He visited to perform a task. This world which He created was His literal home for some time as He became one of us even as He retained His dignity and power as God.

Angels can wield great power. They are described here as being akin to lightning. This is one of the most potentially destructive forces in nature. Paul was describing one of the strongest forces to be seen in this early age. Yet he also describes Jesus as more powerful and more glorious than the angels could ever become.

This brings up an important consideration from Galatians 1:8. "But though we, or an angel from heaven, preach any other gospel unto you than that which we have preached unto you, let him be accursed." Quite simply put, Satan can assume the form of an angel. II Corinthians 11:14 gives us this warning – "And no marvel; for Satan himself is transformed into an angel of light."

If this is true, how can we be certain that we are following the Words of God rather than the path of Satan? We have a Guide Book called "The Bible." Any doctrine, and teaching – this includes my own!! – which does not stand true to the inspired and preserved Words of God is false. Every time! Without exception!

If we are not standing upon the inspired and preserved Words of God we can have no idea where we are standing. In this Book, only in this Book, are the true Words of life which give us leading from the spiritual and eternal realms. No man, not even any "Bible translation," can be trusted which is not standing true on the Truth.

Keep in mind that a "Bible translation" is always a work of man. The only validity any translation may have is connected to two things. The first, and most important, of these is the basic text from which the translation is made. This text must not be a man-constructed text but the actual inspired and preserved Words of God in their original languages and word order.

Second, those who translated must have an abiding faith in the fact that they are actually handling the very Words of God. Those translators cannot be convinced that Scripture is simply another book from antiquity which is subject to decay and error. A text such as the Critical Text, which is based on the assumption that God either could not (questioning His power) or would not (questioning His love toward His created humanity) preserve His Words to man is a text based on a lack of faith in the power and purpose of God. Any translation from such a text is rooted in unbelief and cannot be properly considered as a true translation of the eternal Words of God.]

1.8 *But unto the Son he saith, Thy throne, O God, is for ever and ever: a sceptre of righteousness is the sceptre of thy kingdom.*

[In this passage we see that the Father said of Jesus, the Son God. "...Thy throne, O God..." This would be an amazing inconsistency if the Trinitarian understanding of the Triune Godhead were not an established Scriptural truth.

The Father spoke of the Son in this passage as righteous, i.e. Holy, in all things and at all times.

In the first seven verses of this chapter from Hebrews the Father had shown His Own mighty works and spoke of the glory of the Son. Now, lest there be any doubt from what has gone before, the Father addresses the Son as "God."

The fact that the throne is "for ever and ever" also speaks of the eternality of God as a trait of Jesus. Note that this is not a bestowed or applied eternality. This is an eternality of eternal possession by He Who IS God.

There are many who are dissatisfied with our present president in this nation. It matters not when you might read this words or what location your nation might occupy. There are always some who are dissatisfied with their present temporal ruler. That is simple human nature. But, Jesus will exercise dominion and rule throughout eternity to the delight and joy of the inhabitants of eternity.

Adam Clarke (Adam Clarke's Commentary) sees that some argue for a reading that says "God is thy throne forever." This reading would deny the Deity of Jesus as He is only seen as seated in the Throne of God rather than seated as God on the Throne of God. This is a reading based on the theology of the critic rather than on the true reading of the text.

Clarke states that, "It is a rule of the Greek language, that when a substantive noun is the subject of a sentence, and something is predicated on it, the article, if used at all, is prefixed to the subject, but omitted before the predicate. The Greek translators of the Old, and the authors of the New Testament, write agreeable to this rule."

We must note that when Clarke speaks of the Greek translators of the Old Testament he is speaking of the LXX. Since there is no complete text of the Old Testament in Greek until the third century it is presumptuous to any underlying Old Testament text in the Greek and attribute such to the New Testament penmen. This becomes an exercise in illogic.

There is ample proof that several passages of the Old Testament were translated into the Greek. Consider the above paragraphs concerning translations in this light. There is, however, no real proof that the entire Old Testament was ever completely translated into the Greek. The ancient "proof" of such a translation is littered with fantastic tales such as attended the myths of the ancient Greek "gods."]

1.9 *Thou hast loved righteousness, and hated iniquity, therefore God, even thy God, hath anointed thee with the oil of gladness above thy fellows.*

[Once again, as we have noticed before, the Father was speaking of the Son in reference to the Office of Jesus as the substitute for sinners. As such Jesus was fully human. As to the eternal makeup of Jesus, He is God and fully so. But in His Office as the substitute for sinners the Bible will consider the humanity which He took upon Himself in the incarnation.

Many false doctrines have come because Christians have not considered that Jesus is fully God while being fully human. The Bible will often make a distinction between the position of His Office as Savior - which He willingly assumed in the Kenosis (see Philippians 2:6-8) - and His Deity in which He is the Creator of all (see John 1:1-3).]

1.10 *And, Thou Lord, in the beginning hast laid the foundations of the earth, and the heavens are the works of thine hands.*

[In verse eight, above, the writer had given the identification of whom he was speaking. "But unto the Son he saith, Thy throne, O God, is for ever and ever: a sceptre of righteousness is the sceptre of thy kingdom."

This eighth verse hearkens back to Psalm 45:6. "Thy throne, O God, is for ever and ever: the sceptre of thy kingdom is a right sceptre." This Psalm is a prophecy of the Messiah. Jesus is that Messiah. The human penman of Hebrews is, once again, ascribing the entire creation to the work of Jesus. Therefore, Jesus is God.

That phrase, "in the beginning," is often used in the Scripture. As a general rule this refers back to eternity when the creation was first considered by God. To use a basketball illustration, "in the beginning" would not refer to the opening jump ball. It would refer back to before the time Dr. Naismith invented the game.

"In the beginning" refers back to when there was nothing yet of the physical created universe.]

1.11 *They shall perish, but thou remainest; and they all shall wax old as doth a garment;*

Psalm 102:24-27

[vv. 1-12. Note the phrasing. The writer is clearly using Old Testament prophecy (Psalm 102:24-27) and imagery to show that Jesus is God. The meaning is the same in both as both are describing deity.

The concept that "they" shall change could well be prophecy of the New Heavens and the New Earth as prophesied in II Peter 3:7 and Revelation 21:1. I believe, however, that this is a secondary application. The primary prophetical application seems to relate to the life times and generations of humanity.

Messiah will have an eternal throne. Never throughout the ageless ages of eternity will His Person or His dignity ever change or even decay.

I am about three weeks from my 66th birthday. Even at this age my body will constantly assault my dignity. I cannot do that which I often wish to do. I went on a short walk yesterday to do some church "cold calling." I went to some stranger's homes, introduced myself, and invited them to church. After only a couple of blocks of walking I was very glad to find my car. I was exhausted! This old body let me know just how old it is! Such a thing will never happen to the Lord of Glory. He does not change.

I was listening to some old music on the internet a few days ago. I enjoyed many of the groups from the "war years" of the forties. These were major "stars" in their day. Their day is long past. Very few remember them. Just last Sunday I mentioned "Will Rogers" during a sermon and was met with many blank faces who had no idea about whom I was speaking. Fame and the power of popularity fail. Such a thing will never happen to the Lord of Glory. He does not change.]

1.12 *And as a vesture shalt thou fold them up, and they shall be changed: but thou art the same, and thy years shall not fail.*

[vv. 10-12. Once again the very same thing is said of Jesus in the New Testament as was said of God in the Old Testament. (See Psalm 102:25-28.) Therefore it seems quite obvious that These are both God. Since God is One this is an intimation of the Triune Godhead. There is but One God eternally existent in the Father, the Son, and the Holy Spirit. It is beyond our finite understanding to comprehend this fact. The fact that is clear is that the Son is spoken of with the same concepts of His essence as is the Father. Therefore it must follow that the Son is God.

In the Book of II Peter we are told, "But the day of the Lord will come as a thief in the night; in the which the heavens shall pass away with a great noise, and the elements shall melt with fervent heat, the earth also and the works that are therein shall be burned up." (II Peter 3:10) This event is also foretold in Revelation 21:1. "And I saw a new heaven and a new earth: for the first heaven and the first earth were passed away; and there was no more sea."

It is important to note that these passages are not speaking of the Heaven of God's abode. These verses speak of entities of creation. In this event the sin of Adam, which polluted the entire creation (consider Romans 8:22), will be purged and purified. This could present a scenario where all humanity would be purged as well. Such is not a prospect for the children of God as we are comforted that "The children of thy servants shall continue, and their seed shall be established before thee." (Psalm 102:28)

As to the rest of humanity - those who are not the redeemed of the Lord? Revelation 20:10 says this, "And the devil that deceived them was cast into the lake of fire and brimstone, where the beast and the false prophet are, and shall be tormented day and night for ever and ever."

Some may argue that this verse speaks of spiritual beings being preserved in the torments of Hell for all eternity. Those who thus argue could make the claim that there is an annihilation of the souls of the human wicked. I would caution those who hope for this to consider that the beast and false prophet, although energized by Satan, are of human essence. These will suffer the same fate as does Satan.

To those who would argue that such eternal torment is only for those listed in the above verse, I would also note Revelation 20:15. "And whosoever was not found written in the book of life was cast into the lake of fire." It would behoove all of us to consider this certain future and heed the words of II Corinthians 6:2 - "...now is the day of salvation."]

1.13 *But to which of the angels said he at any time, Sit on my right hand, until I make thine enemies thy footstool?*

[Paul was a trained theologian and a Pharisee. This particular Book, Hebrews, is written to the Hebrew Christians and explains that Jesus is Messiah with argument and illustration from the Old Testament Scriptures. In this first part of the Book, Paul is explaining that Jesus is more glorious than even an angel. Since the angels were held in high esteem by the Jew, to show Jesus was more than them is to point towards both His office as Messiah and His reality as God.

In verses 5, 6, 7, 8, 10 and 13 of this first chapter of Hebrews, the arguments are put forth that Jesus is superior to the angelic hosts. The angels are ministers of the will of God. Jesus is the God of that will as He orders the angels as they are His subjects. Angels are never said to have any reign such as is promised to Jesus. This reign is a prerogative of God; for Jesus to share in this reign is to say that Jesus is God.

Jesus was said of David to be invited to sit at the right hand of The Father. The "right hand" of the ruler is a place of power. It is a place of honor. That quotation, from Psalm 110:1 is applied to Himself by Jesus in a discourse with the Pharisees. (Matthew 22:44)

Both Acts 2:35 and I Corinthians 15:25 attribute the final victory of God over the forces of evil to be accomplished by Jesus. Joshua 10:24 gives a picture of this concept of conquered enemies becoming as "footstools" to the conqueror. This is a sign of the subjection of the defeated and the supremacy of the victor. It is interesting to note that even the Law is a defeated enemy in that its power to lead toward enmity with God (see Romans 7:9-11) is removed from the redeemed.

We might also note that the fact that Jesus is "sitting" at the Father's right hand is symbolic of His defeat of sin and the accouterments of sin; His sittings is symbolic of His already accomplished defeat of sin and the wiles of Satan. Only the formalities of the defeat of Satan are reserved for the ending of time and the final judgments. The cup of iniquity is not yet full for the draught of judgment to be finalized. It has already, however, been determined.]

1.14 *Are they not all ministering spirits, sent forth to minister for them who shall be heirs of salvation?*

[While Jesus is described above as the Ruler Who sits in the seat of Power, the angels are identified as spirits. All of them are thus described.

A spirit is an incorporeal being. They are allowed and empowered to assume the appearance of humans when it serves their assigned purpose.

God is also Spirit. Jesus told the woman at the well that God is Spirit. (John 4:24) These angels have their being in the spiritual and eternal domain. They are still created beings who are subservient unto God. They are not of His eternal order but had a beginning at their point of creation. The creative acts of God are not limited to the created universe but extend further into all. The Words of God are Supreme in any area.

That the angels are called ministering spirits will itself point to their subservient position under the rule of Jesus. This is a term which was commonly used of those who ministered to the princes of this world. Paul used the phrase to further point out the contrast between the all-powerful and eternal Jesus, who has always existed as God throughout all eternity, and the created angels who are His servants. We note that He rules while the angels serve.

The angels also serve, but only on the order from their Commander, those who are the redeemed of the earth. (Daniel 9:21-23; 10:11) While the phrase "ministering spirits" points out that the angels minister to God in the eternal realm, they are also sent forth to minister to the elect. These are two distinct areas of ministering but are both controlled by the Words and Commands of God.

The redeemed of the earth are called "heirs of salvation." We are adopted into a "son ship" relationship with God (consider John 1:12) at the point of our salvation and thus are considered as "heirs of salvation." Note the differential between the Divine Son of God as God incarnate, and the Christian as sons of God as the redeemed of the earth due to the work of the (singular and imperative) Son of God. We do not inherit any divinity. That this could be so was part of the lie of Satan in the third chapter of

Genesis. Such is never promised in the inspired and preserved Scripture of God with the exception of the lie of the deceiver.]

HEBREWS - CHAPTER TWO

2.1 *Therefore we ought to give the more earnest heed to the things which we have heard, lest at any time we should let them slip.*

[Since Jesus is truly better than even the angels, since Jesus is truly the eternal Son of God, since Jesus is truly eternal God incarnate, we have a certain need to hold fast to these things we have learned of Him.

Not only do we have a need to hold fast to the things we have learned about Jesus, the Messiah of God, we have a need to pay heed to that message. I have just returned from a short trip to *Chez Golden Arches* where I bought some cold soft drinks for my grandson and myself. That phrase "bought" carries a very similar thought to the "heed" of this verse. In order for the girl at the counter to put the soda cups in our hands I had to first give her a green piece of paper with a picture of Abraham Lincoln on it. She, in turn, gave me some small pieces of round metal with other images upon it.

The paper was the price of the object I desired. The metal was coin she returned to me was above the price needed.

When my wife and I bought our first car it was necessary the company from which we bought the car be given an *earnest* payment until such time as all of the forms were completed and the automobile became our property. This earnest was to secure our desire to purchase the car.

When we give "earnest heed" we are giving the "price" of our full attention and devotion to Jesus. Our faith and love, thus offered, is always accepted since the true cost of this transaction was paid by Jesus Himself at the cross. The "change" we receive comes in the form of blessings in this present life.

The analogy breaks down as we consider that Jesus is the one Who has purchased us by buying us out of slavery to sin and into the glorious light of Salvation. Besides this we receive salvation from our sins, a renewed relationship with God, and the promise of a home in heaven.

The knowledge of these things comes through revelation from the Words and Spirit of God. In the earlier times God spoke wondrous things through holy prophets. The doctrine of the Person of Jesus has come via His Own Words and the witness of the Holy Spirit.

Paul was writing to a group of people who were in danger of slipping from the Words of Free Grace and back into the Law of Legality. The dictates of this Law of Legality have already been met and fulfilled by the life and sacrificial death of Jesus Christ. The concept of receiving again the Law would be to reject the Grace of Christ.

In I Corinthians 11:30 Paul speaks of the spiritual principle of those who are the saved of the Lord who make a case to reject the concept of His Grace alone and desire that obedience to the Law be partnered therein. "For this cause many are weak and sickly among you, and many sleep." Their souls, purchased already by the Blood of Christ and therefore His property, may see tribulation and even death. These souls, sanctified by salvation and disciplined by Divine Love, may leave this earth so that the cause of Christ not be harmed by the deformed "testimony" of deficient saints.

The unsaved who make this choice have removed themselves from the testimony of salvation. They are doomed by their own decision. "...he that believeth not the Son shall not see life; but the wrath of God abideth on him." (John 3:36b)

The concept of "slip" in this passage is of a vessel which will not hold liquid. It is useless as its contents flow away from it through cracks in the vessel.

The warning is that we will allow the pure doctrine of Christ to slip away from us by our own inattention to the "dribble glass" of our youthful enthusiasm or our elderly rigidity – or any other possibility. Our faith, founded in the inspired and preserved Words of God must be kept elastic to the leading of the Spirit and solidly founded on the faith that God has given his Words without recall.]

2.2 For if the word spoken by angels was steadfast, and every transgression and disobedience received a just recompence of reward,

[There was a tradition among the rabbis that the law was given by Jehovah but communicated to man through His messengers the angels. (Deuteronomy 33:2; Acts 7:59; Galatians 3:19) The argument in this place is simply that if the angels had a hand, even ever so slight of a hand, in the giving of the Law, and Jesus is far above the angels in His person, prestige and power it must follow that the Gospel of Jesus is far above the Law in all respects.

If this were true, it must also follow that we are under the requirement of following the Gospel even above submitting unto the Law.

The word "transgression" points to a willful sin against God in relation to the dictates of the Law. The word "disobedience" points to a failure to do the duties which were assigned by that Law. Paul, in the third chapter of Galatians, compares the Law to a "schoolmaster" whose purpose it was to lead us unto faith in Jesus. It was resolute in its demands made upon the children of man. To run afoul of the Law was to invite punishment from the ultimate Giver of that Law.

Although the Law was purposed to lead us to Christ, it was never a road to righteousness. The Law was more of a picture of the wreckage of those who had strayed from that road. Its message was that man could not fulfill the requirements of the Law and by this to point out the just punishment which would fall upon those who failed to completely follow God in that dispensation.

The need was shown that there was a necessity that it would take an act of God to pull man from the wreckage of the Law and unto the Safety of the Lord. It was not that the Law was wreckage but that the lives of humanity could not "break through" the fact of the Law and gain the favor of God without the sacrifice of Jesus to carry us from our failure in relation to that Law and the fact that Jesus has already perfectly kept all the Law and offers to us a "hand up" past our own legal failures in reference to the Law. In Him we are counted as victors over the Law. His righteousness has secured the Father's forgiveness and the abrogation of our sin under His Own perfections and sacrifice.

Therefore we have no more duty toward the Law. "But after that faith is come, we are no longer under a schoolmaster." (Galatians 3:25) We do, however, have a responsibility to remember the lessons which the schoolmaster has given to us. We are not free to violate the Law at our whim. The "cane" of the schoolmaster may no longer haunt our every misdeed. But the love we owe to the Lord for the Great Salvation given in the Gospel, compels our every attendance to fulfill that Law, not in fear of retribution but under the higher duty of our Love for the Savior as well as in thankfulness for His love toward us.]

2.3 *How shall we escape, if we neglect so great salvation, which at the first began to be spoken by the Lord, and was confirmed unto us by them that heard him;*

[The question applies to all humanity. For the sinner, to neglect appropriating the offered gift of salvation will result in that one continuing on a path to eternal perdition. My father was a tree surgeon. I remember him telling a story once of a rotting tree limb giving way as he ascended his ladder. He fell about thirty feet before the safety rope kept him safe. Had he not used that safety rope he would have continued to fall. The rope did not cause his fall; it merely averted the danger. One who does not accept Christ fails to grasp that which will offer him safety in a spiritual fall.

The verse speaks more fully to the Christian. The "we" of Paul is an indication that this is written to the saved individual. To neglect our salvation is to ignore it. This, sadly, is the case with the vast majority of Christians in our time. They are like the deserter from a military outpost. They are neither doing their sworn duty nor even protecting themselves. This is an invitation for judicial punishment from the world's militaries.

We do not "lose" our salvation. We do lose the joy of our salvation. We do lose the eternal rewards of our salvation. We do lose the joyful power of our salvation in regards to the work which the Lord has appointed us. We lapse into a state where we are contented with the dry sand of the world even as we cannot fathom the great cache of joys which God stands ready to provide to those that love Him.

We also "gain" the displeasure of God and invite the chastening which He reserves for His children in this world. (Proverbs 3:12; Hebrews 12:6)

The offense under the Law was high in rejecting the leading of the Law of the Lord. The offense under Grace is much higher in that it is rejecting the Lord, Himself. To the sinner this is in relation to his refusal to accept that Grace. In the case of the Christian this is in relation to a refusal to return to God the great love which God has bestowed upon him. It is also a dereliction of duty. It is a desertion from the position of our love of Christ in that our love toward Him is not displayed.

I am presently pastoring a church. This, believe it or not, was not something I had strongly desired. In point of fact, I rejected this *assignment* from God for a long period of time. I have not seen great results as the world would count results. I have, however, felt great results in my soul as I follow the will of God. Jonah also argued with God. In following God there was revival in the city of Nineveh. I have felt great revival in my heart as God gives blessing to those who do His will. It is never our work; it is His work in which He allows us to share. We have the blessing of the offering to be co-workers with God in this world.

This is designated as "Great Salvation." Thus, our experience with Grace even outshines the Old Testament examples of the Old Covenant. The Old Covenant was given primarily to the Jew. This New Covenant has been spread to the entire earth. Humanly speaking, it is only our laziness and dereliction which has prevented the joy of the Lord to be experienced by many more people.

The Old Covenant contained many types and shadows of which the New

Covenant has supplied the reality.

The Old Covenant looked to outward forms of piety which could be seen of men. The New Covenant looks to inward forms of piety which are seen of God.

The Old Covenant referenced temporal happiness as it spoke of blessings concerning time. The New Covenant references the joys of eternity as it speaks of an eternal abode.

Moses was the "CEO," as it were, of the Old Covenant. Jesus Christ, the Lord of Heaven and the God/man is our Leader. He spoke of this covenant of grace and bought it with His Own Blood.

The Old Covenant is a man centered religion which directs worship to Jehovah. The New Covenant is a Heaven Centered reality as it looks to the glorified Lord Who died in time so that we could live in eternity.

The Age of Grace is truly a fact of A, singular and imperative, Great Salvation. "Neither is there salvation in any other: for there is none other name under heaven given among men, whereby we must be saved." (Acts 4:12)

Salvation is Great when one considers the Author of that salvation. Salvation is Great when one considers the great sin of mankind which is forgiven and forgotten due to the Great Sacrifice of Jesus. Salvation is Great when one considers the great dangers awaiting the unsaved. Salvation is Great when one considers the Great promises of freedom from sin, fellowship with God and an eternal home in Heaven. Salvation is great when one considers the Great Power of the One Who offers this Great Salvation to us.

All of this has been confirmed by the inspired and preserved Message of the Scripture of God, the Old Testament prophets who spoke of the coming Messiah, the message of John the Baptist, the teaching of Jesus in the New Testament, the message of the apostles, the history of changed lives in the history of the churches and the history of the world, and the ministry of The Holy Spirit within our own hearts and lives.

Those who knew Jesus best were willing to suffer martyrdom to attest to the truth of the Gospel of Jesus. Consider that this last sentence does not refer merely to the apostles of the first century but to the Blood Bought Believers of the ages who faced fires, wild beasts, sword, depravation and more to give us the chance to hear the message of the Love of Christ. I would remind us all that this same martyrdom continues even today. The world hates the true message of Christ. The world hates those who would spread this message of full salvation, or even try to simply live in peace with others as Children of the King.]

2.4 God also bearing them witness, both with signs and wonders, and with divers miracles, and gifts of the Holy Ghost, according to his own will?

[Not only did the apostles confirm the message of Jesus, so did the Power of God. We could speak of His Own power as God in that these same miraculous sign gifts of the early church were also demonstrated in the earthly ministry of Jesus. The difference between those sign gifts of the apostles and the use of those same signs by Jesus lays in the fact that the apostles were empowered for their tasks while Jesus *was the power* that performed those gifts in His earthly ministry.

At the beginning of each of the dispensations there are miraculous manifestations of the power of God sent to confirm the expanded teaching of the new dispensation. Once again, I cannot emphasize this fact too often; strictly speaking there is no new teaching given from dispensation to dispensation; there is an expansion of understanding given concerning that earlier teaching.

God does not change. His Truth does not change. But, with the expanding teaching of each dispensation we are allowed to learn more of Him. We are not instructed differently; we are instructed more deeply into the Truth.

The purpose of these sign gifts is to confirm the Gospel Message. This Gospel Message was an expansion into the entire world, which was the charge given in Matthew 28:19-20, of the Truths which were previously held primarily by the children of Abraham. "What advantage then hath the Jew? or what profit is there of circumcision? Much every way: chiefly, because that unto them were committed the oracles of God." (Romans 3:1-2) These are manifestations of the power of God, not of man, and are thus given the "stamp of approval" of God concerning these expanded teachings.

The signs are miraculous events which illustrate spiritual truth.

The wonders are events which incite an astonishment which brings the mind to feast upon the Truths so represented.

The miracles are manifestations of the Divine power. That they are diverse gives further proof that they are of God. Some "thing" might be counterfeited by man. Speaking of the beast and false prophet of the Tribulation era, John informs us: "And he doeth great wonders, so that he maketh fire come down from heaven on the earth in the sight of men," (Revelation 13:13)

May we never forget that Satan is a powerful spiritual foe. We dare not stand without the spiritual armor given us as Christians. (Ephesians 6:10-18) Even here we must always stand close in the fellowship of the Lord. Only therein is the reality of Spiritual peace and power.

There are several instances where God sent fire down from heaven in the Old Testament. Each of these was to incite worship of the True God rather than as a "show time" to simply glorify any man. Past this the miracles spoken of in this verse were all to defeat the hold of sin on the earth. Each of the miracles of healing was designed to return the body of some person to the "factory specifications" of the original physical creation before the advent of the sin of Adam.

The true miracle of God can reach any situation (diverse) but will always serve to bring glory to God and detriment to sin.

Note well that each of this sign gifts mentioned was activated by the will of the Holy Spirit. Even those acts which seemed to be initiated by the individual, such as the gift of tongues on the Day of Pentecost, were activated and allowed by the ministries of the Holy Spirit. He gave the power when humanity provided the vessel for Him to use. Even that vessel was available only because of the prior salvation of any individual; even here we must appreciate the fact of the Convicting Hand of the Holy Spirit which led to such individual's salvation in the acceptance of the Holy Sacrifice of the Lord, Jesus Christ.

These gifts, as accepted and as used, were given by the Spirit on an "as needed" basis. Our work, much like the angels in this sense, is initiated by Him. We are the vessels He uses to reach His will into the world.

There is a difference between what might be accomplished in our ministry and that which was accomplished in the earthly ministry of Jesus. We act as the Spirit gives leading and power. Jesus acts on His Own authority as the Divine Son of God.]

HEBREWS: Chapter 2

2.5 *For unto the angels hath he not put in subjection the world to come, whereof we speak.*

[I am severely tempted to place this verse as speaking of the millennial kingdom. The Jew of the day of this writing was disposed to see the phrase "the world to come" in relation to the reign of Messiah. Paul, however, uses the phrase "whereof we speak" in relation to the teaching of this verse. The previous verses speak of the Gospel message as superior to the Age of the Law. Therefore we must consider this verse as speaking of the Church Age.

In the Church Age, this present Dispensation of Grace, Jesus remains the head of the church. The angels have not been given to assume this position. This role of supremacy, which is the property of Jesus, even in this Church Age shows Jesus to be above the level of the angels.

He rules while the angels remain His servants. (Revelation 22:9)]

2.6 *But one in a certain place testified, saying, What is man, that thou art mindful of him: or the son of man, that thou visitest him?*

[As mentioned before, Paul was writing to defend the Gospel among a group of Jewish Christians. There had been a great controversy among these believers as to how much of the baggage of Judaism they should bring into the Gospel of faith in Jesus.

A council at the Jerusalem Church had already decreed the extent to which the Gentile Christians need follow the dictates of Judaism. "That ye abstain from meats offered to idols, and from blood, and from things strangled, and from fornication: from which if ye keep yourselves, ye shall do well. Fare ye well." (Acts 15:29) It is to these Jewish Christians which Paul now writes.

These Jewish Christians were well versed in the Old Testament. Paul was not speaking from ignorance when he said, "...one in a certain place testified..." Paul was showing a proper respect to both David and the Scripture in using this phrase in the context of speaking to Jewish Christians.

It is Psalm 8:4ff which is used as a point of reference in this place. The extended passage refers to the dominion which was given Adam over the animals of the earth. This dominion had been complete. Sin has interfered with that dominion. This is a year where we have been reminded often of the lack of true "dominion" over the fish of the sea. The newspapers have carried many stories of "shark attacks" this summer.

The fact that this dominion is undiminished in this Psalm would tend to, along with this use from Hebrews, stamp this as a "Messianic Psalm." This Psalm speaks of perfect, not fallen, man. Jesus is our Perfect Savior. Although He is fully human, He is not touched by the stain of either original or experimental sin.

Verse five from this eighth Psalm will argue that Jesus is "made him a little lower than the angels" in His humanity as He has thus clothed Himself in order to identify with us in offering us salvation. This verse also says in the very next clause that He "hast crowned him with glory and honor."

In John 17:5, as Jesus is ready to offer Himself up as The Sacrifice for the remission of the sins of humanity, prays, "And now, O Father, glorify thou me with thine own self with the glory which I had with thee before the world was." He is ready to receive once again that glory which He had laid aside in the Kenosis.

Thus we see that this is a prophecy of Messiah and yet another proof to these Jewish Christians that Jesus is above the angels and is their promised Messiah.]

2.7 *Thou madest him a little lower than the angels, thou crownedst him with glory and honour, and didst set him over the works of thy hands:*

[Jesus was made in His Virgin Birth as a human man. In this He was counted, in rank not in Person which remained Divine, as a little lower than the angels.

Some commentators argued that the fact that man is a little lower than the angels was because man was a dying creature. If this verse were to refer to mankind as a whole, such could not be the argument. Man was originally a creature made in the image of God. The Breath of God inserted an eternity of existence into the race of humanity. Even after the sin of Adam destroyed the eternity of the human body, the eternity of the soul was not affected. Only the final disposition of that soul, either in bliss with the Father in Heaven or in agony with the tempter in the Lake of Fire, remained in doubt. The eternity of the soul was never in question.

The original creation of man saw him as the crown jewel of the creation of God. He was given dominion over the creation. This is why the sin of Adam had such a far reaching effect upon the rest of creation. (Romans 8:22) The age old question has been, "Why is there so much evil in the world?" The answer is, quite simply and correctly, "Because man brought sin and misery into the world with the sin of Adam."

I read this verse, especially in its setting in Hebrews, as concerning Jesus, not Adam. Jesus was made a little lower than the angels. Being "made," in this sense, presupposes a previous existence of Jesus before the events at Bethlehem. He IS, such has never been not true, God. He took upon Himself the body of humanity so that He could be our substitute for the remission of our sins. In doing this He laid aside the glory of, NOT THE REALITY OF, His Divinity for a short time.

To better understand this duality of nature it might be helpful to read John 3:13 where Jesus says of Himself that He is in Heaven even as He speaks with Nicodemus in Jerusalem. Jesus is the Great God of Creation. He may have inhabited His Own human body but it was the Glory of God Who was tabernacled therein.

After He willingly died on the Cross, the human body of Jesus rose from the dead. After forty days He ascended into Heaven and regained all the Glory that was rightfully His. He reassumed that position of power which was rightfully His.]

2.8 *Thou hast put all things in subjection under his feet. For in that he put all in subjection under him, he left nothing that is not put under him. But now we see not yet all things put under him.*

Psalm 45:6-7

[Vv. 8 – 10. Let's look at the declarations of this passage. First, "...he left nothing that is not put under him..." If "nothing" was not put under Jesus that means that "all" is put under Him. That makes Him to be the Lord of all; there is no other reasonable conclusion than that this is a reference to the Deity of Jesus.

While retaining this supremacy, we also see that Jesus was made "...a little lower than the angels..." We also see that this was for the specific purpose of effecting the salvation of individual humans. Not all have accepted His Lordship; these are the "...not yet all things put under him..." This simply reminds us that not all are born again. Some remain in their sins.

The last part of the verse uses the word "perfect." This is an old English word which properly means "complete." I see this as a twofold statement. One, it speaks of Jesus completing the Work to offer salvation. Two, I think it also has a reference to those who accept Him in that we are completed, in our salvation, through His sufferings.

Either interpretation speaks of the Glory and Majesty of Jesus.

The writer of Hebrews, via inspiration, has written that Jesus, the Son, is that Messiah prophesied in the Old Testament. Since Messiah is God, and Jesus is that Messiah, Jesus is God.

We also see that the human penman of Hebrews quotes from the Old Testament Book of Psalms. This means, of course, that this writer considered that the Old Testament Book had been preserved and was, thus, authoritative. This also means that this concept of Jesus being Divine was not the province of some New Testament "followers" of Him. This verse fully puts the imprint of Divine authority into the New Testament belief that Jesus is "very God while being very man."]

2.9 *But we see Jesus, who was made a little lower than the angels for the suffering of death, crowned with glory and honor; that he by the grace of God should taste death for every man.*

[We've already discussed that the phrase "Jesus was made" applies to His voluntarily submitting to the Kenosis. The only sense in which it could be argued that this was required of Jesus would be to access the reality of His great love. This is something He desired to do because of His great love for His created beings. Sin could only be forgiven by the One to Whom the offense was directed. That was God. Once again, we find the inescapable conclusion that Jesus is God.

Jesus came into the world with the express purpose of dying on the Cross of Calvary. There were times when the leadership of the Jews sought to stone Him to death and He just walked away from them. This time He willingly went with the soldiers and endured the trial and humiliation of the pre-crucifixion floggings because of His love for us. He died on the cross in time so that we would be allowed to live in eternity.

One of my sources, a well-known theologian whom I respect greatly, argued that this verse means that the glorification of Jesus was because of His death on the Cross. I would only say one thing as to this: Ridiculous! Jesus is The Lord of Glory. This "crown of glory and honor" was His. He simply picked up that which He had laid aside.

This is the entire point which Paul has been making. Jesus may have accepted a diminished status – a little lower than the angels – for a short time. This was not in order that He would be able to gain glory at a later time due to His work on earth! The glory was His already. The crown was His already. This are enumerated so that we may more fully understand the Wonder of our Wonderful Lord.

Even had He not gone to the cross He would still be due our unending praise and veneration. The sad thing is that if we were still in our sins we would fail miserably in offering this to Him.

The Truth is that all will eventually offer this praise to Him. Romans 14:11 reminds us, "For it is written, As I live, saith the Lord, every knee shall bow to me, and every tongue shall confess to God." It is wonderful that because of His sacrifice for us, we are allowed to bask in the warm glow of His Love as we have the privilege of agreeing that He is both Lord and Savior!

He tasted the penalty for our sins so that we would not have to do so. Our sins have been judged at the Cross and we are free of that judgment. It is all of God. It is all due to His great love! It is all grace. As the old child's memory help reminds us, grace is a matter of receiving "God's Riches At Christ's Expense."]

2.10 *For it became him, for whom are all things, and by whom are all things, in bringing many sons unto glory, to make the captain of their salvation perfect through sufferings.*

[There was a fitness of consummation for Jesus to suffer and die. This had been His plan and purpose since before the world had been created. (Revelation 13:8) He is the all in all of all from eternity to creation. He both created and upholds all things in the created realm and is the Glory, Holiness, and Power of the eternal as well.

His perfect purpose in designating the Cross was the salvation of humanity. Sin could not enter the Heavenly abode of God. Man had sinned in the Garden. The purpose of God in the creation of man was to produce a creature with which He could fellowship and display His great attribute of love into His creation. Therefore, there needed to be an antidote for the problem of sin in order that the purpose of God in His creation would be fulfilled.

His purpose in the Crucifixion was more than the salvation of sinners – who would be perfected, completed, as the crowing jewel of His creative activity. In doing so He would also display His love and flawless holiness to both the eternal and created realms, to all orders of angel and humanity. Even the tempter who had authored the atrocity of sin would have to admit the great glory and perfections of God at the last judgment.

In His "bringing of many sons to glory" (John 1:12) He would also become the "Captain," or Chief of this salvation. Salvation is of Him, by Him, ultimately for Him, and prepared by His plan and actions. His Kenosis had led to His identification with the sinful creature – yet without sin on His part due to the Virgin Birth. Eve was fashioned before Adam had sinned. She thus enjoyed the eternal benefit of the "Breath of God" which had fashioned Adam as an eternal being.

Adam, created first, had been given the responsibility of being the possessor of the dominion of the earth. This was his obligation under God. The sin of Adam was thus an infection which sullied the entire earth.

Eve, meanwhile, was not given this obligation. Her sin damaged her own soul and sentenced her to physical death – as had Adam, himself, with his own sin. But, the sin of Eve was her own. It was the sin of Adam which infected the entire created realm. (Romans 8:22) It was through Adam that the sin became part of every person born of man and woman down to the present time. The results of this sin of Adam still infect us in this day.

Thus the virgin birth of Jesus meant that His physical body was fully human but untainted by the stain of sin in any manner. Further, as God, His person was impeccable, or incapable of sin in any form. Thus, He had the unique ability to die as one of us, and for each one of us, as the antidote to the infection of sin in our lives. On this account we could be presented before The Father in the Person of the Son. We were allowed to become, even in a somewhat inferior status while still on this earth, the originally intended creature of fellowship with God.

Therefore, we can see that Jesus had perfected, or completed, all that is necessary for our salvation. To refuse Him and seek our own perfection in some other way is to inject the same concept of sin, the desire of Satan to overtake the throne of God, into that relationship. This is why salvation is only through Him. There is no other means of finding fellowship with God or an eternal home in Heaven.]

2.11 *For both he that sanctifieth and they who are sanctified are all of one: for which cause he is not ashamed to call them brethren,*

[The concept of sanctification is not a mystical mystery. To be sanctified is to be set apart for a special – or specified – purpose. We who are the saved by the precious Blood of Jesus are set apart from the general population as the children of God. We each have a purpose in the economy of God. We each have some sort of "chore" in which we are to be engaged by The Father.

Both we and Jesus are considered of one family. The verse above (10) speaks of "many sons." Let us be very certain to understand that this does not give us equality with Jesus. Far from that! Ephesians 5:23 and Colossians 1:18 remind us that Jesus is the Head of the Church. We, adopted sons of God by the atoning grace of Christ, are to be under subjection to Him. Although He took upon Himself a body of clay in order to identify with us so as to be our Perfect Sacrifice, He yet remains The Very God of the Universe.

Jesus took this mantle of humanity upon Himself. In that He was able to die as the Perfect Representative of fallen humanity. "For he hath made him to be sin for us, who knew no sin; that we might be made the righteousness of God in him." (II Corinthians 5:21) Make no mistake. Jesus did not become a sinner. Rather, He took fully upon Himself the weight of our sin and died to make the atonement for us. This we could never have done for ourselves.

We were sinners by nature and had no "goodness" by which we might have approached God to beg forgiveness. Jesus, who had no sin, was able to act in the office of Mediator. He approached the Throne of Grace on our behalf and applied His shed blood to our account. He stands before The Father and pronounces us forgiven and cleansed. We are no longer of a sin nature; we are considered perfect in the nature of Christ.

If we are honest with ourselves we will say that we are not perfect. Jesus disagrees with our assessment. He says that His Blood has cleansed us from all sin and we stand perfect, even within our faults, because of Him when we have accepted Him as our Savior. "...the blood of Jesus Christ his Son cleanseth us from all sin." (I John 1:7)]

2.12 *Saying, I will declare thy name unto my brethren, in the midst of the church will I sing praise unto thee.*

[I would invite the reader to read the entire twenty-second Psalm from which this quotation is taken. As with the fifty-third chapter of Isaiah, there can be no doubt but that this Psalm applies little to David. This is a Messianic Psalm which prophecies of the Savior.

The first part of this Psalm recounts the sufferings of Jesus while He was upon the Cross. Here in the twenty-second verse, as quoted, the Savior begins to exalt in His victory at the Cross of Calvary.

Once again, Paul was writing an "apologetic." This is a theological term which refers to a defense of a Biblical position – it is not to be confused with any sort of "apology." The position which Paul was defending was that Jesus had taken upon Himself a human body during the time of His earthly ministry. This was a necessary accouterment for Him to die as The Perfect Sacrifice for mankind.

The Jew, looking from his Old Testament trained view of spiritual reality, would have trouble understanding this concept since he would view the angels as superior to men. They, after all, had access to the Heavenly realm of eternity. This, coupled with the purpose of the angel to be a messenger for God, made it difficult for them to understand the incarnation of Jesus.

Paul could have used New Testament words of Jesus (examples: Matthew 25:40; 28:10; Luke 8:21; John 20:17) to support this claim. Instead, in deference to the trained Jewish mind of the time, Paul appeals to an Old Testament passage to bolster his teaching about the incarnation of Jesus.

Psalm 22:22 records this statement as prophetically attributed to Jesus: "I will declare thy name unto my brethren: in the midst of the congregation will I praise thee." Here in an Old Testament passage Jesus claims redeemed humanity as His brethren. He identifies with us.

Both "congregation" (Hebrew: qahal) and "church" (Greek: ekklesia) mean assembly.

Jesus did praise His Father (example: John 17:26 during His "high priestly prayer") often and in public. Since there was a hymn sung after the establishment of "the Lord's Table," (Matthew 26:20) there seems to have been a habit of praising the Lord with song. (Psalm 28:7; 40:3; 69:30; 108:1; 149:1; Isaiah 42:10)

As an addendum, I do strongly believe in the primacy of preaching. When properly administered this is both a call to the unconverted and a calling to the Christian to learn more of God and to equip for service in the Lord.

However, as a practical matter I believe that the worship service is the song service where the congregation is engaged in praising the Lord. By this I do not mean the "Praise Service" of the modern churches. I've been in churches where the "Praise Band" serves more as entertainment than as worship aid. I speak instead of the music service where the congregation is involved. The praise of their lips is truly a personal worship in a public setting.]

2.13 And again, I will put my trust in him. And again, Behold I and the children which God hath given me.

["And again" is mentioned twice when referring to Scriptural passages. There is a lesson in this place for anyone who presumes to speak the Words of God into the world of men. Never "skimp" on the Scripture. Therein is the power of God. (Romans 1:16)

There is a mode of travel used in many sports called "the boxer's shuffle." It is to slide the feet from side to side while never "crossing" the feet. To "cross the feet," or to put one foot behind the other in close proximity, is to lose the solid balance of proper footing. When the boxer does this it becomes easier for his opponent to knock him off his balance. When the football or basketball player does this it is much more difficult to hold balance while shifting position.

The solid ground of Scripture is our "point of balance" in all things spiritual. Our own words and devices are easily overcome by the adversary. He can "trip us up" in our testimony and witness. When we stand firmly on the solid ground of Scripture we become unassailable. We become useful to our Lord. Even the seeming setback when we are "on point" in Scripture will witness rewards at a later time as the Lord blesses His words.

Isaiah 55:11 tells us, "So shall my word be that goeth forth out of my mouth: it shall not return unto me void, but it shall accomplish that which I please, and it shall prosper in the thing whereto I sent it." The Scripture is the very Words from the Mouth of God. The Scripture is not a nebulous "concept" which is subject to the whims of the interpretation of man. The Scripture is the very Words of God.

It is not the construct of mysticism to say that when we speak Scripture we speak the very Words of God. It is spiritual reality.

The passage in this verse pictures the duality of the Divine/human nature of Jesus. In His humanity He always exhibited a full trust in The Father.

The concept is illustrated at the grave of Lazarus. In the eleventh chapter of John, verses 41 and 42 Jesus says this, "Father, I thank thee that thou hast heard me. And I knew that thou hearest me always: but because of the people which stand by I said it, that they may believe that thou hast sent me."

Jesus was actually in a body like unto our own. While He was in this human body He always acted as an example of the way in which we should act and react. This explains the second passage (Isaiah 8:18) to which Paul referred in this verse. The redeemed children of God (see verse 10 above), are shown to also be able to act in this manner as did Jesus as they are energized by the Spirit.]

***2.14** Forasmuch then as the children are partakers of flesh and blood, he also himself likewise took part of the same; that through death he might destroy him that had the power of death, that is, the devil,*

[Jesus came to this earth to defeat death. He defeated death on that first Easter Morning when He simply walked out of His tomb. He has also defeated death for us. Death looms as a big terror. We spend hours and years dreading its visit. Why? It is through the medium of physical death that we move to the spiritual realm where we can never die.

I didn't tell my wife when I was coming home from the war in Viet Nam. I wanted to surprise her. But, when the airplane touched down at the little airport in our town, there was Linda waiting for me in the terminal. "How did you find out I was coming home tonight?" I asked her. She replied, "I didn't. I just knew you'd be coming home soon so I've been coming out every night to meet you." Death is the airplane that takes us to the waiting Savior. Better, He is our Companion through the flight.

In the incarnation Jesus took upon Himself a real body. This was, of course, so that He could become the representative sacrifice for us all. His body was so real that He was able to die. Through this death and resurrection Jesus was able to defeat death for all who would accept Him as Savior.

Jesus became man for us. He was tempted just like us. But, He did not sin. That gives Him the standing to be our Savior. Still, the fact that He was tempted gives Him the unique ability to understand our problems as He has shared our humanity.

Jesus is shown as having had an existence prior to Bethlehem. That He took upon himself "flesh and blood" means that He was existent in a form which was not "flesh and blood" at some point prior to His humanity. Carrying this point out to the logical conclusion we must admit that Jesus had the power to modify, or expand, His mode of existence at His Own volition. This demands that we must consider Jesus as God. As we have seen in the pages from Scripture, that point prior was eternity and that other form was, and still is, as the God of Creation.

For the God of Creation to take upon Himself the body and likeness of humanity is called "the mystery of Godliness" in I Timothy 3:16. Jesus came into humanity with the express purpose of giving up the life of that humanity as a sacrifice for fallen humans. He gave us the opportunity to be saved from our burden of sin and to have peace and fellowship with God. He then took up once again the life of that mortal body to fully defeat the power of sin, Satan, and death. Jesus Christ died in time so that we could live in eternity.

Such a construct is only possible for One Who is the Son of God and God, the Son.]

2.15 *And deliver them who through fear of death were all their lifetime subject to bondage.*

[Here is shown the power of the sacrifice of Jesus. He became a man so that He could deliver us from the curse of sin. All mankind, the Jew with the knowledge of revelation and a law which was beyond his capacity to fulfill, and also the Gentile who had no real revelation of God; that Gentile saw his view of God as a vindictive tyrant waiting any chance to pounce upon the defenseless man, dreaded the eventuality of certain death.

The atheist will argue that when the electrical processes of the brain cease there is oblivion. Yet he still finds a compelling need to rant against the very God which he denies exists. Even the atheist knows in the dark recesses of his intellectual dishonestly, that God exists and life continues past the signing of the "death certificate" by the attending physician.

There remains in this day a dread of the process of death. We dread the physical pain and the emotional pain of the experience upon ourselves and our loved ones. The unsaved dread the unknown loneliness of the grave. Even the most altruistic of the unsaved understand on some level that they are going unprepared to a judgment at the bar of God.

These dreads, which are a bondage of fear and dismay are benevolent in their processes. By these men may be lead to find a preparation for the certain eventuality of his soul's departure. This is also a dread which will serve to detour the likelihood of suicide during the severest trials of life.

Religion serves as a crutch for many as they deal with the certainty of their own mortality. Sadly, the religious rites and ceremonies of man's religion will only fail in their attempts to still the guilt of the heart. Worse, these will fail to offer succor at the judgment seat of Christ.

Atheism is another form of "religion" generated by mankind. It can provide neither answers to the reality of mortality nor any real hope. Like the small child who hides behind his hands, "If I can't see you, you can't see me!," atheism is a cruel hoax which lacks reality. It is a philosophy of life which is based only on a negative. "If God does not really exist I can live with impunity toward others and myself."

Ah; but God does exist. We are to be righteously judged by Him. The concept of our impunity is a cup filled with an elixir far more deadly than the hemlock offered Socrates. In this cup there is a poison which will send a soul to a state of eternal misery and regret.

Religion can never help. Only Jesus offers and escape from the endless "hamster wheel" of dread over sin. He, Alone, can set us free.]

2.16 *For verily he took not on him the nature of angels; but he took on him the seed of Abraham.*

[Vv. 16 – 17. As an angel, or in His full Glory of Deity, Jesus would not have been representative of us. He came as a man, to minister to man, so that He might become the Perfect Sacrifice for the sins of man.

Angels are created beings of the heavenly and eternal realm. Some of the angels did sin in relation to the sin of Lucifer. There is no salvation offered them. There is no sacrifice given for them. There is no hope for the angels which left their first estate as created beings who were to be dedicated to the service of their Sovereign Lord.

Humanity is a created being of the realm of physicality and time. He also sinned against The Holy God. This same God, in the human/Divine Person of Jesus, the Christ, became one of them – although completely without sin or even propensity to sin – in order to become the only possible effective remedy for sin.

"But when the fulness of the time was come, God sent forth his Son, made of a woman, made under the law, To redeem them that were under the law, that we might receive the adoption of sons." (Galatians 4:4-5) Jesus came into the world as fully a human being in order to identify His great sacrifice with us.

Jesus came voluntarily as a "son of Abraham" – a Jew. He placed Himself under the Law of Moses so that He could perfectly fulfill that Law. He died completely guiltless under the Law in order that He might apply His perfections to our lives.

At the cross, having given our sins to Jesus, we – the guilty – are considered as not guilty at the judicial bar of the judgment of God. We are free because Jesus obtained our freedom by taking our place at the Cross of Judgment.]

2.17 *Wherefore in all things it behoved him to be made like unto his brethren, that he might be a merciful and faithful high priest in things pertaining to God, to make reconciliation for the sins of the people.*

[Once again, we see that Jesus came to offer sacrifice so that we could be saved. In order for Him to do this, He became one of us. He died in our place. In order to do this, it was necessary that He be one of us.

Jesus came to this earth to understand mankind. Now, there is no question that God understands man and always has. After all, God is the Creator of mankind. This of which we are speaking at this time is more for our benefit. Jesus actually experienced those things, and those temptations, which we experience. He was tired. He was hungry. He was betrayed and deserted by those closest to Him. He knows our problems and when we take our hurts and needs to Him, He is able to give us comfort. We needed this.

As an angel, or in His full Glory of Deity, Jesus would not have been representative of us. He came as a man, to minister to man, so that He might become the Perfect Sacrifice for the sins of man.

The purpose of a priest is to bring the needs of man to God. It is the prophet who brings the Words of God to man. Jesus has fulfilled, of course, both offices.]

2.18 *For in that he himself hath suffered being tempted, he is able to succour them that are tempted.*

[Jesus was willing to take upon Himself this human body so that He might offer salvation to humanity. "Oh, How He loved you and me," the old song says. We cannot fathom a percentage of His great love!

Jesus was tempted. He was tempted in a state of physical weakness after a long fast. As we read the incident of His temptation in the fourth chapter of Matthew we are struck with the fact that Jesus never simply said "Be gone" to the tempter. He had the full authority of His Divinity at His command. He could have done so but did not do so. Rather, Jesus reacted in His humanity. He answered as an example of the way we must also answer temptation. He appealed to every temptation with an appeal to the inspired and preserved Scripture.

For us to be so familiar with the Scripture so as to be able to quote a pertinent passage at a pernicious time would be well for us. Let us study the Scripture, as directed by that same Scripture, in order that we may always emulate our Savior. (II Timothy 2:15)

He lived as a man to be our example. He died as a man to be our Savior.]

HEBREWS - CHAPTER THREE

3.1 *Wherefore, holy brethren, partakers of the heavenly calling, consider the Apostle and High Priest of our profession, Christ Jesus;*

[vv. 1-4. Some may see some confusion by the title of "Apostle" being given to Jesus. The word "apostle" simply means "one who is sent." Since Jesus was sent forth by the Father the term is properly applied. The term is higher than "messenger" however. The term is used of one who is an "ambassador." He is still sent; but the designation is higher than that of the Angel who was sent as mere messenger.

Having already described Jesus as superior to the angels, Paul now begins to show that Jesus also superior to Moses. While Abraham is always considered as the "father" of the Jewish race, it is Moses who is considered the great law-giver of the Jew.

Moses was a faithful worker in the house, that is the church (Both the Old Testament Jewish and the New Testament Christian assemblies are "churches" in the sense that they are "called out" of the world for a specific purpose by God.), but Jesus built the house as He is the Creator, or Ultimate Builder, of all things. In this verse the human penman of Hebrews clearly and plainly shows Jesus to be God.

Aaron was the priest. With the death of Moses it was the prophets who assumed the God-given responsibility of presenting the Words of God to the people of God. With the death of Aaron it was his sons who took up the duty of petitioning God for the people. Jesus is shown to be superior to both by His assumption of the role of both prophet, in that He instituted the knowledge and fact of the Christian religion into humanity, and priest, in that He is the mediator between the people and The Father.

The Jew to whom Paul wrote would have considered the High Priest to also be the "Apostle of God" in that his office was considered as placed upon him by God. Paul uses this symbolism which was familiar to his audience; in this he further shows that Jesus is the High Priest, or "Minister," of our own calling in salvation.

Note that the beginning of the verse speaks of "holy brethren." Paul has been arguing against some deeply held beliefs of his intended Jewish audience. Still, he acknowledges that they are brethren in the faith. Since Paul was "brother" in his Jewishness, he adds to word "holy" to highlight the fact that his argument has to do with the Christian. He further emphasizes this fact by acknowledging that they are also partakers of the heavenly calling of the Christian. Thus the religion of Jesus in the New Covenant is shown to be superior to the religion of the Jew of the Old Covenant.

The Old Testament system of obeying the Law in minute detail has been superseded by the fulfillment of that Law, every jot and tittle thereof, by the New Testament Law of freedom given to the converted soul at the Cross of Calvary and the resurrection of Jesus from the grave. This is further shown by the superiority of Jesus to Moses.

This is needful in that the Jew considered himself as a member of a called people due to their special relationship to the Law and God through Abraham. However, the calling of the Jew from the bondage in Egypt was an earthly calling. The Christian is the possessor of a heavenly calling from the bondage of sin.

We are asked to consider, or think upon, the glories of Jesus. He is dignified by His glory as God. He is Holy beyond that of any other person; even the most "religious" person cannot equate the holiness of Jesus. We should consider His sufferings, His death for us, His resurrection, His ascension, His present position of power at the right hand of The Father, His office as Mediator for us, and more! In doing this we will find ourselves drawn to Him. This, in turn, will cause us to grow in grace.]

3.2 *Who was faithful to him that appointed him, as also Moses was faithful in all his house.*

[Matthew 26:30 is one of the most precious passages in all of Scripture. Jesus was in the Garden with His apostles. His purpose seems to have been to have a "fellowship prayer meeting." The apostles slept as Jesus awaited the coming of the troops to take Him captive and deliver Him up to the tender mercies of the Sanhedrin.

He knew that the next few hours would see Him deserted by those closest to Him. He would observe that Peter would deny Him. He would endure a physical torture that would only end with His death upon the Cross of Calvary. Before this there would be merciless beatings and taunting. He would see His mother horrified by the events.

In His agony at these prospects Jesus said, "If it can be done, let the cup of these atrocities pass from me." In His humanity Jesus balked at the stark reality that would engulf Him. Then, in His humanity, Jesus looked at the need of the world – at our need – and said, "Not my will but thine."

Jesus did not go to the cross whistling a happy tune. Jesus knew that horror that awaited Him. He went anyway. He went for you. He went for me. He went, in His humanity, in deference to The Father's will.

He was faithful to His assigned and accepted task which had been set before the first man had even been created. (Revelation 13:8) That was a mere day in eternity. It must have seemed an eternity in the Day of His Affliction.

When comparing Moses with Jesus, Paul did not spare any of the honor due Moses. Paul admitted that Moses was a great man. When Paul says that Moses was faithful in all his house he is looking at Numbers 12:6-8 – "And he said, Hear now my words: If there be a prophet among you, I the LORD will make myself known unto him in a vision, and will speak unto him in a dream. My servant Moses is not so, who is faithful in all mine house. With him will I speak mouth to mouth, even apparently, and not in dark speeches; and the similitude of the LORD shall he behold: wherefore then were ye not afraid to speak against my servant Moses?"

Moses is higher in dignity than any prophet of any time. Even in understanding that all Moses did was under the assignment and control of God, we see Moses as the giver of the Law, the ceremonies of the Law, the civil law of the nation of Israel, and the leadership which forged this group of runaway slaves into a mighty nation under God.

Moses was faithful to his *house*. This was not a house of wood or brick. This was a people. They were the house of Abraham, the house of Isaac, the house of Jacob and his twelve sons... This was the house of God into the world at large.

Moses even prophesied that God would send another "Moses" to these people. Deuteronomy 18:15 records, "The LORD thy God will raise up unto thee a Prophet from the midst of thee, of thy brethren, like unto me; unto him ye shall hearken."

Jesus was the Prophet to come. Jesus taught the laws of His Religion. They were the fulfillment of those ceremonies as shown by Moses. Jesus taught but two ceremonies for His Church. One is baptism which is not a ceremony whereby favor with God is gained but a picture whereby the favor which God has already shown is displayed in this picture of the death, burial and resurrection of the Lord Jesus Christ.

The only other ordinance of the churches which Jesus founded is The Lord's Table. Once again, this is not a ceremony whereby one gains any grace from God. This is, as is baptism, a ceremony of remembrance of the great grace God has already displayed in the Sacrifice of Jesus on the Cross of Calvary. It is a picture of His body broken for us and His blood shed for the remission of our sins.

Moses did not sacrifice. Aaron was the priest who, with his lineage, prepared and performed sacrifice for the people. Jesus sacrificed Himself for our sins.]

3.3 *For this man was counted worthy of more glory than Moses, inasmuch as he who hath builded the house hath more honour than the house.*

Genesis 28:3; Acts 7:35-38

[You will note that Moses is given his full respect and due. He is called a great man. But, he is shown to be inferior to Jesus. Notice the difference between Moses and Jesus. Moses, a human instrument of God, is credited as being part of the "house" of God. This is in reference to the house of Abraham.

Jesus is cited as the "builder" of the house. In other words, Jesus is shown to stand outside the structure of even Israel. He is shown, although born into the race of man as a Jew, to be the Founder and Constructor of the Jewish people.

This trait shows Jesus to be more than simply another human being. He is shown to be God.

In this passage Jesus is said to have more honor than Moses. Moses was a great leader of Israel. Jesus is the Creator of Israel. This puts Jesus in control of the affairs of man about fifteen hundred years before the events of Bethlehem. This passage speaks both the eternality of Jesus and His power to dictate the affairs of men and nations. Therefore, Jesus is God.]

3.4 *For every house is builded by some man; but he that built all things is God.*

[First a little history from the eleventh chapter of Genesis: Noah begat Shem. Shem begat Arphaxad. Arphaxad begat Salah. Salah begat Eber. Eber begat Peleg. Peleg begat Reu. Reu begat Serug. Serug begat Nahor. Nahor begat Terah. Terah begat Abram. Abram begat Isaac. Isaac begat Jacob. When we speak of the sons of Abram, or the house of Abraham, we are considering him as the founder of a line of people. But, we are overlooking the fact that Abraham was the son of Terah, etc., etc., etc.

When we say that the kingdom of Judah always had a man from the house of David to sit upon their throne, where do we consider Jesse, the father of David?

Every "house" – when considered as a lineage which is the meaning of the word in this passage – was built by someone else back to the time of Noah and his three sons. Extrapolating further back we must begin at Adam.

Moses must be given his great honor in his labors in the house of Abraham. But greater honor must be given to Jesus. Of Jesus it is said, "All things were made by him, and without him was not any thing made that was made." (John 1:3) As Creator

Jesus founded every house of man in the created world of humanity.]

3.5 *And Moses verily was faithful in all his house, as a servant, for a testimony of those things which were to be spoken after;*

[Moses was completely faithful to the task to which he was appointed. The Old Testament Scriptures constantly refer to Moses as "the servant of God." (examples: Exodus 14:31; Joshua 1:1; 9:24; I Kings 8:56; II Kings 6:4; II Chronicles 24:9; Nehemiah 10:29; Psalm 105:26; Daniel 9:11) Moses is never described as founder or owner of the Hebrew people.

Every ordinance given by Moses was first given to him by God. Moses did not originate the Hebrew religion; he only transmitted it faithfully from God. Moses only spoke the Truth as God gave the Truth. This Truth was part of the progressive revelation of God and thus was later expanded, not overcome or denied, by the reality of Jesus as The fulfillment of those ordinances and prophecies of Moses. Every ordinance was a type of the ministry of He Who was to come.]

3.6 *But Christ as a son over his own house; whose house are we, if we hold fast the confidence and the rejoicing of the hope firm unto the end.*

[Moses was a servant who worked in the house of another. Jesus is the Son, the heir, to Whom all belongs. Jesus is not a servant in His Own house. He is the Lord, Master, and Heir of all.

Paul was writing to Jewish believers. When he mentions that we are of the house of Jesus he has issued a twofold statement. First of all, as Jews the people – Paul included – were of the house of Abraham and thus the chosen people of the Covenant of God. Secondly, through the new birth, they were all the adopted children of God by reason of the death, burial and resurrection of Jesus, the Messiah.

Commenting on this verse, Barnes has said that, "No evidence can be strong enough to prove that a man is a Christian, unless it leads him to persevere to the end of life." This is not a statement to suggest that salvation could be lost. Salvation is all the work of Jesus Christ. To argue that a man could "lose" his salvation is to argue that man has control over salvation rather than God exercising that control. (John 6:27; II Corinthians 1:22; Ephesians 1:13; 4:30)

Since Scripture cannot be made to argue against Scripture. God has decreed that salvation is fully His Own Work. (Ephesians 2:8-9) Any work done for God is only possible after salvation. (Ephesians 2:10)

What Paul is referencing in this verse is the propensity to apostatize from the faith. That is "from the faith" not removing oneself from the Hand of God. "And I give unto them eternal life; and they shall never perish, neither shall any man pluck them out of my hand." (John 10:28) The phrase, "no man" would have to include an individual's own actions. If this were otherwise the phrase would be "neither shall any but a man himself pluck himself out of my hand."

Consider that in the eleventh chapter of I Corinthians, verse 30, Paul is speaking of those who would dishonor the Lord's Table. "For this cause many are weak and sickly among you, and many sleep." This points up the Spiritual Principle of God's discipline of His saints. (Deuteronomy 8:5; Proverbs 13:24; Hebrews 12:6-7) When we consider that the Christian has been reborn as an adoptive child of God (John 1:12,

Romans 8:15; 8:23; 9:4; Galatians 4:5, Ephesians 1:5) we can easily see two things. First, we are become the children of God at the moment of the washing of regeneration at the Cross. (Titus 3:5) The Blood of Jesus cleanses us from our sins to the extent that there is no more condemnation. (Romans 8:1)

Second, we are judicially children of God due to that adoptive action. Therefore He is righteous, and considers it to our own spiritual good, in this discipline He brings forth upon us due to His displeasure with us over our shortcomings. Note that this is discipline, not banishment. This disciple will either follow a return to proper conduct and actions on our part as a Christian or will lead to God removing us from this life in order to spare our soul further discipline and to keep pure in light of His Own purposes of calling others to salvation. We do not have the right to attempt, by our own actions, to impede His holy will and purposes.

Those who do not see this discipline in their lives are not saved. God, not being in such a case their adoptive Father, will not discipline but allow them to "fill the cup of their own iniquity." One of the proofs of His love for us is shown in the "woodshed experience." (Proverbs 3:12; Hebrews 12:6)]

3.7   Wherefore (as the Holy Ghost saith, To day if ye will hear his voice,

[One of my sources argued that everything between "wherefore" and the beginning of verse twelve is not essential to the primary purpose of Paul in this place. Folks, all of the Words of God are always important. Milton Bearl, the great personality of early television, once said that it was not necessary that every joke be a good joke. "You can slip in a little 'slurp' and the people will laugh at it because they are in the mood to laugh. It's just 'filler' that tends to fill the time for the show."

The Words of God are concise and important. Every single one of those Words of God is important. God does not use "filler." The inspiration of the Words of God gives the very Words of God. All of them are important.

The "wherefore" used here is an allusion to the fact that the Gospel of Jesus is superior to Moses and the Law. This is something to which we must pay attention. This is more than a matter of politeness in listening to the Spirit; this is a matter of importance to our own souls and lives.

Nonetheless we have a need to realize that Paul is accessing an Old Testament event to teach a New Testament principle. This is important. Nearly every event in the Old Testament is a physical picture of a spiritual truth we need to understand.

The concept of "today" is an important concept. We do not know when yesterday will have been our last day on earth. As I was driving my grandson home from his "cross country" practice we passed an area where people had erected a memorial to a nineteen-year-old boy, barely out of high school, who had died a few weeks prior in a traffic accident.

None of us have any guarantee of another day in this life. It is vitally important that we listen, and heed, the Gospel message today. Tomorrow may be much too late. Tomorrow may have seen the Rapture take place. Tomorrow is not promised to us.

It is interesting to note that this passage is a quotation of Psalm 95:7. This is a Psalm of David. Paul says that the Holy Spirit spoke these Words. Folks, we do not have the option of "picking and choosing" which Words and passages of Scripture we accept. It is all from God and it is all to us for our instruction in the faith.

We must accept all of the Scripture or refuse part of the leading of God. Either we follow Him fully or we reject Him fully. There is no middle ground.]

3.8 *Harden not your hearts, as in the provocation, in the day of temptation in the wilderness:*

[A recurring theme in Hebrews is the warning against apostasy. Apostasy is not mere unbelief. It is to consider the things of God, perhaps to be moved by the thought of His grace, and to depart from this. It is to renounce the leading of the Spirit and reaffirm allegiance to Satan.

This is illustrated by the Israelites in the wilderness. They had seen the mighty power of God in the defeat of Pharaoh's armies at the Red Sea. Despite this they were constantly murmuring against God and Moses throughout their journeys toward the Land of Promise.

The children of Israel murmured about not having bread in Exodus 16:4. In response to this need God provided them Manna to eat. This is a picture of His provision.

The children of Israel murmured about being thirsty in Exodus 17:2-9. In this they actually questioned whether God was really with them. God responded to this by supplying water out of a rock. We do note that the rock was struck by the rod of Moses. This points out the flow of the Spirit into the Church. The water came from the rock that was smitten by the rod of Moses. Likewise, Jesus was wounded (Isaiah 53:4-6) for our sin. He both meets the needs of our soul and has sent the Holy Spirit to lead and guide us. From the "Rock of our faith" came the Comforter in our faith.

The children of Israel built an idol of a golden calf. This particular idol was a symbol with which Israel would have been well familiar as this was one of the "gods" of the Egyptians. This sacrilege of the people was met with the further revelation of the Decalogue. God provided the means of proper worship to a people seeped in a false worship. Once again we see God calling people from the false and to the true.

Even with the ongoing miracle of the manna the children of Israel cried that they had no meat to eat. (Exodus 11:4-5) God sent them their hearts desire by sending quail for them to eat. Along with their choice of food God sent a plague upon them. (Exodus 11:33) This is definitely a lesson for the Christian of this day. When the people reject the spiritual food of God He may allow them to feed upon the food of their choice. This rejection of God's plan for man's plan will cause spiritual illness to follow.

This is a thing to be considered when we reject feeding on the inspired and preserved Words of God and begin to stuff our spirit with the empty calories of the words of man in the weak translation of the false texts of man. The true Meat of the Word is found only in the Manna of God's gift to us. It will never be found, in its fullness, in the quail gathered only by the hands of man.

We may recall that God did allow Pharaoh to harden his heart to the things of God. (Exodus 8:15) We must consider that God did not force Pharaoh to reject the Words of God. That predisposition was already within the heart of Pharaoh as it is in the heart of every man born of man and woman. The nature of sin, inherited from Adam, is an assurance that this will always happen. It is only the acceptance of the leading, and the acceptance of the wooing, of the Holy Spirit which may overcome this inclination of man.

It is this rejection of the Holy Spirit which causes the hardening of the heart toward the voice and leading of God.]

3.9 *When your fathers tempted me, proved me, and saw my works forty years.*

[The next provocation of Israel was in their refusal to accept the commission of God to move forward and march into the land of His promise. Their refusal was predicated upon their fear of man being stronger than their trust in God.

Twelve spies had been sent into the land. This is a wise move. It is always a wise move to consider the enemy and be prepared under prayer to meet and defeat him. Ten of the twelve spies considered the enemy and found him stronger than God in their estimation. The other two, Joshua and Caleb, found the enemy strong but found God to be stronger.

There was a total refusal to follow the order of God to move into the land. The result of this was that the entire generation was not allowed to enter into the land which the Lord had promised and prepared for them.

It is very important to realize that those who died in the wilderness remained of Israel. Their loss was of the reward of the rest in the Promised Land. They were not "disfellowshipped" from their national identity. They remained "of the people" even in their sin and loss at their lack of faith. Born into the "house of Abraham," they did not lose the distinction of their national identity even as they did suffer the loss of the reality of the promise in their own lives.

The purposes of God were worked out in the discipline of this generation. A new generation arose which saw the power of God and counted His power as the power in which they would march into His promises.]

3.10 *Wherefore I was grieved with that generation, and said, They do alway err in their heart; and they have not known my ways.*

[We can argue that God is not touched by like emotions as are humans. This is so, of course. But, we must consider that one of the paramount things in relation to the attributes of God is His great love. After God had prepared so much for the people of Israel their rejection of Him and His preparations would serve to grieve Him. Consider Ephesians 4:30 in context with this.

This particular generation had strained their relationship with the God of the Covenant. It is said that they do "alway" err in their heart. This is more than a simple "life-style" which is opposed to the things of God. This is such a constant error that it has crowded out any consideration of responding in faith to the love of God. It is even deeper than "always;" it moves beyond the simple always of time and becomes a consistency of the purposes of their lives.

We may look at this phrase "they have not known my ways" in two considerations. First, they had never taken the time to actually attempt to walk in His ways. They had not known what it was to walk in the paths of the Lord.

Second, they had never even tried to understand just what His ways were. This is a lack of even a basic consideration of God, Himself. This reality points out a lack of searching the Scripture. When we fail to consider the Words of God as worthy of perusal we can never find any real understanding of what it is that we should do in relation to our walk with Him.

As an illustration of this reality I would ask that we consider the persecution of Christians in the world today. We of my native land have never experienced real persecution. We might have read about this reality in a book or in a news report. But, we have never known it for ourselves.

I firmly believe that the day is soon coming in which we will suffer real persecution. I am not considering the jeers of man and the excesses of state. I am considering real persecution where the blood of the saints will run in the streets. If things continue as they are we will be "re-educated." Our children will be indoctrinated to hate the things of Christ. They may be removed from our care as a state sponsored "antidote" to our teaching of things Biblical. We may even suffer actual martyrdom. Most of these realities are probable with the current situation of our nation and world. Martyrdom is a serious possibility if present trends continue. We need to dedicate ourselves to Scripture and serious prayer. We need to stand for the Lord.

Failure in these things is not a viable option for the Christian.]

3.11   So I sware in my wrath, They shall not enter into my rest.)

[Many of the commentators I consulted considered this rest to be typical of Heaven. I disagree. The purpose of coming into the Land of Promise was to be a rest. But, it was to be a rest on the realized promises of God to direct, protect and empower His people. To see this as a type of Heaven is to misrepresent the entire exodus experience.

Egypt had been a type of the bondage of the human to sin. Sin had so enslaved the people that they could not but petition the Pharaoh for permission to leave. That this permission was only granted via the lie of Pharaoh is evident by the actions of Pharaoh's "palace guard." This was his "personal army" but it was not the entire army of Egypt. Some of these troops were stationed at remote outposts near the boarders. This palace guard followed after the people of Israel with the intent of returning them to servitude or death.

That the people were released at all was not of their own doing. Exodus 7:1 says this of Moses: "And the LORD said unto Moses, See, I have made thee a god to Pharaoh: and Aaron thy brother shall be thy prophet." For a sinner to be removed from the bonds of sin it is necessary that the Words of God (the inspired and preserved Scripture) be preached in some manner. (Romans 10:17) When the Spirit quickens the soul, a person is then able to respond to those Words of God.

The initial exodus was a picture of a person who has been freed from the curse of sin. He is not perfect in himself even as the Israelites failed God over and over in their journey. The entrance into the Land was neither the entrance into salvation (this was already effected in the initial exodus) nor the entrance into Heaven.

Moving into the land the people were expected to fight and defeat the inhabitants of the land. This is not a picture of the "rest" of Heaven. This is a picture of the dedicated Christian life where we dwell with men who would harm our testimony. We fight to overcome the negative testimony which is continually laid in front of our walk. We fight to obtain the good calling and smile of God upon our lives. This is part of our preparation for the greater rest of the Kingdom of Heaven.

The "rest" of these people was a rest from journeying in the wilderness and the rest of fighting the battle of faith, with the leading of the Spirit, to subdue this life under the victory which is given the true soldier of the faith. They no longer had to wander for they had found the land which was promised of God in which to settle.

The argument could also be made that the original group leaving Egypt were not all the "children of God." In this the ones who were not allowed to enter into the rest were not possessors of the promise but only cultural fellow travelers. In this the land of rest would be a type of Heaven only available to those who were true "soldiers of the cross."

I would reject this latter application due to the above considerations of Heaven as a place of rest. Further, I would reject this application because while it is evident that there were some among the group who were not the children of Abraham, these were not the one's expressly refused entrance into the Land. Those who died in the wilderness due to their unbelief in fearing the original inhabitants of the land were of Israel. Their physical deaths did not abrogate this truth. Rather than suggesting that their "salvation" was lost due to their actions, this seems more a prophecy of I Corinthians 11:30.

God does not withhold heaven from His adopted children. He does sometimes call us "home" when we have shown ourselves unfit to witness of Him into all the world. God will disciple His adopted children. In this we must remember that our sins have been so judged at the cross that, "There is therefore now no condemnation to them which are in Christ Jesus, who walk not after the flesh, but after the Spirit." (Romans 8:1)

The very next verse explains that those who have been born again are walking in the Spirit. They no longer walk according to the Law. "For the law of the Spirit of life in Christ Jesus hath made me free from the law of sin and death." (Romans 8:2; see also II Corinthians 5:17)

Obviously, the death spoken of is not physical death. The death spoken of is spiritual death. The Christian, born of the Blood of Jesus Christ into a new life, is free from this consideration. The penalty has already been paid.]

3.12 *Take heed, brethren, lest there be in any of you an evil heart of unbelief, in departing from the living God.*

[We must consider that Paul is speaking of apostatizing from the Truth of the message of God. It is possible to apostatize from the faith only if our ultimate definition of "faith" is something which we hold. Indeed, there are many days that we might not "feel" very saved, or close to God.

A baseball player may be a very good baseball player by everyone's standard. However, he may go 0 for 5 with five strikeouts on any given night. Would this mean that he was no longer a professional baseball player? Of course not. One bad game does not change the fact that the man has a contract which pays him x amount of dollars to put on the uniform and play the game. His feelings have nothing to do with the fact shown by the man who holds his contract.

Brethren, God holds our contract of eternal life. It is issued upon the full credit of Jesus Christ as issued by His Blood on the Cross of Calvary. If we have signed that contract by accepting Him as Savior we are bound by the contract. Let us never overlook the fact that He is likewise bound by His Own honor to that contract. Let us never be in the position of demeaning God by doubting His honor. Our salvation is eternally secure because the Words of God are always eternally secure.

Looking back at the Old Testament illustration, what was the root cause and result of the unbelief of both the ten spies who brought an evil report and the generation of Israel which "bought" the evil report?

The cause was to look at the men who would oppose them and believe that they were so strong as to do battle with and defeat the God of Israel. It was a fear that, as J. B. Phillips once put it, "Their God was too small." Was God too small to defeat the enemy? Of course not? The false belief of the "lost generation" simply refused to look at all the facts and accept that God is All and over all!

The result was that this lost generation was denied the possibility of facing this arrayed enemy and defeating him in battle. Such fear, among the army, would grow and affect other soldiers. It could not be tolerated in the time of battle. Therefore, these were not allowed to go forward into battle. The army of Gideon is another example of this same paradigm of faith. Simply put: doubt tends to weaken faith. Unbelief is a lack of confidence in the God of the Universe.

The problem at the time Paul was writing, especially among the Jewish Christian congregations, was a refusal to consider that all of those Old Testament services and types had been fulfilled in Christ and were no longer part of the economy of the Age of Grace. There was a dangerous tendency to downgrade the sufficiency of Jesus by adding again those symbols and types to the pure religion of the cross and resurrection.

This would have added the works of man to the concept of faith in Jesus. Such would disallow saving faith which is predicated on the completeness of the sacrifice of Jesus on the Cross of Calvary.

In doing so the church would have removed from Jesus His honor. This is, by definition, a departure from God. (John 12:44)

This unbelief is recognized as an "evil heart." This same phrase is used in Jeremiah 16:12. "And ye have done worse than you fathers; for, behold, ye walk every one after the imagination of his evil heart, that they may not hearken unto me." This will keep one from God. But, by extension of the influence of such a one upon others, this will impede the Message of salvation among the wider world. Our doubts destroy not only our own peace but also destroy the very concept and conduct of our witness into the world. Unbelief does more than dilute any witness to faith; it destroys any compulsion to carry forth that witness.

Our current widespread unbelief concerning the preservation of the Scripture has destroyed the faith and practice of the churches. We no longer see any "church calling nights" partially because we do not recognize a compelling faith. Neither do others see a convicting faith within the churches. The church has lost her power.

The Christian, for the vast majority of those who still bear the name, are denied their entrance into battle by their own lack of Biblical faith. As churches in these "post Christian" times, we are no longer winning ground; we are treading water!]

3.13 *But exhort one another daily, while it is called To day, lest any of you be hardened through the deceitfulness of sin.*

[When we hear this word "exhort" we are tended to translate it in our minds into "preaching." No. To exhort is to help others to be enthusiastic in their faith. I haven't been to a basketball game in probably twenty years. When I used to go I generally sat quietly and tried to analyze to moves made by the players and the coaches. I was a terrible fan. Others in the stands would jump up and shake their fists at the referee's calls against their team. These types of fans would incite others to get more involved in the game.

Generally speaking a sporting event is a group event. This holds true for the fans in the stands as much as for the players on the floor or field. That is why the cheering is so loud. This, in turn is why some people go back over and over. They enjoy the comradery of the crowd.

Most people are like that.

It is the same in the assemblies of the Lord. Enthusiasm begets enthusiasm. It is somewhat this concept which is being urged in this verse. We are to encourage others in the faith. That is not just "cheering." Much of this is simply conversation with others. That is a large part of the worship involved in a church service. Christian conversation with others of like faith is an important part of our services.

Paul asks here that we use this fact to encourage others in the doctrines and practices of our faith. Encourage others to see and enjoy the facts of the Lord. This will lead us to enjoy and apply these things to our relationship with Him. Paul asks that we be faithful in this.

This verse presupposes that we are faithful in our church attendance. This is probably one of the most important events in our lives. I was going to write "Christian lives," but I thought better of it. True, worshipful Christianity should never be just a part of our lives. We need the attitude of living for Christ, and with Christ, and in Christ, daily.

By saying "today, while it is called today" Paul is saying that we use whatever resources we have to encourage others in the faith even as we encourage others to come to the faith. Each day will give new opportunities for us to be found useful for the Master.

The problem is that we tend to become hardened to these things. It is so easy to just "sleep in" on one Sunday morning. Then a second Sunday morning. Then a third... It is easy to critique the pastor's sermon. It is easy to just pick up the Sunday school quarterly before church and then put it down. We become jaded. It is so easy.

I saw a man last winter who was shoveling the walk at his home during a blizzard. "It's a losing proposition," I told him. He said, "Yeah; but if I don't keep it up it will be all the harder to do later."

Wise man. He was dedicated to his desire to have a clean walk in front of his house.

Do we even have a dedication to serve the Lord? Is this just something we do because we've always done it?

Paul says that Christians can be hardened by the deceitfulness of sin. The deceitfulness of sin is partly in that it seems so innocuous. It's just a little, one time, thing. Well, maybe we might do it again.

I am diabetic. I should watch this very closely since my grandfather died from the disease. I don't. Just one cinnamon roll. Well, maybe one more. Six cinnamon rolls later I get ready to check my blood sugar. Wow! What happened? Six cinnamon rolls, one at a time, is what happened.

Sin tends to "snowball" unless we flee to the Scripture. Sin tends to overwhelm unless we find our prayer corner. Sin tends to eventually conquer us unless we meet the Master, confess, repent and begin to rejoice in His fellowship.

From the tiny acorn a mighty tree will grow. From the tiny cinnamon roll, repeated over and over, a bathroom scale is ignored!

Let us beware of sin even as we "be wearing" our robes of righteousness as we walk with The King! Take heed that we depart not from the prayer closet, the Scripture reading room, and the fellowship with the Savior. Neither should we neglect fellowship with others of like precious faith!]

3.14 *For we are made partakers of Christ, if we hold the beginning of our confidence stedfast unto the end;*

[We are made partakers of many blessing in Christ. Some of these are temporal: His daily guidance, the closeness of fellowship with Him, His invitation to prayer, peace beyond the world's standards, the call to work with him (consider Peter and Cornelius in the 10th chapter of Acts) in the work of bringing souls to salvation in Christ, the empowerment of the Holy Spirit in times of need, and much more.

These are all dependent upon our obedience and walk with Him. Those of the eternal realms, eternal life, fellowship with God in Heaven, an eternal home in the bliss of Heaven are unconditionally given through our adoption as sons of God.

The idea of holding forth our confidence is a work of man. Such can have no bearing on eternal life. When man sinned in the Garden there was set in motion a series of events predicated on the fact of sin in the creation and perfection in the holiness of eternity. Man cannot access the holiness of God while in a body of the construction of a sin polluted natural world. If such were to happen all hope of salvation would be lost. (Hebrews 6:6) We would become a most desperate and doomed creature. Our only possibility of renewal from sin is the perfection and holiness of the eternal realms to be somehow restored to us in the realm of time and physicality.

Although the fact of perseverance as a "practicing" Christian is the best evidence of a renewed heart, the reality of this evidence is dependent upon the renewing of our hearts at the point of real, Biblical, salvation.

A pious attitude and walk may be indicative of salvation; it is not necessarily the result of such salvation. Many are pious and lost. Many are "religious" and lost. Many are altruistic and lost. Many are genuinely "good" people as the world counts goodness and lost. I could name many cults to which people are attached and committed; they are still lost.

The only certainty of an eternal salvation is the Sacrifice of the eternal Son of God. When we accept Him in faith, He accepts us for eternity. While our life choices may cause us to suffer discipline from The Father, the power of The Son is our assurance of eternal life. Our power of trying to persevere on our own would be to fail miserably.]

3.15 *While it is said, To day if ye will hear his voice, harden not your hearts, as in the provocation.*

[It is a serious thing to ignore the calling of the Holy Spirit. I would not claim the mantle of "five point Calvinism;" but we are not saved of our own choice. No man will willingly come to God while he is still in his sin. (Romans 3:10-12) We are

HEBREWS: Chapter 3

responders to the calling of the Spirit in our salvation. (John 15:16-19; Ephesians 1:4; II Thessalonians 2:13; I Peter 1:2; 1:22; 2:4; Revelation 17:14)

The Holiness people have a phrase, "Crossing the dead line" and "Sinning away the day of grace." I would not say that I completely agree. But, I do know that the reality is that we are saved only when we respond to the calling of the Spirit. We do not approach God because we are sinners and His purity is anathema to our basic nature as human beings. So is our sin nature to Him anathema.

But, His grace is such that the Death of the Savior on the Cross of Calvary has set in motion God's plan of the redemption of many. Not all will be saved. But those who are the called of God are given the opportunity to respond in faith to His call. Even that faith which we are privileged to exercise is a gift from Him. (Ephesians 2:8-9)

Remember the illustration given earlier in this chapter. Not all of Israel was allowed to enter into the land of God's promise because they failed to trust Him. That is a physical event which shows us a spiritual truth. When conviction is felt upon the heart it is time to respond to the Love of God. Tomorrow is another day and we are not guaranteed the Spirit's conviction upon our heart!]

3.16 *For some, when they had heard, did provoke: howbeit not all that came out of Egypt by Moses.*

[It is interesting that Paul says that "some ... did provoke" after hearing the reports of the spies. Read from the simple history of the event almost all were among those who provoked God with their unbelief and lack of trust in His Divine protection and provision.

Clarke champions a change in the text at this place. "There is a various reading here, which consists merely in the different placing of an accent, and yet gives the whole passage a different turn ... But who were those hearers that did bitterly provoke, but all those who came out of Egypt by Moses?" Barnes joins in this supposition.

Sadly, this is the predisposition of far too many theologians and textual critics in our time. "If the plain Words of Scripture seem to cause our human minds to rebel we must change those words to reflect our own scholarship." This was the error of Origen and others who worked to change the pure Scripture into their image rather than changing themselves to reflect the Scripture. It is an error to suppose that Scripture must never speak that which our mortal minds cannot fathom. Are not God's ways above our ways?

Moses changed the Words of God at one point. He struck the rock with his rod to bring forth water for the people. He had done this before at the express command of God. (Exodus 17:6) The problem was that this time the command of God was to speak to the rock. (Numbers 20:8) For this betrayal of the express Word of God, Moses was prohibited from entering into the land of promise. (Deuteronomy 32:49-51)

Moses "knew what to do." So he did it. The problem was that he did in anger what was not the command of God. He followed what he thought was right rather than listening to the Words of God and actually doing what was right.

That is the same problem with the "Bible correctors" of our day. They want a better word than what God has given so they search out a "new" translation from an "old" copy of a long neglected text. Why had the text been neglected if it was the text which was actually blessed of God? Could it be that it is not the text of God. Simple consideration of the purposes of God will find that the God of Love would not have withheld His true text while allowing a false text to reign supreme for a thousand years. Neither would He bless a false text but see His full blessings withdrawn from society when a "corrected" text is raised as the "new standard" in His churches.

Folks, can we really argue that God is blessing society through the "salt" of our witness more in this day than fifty years ago, more than four hundred years ago, when the text of antiquity, the Textus Receptus which underlies our King James Bibles, was held supreme in the pulpits of the day and the hearts of the believers?

We are still left with the question as to why the text says that "some" provoked God when the vast majority were involved in the same sin. I would argue that the purpose is the love of God for His servants. Caleb, Joshua, and most of the Levite class who labored in the Tabernacle did not sin against God by doubting Him. God sees and honors those who see and honor Him.

Even a very few, when they are on the side of God, are the majority. The "some" of unbelief remain in a spiritual minority in their sin.

Not all who came out of Egypt with Moses were allowed to enter the land of rest. Neither was Moses. It is the degree of our faith and willingness to follow God which determines our opportunities for usefulness by Him in the great spiritual warfare of the day. It is His inspired and preserved Words which He uses to prepare us for such empowerment. We are either faithful to Him, and His true Words, are we are provoking Him with unbelief.]

3.17 *But with whom was he grieved forty years? was it not with them that had sinned, whose carcases fell in the wilderness?*

[I can see the crowd of the children of Israel when the spies come back from their inspection of the land of promise. It was wise to send out spies to see what was waiting for the troops when the entered the land.

Two of the spies stand before the group with an anxious look; they are anxious to get back in that land with the rest of the army. "Folks," they cry out, "This is the best-looking land we've ever seen. God has promised to give it to us. All we have to do is walk in and take it. It is already ours because God has promised."

The other ten spies look a little more somber. "It's a great land; no doubt about that! But there is a little problem. These people are giants in there. They are going to kill every one of us if we so much as show our faces."

Ten to two is the score. The people say, "Nope. We can't believe God would send us on such a 'fool's errand.' This wandering has been working out pretty well for a long time. Let's just keep on keeping on. I want my draft deferment because I ain't going!"

I can see the local bands and singers all hurriedly writing protest songs. Look, there's some actress sitting on a Canaanite chariot. She's pretending to shoot arrows at those Hebrew invaders. Papers are being writing about the inadvisability of taking the Word of the Lord to these people; they've got their own gods. They really seem happy in their perversions. There is a group of young Hebrews chanting, "Oh no, I won't go!"

God has judged the "cup of iniquity" of the Canaanites to be full. He is ready to judge them for their sins and immorality. The Hebrew people say, "Not so fast. Sure these people will engage in temple and personal immorality. Sure these people will offer their young children to be burned as sacrifices to their gods. Who are we to judge? They are just making their own life style choices."

The two spies who wanted to follow God are drowned out in the reasonable arguments of those who really didn't want to follow God. "It might be dangerous. It is too hard. It's not too late to head back to Egypt."

This sin was both a lack of trust in the ability of God to fulfill His promises and a lack of conviction that the way of God was the right way. The people had been a sinful group ever since they had crossed the Red Sea on dry ground. They had seen the power of God. They had seen the provision of God in the manna they ate daily. God had always taken care of them.

And, they had always complained that He wasn't taking care of them in the manner to which they wished to become accustomed. Oh, they could do that "Tabernacle thing;" the show was worth the price! But, to really trust God to move into the land of promise? That was a whole 'nother situation!

The "cup of iniquity" of the Hebrew people had just filled itself to the brim. All of that group which had been freed from bondage in Egypt was to perish in the wilderness. Only those men who were under the age of twenty would survive to enter the land.

God was grieved by the attitude of the people. They not only argued with His leading, they argued with His ability to lead. They doubted His power to produce His promises concerning the land of promise.

Despite the lack of faith of these people the program of God continued. However, the program of God continued in the lives of other people. Galatians 5:7 says, "Be not deceived; God is not mocked: for whatsoever a man soweth, that shall he also reap." The crop of a lack of trust in God does not find the fruits of the Spirit. It must be also admitted that the fruit of man is temporal and will rot on the vine.

When a people turn from the true worship of The True God they will find decay in society, government, and in the churches. We will always reap what we have sown. That is a spiritual principle of God. We may not always die in the wilderness but we will never walk in the blessings of God when we sin so deeply as to grieve the Holy Spirit. (Ephesians 4:30)]

3.18 *And to whom sware he that they should not enter into his rest, but to them that believed not?*

[Who were the ones who were not allowed to enter in the land of promise? It was those who did not believe that God had the power to keep His promises or to subdue the enemy. This was a lack of faith in the goodness and power of God. Note, as the last verse indicates, that this was not the first time these people had failed the test of faith. Despite the proven power of God from the plagues of Egypt, past the dry path through the Red Sea, and all during the sojourn to this point, these people had continually failed to put their complete faith and trust in God.

They constantly complained that nothing was good enough except the "good food of Egypt." After all, they had been safe and comfortable there. It seems that had short memories of the inhumanity of slavery and very acute misconceptions of the great grace of God.

Several of the commentators continue to equate this loss of access to the land of promise with the loss of salvation and a home in Heaven. Read my commentary on verse eleven above. The land of promise is not symbolic of Heaven. The land of promise was a land of rest from their travels but it was also a land of warfare. This is not the picture of Heaven but the picture of a victorious Christian life. Jesus said, "Peace I leave with you, my peace I give unto you: not as the world giveth, give I unto you. Let not your heart be troubled, neither let it be afraid." (John 14:27)

The peace of God is often a peace given in the midst of trial and temptation. It is a peace of trust and faith in the Lord. Even Noah was not saved from the flood in its entirety. He was given a place of rest above the waters of judgment. This rest was not a lack of work. There was plenty of work to do in caring for the animals which God was using Noah to save from the judgment of the flood. In this world we are called to work in the fields of the Lord, seeking those to whom we ask the Holy Spirit to send conviction upon that they may also enter into this land of peace and rest.

Such was the task of the children of Israel within the Promised Land. Even as they would later feel the pain and judgment of God upon their own national sins, given through the Assyrians and Babylonians, so were they to be used as the instruments of God's justice on an immoral and irreligious people in that Promised Land.

The cup of iniquity is a poison whose only antidote is the shed Blood of the Savior Who has taken our punishment upon the cross. The Old Testament examples are pictures of the power of God to save His Own. As He swore the title of the Land of Promise to Israel, so He swore the punishment to those who refused to trust Him.

God is The God of Love. He is also The God of Divine Justice. It is His love which administers His judgment for our benefit and instruction in righteousness.]

3.19 *So we see that they could not enter in because of their unbelief.*

[Once again we must consider what it was to which they could not enter in. They could not enter into the land of promise. This does not equate with Heaven, or salvation. This is typical of the deeper things of the Christian life. These who did not enter in were not dislocated from their status as Israel's children. They were denied the fullness of the promise of the land; this is an indication of a loss of temporal blessing.

If we argue that this is a departure from saving faith we have misread the meaning. To make the land of promise Heaven and the lack of being allowed to enter into it the loss of one's chance at Heaven we must pronounce Moses and Aaron as lost sinners. Neither of these were allowed to enter.

Actually, the situation of Moses and Aaron is indicative of one who has lost his place in the service of God. The age, although great, of neither one compelled them to die on "the other side of the river."

The point was made that salvation must be accepted now. I would not argue with that at all. This is an imperative since salvation is, I believe, available only when the Spirit calls us to salvation. This is not something we can do on our own. Our sin nature, inherited from Adam, will serve to make us opposed to the things of God except under the conviction of the Holy Spirit.

To this, especially with the consideration of Moses and Aaron, I would only add that our decision to dedicate ourselves to the service of the Lord is a present necessity.

We can never walk too close to our Savior. His love for us will compel us to consider His love for others as well. In this, again under the influence of the Spirit, we will be drawn to accept His assignments and look for places of service in His perfect will.

One of my sources actually made a rather large point that "so" in this verse should be "and." I see no real difference in the meaning. I do see a real difference in our attitude toward the Words of God. If we honestly love God and His Word we will not seek to change that Word to fit our own image. Rather we will be changed, by that inspired and preserved Word, to change ourselves further into His image.

One of the greatest faults in the churches, and in many Christians, in our day is a lack of faith that God has spoken. This is very germane to the situation in this chapter. A lack of faith in the Words of God – as given by Inspiration and preserved by the Holy Spirit! – will sap our spiritual vitality and cause us to veer toward the world. This is the very sin of those who were denied entry into the land. They did not trust the Words of God; instead the trusted the words of the doubting spies vision of the world.

Again, one of my sources said that the people were denied entry into the land even though they desired such entry. I strongly disagree. They did not want to enter the land because of their fear. A realization of the love and power of the Lord will drive out fear and cause us to desire His Will above any other. "There is no fear in love; but perfect love casteth out fear: because fear hath torment. He that feareth is not made perfect in love." (I John 4:18)

When we come to the realization of the perfections of His completed love toward us, in the cross, in the world, in our witness, in our fellowship with Him and His people, we realize that we have no need to fear the powers of principalities or human antagonists. "Nay, in all these things we are more than conquerors through him that loved us. For I am persuaded, that neither death, nor life, nor angels, nor principalities, nor powers, nor things present, nor things to come, Nor height, nor depth, nor any other creature, shall be able to separate us from the love of God, which is in Christ Jesus our Lord." (Romans 8:37-39)]

HEBREWS - CHAPTER FOUR

***4.1** Let us therefore fear, lest, a promise being left us of entering into his rest, any of you should seem to come short of it.*

[Did you notice how Paul did not "preach down" to the recipients of his letter? There are too many preachers who have installed themselves as "lord over their congregations." We are not the master over the Lord's garden. Neither are we hirelings. We are only servants appointed to the task by the Lord of the Harvest.

I understand the need for the minister to attempt to install standards and doctrinal understanding among the people who sit in the pews. This is our job. But, the manner of completing these tasks is to teach the Scripture. Done properly this will allow the Lord to establish His standards and doctrine. We, as ministers, are not greater than the inspired and preserved Words of God. We are not to apply our, or the denomination's, standards; we are to apply the standards of God in our preaching and trust the Spirit of God to move the people when they have a need to be moved.

There is the phrase once again: "entering into his rest." Properly understood this is a call to enter into the service of God. This land is entered in faith. Dereliction of duty in this area may inhibit our ability to be serviceable for God in one certain capacity.

An example of this is a man I once knew who was a very good Bible preacher and expositor. He could preach rings around me. But, something happened in his life at one time. I honestly do not know the particulars. I only know that he was "disinvited" to preach at a certain church. To my understanding he moved into a type of "street corner" evangelism in which he approached people with the gospel as a Christian rather than as a pastor. He didn't "resign his commission" but accepted another assignment for God.

I've known others who have refused to resign from pulpits when they've continued to harm the cause of Christ with their actions. Continuing to claim the title "Rev." does not always imply one in the service of God. It is often pride, not piety, which is in the pulpit. This is not service to God.

Paul uses an analogy from an Olympic footrace. In these races anyone who was not the first over the finish line, the winner, was spoken of as having "come short of the mark." They may have raced but they did not win the prize.

Be careful not to misinterpret the phrase "rest." It is neither the rest of Heaven nor of inaction. It is the rest of being within the known will of God. In Matthew 11:30 Jesus says, "For my yoke is easy, and my burden is light."

The people who "entered into this rest" were used as the agents of God in delivering His Judgment upon a sinful people. Unless we understand this concept we are very apt to view the redemption of the land by the Hebrews from a twenty-first century mentality which might look unkindly on the concept. Much of the Old Testament concerns historical incidents which portray spiritual truths we need to learn.

The Truth here is that God hates sin and what it has done to His Creation. He will judge this sin and those who commit such. In just a few centuries the Hebrews would find this same lesson played out upon the slate of the divided kingdoms by the Assyrians and the Babylonians.]

HEBREWS: Chapter 4

4.2 *For unto us was the gospel preached, as well as unto them but the word preached did not profit them, not being mixed with faith in them that heard it.*

[The verse simply speaks of the Word being mixed with faith. Compare Romans 10:17. "So then faith cometh by hearing, and hearing by the word of God."

When I was a Freshman at the first college I attended we were all warned not to attend a certain liberal church in the heart of town. A freshman, of course, would hear this warning and assume that this was the very place he must go. When we went we heard a "sermon" that was really quite good. It was on morality and the work ethic. But it had nothing about the Blood of Christ. There was a call to live righteously before men but no call to accept the Savior as Lord. This type of preaching, while very good on a Tuesday night, is a wasted opportunity on a Sunday morning. We need, honestly and spiritually NEED, to hear a message from the Bible. That is the voice of God speaking to us from the inspired and preserved Words He has spoken for our benefit.

The verse also says that this was the same message which was preached to the people of the exodus by Moses. The human mind will answer that assertion with a single word: "What?"

The Bible is a Book written by a single Author. There may have been about 40 penmen of this Book. The Book may have been written on three continents over a period of 1,500 years. But, it is the work of One Author. God has inspired the Words, not just the concepts such a construct as "concept inspiration" is an invitation to unbelief and confusion, of the Scripture for our benefit. All of the Words are important for they are all interconnected. The teaching in one area will generally be expanded in another area but it is all of teaching but One Truth.

Those ceremonial laws which Moses relayed to the people of the exodus will speak of Christ. Indeed, He fulfilled those prophetic pictures of His work in His earthly ministry. Scratch the Bible in any place and it will bleed red with the picture of the Blood of Christ.

The sacrificial system saved no one. Hebrews 10:4 informs us that, "For it is not possible that the blood of bulls and of goats should take away sins." I am fairly certain that there were many who did not mix faith with these ceremonies and sacrifices. They merely fulfilled a civic duty.

Many others had faith in the Words of God concerning these things. They did them in faith to those Words of God. These obtained a salvation which was based, although they had no real understanding of it, on the Sacrifice of Jesus Christ at the Cross of Calvary. (Revelation 13:8)

Likewise, we do not have to understand every point of Scripture. We never will. One of the present roles of the Spirit is to illumine our hearts with the meaning of Scripture. He will open the Scriptural Principles that allow us to see more of the meaning of God within the Divinely inspired and preserved Scripture. We are also commanded to study those Scriptures to find all that God has for us. (II Timothy 2:15)

I watched my grandson try to put sugar in a glass of ice tea yesterday. He stirred up the liquid and watched the granules of sugar float to the bottom of his glass. If one wants "sweet tea" he must add the sugar while the tea is hot. That way the sugar will melt into the tea.

Hearing the Words of God is not enough. An atheist can hear the Words without effect.

Our need is to hear those Words and unite with them in faith. The faith is placed in those Words of God. Faith is more than simply trust. It is a firm belief in the words mixed with the realization that those are the Words of God; therefore those Words are fully trustworthy because God is fully trustworthy. We are to react with faith in God and His message to us. In this we realize that we must accept Jesus as Savior. There is no other way of salvation. "Neither is there salvation in any other: for there is none other name under heaven given among men, whereby we must be saved." (Acts 4:12)]

4.3 *For we which have believed do enter into rest, as he said, As I have sworn in my wrath, if they shall enter into my rest: although the works were finished from the foundation of the world.*

[Paul has been bringing illustrations from the exodus to help explain the Christian walk to a group of Jewish believers. Once again he includes himself among them. "...we which have believed."

By saying "we which have believed" Paul also implies the negative. Those who have not believed may not enter into this rest. Once again, this rest is not indicative of Heaven. It, as was the rest of the entrance into the land by the Hebrews, does not indicate Heaven but the faithful adherence to the cause and purposes of God in this present life. This is not to say that full faith in the shed blood of Jesus Christ has nothing to do with our Heavenly promise. We gain our salvation through this faith. This allows us to walk in the rest which is given in this life. It is this salvation faith which is our surety of the eternal favor of God.

Once again we must consider that the Jewish people are the Covenant People of God. These covenants which God made with them are still valid as they are based upon the Honor of God. The promises to the Jew are earthly promises. These will be literally fulfilled upon this earth – Just as God promised!

The fact that God does keep His promises to the Jew is just one of the reasons why we can have faith that He will also keep His promises to the Christian. We are the people of the "New Testament in His Blood;" therefore His promises to us concern the Heavenly and eternal realms. They will also be fulfilled in the Heavenly and eternal – Just as God promised!

Further, as for the Christian, the fact that God does not immediately translate us to Heaven upon conversion is indicative that He has a Heavenly purpose for us to fulfill while we are upon this earth. That Heavenly purpose is that we labor in the Masters fields as true bondservants of His. It is with our effort, with the support and empowerment of the Holy Spirit, that God raises a new "crop" for Heaven with each passing generation. Our labors within this realm are the rest to which we are called within this life even as the subjugation of the Promised Land was the rest to which those of the exodus were called.

It was the righteous wrath of God which judged those of unbelief as not competent to enter into the "rest" of the Land of Promise. They were not faithful unto their task. This faithlessness was counted as unbelief.

Likewise the lack of trust and faithfulness of the Christian to embark upon His duty to His Lord will cause us to miss all of the blessings God has for those who are faithful to Him and His reasonable call upon our lives in these times. Make no mistake;

the cause of Christ will be completed. It is we, through our lack of trust or initiative when we refuse His call to service, who will suffer loss.

The eternally founded plan of God will continue to be revealed and commenced and completed. The determinative will of God is established as though it were already accomplished. It will come to pass. His rest on the seventh day of creation is proof that all His Will will be accomplished within this creation.

The determinative will of God to provide salvation for a people He had not yet created was furnished to humanities historical accuracy at Calvary. (Revelation 13:8)]

4.4 *For he spake in a certain place of the seventh day on this wise, And God did rest the seventh day from all his works.*

[The "certain place" is Genesis 2:2 where God rested from the work of creation. This does not mean that God was tired. It means simply that His work of creation was completed. He ceased from this particular work. When Jesus said, "IT IS FINISHED," on the Cross (John 19:30) the matter of provision for the salvation of humanity was finished. There was nothing to be added thereto. Anyone who would attempt to supply his own work in an effort at obtaining salvation has denied the Words of the Lord. The same could be said of religious devotion or sacrifice. Jesus said "It is finished;" we have no right or purpose to dispute His Words.

The rest of God from Creation does not mean finding and easy chair and watching a celestial television to see what was going to happen. Colossians 1:17 speaks of the eternality of Jesus. It also shows Him to be working in His creation in the holding together of that creation. "And he is before all things, and by him all things consist." John 1:3 shows us that Jesus is the Creator of all things. He has retained an interest in His creation.

We might notice that at the end of the first six days of creation the ending of that day is recorded. However, there is no record of the ending of the seventh day. This is a picture that God has finished fully with His creative acts. There will be no more.

What this does not mean is that each of the days was of indeterminate length. One of my sources used this fact of no recorded end to the seventh day to argue for the "day / age" theory. He remarked that this would show that there is no 24-hour day indicated. But, the seventh day was a cessation of creation while the earlier days were concerned with that creation. Therefore no such conclusion can be reached from entities which are not parallel.

The rest promised in the exodus cannot be considered the Sabbath Day rest as the establishment of the Sabbath Day rest had already been instituted and enjoyed before the entrance to the land of promise was considered by the people.

The lack of faith, once again, in the power, leading and sufficiency of God did not dismiss the people from their status as children of Abraham. I believe that they did lose much of the blessing of that status, they were unbelievers. But, what they lost – from the Scripture – by this unbelief was the ability and permission to enter into the Land of their Covenant. More could have been lost. I do not deny this. But, from the Scripture, the only loss we find is the loss of the entrance into the Land. Once again, we must consider that neither Moses nor Aaron were allowed this privilege of entering the land.]

4.5 *And in this place again, If they shall enter into my rest.*

[Once again the place quoted is from Psalm 95, this time verse 11. The reference remains to the entry into the Promised Land during the time of the Exodus. The spiritual principle involved remains the entry in the rest of obedience. The reality of Heaven is not in view due to the fact that the conquest of Canaan speaks of the Christian walk of warfare with the adversary. "The rest" is the rest which the world can never comprehend. It is resting in the will and favor of the Savior.

The rest refused deals with the entering of the land in obedience to the invitation and command of God.

It is possible to consider this rest and the rest of eternal salvation in this picture of disobedience. God does not force anyone to be saved. The Spirit woos and calls; it is for the sinner to respond in faith – the faith also being supplied by God's graciousness. (Ephesians 2:8-9)

This is, however, a secondary application. This breaks down when this group of Israelites are denied entrance into the land even though they remain Israelites. They were still children of the covenant. This does not, obviously, mean that they received the full blessing which God had available for them to receive. They lacked possessing the land.

Likewise, the Christian who fails to move into the "service mode" is denied all the blessing which could have been his had he moved forward into the "land" of spiritual conquest. The Christian of such carnality is still a Christian. He is still an adopted child of The Father.

He still enters into the "rest" of eternity. He does so, however, lacking the blessings he might have laid up for eternity. (I Corinthians 3:15; I Peter 4:18; II John 8; Jude 23)]

4.6 *Seeing therefore it remaineth that some must enter therein, and they to whom it was first preached entered not in because of unbelief:*

[Though there be many who perished in the wandering because of their unbelief, yet there were many who did enter into the land. Likewise, there are many who enter into the deeper walk with God even though many will balk at this point and turn away from any concept of service toward God.

There are several terms used to describe this deeper walk. To the Holiness people this is entire sanctification. To the charismatic this is the baptism of the Spirit. To the fundamentalist this is the dedication of one's life to the Lord. Each speaks not of a second work of grace, although many will apply that term, but to a deeper commitment and walk with the grace of our Lord Jesus Christ. The great evangelist D. L. Moody explained it by saying (I do paraphrase here.) "The world has never seen a man who was wholly dedicated to the things of God. By His grace I will be such a man."

I hired some men to do some yard work for me. One of them asked for a certain amount per hour. I offered at sum of $300.00 for the entire project. He accepted by offer. The "sold out" Christian will count the cost of serving God. That cost is one's entire life as a sacrifice to God. It is not that we give up control of our lives. It is that we give the controlling of our lives over to God. He says to do. We do to the best of our abilities and with the best of His assistance. It is a task where we can never lose. (Romans 12:1)

It is a decision where we can only be victorious. (I Corinthians 9:19; Philippians 1:21; 3:7; I Timothy 6:6)]

4.7 *Again, he limiteth a certain day, saying in David, To day, after so long a time, as it is said, To day if ye will hear his voice, harden not your hearts.*

[God is our Constant Contemporary. His day is an eternal now. Thus the day of decision of the people of the exodus to consider a trust in the Words of God still equates to a day of decision for us. David wrote the Psalm which Paul has been accessing hundreds of years after this call to enter into, and subdue, the Land of Promise.

The day of trust of which God spoke at the earlier time was still the day of trust in the time of King David. The day of trust remains in our day; each day down to the present is the day of trust. We are still warned to listen to the voice of God. This seems to limit the concept presented here to those who are the saved of the earth. Only the saved will listen to the voice of God.

Sadly, not even all of the saved will both hear and heed to words of God. I could access something in my own life just a day ago where I did not heed the words of God. This sort of thing will impede our ability to live fully in His will.

The town where I live seems to be completely "under construction." Someone has made a lot of money selling barricades which limit the traffic to "One Lane Ahead." A lack of the trust in God which causes us to live in His will is an impediment to His perfect will for our lives. When we refuse to repent of such, when we "harden our hearts" to pursue a path other than the path of God there is an impediment erected between ourselves and the ability to fully follow His will. To not fully follow His will is to place ourselves outside the perfect will of God.

We remain the adoptive children of God but we deface His work in the world with our carnality and lack of complete obedience. It is not that He is defaced by our lack but that we are the producers of such defacement in being petulant adoptive children of our Heavenly Parent. Our place of service to Him may be forfeit. Others will gain the rewards which were to be our crowns in Heaven.

The warning is to choose each day, each hour, each minute, to follow our Savior and to trust His Word and leading.]

4.8 *For if Jesus had given them rest, then would he not afterward have spoken of another day.*

[The first thing I noticed in this verse is that Jesus had given the rest of the entry into the Land of Promise. This is another statement of the Divinity of Jesus. Ussher has dated the writing of Hebrews at about 64 A.D. This is within a single lifetime of the witnesses to the death, burial and resurrection of Jesus. Therefore, this is yet another proof that the early church, and the apostles, accepted the full divinity of Jesus. The belief that Jesus was God incarnate is not a late addition to the churches doctrine as some have argued.

Jesus is the Greek word equivalent to the name of Joshua, the son of Nun in the Hebrew language. Looking from this perspective – which seems by the context to have been the meaning of Paul – we see that there is a later rest promised to the children of Israel.

Both we, and the Hebrews of old, find our full rest in the service to God. Heaven is our reward but it is not properly a simple time of rest for we will be "employed" as servants, as adopted sons, as the Bride of the Son, during this timeless time of eternity.

However, for the Israelites there will be a yet further time of rest. The conquest of the land was incomplete. It was fully promised by God; (Joshua 1:3); it was not fully realized by the Hebrew due to his unwillingness to fully follow God in all matters.

There is a coming time of national rest for Israel. During the Millennial Kingdom, where Jesus Himself will sit upon the literal throne of David, the promises given to the sons of Abraham will be fully realized. This is their later, physical and earthly, fulfillment of the Divine Promises made to Abraham. The rest will be unending even as it remains an earthly rest concerning the New Heavens, the New Earth and the New Jerusalem. (Revelation 21:1-3)]

4.9 *There remaineth therefore a rest to the people of God.*

[For Israel there is a rest that will follow the rest from their wanderings in the Land of Promise. These are, after all, the People of Promise. Based solely on His Own honor God will perform those ancient promises to Abraham and his descendants.

In this is further shown the exaltation of Jesus above even Moses. The offer by Moses, through Joshua, was a land wherein the people might cease their wandering and establish a homeland for them and their children. This was the promise that God had given. Moses relayed this promise to the people as the spokesman for God in their midst.

Since David was writing hundreds of years after the time of the entrance into the land of promise it is obvious that this is not fully what he had in mind. Looking down through the ages the Spirit of inspiration gave David the view of a Sabbath type rest which was everlasting. It would be a time when the subject of worship would not belong to just a single day; it would be an ongoing reality.

To the son of Abraham this Sabbath of rest would be in the everlasting kingdom of David, with Jesus on the throne, in the New Jerusalem.

To the adopted son of God, the Christian, this rest is available now as we labor for the Lord while resting in His love.]

4.10 *For he that is entered into his rest, he also hath ceased from his own works, as God did from his.*

[When God "rested" on the seventh day the picture is not of Him kicking off His shoes and sitting back in a recliner. The simple meaning is that this rest was a cessation of His work of Creation. This work was complete. This does not suggest a lack of effort. The creation may have been completed but the oversight and holding together of that creation continues. (Colossians 1:16-17)

The idea of theistic evolution, whereby God created and then sat back to see what was going to happen, is an untenable belief. God is still very active in the upholding of His creation and the guidance of the history of this planet toward a predetermined conclusion.

The fact that the one "resting" is ceased from his work is indicative of the truth that true rest in the Savior, for the Christian, is to be involved in doing the will of God upon this earth. We rest from our work as we rest in doing His work.

This does not suggest any mindlessness on our part as Christians. As Jesus is involved in the Creation so ought we to be in the doing of His work on this earth. We may plan – we should! Understanding that His is the Ultimate Power in any work we might attempt, we should make every effort to perform to the ultimate of our abilities. He will supply whatever it might be that will assist us in that work as we pray His blessing upon our efforts for Him.]

***4.11** Let us labour therefore to enter into that rest, lest any man fall after the same example of unbelief.*

[There are two things we must understand in reference to this verse. What is the rest? What was the nature of their unbelief?

The rest, to these wandering people, was a rest of entrance into the Promised Land. This land is not typical of the Land of Heaven. It is typical of the walk of the Christian in this world.

In order for these people to possess the land, these people needed to go in and subdue the land by conquering the people who then possessed the land. Also, we must note that they entirety of the land promised by God has never yet been totally possessed by the sons of Abraham.

This is not a picture of Heaven as many have argued. We do not have to fight anyone to gain Heaven. As a matter of plain fact, there is nothing we can do to gain Heaven. This is a gift from Jesus; He purchased this for us with His sacrifice for us on the Cross of Calvary.

Those who were displaced were under the judgment of God for their many, and gross, sins. The land was to be purged of their sin. This, the eradication of our sins was accomplished at that Cross of Jesus. Because of His work on that cross we are already counted in His perfections.

There is no one to be displaced in order for us to enter Heaven. Lucifer has already been expelled along with the angels who fell with his sin. (Jude 6)

The entirety of the Heavenly estate is promised to those whose sins have been forgiven by the Blood of the Lamb. We do not have a need to attempt to gain all that is promised by God for it is His gift. The gaining is simply given us as adopted sons.

The nature of the sin of these people was twofold: First, they did not believe that God could perform that which He had promised. Second, they feared the people of the land more than they feared God.

Our salvation is predicated on a complete trust that the work of Jesus is all that is needed for that salvation. We have no work we can offer to purchase our own salvation. We can only accept that which He has offered. In this we do display the faith which says that Jesus paid the entire price. I need no other argument. I need no other work. Indeed, to attempt to substitute our own work is to be guilty of the sin of unbelief.

Ephesians 2:10 plainly says, "For we are his workmanship, created in Christ Jesus unto good works, which God hath before ordained that we should walk in them." Salvation is the work of Christ Jesus. We can produce no good works, spiritually speaking, until He has endowed us with His salvation. At, and after, that point we are expected to walk into a life of the good work of following the Lord in the fields of His created but lost humanity with the message that Jesus died in time so that they could live in eternity.

One of the things that prevent most of us from fully experiencing the thrill of working for the Savior is our fear of what others might think, or say, of us. The other preventative is ourselves. We feel our inability and do not fully access His full ability. The fear of man, even if that man be ourselves, is the sin of unbelief as well. It is a matter of not fully trusting the Lord in the same manner as the Hebrews had not fully trusted Him in the entering of the Land.]

4.12 *For the word of God is quick, and powerful, and sharper than any twoedged sword, piercing even to the dividing asunder of soul and spirit, and of the joints and marrow, and is a discerner of the thoughts and intents of the heart.*

Acts 20:26-28; Romans 1:16; 10:17; II Timothy 2:4

[My grandson has watched some "Star Wars" movies. He wants a "real Light Saber." He just isn't content with a toy replica. At five years old he is certain that his dad is mistaken when he tells the little one that there are no "real" Light Sabers on the market!

Folks, we need a real sword to do battle with a real Satan and to worship the Real Savior. I am afraid that a nice sounding shinny toy just won't do for the intended task. It would even be dangerous. Satan ain't playing.

Sadly, too often in our day of "easier to read," Reader's Digest style, translations based in a lack of faith, we - the Christian - can only play. We lack the real ammunition God has supplied if we are to be true participants in the Spiritual battles of the day!

Several years ago my wife and I met the President of the United States. I try to work that into the conversation from time to time! The truth is, however, that any Christian has better access than this. Any blood bought believer in Jesus Christ can go to the Throne of Glory and talk with the Creator of the universe.

It is also possible that this verse refers to Jesus in the sense that John 1:1 calls Him the Word. In such an interpretation we would see the Divine judgments of Jesus and His complete understanding of humanity.

The judgments of Jesus are not based upon the testimony of men. Jesus fully understands man and his thought and active processes. The just judgment of Jesus is based on the reality of the situation of unregenerate man. The comprehensive knowledge of humanity is also concerned with the just discipline of the believer as an adoptive child of God.]

4.13 *Neither is there any creature that is not manifest in his sight: but all things are naked and opened unto the eyes of him with whom we have to do.*

[There is not a thing that we are able to hide from God. He knows all of our imperfections and flaws. We may hide something that we've done from the world at large. Maybe no one knows the dark secrets of our hearts. Well, God knows.

How can we not be afraid to stand at the judgment bar of God! We can have no defense. God knows even those things that are hidden deep within the recesses of our minds. What we have hidden God will make known. Eternal justice is a real fear. What can we do?

I John 2:1 says that, "...we have an advocate with the Father, Jesus Christ the righteous."

Jesus is our defense counsel as we stand before the justice of God! He will plead the case for us! But, we do need to accept Him as our Savior. Have you done this? Why not just accept Jesus as the One Who has already paid the price for your sin?]

4.14 *Seeing then that we have a great high priest, that is passed into the heaven, Jesus the Son of God, let us hold fast our profession.*

[The theme of the Book of Hebrews is that Jesus is more excellent than any other. The problem of the Book of Hebrews is apostasy. The leadership of the Jews was very adamant in their attempts to stamp out this religion of Jesus. The made every attempt to explain why the Christian religion of Jesus was false.

Over against the warmth of the Christian fellowship of believers was the cold formality of the Jewish religion of the day. The ceremonies must be followed to the letter. The Law must be followed to the letter. The sacrifices must be offered according to form and practice.

With all of this pageantry to seduce the weak there was added the "proofs" of their religious observances. The Jews had a high priest to bring their problems and needs to God. The Jews had a tabernacle in their past by which God led them through the wilderness. The Jews had a Temple which was the House of God. The Jews even had a sacrificial system to pay for their sins. Without all of these the argument was that the Christian had no real religion.

But the Christians did have a High Priest; this was Jesus. The Christians had the leading of the Holy Spirit to lead them through their walk in this world. The Christians had a temple not made with hands. It was to the Lord that the Christian prayed. He was their temple. The Christians had no need for a sacrificial system for the Lord was, and had performed, all the sacrifice they would ever need. His Blood bought them remission of their sins.

The Old Testament High Priest, on the Day of Atonement would take the blood of the sacrifice. He would walk away from the area where the people were assembled. He would continue His walk. He went into the Holy Place, passed through the veil. He was out of the sight of the other priests. He would then pass through into the Holy of Holies. Here he would come to the mercy seat and sprinkle the blood of sacrifice for the sins of the people.

Likewise Jesus, at the mount after His resurrection, ascended out of the sight of the people assembled to worship Him. He would come to the clouds and pass through their "veil" to move out of the sight of the Apostles.

The Jew at the time believed that there was a blue curtain which served as a dome over the earth. Beyond this dome were other heavens and, finally, the throne of God. In the eyes of the people it seemed that Jesus passed this curtain as well. He entered into the Throne Room of God. There, at the Heavenly mercy seat – of which the earthly was only a pale copy – He sprinkled His Own blood, the Blood of the Lamb of God, onto the Heavenly mercy seat. This was the Blood which did not cover the sins of the people of God. It eradicated those sins. They were gone!

The earthly High Priest had access to the blood of the sacrificial animals which could only cover the sins of the people. The Blood of Jesus was sufficient to cleanse the sins of the people. (I John 1:7) This is still the case as the sinner who comes to Jesus will have his sins cleansed even in this day. Jesus cleanses our sin and gives us access to The Father. (Ephesians 2:18; 3:12) In verse sixteen, below, we see that this Blood of Jesus even gives us access to the throne of God. We are invited, nay – we are commanded to come to the throne of God and commune with our Savior.]

4.15 *For we have not an high priest which cannot be touched with the feeling of our infirmities; but was in all points tempted like as we are, yet without sin.*

[This passage, as does the Temptation on the Mount, shows that the human Jesus was tempted. Yet, He was without sin.

As a human Jesus was tempted. He is well able to understand our trials and tribulations. Yet, He remained without sin. Jesus is our Great Example of how we ought to live as human beings, as well as our Savior.

There are some misconceptions about the humanity of Jesus. One of these is the error of Docetism. Their error lay in teaching that Jesus was not really human. They consider that He only appeared human. Among their doctrines is a teaching that Jesus did not really die on the cross but only apparently did so.

One of the errors of this doctrine is that it removes that special relationship which He has with His created beings. The view of the Docetist would make Jesus unfamiliar with our suffering. He is not. His suffering on the cross was real. This is evidenced by His agony in the Garden. This is one of the most precious passages in the Scripture. Jesus knew the horror that awaited Him. He seemed to nearly recoil at the thought of this ordeal. Yet, knowing all He knew, He continued to the Cross because He loves us.

What a sweet picture this is to me!

Also, this doctrine of the Docetist would remove the entire basis for our salvation. A representative of the human race died as punishment for the sins of our race in order to offer the way of salvation. Remove the full humanity, the full divinity, or the sacrificial death of Jesus Christ on the Cross of Calvary and we are left with no basis for our salvation.]

4.16 *Let us therefore come boldly unto the throne of grace, that we may obtain mercy, and find grace to help in time of need.*

[One of the best things about our salvation is not necessarily the idea of a home in Heaven. Don't misunderstand; that a pretty good thing to consider! But, this is for later. For now we can have that fellowship with Him. We can approach the Throne of Grace; we are even encouraged to do so.

The rest of the world might just approach hard liquor when they have a problem. When they awaken in the morning the problem will still be there. Only, on top of the problem they will have a head ache!

We have the option, invitation really, to approach God with our problems. We can continue to talk with Him as He works to resolve our problems for us as the Father does for the sons and daughters. We can approach Him constantly and never get a head ache; we are heart blessed, instead!

All of this was included in the price which Jesus paid at the Cross of Calvary. His great salvation is even much more glorious than we often consider because He works through this to provide for our need.

We needed salvation. He provided that for us.

We needed a way to restore a relationship with the Creator. He provided that for us.

We needed to find purpose and meaning in this earthly life. He provided that for us.

We needed to find a way to feel real peace about the loss of loved ones from this earthly life. He provided for that for us.

We needed the assurance that this short life was not all that there was. He provided that for us.

He provides for our every need if we will simply trust and find that His grace is sufficient!]

HEBREWS - CHAPTER FIVE

5.1   For every high priest taken from among men is ordained for men in things pertaining to God, that he may offer both gifts and sacrifices for sins:

[This is a continuation of the thought from the ending of the fourth chapter. Jesus is there called the Christian's High Priest. (Hebrews 2:17; 3:1; 4:10-15) Paul begins by examining the duties and realities of the human high priest of the Jewish religious system. Every consideration of the human high priest is a prophecy of our Heavenly High Priest.

The high priest was from the family of Aaron. That was the first requirement. Although this was sometimes ignored under the rule of Rome, this was the requirement of the Law as given through Moses.

With this thought we are reminded that Messiah was to be King over the Jew. This fact points to the lineage of Jesus. He was, through His earthly "step father" and His earthly mother, doubly of the house and lineage of King David. Lawfully, Jesus had perfect right to the Throne upon which He will sit in the ages to come.

The Roman rule had reduced the tenure of the High Priest to a yearly "election" to the office. (John 18:13) This was not so in the original as is shown by the High Priest leaving his office upon death. (Numbers 23:25-28) Jesus had died and then risen from the dead. His "tenure of office," if we may use the term, was permanent as He is eternal. (Hebrews 6:20)

The high priest was chosen from among his people, the Levite tribe of Aaron. Jesus also came from the race of humanity. An angel, or a created man such as was Adam, could not have been our Savior. Jesus came as one of us to purchase our salvation for all who would believe.

The high priest could enter into the "Holy of Holies" once a year, only on the Day of Atonement, in order to sprinkle the blood of sacrifice upon the mercy seat. It is interesting to note that this priest had a rope tied to his leg as he went about these duties. An unworthy priest could have been struck dead had he walked in his sin for which he had not offered full sacrifice into the symbolic presence of God. The rope was to pull him out without sending another into the Holy of Holies.

Jesus took the Blood of His perfect Sacrifice into the Tabernacle of Heaven. This He offered for the sins of all who would accept Him as Savior throughout the ages of time. This He did once. The Sacrifice of Jesus was taken and accepted as the full payment for sins unto those who believe. There is no need for Him to enter into the Heavenly Sanctuary yearly. The Sacrifice considered as complete before the foundations of the world (Revelation 13:8) is completed in reality as it had been shown in the Temple ceremonies. They were a picture of that which has been completed. (Hebrews 9:12-14)

The veil which has separated man from the mercy seat is gone due to the perfect Sacrifice of Jesus. (Mark 15:38) Our access to the Throne of Grace is accomplished for those who have accepted Jesus Christ as eternal Savior. (Hebrews 4:16) This is not simply a privilege or invitation. This is a Biblical command for the believer.

I live near the "projects." Some of the best people in the natural live just across the street from me. They have so many problems, and often poverty, of their own that they have a real feeling for others. They both identify and sympathize.

The earthly high priest was chosen from among his brethren. He was a man of like passions as were others. He understood the problems of the people. Jesus is such a High Priest. "For we have not an high priest which cannot be touched with the feeling of our infirmities; but was in all points tempted like as we are, yet without sin." (Hebrews 4:15)

The verse above may seem a contradiction. James 1:13 says, "Let no man say when he is tempted, I am tempted of God: for God cannot be tempted with evil, neither tempteth he any man." Jesus is God. But, He was tempted on the mountain in His humanity; we have the event recorded in the fourth chapter of Matthew, verse 1 through 11.

What is so often overlooked is the fact that Jesus is Fully God; He is also fully man. Jesus was tempted in His humanity. We see in Matthew 4:1 that this was in the plan of God. I believe that the primary purpose of His temptation was for us. Look carefully at this eleven verse passage. Every answer Jesus gave to Satan was a quotation from the inspired and preserved Word of God.

Jesus was tempted in His humanity to show us the means of resisting temptation in our salvation. We have no promise outside the Lord. The seven sons of Sceva in Acts 19:14 and following attempted to use the name of Jesus as an occult talisman. It didn't turn out well for them. Neither does one who has not accepted Christ have the right to expect protection from God simply because that person might read a verse here and there. That person's quotation from God Word is in his own power. It is, as they say in financial matters, "a misappropriation of funds."

Don't misunderstand. God does honor His Words every time. But, He is not bound to do so with a person who is outside the protection of the Blood of Jesus Christ. Simply reading about salvation is not equal to accepting that salvation.

The earthly high priest, in his ordained office, was to serve as a mediator between God and man. That priest offered both gift and sacrifice in in the name of the people. He also was bound to offer sacrifice for his own sins. Jesus had no such need to offer sacrifice for His sins because He had none. He is our Mediator with The Father.

The distinction is made in the verse between bloodless gifts to God. Even these were only in answer to His commandments, and the blood sacrifice of those animals for the sins of the people.

As an aside, no minister of the Gospel has the right to be called a priest. He is not. A priest is one who offers sacrifice to God. The priests of the Roman Church are properly using the term but not the reality. Their doctrine dictates that the elements of the Lord's Table are, upon their consecration, the actual Body and Blood of Christ. They offer these daily in their Mass. They do it in eternal error. Hebrews 9:28 argues that Jesus was only offered once. There can never be another sacrifice of His body and blood. "So Christ was once offered to bear the sins of many; and unto them that look for him shall he appear the second time without sin unto salvation."

We must also note that there is no priest who has the standing to offer the body and blood of Jesus as a sacrifice. This He has done of Himself. (Hebrews 7:27)

The Lord's Table is not an offering. It is a memorial service. (Psalm 111:4; Luke 22:19; I Corinthians 11:24-26) There is neither saving grace nor mysticism in this memorial service. By this we celebrate the fact that Jesus Christ died in time so that we could live in eternity.

Hebrews 10:2-14 expands on this theme with explanation that the simple fact that Jesus was ONCE sacrificed is an indication that His death is effective eternally while the Old Testament sacrificial system was temporal in scope and duration.]

5.2 *Who can have compassion on the ignorant, and on them that are out of the way; for that he himself also is compassed with infirmity.*

[In this place the physical high priest of the Hebrew religion is shown to be a foreshadow of He Who came as Messiah and High Priest of our Christian faith. The high priest was judge and jury, as it were, to the people of God. He was to be a man of compassion, pity and understanding of the people he represented before God. His own understanding of himself as a mere man who fulfilled an office would give him understanding of the people because he was subject to the same temptations and failures as were they.

The burden of the sin nature is laid upon all. Considering this as a mitigating circumstance, the high priest could consider the needs of the people of the congregation and be understanding toward them.

This understanding was not allowed to remove the Law of God. The wise and compassionate high priest was bound to obey, and to enforce, the Law of God. His personal compassion could alleviate where possible but would need to stand aside when his own feelings were "overruled" by the standards of the Law of God.

There was a sacrifice for the man who sinned unwittingly. An "oops" does not remove the penalty of disobedience toward God. Man remains guilty and even this unwitting sin must seek atonement. Leviticus 5:1-19 speaks of this.

All of the Law must be applied evenly to both Israelite and "foreigner in the midst of the people." (Numbers 15:29)

The spiritual truth we can learn from this is that even the seeming "best" of the human race stands in need of the forgiveness of sins offered by Jesus at the Cross. No human is exempt from the sin nature. No human is exempt from the need of salvation.

As for any willful sin, we must understand that willful sin has no sacrifice. (Numbers 15:30-31) The spiritual application at this point would apply to one who has never accepted, which is in essence to refuse, the salvation in Jesus Christ and His atonement will die in his sins. There is no sacrifice other than faith in the shed Blood of Jesus that will cleanse our sins.]

5.3 *And by reason hereof he ought, as for the people so also for himself, to offer for sins.*

[The high priest, as a human, did not become "super priest" when he was ordained to his office. He was still a fallen human being who had a need to follow the same Law which he prescribed for others. There was even a sacrifice specifically given for the priest who sinned. (Leviticus 4:3)

Moses sent Aaron to make atonement for himself before Aaron was to offer sacrifice for the people. (Leviticus 9:7) In this we see the reality that God demands a sinless advocate for the sins of the people. We cannot argue that Aaron was sinless at this point; the best we can argue from the position of fallen humanity was that Aaron had his sins "under the blood." This was not the Blood of Jesus. Hebrews 10:4 reminds us that the blood of the Old Testament sacrificial system could not obliterate sin. That blood, sacrificed in faith to the revealed Words of God was a covering for sin.

It is this faith in the revealed Words of God which has been required of man throughout all the dispensations of God. These all looked forward, though the people did not understand this truth as it had not yet been revealed to them, to the death of Jesus Christ on the Cross of Calvary. His Sacrifice of Himself does remove sin from the believer. (I John 1:7)

This Sacrifice of Jesus was counted as complete from before the foundations of the earth. (Revelation 13:8) The actual Sacrifice, counted as complete and therefore effective to all the blood of animals to cover sin, was completed on Calvary. David prophesied this in Psalm 68:18. In Ephesians 4:8 we find the reality of which the prophecy spoke.]

5.4 *And no man taketh this honour unto himself, but he that is called of God, as was Aaron.*

[There were none in ancient Israel who were allowed to appoint themselves as High Priest. This was a limited access office. Aaron was first appointed as the high priest by God, via the mediation of Moses. The sons of Aaron, his posterity, were then appointed to follow Aaron into the office.

I am a Baptist. One of the hallmarks of the Baptist churches is that they are each independent churches. We may join together in associations, conventions, brotherhoods and the like; we still remain independent Baptist Churches. The point is that we have no hierarchy except the leading of the Lord. That is a good point; it is Biblical.

However, as with any of the good things of God, we see the hand of Satan working to sully the work of God. Anyone may claim the mantle of "Baptist." Not all are Biblically so. I am thinking of one specific independent Baptist, claimed as such, Church. They seem to have styled themselves as Old Testament prophets of doom. In my own dealings with them, slight – just from the local newspaper accounts as they came to dishonor some local fallen soldiers – I have seen little to identify them as a New Testament Church of the Lord.

Since they appear to be "five-point" Calvinists – not necessarily a bad thing at all times – they seem to never preach salvation. The judgment of God seems to be their only theme. I have never heard them, or read of them, speaking of either personal repentance or the mercy of God though the Cross of Christ.

The Great Commission Mandate as given in the last few verses of the Gospel of Matthew to the Church and to the membership of those churches seems ignored.

Folks, we do not have the right to "pick and choose" among the garden of the Lord's spiritual fruits. If we are to be true followers of Jesus we must follow Him in all areas. We may, should, hate the sin which binds our fellow human beings. We have a Christian duty to love those with whom we disagree. (Matthew 5:44) We must never love them to the extent that we would love them into Hell. Our need is to love them with the Savior's love which calls all men to repentance.

Should they then refuse the Lord's salvation we have heaped "coals of fire" upon their unrepentant heads without dishonoring our Lord before the world. (Romans 12:19-21) We must strongly assert the truth in this verse: We do not do harm to anyone in the Name of Christ. We must acknowledge that whatever harm may come is a result of the Lord's doing. Such must never be of our doing; we have neither the right nor the command to do harm.

What I have done above is to offer a spiritual application of the verse in Hebrews; for the verse speaks neither of the "church in the wilderness," nor the New Testament churches. The verse does give application that we are bound to listen to and for the leading of God. We could also apply this same spiritual principle to the role of minister. This is not a hereditary role. I could name sons of well-known preachers who simply took over "the family business" and led the people of God into the apostasy of self-glorification. Conversely I could name the sons of well-known preachers who exceeded their father's ministry as they followed the same God given paths further down the road for God.

The point being that Jesus is in charge of His Own Church. God will bless the faithfulness of the servant who labors in His field. No such blessing is promised for the hireling whose chief purpose is to put the title "Rev." in front of his name.

The primary point of the verse, however, speaks of the succession of persons into the office of High Priest. Jesus has become the High Priest of our Christian convictions. No one can follow Him into that office as He now lives forevermore. This obviously means that no man can sit as a "vicar of Christ" since Jesus calls whom He wills and empowers that person who follows Him. There is no need of an intermediary because Jesus is the Mediator, Himself. (I Timothy 2:5)]

5.5 *So also Christ glorified not himself to be made an high priest, but he that said unto him, Thou art my Son, to day have I begotten thee.*

[This is a quotation from Psalm 110:4 and Psalm 2:7. Psalm 110 speaks of Jesus being a priest after the order of Melchisedec. We will access this a little more in the next verse. We might note here that Jesus did not glorify Himself into this office. We can read in Philippians 2:6-9 that Jesus emptied Himself of the outward glory of His Essential Deity in order to be our example, our Savior, and our Mediating Priest. He did not seek glory for He already possessed the Glory of His Eternal Godhood. Instead He focused on service to fallen humanity. Such was His love for us.

"Thou art my Son, to day have I begotten thee" is a quotation from Psalm 2:7. Both of these Psalms are Messianic Psalms in that they speak prophetically of the coming Messiah of the Jew and Savior of the world.

The simple fact that Paul accessed two different Psalms in one sentence is an example that we must not look at one passage to build doctrine. We need a picture of the entire Bible if we are to understand the Words which God has given us about Himself from the inspired and preserved pages of Scripture.

The picture of Jesus given in the New Testament is one of a Man Who displayed the power of God in His ministry on this earth. I understand there are many, the disciples and the Old Testament prophets come quickly to mind, who also displayed this power on occasion as the Spirit gave them power in a specific situation.

In the second chapter of Mark we see the familiar story of the man who was let down through the roof in order to be healed. Jesus also forgave this man's sin at this same point. The religious leaders didn't really care for that. Jesus knew what they were thinking and showed His ability to forgive sin by bidding the man to take up his bed and walk away.

Only God can forgive sin. It is only He Who has been offended by sin. No mere "prophet" could forgive sin. Only the One offended can pardon the one who offended. This is the difference between Jesus and the mere prophet, priest, apostle, or even preacher. All these have been affected by the sin of Adam and the world. To none of them was the offense directed.

Therefore, we cannot read this verse, "This day have I begotten thee," and consider that Jesus had a beginning at any time in His Eternal Essence. Isaiah wrote this as a prophecy of Jesus: "For unto us a child is born, unto us a son is given: and the government shall be upon his shoulder: and his name shall be called Wonderful, Counsellor, The mighty God, The everlasting Father, The Prince of Peace." (Isaiah 9:6)

A child was born but a son was given. The physical Jesus, Who was to offer up Himself on the Cross of Calvary, was born on a specific day in Bethlehem – A Child was born. But Jesus, "The mighty God," was a Son given to humanity. This is the dual nature of Jesus. He has always been God; but for us He became a human being so that He might offer Himself as a cleansing Sacrifice for our sin – A Son was given.

Some of the commentators referred to Romans 1:4, "And declared to be the Son of God with power, according to the spirit of holiness, by the resurrection from the dead," as the place where He was "begotten" as noted in this verse from Hebrews. I strongly disagree. Jesus was not begotten at that time. His Deity was proved by the resurrection. His Sonship is an eternal Sonship. He is considered at the Lamb slain before the foundations of the earth. (Revelation 13:8) He is the Creator of all. (John 1:3) He is, therefore, no created Being but God, eternal. He is of One Essence with the Father and the Holy Spirit. (Philippians 2:6)

It was The Father which appointed Jesus to the Office of the High Priest of our profession. This protocol was necessary in order to be true to the Words of God as given to Moses. Jesus was not from the lineage of Aaron and thus, to be true to His Own Words, necessitated that Jesus would be appointed High Priest from outside the line of Aaron.

In the determinative counsels of God He has exalted His inspired and eternal Words of Scripture above His Own Name: "I will worship toward thy holy temple, and praise thy name for thy lovingkindness and for thy truth: for thou hast magnified thy word above all thy name." (Psalm 138:2) How dare we mere men argue that God has lost control of, or hid from man, or only inspired the general concept of His Words? The Words of God remain eternal even as He is eternal. (Psalm 119:89)

God remains true to His Word. His Word is His bond, His dignity, His truth. We sit in a dreadful place when we demean and deny His Words of Truth.]

5.6 *As he saith also in another place, Thou art a priest for ever after the order of Melchisedec.*

Genesis 14:18-20; Psalm 110:4; Hebrews 7:1-10

[This "other place" is from the Psalm 110:4. We would note that Jesus quoted the first verse of this Psalm (Matthew 22:43-45) in relation to Himself.

Note that Melchisedec is called a priest rather than a high priest as Jesus is called in verse five, above. Jesus is not an unauthorized or self-appointed priest. Jesus, in His humanity as our Representative, is commissioned by the Father.

As Melchisedec is not Jewish, as were the priests of Aaron, so is the appeal of

Jesus to the entire world of humanity.

Melchisedec was also the King of Salem. It was not allowed that the King among the Hebrews be also a priest. I Samuel 13:9 records King Saul appropriating the role of priest and offering sacrifice. This was counted as a great sin in the life of Saul. His kingdom would be taken from him and his house.

It is instructive to note that Melchisedec was a priest before the establishment of the Aaronic priesthood. Part of the meaning here is that Jesus predates all other priests. This is not to say that Melchisedec was a preincarnate Jesus. This was obviously not so as Melchisedec did not bless Abraham; he only asked that God bless Abraham.

As for Melchisedec, both his mother and his father were unknown. He lived the life of humanity but there is neither record of his birth or of his death. Melchisedec is a type of Christ in that his ministry predated Aaron and there is no recorded beginning or ending of his days. We can look at these things in the life of Melchisedec and relate them to the coming Messiah.

There are differences between the priest and the High Priest. The priest is an underling but the High Priest is the supreme ruler of his domain. Jesus is both High Priest and King over His Church and His Creation.

The duties of the priest and the High Priest differed in location as the priest labored primarily in the court-yard of the tabernacle while the High Priest entered into the Holy Place. We can see the earthly ministry of Jesus as contrasted with His ascension and Heavenly Ministry.

The priest of the Temple busied himself with the offering of many sacrifices. Jesus only offered Himself one time. The Blood of Jesus was sufficient for eternal salvation and that Sacrifice needed not to be offered another time.

Also, as the High Priest took the blood of sacrifice to the Holy Place, we see that Jesus ascended into Heaven where the Heavenly Mercy Seat abides.

As Jesus was clothed in humanity for His Work on this earth, so was the clothing of the priest simple and utilitarian. The clothing of the High Priest was much more ornate. Jesus is now clothed in His Glory of Deity.]

5.7 *Who in the days of his flesh, when he had offered up prayers and supplications with strong crying and tears unto him that was able to save him from death, and was heard in that he feared;*

[This verse speaks of Jesus. Specifically, I believe it speaks to His time in the Garden of Gethsemane. It was here that He looked at His coming ordeal. He didn't blithely look at the coming horrors and say, "Well, by this time tomorrow it'll all be over."

Jesus looked at the pain and looked beyond it. I really believe this. Jesus was not a weak man. He was a rugged man well able to endure the pain – although it was a great pain. He may well have recoiled at this prospect.

The emotional pain would also be great. These men who were with Him would scatter in fright from the coming actions. Peter would deny Him. Judas had already betrayed Him. The plot was already in motion. Once the "trip wire" was set these friends, they had been with Him for over three years, would scatter in fear. He had a deep and abiding love for them. They professed such for Him. They would all, except for John, desert Him. His closest friends would leave Him in His terrible hour of need.

Jesus would watch His mother, who had seemingly followed Him throughout His earthly ministry, see the son of her youth tortured and dying in a public spectacle. This emotional pain would be agonizing to any human. Jesus had willingly taken upon Himself a human body specifically for this task.

The worst pain was that Jesus knew the time was coming when He would cry out, "My God, My God, Why hast Thou forsaken me?" Of one essence with The Father, Jesus had never experienced a single split second of separation from The Father. But, on that cross He would suffer the full penalty for the sins of the world. This, I believe, was His greatest agony. His fear was not fright. His fear was His devotion to The Father. In the human this was a Godly Fear.

Jesus asked for the cup of this death to be taken from Him. Then, quickly, He added, "Only if it is Your Will." An angel was sent to strengthen Him as He steeled Himself to do that for which He had come into the world.

Jesus is a High Priest Who understands our deepest worries and pains. He has suffered them. He stands with us as we suffer them. He is The High Priest Who has compassion and love for His people.

Jesus was obedient to the task set before Him. The glorious truth is that He understands that we may sometimes be hesitant. He understands and is ready to strengthen us for the task which is set before us.]

5.8 *Though he were a Son, yet learned he obedience by the things which he suffered;*

[Jesus is, always has been and always will be throughout the ageless ages of eternity, the Son of God. In His Kenosis Jesus had laid aside many of the glories of His essential Deity. (Philippians 2:5-8) This time in the Garden was time of trial for Jesus. Through the experience of this trial Jesus learned the lesson of obedience to a father. Jesus had always done as The Father directed during His earthly ministry. (John 8:29) He was now presented with a test. There was no chance that Jesus would falter during this test. He remained God in His essence and that fact precluded any possibility of failure. But, His suffering in this experience in His humanity would serve to give Him an even greater understanding of the trials and tribulation of humanity.

This was part of His purpose in being the Great High Priest of our salvation.]

5.9 *And being made perfect, he became the author of eternal salvation unto all them that obey him.*

[The phrase "being made perfect" has nothing to do with physical or moral perfection. The phrase has to do with completion. Jesus went to the Cross in order to finish the course which was His. He rose from the dead as a proof of His completion of that course. Jesus did everything perfectly to purchase our salvation.

That He is the "Author" of eternal salvation is that He – and only He – has the ability to save anyone from their sins. We can't do it ourselves. No "religious leader" can guarantee our home in Heaven and peace with God. I understand that there are a myriad of "faith systems." They are trying to plagiarize the work of Christ. We need the original work not an ersatz "copy" which has no real power.

I have written several books. Anyone can easily buy one and copy my work word for word. They can even sale them. I won't get a single cent of royalty payments on those copies. They may look a lot like mine; they are not.

Likewise, anyone can claim to offer salvation. Any religious system can claim to offer salvation. The royalty check on these will burn in the fires of Hell. They are false ways of salvation. Only full trust in the finished work of Jesus Christ is "the real deal." It is necessary to meet Jesus at the Cross to gain real salvation. Every time!

If you desire the "royalty" of Heaven you need to look in His Book and find Jesus.]

5.10   *Called of God an high priest after the order of Melchizedec.*

[Melchisedec is a mysterious figure to us. One thing not mysterious is that he worshiped the true God, Jehovah. We are tempted as we read the story of Abram to consider that Abram established the worship of Jehovah into the world.

He did not. Such an act would have elevated Abram above Jehovah. It would have nearly seemed that Abram had *invented* the worship of Jehovah if he had *introduced* Jehovah into the world of man. This is a very low view of the Creator God!

That Melchisedec was a priest unto Jehovah is proof that there were many scattered around the ancient world who did understand and preach of the True God. The ancients had a tradition that Melchisedec was Noah's son, Shem. I don't subscribe to this view but it would be understandable that a son of Noah would understand and worship the True God of the Heavens and Earth.

So would it be that even the sons of Shem would understand the true worship of the True God. It was sin in the life of humanity which had jettisoned this true worship of the True God from so much of human culture. (consider Romans 1:28)

The verse says that God "called" Jesus a High Priest. I do believe that this was a judicial appointment of the God of the sons of Abraham. However, the meaning here is more likely that The Father God called Jesus in the sense of recognizing the position of the Son as the Eternal High Priest of our profession.

That word "eternal" is indicated in Psalm 110:4 which is the full quotation from which Paul was arguing at this point. "The LORD hath sworn, and will not repent, Thou art a priest for ever after the order of Melchizedek." "For ever" is a comparable phrase to "eternity." For Melchizedec there is no recorded birth or death. Neither his father nor his mother is ever mentioned. In this sense the tenure of Melchizedec as a priest unto God was without beginning and without ending.

We do know that Melchizedec had both a birth and a death. We are only considering the literary picture which God has given of this man in the Scripture. Melchizedec was a type of Christ, Who is eternal in actuality.

The priesthood of Melchizedec predated the Aaronic priesthood. Therefore, it is not simply parallel; the priesthood of Melchizedec was superior to that of the sons of Aaron. As we shall see in the seventh chapter of Hebrews, the fact that Abram gave tithe to Melchizedec as the priest of the true God, means that Abram placed himself in a sense of spiritual subjection to Melchizedec.

Couple this with the realization that in Abram, even Aaron, would be considered as inferior to Melchizedec both in the paying of the tithe and in the accepting the blessing of God through the mediatorial office of Melchizedec.

Melchizedec labored hundreds of years before Aaron was born. Thus Melchizedec cannot be considered as of the lineage of Aaron. His priesthood was of

God. It was not of God via the mediation of Aaron.

Neither is Jesus of priestly lineage. As with Melchizedec, Jesus is a High Priest to the entire world of humanity rather than simply to the sons of Abraham.

Melchizedec was also the king of Salem. This is Jerusalem. Reading the meaning of the name of Salem we find that Melchizedec was "The King of Peace." Jesus is called "The Prince of Peace" in Isaiah 9:6. This does not mean that Melchizedec was a preincarnate appearance of Jesus. This does mean that Melchizedec was a type of Christ. We can learn some things of Christ by considering Melchizedec.

Melchizedec sat on the throne in Salem – Jerusalem. Jesus will sit on the throne of David in the city of the New Jerusalem. Melchizedec gave comfort and provision to the armies of Abram even as Jesus gives comfort and spiritual provision to the soldiers of the army of Jesus in this world.]

5.11 *Of whom we have many things to say, and hard to be uttered, seeing you are dull of hearing.*

[I understand the term "writer's block" where one just can't seem to continue for a lack of what words to write. Paul didn't have that problem. He had many things yet to illustrate from the typology of Melchizedec. There was much yet to learn of Christ by the study of this Old Testament example.

It wasn't "writer's block" that caused the consternation which Paul felt at this place. It was "hearer's block." The people were not prepared to hear and understand all that had been placed before them in the inspired and preserved Scripture.

These were not novice Christians. They were trained Jews who had converted to the religion of their Messiah. Unfortunately they understood Judaism so well that they were nearly apostate from the Christian message as they wandered back to the old familiar things rather than moving on into the message of Messiah.

We have the same problem in our day. Garner has listed five things which impede our ability to process the Biblical message. The first of these is a lack of devotion to the things of God. We were recently doing some "deep cleaning" at home. A letter from a girl I had dated nearly fifty years ago surfaced. Fifty years ago this letter was a precious thing to me. Today this lady, a wonderful person, and her letter which was hiding within an old book, meant little to me. I no longer had the deep love for her I once had. I had found much better with my wife, Linda.

Have we left our first love? (Revelation 2:4) I don't mean to ask if we have moved away from the faith in Jesus Christ. I mean to ask if we have found a shiny new toy of intellectual endeavor. Has our love for Christ waxed cold as we have found a love of searching out theological considerations? What is it that stands between us and that deep passion we ought to feel for our Lord and Savior? It isn't "better!" It may even be, from the standpoint of the world – and from the world of *churchy circles* – a seeming "good" thing. Folks, it is still an idol between us and God. Get rid of it and get back to God!

The second is a carelessness of divine matters. I see this in most of our attempts as "saying grace." For the most part this ritual, three times a day and nearly eleven hundred times a year, has become more pattern than true praise. Preachers handle the sacred every day; it should never become routine but should always be refreshing to our souls.

DeWitt on the GENERAL EPISTLES

Preacher, do you remember how it felt the first time you walked into a pulpit? How do you, do you even still realize what you do when you, approach the sacred responsibility to represent God to the people of God – every single time?

The third point is that we tend to become worldly minded. I don't mean that we put the world's needs before our duty to God. I mean, do we consider the Lord as paramount or do we root for the Packers? Rooting for the Packers is not a bad thing; my son is a rabid fan. This is a consideration of our priorities. If we do not keep God first in our lives He will soon be dismissed from our lives.

The fourth point is prayer. Do you? I don't mean, "Now I lay me down to sleep..." That isn't prayer. That is recitation. We had a good man preaching at this church for a while. He was brought up Lutheran. He preached the Gospel. But, he read his prayers. They were good prayers. They didn't get as high as the ceiling. I'm surprised he didn't trip over them on his way out. Prayer, real prayer, is conversation with God. I might have read books to my children when they were young. Prayer is talking with God. Do you? Do you really? Do you with fervor?

The fifth thing was a neglect of Scripture. I know that every preacher, even those who get their sermons from the internet, read the Scripture almost every day. But, do we really read it. My son has been working on a project with his son. He has read and reread the instructions. He doesn't want to get things wrong.

Without a private time of reading Scripture, not for "work" but for fellowship with the Lord, we will soon become dry and methodical spiritually. I recall the words of a man who said, "God couldn't get into that church if He had a pass key." The people all read their Sunday School Quarterlies. The preacher led in the "call to worship" from the back of the song books. But, no one had the slightest idea what direction God was moving because they dismissed His Book as a simple "tool of the trade" of being *churchy*. If we never take the time to hear God speak we will never be able to locate Him in an hour of need. We won't know where He is.

I'm going to add a sixth thing. Physical sloth keeps us from fully engaging with God. If I am so sleepy that I fall asleep while I'm typing, I either need to get more rest (not likely!) or more exercise so I can be alert to the leading of God. A little less gluttony wouldn't hurt, either! The purpose of food is to keep us alive. Too much may buy us a ticket out of the will of God! It will also tend to diminish our usefulness for God. An out of shape, overweight 70-year-old preacher presents a picture of a man of God that advertises he can't control himself. What does this say about that man's commitment to follow God?

What does this say about God's choice for spokesmen? May we begin to seek to never dishonor Him with our obese appearance.]

5.12 For when for the time ye ought to be teachers, ye have need that one teach you again which be the first principles of the oracles of God; and are become such as have need of milk, and not of strong meat.

[Vv. 12 – 15. The Scripture is the children's Bread of Life. The writer of Hebrews desires that we feed on the Word of God. He wants us to move from the elemental things on to the deeper things of God. We see the desire that we move on from the "milk" of the Word unto more meaty subjects.

The imagery used is of an infant and an adult. An infant will be fed milk. His system could not digest the meat even if he had the teeth to chew it. Likewise, there are many Christians who have never moved on into a study of the deeper things of God. They are deformed, malformed, in their spiritual lives.

It is through the Word that we are able to begin to understand and assimilate some of those things that God would have us to know. The Spirit guides us as we study the Words of God. We become less carnal in our attitudes and deportment and more spiritual in our outlook into the world about us.

If we were never intended to learn more of Him, if the salvation experience was all that He has for us, He would not have commanded us to study His Words. "Study to shew thyself approved unto God, a workman that needeth not to be ashamed, rightly dividing the word of truth." (II Timothy 2:15)

Our salvation is the greatest thing, to be sure. Without that base of salvation our spirit can never be rejuvenated unto the things of God. But, once that salvation has renewed our soul, God expects us to move forward.

The people to whom this Book was addressed were not recent converts; they should have been fully functioning teachers of others about the things of God.

The reference to "oracles" was a reference to pagans who would always consult their oracles for guidance in all matters. The Christian has an oracle which should always be teaching him the things of God. This is the Scripture. We should be often engaged in searching out the will of God for our daily lives. (II Timothy 2:15)

The milk of the Word is the rudiments of the Word. Even these had become bypassed. In accordance with the general thrust of the Book, and the phrase "are become," suggests that these people had experienced an incipient apostasy of indifference to the things of God. They cared less, and consequently searched less, for things of God than they had at one point.

The Christian life has been likened to a greased pole. We have the rope of fellowship with the Lord that eases our climb to grow in Him. When we forgo this rope for anything else, education, piety, church, we tend to begin to "back slide." We can never hold our position, much less move forward, when we do not hold tightly to the Savior.

We might look at the food. When my son was a baby we mentioned to his pediatrician that his sister had been hard to "break" from her bottle. The pediatrician said, "Never give him anything but formula in the bottle. Juice and water should come from a cup whenever possible. Some day he'll simply throw that bottle away." We did. And, he did.

Within the "meat" of the Word there is a great variety. Paul was beginning to show this with an appeal to the typology of Melchizedec. Preachers always need to preach the entire Bible. Our favorite verses may be comfortable but we need to always move forward. The people of God will follow the leading of God when He is allowed to be seen.]

5.13 *For every one that useth milk is unskillful in the word of righteousness: for he is a babe.*

[A pious person may pontificate that he is only interested in seeing souls saved. This will generally be a person who has no real desires to see God glorified.

A kindergarten teacher may love those young charges. The teacher may hate to see them graduate to the next level. The teacher misses the little ones. But, this teacher does realize that a 17-year-old who is only able to do the work of a kindergarten student is a tragedy. Such is a case of an arrested development of a person who will never fulfill his own life in the world. The kindergarten teacher has completed the task when that student is able to move to first grade and be successful.

Likewise we do need to see souls saved into the Kingdom. We fail these souls if we do not prepare them to move beyond the first principles of salvation and move into a useful life for the Lord. It is this which will insure another "crop" of converts, saved from sin and unto glory, through the ministry of these earlier converts. They are then no longer "babes in Christ;" they have become laborers in the fields of their Lord.

This expanded knowledge will allow us to see the glory of God, expanded and fulfilling, as we move forward in Him.

Paul, once again, was writing to Jewish Christians. It is possible that they had latched on to some of the rudiments of the faith by considering the Jewish sacrificial system. It is possible that some of these were converts from that first Day of Pentecost. These had much to learn of Jesus. A self-satisfied smugness in "finding the way" does not equate with a Soldier of the Cross who seeks to win, and teach, others of Christ.

A babe is unfit for spiritual warfare; he is an easy target for the enemy of our souls.]

5.14 *But strong meat belongeth to them that are of full age, even those who by reason of use have their senses exercised to discern both good and evil.*

[As in the above verse, it is not the province of a human to remain a baby. The natural progression is to move from baby to toddler, to child, and finally to adult. One who does not follow this progression is said to be "disabled." Let us not be disabled Christians! God decreed better for us than this.

Rather than continuing to depend on others for all things in the Christian life we are to so grow in the graces of God that we begin to understand the higher things God would have for us to understand. In this way we become more and more useful for the Master and for others who have a need to come to, and grow in, that same Master.

My grandson delights in trying to get me to play catch with him. Just a few days ago I had a cataract removed from my left eye. Since I am currently wearing an eye patch over that eye (Only for ten days.), I have no real depth perception to see when the ball is near enough to catch it. Paul is comparing our physical senses to our spiritual senses in this passage.

Once upon a time I played right field for our elementary school Cub Scout baseball team. To say I was only terrible would be to brag that I was better than I was. If my memory serves me correctly (And if it didn't there are those who would remind me!), I went two years without a hit. I continued to practice. Eventually I became a good enough hitter that I no longer embarrassed myself.

Childhood sports are the cause of almost all male neuroses.

The same set of rules applies to our spiritual knowledge. There are things we learn as we continue to follow the command of God to study the Scripture. Some things we will never learn. As we continue to grow in the Lord there will be more things about Him which we will want to learn.

One of the problems for those who have never made the effort to learn more of Christ is that they become "easy pickings" for the cultist. The cultist will advertise a "Bible Study" which will turn into an indoctrination session. In these the unarmed Christian is in danger. He still will not learn of Christ; he will learn the tenets of the cultist.

Paul wants those to whom he writes to be able to discern the difference between good and bad, between righteousness and sin. We do this by a study of the Scripture; a consistent and directed study will allow us to learn those things God has for us to learn. Never simply trust a preacher or a religious writer; always trust the inspired and preserved Word of God as the Spirit illumines such to us.

One caution in this study: It is necessary to consider the entire Scripture. We can never build a doctrinal base on a single Scripture. God's method of inspiration of that Scripture includes the concept of progressive revelation. His Words were never false; they are always His Words of Truth given to humanity. However, through the various dispensations of human time we do see God expanding His teaching. The truth only deepens in reality as He leads mankind into the spiritual principles which underlie, and are explained by, the inspired and preserved Word of God.]

HEBREWS - CHAPTER SIX

6.1   Therefore leaving the principles of the doctrine of Christ, let us go on unto perfection, not laying again the foundation of repentance from dead works, and of faith toward God,

[One of the reasons I believe Paul was the human penman of Hebrews is that he was a well-trained Pharisee. (Acts 22:3; 23:6) The writer here displays the training of a "Doctor of the Law" in his arguments to people who were seeped in the things of the Jewish religion. I tend to believe that many of those to whom this Book was intended were devout Jews converted during the Day of Pentecost revival.

These were men who knew and revered the Old Testament Law to such an extent that they came from great distances to be in the Temple on that day in reverence to the Jewish holiday. They were also men who were converted to Jesus and "stayed on" with the Jerusalem church displaying that same religious devotion toward Messiah.

The argument of Paul was that they had simply "stayed on." They had not progressed in the Christian Religion as they ought to have done.

The first large problem which comes to mind is in reference to the Gnostic teachers of the early church age. Note that I did not say "early church;" I said "early church age." Many who would make a claim to teach Christianity are not teaching the Christian Religion.

In this I would note that the Gnostic teachers believed that much, or special, learning would allow them to reach a state of salvation. Paul argues for people who have already received salvation to learn more of their Lord. The purpose was not to gain salvation but to grow in the salvation they already possessed.

Christian growth is geared toward a greater awareness of the glories of God. It is a quality which is directed toward the greater glory of God and His Person than toward ourselves for personal gain.

The meaning of Paul, as evidenced by the use of "milk" in the verses 12 and 13 of the previous chapter, is the "completeness" of maturity. "More about Jesus would I know, More of His grace to others show; More of His saving fullness see, More of His love who died for me." So goes the old Hewitt Hymn. That hymn could well be our prayer as we follow the Words of Paul in this passage.

Paul bids us move from dead works to a living faith.

The writing was to New Testament Christians who still clung to their Old Testament theology. They understood the concept of faith and repentance. They still tended to see them in the light of Old Testament example rather than in their New Testament fulfillment and reality of the work of Messiah. Messiah had already, as no mere man could due to the incipient sin nature within, fulfilled an obedience to the entire Law of Moses. In Him we have received a freedom from that Law. It isn't that we do not seek to live by the principles of that Law. It is that we live in freedom from the penalty of that Law.

The Christian life is alive in the reality of the Love of Jesus, the Christ. His sacrifice has been completed. Our salvation is assured. Let us move on from the dead work of a fulfilled Law and live in the freedom that is in Jesus. We need not *obey* the

Law in fear of retribution but rather, *respect* and follow the principles of that Law from our love in reciprocation to the Love which Jesus has shown to us.

In Leviticus 16:21 and following, we have a picture of that "laying on of hands" by Aaron upon the head of a goat. Symbolically this goat would carry the sins of the people away from the camp. Jesus, by His sacrifice, has carried away our sin as far as the East is from the West. (Psalms 103:12)

As an aside: How did David know that east and west never meet? On the great globe of the earth if one is standing on the North Pole every direction is south. Likewise a person standing on the South Pole would find every direction as north. But the east is always fleeing from the west as the earth turns on its axis. How did David understand this principle?

The answer is that David did not understand this. It was just a phrase that came from the mind of God unto the pen of David. The inspiration lay on the Word of God not the concept of David.

We would also note that the concept of the laying on of hands was a part of the initiation of a person into the fellowship of the early church. It was a symbolic transfer of the power of the Spirit into the membership of that early church.

In a more modern term we might argue that Paul was saying, "Don't keep standing on the promises. Carry them out in the world which stands in need." The sanctuary of the church is a clinic for the Christian to learn his responsibility to the Lord. The world around that church is the area of operation for the Christian to discharge his responsibility to the Lord.]

6.2   Of the doctrine of baptisms, and of laying on of hands, and of resurrection of the dead, and of eternal judgment.

[Although the concept of the breaking of the Scripture into verses is not part of the original reality of the inspiration of the Scripture, it is worth noting that the idea of repentance and saving faith is separated as a foundational issue from these others. The repentance which comes with faith and the faith which comes with repentance are similar. They are indicative that one has received Jesus Christ as Lord and Savior.

Unless we see ourselves as in need of a Savior we will be loath to repent of our natural bent toward day-to-day life. The poet Robert Burns wrote, I paraphrase, "Would the gift be given to see ourselves as others see us." When we see ourselves as God sees us we will be led to repentance from our sins. At this point we become willing, anxious, to access faith in the risen Savior as an atonement for our sins. The one seems to rest within the other.

The things illustrated in this second verse were often practiced by those from without the household of faith.

Since the very meaning of the "Baptism" means to dip or immerse, we can consider that the Jewish rights of many washings were a type of baptism. They were part of the Levitical Law but they could not offer salvation.

This verse does not suggest that there are various "modes" of Scriptural baptism any more than it assigns grace on behalf of any baptism. The concept of Grace is only because of the Cross. Any unsaved persons baptism will make him wet, not regenerated.

Neither can any baptism in the Christian Church offer salvation. This was a church ordinance which displayed the death, burial and resurrection Jesus as the person baptized was dipped below the water and then raised back. This is an illustration of the converts acceptance of Jesus as Lord and Savior. The only salvation within this ordinance is the salvation which has already been claimed by the penitent. It is a picture to the world, and to the church, that this person has taken Jesus as his Savior.

Among the Christian churches there was also the Baptism of the Holy Spirit. (Matthew 3:11)

As for the laying on of hands, this was a familiar thing among the Jewish religion. In Matthew 10:13 we see Jesus laying His hands upon the children as He blessed them.

Among the "sign gifts" of the early church the laying on of hands was used in healing, (Acts 28:19) ordination, (I Timothy 5:22) and the imparting of the Holy Spirit.

While God is Sovereign, as a general rule these "sign gifts" ceased operation at the close of the impartation of the inspired and preserved Words of the New Testament. I do acknowledge that God can well do as His wills without violating my own theological view. Still, I think it very obvious that the sign gifts are no longer in general operation.

The belief in the resurrection of the dead is two fold. The Old Testaments prophets, I think primarily here of Job (Job 19:26) and Daniel (Daniel 12:13) as obvious examples of this belief.

This was another seminal doctrine of the early church. The Sadducees did not agree with this doctrine (Mark 12:18) although the Pharisees did in principle if not in full concert with the church.

Neither did the Philosophers to whom Paul spoke agree with this doctrine. (Acts 17:32)

Paul also mentioned the concept of eternal judgment. When God breathed the Breath of Life into Adam the entire human race was endowed with an eternity of existence. We will all exist forever. The Christian will live an eternal life of bliss and blessing with our Savior. The person who has never accepted Jesus as Savior will have an eternal existence of suffering over his unforgiven sin.

Our job is not to learn all. Our purpose is that we learn more of Jesus each day that we will be useful ambassadors of His to those who are lost. We pray that the Spirit will convict as we issue the Good News that Jesus Christ died in time so that we could live in eternity.]

6.3   *And this will we do, if God permit.*

[The plan of Paul is to begin teaching the deeper things of God.

Paul seems to say the he intends to look at the Old Testament truths and see New Testament facts about God and the Christian religion.

It is interesting that Paul, while he is writing down the inspired and preserved Words of God in this instance, still voices his own dependence upon God. Paul, arguably one of the smartest men to ever live, voices his own complete dependence upon God.

This is a place where we ought also to abide. (James 4:13-15)

There is a sublime interconnectedness within the inspired and preserved Scripture. Over forty men took pen in hand to write the Words of this miracle Book. Only One Eternal God was the ultimate Author. This shows throughout the text.

HEBREWS: Chapter 6

This fact alone should be enough to convince any serious inquirer that the Bible stands through the years of time as the unassailable testament to the Love of God for His creation!]

6.4 *For it is impossible for those who were once enlightened, and have tasted of the heavenly gift, and were made partakers of the Holy Ghost,*

Matthew 24:3

[Some have mistakenly concluded that this extended passage teaches that a person can "fall" from grace. Reading the fifth chapter immediately preceding this passage we see that the writer of Hebrews is speaking of the picture of the High Priestly duties of Jesus. Paul wishes to move beyond simple doctrine (the milk of the Word - 5:13) and move on to a more mature discussion of doctrine (the meat of the Word - 5:14). But (6:3) it is still necessary to consider the rudimentary things of the faith. Under this heading the writer says that "if it were possible...to fall away."

The very fact that this phrase is used makes it clear that it is NOT possible to fall away. Had this been a real possibility the writer would have used the phrase "when one falls away," rather than "if it were possible." Later (7:26-28) the writer explains the all sufficiency of Jesus Christ. For one to be able to fall from the faith (i.e. lose his salvation) it would mean that Christ was, Himself, ineffectual. It would mean that Christ must be sacrificed often when He was sacrificed but once. Rather than teaching that one may fall from grace, this passage, when viewed in its complete context, is a ringing affirmation that Jesus is "able to save them to the uttermost that come unto God by him, seeing he ever liveth to make intercession for them." (Hebrews 7:25) Jesus, the writer of Hebrews informs us, is even more than "the author and finisher of our faith," (Hebrews 12:5) He is the Active Sustainer of our faith. Our salvation comes by Him and He, Himself, is the Guarantee of that salvation. The very phrase "author and finisher" would argue that salvation, even the "keeping" of it, is of Christ since all of it from beginning to end is of Him.

One of the first basics of hermeneutical study (One of those "theological" words. It simply means the attempt to understand what has been written.) is to ascertain to whom the writer was addressing. In this case it was Jewish Christians who had not fully separated from their Jewish roots. Although they had begun to understand, and accept, the reality of the New Testament of the Blood of Jesus, they were still bound by their Old Testament understanding of the Law and Ceremonies as propagated by Moses.

These were people to whom Paul had been addressing in regards to apostasy. One cannot simply become apostate from a concept. The very term connotes to apostate *from* something. With this in mind we must argue that this verse speaks of those who have been baptized, an initiation rite, into a local church – presumably the church in Jerusalem. These are professors of the Christian religion. But, it is obvious from this verse and those following that they are not possessors of true salvation.

"They were once enlightened:" They had been led to understand that faith in Jesus, the Messiah, was not a departure from Judaism. This faith would lead to a deeper walk with the God of Abraham than even the walk with Moses had been. They even understood the concept that in Jesus all of the Old Covenant types and ceremonies had found their fulfillment.

"They have tasted of the heavenly gift..." Sadly, this does not say that they have ingested the heavenly gift. First, what is the heavenly gift? It is true salvation whereby one has had his sins forgiven and is now blessed with an eternal destiny of heavenly bliss with the Savior.

Second, this means the infilling of the Holy Spirit. This is the fact of the Spirit taking up a residence within the body of the believer. This is not the same as being baptized with The Holy Ghost. The first speaks of the fellowship of the believer with the Savior. The latter has to do with the power of the Spirit imparted to a functioning and committed believer.

The one speaks of honest salvation while the other speaks of dedication and commitment within that salvation.

There is a third phrase in this verse. "Made partakers of the Holy Ghost..." This is separate from the previous phrase. To be a partaker of the Spirit is not the same as being enlightened by the Spirit. To be enlightened is to be taught by Him. This is the illumination of the inspired and preserved Scripture. This had been experienced by these who were not yet saved. It was part of the process by which the Spirit called them unto true repentance and conversion.

These had partaken of the Spirit in that His convicting power was upon them in those arguments concerning Christ as shown by the Hebrew Scripture. But, they had only tasted of these truths. Nowhere is the suggestion made that they had received these truths into their lives. They may have assented in their minds. This assent gave them an entrance into fellowship with the saints. This mere understanding did not bring them in true repentance and faith to the Cross of Jesus.

Jesus told a parable about a man who sowed a field in Matthew 13:3-8. Some of the seed fell upon good ground. It brought forth fruit. This is a picture of true conversion. Some of the seed fell into land overgrown with weeds. This seed was strangled by the weeds and did not blossom. Some of the seed fell into stony ground. It blossomed but soon died out because there was no root system. It was not connected to the ground which would have given it life.

Any gardener understands this parable. So does any pastor who has preached salvation and seen all three responses. Some are saved. Some are interested in the concept but refuse the reality. Some are real "fire crackers." They set off sparks but soon tumble back to the earthly.

The people to whom Paul alluded were "fire crackers." They may have put on a good display but they were only energized by their own gun powder. They looked real but they did not have the power of a true profession.

These were the ones who scurried back to their "religion" even after hearing, and even seeing in others, the power of God.

Paul is warning the readers not to be deceived by the example of others but to be empowered by the Spirit of God.]

6.5   And have tasted the good word of God, and the powers of the world to come,

[Continuing on from the last verse we see that these are people who have tasted the good word of God. Do you understand that the Old Testament is the Word of God? We, as Christians, tend to major on the New Testament. The completed New Testament was not yet finished in the realms of time and available. But, these Jewish people were those who greatly loved the Words of God as given by Moses and the Prophets.

Make no mistake, these Old Testament Scriptures taught Jesus. What a thrill it must have been to these devout Jewish men to read of the promises of Messiah in the Hebrew Scriptures and then see these same Scriptures fulfilled in their Messiah, Jesus.

Not only had they tasted the Word of God from the Old Testament, they had also tasted the reality of the Word of God in the Person of Jesus. In His Name they saw prophecy revealed and bodies healed. It was a thrilling confirmation of their Jewish identity.

Oops! Problem here. There was a real consideration to fall back into their Jewish identity and reality. This is the problem which Paul was warning about.

We look at this verse and see the phrase "world to come." We see Heaven. We see the doctrine of death and resurrection. These men look at the same phrase and see it from the Jewish perspective of the day. "World to come," to them, spoke of the coming Messiah. They saw the restoration of Israel. We look and see the Church Age.

Going back just a few chapters, these men looked at the coming age in the light of the "rest" offered by Moses and Joshua in the Land of Promise. A false view of a false reality will always bring an erroneous view of Truth.

These men to whom Paul is writing would have been recipients of much of the genuine outward signs of a born again person. They had been enlightened to the realities of Jesus as the Messiah as He fulfilled the prophecies of Old Testament prophets as to His Office. They heard His teaching and heard the "ring of truth." They had even, probably, been well aware of John the Baptist as he prepared the way.

They had tasted of the things of God and had intellectually accepted them as agreeable to their Old Testament religious outlook.

They had partaken of the Spirit in that they had felt His tug upon their heart-strings with His convicting voice.

They had an honest and abiding love for the Words of God in their Old Testament Scriptures.

They may have even participated in the powers of God. They may have been physically healed by the power of the risen Christ. But, they had not participated by accepting that Jesus, and only Jesus, is the answer to the sin problem.

They were wont to go back to the comfortable sacrifices of their old lives. In this, returning to their Jewish roots and the religion of Moses, they had rejected the Person of Jesus as Savior. True Christianity has never been a religion. It has always been a relationship with the Lord of Glory.]

6.6 *If they shall fall away, to renew them again unto repentance, seeing they crucify to themselves the Son of God afresh, and put him to an open shame.*

[Genesis 6:3 says, "And the LORD said, My spirit shall not always strive with man, for that he also is flesh: yet his days shall be an hundred and twenty years." This was before the flood. The great age of the pre-flood patriarchs diminished after the flood due to the sin of man. Psalm 90:10 speaks of a further reduction of the age of man. Make no mistake, sin kills and harms the creation and the humans of that creation.

Note well the word "if." This is not a pledge that men will fall away from the teaching of God but is a warning least one apostatize from the faith as these "professors" were in danger of doing. I find here an example of a spiritual principle. It is not possible that one who has been brought to the brink, as it were, of salvation may ever find himself so close to God at any future moment.

I think of a girl I dated in high school. I had not seen her in about twenty years when she appeared at a gas station where I was working. I invited her to church. She said, "Oh, I still believe all those things from back then. But, I don't go to church any more." I've known many people like this. The person who once attended church and seemed so spiritually minded slowly drifts away. Years later he may profess to "still believe" but every issue of his life suggests differently.

The Holiness people have two phrases I try to always remember. One is "God is a Gentleman. He forces His way on no man." The second is "Crossing the deadline." The meaning is that God does not promise to always strive with man. The deep conviction of one day may become the memory of another day. We need to accept salvation when the Spirit lays the message upon our heart. We can come to God only when He calls us. Salvation is completely His Work. Even our acceptance is predicated upon His calling. I honestly believe that it is possible to, again as the Holiness people would say, sin away our day of grace.

There is a story of a young man who asked a certain girl out on a date. She said, "I wouldn't go out with you unless you were the last person alive on earth." The young man said that her indecision gave him hope. But, after having seen her go out with too many other men, he thought that it would be best if he dismissed her from his mind.

May no one ever refuse God's gracious call so often as to see Him no longer call!

Paul does give a reason that the man who has apostatized may not return to the state where he would seek salvation. Such a person, as the one above in verses 4 and 5, has felt the glory of God upon his spirit as the Spirit called. In refusing to respond to the convicting call of God this person has said by his action of refusal that God is not worthy of him. That is the picture given to the world.

We can also consider that one who was once saved, and has fallen from grace – were it possible – would need to return to the first elements of salvation which is the Cross of Jesus. Jesus has been ONCE sacrificed. There is no return to those first elements for one who has – if it were possible – renounced or lost his salvation. Jesus has once suffered for the sins of the world. There is no more sacrifice available to one who counts this as a small thing.]

6.7 *For the earth which drinketh in the rain that cometh oft upon it, and bringeth forth herbs meets for them by whom it is dressed, receiveth blessing from God:*

[There are thunderstorms in the forecast for today. It could be worse. There are flash flood warnings for the state north of us. I really haven't heard how much moisture we are going to get. The forecast is for five inches to the north of this location.

There is a difference between what we are expecting and what they are expecting. We will see a rain that soaks into the ground and brings life to the crops of farms and gardens in the area. In the North they are going to see so much water as to hurt the crops, cause erosion and keep the farmers from their fields.

HEBREWS: Chapter 6

One is good and one is not so good. For us the water will come down and refresh the land as it soaks into the soil. For those north, the water will probably cause more harm that help! It's all in the manner which the earth reacts to the water given.

The same blessing of rain will overwhelm one area even as it gives food to another.

It is the same, in Paul's parable, with the graces of God. For the truly repentant the blessing will be accepted into the life and cause a growth for God's use. For the apostate there will be no real blessing. Blessing is available to the apostate but he allows it to "run off" and actually harm him.

The reason for the dichotomy? One will internalize the blessing and use it to grow in the Lord. The other will not only refuse – the "run off" – but will somehow resent the blessing in such a way as to not see God's goodness but to reject God's power and leading.]

6.8 *But that which beareth thorns and briers is rejected, and is nigh unto cursing; whose end is to be burned.*

[Moving beyond the good ground we see the desert land of thorns and briers. This is a parable of those who will become apostate from the faith and follow after human religion.

I was stationed at one point in Ft. Bliss, Texas. This particular base is basically within the city of El Paso. This area in West Texas is nearly desert land.

At one place I noticed a bridge over a small dry stream bed. I didn't think much of it until there was a storm up in the mountains. The area gets so little rain that the ground is hard; it does not drink in the rain. That dry stream bed became a raging river before I even realized there was a storm. God warns these people not to let go of His Words; these are words of warning.

Some argued that this were words of warning about the impending judgment upon the city of Jerusalem. Jerusalem was the capital of the Jewish religious system. It was there that Jesus was judged "criminal" and "heretic" by the leadership of this religious system. It was there that Jesus was sacrificed and put to death. Jerusalem was judged for the sins of both Jew and Gentile in 70 A.D. by the same Roman army which had nailed the Son of God to the Cross of Calvary.

While I would agree that Jerusalem was judged, I do not agree that this was the thought in the mind of Paul as he wrote this epistle.

Instead Paul was warning the people of the Jewish church about their mishandling of the blessings of God. He was warning to turn fully to God. The previous verse explained the suitable place for their faith the operate; it was within the will and directive of God. Those "herbs" which the good land grew were not only tasty additions to the diet; they were also medicinal in nature. They would keep the human body in good shape. This is a reminder that a proper relationship with the Creator will keep our souls in better shape!

As to those who would apostatize, they were those who brought forth spiritual briars and thorns. There is no real food value in briars and thorns. They will even tend to crowd out the good crops which might have been grown in the lives of these people.

This land was a rejected land because of the poor yield of the land allowed little for useful crops. Can we actually expect the smile of God upon our lives if we spend them outside His will? We are become useless to His eternal determinative will when we display briars and thorns rather than the wheat and barley of consecration.

The land must have seemed cursed because other land would yield good crops but this land was less than useless. It was actively arrayed against good cultivation. Therein is the base problem of the person who rejects the blessing and leading of God. In this we are arrayed with the enemy of our souls against the purposes of God.

I am a city boy. It's a small city but my only method of harvesting corn has to do with visiting the local grocery store. I have no clue!

When my wife and I were in Louisiana we saw a field on fire. I ran to the farmhouse near the field and reported what I'd seen. The farmer wasn't there; he was "working" the fire. When I reported the fire to his wife she looked at me like I was a complete idiot. Well, maybe not "complete" but pretty close. "If we don't burn off the stubble we will not be able to grow a crop."

The Romans, and others, also did this on fields that gave only thorns and briars. The intent was to kill the seeds of the weeds so they could grow better crops of real food stuff.

I won't elaborate but, the one who leaves the things of Christ for the things of man is also in danger of feeling the flames of the fires of Hell upon himself.]

6.9 *But, beloved, we are persuaded better things of you, and things that accompany salvation, though we thus speak.*

[Paul admits that he has been speaking harshly. He now modifies this by reminding the Hebrew believers that they are his brethren, both in the flesh and in the Spirit. He has been warning them of an apostasy from the pure faith and back into the bondage of the Law.

There was no doubt those among them that there those who were actors; these may not have even understood their place of danger. These were those who were close, as in verses 4-6, to having obtained actual salvation. They were so close as to have fooled not only the others but also themselves into believing that they were saved. God knew their heart. Paul had appealed to them to make certain that their faith was in God rather than in Religion. These, like an ocean liners anchor attached to a rowboat, would have dragged down the effectiveness and testimony of the Church. Our true "good works" lay neither in good intentions nor even in seemingly – from the worlds standpoint – good results. The only True Good Works always lay in the will of God directed out into the world as a testimony to His Glory and mercy. These good works are only such as accompany true salvation within the heart of the believer.

Paul compliments the true Christians with his remark that they are not as the ones spoken about in the preceding verses. They are the good and productive ground rather than the worthless and cursed ground.

Paul had said some hard things in this letter. His purpose may be summed up by II Peter 3:9, "The Lord is not slack concerning his promise, as some men count slackness; but is longsuffering to us-ward, not willing that any should perish, but that all should come to repentance." Paul issued warning that the believers and the seeming believers should "Examine yourselves, whether ye be in the faith; prove your own selves. Know ye not your own selves, how that Jesus Christ is in you, except ye be reprobates?" (II Corinthians 13:5)

HEBREWS: Chapter 6

The warning of Paul was of the judgment of God upon those who were not truly saved by the Blood of Christ. Faith, true saving faith, is not a matter of what we might know or even teach. It is a matter of Who we know in that faith relationship. We must know Jesus as Savior to have become true adopted sons of God. "That your faith should not stand in the wisdom of men, but in the power of God." (I Corinthians 2:5)]

6.10 *For God is not unrighteous to forget your work and labour of love, which ye have shewed toward his name, in that ye have ministered to the saints, and do minister.*

[As the proof of his reason for faith in these people, was Paul's greater faith in the mercies and glory of God. Further, Paul does take time to compliment these people on their abundance of Christian love in action. They may not have learned the intricacies of all of Christian doctrine but they have learned, as shown by their actions, that they have learned the need of Christian service.

God would not forget their true service to Him. His promises of judgment are frightenly true; so are His promises of blessing. As these people had blessed others in their need, so also would these people be blessed in their own hour of need. (I Corinthians 16:1; Romans 15:26 ff)

We must pause at this point and understand the blessing of God is never a promise of wealth as the world would count wealth in money and possessions. Most of us would have real problems in administering wealth in a Christian manner; this is a gift of God which is shown to bring Glory to the Lord and converts to their own salvation. The promise of God is for our daily sustenance as was the manna for the children of Israel in the wilderness. (Matthew 6:30) Note that this promise is based on His grace rather than our merit.

I would also emphasize the change here from speaking of professors of religion and the possessors of true Salvation. Paul mentions in verse nine that these blessings of verse ten are the things that accompany true salvation. The work of the people which is mentioned is a work that is both performed *in* the fact of their salvation but is also the work performed *because of* or flowing *from* that salvation. (Ephesians 2:10)]

6.11 *And we desire that every one of you do shew the same diligence to the full assurance of hope unto the end:*

["We." I do not believe that Paul was using the "imperial we" of monarchs. Such a construct would suggest that Paul considered himself as above the church to which he was writing. I understand this "we" as twofold. First, those who were fellow-laborers with Paul would have felt the same desire to see these Jewish Christians both stand fast in the faith of the Lord. But, secondly, all Christians are encouraged by the growth of other Christians. One of the values of a local church body is that each of the church will tend to build up one another in the faith. Any action of faith of one will strengthen the other within the faith.

The object was to show Christian love in supporting one another. This Christian benevolence would also be noticed by those outside the household of faith. A constant testimony of care is a continuing testimony to the enlivening power of the Spirit. This will serve as one means of drawing others to the Savior.

The hope here is the full assurance that Jesus keeps all of His promises. We can hold this type of hope dear to the end of our earthly lives. The churches can hold this type of hope dear until the end of the Church Age when we meet Him in the clouds. This hope is not an opinion but a reality of Assurance based on the power of God to give such assurance to the people who are in Christ, Jesus.]

6.12 *That ye be not slothful, but followers of them who through faith and patience inherit the promises.*

[Paul exhorts these believers not to be slothful, that is timorous, frightened, or negligent in waiting for the promises of God. His primary thrust is toward those Old Testament patriarchs as is shown by the following verse and the previous references made to the people of the exodus from Egypt.

God has given us many examples from the Old Testament which are teaching us things we need to understand of the spiritual in the New Testament. Abraham was given a promise. He didn't live to see most of the fulfillment of that promise but he didn't waver in his trust in the God of that promise.

Isaac and Jacob, and those of following generations, did not see the fulfillment of the Promise of God. Eventually, as Paul had spoken of earlier in this Book, the people of Abraham did enter into the Land of the Promise. But, even after the Kingdom had been established they did not see the promised Messiah. This was a hoped-for fact but was not realized for hundreds of years until Jesus came to live among men. (Luke 10:24)

This was the primary meaning of Paul in this passage. However, I think that it does no violence to the passage to consider it also in the sense of the New Testament Church. There were examples of persecuted Christians. There were examples of blessed Christians. These could also be seen by the people to whom Paul wrote. Their testimony would be a blessing to each other. So could these men to whom Paul wrote become a testimony of blessing to others.

Speaking of the blessing given by example of the patriarchs and others, Burkitt has noted that, "Heaven is not ours by purchase, but by promise." The exhortation was to trust God in all things.]

6.13 *For when God made promise to Abraham, because he could swear by no greater, he sware by himself,*

[God made certain promises to Abraham; one of these was to bless the entire earth through the seed of Abraham. (Genesis 12:3) This is a reference to Messiah, which is Jesus Who became the sacrifice for sin unto all, son of Abraham and Gentile, who would accept the salvation He made available through His Sacrifice on the Cross of Calvary.

Paul was specifically speaking of the passage in Genesis where Abraham was prepared to offer his son in sacrifice should this be the desire of God. (Genesis 22:15-18) Paul did not quote the entire passage. He was certain that his audience would be sufficiently familiar with the passage to understand the meaning.

Why was the very portion which spoke of Messiah left of in this quotation by Paul? I must confess that I do not understand. It could be that it was so there would be no hint that Messiah had transferred all the promises to Abraham, and his progeny, unto another. These promises which God made in covenant with Abraham were never to be transferred from Abraham to the church – or to anyone else!

There is a theology current among men whereby it is postulated that all the promises to the Jewish people were removed from them and transferred to the Church. Such is not the case! God made certain promises to Abraham and swear on His Own honor that He would perform these things in reference to the sons of Abraham. God has never gone back on His Word. The promises to Abraham and his sons are the property of Abraham and his sons. This is the inviolate Word of the Lord. As Christians there are some of which we may share in; but the primary promise is to the sons of Abraham.

God has said that His promises are secure. They are guaranteed by Himself on His Own eternal authority and honor. It is His certainty among those promises to Abraham that are the guarantee of His promises to us of the churches. One certainty secures the other certainty.]

6.14 *Saying, Surely blessing I will bless thee, and multiplying I will multiply thee.*

[This is a partial quotation from Genesis 22:15-18. Paul, writing to Jewish men, would have expected them to be so conversant with the Old Testament Scripture as to understand the entire passage from the "snippet" he supplied. This was the salient part of the passage in regard to the argument of Paul. The argument was that God had made, and obviously kept, promises to Abraham. Thus, the promises to the Christians were also guaranteed of fulfillment by God.

It is worth noting that the passage in Genesis reads, "I will multiply thy seed." The meaning remains the same. But, still this presents a problem unless we consider that the Same Spirit which inspired the Genesis account also inspired the passage in Hebrew. Thus, in a sense, the Hebrews passage was a *version* or *translation* of the Genesis passage. The Holy Spirit has every right to refine His Own Words. The purpose of the Hebrews passage is that men see that God had kept His promise to Abraham.

We could argue that the seed of Abraham was contained within his own self so "his seed" multiplying is not different from Abraham multiplying. That is true, of course; but it is not satisfying on some levels.

It is my feeling that the "law of double fulfillment" is in order in this place. This law of Biblical understanding is that prophecy may refer to a local event at the time of the writing and at the same time to an event in the distant future.

We see this law in operation quite often in reference to Messiah. Isaiah 7:14 concerns Syria and Remilah. The "virgin" was a sign to Ahaz of deliverance. The word translated "virgin," from the Hebrew at this point, could mean "young woman;" it contained both meanings. However, in Matthew 1:23 the Holy Spirit quotes this verse and uses a Greek word which can only mean "virgin." He applies the verse to Jesus. Thus, we have a double fulfillment of the verse from Isaiah.

This fact is given by the Holy Spirit in His Words and Inspiration.

We may see the same thing here. This is conjecture on my part so I would not consider this too strongly. But, there is a need for people in this day to understand that no translation can bear the mark of inspiration upon it except by appeal to the underlying text from which that translation was made. It is under this rational that I accept the King James Bible as the Standard for the English Speaker. The underlying text from which the King James Bible was translated is a faithful transmissiom of the originally inspired and providentially preserved Words of God. These are the words translated in that King James Bible.

The underlying text of almost all contemporary English translations is the Critical Text which is founded in a lack of faith that God could, would, or did preserved His Words to mankind. This lack of faith disqualifies, in my mind, those efforts based upon the Critical Text.

In the passage in Hebrews the Holy Spirit inspired what He intended to bring to humanity. We rest on faith in Him.

The idea of "multiplying, I will multiply" is a Hebraism which carries two meanings. The first is that of exceedingly great multiplication. The other is a continuation which does not end. Therefore it states an eternal promise. The same could be said about the phrase "blessing" and "bless." The continuation at this point argues against the concept of "Covenant Theology" which argues that the Church has taken over the promises which God has removed from the Jew. The certainty of continuation of the blessings upon the people of Israel is promised in the oath and covenant of God to Abraham.]

6.15 *And so, after he had patiently endured, he obtained the promise.*

[Abraham was first given the promise when he was in Haran. He was seventy-five years old at that time. Abraham followed God for twenty-five years throughout the Land of his Promise and into Egypt. He failed God several times but he never gave up on his belief that the promise was sure.

Abraham wavered in Egypt in regards to his wife. He lied to the Pharaoh out of fear of his life over his wife. Nonetheless Abraham persevered. He returned to the Land where God had called him and waited upon the promise.

Abraham had another relapse. His wife gave Hagar, a maid, to her husband. The result of this union was the birth of Ishmael. Ishmael was not the child of promise and eventually was sent away. How this must have torn at Abraham's heart.

Abraham was so anxious to see the promise of God fulfilled that he once even offered one of his servants to God. He wanted God to fulfill the promise in this man. Still Abraham waited for the promise of God. He waited expectantly. Although he waited amiss from time to time, Abraham never gave up his faith that God would complete His promise as He had said.

Finally, when Abraham was 100-years-old and his wife was 90, when it was physically too late for them to have children, Isaac arrived. The promise of God was kept in the form of a miracle. Our understanding may be faulty but the Word of God stands triumphant and secure.

Although he waited many years, the faith of Abraham was fulfilled in the time of God's choosing.

There were facets of the promises which Abraham never saw. But, the miracle birth of Isaac was the pledge that all the promises would be fulfilled. Abraham died having seen the promise of the promise of God. He still trusted the Lord of miracle and faithfulness.]

6.16 *For men verily swear by the greater: and an oath for confirmation is to them an end of all strife.*

HEBREWS: Chapter 6

[The concept of an oath in this place is much akin to the idea of signing a contract. It is an affirmation that the parties involved have agreed to the terms involved. Before the invocation of an oath of agreement the parties involved may have been involved in strife over the responsibilities and duties of each.

Paul was seeking to "build up" that faith of these Jewish Christians by reminding them of the promises which God had kept in regards to the natural offspring of Abraham.

In matters of religious duties there was a natural strife between man and God. The sin nature within man made him predisposed to go left any time God might have said "go right." The temperament of the natural man is opposed to the things of God. Paul puts it this way in Romans 8:7 – "Because the carnal mind is enmity against God: for it is not subject to the law of God, neither indeed can be."

The concept of enmity is hostility. Because of the cross this enmity has been removed. "Having abolished in his flesh the enmity, even the law of commandments contained in ordinances; for to make in himself of twain one new man, so making peace; And that he might reconcile both unto God in one body by the cross, having slain the enmity thereby" (Ephesians 2:15-16)

The oath which God attached to His promises to Abraham, on the basis of His Own Good Name, is a guarantee to the Christian that our blessings are secure in Him. As God has kept, and will keep, every promise made to Abraham and his natural generations, so will God keep His Oath and Covenant with the Christians.

These Jewish converts could well see that God had kept His promises through the Law. This is a spiritual principle which carries forward the Glory of the Truth of God. He always performs that which He has pledged.

The oath of God based upon His Own Name is the greatest guarantee which can be given that His determinative will is secure and final.]

6.17 *Wherein God, willing more abundantly to shew unto the heirs of promise the immutability of his counsel, confirmed it by an oath.*

[When God made an oath to do a thing, He swore it on His Own immutability (unchangeableness). This was His guarantee that this promise would be carried out. An oath, here, is simply a guarantee of His promise.

In His great love and graciousness God gave us guarantee of His already perfect and unchangeable Word. His Word is firm and perfect because it is His Word. As He is perfect and not given to change, so is His Word to us. The present plea to find new *lost* texts of Scripture to *correct* what we have is an insult to the God Who gave His Word to us. It is to postulate either a weak, unable to providentially preserve, or a capricious, unwilling to providentially preserve, God Who really didn't mean it, obviously, when He gave His Words to humanity. If He were to think so lightly of His revelation, what are we to assume of the eternal importance of that revelation?

As to the promises which God made to Abraham we are left with the same question. Has God withdrawn His promises to Abraham and reassigned them to the church? If God would act in such a variable manner in regard to His promise to Abraham as to change His mind as to the recipient of these blessings, what are we to consider in regard to His promises to us of the Church Age?

The promises to Abraham were to a man of faith. To suggest that a later failure on the part of Abraham's sons would abrogate the fact of the promise made to Abraham is to suggest an unbecoming caprice on the part of the Promised Word of God. Such is to suggest that God counted as a small thing the faith of Abraham. It is to suggest that, just possibly, God should have made a better choice than Abraham.

True, some of the later promises were conditional. But, the great promises of a national revival of Israel in the latter days must also be factored into this discussion. God will keep His promises even to national Israel as they are, generationally, in Abraham and it is according to his faith that the promises were made.

That the church shares in these promises is not an argument to disinherit Israel from the promises made to them in the name of their father, Abraham. The pledge and the oath of God are guarantee that He will perform that which He has said.]

6.18 *That by two immutable things, in which it was impossible for God to lie, we might have a strong consolation, who have fled for refuge to lay hold upon the hope set before us:*

[When the verse says that God cannot lie there is no hint of any weakness or inability within God. This points to a strength within God that His Word is always "yea and verily." To tell an untruth is an action that is foreign to the nature of God. His Word is eternal as is He.

In the first chapter of Genesis we see God speaking the universe into existence. Therefore, His promises to Abraham and Abraham's descendants are certain. What God says will always come to pass.

Even with this certainty we find that God, in His graciousness, gave Abraham an oath to assure Abraham of the truth of these promises. This was not necessary as the Words of God are always the Words of Truth. This was a picture of God giving more to man who stands in weakness.

The picture of fleeing to refuge is a picture of the ancient Hebrew fleeing to the cities of refuge in ancient Israel. If a man had accidently slain another he could go to one of those cities and find peace from the family of the slain man. He was allowed to stay, unmolested, in one of those cities until the death of the high priest. By that time the original tempers may have cooled and the truth of an accidental slaying could have been established.

Noting the above, we flee to Jesus, our Refuge. He is the High Priest Who will never die. We are, therefore, eternally safe in Jesus. Our sins are forgiven and forgotten. We have an eternal salvation that is dependent on the life of the eternal High Priest of our profession.

The two immutable, unchangeable, things are the promise of God which can never fail unless we were to argue that God is capable of failure. He is not. The promises are secure. The oath, based on the eternal Name of God is likewise unchangeable as He is always perfect in all ways.]

6.19 *Which hope we have as an anchor of the soul, both sure and stedfast, and which entereth into that within the veil;*

[Paul describes the Christian as a ship out on a tempestuous sea in a storm. This physical metaphor is used in the Gospels. At one point the disciples were in a small boat in the midst of a large storm. Jesus was calmly sleeping until they awakened Him. He saw their worry, not their danger as He was with them through it all, and calmed the seas and the wind. Where Jesus is there is calm among the disciples.

On another occasion the disciples were out on the sea at night when they saw Jesus coming to join them. He was walking on the water. That which held up their little boat, and could have easily drowned them had the sea have been in storm mode, was the very walkway which Jesus used to show them His presence.

The picture Paul uses at this place is of a ship out on the sea which is unable to get to the port on its own. The waves are too high. The wind is too daunting. The world does this to us. Either the dangers are too great and the persecution too strong for our feeble persons or the waves are so calming as to lull us to sleep. Always we must point our ship to Jesus.

In the case of this parable of Paul, the ship was in danger. It could not make port through the storm. Rather than be driven back out into the sea, the anchor was tossed out. If all went well this anchor would attach itself to the rocks below and hold the ship secure. The crew would find their landfall when the storms ceased and the fury of the sea was forgotten in the safety of the port.

It is interesting to note that the anchor was useless when it was within sight of the crew. The anchor needed to go swiftly past the winds, the waves, the water and find the secure bed of the sea. With the anchor nestled in this place the ship was secure. The anchor was not seen as it did its work. It was still, though not seen, the thing which kept crew and ship unmovable, to an extent, within the tempest of the sea. It may well be that the storm would not abate. Nevertheless the anchor gave safety through the storm.

This anchor in the parable did not go to the depths of the sea but to the Heights of Heaven. It went through the "veil." This was symbolic of faith going through the Temple and into the "Holy of Holies" of the Mercy Seat of God. To the Jewish mind of the day this was the symbolic presence of God.

That Heavenly Mercy Seat was the place where Jesus had sprinkled the Blood of His Sacrifice. The call was to rest in Him and His finished work. Our souls are secure in the salvation He purchased.]

6.20 Whither the forerunner is for us entered, even Jesus, made an high priest for ever after the order of Melchisedec.

[The forerunner was a scout, or a spy, among the Roman armies. He went into the new land first and reported what he had found so the remaining army could prepare to join him in this land.

Jesus is the "Forerunner" in the sense that He is the First Born of the dead. (Colossians 1:18) This is not a processional "first born." It is a positional first born in that the first born among the society of the day was the son who was the inheritor of all. He was the head of his family. To say that Jesus is the "Forerunner" is to say that He is the Head of the Church.

Paul moves even past this and announces that Jesus is our eternal High Priest. He entered into Heaven to mediate on our behalf as He sprinkled His Own Blood on the Heavenly Mercy Seat. He is not of the Aaronic priesthood. They ministered under the Law and only to the Hebrew. Jesus is of the order of Melchisedec; His Priesthood is eternal and to all who believe – both Jew and Gentile.

It was not necessary for Jesus to go to the mercy seat on His Own behalf as did the Priests under the Law. Jesus went for us and our needs as our Great High Priest.

Jesus is our eternal Mediator. There was none before Him. There will be none after Him as He is the Eternal Priest of the redeemed. He continually prepares for us a place of holiness and happiness in the presence of the Father, the Son, and the Spirit.]

HEBREWS - CHAPTER SEVEN

7.1 *For this Melchisedec, king of Salem, priest of the most high God, who met Abraham returning from the slaughter of the kings, and blessed him;*

Genesis 14:18-20; Psalm 110:4; Hebrews 5:6; 7:2-10

[The phrase "Order of Melchisedek," as opposed to the "Order of Aaron," is typical of the Priesthood of Jesus. Neither is Jesus only Priest to the Jewish nation as were the priests of Aaron. The Priesthood of Jesus is universal in that it covers all humanity.

The following verses show Melchisedek as greater than Abram. This is not with reference to the further glory but in deference to his office of priest. Melchisedek is the only priest of his line mentioned in Scripture. Melchisedek is mentioned as a type of Christ. The fact that he was both a Godly king and priest are the most important ingredients of his "shadow image" of He Who was to come. The lack of a recorded linage of Melchisedek also speaks to the true eternity of Jesus. Again, this is simply a physical echo of what is true in the spiritual.

As a man it is evident that Melchisedek had both mother and father. But, in his office as priest he had neither predecessor nor successor mentioned. Thus the priestly line of Melchisedek had one person – Melchisedek. The name "Melchisedek" means "righteous king." This speaks in type of Jesus Who is our Righteous King.

This Melchisedek reigned as king in Salem. The word means "Peace." Therefore it is proper to speak of Melchisedek as the righteous king of peace. Again, this speaks in type of Jesus. Jesus is our Righteous King and brings to us a peace which can never be understood by the world at large.

Note well that Melchisedek was king in Salem. This is the same Jerusalem from which Jesus will reign as King of kings from the throne of His father, in the flesh, David.

Some would argue that Salem, here mentioned, was Shechem. I would note of this city that it was the site of a great congregation of the children of Israel. Joshua spoke to them from this place. It seems that Shechem would not be the correct site. I would still argue that Melchisedek was the King at what would later be known as Jerusalem.

Yet another similarity to Jesus is that Melchisedek gave refreshment to Abraham and those fighters under him as they came from defeating the kings who had abducted Lot. Melchisedek gave refreshment to those fighters under Abraham. Jesus has not only rescued us from the clutches of the enemy of our soul, He also gives us a refreshed spirit.]

7.2 *To whom also Abraham gave a tenth part of all; first being by interpretation King of righteousness, and after that also King of Salem, which is, King of peace,*

Genesis 14:18-20; Psalm 110:4; Hebrews 5:6; 7:1; 3-10

[It was an ancient custom that a tithe was to be given to the provider of the victory. In this Abram acknowledged his subservience to the priest of God as the priest was in the office as a representative of God. Christ owns His Own superiority over the Levitical priesthood of Aaron.

We do not know who Melchisedek was beyond the few verses which speak of him. He was probably a Canaanitish king. What we do know of Melchisedek was that he worshipped and represented the True God of Heaven. Consider Romans 1:21: "Because that, when they knew God, they glorified him not as God, neither were thankful..." Early humanity knew of God. The sad fact is that they, even as so many in our day are departing from the culture of a godly heritage, simply rejected Him.]

7.3 *Without father, without mother, without descent, having neither beginning of days, nor end of life, but made like unto the Son of God, abideth a priest continually.*

Genesis 14:18-20; Psalm 110:4; Hebrews 5:6; 7:1-2; 4-10

["Like the Son of God" speaks to the typologically. Melchisedek resembled Jesus in certain aspects. "Made like" is a reference to the eternal Priesthood of Jesus since there is no recorded birth, death or genealogy of Melchisedek. Humanly speaking, as a man Jesus had no father. Spiritually speaking, as God Jesus had no mother.

With Melchisedek as a "type" we are shown that it was not necessary for Jesus to be from the line of Levi and Aaron to be Priest. The Jews of the time Hebrews was written were especially concerned with genealogies of the priests. Jesus had no genealogical record as a Priest. Unlike the Levitical priests, who served from age 30 to age 50, Melchisedek was a priest for his entire life. This is a conjecture from the fact that Melchisedek was also the king. The likeness between Melchisedek and Jesus was not in the man, Melchisedek. The likeness lies in the Scriptural representation of office and (in Melchisedek's case "seeming") eternality.

We are struck with the eternality of the Priesthood of Christ. Did it have a real beginning only after His crucifixion? We could argue against that. Revelation 13:8b speaks of Jesus as "...the Lamb slain from the foundation of the world."

I disregard the first part, for this study, of this verse in Revelation as it speaks, in contrast to Jesus and those who truly worship Him, of those of the tribulation era who worshipped the beast and false prophet. Jesus is shown to be above these in His description as the Lamb.

The word "foundation" suggests that Jesus was slain before the world had even been created – at the conception of the world. Following such a consideration we would see Jesus as the Ultimate Savior of the world. The Old Testament sacrifices, which could not save man, (Hebrews 10:4) could only serve to allow a man considered as righteous due to his faith in the revealed Words of God at that point in time, to have his sins covered rather than ultimately forgiven. This awaited the actual sacrifice of Jesus. Only then could the natural "righteousness" of man become an available righteousness on spiritual grounds. Old Testament saints were saved in the grace of God by the anticipation of the sacrifice of Jesus on the Cross of Calvary.

In this scenario we could consider that Jesus had assumed the Priestly Office for sinful humanity from before the world, or man, had even been created. We would therefore consider Him as the Priest forever from the time of His acceptance of His role of sacrificial Lamb. Jesus is, therefore, The Eternal High Priest of our salvation.

To those who might disagree with my time-line, I accept the criticism. I may well be wrong in this but I believe this to be true nonetheless due to the awfulness of sin and the amazing grace of God.]

HEBREWS: Chapter 7

7.4 *Now consider how great this man was, unto whom even the patriarch Abraham gave the tenth of the spoils.*

Genesis 14:18-20; Psalm 110:4; Hebrews 5:6; 7:1-3; 5-10

[Melchisedek stood, in his office of priest, between God and Abram. This is shown in that Abram honored God through the office of Melchisedek. Abram gave witness to the piousness and righteousness of Melchisedek in accepting his priesthood.

Considering the Levitical priesthood, Melchisedek was shown to be above this even as Christ is above Melchisedek. The grandeur of Melchisedek was in his office as priest. This office was important in that it brought Glory to God.

The Jewish men greatly regarded Abraham. And, well they should for Abraham was the one to whom the great promises of land, posterity, and the blessing which would be upon the entire world. Yet, this same Abraham, a prophet in his own right, offered a tenth of the best of the spoil of his battles to Melchisedek. In doing so Abraham acknowledged his standing below Melchisedek. Melchisedek was a priest unto the True God. Abraham agreed that this was the case and offered a tithe to God by the office of Melchisedek.

Since Melchisedek was a great man, in his office above even the father of the Jewish race, how much greater is Christ of whom Melchisedek was only a type.]

7.5 *And verily they that are of the sons of Levi, who receive the office of the priesthood, have a commandment to take tithes of the people according to the law, that is, of their brethren, though they come out of the loins of Abraham:*

Genesis 14:18-20; Psalm 110:4; Hebrews 5:6; 7:1-4; 6-10

[The tithe went to the priest who then had the duty to bless the giver.

The Levitical priest had the right to the tithe via the Law of Moses. Melchisedek received the tithes of them via Abram. These Levitical priests had no rank above the other Jews; they only had the office of priest bestowed upon them. Only those Levites who were of the house of Aaron had this office bestowed upon them.

In the order of "ranking," the Levites were under the priests of the house of Aaron. Those priests were under Abram as he was Patriarch, or head, of the family line. Abram placed himself as under Melchisedek as typical of Christ. But, Melchisedek is under Christ in authority and power as Jesus is God and Melchisedek served as a priest under Him.

Not all of the descendants of Levi were priests. But, all the priests were descendants of Levi who had this office conferred upon them. All of the descendants of Levi were, likewise and primarily, descendants of Abram.

When the people of Abram entered the Land of Promise during the exodus, the priestly line did not receive an inheritance of land to sustain them. They were maintained by the tithe given to the priest by the other tribes.

Since Melchisedek was a king, he did not receive "maintenance" from the tithe of Abram. He had no need of such sustenance. The tithe which Abram gave to Melchisedek was completely considered as an offering to the Lord. Abram's acceptance of Melchisedek as the priest of God was long before the line of Aaron, or the Levites for that matter, had come into being. These lines, being fathered by the Patriarch Abram, were themselves under Abram and thus paid tithe to Melchisedek through Abram thus placing themselves under Melchisedek.

Melchisedek remains under Jesus although the humanity of Jesus was through the agency of Abram. It was, however, to the Divinity of Jesus that Melchisedek exercised his own priestly office.]

7.6 *But he whose descent is not counted from them received tithes of Abraham, and blessed him that had the promises.*

Genesis 14:18-20; Psalm 110:4; Hebrews 5:6; 7:1-5; 7-10

[Melchisedek blessed Abram even though Abram was the recipient of many promises of God and was the beginning of the line which would include the Savior of the world.

Melchisedek was not of the blessed line of Abram. He was a true priest though he was not of the line of the people of the promise via Abram. In this sense he was above Abram, not in promise but in office. Thus the groundwork is laid to consider Jesus as also above Abram, not in His humanity – although the humanity of Jesus was a perfect and sinless humanity – but in His Office as High Priest to all nations as Melchisedek was a Gentile high priest even before there was an established Abrahamic line. Melchisedek was a potential priest to the entire world of humanity.]

7.7 *And without all contradiction the less is blessed of the better.*

Genesis 14:18-20; Psalm 110:4; Hebrews 5:6; 7:1-2; 4-10

[Without any argument allowed, the greater in office as standing as a priest before God, blessed the lesser. The same principle is shown when the father (ex. Abraham, Isaac, Jacob, etc.) gave blessing to their sons.

The priest is acting in the authority of God when he gives a blessing. This, of course, is only true of true blessings and true priests.

It was Abram who had the promises of God bestowed upon him. This was evidence of the great favor which God had given to Abram. Nonetheless, in acknowledging the superior office of Melchisedek as priest, Abram was accepting a lower station that that held by Melchisedek.

The one of lower station may offer "good wishes" to one of a high station but the blessing of God is bestowed by the higher upon the lower.

This point may be considered as a sub-text consistent with the Kenosis of Jesus as a human being in His incarnation.]

7.8 *And here men that die receive tithes, but there he receiveth them, of whom it is witnessed that he liveth.*

Genesis 14:18-20; Psalm 110:4; Hebrews 5:6; 7:1-7; 9-10

[Melchisedek "liveth" in Scripture, God's Eternal Words. So, too, does Christ. But Christ is superior. Christ lives in eternity in the eternal reality of non-ending life. Melchisedek "lives" in the pages of Scripture but he did die and now resides in Heaven. Jesus died as The Sacrifice in time. But Jesus rose from the dead in time. He now lives in eternity but will someday return to this earth to reign from the Throne of David in this same physical world. As God, Jesus will continue to reign even during this time, to reside in the eternal and spiritual Heaven. (consider John 3:13)

The Levitical priests all die or retire and die. No mention is made of either in relation to Melchisedec. Paul, speaking of the time he was writing, noted that the paying of tithe to the priests was unending. But, the death of priests would mean that new men would receive the tithe Thus the Levitical priesthood is changing. Jesus never changes. (see Hebrews 13:8)

Melchisedek lived when he received tithe of the Jews in the person of Abram. Jesus "ever liveth." (see Hebrews 7:25)

The "here" was the then present Levitical priesthood. The "there" is the Biblical record of the priesthood of Melchisedek. Make no mistake; Melchisedek did die as must all mortal men. Since neither the birth nor death of Melchisedek is recorded we have a picture of man who, in the literary sense, lives forever. This is, of course, a type of Jesus Who, in actuality, does live forever as our Great High Priest.

The one, Melchisedek, only suggests the Other, Jesus as the Ultimate Reality. Thus we see that the Levitical priesthood was temporary in that each succeeding priest died. The eternal Priesthood of Jesus is shown to be superior as not temporary but continuing.]

7.9 *And as I may so say Levi also, who received tithes, payed tithes in Abraham.*

Genesis 14:18-20; Psalm 110:4; Hebrews 5:6; 7:1-8; 10

[As the head of his "race," Abram placed the entire "house" of the Jew under Melchisedek when he submitted tithe to him. When considering this we may also consider that Adam, as the federal head of humanity, placed all people under the yoke of sin.

Levi and his entire line symbolically paid tithe in his father, Abram. Levi includes his entire line to embrace even the priestly house of Aaron.

Melchisedek took tithes as immortal in the sense that there is no record of the death of Melchisedek. As a type of Christ, then, we are able to see that Christ is truly immortal. If Melchisedek is above the Levitical priesthood, how much more is Christ above both Melchisedek and the Levitical priesthood.]

7.10 *For he was yet in the loins of his father, when Melchisedec met him.*

Genesis 14:18-20; Psalm 110:4; Hebrews 5:6; 7:2-9

[The fact that the natural descendants of Abram were inferior (symbolically speaking) to Melchisedek does not apply to Jesus, Whose Father is God. While the priesthood of Melchisedek may be said to be "like" Jesus, it is inferior to Jesus as it is only a shadow and type of the reality of Jesus.

Only those born naturally, under sin, have need to receive blessing from, or to pay tithe to, a priest. Therefore, Jesus is not under Melchisedek. A priest, even as a "Melchisedek" of God is always under God. Jesus is God in the flesh.]

7.11 *If therefore perfection were by the Levitical priesthood, (for under it the people received the law,) what further need was there that another priest should rise after the order of Melchisedec, and not be called after the order of Aaron?*

[Psalm 110:4 is a Messianic Psalm. It says, "The LORD hath sworn, and will not repent, Thou art a priest for ever after the order of Melchizedek." Paul asks that we note that Messiah will not be a priest of the order of Aaron.

Paul also asks why it is necessary that a priest come of a different order than that of Aaron. If this priesthood, and the Law which was attendant with it, were able to bring men to perfection before God, why must it change?

We can look from our New Testament perspective and argue that all was fulfilled in Christ. The perfect sacrifice was given in Jesus. The ceremonies, the holy days, the ordinances were all pictures pointing to Jesus; they were fulfilled and superfluous. The day of these things had come and gone. The reality had replaced the shadows and types.

But, there is more. There was no perfection allowed under the Levitical priesthood. The priests, as good as they were, were failed men in themselves. This is proven by the fact that they needed to offer cleansing sacrifice for themselves as well as for the people. There was no real inward change in anyone under the system of the Levitical priesthood. It was necessary to come back with sacrifice often for the continued failing of the people.

It would also be argued that the many High Priests, each succeeding one another, gave no real permanence to the system. There was needed a Single High Priest, not one appointed to carry out the duties in his life time and then followed by another of the same duration. Jesus, as the Single High Priest lives forever to carry out His duties for the believer.

It is to be noted that the Levitical priesthood came after the Law had been given to show mankind the sinfulness of sin. (Romans 3:20) But, as the continual sacrifice and ceremony displayed, sin was not overcome by either the Law or the ministrations of the priests.

The very Mercy Seat which the High Priest could only approach one day each year to offer the blood of sacrifice for the sins of himself and the people was not approachable by man. It was "off limits" under the administration of the Levitical priesthood. The veil which separated the Mercy Seat so that only the high priest, and then only once a year, could access that room, was torn in half at the crucifixion of Jesus. (Mark 15:58) Now, because of the offering of the High Priest of our profession, Jesus, we have direct access to The Father and the throne of Grace.

A better High Priest has come. He has offered His Perfect Sacrifice one time for the sins of many. (Matthew 26:28) The Blood of the Sacrifice of Jesus has given us the remission of sins where the former sacrifices of created beings could only cover that sin.

In the time of Abram the priesthood of Melchisedec was shown to be superior to that of the Levitical priesthood. Now, in Jesus, the Perfect Priesthood of the Perfect and Eternal Sacrifice has come.]

7.12 *For the priesthood being changed, there is made of necessity a change also of the law.*

[The Law and the Levitical priesthood were closely interconnected. With the change in the priesthood there must be a resultant change in the Law. One of those things was the transfer of the line of the High Priest. Under the Law this had been of the tribe of Levi and the family of Aaron. The Great and Permanent High Priest would also be King. Therefore, the High Priest is now Jesus, "The Lion of the Tribe of Judah." (Revelation 5:5)

We see Aaron stand aside as he welcomes the perfections, which were never available in his line, of Jesus. There is a High Priest forever.

We might note that history records the destruction of the last Temple at Jerusalem within a generation of the offering up of Jesus. There is no longer any purpose to be served in a human high priest going yearly into the Temple made with hands. Jesus has completed His Own work at the Heavenly Mercy Seat.

Having abolished the Law by the fulfillment of that Law, Jesus now reigns as King and High Priest of our profession of faith. (Ephesians 2:15)

The Levitical Law was concerned with washing and ritual cleansing. The Law of the Gospel is concerned with spiritual truths. "Not by works of righteousness which we have done, but according to his mercy he saved us, by the washing of regeneration, and renewing of the Holy Ghost" (Titus 3:5) The "washing of regeneration" is not a ritual bath or baptism. It is the cleansing of our sins by the shed Blood of Jesus Christ. (I John 1:7)

We live by a newer and higher standard. This is not to say we would ignore the Ten Commandments or the moral law. These are spiritual principles by which we ought to live. Our relationship to them is no longer one of fear that we might fail. Our relationship is one of love in that we might serve our Lord Who died for us.

We are no longer bound by the ceremonial and sacerdotal laws of the Old Covenant. Jesus has fulfilled these and our life is in Him and His offered salvation. We look at these and find Jesus in them. They were sign posts and types of our Great High Priest and Lord.]

7.13 *For he of whom these things are spoken pertaineth to another tribe, of which no man gave attendance at the altar.*

[Be very careful here. The Old Testament Law was not abolished in the sense that we see abolition as destruction. The Old Testament Law was fully fulfilled in the Person of Jesus. Therefore, as a law of worship it is no longer binding on anyone. As a point of fact, one who would attempt to keep the Old Testament Law, ceremonial or otherwise, has rejected the finished work of Christ in a return to that Law and a movement away from God.

This was the apostasy of which Paul continues to warn these Jewish believers. Jesus had removed the fear of the Law and replaced it with the love of being able to obey God. The spiritual principles of the law (small case) continue as a way of life but not as a way of worship. The New worship of the New Covenant of the Blood of Jesus has no earthy temple. The churches are not temples but meeting places where the ordinances of the New Testament are carried out as the worship centers on the risen Lord.

The church ordinances of Baptism and The Lord's Table are not laws of the church. There is no grace available in them. These are memorials of the wonderful work of Jesus as He died, was buried, and rose again to save us from sin in a perfect way that even the temple sacrifices could have never done.

The tribe of Levi has no place in the administration of this New Covenant. They have completed their job. They were forerunners in somewhat the same sense as was John, the Baptist, in preparing the world to understand and accept the sacrifice and redemption of Jesus. It is now the Lord, Himself, Who labors as our High Priest and King.

Since David has, by inspiration, prophesied that Messiah would be a Priest forever – and the line of Levitical priests had a beginning in time – it is obvious that the Levitical priesthood was never intended to be a permanent institution. Further, Messiah was prophesied to be of the tribe of Judah. (Genesis 49:10) Since the prophecy of David was that Messiah would be a Priest forever it would be necessary that the line of Levi would be superseded in their priestly duties by a man from the tribe of Judah.

David said, "The LORD hath sworn, and will not repent, Thou art a priest for ever after the order of Melchizedek." (Psalm 110:4) It is said that Messiah will be of the priestly order of Melchizedek. It is not said that Messiah will be of the line of Melchizedek.

There were many priests who served under the Levitical high priest. The fact that Jesus is said to be a priest "after the order of Melchizedek" does not make Jesus subservient to Melchizedek. The meaning is only that both were of the same "order" of priests. Both, as priests, are priests to all of humanity rather than primarily to the Israeli people. That is the simple meaning. An added, identifying facet is that there is no mention of the birth or death of – or of any successor to – Melchizedek.

The eternality of Jesus, as God, when coupled with His being Priest "forever," would also serve to place Melchizedek as a priest subservient to Jesus. They may be said to be of the same order; but, they are of vastly different rank within that order. Jesus had been appointed High Priest, not of any priesthood of man obviously, before the foundation of the world. His appointment came from The Father as Jesus accepted the role of both Sacrifice and Priest for the redeemed of the world to come.

Where the Old Testament priests had sacrificed animals of creation for a sin covering for both themselves and the people, Jesus sacrificed Himself – The Creator of Creation! – for the sins of those redeemed of the world to come.]

7.14 *For it is evident that our Lord sprang out of Juda, of which tribe Moses spake nothing concerning priesthood.*

[In His maternity, humanity, Jesus was from the tribe of Judah – a direct descendant of King David. As far as the social law of man was concerned, Jesus was also from the tribe of Judah through His "step-father," Joseph. Again, He is legally, by the social law of man, a direct descendant of King David. No one, then or now, has ever successfully disputed this simple fact. Had there been any argument raised about this fact in the early days of the church, this would have been strongly raised to dispute that Jesus was Messiah. Other arguments may have been attempted but we have no record of this argument ever being used.

The Jews kept meticulous genealogical records. Matthew records the genealogical background of Joseph while Luke gives the history from which Mary sprang. It is my guess that these were destroyed when the Roman armies sacked and burned Jerusalem in 70 A.D. since to the best of my knowledge there has been no mention of these since that time.

Paul argues that such a change is necessary due to the inspired and preserved Scriptural statement of David in Psalm 110:4. Messiah, from the tribe of Judah, could not be a priest as God had promised would be the case. Yet, those promises of God are unbreakable.

There had never been a true priest from any but the tribe of Levi. God's Word said that Messiah would come from the tribe of Judah and be a priest. Since the Word of God cannot be broken (John 10:35) it would be necessary that the Old Testament Law would be superseded by a superior law. This would also necessitate that the Old Testament Law be either fulfilled and made of no effect or changed.

Jesus fulfilled the Law for the believer and brought in a New Covenant in His blood. The world is no longer required to sacrifice elements of the creation because the Creator has become the Eternal Sacrifice for the sins of many.]

7.15 And it is yet far more evident: for that after the similitude of Melchisedec there ariseth another priest,

[Setting aside all the arguments that Jesus is Messiah, we look simply at David's prophecy and realize that it is necessary that a priest not of the order of the Levitical be established. This must be Messiah, of course. But, more importantly, this simply must be. The prophecy of God demands this be so.

In "the similitude of Melchisedec" two things are obvious. The first is that this coming priest will not be of the tribe of Levi nor of the family of Aaron. Melchisedec predates both. The second thing is the consideration that he stands superior to the Law of Moses in regard to the priesthood.

This does not mean that Jesus is like Melchisedec. The reverse is true. Melchisedec is a type of Christ. A type anticipates the reality to come. The important point which Paul is making is that Melchisedec is not of the priestly line. Neither is Messiah from the priestly line.

In His Deity Jesus is from no human line. In His humanity Jesus is from the line of Judah. As such He is from, again humanly speaking, the Kingly family of David and the line of Judah.]

7.16 Who is made not after the law of a carnal commandment, but after the power of an endless life.

[Each high priest was appointed by ceremony and rite as prescribed by the Law of Moses. His appointment depended upon his family and his rank within that family. It had to do with human facilities.

Indeed, the entire Law was such. All things attendant to the Law, to include the assumption of the office of high priest, had to do with outward ceremony rather than inward character.

The very office could not be considered as eternal because it was relinquished upon the death of that office holder. Each man died in turn.

Jesus did not assume the Office of High Priest by the ministrations of any man or set of rules. He was eternally appointed to the office by His Father. His is not an office in which He will be succeeded by anyone because "He ever liveth." (Hebrews 7:25) His duty as the High Priest of our profession was conferred upon Him by The Father.

The rituals of the Law had the power of giving commandments to man. Only Jesus can give life to man. He has also given life, or reality, to the law of love. As we live within the salvation which Jesus brought to us by His sacrifice and our simple acceptance of the Spirit's wooing, we realize His love to us and respond by a strong desire to return His love in our obedience and eagerness to display our love to Him. (I John 4:19)]

7.17 *For he testifieth, Thou art a priest for ever after the order of Melchisedec.*

[Paul returns to his "text verse" on this point. It is worth restating that King David wrote the original words of this verse which Paul quotes at this place. However, the inspiration of God lies upon these words; they are therefore the Words of God. It is He Who has testified to the fact that His Son, Messiah, will be a Priest throughout eternity.

Since there is no record of the birth or death of Melchisedec, we can argue – from the literary standpoint – that Melchisedec was never born nor did he ever die. We know that Melchisedec, a human man of history, did both. He was born and he did die. But, it is that literary example which is applied to Jesus.

Jesus in His humanity experienced both birth and death. In the reality of the Divine nature of Jesus He had always existed and will always exist. His human death, recorded in Scripture has no bearing upon His eternal existence. Jesus existed before the events of Bethlehem. He was born into the world in His humanity but He existed from eternity before this reality which He accepted for our salvation.

Likewise, Jesus died – in His humanity – in a real sense upon that cross in order to gain our salvation. Both were decisions of love. Both were overridden by the reality of His eternal existence. That eternal existence is the emphasis of this verse.

Hundreds of years before the birth of Jesus God spoke to Him and made the vow of an eternal priesthood. About forty years after the death of Jesus on the Cross of Calvary we see Paul writing inspired Scripture. Once again, via the medium of inspiration, God repeats the vow to Jesus of His eternal priesthood.

This is a priesthood, that of Melchisedec, which is outside the line of Aaron, Moses, Levi – any of the sons of Abraham. Melchisedec predates all of these men. Melchisedec even predates the giving of the Law and Ceremonies of the religious life of Israel.

Jesus is a Priest in like, but far superior, manner. He stands outside of, and superior to, the establishment of both Israel and the Levitical priesthood.]

7.18 *For there is verily a disannulling of the commandment going before for the weakness and unprofitableness thereof.*

[With the replacement of the priests of the order of Aaron, the entire system of the Law failed. The one was inseparably entwined with the other. It was the priestly class who had administrated the ceremony and sacrifice of the Law.

The word "disannulling" is rendered as "complete cancelling, annulling, nullifying" in the Defined King James Bible. With regards to this concept it might be good to review our old history lessons. In the decades leading up to the War Between The States there were laws and tariffs passed in Washington, DC, which were not accepted by some of the states. Sometimes the state legislature would pass "Articles of Nullification" which would declare that those laws and tariffs were "null and void" within their jurisdictions.

When God made the office of the Levitical priesthood "null and void," so too were disannulled the precepts of the Mosaic Law which they had administered.

The purpose for this nullification was that the Law had already fulfilled its purpose. It was established to point toward the coming Of Jesus and His perfect Sacrifice. As the new age of grace was established it would be necessary that the old age of the Law be dismissed. The purpose and procedures of the two systems were mutually incompatible.

The Mosaic Law was the "commandment going before" the Church Age of Grace. This "Law System" is said to have an inherent weakness within it. What the Law lacked Grace has provided.

The Law could not provide full pardon from sins. Jesus, as the High Priest of our profession, has the right and the power to fully pardon on the basis of His Sacrificial death on the Cross of Calvary.

The Law could not change the heart of man. Jesus has the power to make us a "new man." (II Corinthians 5:17)

The Law simply found man guilty of sin and left him in that place. Jesus calls us to walk a new walk. (John 8:11)

The Law made demands in its commandments but offered no assistance to live a new life. (John 14:16)

The Law has no Spirit to guide and uphold. (Ephesians 4:30)

The Law had no energy to impart life. (John 10:10b)

The Law was completed by the work of man. Indeed, the Law only showed man the sinfulness of his own sin. Man cannot aspire to any "good work" to bring himself before the throne of God. (Psalm 53:1; Proverbs 21:4; Ecclesiastes 7:20; Isaiah 53:6; 64:6; Ephesians 2:10)

The weakness of the Law is contrasted with the power of the Gospel. (Romans 1:16)

The Law was good in that it pointed toward Jesus. It was weak in that it required works on the part of man. Only the Work of Jesus has ever been able to save anyone from sin. (Revelation 13:8b) The Law asked man to do what he could not. Grace now asks man to accept what Jesus has powerfully done for us.

Those who responded to God through the Law had no concept of the suffering Savior. They did know that which God had asked them to do. This is what they did in answer to the demands of God and in faith in Him and His words. (Romans 4:5)]

7.19 *For the law made nothing perfect, but the bringing in of a better hope did; by the which we draw nigh unto God.*

Galatians 2:16: Romans 8:3

[The bringing in of the Law was a guidepost to point toward the coming Savior. It made nothing perfect. Not just man, nothing was perfected by the Law. It was a shadow of Him Who should come with the New Covenant of His Blood. (Matthew 26:28)

This New Covenant was perfection. Looking at the old English meaning of "perfection" we find the idea of completion. The Mosaic Law was not the final plan of God for the redemption of fallen humanity. It was instituted to show man his own sinfulness and inability to pay the price for his own sin and rebellion.

It allowed man to consider that it took the very life blood of a substitute, an innocent substitute, to cover his sin. That this was not a completed solution was made evident by the many sacrifices and ceremonies of the Mosaic Law.

It taught man that his own unrighteousness made it impossible for him to enter into the presence of the Holy God. Only the high priest could enter into the Holy of

Holies – and that just once a year after having offered sacrifice for himself. Even the high priest of the Old Covenant was a sinful man.

Sin was pervasive in the human race.

The completion of the Law would wait until Jesus perfectly fulfilled all the rites, ceremonies, and commandments of the Law. His perfection was counted as man's completion of that Law. In this He was able to offer Himself, sinless and perfect, as the innocent substitute to remove sin from those who would accept His offered salvation.

With the perfection of Jesus applied to those who call Him, Savior, Jesus now offers all Christians the right to approach the very Throne of God. (Hebrews 4:18) This is more than merely an offer. Man was originally created to have fellowship with God. Consider God coming to man in the original Garden. (Genesis 3:8) This fellowship was broken until spiritually restored by the death, burial, and resurrection of Jesus.

The earth is still under the curse of sin. (Romans 8:22) The day of the restoration of the earth is yet future; it is assured. (II Peter 3:10-11) Either in the great rapture of the church, or our own passing through the valley, will allow us to see face-to-face our Savior. (I Corinthians 15:51-58) Until that time we commune with Him through His inspired and preserved Words to us and in the prayer closet as we approach the Throne of His Grace.

This promise is surely a better thing than the continual offering of the animals of creation for the sin of man. Such was good in its appointed time. It was the Word of God for the need of man. The man who experienced faith in that Word of God and acted in obedience was counted as righteous. It was the Cross of Christ, though the man did not understand this, which was the basis of his ultimate salvation.]

7.20 *And inasmuch as not without an oath he was made priest:*

[God only pronounced an oath about a thing five times. The Words of God are always immutable. At these times He condescended to humanities imperfections and graciously added an oath to further point out the certainty of the things He had spoken. They would surely come to pass.

Abraham, being old along with his wife, may have had cause to doubt the promise of God that all the earth would be blessed from the issue of his seed. Abraham had doubted twice, it appears. He allowed his wife to influence him in the matter of Hagar. Ishmael was not the seed of promise although, as the son of Abraham there were promises of God given to him. (Genesis 17:20)

Abraham also wavered in the matter of his servant, Eliezer. (Genesis 15:2-4) God responded with an oath that the seed of this promise would be of Abraham's issue. (Genesis 22:16-18)

When the people of the exodus balked at following the direction of God to enter into the land of their promise, God disallowed them from entering in at all. Their lack of faith and trust in the God of their Exodus prohibited them from entering into the land. God sealed this refusal with an oath. (Deuteronomy 1:34-35)

Even Moses, the great leader and lawgiver – under God – of the people was denied entrance into the Land of Promise. Even though Moses was allowed to see the land, (Deuteronomy 34:4) God denied Moses the opportunity to enter into the land. (Deuteronomy 4:21)

God had narrowed down the family line of the coming Savior of mankind to the family of Abraham. This line was narrowed to the line of Judah in Genesis 49:10. Saul was chosen to be the first king of Israel.

We could consider that Saul was a type of all Israel. He was the best that the earthly had to offer. He was a physical choice. (I Samuel 9:2) Saul, chosen as king, could not be the ancestor of our Lord. Messiah was to come through the family line of Judah. (Genesis 49:10) Saul was of the family line of Benjamin. (I Samuel 9:21)

In a picture strikingly similar to the replacement of the Levitical high priest, as Paul has been speaking, with our Heavenly High Priest, Saul and his family were disallowed the kingdom. The replacement was King David. David was of the line of Judah. Whereas Saul had been ordained king under an earthly consideration, David was ordained king with a Heavenly consideration as purposed.

God had winnowed His choice of lines to produce Messiah. Genesis 3:15 had spoken of the entire family of humanity. This was narrowed, in that verse, to the women of that family of humanity. The line was further reduced to the line of Abraham's descendants. A further narrowing was the choice of the family line of Judah. Now God promised that the line of the family of David would always be the royal family. (Psalm 89:4) This oath was token that Messiah would come from the royal line of David.

Finally we see that God made an oath that Messiah would be a Priest in an eternal sense. As there was no recorded birth or death of Melchisedek, so does Messiah, Jesus, have no beginning nor ending either in His eternal Person of Deity or in His eternal Office of High Priest. (Psalm 110:4) The "type" of Melchisedek gives way to the Reality of Jesus, Messiah.

The argument of Paul that the oath given by God as regarding the Priesthood of Jesus is a higher confirmation than the simple ceremony and ordinance which was performed by man under an Old Covenant. That Old Covenant has been annulled with the establishment of the New Covenant of the Blood of Jesus Christ.]

7.21 *(For those priests were made without an oath; but this with an oath by him that said unto him, The Lord sware and will not repent, Thou art a priest for ever after the order of Melchisedec:)*

[Not only did The Father say that Jesus would be High Priest forever, He attested to this statement by an oath. Further, to "seal the deal," The Father said would never repent (turn from) this decision. That is three affirmations corresponding to the Divine Trinity of God.

Moses has been called "the Great Law Giver." He was. But it is important to keep in mind that the Law which Moses gave was that which he had received from God. Exodus 40:16 tells us that "Thus did Moses; according to all that the LORD commanded him, so did he."

Considering the imprint of inspiration upon the Words of Scripture we could almost argue that the words of Moses were a "version" of the Words of God. With this general thought in mind we note that there was no oath given at the investiture of a man who became the Levitical high priest. It was a hereditary office with son succeeding father.

The argument of Paul is that the simple line of human succession does not begin to compare with the majesty of the Oath of God whereby Jesus was High Priest. In the lacking of a Divine oath for the Levitical high priest, this becomes a situation of one created man simply replacing another created man at the death of the former. Although there is a means of continuity there is no real eternity in the Levitical priesthood. This lack of eternality argues that the Levitical priesthood is not permanent and may be abrogated or changed.

The eternality encased within the Oath of God pertaining to the Priesthood of Messiah shows an unchanging reality of the Priesthood of Jesus.]

7.22   By so much was Jesus made a surety of a better testament.

[The Oath of God concerning Messiah as High Priest forever makes the New Covenant a better covenant than the Old.

The Jewish blessings under the Mosaic Law were temporal blessings concerning time. The blessing given the believer under the New Covenant are spiritual and of eternity. There is a pardon of sin rather than just a covering of sin. There is the promise, firm and certain, of Salvation. The New Covenant applies to the entire world of humanity rather than just to one nation or family.

The priests of the Old Covenant were dying men. Each would pass from the scene only to be replaced by another of the same physicality. The offerings they made could never eradicate sin nor even cleanse the heart of anyone. The rites were available only to the people of Israel and proselytes to that faith.

Jesus is an eternal High Priest for, and to, the believer; He will never leave His Office by death. He is infinite in His power, knowledge and wisdom. Rather than sacrifice a creature of the creation, He sacrificed Himself, the Author of Creation. In doing this He opened the door of grace to all.

The Words of God are always certain and true. In the giving of this oath to the society of humanity is a gift to fallible men in that we can see this as of a higher order than the simple succession of office of the Levitical priest.

The terms of the New Covenant are simple and so easy to understand that a child can learn them.

The ordinances of the New Covenant, baptism and the Lord's Table, are more meaningful to the minds and souls of men as these are not mystical things to gain grace but memorials of the grace which He has already given.

The simpler ordinances of the New Covenant are must easier to perform. They do not require elaborate or expensive settings. They are easily within the reach of even the poorest of Christian assemblies and people.

The New Covenant offers the benefits of the Grace of God to all people everywhere. There is no need to become a proselyte of another religion in order to become a follower of Christ.

The New Covenant is not administered by fallible and fallen men. We have the certainty of our soul's renewal because the Administer of our faith is the Perfect Man, and Perfect God, Jesus Christ.

Since the installation of the New Covenant by the acts of Jesus, the Old Covenant has fallen into disuse. The power of the Old Covenant was in its teaching of the New Covenant. Since the arrival of Jesus and His death, burial, resurrection and ascension back into the Heavenlies, the Old Covenant no longer has the power to do other than convict men of their sin. The Old Covenant is a mirror to show our need for trusting Jesus.

HEBREWS: Chapter 7

The New Covenant is based on better principle. The Old Covenant demanded that man perform acts of contrition with reference to his own sin. The basis of the New Covenant is the Jesus has done all the work to eradicate our sin. His death on the Cross was in full payment for our sins. Our only duty in regard of the New Covenant is to trust that Jesus has done all the work, already!

Jesus is the Surety of the New Covenant. The surety was a witness to the conditions of a covenant between two parties. His duty was to witness the agreement and assure that the duties of both parties be carried out. Incumbent with these duties the surety would assume the position of guarantee of the contract.

Jesus has guaranteed our salvation with His Own blood. He mediates to The Father that we are saved, secure and, positionally, sinless. (I John 1:7; 9)

Jesus mediates from The Father that we have peace with God. (John 14:27) The parental punishment from The Father which is made necessary because of our shortcomings and lacks, (Hebrews 12:6) stands as a surety of that peace with God.]

7.23   And they truly were many priests, because they were not suffered to continue by reason of death:

[According to Burkitt there were 83 high priests during the entire period of Hebrew residence in the Land. He argued that 13, beginning with Aaron, served in the Tabernacle, 18 served at Solomon's Temple and 52 at the Second Temple, ending with Phineas who died in the destruction of the Temple in 70 A.D. I would assume that this includes the Herodian Temple of the time of Jesus as an extension of the Temple built by the returnees from the Babylonian captivity.

Taking round numbers, this would total 83 High Priests in 1470 years (Using Ussher's Exodus at @ 1400 B.C. and adding 70 years to account for the Roman sacking of Jerusalem.) this would amount to about 18 years per high priest.

All the above is interesting but the only thing we can take from it is that there were a "whole lotta" high priests. They each gave up their office upon their death and were succeeded by their sons. During that entire time frame since that time there has been but ONE High Priest of our profession, Jesus. If we compute from 33 A.D. (Admittedly a highly unlikely year!) as the time of the Crucifixion of Jesus until 2015 we come up with Jesus in His Office for 1,982 years – and counting!

I yield to Burkitt again to argue the obvious, those 83 Levitical high priests all "resigned" their office upon their death. Jesus, at His death on the Cross of Calvary, was performing the duties of High Priest as He died. He was offering up His Own body as a payment for sin as He died. Since Jesus is eternal in His Deity, it is obvious that He never spent a time when He was not performing those priestly duties on our behalf.

This speaks to a much superior High Priest, in the Person of Jesus, to any – or all! – of those 83 who served from the time of the establishment of the Levitical priesthood until about 40 years – from the crucifixion, burial, resurrection and glorification of Jesus until to Roman army destroyed the last temple.]

7.24   But this man, because he continueth ever, hath an unchangeable priesthood.

[Jesus is an "unchangeable" High Priest for there is never a need that He be replaced with another. He lives, and serves, forever. This is a confirmation of the prophecy of David from Psalm 110:4 – "The LORD hath sworn, and will not repent,

Thou art a priest for ever after the order of Melchizedek."

An objection has been raised that the dismissal of the Levitical priesthood points to a variableness within the determinative will of God. Not so. The concept of permanence was never part of the concept of the high priest during the period of the Mosaic Law. As discussed above, verse 23, the average tenure of the High Priest was under twenty years. There was even provision in the Law of Moses for the succession of high priests. (Deuteronomy 10:6)

The entire process of the Law of Moses, and the Levitical priesthood who administered it were always to be temporary. They are a type of our Lord. The entire Old Covenant Law points to Jesus. When Jesus had fulfilled that Law, and offered up Himself as a sacrifice for the sins of the world, the Law ceased to have meaning.

John the Baptist was a great prophet and preacher. His entire purpose was to point to the coming Savior. Soon after the public ministry of Jesus was begun we begin to see John the Baptist begin to fade from the view of history. His time had been fulfilled and his job was finished with the coming of the Lord.

It is the same with the Mosaic Law. We may never pass beyond the spiritual and moral truths in that Law. But, we are no longer bound by the ceremonial and sacerdotal aspects of that Law. The type has been replaced by the reality of the Savior.]

7.25 *Wherefore he is able also to save them to the uttermost that come unto God by him, seeing he ever liveth to make intercession for them.*

[This particular verse can seem confusing at first glance. The appearance is there that God and Jesus are separated. This is not so. The Trinity of the Godhead is three distinct Personalities Who eternally exist as One. In this verse Jesus is being spoken of in His office as Savior. Thus, sinners come to Him in faith and He presents them to the Father as saved individuals.

Since the verse also says that "he is able also to save them," making the salvation experience under the power of Jesus, we see that He is God - even in this verse. Only God has the privilege of pardoning the sin of the sinner.

We might well note that this salvation is "to the uttermost." Jesus continues to work His work of salvation – not in that we are progressively saved, we are "Once Saved" – all the way through to its completion. We can never "lose" our salvation as Jesus is ever powerful to hold us, and ever mediating to call us. There is no "brink" for us to pass. Jesus is all powerful to hold us to Himself.

I left the power on to my coffee pot on last night. The bottom of the coffee pot is now stained with burnt coffee. I don't know if I will ever be able to clean the pot to its original condition. Our souls are stained with sin. We can never clean them to the point where they would be clean unto God. Jesus has offered the Cleansing Agent of His Own Blood to clean our souls. Our condition will remain besmirched and sinful unless we meet Him at the cross and accept Him as our Savior.

There is no need for any to die in their sin. Jesus will cleanse sin.]

7.26 *For such an high priest became us, who is holy, harmless, undefiled, separate from sinners, and made higher than the heavens;*

[The Holiness of Jesus, however, is part of Who He Is. His very nature is Holy.

This verse reminds us that Jesus is Holy. When speaking of His Office as High Priest, the following comment is made. "For such an high priest became us, who is holy, harmless, undefiled, separate from sinners, and made higher than the heavens."

This verse speaks of Jesus. We must note that the "was made" does not refer to a promotion, His being created, or His sudden ascension to a post. The meaning has to do with His innate status of Creator God. The "was made" speaks of His humanity united with His Deity.

Of course, the fact is emphasized that Jesus is holy. We can also consider that Jesus is our High Priest. Jesus is also Prophet, of course. The office of prophet is to deliver the Words of God to man. Every pastor should be a prophet rather than a mere moralizer. But, the office of priest is to bring the needs of the people before the throne of God.

Jesus brings the needs of the people before God in a way that is both unique and singular. His Priesthood is unique in that He is the Only Begotten of God. He is the promised Messiah. He is the Savior Who died in our place. He is God with the authority and power to bring our needs to the Throne and to provide the answer to those needs.

His Priesthood is singular in that He is the only mediator. "For there is one God, and one mediator between God and man, the man Christ Jesus." (I Timothy 2:5) This verse, of course, speaks of Jesus in His mediatorial office as the Representative of humanity. The salient point is that He is not only the Only Savior; He is also the Only Mediator.

A pastor, or really any Christian, may pray for a person. We can invoke the Spirit to work upon their hearts and needs. But, neither the man in the pew nor the person in the pulpit, or denominational headquarters, can ever pray in place of a person. That personal relationship between the Spirit and the people is one of the principles of God.

Likewise, no person can take his petition to a church official, a Christian brother or sister, a pastor, or anyone else with the expectation that the prayer of those other people will relieve that person of the responsibility of approaching the Throne of Grace on his own behalf.

Only Jesus is authorized to act as Mediator between God and man. To ask another to take that responsibility is against the principles of Scripture and an attempt to lead another to sin as it is asking them to take the place of Jesus.

We can pray for others, and we should. But we can never remove our own responsibility, as individuals, to take our cares and needs to Jesus for ourselves. Group prayer is good and effective. However, private prayer is needful and a blessing to the petitioner. Private prayer is also Scriptural!

Looking back at the verse. Jesus became us. The meaning here is much like a man much in love with his wife who will say, "She completes me." Jesus became all we ever need in the spiritual and, in His fulfilling our needs as created beings, in the physicality of our daily lives.

Jesus is separate from sinners. He is perfection personified. Sinners are dereliction or sin personified. The perfections of Jesus set Him completely apart from sinful humiliation. Yet, He calls sinners to Himself that He might cure that spiritually damning malady.

It is the incarnate holiness of Jesus which allows Him to impart His Own perfections to those who accept Him as Savior.

He is harmless. Although men revile Him repeatedly, He continues to love them to the last drop of His precious blood at the Cross of Calvary.

He is without sin. In His humanity Jesus was perfect humanity as God had created man to be. His was a pre-Adamic perfection untainted by the stain of the sin of Adam. In His divinity Jesus was not capable of sin. Sin remained anathema to Jesus. It would not be in His divine nature to even consider sin.

When Stephen, the first martyr mentioned from the Church in the Scripture, was dying he looked up into the Heavens and saw Jesus. Jesus is exalted beyond the Heavens. He is the God of Heaven.]

7.27 Who needeth not daily, as those high priests, to offer up sacrifice, first for his own sins, and then for the people's: for this he did once, when he offered up himself.

[The Levitical priests had a six day work week. They continually, daily, offered animal sacrifice to the Lord. Had these sacrifices been sufficient for the remission and removal of sin they would not have had to continually offer them up.

It is worth noting that before offering up a sacrifice on behalf of someone else, the priest would offer up a sacrifice for himself. The old phrase quoted to people who try to show us how to do things is, "Physician, heal thyself." The Levitical priest could not find a way to remove his own sinfulness. He "continually" offered sacrifice.

Jesus, however, offered no sacrifice for himself as our Great High Priest. Jesus offered up Himself as a sacrifice for the sins of the world. He only needed to do this one time for it to wash clean the sins of the world.

Read that carefully. "...he did this once, when he offered up himself." The Church has a memorial service called, "The Lord's Table." We, some more often than others, do not offer up Jesus again. We celebrate a memorial that He offered up Himself.

The animal sacrifices were repeated and repeated and repeated and... Even at that often offering up they had need to repeat them again on the next day. Jesus offered Himself once and that Offering was so powerful that there was never a need to do it again.

Jesus sacrificed Himself. It was no error or tragedy that Jesus went to the cross and suffered the death by crucifixion. It was the plan of Jesus to offer up Himself.

The song says it all: "How wonderful, How glorious..."

Unlike the Levitical priests, Jesus had no need to make an offering for Himself. He was not, is not, a sinner. He is "separate from sin." Jesus offered only a sacrifice for others.

Neither did Jesus take an animal of a created order to sacrifice. Jesus gave of Himself, the Creator, to be sacrificed. It is not possible that any entity from the created order could be a proper sacrifice for sin within the created order. The entire created order is stained by the horror of sin. (Romans 8:22) It was the Creator, Himself, Who offered Himself to the tender mercies of the cruelty of the Roman soldiers, Who offered Himself as the (Singular and emphatic for there is no other!) sacrifice for the sin of the world.

The soldiers did not crucify Him. The crowds were not responsible for His death. We, sinners all, were responsible for the fact that Jesus offered Himself as the sacrifice for our redemption. (John 3:36)

Finally, unlike the Levitical priests, Jesus did not die for the sins of the nation. He died for the sins of the world. Anyone may accept the Salvation which Jesus has already purchased at the Cross of Calvary.]

7.28 *For the law maketh men high priests which have infirmity; but the word of the oath, which was since the law, maketh the Son, who is consecrated for evermore.*

[Under the Mosaic Law there were men appointed to be High Priest. These men were fallible and afflicted with all the maladies common to humanity. These included both physical and spiritual failings. The only distinguishing factor of the priestly caste was their office as priests unto God. In all other aspects they were subject to infirmity.

This fact was proven on two counts. On the first, it was necessary for these priests to offer sacrifice for themselves even before they were allowed to offer sacrifice for the general population.

Second was the fact, supported by the laws of succession, that these men were also subject to death. Their service in administering the law did not change that truth.

The Levitical priests would point to their genealogies to support their claims to the priestly office. Jesus need only point to the Oath of God concerning His higher appointment.

They were of temporal families and generations. Jesus is eternal in His Own generations.

The Levitical priests received tithes from their brethren to support themselves. Melchisedek, as a king did not need support money but he did receive tithes from Abraham, the father of the entire line, in his office as priest. Abraham thus showed his own subservience to Melchisedek.

Jesus does not personally receive tithes. He, rather, supplies the needs of those who come to God through Him.

The Levitical priests would pray for blessings upon the people. Jesus simply blesses those who are His.

The Levitical priests were insufficient for their tasks. They never ceased offering sacrifice for themselves and others because they never found sin removed from anyone. The curse remained. As Eternal High Priest Jesus is ever living and ever sufficient. His sacrifice removed the fact and nature of sin in those who come to Him.

The tenure of the Levitical priest was for his own lifetime. Jesus has no successor in His Priesthood for He is eternal and will never die.

The Levitical priest was sinful and fallible. Jesus is Holy, Undefiled, and able to save all who come to Him. (John 6:37)

The Levitical priest served in his infirmity. Jesus serves in the power of His glory.

It must also be noted that Jesus, serving as Eternal High Priest after the order of Melchisedek, serves in a capacity which both precedes and continues after the Levitical Priesthood. This is but one more instance of the superiority of Jesus as High Priest of our Profession.]

HEBREWS - CHAPTER EIGHT

8.1 *Now of the things which we have spoken this is the sum: We have such an high priest, who is set on the right hand of the throne of the Majesty in the heavens,*

[Jesus is not only our High Priest, He is also The Magistrate of our Judgment. Too often we dwell on the wonderfulness of His humanity and fail to appreciate the Glory of His Divinity.

Paul argues that Jesus is the Sum of all the good and greater things which set Him apart as the High Priest of our profession. Jesus is of a Higher Order, as pictured in Melchisedec, than the entirety of the Levitical priesthood. Unlike the daily and yearly sacrifices of the old order, Jesus has presented One Sacrifice of Himself which is sufficient for the salvation of all who would come to Him. His sacrifice is sufficient and effective. This is the sacrifice which has been accepted as a pardon from sin by The Father.

This might be a good place to consider the Three "Persons" of the Trinity. We must not mistake Jesus as a "lower god" for He is fully God in His Divine Person. Jesus is neither The Father nor The Spirit. There is but One God of One Essence; yet, that Eternal Essence is incumbent within Three distinct "Persons" of that One Divine Essence. This is not a picture of Three Gods.

This is not a picture of Three separate appearances such as one man being seen as father, husband and co-worker by three different people. The picture is more of a cup of coffee with cream and sugar. There is but one essence of beverage within the cup. The cream adds a distinct taste. The sugar adds a distinct taste. The coffee adds a distinct taste. The three are easily recognized as differing in their purpose but as one in their application. They are indivisible within that cup.

The Father seems to fill the office of Administration although He may Adjudicate or Announce at His good pleasure and purpose. The Son seems to fill the office of Adjudicator in that He is both Mediator for the righteous and Judge to the unrighteous. He may also fill the office of Administrator or Announcement at His good pleasure and purpose. The Spirit seems to fill the office of Announcer although He may fill the office of Administrator or Adjudicator at His good pleasure or will.

The point seems that God is of but One Essence of which there are Three distinct "Persons" Who work in complete and total harmony as The One God of Eternity.

Therefore, we can see that Jesus does have all power in Heaven and on Earth. With this power, and based on His Sacrifice of Himself on the Cross of Calvary for the remission of sins, He is able to save all who come to The Father by Him.

We must note that unlike the temporal high priests of the Levitical order, Jesus did not depart the Holy of Holies after His Work of Redemptive Sacrifice. He still abides to mediate for the Christian as He remains our Great High Priest and Continual Mediator. He is sympathetic to our weakness and continues to uphold us beyond our power to stand.

Jesus remains sinless and unchangeable. He will never not be either sinless in His Own Person or unsympathetic to our plight as weak humanity. He is Divine and of Eternity.

And, yet, the verse says that He is set at the Right Hand of God. That word "set" (Kathizo 2523 in Strong's) carries the meaning of "sit," as well. The "Right Hand of God" is not a word of spatial consideration but of symbolic and actual power. Jesus sits in the seat of Power. The fact that He is shown as sitting is a statement that His work has been completed. It gives the same picture as of God "resting" in the seventh day. The job is done. "It is finished." (John 19:30) Nothing can be added to the finished work of Jesus on the Cross of Calvary.]

8.2 *A minister of the sanctuary, and of the true tabernacle, which the Lord pitched, and not man.*

[Jesus is called a Minister of the Sanctuary. The Levitical priest, as a minister, was a public servant to the people. His "job" was to offer the sacrifice on behalf of the people for their sins. Once a year the high priest would sprinkle the blood of sacrifice upon the Mercy Seat in the Holy of Holies. He would first offer sacrifice for his own sins so that he might approach the symbolic presence of God in pureness in order to offer for the sins of the people.

The Tabernacle in the Wilderness was in the structure of a tent. It was to the specifications of this Tabernacle that the Temple was built. The true Tabernacle was the Heavenly form of which the Tabernacle in the Wilderness, and the Temple, were types and shadows.

John 1:14 tells us this of Jesus: "And the Word was made flesh, and dwelt among us, (and we beheld his glory, the glory as of the only begotten of the Father,) full of grace and truth." The word "dwelt" is 4637 in Strong's; it carries the context of a tent. It speaks of the Tabernacle in the Wilderness.

This Tabernacle, and the Temple which followed it, were each the place where the Israelite understood God to dwell. The mercy seat in the Holy of Holies was the place of His Throne. With this in mind we see that the human Jesus was the place where the God of the Universe dwelt. The shadow of the Tabernacle gives a view of the reality of the Person of Jesus which the Tabernacle foreshadowed.

The same word is used to describe the temporary booths set up for ceremonial services. Those were not kept up at all times. Jesus came to save us and then to depart to serve us in the Heavenly Tabernacle.

At the time of His earthly ministry there was no plan for Him to remain on earth. His purpose, after His sacrifice at Calvary, was shadowed by the earthly high priest of the Levitical order. He returned to the Heavenly Sanctuary to sprinkle His Blood of Sacrifice on the Heavenly Mercy Seat.

The Temple had "outer courts" within the structure. The Tabernacle also had a courtyard which could well be considered typical of the world at large. The penitent approached the altar and sacrificed unto the Lord even as Jesus offered Himself as the True Sacrifice for Sin in the "courtyard" of the world at large.

Within this courtyard was another structure. The first part of this, behind a veil and not accessible to all was the Holy Place. This would be indicative of the redeemed of the Church. Behind another veil was the Holy of Holies which could only be entered by the high priest – and then only on the Day of Atonement. In this place was the Mercy Seat of God upon which the blood of the sacrifice was sprinkled.

This "holy of Holies" would be indicative of Heaven. Jesus, our Great and Eternal High Priest has entered this place to sprinkle the Blood of His Sacrifice upon the

Heavenly Mercy Seat in a Tabernacle not made with hands. At His offering of Himself on the Cross, when He died that veil between the Holy Place and the Holy of Holies – indicative of the presence of God – was torn from top to bottom. We are bade entrance into the presence of the Throne of God in prayer and as we pass from this life to the next as Blood bought believers.

This is not due to any righteousness on our part. This is completely due to the Sacrifice and Mediatorial Office of Jesus as He applies the sacrifice of Himself to cleanse our sin and offer us peace with God and an eternal life of bliss with our Savior.]

8.3 *For every high priest is ordained to offer gifts and sacrifices: wherefore it is of necessity that this man have somewhat also to offer.*

[The purpose of a priest is to make an offering to God on behalf of man. They were ordained, or set apart, for this very purpose. Paul now begins to elaborate on the fact that Jesus is the Great and Eternal High Priest of our Profession.

The purpose of the Law of the Old Testament was to show two things. First, the Old Testament Law was established to point to Jesus, of course. But, in doing this the Law also showed the complete depravity of man. Man was always, still is!, unable to approach the standard of God. Even the Levitical priests had to offer sacrifice for themselves.

Second, in showing the utter depravity of humanity, the Old Testament Law was able to point out the transcending holiness and glory of God.

In the grace of the New Testament we are shown the complete inability of man to secure any favor with God. We are also shown the all sufficiency of the grace of God.

The gifts offered by the priests were tokens of man showing his own favor toward God. The sacrifices were able to show the fact that God held humanity in general disfavor because of the sinfulness of man. From the standpoint of man, this was the purpose of the sacrifice of those animals of creation. But, there was much more as God intended these temporal sacrifices to be a picture and prophecy of the Cross of Calvary.

It was necessary for Jesus to have a body to offer as a sacrifice for the sin of humanity. It was to this duty which the priest was consecrated. One of the meanings of "consecration" is "to fill the hand." Man has no innate goodness within Himself to approach The Holy and Pure God of Creation. Thus, there is the need of sacrifice. This was to be a total sacrifice to illustrate the total depravity of lost humanity. This both an agreement of man with God as to the state of the sinner, and a picture of the surpassing Holiness of God – especially so when compared with that sinful character of created man. The was the sacrifice which the Priest took in offering to God.

Jesus came to fill a perfect human body so that He might shed the very life blood of that perfect human body as an atonement for the sins of others who, likewise, had a human body – albeit a human body which had been diseased and spiritually disfigured by sin. They, sinful and disfigured, could not approach The Holy God to make a plea for grace. He, alone of a perfect human body without the taint the "sin gene" sent down through the generations via the sin of Adam, could offer His Own Perfect Body as The Perfect Sacrifice for sin.

By accepting this sacrifice as having been offered on their behalf, humanity could share in the perfections of Jesus and have their own sins washed away in the blood of the Lamb of God.

    Christian ministers are not priests. We cannot be because we have no sacrifice to offer; Jesus has already completed the only perfect and available sacrifice for sin. We are only, at our best, able to point toward the perfect and total sacrifice of Jesus and pray the Spirit's conviction upon others that they would accept that Sacrifice for the remission of sin.

    While the priests had to daily offer the sacrifice of the animals of creation to cover the sins of men, Jesus Once offered His Own Body as The Creator; this is the perfect and complete sacrifice for sin.

    The priests carried the blood of created animals into the Holy of Holies on the Day of Atonement. Jesus entered the Holy of Holies of the Heavenly Tabernacle, built by God and not by the hands of sinful humanity, with His Own Blood as the Creator. In this He purchased full and complete salvation to all who would accept Him.]

8.4   *For if he were on earth, he should not be a priest, seeing that there are priests that offer gifts according to the law:*

    [If Jesus had not ascended into Heaven He could not have been our Great High Priest. At His incarnation Jesus was "made under the Law." (Galatians 4:4) In the Kenosis He had voluntarily placed Himself under the Mosaic Law. This Law was not abrogated until He had fulfilled that Law in all its particulars. As actual High Priest, He offered up His Own Humanity as an offering for sin. It was necessary that the Blood of His Sacrifice be sprinkled on the Heavenly Mercy Seat as fulfilling His duties as High Priest on the Day of Atonement. This was done in the Heavenly Sanctuary of which the earthly was only a type and shadow of that spiritual and eternal reality.

    As the Law was completely fulfilled at this point it was no longer needful that He, or any of the redeemed of the Lord, should be under the Law. The duties of the Mosaic Law were fulfilled and discarded as a no longer functioning picture of the reality which had come to pass. The Spiritual truths and moral obligations of the Law remained as they continued to teach the concept of the depravity of man. The rites and ceremonies of the Law, completely fulfilled in the life and death of Messiah, were no longer duties to be fulfilled by man.

    Spiritual principles remain. Slavish obedience to the types are given way to grace and love as administered by the Savior in His role as perfect High Priest of our profession. Reality has replaced typology.

    At the time of the penning of this Book the Temple still stood. It had not yet been destroyed by the Roman armies. It is interesting to consider that the same Roman army which brutally put the Savior to death in order for His Sacrifice to bring freedom from sin and full salvation to mankind, also brutally removed the last vestiges of the duties of the offering of temporal sacrifice by the Levitical line of priests.

    Up until the point of the destruction of the city and Temple, there were still offerings being made of the beasts of creation. These were no longer authorized by the defunct system of Mosaic Law; they were only offered by human priests who acted in their own, and in traditional, authority.

    Under the Mosaic Law Jesus could not be priest. He was, humanly speaking, of the line of Judah while only the descendants of Levi, and of the family of Aaron, could be priests and offer sacrifice under the Mosaic system which Jesus replaced with perfection of His complete fulfillment of that superseded, and centered on the works of man, system.

Under the Law of Grace the concept of animal sacrifice is no longer allowed. To consider the keeping the ceremonial law of Moses is a direct insult to the Savior Who died in time, fully fulfilling and disannulling the Mosaic Law, (Hebrews 7:18) that all might come to The Father by Him. True and eternal salvation is in Jesus. (Acts 4:12) It is to Him alone we must flee for salvation from our sin, peace with God and an eternal home of bliss in the presence of the Savior.]

8.5 Who serve unto the example and shadow of heavenly things, as Moses was admonished of God when he was about to make the tabernacle for, See, saith he, that thou make all things according to the pattern shewed to thee in the mount.

[Moses received these instructions directly from God while he was on Mount Sinai. These instructions came at the same place as the giving of the Law. I would submit that this strongly suggests the force of the Law of God upon these instructions.

These things were a vague, but importantly distinct, representation of the Heavenly pattern. These things were vague in that they were a representation in time and physicality of those things which are eternal and spiritual in their very essence. They were distinct in that God explained the unknowable to the unknowing. (John 3:12) For there to be any semblance of eternal reality within the pattern of the Tabernacle it would be necessary that Moses exactly follow the directions given by God. What Moses might view as a small deviation might be a great deviation. Moses, a human man on earth and in time, had no way of understanding the eternal spiritual realities of Heaven except as God gave him instruction.

The human priests of the Levitical order followed their instructions from the Mosaic Law to the best of their abilities; even though they might not understand all. They did understand to do all.

Consider, in light of this, the giving of the Words of God by the inspiration of God. These are Words of eternal and spiritual significance. If it were true that those Words had been lost at some point in time it would not be possible to "reconstruct" in a manner pleasing to God that which was lost. Humanity could not have the knowledge of the spiritual and eternal except it come from God. If it were possible that these words were lost, humanity would be left adrift upon a sea of uncertainty and human reasoning. It is not possible to reconstruct that which mankind cannot conceptualize.

The Words of God are perfectly kept in Heaven. (Psalm 119:89) Since God gave them to humanity it is logical – with our imperfect and incomplete knowledge of the spiritual and eternal – that God would oversee His intended Message to man in such a way as to insure those Words of instruction and edification would be kept intact.

Since it must be admitted that God has this power, can we argue He would not do so. When we look at His prohibition to changing the Words of the Mosaic Law in any instance, (Deuteronomy 4:2; 12:32; Proverbs 30:8) and His repeating of such prohibition to changing the Words of His Law of Grace, (Revelation 1:3; 22:18-19) we must conclude that He jealously guards His eternal Words from any destruction in time.

This is not to say that there were not copies of these eternal Words which were sullied by the hands of ungodly men. Satan tempted the Living Word of God soon after

Jesus had assumed His public ministry. But, Satan could not overcome Jesus. It is reasonable to conclude that Satan would also attack, by alteration when possible, the Written Word of God. But, Satan does not have the power to overcome the eternal Words of the eternal God.

It is a spiritual principle that the Authentic Words of God are available at all times to His Church and His people. This is displayed in the shadow and type of the Tabernacle. The Tabernacle was the presence of God with His people in a manner which typified His Sacrifice for all Humanity. His Word to us is that which allows us to see the Glory of Christ and the perfections of God as contrasted with our sinfulness and spiritual weakness as human beings.

To disallow this is to follow the pattern of the priest who continued to offer animal sacrifice after the time of the Crucifixion of Jesus. It is an attempt, perhaps unwittingly, to put the words and works of man as of more importance than are the Words and Works of God. It is to doubt the goodness, power and love of God that He would give His Message to man and then allow it to be withdrawn. This concept would leave us rudderless in a sea of danger without even the knowledge of the sea.]

8.6 *But now hath he obtained a more excellent ministry, by how much also he is the mediator of a better covenant, which was established upon better promises.*

[We look at Jesus as our Great High Priest and see that His ministrations upon our behalf are more glorious than were those of the Mosaic Law. The concept of the Old Covenant was a picture of a Covenant which had been primarily secular and transitory. It was concerned with the sons of Abraham. It faded away when the Light of the Word came to show its weakness and fulfill its demands.

This New Covenant speaks primarily of the spiritual and the eternal. The Old Covenant had been merely a shadow, an outline of indistinct borders, of the reality which was ushered in by the New Covenant of Jesus.

Jesus has become, as our Heavenly High Priest, the Mediator of this New Covenant of grace.

While the Old Covenant promised a long life and the length of days to the righteous, the New Covenant spoke of an eternal life to redeemed sinners.

The ceremonies and rites of the Old Covenant were administered by the priests who were part of sinful humanity in their own right. They had to offer sacrifice for themselves as well as for the people. These sacrifices and offerings only gave the promise of a chance to do the same in another day. Jesus came to offer the New Testament of His Blood which would give us full peace with God and the chance to serve Him.

The Old Covenant offered regular seasons of rain and harvest. This was good as it allowed the people to properly order their lives in the Land of Promise. In the New Covenant we are offered the perfect "home" of Heaven where all of our needs are supplied by the Lord.

A benefit of the Old Covenant was peace with the neighboring nations. In the fidelity of the people to the worship of God, there would be no successful warfare instigated against them. The New Covenant offers us peace with God. Although Satan may attack us, we are assured that, "Ye are of God, little children, and have overcome them: because greater is he that is in you, than he that is in the world." (I John 4:4)

The people of the Old Covenant looked forward to the day when Messiah would come. Those of the New Covenant are promised a relationship with Messiah, Who has already come; We are offered peace and fellowship with Him due to His Sacrifice and mediatorial office on our behalf.

In the Old Covenant the concept of hope was contained within the obedience to the Law and its ceremonies. In the New Covenant we have faith that the sacrifice of Jesus has already purchased our salvation and made us adopted into the family of God. (John 1:12)

Under the Old Covenant the people had the Law and the Prophets to lead them. In the days of the New Covenant the entire Canon of Scripture has been completed and preserved for us. Beyond this we have the promise of the Spirit to illumine those inspired and preserved Words of God for our instruction and fellowship.]

8.7 *For if that first covenant had been faultless, then should no place have been sought for the second.*

[Paul states the obvious: If the Old Covenant had been perfect there would have been no need for this New Covenant. (see my note at Hebrews 7:11)

This is another place where we need to tread softly. The Old Covenant was not imperfect. The fault did not lie within the covenant of the Mosaic Law. Its demands of perfection were beyond the reach of any human person. The Law was never completely fulfilled, in its entirety, until Messiah came and fulfilled all of the Law and the Ceremonies.

Nonetheless, there was a lack within the Law. It demanded a complete fulfillment. No one but Jesus has ever done so. That was not the problem. The Law was not deficient in its demands; it was deficient in its rewards. There was no means within the Law to justify and give salvation to mankind. (Romans 8:3) The requirement of exact obedience was hampered by the lack of assistance to do so.

The fact is that the Law was deficient in that it did not go far enough. It lacked the mechanism of Grace which would allow full salvation. The person who fulfilled the sacrificial requirements in faith, trusting the Words of God in this manner, was able to gain status as "righteous." (Romans 4:3) But, his sins remained. His true salvation was dependent upon obedience, faith in the words of God, and the coming sacrifice of Messiah on the Cross of Calvary.

This Sacrifice of Jesus was always the means of true salvation. (Revelation 13:8) This was the complete plan of God from before the foundation of the world. Though the ancients did not understand this dynamic of God, although prophesized in places like the 53rd chapter of Isaiah and the 22nd Psalm, this was the basis of their salvation in the same way that this is the basis of salvation in the New Covenant. (See my notes at Luke 16:9)

The Mosaic Law was perfect in its intended purpose. (Galatians 3:24-25) I was talking with a young man a few days ago. He asked how we knew that Jesus is the True Savior. One of the infallible proofs of Scripture is the Law which prophesied of Jesus through the ceremonies and rites of the Law and the prophecies of the prophets who prophesied about Messiah. The Law was perfect in its intention of introducing us to the Savior.]

HEBREWS: Chapter 8

8.8   For finding fault with them, he saith, Behold, the days come, saith the Lord, when I will make a new covenant with the house of Israel and with the house of Judah:

[There is disagreement with just "who" the fault was found. I believe it threefold.

First, there was a "fault" with the Law. It was never intended to be permanent as the death of Christ quite evidently shows. Had the Law been a permanent way of redemption there would have been no need for Jesus to die on the Cross. The fact that He went to the Cross, and was considered as slain before the Law was even given, is a proof that God intended the Law to reign only so long as Messiah tarried His coming.

Second, there was a fault with the priests who were the administrators of the Law. They had to offer sacrifice for themselves before they could even begin to assume their daily duties. Sinful men cannot offer absolution to other sinful men. Only the perfections of Jesus in His humanity and in His Deity allowed Him to stand above the sin incumbent within others so as to be a fit substitute to offer full and complete salvation from sin.

Third, the people seemed constantly to be sliding into the idol worship of the nations around them. They lacked a real zeal for worshipping the God of Creation. Past their idolatry the people also succumbed to the sin of believing that they were above other people simply because they were the sons of Abraham.

Paul appeals at this place to Jeremiah 31:31-34 to make the case that the New Covenant is both of God and necessary.

Since both the Kingdom of Israel and the Kingdom of Judah are mentioned we are informed that there will be a time when all the sons of Abraham are again "center stage" on the agenda of God for this world.

My belief is that this will happen during the Tribulation Era. The Church has no place in this time of tribulation. We have already been raptured from the earth when this tribulation begins. Jeremiah 30:7 informs us that this time of tribulation is a time of Jacob's trouble. Since Jacob was father to each of the twelve tribes this phrase would include all the sons of Abraham.

In Revelation 7:5-8 we see that each of the tribes is mentioned along with a group called out from them to evangelize the world during this tribulation.

As to this renewal of all Israel during the latter days we would note a few things. First, this is because they are convinced that He is The Messiah as promised. Zechariah 12:10 makes reference to Jerusalem and the house of David in relation to this renewal. "And I will pour upon the house of David, and upon the inhabitants of Jerusalem, the spirit of grace and of supplications: and they shall look upon me whom they have pierced, and they shall mourn for him, as one mourneth for his only son, and shall be in bitterness for him, as one that is in bitterness for his firstborn."

Considering that Jerusalem was the place where Jesus was offered up for the sins of the world, this verse seems very appropriate.

Second, the people will be freed from the burden of the Law as they are brought into the spiritual religion of Messiah. The Holy Spirit will offer His enablement's to the people unlike the period of the Mosaic Law.

Third, unlike the transitory nature of the Mosaic Covenant, this will be an eternal Law of Grace which is visited among the people.

Fourth, I find the phraseology of "they shall look upon me" and "they shall mourn for him" as a statement of the full Divinity of Jesus Christ. "They shall look upon me," makes Him to be the Agent of Inspiration in this place. "They shall mourn for him," marks this Man of Deity as the Only Savior of the world. Jesus is the Initiator of the Covenant of Grace.]

8.9 *Not according to the covenant that I made with their fathers in the day when I took them by the hand to lead them out of the land of Egypt; because they continued not in my covenant, and I regarded them not, saith the Lord.*

[Paul is here quoting from Jeremiah 31:32, "Not according to the covenant that I made with their fathers in the day that I took them by the hand to bring them out of the land of Egypt; which my covenant they brake, although I was an husband unto them, saith the LORD"

We well note that this is not an exact quote. This is allowed under the concept of inspiration since it is the Spirit illumining the Words of preserved and inspired Scripture for His Own purposes. The passage in Jeremiah referred to a time yet future, regarding the Covenant People of God of the Abrahamic Covenant, at the penning of the words. The passage in Hebrews spoke of a present reality pertaining to the Christian Church.

Sometimes the small variations in the quotation of passages from the Old Testament by the New Testament penmen may be the necessary result of transferring the Words from Hebrew to the Greek. Such variations as these cannot be considered as translations; the same Spirit of inspiration was involved in both at this time. Both, therefore, are to be considered as the inviolate Words of God.

Since the above is true only of God, no translation made by man may be properly considered as inspired. At its best a translation can only be, as the moon reflecting the greater light of the sun, a reflection – accurate in the view given of the substance of the original but of lesser quality and intensity – of that which is the originally inspired and preserved Words of God. No man or translating committee can ever be confused with the Authoritative Spirit of God within the work of that man or committee.

The phrase "saith the Lord" at the conclusion of this passage is important. No one can speak for Him. No one can speak as Him. The majesty of His Words is what allows us to see the Majesty of Him.

Note that the New Covenant is different from the Old Covenant. The Old Covenant was man centered in its requirement of sacrifice and ceremonies as performed under the Levitical priesthood. The New Covenant is Christ centered as it is His Sacrifice of Himself which brings us to a place of favor with God. But, may we never overlook the fact that both the Old and the New Covenants are based on faith in the Words of God to man. Both are based on obedience to those Words of God to man. And, though we often overlook the fact, the basis of both remains that Sacrifice made by Jesus on the Cross of Calvary – future and not fully understood by those under the Old Covenant and foundational and rarely fully considered in the majesty thereof, by us of the New Covenant.

The United States Declaration of Independence took effect, provisionally at least, on the 4th of July in 1776. Some years later the Constitution of the United States was ratified by Congress and the States in the name of the people. I have never signed either; I am nonetheless bound by the constraints and freedoms of both.

Likewise, in Joshua 24:21-25 the leadership of the people of Abraham bound themselves by oath to worship God – and God, Alone. The refusal of the people of that nation to continue in that Covenant which they had made with God resulted in a spiritual rebellion against Him and His protecting Hand. The prophecy of Joshua 24:20 was fulfilled upon the rebellious people.

Assyria and Babylon became the instruments of God which punished His Covenant people. Note that they have not been eternally cast aside. They are still the people of His Covenant. The purpose of His punishment has been to restore them to Himself.

We can look to our own "War Between The States" to help understand this reality. The eleven Southern States seceded from the union of the United States in 1861. The Northern States did not accept this was proper so a war was fought to compel the States of the Confederacy to return to the Union. The War being successful, the Southern States were readmitted to the Union and today enjoy all the rights and benefits of such union as though they had never rebelled.

Of such a nature is the correcting rod of God upon the rebellious sons of Abraham. The New Covenant will return them to His good favor. They will be restored to their full status as The Covenant People of God as though they had never rebelled in their apostasy.

The "rebellion" of these sons of Abraham was to follow after, to worship, false idols in a rejection of the pure religion of Jehovah. Later, their rejection of God, in the Person of Jesus Christ – Messiah – led to a rebellion from God and into the dead tradition of the Old Covenant when Jesus had fulfilled that Covenant and instituted the New Covenant of His Grace.

God had taken the sons of Abraham by the hand to lead them from the slavery of Egypt into the nationhood of the Land of Promise. This is an illustration of a tender and protecting hand leading a child to a place of safety and plenty. The people had brushed aside this Hand of Mercy in their reaching for the weak and lifeless hands of dead idols.

In their breaking of the covenant of Joshua 24:21-25, the people had rejected God. He treated them, in their rebellion and apostasy as "not His Own." In other words, we could argue that He allowed them to see what it was like to stand on their own without His Divine assistance.

The punishments meted out by the Assyrians and Babylonians were an example to His people that their true peace and safety was available only under that protecting hand. They were not "special;" their God was powerful to save.]

8.10 *For this is the covenant that I will make with the house of Israel after those days, saith the Lord, I will put my laws into their mind, and write them in their hearts and I will be to them a God, and they shall be to me a people:*

[Paul accesses Jeremiah 31:33 to explain this New Covenant which will descend upon all Israel. "But this shall be the covenant that I will make with the house of Israel; After those days, saith the LORD, I will put my law in their inward parts, and write it in their hearts; and will be their God, and they shall be my people."

Although the verse from Jeremiah speaks of a time in the future, Paul will peg the truths of this verse to the present dispensation. The Gospel is now available. Paul's argument is with Jewish men in a Christian Church; he is arguing the benefits of the New Covenant over the Old Covenant to a group of men who seem willing to cling to the tradition of their *religion* even while being confronted with the claims of Jesus concerning this New Covenant.

The phrase "after those days" is in somewhat dispute. Some attribute the phrase to the present Gospel dispensation by pointing to the operating of the New Covenant within the hearts of the believers within the Church. Others point to the beginning of the Millennial Kingdom when Jesus will sit as ruler of the world from Jerusalem upon the literal Throne of David. A third argument is that this refers to the time frame after the "days of the Gentile" has been ended.

I would hold to that last argument. The tribulation era, as we have seen, is described as the "time of Jacob's trouble." (Jeremiah 30:7) The phrase "after those days" is speaking of a time after the times of the Gentiles when God's attention returns to the people of the Abrahamic promises.

The times of the Gentiles began with the subjugation of Judah by the Babylonians. The Temple was destroyed at that time. Although there was another Temple built, and the Temple sacrifices begun again, the primary focus has been upon the Gentiles rather than the Jew. Any reading of the histories of the Book of Daniel will reveal this.

"After those days," that is after the times of the Gentiles has culminated we see in this verse that there is a covenant with the house of Israel. This, "house of Israel," as previously noted, is a phrase which speaks to the entirety of the nation of Abraham. The fact that there are sons of Abraham from all the twelve tribes mentioned in Revelation is another indication that we have returned to the time of Israel as center stage in the program of God upon this earth.

The Kingdom of Israel, as opposed to the House of Judah, seems a type of the erring Christian. Their identification as sons of Abraham has been lost in the sands of time. Even they, for the most part, do not realize their position as heirs of the promises of God. But, God has never forgotten who they are. At the perfect timing of His infallible will He will call them back to Himself. They will cease their wanderings of judgment. This isn't because they have "earned" this calling back. This is because of who, in reality, they are. They are the sons of Abraham to whom the promises of God were given. His Word and His promise never fail to conduct the benefits of the great grace, mercy, and love of God.

So, too, the erring Christian, the honestly Blood bought believer in Jesus, is known as the adopted child of God. He may be called back through judicial punishment as will be these Hebrews of the Diaspora. He may be called back through the death of his body. We would pray that he would be called back by the same wooing of the Spirit as he was first called to the Savior. The point is that the power of the promise of God is even stronger than the backslidden true believer. (John 18:9)

I might note that "the house of Israel" refers to the entire group of the sons of Abraham. "The Kingdom of Israel" refers only to those of the break-away kingdom after the death of Solomon. "Jew" refers to those of the tribe of Judah. We use the term as a handy, "shorthand," especially since the destruction by the Romans within the area of Judah, but – properly speaking – the term speaks only of a person from the tribe of Judah.

God will renew His provisions to the house of Israel. The New Covenant of grace will finally be seen by them as having supplanted the Old Covenant of the Mosaic Law. This will result in an inward change within these sons of Abraham. Their worship will no longer center around outward symbols and rites as they will come to realize the true Messiah. Their worship will be inward within their hearts which are affected by the indwelling power of the Spirit.

Their hearts will be renewed to understand the great truths of The Great High Priest of our and their, profession.

They will then fully recognize the great privilege and possessions which are theirs through Messiah. That torn veil between the Holy Place and the Holy of Holies, symbolizes their access to God through Messiah. He is now their High Priest even as He is the same for the other Christians. Yes, they will be Christians. They retain their position as sons of Abraham even as they glory in that Son of Abraham by whom all the world was blessed.

He is truly their God. They are truly His people on this earth.]

8.11 *And they shall not teach every man his neighbour, and every man his brother, saying, Know the Lord: for all shall know me, from the least to the greatest.*

[In the next two verses Paul accesses Jeremiah 31:34 – "And they shall teach no more every man his neighbour, and every man his brother, saying, Know the LORD: for they shall all know me, from the least of them unto the greatest of them, saith the LORD: for I will forgive their iniquity, and I will remember their sin no more."

Under the Old Testament Mosaic Law there was no provision made for formal teaching of the Law. The few instructional instruments available, such as "the schools of the prophets" were severely limited as to their outreach. The prophets spoke to crowds but not in formal session, as it were. Both the Tabernacle and the Temple were properly places to offer sacrifice but not suited for instruction.

When the Synagogue system was inaugurated, it was a place to read the Law but, again, there was scant attention given to study of that Law except by small conclaves of rabbinic students.

It was into this void that individuals would teach each other of the things of the Lord and Law. This began to change near the time of John the Baptist; but in the earlier days it was not so. The heart that has been changed by the Lord will desire that the mind learn of Him in all things and ways possible. (II Timothy 2:15)

The Old Covenant had been a national religion. The New Covenant is an individual relationship with the Lord of Glory. This, properly speaking, will lead to a more intimate desire to fellowship with the Lord. Whereas the Old Covenant only called to obedience, the New Covenant moves even past this and calls to fellowship.

From the least to the greatest seems a New Testament consideration. The Gospel Message is not hard to understand; the Message of the Gospel is so deep that the wisest men in history have spent years of study and have not begun to find the depths of knowledge of the goodness and glory of the Lord. His Ways are beyond our ways. But, even those most "simple" of humanity are able to grasp enough of the gospel, to find salvation in the Lord.

There are things that we will never understand about this miracle Book of inspired and preserved Scripture. It is then that we fall back to the earliest days of our salvation and repeat, "Lord, I believe. Help thou my unbelief." (Mark 9:24) Lord, I know but I know so little. Thank you for the faith to understand that You are The Lord and I am Your servant. I do not have to know. I do need to obey!]

8.12 *For I will be merciful to their unrighteousness, and their sins and their iniquities will I remember no more.*

[This is grace with a purpose. That purpose is love. The Spirit in that Day will come upon His people of His promise. For them to truly be His people it is necessary that they become a pure people. For this to be a reality it is necessary that their sins be adjudicated and forgiven. This necessitates their acceptance of the Sacrifice of Messiah.

There is no other means of Salvation. Certainly, the sacrifices of the Mosaic Law could not atone for their sin. This is proven by the many daily and yearly sacrifices. Only the Holy Sacrifice of their sinless Messiah could both access the Grace of God's love and adjudicate the guilt of man's sin.

This mercy extended on behalf of Messiah's Sacrifice is not just a "free pass from sins" situation. This mercy extended on behalf of Messiah's Sacrifice is an acceptance of a paid receipt for the punishment of sin; Jesus accepted this punishment on His Own part and applies that this punishment has been paid on behalf of those who have accepted Him as Savior. We are then called to walk in newness of life. Consider Ephesians 2:10.

In a modern consideration we might argue that Jesus' Sacrifice paid the "fine" which we owed on account of our own sins. We are free because He has freed us by His Blood of Sacrifice.

It is the Holy Spirit Who awakens the soul to the need for repentance and then stays to strengthen the soul to live in newness and learn of Messiah. We see this today. Paul was speaking of this present reality. But, in accessing the verses from Jeremiah 31:31-34, Paul sees those same words and concepts applied to the entire people of Israel at that Day.

The marvelous grace of God flows past the sin of man. Man's sin has set him against the rule of God. For humanity this rebellion has become a rule of life. The graciousness of the Holy Spirits leads these sons of Abraham from their place of rebellion and into the place of repentance.

This is the fundamental promise of God which is stated as even now available to all who come by faith to the Cross of Messiah.]

8.13 *In that he saith, A new covenant, he hath made the first old. Now that which decayeth and waxeth old is ready to vanish away.*

[The Old Covenant is subject to corruption. It was, as previously noted, never intended to stand as a permanent means of religious observance. All of the rites, ceremonies, and even administration are contained within the acts of fallen humanity. These are under the direction of God, to be sure. But they are carried out by sinful men; as such the acts of the Mosaic Law could never attain to the status of a true relationship with the Transcendent God of Creation.

First, the Old is short of His glory in its application. Even the sacrifice contained within this Old Covenant speaks of the sin nature abounding in humanity. The very objects of these sacrifices are of creation themselves and thus of a fallen nature. (Romans 8:22)

Second, the Old is short of His glory in its appreciation. The ceremonies of the Mosaic Law were shadows and representations of the True to be fulfilled in the Person of Messiah. Since these are only shadows and representations given in the physical aspect of time, they can never equal the reality of sinlessness and completion attained by the eternal and perfect Messiah. These ceremonies may give a glimpse and shadow but they can never give the spiritual substance of that which they suggest.

Third, the Old is short of His glory in its administration. We note that even the high priest lacked the perfection to offer atonement for the people. The high priest was a finite person. It was necessary that he be succeeded in office by others due to the death of the men who filled this office.

Also, it was necessary that the high priest offer sacrifice for his own sins before he could begin to officiate for the sins of others. This may have given him understanding of the sin in the lives of the people but it gave him no standing to officiate the abolition of their sins.

Also, it was necessary that the sacrifices offered would be repeated over and over again. Thus it was shown that the sacrificial system of the Old Covenant did not remove the sin of the people.

Fourth, only the aspirations of the Old Covenant even pointed to the glories of God. The purpose of the Old Covenant was to show the weakness of humanity in their sin and failure as juxtaposed to the Power, Glory, Righteousness and Holiness of God. In this mankind was shown his need for a True Savior Who would be outside of, and above, his own weakness.

The strength of Law was that it pointed up this need even as it pointed toward the Ultimate Savior of Messiah. Now that the Messiah had come the Mosaic Law, except as a moral guide as showing the spiritual principles therein, had become an unnecessary burden upon the people. That Mosaic Law had been replaced by the eternal Law of Grace.

This Law of Grace was superior in all points to the Mosaic Law and thoroughly superseded it.]

HEBREWS - CHAPTER NINE

9.1 *Then verily the first covenant had also ordinances of divine service, and a worldly sanctuary.*

[The British Family Bible argued that the Jewish notion of the Tabernacle, and thus the Temple which was patterned thereon, was to represent creation to the entire world. The outer court would then represent the world at large as familiar and reasonably placed. The first part of this inner sanctuary, the Holy Place, would then represent the redeemed of the ages as we come into the presence of our Savior. The imagery of the Holy and Holy of Holies, would then represent Heaven as unseen, real but unknowable and inaccessible.

It is argued by some that the above is what Paul had in mind when he mentioned "a worldly sanctuary." It is more likely that the meaning has to do with the material from which the Tabernacle had been made. A reading of the pertinent passages from the Pentateuch would show that the people gave the best of what they had in the building of the Tabernacle in the wilderness.

The gifts were considered as given to God when they were applied to the building of the place where the Old Covenant worship would be centered.

Despite being built with the greatest of care and the costliest of materials, this Tabernacle and the Temples which followed it have all fallen into ruin. The sands of time have overcome the worldly Tabernacle but the stasis of eternity sees that the Heavenly Tabernacle stands firm and perfect.

Still, it must be argued that the form and plan for both the Tabernacle and the Temples sprang forth from a Heavenly template. They were divine in their purpose and plan as given by God to His servant Moses.

The same must be said of the holy ordinances and services which took place within these structures. They served a Divine and Holy purpose among men. They pointed toward the Holiness and Majesty of God even as they displayed the sinfulness and depravity of man. The Mosaic Law taught man of his need for a Savior.

In doing this the Old Covenant gave picture and type of Messiah. The plan of the Tabernacle and those ceremonies were such as to show the need for and the person of Messiah.]

9.2 *For there was a tabernacle made, the first, wherein was the candlestick, and the table, and the shewbread, which is called the sanctuary.*

[This particular passage could be misunderstood were it not considered carefully. The next verse gives the context of the second. This speaks of the Tabernacle which was within the Tabernacle. The word "tabernacle" simply means "tent." Inside the great tent of Outer Court of the Tabernacle was a smaller tent. This was the "Tent of the Covenant."

This Tent of the Covenant was divided into two compartments. The first, or outer section, of these compartments was the Holy Place. The second, the Holy of Holies, was about one half the size of the Holy Place. Although limited to just one day of entrance per year, and that by the High Priest on the Day of Atonement, to the Holy of Holies, the outer part of this Tent of the Covenant was entered daily.

The first thing encountered in the Holy Place was the Golden Candlesticks. These were lighted at sundown and allowed to burn all night until they were extinguished at sunrise.

This Golden Candlestick had seven lamps at the end of "arms" extending from the top center of the candlestick. There were three on each side and one lamp on the middle. The familiar menorah of Hanukah is the general pattern of this Golden Candlestick. There was no provision for windows within this interior tabernacle. These lamps were a light shining in darkness.

I am tempted to state a spiritual significance at this place. Since Paul supplied no such imagery, I probably should not. Still, I cannot help but see Jesus, the Light of the World, portrayed in this situation.

Looking back at that concept of the Light of the World, it is not hard to envision entering into this portion of the Tabernacle as representative of the penitent of the Church Age of Grace coming into the presence of Jesus.

The next object encountered is the table. This is a wooden table overlaid with Gold. Once again it is apparent that this may be a reference to Jesus. Jesus was seen during His earthly ministry as a human man. That, by His eternal choice, He was. But, the reality of His essence is Deity. Jesus is God Who chose to lay aside, for a time, His Royal Robes of Deity, not His essential Deity for that is the essence of Who Jesus in reality is, in order that He might perfectly offer Himself as the Ultimate and Actual Sacrifice for the sins of fallen humanity. He has since restored that Glory to Himself.

Upon that Golden table was the show bread. There were twelve loaves, divided into two piles of six each, placed on that table each Sabbath. These loaves represented the twelve tribes of Israel. Those loaves stayed there until the following Sabbath.

It is interesting to note that six is the "number" of man. We can't go too far off into the quagmire of "Biblical Numerology," but it is interesting that this represents, in the two piles, that the Salvation offered by Jesus is available for both Israelite and Gentile.

I would caution that Paul made no argument for what purpose these elements stood. However, it is my belief that everything in the Old Testament has a picture of a spiritual reality. In point of fact, this is what Paul is arguing in reference to much of the Old Covenant in its relationship to the New Covenant.]

9.3 *And after the second veil, the tabernacle which is called the Holiest of all;*

[This second veil was the one that was "rent in twain" at the Crucifixion of Jesus. Only the high priest, and he only one day a year, was able to pass through this curtain. He went in to sprinkle the blood of sacrifice upon the Mercy Seat.

There was one veil as the priest entered into the Holy Place and another as the high priest, once a year, would go into the Holy of Holies. Paul notes that this place, the symbolic abode of God on earth, was the Holiest of all.

God is Omnipresent. That is one of those "big" theological words. All it means is that God is not limited in a spatial manner. He fills the universe. Consider Psalm 139:7-18 where the Psalmist finds there is no place where God is not able to see him. If you have a King James Bible you may wish to consider John 3:13 where Jesus declares Himself to be in Heaven even as He is speaking with Nicodemus. But the place in the Holy of Holies was considered the "special" abode of God during the Tabernacle and Temple period.

This is a passage deleted by most versions which use the Critical Text of man as a basis for their translation work.

The Holy of Holies was the place where Divine Presence of God, the Shekinah, dwelt between the cherubim on the Mercy Seat.

The parting of this veil at the time which Jesus offered up His Body for sin, gave the Truth that man no longer needs to be separated from God. Jesus has given us access through His Blood to the Mercy of God's forgiveness. There is no mediator allowed except Jesus to perform this work of grace. "For there is one God, and one mediator between God and men, the man Christ Jesus..," (I Timothy 2:5) This verse does not equate Jesus as simply a man; it notes that He purchased our salvation in His humanity on the cross.

Paul notes only that this was "called" the Holiest of all. He is allowing in his argument that this was "called" such but that the True Holiest of All was at the Heavenly Tabernacle which was not made with human hands. The entirety of the Tabernacle, both the Outer Court and the Holy Place, were merely a humanly constructed – albeit in accordance with the exact plans which God had delivered to Moses – Tabernacle which gave a human view to the Heavenly template which Jesus entered with the Blood of His Sacrifice as our Savior and Mediator.]

9.4 *Which had the golden censer, and the ark of the covenant overlaid round about with gold, wherein was the golden pot that had manna, and Aaron's rod that budded, and the tables of the covenant;*

[I add the following from *Adam Clarke's Commentary*: "It is evident that the apostle speaks here of the tabernacle built by Moses, and of the state and contents of that tabernacle as they were during the lifetime of Moses. For, as Calmet remarks, in the temple which was afterwards built there were many things added which were not in the tabernacle, and several things left out. The ark of the covenant and the two tables of the law were never found after the return from the Babylonish captivity. We have no proof that, even in the time of Solomon, the golden pot of manna, or the rod of Aaron, was either in or near the ark. In Solomon's temple the holy place was separated from the holy of holies by a solid wall, instead of a veil, and by strong wooden doors, 1Ki 6:31-33. In the same temple there was a large vestibule before the holy place; and round about this and the holy of holies there were many chambers in three stories, 1Ki 6:5, 6. But there was nothing of all this in the Mosaic tabernacle; therefore, says Calmet, we need not trouble ourselves to reconcile the various scriptures which mention this subject; some of which refer to the tabernacle, others to Solomon's temple, and others to the temple built by Zorobabel; which places were very different from each other."

From this I would infer that the people's relationship to even the Mosaic Law had wavered over time. This is the state of human religion about which Paul has been speaking. Once again, when we are speaking of the Old Covenant we are not speaking of an eternal covenant but a transitory covenant whose purpose was to show the sinfulness of man in juxtaposition to the eternal holiness and perfections of God.

This lesson would have been further heightened by the lack of care taken by the priestly caste to properly follow the heavenly instruction. Nonetheless, the central teaching remained whereby the sacrifice of the created animals was offered to God on behalf of the people.

The Church which Jesus founded has likewise not completely followed His plan. This is evidenced by the spilt into denominationalism. God intended that His churches be under Him and under Him alone. There is no real provision given in Scripture for the idea of a "Super Church" which exercises "ownership" or control over the local bodies of fellowship. These local bodies are to be autonomous under the headship of Christ.

Even among the various local churches which are true to Christ, be they denominational or baptistic, the vast majority – although differing in special doctrinal and church policy issues – these churches were begun, and continued for a time, under the seminal doctrine of Christ and the Blood Atonement as the sole means of salvation.

I would caution, from the above citation from Adam Clark, that he seems to be very weak on the subject of preservation of the Scripture. Over and over in his commentary there is a search for "alternate readings." In his writings this seems to be more a doubt of faith in the ability of God to preserve His Own words than of an attempt to truly search out the meaning of the words which have been preserved.

The "golden censer" is mentioned as being in the Holy of Holies. Moses made no such requirement that such be there. It would not have been possible for such a censer to remain behind the veil. The purpose of the censer was to carry fire to burn incense. This would have only been done once a year by the high priest on the Day of Atonement. It may have been that such censer was carried in yearly by the priest. It could have been that the censer was left inside the veil to be brought out and prepared for its intended purpose. Although this last seems unlikely unless it were left one the ground, so to speak, so the high priest could reach under the veil and retrieve it each year.

In any case, the golden censer would have entered with the priest and thus have been the first part of the furniture of the room.

The central part of the Holy of Holies was the Ark of the Covenant. It contained the original stone tablets on which Moses had received the Commandments from God on the mountain of Sinai. It was made of wood and overlaid with gold. It originally contained a "pot of manna," which would have been easily obtained during the time of Moses and the exodus. This seems to have been miraculously kept from "spoiling" as any manna kept for over one day, except for the Sabbath provision, would have quickly spoiled. (Exodus 16:11-31)

Along with these was the rod of Aaron which was the confirmation from God that Aaron was to begin the priestly line. (Numbers 17:5-10)

By the time of Solomon all that was left within the Ark was the tablets of the Law. I would not speculate what happened with the other elements. (I Kings 8:9) All I could add is that the Ark, itself, has been lost to history. The reason lies within the councils of God. My guess, and I emphasize "guess," is that the intent is to discourage making an idol of the Ark. Beyond this I cannot go.]

9.5 *And over it the cherubims of glory shadowing the mercyseat; of which we cannot now speak particularly.*

[Over the ark were two cherubim, one on each side. These were winged creatures, angelic, whose wings touched over the Mercy Seat. They faced each other with their gazes downward toward the Mercy Seat.

Note that these glorious creatures, made of pure beaten gold, looked at the Mercy Seat where the blood of the sacrifice was sprinkled on the Day of Atonement. It was from this seat that God symbolically sat in the Tabernacle to receive the offering for atonement from the high priest.

Paul declines to speak much about this. His gaze moves from the Old Covenant and its types and shadows, to embrace the reality of the New Covenant of Jesus. He was writing to Jewish men who had a deep understanding of the meaning and events concerning the Temple. Paul's purpose is to move the gaze of these men from the picture to the Real.

The glory shadowed the Mercy Seat may have been the reverential attitude of the Cherubim in their worshipful manner. It may also, more likely in my mind, have been the Shekinah Glory of God as He symbolically took His place upon the Mercy Seat in the Holy of Holies.

I would only further note that it was this same order of Cherubim which God used to guard the Garden after the sin of Adam. (Genesis 3:24)

We should probably note that the word "Cherubim" is the plural of "Cherub." The "s" at the end of the word "Cherubim" should not be considered as a mistranslation but as an adaption to better explain the original, while keeping the exact sense of the originally inspired Words, with regard to the English speaking reader.]

9.6 *Now when these things were thus ordained, the priests went always into the first tabernacle, accomplishing the service of God.*

[The concept of a thing being ordained is that it be prepared for a specifically intended purpose. That preparation may be an investiture of certain symbolical or real powers or abilities. These articles in the Tabernacle were simply wooden and metal articles. They were of the creation of God but there were in themselves, of the mundane of the everyday world until they were set aside for the sacred purpose for which they were intended to be.

So are we in this world. We are simply members of the race of humanity. We are nothing special within ourselves. In the grand scheme of things our abilities and attributes are not so much different than are countless others. We are not special. But, He who has called us to salvation is the Creator of this world. He has called us to be set apart from sinful humanity in special service to Himself.

That is the great glory of a Christian. We are simply mud. But we are the abode of the Creator and Author of the Universe. The power and abilities which lie within our poor mortal bodies, as these are energized by the Lord of our salvation, is such as can do wonders for our Lord.

I have a computer on the desk in front of me. It is a simple arrangement – O. K. Not so simple! – of wires and plastic. But, the one who constructed this machine has made it possible that the machine can do wonders unheard of by anyone just a few hundred years ago. Whether this machine is used for good or evil is not within the power of the machine to decide. It simply reacts to the touch of fingers, mine or someone else's fingers, and it responds as directed.

God has given us the great ability to exercise our "free will." Unlike this computer we can decide where we wish our ability to carry us. May we yield ourselves to the Master. May we allow His eternal purposes to flow through our lives. Without Him we are just here. With Him we can be tools used by the Master of the Universe to shape an eternity of bliss in the lives of others as we repeat the old, but ever new, refrain that Jesus Christ died in time so that others could live in eternity.

Each day, habitually, the priests were busy in the worship of God on behalf of the people. They did much in the outer courtyard; they also ministered within the Holy Place, the first "room" of the Holy Tabernacle in the midst of the Tabernacle. The public was not allowed into this place even as the general priests were not allowed into the second room, The Holy of Holies.

These prohibitions served to keep the "mystery of holiness" beyond the reach of the people. How different, and better, is the New Covenant wherein we are called to the Throne by the High Priest of our profession. The sin which had kept the people of the Old Covenant from the fellowship with God has been washed clean in the Blood of the Lamb.]

9.7 *But into the second went the high priest alone once every year, not without blood, which he offered for himself, and for the errors of the people:*

[Going into the second room of this Tabernacle within the Tabernacle was restricted to the high priest. He was only allowed to make the trip one day a year. It is more than likely that there were several trips into the Holy of Holies during that one day which was the Day of Atonement. This was on the 7th day of Tisri. Interestingly enough, Tisri was the 7th month of the ecclesiastical calendar but the first month of the civil calendar.

The Jewish tradition was that the high priest would enter four times into the Holy of Holies on the Day of Atonement. First, he would enter to burn incense. (Leviticus 16:12) Second, he would enter to sprinkle the blood of a bullock upon the Mercy Seat as an offering for his and his family's sins. (Leviticus 16:14)

It is interesting to note that there was no other priestly work done on the Day of Atonement except that done by the high priest. (Leviticus 16:17) Jesus is The Only Savior of mankind. There is no need for any other work to be accomplished than that which He has already done!

Then the goat would be sacrificed (The 16th chapter of Leviticus gives explanation here) after which the high priest would re-enter the Holy of Holies for the third time in order to sprinkle the blood of the goat upon the Mercy Seat. (Leviticus 16:15) The fourth and final entrance into the Holy of Holies would be to retrieve the golden censer. This was the tradition of the Jews as to the four entrances on the one Day of Atonement by the high priest into the Holy of Holies.

There was another goat considered on this day. This was the "scapegoat" which symbolically removed the sins of the people from the camp of Israel. (Leviticus 16:8-26) We might consider this goat in conjunction with the willful sins of the people. The sacrificial system was for "accidental sins." These were true sins. There is no question as to this fact. But, these were not premeditated sins. They may have even been committed unknowingly but were nonetheless real.

There were also premeditated, willful, sins. This would be sins which were committed because one had a disregard for the Law, and more importantly the Person, of God. Numbers 15:30-31 speaks of this type of sin. "But the soul that doeth ought presumptuously, whether he be born in the land, or a stranger, the same reproacheth the LORD; and that soul shall be cut off from among his people. Because he hath despised the word of the LORD, and hath broken his commandment, that soul shall utterly be cut off; his iniquity shall be upon him."

These are sins which argue against the rightful rule of God. An easily seen illustration of this concept is the recent ruling by the Supreme Court regarding same sex marriage. Corollary with this is the argument by one of the leading contenders for the nomination for president who argued that we must be willing to change our belief system to accommodate this civil ruling. This is an argument which says that the eternal Law of God is subservient to the temporal law of human governments. "It is a fearful thing to fall into the hands of the living God." (Hebrews 10:31)

To be "cut off" could speak, and often does, of capital punishment being administered. There is another meaning whereby the person was dismissed from the company of the camp of Israel. He was no longer allowed to journey with the group so that his sin would not be a contagion among the rest of the people. This meaning seems more in line with the concept of the "scapegoat." The scapegoat could no longer remove the sins of the people than could the sacrifices of the animals of creation. (Hebrews 10:4)

The picture of the scapegoat is more closely attuned to the concept of ecclesiastical separation. "Wherefore come out from among them, and be ye separate, saith the Lord, and touch not the unclean thing; and I will receive you" (II Corinthians 6:17)

I realize that the illustration seems to have broken down in that the scapegoat is removed from the camp in Leviticus 16 while the Christian is to remove from sin; but the spiritual principle remains that light and darkness cannot comingle. When we consider that the camp of Israel contained the people of the Covenant of God while the scapegoat was the personification of sin, we see the same truth. Sin ought not to be given place in the midst of the people of God.]

9.8   *The Holy Ghost this signifying, that the way into the holiest of all was not yet made manifest, while as the first tabernacle was yet standing:*

[One thing stands out in this verse. Although the New Covenant is superior to the shadow and types of the Old Covenant, we must still consider that the Old Covenant has the imprimatur of the Holy Spirit upon this system. The Holy Spirit authorized the teaching of the Old Covenant as a manner of imparting divine truth to the people of God.

The primary teaching was that this Old Covenant system could not give a way for the people to aspire to the Heavenly standards of God. Even the high priest of this system was only allowed one day a year in which he could enter the symbolic presence of God in the Holy of Holies. It was necessary for even this high priest to offer sacrifice for his own sins before he could attempt to mediate for the people.

As long as this tabernacle system remained that lack would remain. This was a "built in" feature which the Holy Spirit intended to prepare the way for Jesus to institute the New Covenant of His Blood.

The Old Covenant was Divinely appointed but was not Divinely anointed with the

Blood of The Perfect Sacrifice of the Lord of Glory. Men had no way of approaching God through the carnal sacrifices of created animals, presided over by carnal men, and offered fully of the earthly which was itself cursed by the sin of Adam. (Romans 8:22)

Further, the Old Covenant was open only to the sons of Abraham or to proselytes to that religious system. This was not the fulfillment of the promise of God to Abraham that through him all the world would be blessed. (Genesis 22:18)

Rather than blessing all nations through Abraham, the Old Covenant of the Mosaic Law separated people into classes. There were the sons of Abraham and there were the Gentile nations seen in Moses. Further, even the sons of Abraham were divided under the Old Covenant. These Israelites were divided into the people, the priestly caste, the priests and the high priest. Each was given duties and responsibilities under the Law. There was no aspiration to go beyond the place into which they were born.

Such is not the situation under the New Covenant. We are all, those who accept Jesus as Savior, brothers and sisters in the same family of faith. True, we are to be separate from sinners. This is a spiritual principle as old as Cain and Abel. This is simply the difference between the people of God and the people who are not of God. The separation is only among saint and sinner.

The "laity" is not above the "clergy" for we are all priests unto God with Our Great High Priest Jesus as our Eternal Mediator. (I Peter 2:9) It is true that God has given to each Christian a responsibility within the body of believers. (I Corinthians 12:4-31) This does not place one above another in any sense. We are to complement each other that we may be an effective witness for Jesus and unto the world of humanity which stands in need.]

9.9 *Which was a figure for the time then present, in which were offered both gifts and sacrifices, that could not make him that did the service perfect, as pertaining to the conscience;*

[Albert Barnes says this of the Old Covenant sacrifice and ceremony: "They could not expiate guilt; they could not make the soul pure; they could not of themselves impart peace to the soul by reconciling it to God. They could not fully accomplish what the conscience needed to have done in order to give it peace. Nothing will do this but the blood of the Redeemer."

I remember one time when my daughter was very young she used the little net we had for cleaning out a fish tank to take one of her favorite fish out for a walk. "He was really happy when we started. He was just jumping up and down. But, he's tired now so he's sleeping."

Burial at sea. Flush.

I used to watch "old people" as they struggled to climb a flight of stairs. I now is an "old people." Those stairs are really hard to climb!

Since all we have ever experienced is that of time and physicality we tend to think that this is all there is. Well, for us it may be. But, that will not always be the case. Time and physicality are both a subset under the true reality of the eternal and spiritual. We tend to not realize this since we've never experienced anything except that which we can see, feel and experience in the created world.

The people of the time of the Mosaic Law probably could not understand that all of these rites and ceremonies could never take away or alleviate their sin. These could never give them the "standing" to experience the removal of sin.

These things of the Mosaic Law were simply object lessons to explain the realities of the eternal and spiritual. They were used, by God as they were ordained of God, to supply a sense of true spirituality.

Gifts were offered as thanks to God for His many temporal blessings. Sacrifices, the very life blood, of certain of the animals of creation, were given to show the horror of sin and its consequence. But, nothing which the people did, or which the priests did for them, could offer any expiration of their sins. The people continued to sin and feel the convicting pang of this short coming upon their souls. All of these things were only lessons in the classroom of the Spirit to lead to the yearning for the coming of Messiah Who would remove those sins by His Own Sacrifice of Himself upon the Cross of Calvary.

Take time to read the Pentateuch. Not all of the animals were to be used for sacrifice. Only certain, prescribed, animals could be offered as Sacrifice to The Holy God. Many men have died down through the ages. Some have been martyrs to a cause they saw as greater than themselves. Some died as sacrifices so that others could live. Only One Man, Jesus, was ever offered up as a Sacrifice for the sins of humanity. Only Jesus died in time so that others could live in eternity. Only the Sacrifice of the Perfect Son of God has ever been accepted as the Full and Complete Sacrifice for the remission of sins. Only a full acceptance of Him and His Sacrifice can remove the guilt and stain of sin.

The time of the teaching of the Tabernacle and Temple has passed. We now stand in the reality of the eternal Spirit. Our present need is to accept the Words of God and put our faith in the Son of God for our salvation. Nothing else is asked of man by the leading of God. Nothing else is accepted by God from the need of mankind.]

9.10 *Which stood only in meats and drinks, and divers washings, and carnal ordinances, imposed on them until the time of reformation.*

[Both the picture and the lessons are from those Old Testament types and shadows which pointed the way to Jesus. Those ceremonial washings were often repeated as they did not cleanse fully from sin. It is the blood (sacrifice) of Jesus which cleanses us from all sin. Water baptism is an ordinance which is reserved for those who have already experienced salvation.

The washing of the Old Covenant only cleansed a sinful body. This, once again, was symbolic of the inner cleansing which Jesus offers through His Sacrifice. The sacrifices of creatures of the creation could not offer an inner cleansing for they were part of fallen nature.

This was true of all of the rites and ordinances of the Old Covenant. That which is of the earth can never cleanse that which must experience a cleansing from the eternal and spiritual realms. Only the Sacrifice of Jesus can give this experience for only Jesus is from those eternal and spiritual realms. Only Jesus is God in the body of humanity.

Even the phrase, "meats and drinks," shouts of the carnality of time. This refers to the dietary laws of the Mosaic Law. There were many. In these we once again see the separation of the clean from the unclean. We see what is allowed and what is disallowed.

We need to use more care when we confront the world. We often use a "short hand" of "works" and "non works" when we confront the culture of the world. "A Christian does this," and "A Christian doesn't do that," in our message gives the appearance that we can work for salvation by taking on the trappings of a Christian lifestyle. Ain't so!

Works flow *from* the life of one already born again. There are no good works which can ever save us from our sins. (Ephesians 2:8-10)

The works of the Mosaic Law were an imposition of learning upon the nation of Israel. These rites and ordinances were only in effect so long as the lessons were being taught about the coming of Messiah. At that point there was a "reformation" of the Covenant of God among the people of this planet.

One of the meanings of "reformation" is "restoration." I see this as the proper meaning in this instance. There was given to man a restoration of the Divine intents of the original creation. God created humanity with the purpose of fellowship between Himself and His created beings. The Love of God requires an object for the display of that Love. "For God so loved the world, that he gave his only begotten Son, that whosoever believeth in him should not perish, but have everlasting life." (John 3:16)]

9.11 *But Christ being come an high priest of good things to come, by a greater and more perfect tabernacle, not made with hands, that is to say, not of this building;*

[Our redemption came through the death of the man, Christ Jesus. Our salvation is proven by the risen Lord. Through His resurrection Jesus defeated the power of death. He overcame death as He offered life, eternal life, to all who would believe.

Jesus is now our High Priest. He has performed His Heavenly duties in the manner of the earthly high priest but in The Supreme Demonstration of the Love of God. He did not carry the blood of a bullock into the Heavenly Sanctuary for He had no sin which needed expiration. The Sacrifice of His Own Blood was completely for us.

There are three competing arguments to explain the phrase "perfect tabernacle." The first of these is that the reference is only to the Church He founded. This may be pleasing to our sensibilities as members of His Church in this Church age but I do not find this a satisfying allusion. He is Head of the Body of the Church. The Church is given Heavenly and eternal promises. But, the church is peopled with imperfect humanity and, for time at least, resides here on earth.

The second argument refers to the Body of Christ, Himself. The argument is that He presented His Body, thereby His Blood, in Heaven as The atonement for sin. I can't argue with that but it still seems short of the mark.

I would rather accept the third argument because it gives a certain reality to the Truth of the earthly Tabernacle, and Temple, as patterned after a Perfect Heavenly Template. This argument is that Jesus did present His Perfect and Sinless Body into Heaven as He sprinkled the Blood of His Sacrifice upon the Heavenly Mercy Seat. In this He fulfilled all the types and shadows of the Old Covenant in the institution of the New Testament of His Blood.

When the verse argues that Jesus holds the promise of "good things to come" we see that He is not Temporal as were the high priests of the Tabernacle. He does more than offer a corrective remedy for sins past but also for all of our life here on earth as the Spirit comes to live within us and lead us into Truth. The Old Covenant had offered carnal things which pointed toward Messiah; Messiah offers the performance which the Old Covenant had only suggested.

These are not things, neither is the Heavenly Temple of course, which could ever be made with the created hands of mankind. God, Himself, prepared salvation for a fallen race even before the race of man had been created. (Revelation 13:8b)]

9.12 *Neither by the blood of goats and calves, but by his own blood he entered in once into the holy place, having obtained eternal redemption for us.*

[This speaks of a one time salvation, a one time sacrifice, and the full superiority of the Blood of Jesus in the salvation of souls for eternity. The priests of the Levitical line had to offer sacrifice daily for many things and yearly on the Day of Atonement. These offered the blood of animals of the creation.

Jesus only needed to offer up Himself One time. The human blood of the Creator of humanity is so powerful that it needs never to be repeated as the Sacrifice for the sins of the race of man. Rather than offering the blood of a temporal and ineffectual sacrifice attended by the race of man, Jesus – as a True Representative of humanity – offered up the Pure and Sinless Blood of His human body. It was for this cause that He came into the world as a human man through His voluntary Kenosis.

Jesus acted in His Own Sacrifice of Himself, and acts as our High Priest in Heaven, in a sacerdotal manner for us. His actions and ministry cover even more than our salvation from sin. He made an offering of His Own Blood in the Heavenly Sanctuary. (Hebrews 9:14) He put away sin from our account by the action of His Own Sacrifice on our behalf. (Hebrews 9:26) With His Own Blood He purged our sin. (Hebrews 1:3) He sanctified, or set us apart for His service, with His Own Blood in our salvation. (Hebrews 8:12) He appears before God on our behalf. (Hebrews 9:24) And, He daily makes intercession for us. (Romans 8:34)

The Jamieson-Fausset-Brown Commentary argues that Jesus is represented in His death by the slain goat of the sixteenth chapter of Leviticus. That commentary further argues that the living goat is representative of His resurrection. About the first part of that argument, I would not argue as the goat slain in Leviticus 16:15 was slain as sacrifice for the sins of the people. However, I find no way in which the living goat, the scapegoat, could be considered as representative of the Resurrection of Christ. That goat left the camp and was not seen again. Jesus is our Constant Companion. He has not left the Camp of the Redeemed as He is the Head of the Church.

Rather than symbolizing Jesus, I see this second goat as representing our sin. That goat is gone to never be seen again. Psalm 103:12 reminds us, "As far as the east is from the west, so far hath he removed our transgressions from us." I John 1:17b reminds us, "the blood of Jesus Christ his Son cleanseth us from all sin."]

9.13 *For if the blood of bulls and of goats, and the ashes of an heifer sprinkling the unclean, sanctifieth to the purifying of the flesh.*

[An attempt is made to use the sprinkling of the blood of the animal sacrifices of the Old Testament to teach sprinkling as a proper mode of Baptism. Two things must be noted of such an argument. First, what is the location on which the blood was sprinkled? Are we also to argue that the head of an initiate is holy before God?

Second, the passage is not teaching any form of baptism but, in the extended passage, is teaching that the Sacrifice of Jesus was superior to the sacrifice of these Old Testament animals.

There were two thoughts at work in this verse. The first, the blood of bulls and goats, had to do with the sacrifices attendant to the Day of Atonement. This had been touched upon in verse twelve. This had to do with the sins of the people. Here the focus is on the cleansing of the ritually unclean as pertaining to the human body.

The passage which Paul addresses as to the cleansing of the ritually unclean was from Numbers 19:1-22. Those who were ceremonially unclean were not allowed to take part in the Tabernacle ceremonies.

In order to clean the ceremonially unclean a red heifer (cow) was sacrificed outside the confines of the Tabernacle. We would only make note here that Jesus was sacrificed outside the walls of the city of Jerusalem.

This red heifer was killed and burned completely. It was to be reduced to ashes by the one burning it. A man was then brought in to collect the ashes of the red heifer. These ashes were mixed with water and sprinkled upon the ceremonially unclean as a means of cleansing them so they would be free to enter into the Tabernacle worship.

As to those offering up this red heifer, the high priest who watched the affair, the one who burnt the red heifer, and the one who collected the ashes, were all considered ceremonially unclean. They were to wash themselves and their clothing. These remained unclean until the evening.

Paul asks that we consider that this purification had only to do with the human body. There was no provision made for conscience of the "inner man" in this ceremony. The blood of Jesus cleanses the entire man as His Blood is superior to anything that could be offered by an animal of the creation. Only the Blood of He who is the Creator could cleanse the soul and offer forgiveness from sin.

The dead works of man can never be effective as an offering to the Living God. God used these dead works of man to point toward the Living Work of the Son of God. In that way the works of the Old Covenant were effective in bringing men to the salvation offered by God. These works did not bring salvation in and of themselves.

It was the work of Jesus on the cross which was the basis of the salvation of man even in these Old Covenant times. Faith was exercised in the revealed Words of God by the Old Covenant sacrifice. This was counted as righteousness until such time as the True Propitiatory Sacrifice at Calvary was offered by Messiah.]

9.14 *How much more shall the blood of Christ, who through the eternal Spirit offered himself without spot to God, purge your conscience from dead works to serve the living God?*

[Several of the commentators applied the phrase "eternal Spirit" to The Holy Spirit. I cannot fault them in this. The Trinity always works in concert, One with Another. But, the context of Paul's argument speaks of Christ and His All-Sufficiency. Jesus offered up Himself as THE Sacrifice for our sins.

Unlike the unknowing animals of creation which were sacrificed upon the altar of the Tabernacle, Jesus went to Sacrifice Himself purposely. (Luke 9:51) He knew where He was going. He was going to the death of His humanity in the most painful and humiliating manner available. He knew why He was going. He was going because of

His Great Love for His created beings – for you and me! He knew when He was going. He went anyway. (Matthew 26:31)

The blood of the unknowing beasts of the field was able to cleanse the ceremonially unclean – in their bodies. The Blood of the Creator of those beasts of the field was shed to cleanse our souls.

The red heifer was able to ceremonially cleanse the ceremonially unclean so that they could enter into the symbolic presence of God in the Tabernacle worship. The Blood of Jesus Christ cleanses us from sin so that we can enter into the presence of God in prayer and in our persons as we pass from this life to the next.

In this we are able to not just "serve" God. We are called to be co-laborers with Him in His wonderful work of the salvation of souls. Our part is to witness to the truth that Jesus Christ died in time so that others could live in eternity.]

9.15 *And for this cause he is the mediator of the new testament, that by means of death, for the redemption of the transgression that were under the first testament, they which are called might receive the promise of eternal inheritance.*

[Whether regarding the sacrifices attendant to the Day of Atonement or the sacrifices which allowed for the ritual purifying of the body, the Blood of the Sacrifice of Jesus was superior to any of the sacrifices of the Old Covenant. The effectiveness of these sacrifices of the animals of creation under the Old Covenant were never sufficient to cleanse the inner man of his innate, or specific for that matter, sin. They provided a means by which man might exercise faith in the as yet unseen Sacrifice of Messiah.

The people of the Age of the Mosaic Law could not understand the fact of the suffering Messiah as a means of true and ultimate salvation. They were able to understand the commandments of God under their dispensation. Their faithful exercise of the leading of the Words of instruction which were given to them gave a means to exercise faith in God. From our standpoint of the Church Age we see this as an extremely limited faith – not in the scope of the exercise of that faith but in the scope of a full understanding of the workings of God.

The salient point, as it is throughout the ages of creation, is that exercise of faith in the goodness and power of God. Salvation is always, has always been, tied to the faith which trusts the Words and Wisdom of Creator God and eschews the false leading of created beings. "Wherefore God also gave them up to uncleanness through the lusts of their own hearts, to dishonor their own bodies between themselves: Who changed the truth of God into a lie, and worshipped and served the creature more than the Creator, who is blessed for ever. Amen." (Romans 1:24-25) It seems a matter of to whom, or to Whom, respect, trust and fidelity is given. This is the mark of one who is led by The Spirit rather than led by his own spirit of carnality.

Spiritual salvation has always been ultimately based on the Cross of Christ. (Revelation 13:8) In this the effect is ultimately to return the creation to the state of His original intent. Make no mistake, God is ultimately and eternally in control of His creation. The seeming triumph of sin in the short term of time is not due to a lack of control of God. This is part of His teaching as He allows all creation to view the disarray of sin in counterpoint to the sublime perfections of the Holiness of God.

The mediating office of Jesus is that which, based on His Blood Sacrifice of Himself in His humanity is to reconcile those who accept Him into full fellowship with

God – as man was created to enjoy. The Old Covenant could not properly atone for the sins of carnal humanity. Those sacrifices were from the same nature of creature as was sinful mankind. It would take the death of One from the Eternal Realms where sin is unknown, but performed within the realm of time and physicality – the realm which was sullied by sin – to defeat the devices of sin in the very realm of their seeming superiority. Even the place of the seeming superiority of sin was subject to the Power and Glory of the God of Eternity.

God, in the Person of Jesus the Christ, took upon Himself a human body, untainted by the sin of Adam via the Virgin Birth, in order to offer the Perfect Holiness of Himself as a representative Sacrifice of humanity in order to do what we could never do. He has cleansed the sins of those who accept this Sacrifice as redemption for their souls.

The word "testament" in this verse is identical to covenant. But, this word "testament" carries with it the meaning that one must die for the testament to come into effect. Salvation is dependent upon the offering of a sacrifice. The Perfect Sacrifice which has eternal spiritual power is that Self Sacrifice of Jesus at Calvary. Therein, and only therein, is the possibility of true salvation from sin. (Acts 4:12) A covenant is a promise made; it is an agreement between two parties. A testament is a promise accomplished and given; it is an agreement bestowed upon another by the act of the party who has made the testament.

Some have complained that the word "covenant" should have been used in this place rather than "testament." Their reasoning seems partly to be that there is a Mediatorial Office to be considered under a covenant. The high priest being mediator. These have overlooked the office of executor of an estate. This is a mediatorial office in that it relates to the integrity of the disposal of the articles of the estate. Jesus is the Executor of His Own Estate. Jesus did not die and leave His purposes to another to fulfill. Jesus lives to act as the Executor, or Mediator, of the Estate of His proffered eternal salvation and all of the considerations therein.]

9.16 *For where a testament is, there must also of necessity be the death of the testator.*

[My parents both went to a lawyer some years before their death in order to make a "last will and testament." My mother died first; there was no need to execute a will on her behalf as everything transferred to my father. When my father died it was different. All of the children were of adult age. The "family" of my father and mother expired with their deaths. We children had established other homes and families.

I was established as "executor" of my father's estate. I had no real part in the disposition of the articles of my father's will except to follow his wishes as outlined in that will. This I did to the best of my abilities.

While my father lived I had no authority over his belongings. Even after he died I had no authority over his belongings. The executor of the estate has no authority except to follow the words and intents of the will.

A will is a legal covenant which has no purpose or effect until such time as the author of that will has passed from this life. At that time the will becomes the "final wishes" of the deceased. As such it is the "last word" as to disposition of the possessions of the deceased.

Barnes, Clarke, and a few argued that the word "covenant" should have been used in this verse rather than "testament." The word covenant would not have carried the same connotation to the ears of the English speaker as does the word testament. Thus, to have used "covenant" in this place would have amounted to a mistranslation as to the meaning and intent of the words of Paul at this place.

Both words mean essentially the same thing. To the Jewish ear the word covenant, as considered in the Mosaic Law as administered by the Levitical Priesthood, will carry the necessity of the death of the sacrifice. Testament, in relation to the understanding of the English speaker must contain the necessity of the death of the testator. To argue for the word "covenant" in place of "testament" in this instance would give the impression that the carnal high priest of the Levitical order was the "testator" since it is tied to the operation of the "covenant." It could not be properly argued that it would speak of the animal of creation being sacrificed in the case of the argument of Paul.

Jesus is the Ultimate and Perfect Sacrifice for sin. As our High Priest He offered Himself as sacrifice for our sins satisfying the letter of the Mosaic Law of the Old Covenant. As the Ultimate Testator of the New Covenant of His Blood, He died as that Perfect Sacrifice for sin. His death sealed the provisions of our Salvation. (I Peter 3:18)]

9.17 *For a testament is of force after men are dead: otherwise it is of no strength at all while the testator liveth.*

[Until the man who made the will is dead that will is only a "probable course of action." The living man may change the provisions of his will at any time he may choose. My father did this during his final illness. He changed the provision that I was to administer his finances in the event of any incapacity on his part. One of my sisters was put into this position. It was much easier for her as she had some working knowledge of his financial situation beforehand.

But, upon his death the full provisions of my father's will came into force.

It should be added that I had to formally accept the position of executor of my father's will before I could assume this office. The death of Jesus on the Cross has purchased salvation for all who would accept this Sacrifice as on their behalf. (John 1:12) The salvation offered by Jesus does not come by birth into a specific human family or the acceptance of certain ethical consideration. The salvation offered by Jesus comes only by acceptance of Him as Savior. (Acts 4:12) There must be a time of decision.]

9.18 *Whereupon neither the first testament was dedicated without blood.*

[I would believe that this first testament refers to the beginning of the Mosaic Covenant of the Law. (Exodus 24:1-8) My reasoning is that this was the former Covenant with the people of the Israelite Nation. Before this we could look to the Covenant with Abraham (Genesis 15:9-17) wherein the Covenant of God with Abraham and Abraham's posterity was formalized.

I look to the Exodus covenant because it was formalized with sacrifice. The sacrifices and ceremonies of this covenant were all symbolic of the coming Messiah. Since Paul has been speaking of an "apples to apples" comparison, this seems right in the context of the verse.

The sacrifices of the animals of the Mosaic Covenant were sacrifices of unknowing animals of the creation of God. These, taken from the same sin sullied creation as were the people could never offer a complete sacrifice with a view to the eternal and spiritual environs of the Heavenlies. But, they did give a physical view to the people of their day that there was a coming Sacrifice of He Who was of the Heavenlies. I do not believe that these people looked at this possibility. But, they did look to the known Will of God from the known Words of God. In this they exercised faith which was counted as righteousness until such time as Jesus would come into time and become the True and Effectual Sacrifice for Sin.

The symbols of that first covenant point toward the realities of the New Testament of His Blood. The Old Covenant was a true covenant relationship between God and His people. The New Testament of His Blood is a true Testament, or Will, as it bestows blessings from Him Alone to those who accept those gifts. It is not a "covenant" in that there is no "agreement between parities" in place. Rather, there is a gift based on the death of the Testator which is freely given to the recipient by the Divine Will and Largess of Messiah upon each persons acceptance of that reality for themselves. (Romans 6:23)]

9.19 *For when Moses had spoken every precept to all the people according to the law, he took the blood of calves and of goats, with water, and scarlet wool, and hyssop, and sprinkled both the book, and all the people,*

[Once again we are speaking of an Old Testament dispensation where the blood itself was sprinkled on both the book and the people. We might also quickly note that the writer of Hebrews has already spoken of the ineffectiveness of the Old Testament ceremonies.

Here we see that Moses did as specified by the Law. We need more of this today. We need less individualism in the pulpit and more humility which simply follows God. I spoke by DVD at a Bible Conference this past summer. One reviewer said that this allowed my personality to show through. This was meant as a compliment. No one needs my personality in any pulpit; we have a desperate need to see the Name of Jesus exalted from the pulpit!

We must note that the Scripture Paul is accessing in this place (Exodus 24:1-8) makes no mention of the Book being sprinkled with the blood. Neither are calves, goats, water, scarlet wool, hyssop, and the tabernacle and vessels of ministry mentioned by Moses. The notation as to the tabernacle and vessels of ministry are separated here until Hebrews 9:21. They had not been yet fashioned so their cleansing by blood was also separated from this time. But, the question must still be asked, why are these other things mentioned here?

The Words of Moses in Exodus were inspired of God. So, too, are the Words of Paul writing in the Book of Hebrews inspired. But, there are more words in Hebrews than there are in Exodus. We can easily look here and realize that the Holy Spirit has added more information to the New Testament than was available to the readers of the Old Testament. Still, we must ask, from where did these extra words come?

The general conjecture is that these added words come from rabbinical tradition. I am not one to lay too much emphasis on the traditions of man. Neither am I one to lay too little emphasis on the inspired and preserved Words of God!

We all know that 2 + 2 = 4. This is not something we have derived from the Biblical records. It is still true. Consider our question above in this light. All Truth resides in the inspired and preserved Scripture. But, not all outside of Scripture is not true. This may not be spiritual truth but it might well be historically accurate.

The book of Enoch is not Scripture. But, the inspiration of the Holy Spirit has taken one passage from this book and incorporated it into the Book of Jude. (Jude 14) This does not validate the entire book of Enoch. Inspiration merely records that one short passage from the book of Enoch is historically accurate.

We follow the same reasoning with regards to this passage. Not all of the rabbinic traditions are true. The Spirit has explained that some parts of these traditions are historically accurate and has enshrined them in the inspired and preserved Words of God.

Beyond being inspired, the Words of Scripture are always historically accurate. We may disagree with some of those words. This simply means that we are wrong!

The sprinkling of the Book of the Law points out an important spiritual principle: The Law could never be fulfilled without the Blood of the Lamb of God being shed! Neither could the people be freed from their sins without the spilling of this Precious Blood!

It is possible that Moses sent the "young men" of Exodus 24:5 to assist in the sprinkling of the blood and water mixture upon the entire congregation. It may also be that Moses sprinkled only the leaders of the group, who would have been closest to him, as representatives of the entire congregation.]

9.20 *Saying, This is the blood of the testament which God hath enjoined unto you.*

[Note well the connection between this action by Moses at the institution of the former Covenant and the Words of Jesus at the institution of the ceremony of the communion table for His Church. "For this is my blood of the new testament, which is shed for many for the remission of sins." (Matthew 26:28) Even the initiating ceremony of the Old Covenant was a prophecy of the New Testament of His Blood.

We must note that this is much more than the simple covenant as entered into throughout the society of man. This was not a contract between equals. It carried the full weight of the Author of the Universe. This "covenant" was a Law to follow. It could not be simply disregarded on whim.

Let us fully understand that the New Covenant of Grace is not to be taken lightly, either. We are honor bound, as subjects of the King of Creation, to follow and obey His Spiritual dictates. The Old Covenant with its Law and Ceremony are not for us to follow. We have seen them already completed in Christ. It is, however, for us to live by those Divine Principles which are displayed therein.

To do less is to dishonor our Savior. May we not be guilty of showing disrespect toward our Sovereign God. (Proverbs 13:24; I Corinthians 11:30; Ephesians 4:30; I Corinthians 11:30)

The custom is not in favor as much as it once was, but in times past the most solemn contracts were signed in the blood of the man who made such contract. Let us never forget that Jesus signed His Love to us with His Own Blood!]

HEBREWS: Chapter 9

9.21 *Moreover he sprinkled with blood both the tabernacle, and all the vessels of the ministry.*

[If this verse is to be used to teach sprinkling as a proper mode of baptism we must be prepared to mop the floors when we are finished! To slavishly follow the intent of this passage when "baptizing" by sprinkling we must bring out all of the "religious" items which adorn the area of such "baptism." We must also be prepared to sprinkle the altar Bible. We might also quickly note that the writer of Hebrews has already spoken of the ineffectiveness of the Old Testament ceremonies.

This action is some time later than the events of verse 19. Still, the process of cleansing these articles to set them apart for the worship of Israel is repeated at this time. The spiritual application is that everything needs to be under the Blood of Christ.

Even the best we have to offer is polluted. This is one of the reasons that we cannot attempt to "work" our way into Heaven. We must pass our self-control under the cleansing Blood of the Savior. We have no work worthy of Heaven. It is only after we have received the gift of Salvation that we can begin to complete any work in the service of God. (Ephesians 2:10)

We must also note that it was not just any blood which was sprinkled. It was only the blood of sacrifice which could cleanse and make ready for worship. Again, not just any "blood" can serve to save our soul. Only the Blood of the Sacrifice of Jesus is effective – and This is Eternally Effective!

That the blood of sacrifice was used to cleanse even the utensils of worship in the Tabernacle is indicative of the fact of man's unworthiness. That which we might call "holy" is polluted by the tint of sin. Even our worship is faulty until it is brought under the Blood of The Lamb.

Not only did the "things" need to be cleansed. So, too, did the persons and even clothing of the priests needed to be ritually cleansed. These priests needed to offer sacrifice for their own sins before they ministered for the people.

Preacher! Keep that in mind. Our often familiarity with the Scripture sometimes dulls our own spirits and senses. Keep your eye on the Savior and realize the extreme need to minister only in His power and to His Glory. We have no glory except that which we share with others of the sublime Gospel Message that Jesus Christ died in time so that others could live in eternity! And, the thought of that Glory should humble us to our station. We are servants of the Lord of Glory. Let us always simply be tools in the nail scared Hands!]

9.22 *And almost all things are by the law purged with blood, and without shedding of blood is no remission.*

[Paul hedges at bit here. "Almost all things are ... purged with blood." This had to do with ceremonial cleansing. There were exceptions. Some of the vessels were purified by water or fire. (Numbers 31:22-24) Also, as discussed earlier, the ashes of the red heifer were used to cleanse the ceremonially unclean. (Numbers 19:2-10) All things would have been first consecrated by blood offerings of sacrifice.

Then general rule of the remission of sins required the blood of sacrifice. The people understood their lives to be forfeit unto God because of their sin. Sin the life of an entity, human and animal, was in the blood of the organism, the sacrifice was symbolically gives a life to God as a covering for the sin in the person's life. (Genesis 9:4)

It was a near universal requirement that there be a blood sacrifice to atone for the sin of a person. (Leviticus 17:11) Surprisingly, to many of us, there was an exception to this rule. Leviticus 5:11 allows, "But if he be not able to bring two turtledoves, or two young pigeons, then he that sinned shall bring for his offering the tenth part of an ephah of fine flour for a sin offering; he shall put no oil upon it, neither shall he put any frankincense thereon: for it is a sin offering."

The turtledove and pigeon were the least expensive sacrificial animals available. But, in the case of extreme poverty it might be that even these were out of the reach of a person. God is never willing that any should have to perish. (II Peter 3:9) As with Cornelius in the tenth chapter of Acts, God acts out of His great mercy and love to reach out to the sinner in need. God therefor allowed the meal offerings for the seriously poor.

A popular saying is, "God must love the poor; He made so many of them." The truth is that God loves the poor because it is more often the poor who will cast aside all pretense of self-sufficiency and call upon the Lord in faith.

This concept cannot be carried over into a New Testament setting. It is only the Blood of the Sacrifice of Jesus upon the Cross of Calvary which can save a man from his sin. No person has to supply that which he cannot afford as an offering to God. Jesus has already supplied, with His Own Body, the True Sacrifice for sin. In every single area of salvation we find that Jesus supplies and we simply accept that which He has already offered. (Philippians 4:19)

An interesting consideration is in order concerning the person who might wish to offer the flour of works, religion, piety, altruism, etc. rather than pleading the Blood of Jesus. Consider Cain and Abel. Cain used the best of his crops to offer to God. Cain was a "tiller of the ground." This was the best of his labor which he offered. Abel offered a lamb from among his flocks. God accepted the sacrifice of Abel and rejected that of Cain.

As far back as the third chapter of Genesis we see the concept of animal sacrifice being introduced. The sin offering has always been the blood of the innocent for the sin of the guilty. This is a picture of the Sacrifice of Jesus for our sin. Although the flour offering was allowed by the mercy of God, this was not the picture of the coming Messiah, except as we consider that Jesus is "the bread of life." We do use the symbolism of the wine as type of His blood and the wafer as a type of His body in the remembrance of the Lord's Table.

Let's for a moment consider that someone might have conspired to "game the system." They might reason, "I don't have so much money that I can waste the price of even a turtledove. I'm just going to take some flour to the priest and tell them that I am too poor to pay for some bird just for it to be sacrificed." The man wears some old clothes on this visit. The priests are fooled and the man figures he's got the "discount rate" for his sin.

This type of subterfuge is covered in the fifth chapter of Acts. Ananias and Saphira conspire to look real good at church while keeping the best for themselves. As you read the story you might do well to consider that there was no requirement for these two to sell their land and bring an offering to the church treasury. It seems to me that they wanted to look "super spiritual" and keep the money for "a rainy day."

The sin was in not being truthful before God. (Acts 5:4) They lied to God in reference to this "gift." Both Ananias and his wife, Saphira, were struck dead because

HEBREWS: Chapter 9

of their action. Again, the penalty was not contingent upon their selling, or not selling, their land. The penalty was because they had dishonored God by the words of their action.

Considering the reality of Spiritual Principles, I would assume the same fate awaited the man who brought the flour offering under the Old Covenant with the intent to defraud God.]

9.23 *It was therefore necessary that the patterns of things in the heavens should be purified with these, but the heavenly things themselves with better sacrifices than these.*

[The things of the earthly tabernacle were representations of the heavenly things. They had no innate power of themselves as they were only representative of the Heavenly. They were all intended to point toward Messiah Who would come not as representative but as The Reality of the Heavenly; He has all power within Himself as He is Heavenly in the essence of His Being.

It was necessary that the earthly things be consecrated to the holy purposes for which they were fashioned. This included objects as well as priestly functionaries. The priests were flawed men who were sinful creatures; it is easy to understand their need of purification in order for them to go about their God assigned tasks.

"But ye are a chosen generation, a royal priesthood, an holy nation, a peculiar people; that ye should shew forth the praises of him who hath called you out of darkness into his marvellous light..."   (I Peter 2:9) As we consider the words of Peter, may we also consider that the earthly priesthood of Israel was administered by men of the earth. They were human and sinful. Of such a state of man are we! Our only worth lies in our consecration in salvation as provided by the Lord. We are never special in or of ourselves. We are allowed the privilege of serving the Lord of Glory. It we must glory it should be in the fact that we are sinners saved by grace. We are called to lay our own lives on the altar and accept the will of the Lord in all things.

It is a little harder for us to consider that the objects used in the worship services would need to be purified. We do not consider objects to have any capacity to be tainted by the sin of Adam. Romans 8:22, "For we know that the whole creation groaneth and travaileth in pain together until now," teaches us that the sin of Adam caused repercussions which cast the stain of sin upon the entire creation of God.

The universe has been described as a brutal place where stars live and die, "black holes" gobble up everything in their path, and everything is born only to eventually die. The universe decomposes of its own accord. Wherever sin exists there is ultimate death assured. Sin has so stained the reality of the physical creation that even those physical things await a day of judgement and purification. "Looking for and hasting unto the coming of the day of God, wherein the heavens being on fire shall be dissolved, and the elements shall melt with fervent heat? Nevertheless we, according to his promise, look for new heavens and a new earth, wherein dwelleth righteousness." (II Peter 3:12-13)

The things of the Heavenly Sanctuary are not so. The concept of a "new" heavens and a "new" earth are restricted to the created realms of Genesis. The Heaven of the abode of God has never seen the destruction of sin for sin cannot abide where the righteousness and holiness of God reside.

The Heavenly Sanctuary was never "purified" in the sense of the earthy tabernacle. The Heavenly Sanctuary never had need of purification for it never experienced the disfigurement of sin. It was this Heavenly Sanctuary which welcomed the Risen Savior as He brought the Perfect Blood of His Perfect Sacrifice. This Sacrifice of the Perfect Son of God in His humanity is effective for the removal of all sin. The sacrifice of the animals of creation was a type of Messiah's Sacrifice. The sacrifice of the animals of creation was never effective for the removal of sin; their power lay in their message of the reality of Messiah and the Heavenly Sanctuary.

It is not the Heavenly Sanctuary which was made holy by the Sacrifice of Jesus. The power of His Sacrifice has made us positionally holy. We are not holy; we know this. It is only the Blood of Jesus which has given to us the "standing" of holiness which allows us access to The Father now and to the eternity of Heavenly bliss in His presence after we leave this mortal life.

Notice that the one Sacrifice of Jesus is placed in a plural tense. All of the many sacrifices of the Mosaic Law are not equal to the One Superior Sacrifice of Jesus!

An easy understanding of our position as holy comes from the trial, years ago, of O. J. Simpson. He was accused of killing two people. But, the trial produced a verdict of "not guilty." Therefore, in the eyes of the law of the land, O. J. Simpson is not guilty of killing those two people. I am aware that he was tried again for the same offense and found "responsible for the deaths." That does not change the reality that, in the eyes of the law, he is not guilty of the murders. If our sins are under the blood of Jesus, we are considered as holy in eyes of the justice of God because "But if we walk in the light, as he is in the light, we have fellowship one with another, and the blood of Jesus Christ his Son cleanseth us from all sin."   (I John 1:7)]

9.24   *For Christ is not entered into the holy places made with hands, which are the figures of the true; but into heaven itself, now to appear in the presence of God for us:*

[As a man, the Jesus of the incarnation pleads with the authority of His Own Divinity, the blood of His sacrifice for our salvation.

Jesus never was not God. What we see of Him, in a subordinate role, in the New Testament is the result of the Kenosis whereby He divested Himself of the outward glory of Deity. When Jesus took upon Himself the robes of humanity, in order to be one of us and thereby become the sin substitute in our place, He placed Himself in subjection to the Father as our Representative.

"But we see Jesus, who was made a little lower than the angels for the suffering of death, crowned with glory and honour; that he by the grace of God should taste death for every man." (Hebrews 2:9) Jesus did not lay aside His essential Being. He was never at any point not God. But, He became as one of us. His Person was always Deity; that is Who He is. But, His position was as a human while walking those dusty roads some two thousand years ago.

Let me try to explain this construct. I am a human being beset with all the frailties and faults of humanity. My wife would have said I have a few extra of those! But, when I assume the office of pastor I become a representative of God while I am in that pulpit. I am still me. But, I assume an office. The assumption of office does not make me something I am not. If I fail to properly fulfill the mandates of that office it is I who am at fault.

Jesus assumed the office of humanity, so to speak, via the Kenosis so that He could become the Perfect Sacrifice for sin. He acted in that office as a human, because He was human. But, even while in that office, His essential Personhood was Deity.

It is from this construct that we may begin to understand the dichotomy of Jesus being fully God and yet subservient to the Father. A misunderstanding of this duality of nature is the cause of many errors and the springboard for many cultists.

Jesus laid aside His equity with The Father to purchase our redemption. Let us be very clear, again, on this subject. The lack of equity regarded only the office of Jesus as the representative of humanity. This does not reflect upon the Person of Jesus as Deity in His Own right.

Jesus has not entered into an earthy tabernacle as did the high priest of old. The human high priest removed himself from that earthy tabernacle and returned to his human life. Jesus, our Great and Eternal High Priest, remains our Mediator. He does not "go home and watch T.V. with His dinner." He is ever "on the job" as Mediator and Savior. The human high priest of the Old Covenant only appeared in the Holy of Holies, the presence of God, one day every year.]

9.25 *Nor yet that he should offer himself often, as the high priest entereth into the holy place every year with blood of others;*

[The Levitical high priest entered the Holy of Holies on one day each year. This was on the Day of Atonement when he would come to offer the blood of sacrifice to God. This act was continued by high priest after high priest, each succeeding the other upon the death of that previous high priest.

Thus, not only was the act of sacrifice repeated so also was the administrator of that act. No single sacrifice or administrator was ever essential to the procedure. The one, sacrifice, it was necessary to repeat over and over pointing out the lack of permanent ability therein. The other, administrator, had to be replaced upon his own death pointing out that there was no promise of life within the system.

Jesus came only one time into the Heavenly Sanctuary. He offered Himself as The Perfect Sacrifice only one time. This is evidence that the Sacrifice of Jesus was so powerful as to need no repeating. Jesus lives forever; there is no expiration date on His offer of Full Pardon and Salvation. As long as we live on this physical earth in time we are able to access the benefits of His one time Sacrifice which was offered on this physical earth in time. That He has entered into that Heavenly Sanctuary is our guarantee that we who have accepted Him as Savior will follow Him as His eternal subjects into the Heavenlies.]

9.26 *For then must he often have suffered since the foundation of the world: but now once in the end of the world hath he appeared to put away sin by the sacrifice of himself.*

[The phrase "end of the world" might seem somewhat problematic as this was written nearly two thousand years ago. The phrase does not refer to time but to the duration of the Mosaic Law whereby the Levitical priests administered that Law. Since all of that Law was fulfilled in Jesus and He has given Himself as the Final and Ultimate Sacrifice for sins, that age ended at Calvary.

There has been some discussion of Revelation 13:8. "And all that dwell upon the earth shall worship him, whose names are not written in the book of life of the Lamb slain from the foundation of the world." The first part of this verse is speaking of those who worship the Antichrist of Revelation. Many argued that the phrase "...the Lamb slain from the foundation of the world," spoke only of a time after the fall of Adam. I disagree.

I believe that at the point God considered the creation of the physical universe we inhabit He understood that man would sin. He understood that Calvary would be both the result and the renewal of that creation. His great love created the universe and man who inhabits that universe with the understanding of the reality of Calvary from that point. Jesus was considered as slain for sin long before Adam was created or sinned. The events of Calvary were not the result of, "Look what Adam has done!" The events of Calvary were according to the foreknowledge of God and were, "Look what Adam will do. I will redeem him by My Own act of love."

Therein is the reality of the message of this verse. It was never necessary that Jesus be sacrificed yearly as were the sacrifices of the animals of creation. The sacrifices of the Mosaic Law were effective in showing the coming of Messiah and His great work of redemption; they were not effective in redeeming from the sin spawned by the act of Adam.

Jesus was Sacrificed just once. The Sacrifice of the Divine Lamb of God was infinite in its power to cleanse. The effects of the Sacrifice of Jesus reached back to Adam and forward forever. All humanity can only find salvation in this One Time Event.]

9.27 *And as it is appointed unto men once to die, but after this the judgment:*

[Each one of us has a date with the Author of the Universe. When will your date come?

Several years ago, my wife and I went through another Christmas holiday. We went to a watch night celebration at a local church. We went to the store, to lunch, to work... All of these things are just part of the normal life.

We even were making plans as to what to do on vacation the following summer. We had plans to go down to the town in which we were engaged and just see the old sights.

I went to that town the next summer. Linda did not. In the middle of January, she was diagnosed with a brain tumor. Four months later, to the day, she departed to her eternal home.

You do not know when the time will come for you to keep your scheduled appointment with God. But, you can know how to be ready for this appointment. Trust Jesus as your Savior.

Though there were those such as Lazarus who were raised from the dead by the power of God, the program of God still stands. We are appointed to die one time as a final exit from this mortal coil of clay. After this will come the judgment bar of God. We must either be prepared to plead the Blood of Christ or the work of man. Only the Blood of the Self-Sacrifice of Jesus on the Cross of Calvary can ever mitigate our sins and give us the forgiveness of sin and the eternity of bliss in the Heavenly realm. Our works, done in time and in the clay of human bodies can never count as worthy of the eternal and spiritual. Only the Sacrificial Death of Jesus, carried out in time but applied in the Heavenly Sanctuary of Heaven has the power to redeem us from the sin of time to allow us to share in the perfections of eternity.]

HEBREWS: Chapter 9

9.28 *So Christ was once offered to bear the sins of many; and unto them that look for him, shall he appear the second time without sin unto salvation.*

[In the process of the Virgin Birth Jesus came to this earth as a human. He came to show us the way we should live. He came to die so that we could be given, through the Spirit, the way we could live. He came to be the Sacrifice so that we could have our sins forgiven. Now, we await His return in Glory. He is the Lord of the Universe and He is coming back for us!

This verse contains several facts that have a profound bearing on humanity. We see that Jesus was "once offered." Paul has been making much of this fact. The Mosaic Law specified many sacrifices and ceremonies. These sacrifices had to be done over and over due to the sin of the people. Even the solemn Day of Atonement was repeated yearly. Only Jesus ever fulfilled completely the Law of Moses. Moreover, the ceremonies of that Law were also fulfilled in the life, burial, and resurrection of Jesus. Thus the Mosaic Law and the Levitical priesthood which administered that Law were both made of no effect due to the fulfillment of all of those Laws and ceremonies in Messiah.

More than just this, Jesus also provided a New Testament of His Blood which replaced those ceremonies and laws of Moses. The Self-Sacrifice of Jesus on the Cross of Calvary, and the attendant sprinkling of His Own Blood of Sacrifice upon the Heavenly Mercy Seat meant the salvation of many.

Note that word "many." Jesus did not die for the sins of the world. I John 2:2 tells us that, "And he is the propitiation for our sins: and not for ours only, but also for the sins of the whole world." Provisionally it is true that Jesus did die for the sins of the entire world and history of mankind.. Anyone who desires to partake of the salvation which Jesus has procured may do so. His Blood in Sacrifice is able to propitiate, or appease the sins of anyone who accepts Jesus as Savior. To them the Blood of His Sacrifice is applied. They are saved.

However, in practice we understand that not all will accept Him as their Savior. Two verses after the great salvation verse of John 3:16 the Bible says, "He that believeth on him is not condemned: but he that believeth not is condemned already, because he hath not believed in the name of the only begotten Son of God." (John 3:18) Jesus died so that all who accept Him as Savior have the reality of eternal salvation. The reality of the situation is that not all have accepted Him. Therefore, in practical application we must admit that Jesus died for "many."

Provisionally Jesus died for all. Yes. Those that refuse to accept Him have no part in His offered salvation. In a practical sense we cannot, after the fact, argue for a universal salvation because not all accept the offer of Salvation. Jesus has set a choice before people. They may accept Him as Savior and access an eternity of bliss in the eternal realms of Heaven with the Master. Or, they can refuse to accept Him and suffer the default setting of an eternal existence of regret in a Christless Hell.

Jesus is coming back to offer even more than we have now in Him. We have, today in Him, the completed salvation of our soul and spirit. These are of an eternal essence due to the "breath of God" upon the creation of Adam. (Genesis 2:7)

There is more to come. "In a moment, in the twinkling of an eye, at the last trump: for the trumpet shall sound, and the dead shall be raised incorruptible, and we shall be changed. For this corruptible must put on incorruption, and this mortal must put on immortality. So when this corruptible shall have put on incorruption, and this mortal shall have put on immortality, then shall be brought to pass the saying that is written, Death is swallowed up in victory. O death, where is thy sting? O grave, where is thy victory? The sting of death is sin; and the strength of sin is the law. But thanks be to God, which giveth us the victory through our Lord Jesus Christ." (I Corinthians 15:52-57) When Jesus returns for His Own, our bodies will experience the fullness of His Salvation. The residue of sin in our carnal bodies will be cleansed. We will inherit new bodies, of our old bodies, which are then matched to our heavenly home. We are saved, body, soul and spirit, by the Blood of the Lamb.

When Jesus returns this second time He will not appear as the humble servant of the Kenosis. He will return in His full glory and power as Deity. We shall see Him as He is!

Jesus returns not as a Sacrifice for Sin but as the Power of The Almighty God. In this He displays the full superiority of His Self-Sacrifice over the temporal sacrifices of the animals of creation. The Creator does what those temporal sacrifices of creation could never do. He saves us utterly and completely in a display of His Own power.

Please, do not misunderstand. We are saved for all eternity at the very instant we accept His Sacrifice on our behalf in faith. At His return He gives us even more as He refashions our very earthly bodies in His glorious image. The same spiritual principle which expands our understanding of Scripture without changing that Scripture is shown in our eternal salvation which expands to include our bodies of clay which are reunited in a way I cannot comprehend with our souls and spirits.]

HEBREWS - CHAPTER TEN

10.1 *For the law having a shadow of good things to come, and not the very image of the things, can never with those sacrifices which they offered year by year continually make the comers thereunto perfect.*

[The Law provided a way for the people to worship God. But, in the final analysis, those sacrifices were only prophecies of the coming sacrifice of Jesus on the Cross of Calvary. Whereas the former sacrifices were true pictures, they could not ultimately offer salvation.

These sacrifices, under the law, were acts carried forth by sinful men. They made the sacrifice in their sin and they returned home, after the sacrifice, in their sin. The writer of Hebrews notes that had the sacrificial system done away with sin, there would have been no need to offer sacrifice over and over. Acceptance of the sacrifice of Jesus, however, is the ultimate cure for the ultimate ill of sin.

A shadow is an outline made by an object which blocks the light from shining through. It provides the mere outline of something true which stands between the sight of the person standing in the shadow and the thing which casts the shadow and the True Source of the Light. Such is the Law. An observance of the Law gave a picture that there was something better and stronger which was not seen in its fullness.

These Old Testament saints were saved by following, in faith, the Words which God had given to them concerning sacrifice. But, it is important to understand, that salvation was based upon the coming Sacrifice of Jesus - of which these Old Testament sacrifices were but a shadow.

In the Garden Adam turned his back on God and his allegiance was transferred to Satan. In the New Testament conversion experience, we turn our back on Satan as we accept the gift of forgiveness which Jesus has purchased for us with His Own blood on the Cross of Calvary. In effect, we are returned to God through faith in the Blood of Jesus. The Old Testament sacrifices only pointed to this truth.]

10.2 *For then would they not have ceased to be offered? because that the worshippers once purged should have had no more conscience of sins.*

[Do you see the point being made? The sacrifices of the Old Testament Law were not permanent. They had to be done over, year after year. This was simply creatures being offered on behalf of other creatures. This was a picture of the perfect sacrifice to come. Had these been a perfect sacrifice they would not have needed to be repeated year after year. This very repetition was a picture of the inability of the Mosaic Law to fully give remission from the sins of man.

When Jesus offered Himself as the perfect sacrifice, this was not a picture. This was a fact. This was not a creature being offered for a creature. This was God sacrificed in the Person of Jesus Christ as a payment for sin; not a simple covering. The Sacrifice of Jesus does not have to be repeated because it is a perfect sacrifice. Perfection does not become better by repetition.

Neither does the fulfillment of the type need, anymore, to be repeated because that sacrifice of Jesus was a fulfillment of the Old Testament Law. After the Actual had come in the Person of Jesus Christ to again offer the former sacrificial type would be a repudiation of Jesus. The sacrifice of Jesus was the full perfection of the Law of God. Any other sacrifice would be a repudiation, by the creature - man - of the revealed Truth of the Creator - God.

Jesus did die in time so that we might live in eternity!

There is a two-fold burden of the Law. First, it is something for which its time has passed. We no longer follow the law as a way of life because Jesus has done that in our place. The faith, required of God, is to be placed upon He Who fulfilled that Law rather than on the creature whose only purpose was to point toward that fulfillment.

The second burden of the Law is that we would need to keep it perfectly. History has shown that no mere person has done this. Scripture has shown that no one from the race of Adam has done this. Finally, to perfectly keep the Law we must follow it to its natural destination. That destination is the Cross of Jesus Christ.

Only Jesus has ever kept the entire Law in a perfect manner. Even the ceremonies of the Mosaic Law were fulfilled in Jesus. Thus the very purpose of the Mosaic Law has been fulfilled and it is no longer in force. The true force of the Law, sacrifice and ceremony, was to point to Messiah. Jesus is that Messiah. John the Baptist is called a forerunner of Jesus. That is to say that he came to show the way to Jesus. Jesus came to be the Way to Heaven. (John 14:6) Because of this the Mosaic Law is no longer in force. The purpose of that Law was to point to Messiah. Since Messiah, Jesus, has come to fulfill His purpose, to look toward the Law is to be unable to see the True Salvation of Christ.

The Law, which had pointed toward Jesus, now stands behind Jesus. To place our works under the Law is to put the Law and its ceremonies between us and Jesus. The Law will never allow us to see the Light of the World, Jesus, (John 1:5) as the Law is only a shadow of He Who has already come to offer us remission of our sin.

Simple logic leads us to the conclusion that we cannot be saved by our own good work. Passages such as Acts 4:12 make it very clear that the obedience to God which will effect our salvation can come only by accepting Jesus Christ and His sacrifice. We cannot effect our own salvation; to try to do this is sin because it is in direct contradiction to God's expressed desire.

The lack of "conscience of sins" does not mean that we forget that we are sinners saved by grace. We look at the great grace of Christ and marvel that He died, as the old song reminds us, "for such a worm as I." The great grace of Jesus leads us from a consciousness of sin and into a consciousness of the greatness of His grace toward us.]

10.3   *But in those sacrifices there is a remembrance again made of sins every year.*

[Rather than placing sin behind a man, the continuance of the sacrificial system kept that sin ever before him. Today, as I put finger to keyboard, is Columbus Day. I was reminded of this fact as I entered the local Post Office to buy some stamps on my way to the church office.

I understand that many history revisionists will defame Columbus. The "New World" had been discovered long before 1492. Still, we honor this day as the beginning of a new life for the "Old World." The tremendous Westward expansion of the European nations was not without its flaws and horrors upon the native populations. Still, the

HEBREWS: Chapter 10

expansion brought new ideals of individual dignity, land to produce food for a burgeoning world population, hope for the downtrodden of Europe and – eventually – Asia and Africa, and a new mission field to which the old story could be told that Jesus Christ died in time so that others could live in eternity.

Today we look back and ponder these great changes in population and geography.

Each year Israel would celebrate the Day of Atonement. This was not intended to be a celebration of sin, yet the focus was on sins past. And, in the reality of humanity there must have been a consideration of sins future. The fact that one Day of Atonement followed another was a proof of the fact that nothing changed because of this yearly celebration. There was no true expiation of sin in the lives of the people; there was another Day of Atonement to put on the calendar for the same purpose the following year.

I have no doubt that the celebrations on the Day of Atonement were a true celebration of piety. Yet it was a celebration which understood the futility of all things. Only the True and Abiding Sacrifice of Messiah would eventually allow the True Day of Atonement to come as a result of the Cross of Calvary.]

10.4 *For it is not possible that the blood of bulls and of goats should take away sins.*

Luke 16:23; Ephesians 4:8

[When we read the above verse in its context we see that the Old Testament sacrificial system was effective but it was not permanent. The process had to be repeated over and over. The sacrifice of Jesus on the Cross of Calvary is both effective and permanent. "So Christ was once offered to bear the sins of many; and unto them that look for him shall he appear the second time without sin unto salvation." (Hebrews 9:28)

Moreover, the sacrifice of Jesus is the basis under which the former animal sacrifice's gained their own minimal, and ultimately ineffectual, authority. It was a derived authority looking forward to the actual sacrifice which should come at Calvary. "For Christ is not entered into the holy places made with hands, which are the figures of the true; but in heaven itself, now to appear in the presence of God for us." (Hebrews 9:24)

The Old Testament saints were brought into the rest of Paradise but were not sanctified holy until the Blood of Christ was shed. Those who accepted this sacrifice, which would apply the true grace of God to their lives, were finally made holy in that faith in Jesus Christ.

When this verse is compared with the sixteenth chapter of Luke (The incident of the rich man and Lazarus) we are able to see that the Old Testament saints were waiting the final purging of their sins which was only possible by Jesus as The Representative Sacrifice. His sacrifice would make them fit to enter into the presence of God.

The Blood of Jesus did more than all the Old Testament sacrifices. His Blood did not merely cover, it cleansed and cured sin. Jesus then escorted those Old Testament saints into the presence of God. (Consider Ephesians 4:8b)

See note at Luke 16:19.

Comparing Revelation 13:8 with this verse, we might note that – provisionally at least – Jesus had already been sacrificed. The logical question might be asked, why did not the animal sacrifices of other cultures gather the same atonement for their practitioners as did the animal sacrifices of the Israelite? The answer lies, as it does in every dispensation, in the heart of faith. The Israelite, and he only, was offering sacrifice in response to a heart faith in the revealed Words of God. There were Israelites who were only doing their "civic duty," who did not sacrifice with this heart of faith. To these the sacrifice was not acceptable to the Lord. Mankind is to respond to God in faith believing that "he is, and that he is a rewarder of them that diligently seek him." (Hebrews 11:6b) The first part of that verse reminds us, "But without faith it is impossible to please him: for he that cometh to God must believe..." This is a principle of God.

This verse speaks of the Day of Atonement. That was the day on which bulls and goats were sacrificed. Even this, the highest day of sacrifice, was not a day on which sins were forgiven and cleansed. It was a day, as were the other days of sacrifice, which pointed toward the complete sacrifice of Messiah. The people did not understand all the significance in this day nor in any of the days of sacrifice. They did know to place their faith in the revealed Words of God and in the God of those Words. This was counted as righteousness among the faithful.]

10.5 *Wherefore when he cometh into the world, he said, Sacrifice and offering thou wouldest not, but a body hast thou prepared me:*

[Paul had just told these Jewish men that the sacrifices of the Old Covenant were not effective. This would not have pleased them! His appeal for proof of his statement was to open their own Scriptures.

The passage from the Old Testament speaks of "when he cometh into the world" in reference to Messiah being superior to the sacrifices of the time in which David originally penned this Psalm. This looks into the future and sees Messiah coming. That is what the phrase "when he cometh" would have meant to the Jewish mind of the day in which Paul labored

Psalm 40:6-10 is accessed in this and the following verses: "Sacrifice and offering thou didst not desire; mine ears hast thou opened: burnt offering and sin offering hast thou not required. Then said I, Lo, I come: in the volume of the book it is written of me, I delight to do thy will, O my God: yea, thy law is within my heart. I have preached righteousness in the great congregation: lo, I have not refrained my lips, O LORD, thou knowest. I have not hid thy righteousness within my heart; I have declared thy faithfulness and thy salvation: I have not concealed thy lovingkindness and thy truth from the great congregation."

I think it instructive to note at this place that most of the commentators have argued that Paul uses the Septuagint, rather than the Hebrew, at this place. Their argument is that the Hebrew has become corrupted so Paul uses the Septuagint rather than the Hebrew.

There was a well-known vaudeville couple who hailed from Peoria, Illinois. Their act was called "Fibber McGee and Molly." Molly had a "catch phrase" she used when her husband had made an outlandish claim: "T'aint so McGee." Well, as to the claim that the devout Jew of the day had switched from the Hebrew to the Greek: "Tain't so McGee!" The Hebrew was the only thing allowed in Temple worship.

Greek, also, may have been the "international language;" it was not the day-to-day language of the people. The phrase of Jesus in His agony on the Cross, "And at the ninth hour Jesus cried with a loud voice, saying, Eloi, Eloi, lama sabachthani? which is, being interpreted, My God, my God, why hast thou forsaken me," (Mark 15:34) was spoken in Aramaic, not in Greek.

It is a fact that there is no complete copy of the Septuagint until the third century in the Hexpala of Origen. Rather than Paul quoting from what was at that time likely a non-existent LXX, it is more likely that Origen used the Greek of Paul to "update" the LXX.

As to the wording being somewhat different in Paul than it was in the Psalm is attributed to the Holy Spirit defining and expanding His Own words.

The salient point of interest is Paul's use of "body" rather than "ears" in the sixth verse of that fortieth chapter of Psalms. David, writing prophecy of Messiah at this point, references Exodus 21:2-6 in the reference to Messiah. "If thou buy an Hebrew servant, six years he shall serve: and in the seventh he shall go out free for nothing. If he came in by himself, he shall go out by himself: if he were married, then his wife shall go out with him. If his master have given him a wife, and she have born him sons or daughters; the wife and her children shall be her master's, and he shall go out by himself. And if the servant shall plainly say, I love my master, my wife, and my children; I will not go out free: Then his master shall bring him unto the judges; he shall also bring him to the door, or unto the door post; and his master shall bore his ear through with an aul; and he shall serve him for ever." This is a picture of one who has voluntarily placed himself in subjection to another.

In the natural this has to do with the Kenosis whereby Jesus placed Himself, in His Humanity, in obedience to The Father. John 8:29 has to do with Jesus doing, at every step, the will of The Father. Jesus prayed often. His ears heard the Words of The Father. In that sense the Psalm is accurate in its description of the ears of Jesus being attuned to The Father.

However, the Holy Spirit mentions the body of Messiah at this place. The sense is not that different. However, it is an expanded sense. It was the Body of Jesus which was sacrificed for the sins of many rather than just His ears. Jesus poured out in sacrifice the very life blood of His humanity as the Sacrifice which was better, actually effective rather than a mere shadow of the reality of that Sacrifice, than the sacrifice of the animals of creation even on the Day of Atonement.

In the process of the Virgin Birth (Isaiah 7:14 and Matthew 1:23) we see that a body was prepared for Jesus.]

10.6 *In burnt offerings and sacrifices for sin thou hast had no pleasure.*

[God did take pleasure in the concept of man's obedience to His Words and Directives in the Mosaic Law. But, as to the actual sacrifices of the animals of creation He did not take pleasure in reference to their effectiveness.

The purpose of these sacrifices was never meant to solve the problem of sin in the life of humanity. God took pleasure in the fact that these pointed to Messiah and the True Sacrifice which had been planned from before the creation of the world. (Revelation 13:8b)

There is also the argument that some saw these not as a service to God. These would have looked at the sacrifices either as a civic duty or as a superstitious talisman. There was no true worship attached to the sacrifices in such a situation. The purpose of the sacrifices and ceremonies were never a means toward an end. They were merely the sign post to point to the reality of the Sacrifice of Messiah.]

10.7 *Then said I, Lo, I come (in the volume of the book it is written of me,) to do thy will, O God.*

[Paul adds a parenthesis in this verse to show its relationship to Messiah rather than just to David. The Scripture speaks of Jesus through and through. We note here that Jesus came to do the will of The Father. Once again we would note that this has to do with His Voluntary Kenosis whereby Jesus emptied Himself of His outward Glory of Deity. (Philippians 2:5-8) He did this in order that He could become our example in all things pertaining to righteousness and, more importantly for the first is encompassed within the second, to be The Effective Sacrifice for our sins as He became one of us in His humanity.

We note that Jesus came to do the will of The Father. As early as Genesis 3:15 there was reference to the "seed of woman" which speaks of His virgin birth into humanity. He also came to die in this humanity as The Sacrifice for our sins. (Psalms 22:--; Isaiah 53:10-12) These verses listed at this place give a clear picture of the crucifixion of Christ; they were written hundreds of years before the fact and fulfilled perfectly in the fullness of time.

Jesus came to fulfill the Law of Moses. (Matthew 5:17) When Jesus had completed this task the Law became of no effect upon humanity except as a moral guide to the spiritual principles of God. Even the ceremonies of the Law were fulfilled in the human life of Jesus.

Jesus came to bring a sword of separation. (Matthew 20:34-36) There is a separation between light and darkness. The one can never intrude upon the other. Likewise there is to be a separation of the saints of God and the sinners of humanity. This does not mean that we are never to intermingle with those outside the household of faith. If we were to do this we could not present the Good News that Jesus Christ died in time so that others could live in eternity.

But, our separation to the things of God will preclude our taking part in the rites and ceremonies of false religions as well as those unbiblical amusements of man. We ought never to bring the world into the church in search of a crowd. This will dishonor the Biblical message and lower us to a position below that of our calling. An avalanche never sends snow and rocks upward. Neither will our testimony or faith rise when placed into the mire and muck of the soiled world!

Jesus was sent to the Lost Sheep of Israel until the time of His offering up of Himself in sacrifice to bring the blessings of God to all nations who would receive Him. (Genesis 22:18; Matthew 15:24) This is an indication that those sacrifices and ceremonies of the Old Covenant were not sufficient for salvation. Israel was a nation of lost sheep even as she worshiped at the Temple, note that this was known as "Herod's Temple," in Jerusalem.

Jesus was sent to the lost sinners of the world. (Matthew 18:11) His mission as Messiah may have been to Israel but the promise given to Israel was to bless all nations. (Genesis 22:18)

Jesus was sent to minister the Message of God into the world of man. We are those who are gloriously allowed to assist in this task. It is our purpose as followers of Jesus. (Matthew 20:28) Note that He is given as "a ransom for many." Not all will accept the salvation He offers.

Jesus was sent to preach the Good News of the Gospel of Truth. (Mark 1:38) This is also our task in this world. (Luke 24:46-48) This Gospel is not restricted to preaching at a church service but is a task that is only completed in the farms and metropolises of mankind. Salvation never heard is salvation never accepted. (Romans 10:14-17)

Jesus was sent to save lives. (Luke 9:56) The creation of God consists of much. He is the Author of our very lives. Therefore He knows what makes us all that we should be even in our natural lives. The "owner's manual" of my car gives me much information that can be used to make the car run better and longer. Consider that God created us. He knows what is best for us. The true Christian life-style, culled from the pages of His Book, will cause us to be better human beings even in the natural.

Jesus was sent to seek and to save the lost sinners of the world. (Luke 19:10) As followers of Him this becomes our task in this dispensation.

Jesus was sent to send fire upon the earth. (Luke 12:49) We can look at this with reference to the flaming tongues of Pentecost. (Acts 2:2-3) We have the same "fire" available to us today. We have even more because we have the completed text of the New Testament of His Blood. God inspired those precious Words of Power. More importantly to us in this day, He has preserved His Words perfectly and they are still available to us in their power today.

Beyond this, we must consider that the earth, itself, is reserved to the judgment of God. (II Peter 3:10) Sin will be totally eradicated from the creation of God in order to insure a blissful eternity for His called of this earth.

Jesus was sent to do the will of God. (John 6:38-39) In all things of His humanity Jesus was obedient unto the will of The Father. In this He serves as our example to become obedient unto Him. I used the word "become" in that last sentence because I doubt that any of us are fully obedient to Him.

Jesus was sent to execute judgment upon the earth. (John 9:39) At the Cross of Calvary Jesus took our judgment for sin upon Himself. He sacrificed Himself in order to cleanse our sins. He has applied His Blood of Sacrifice to all of our sins. This includes our own misdeeds, all committed after the Cross, and that sin of Adam which is inherited by all children of man. Only Jesus, born of the virgin, was ever free from the inherited sin of Adam.

Eve was taken from Adam before Adam sinned. Although Eve sinned herself, she was not the titular head of the race of man as is Adam. She did not share in the sin of Adam as do we all. Thus the virgin birth of Jesus allowed Him to become fully human while remaining fully free from any stain of sin. Indeed, as Deity incarnate this was a requirement. Jesus did not sin, and could not sin, in His humanity as the Essence of His Being was Divine.

Jesus was sent to give abundant life. (John 10:10) No man who still bears the guilt of his sin, and thus stands in the impending eternal judgment of God, can possibly live a life to the fullest of his human potential.

Jesus was sent to be The Light into the world of the darkness of human existence. (John 12:46) Mankind lives in eternal spiritual darkness. He cannot find the Light of God as this Light has been rejected from his family of humanity via the sin of Adam. (Romans 3:10-12)

Jesus came to bear witness to the Truth. (John 18:37) The Truth, the Whole Truth, is that man is a sinner who will die and go to an eternity of regret unless that person accepts Jesus Christ as Savior. There is no other way. (Acts 4:12)]

10.8 *Above when he said, Sacrifice and offering and burnt offerings and offering for sin thou wouldest not, neither hadst pleasure therein; which are offered by the law;*

[These things, sacrifice, offering, burnt offerings, and offering for sin comprise nearly the complete Mosaic Law of the Old Covenant. God derived no pleasure in them. It was not that these were wrong as they were as prescribed by God to Moses. The lack of pleasure does not concern the actual actions as done in faith and obedience to the Words of God.

The lack of pleasure had to do with the fact that none of these could actually remove either sin or the propensity to wallow in sin. The Spirit of Inspiration upon the Words penned by David gave a truth which may not have been evident to the people living under the Old Covenant. Their sins were not cleansed by the many rites and ceremonies of the Law. God did not take pleasure in these things to the extent of bestowing His Free Grace upon those who took part in these rites and ceremonies.

These things could never remit sins because they were objects which came from the sinfulness of the sin sullied creation. Only a sacrifice from outside of the created realms, from the realm of the very acts of creation could possibly offer expiation of sin in the life of an individual. Only God, the One Who was directly offended by the acts and attitudes of sin could produce a sacrifice which contained saving virtue.

Jesus was the Active Agent of Creation. (John 1:3) Moreover, Jesus is God; He is the One offended by sin. He has the right to forgive sin. (Mark 2:9) As the earthly sacrificial system was modeled upon the heavenly template, we can see that a total blood sacrifice was, indeed, necessary for sin to be removed from an individual. Only the Pure Righteousness of Jesus could die in His humanity as a representative sacrifice for sin. The death of no created being could complete this task. Therefore, God had no pleasure in the sacrifice of the animals of creation; they could never remove sin for they were from sin themselves.

What these Old Covenant actions could do was to point toward the Cross of Calvary. It was only the Self-Sacrifice of Jesus which could cleanse sin from a person.]

10.9 *Then said he, Lo, I come to do thy will, O God. He taketh away the first, that he may establish the second.*

[Very plainly stated, the first covenant of the Mosaic Law was fulfilled in Jesus. With that finished it was time that the New Testament of Grace was instituted. To illustrate: I just made a pot of coffee. I can't pour any more water into that coffee pot. If I decide that I want pure water rather than coffee, I must either pour out the container of coffee in order to have room for pure water. Or, I must find another container in which to put the water.

The "water" of creation has been stained by contact with the "coffee bean" of sin. The pot in which the water stands is full to the brim of coffee. If I decide I want to drink water instead of coffee I must pour out the coffee – get rid of the coffee and all traces of it by cleaning the pot – and find either a new container or make the first one clean. I would wash the container of coffee with water and soap. We are cleansed of our sin by The Blood of the Lamb.

The purpose for which Jesus came into the world was not simply to be born as a man in order to give us The Holy Example to follow. He came to fulfill the complete Law and Ceremony of the Mosaic Law. But, He came for even more. He came to provide a Sacrifice which would please God and take the fact, consequence, and power of sin from the world of all who would apply that sacrifice in faith to themselves through His Grace.

This Sacrifice of Jesus is pleasing to God.]

10.10 *By the which will we are sanctified through the offering of the body of Jesus Christ once for all.*

[Through the Sacrifice of Jesus as many as access His offered Salvation are sanctified – set apart from the world of sin and unto His Holy Name – as The Father had willed and The Son had accomplished. The ending of the subjection of the Mosaic Law, with the beginning of the Law of Grace through Jesus Christ is shown to be the Will of God.

Before coming to the church office to work on this commentary I went to *Chez Golden Arches* for breakfast. When I was done with that breakfast I took the tray I had used to carry the items of food and put the residue into a trash receptacle and placed the tray on a stack of other trays. I will never eat that particular breakfast again. I may eat one like it; but I will not eat that one. It is done. It is over. Even the residue has been placed in the trash out of sight.

Paul was telling these Jewish men that it was time to clean off the tray of the Old Covenant. It was time to move on into the Grace of Jesus Christ.

The Work of Jesus on the Cross of Calvary has been completed. The fact of Sacrificial death of the Innocent for the guilty has been completed. The single Day of Atonement of Grace has been completed. These events will not again transpire. These works of Deity are complete. We are considered as complete in Him as His Blood cleanseth us from all sin. (I John 1:7)

Someone had said that "all" means "all" and that is all that all means. The Work of Jesus is not flawed as is the work of man. There is no need for Him to be offered up again. His Work of Self-Sacrifice is completed for all eternity.

We are now entered into a new walk whereby the Spirit leads us to spread the Gospel Message that Jesus Christ died in time so that we might live in eternity. His Work of Self-Sacrifice is completed even as His Work of Mediation continues for us.]

10.11 *And every priest standeth daily ministering and offering oftentimes the same sacrifices, which can never take away sins.*

[The former sacrificial system was a teaching tool to prepare the way for an understanding of the sacrifice of Jesus. This is not to denigrate the former sacrificial system. It was effective for the Old Testament saints because they were responding in faith to the revelation which God had given to them. But, in the light of eternity, these sacrifices only covered the sins of the people. "For it is not possible that the blood of bulls and of goats should take away sin." (Hebrews 10:4)

The former covenant of the Levitical priesthood is shown to not be eternally efficient in that the rites and ceremonies must be repeated year after year. The continuation of the stasis of sacrifice and ceremony by a continual procession of sinful – they must often sacrifice for themselves – human men only holding the office of high priest during a mortal life time, is an evidence of the temporal nature of that priesthood and covenant.

Such temporal men and appointments give evidence to the earthly nature of the Mosaic Law. This does not reach the heavenlies as, although as prescribed by God, it is earthly in its essence of application. (I Corinthians 15:50)

The ultimate, legal in the light of eternity, removal of the sin of the Old Testament saints waited for the ultimate sacrifice of Jesus Christ on the Cross of Calvary. The faith of the people of the Old Covenant was counted to them as personal righteousness; but there were those who only performed the sacrifices as a sort of "civic duty." They had no real faith. The faithful were counted as saved for eternity by the sacrifice of Jesus Christ. They might not have understood this; they probably didn't understand at the time. But, God counted their faith and applied the Blood of Jesus to their accounts.

Verse four of this same chapter had said, "For it is not possible that the blood of bulls and of goats should take away sin." This tenth chapter of Hebrews has been showing the superiority of the sacrifice of Jesus over the Old Testament sacrifice. Those Old Testament sacrifices had been effectual in covering the sins of those Old Testament faithful. The faith of those people in the Words of God had made them righteous. They were not sanctified, or set apart holy, until the greater sacrifice of Jesus Christ removed and cleansed those sins. See note at Luke 16:19 for a further discussion on this theme.

The point being made is that only the sacrifice of Jesus is effective in cleansing sin. All who have had their sins cleansed owe that to Jesus. It is only He, as God, Who has the power to remove sins and make any person clean before God.

The sinlessness of Jesus proves His Divinity and saves our souls!]

10.12 *But this man, after he had offered one sacrifice for sins for ever, sat down on the right hand of God;*

Zechariah 6:13

["This man," Jesus, completed just one sacrifice. This Sacrifice was of His human body as a representative of all who would come to Him for salvation. The many human priests of the Old Covenant continued to perform their duties of sacrifice of the animals of creation day after day and year after year. Jesus completed just one Perfect Sacrifice and then sat down signifying His Sacrifice was, indeed, perfect and sufficient for all time and for all who would call upon the Lord.

The verse says that Jesus sat down on the right hand of God. This concept hearkens back to John 1:1-2. "In the beginning was the Word, and the Word was with God, and the Word was God. The same was in the beginning with God." Zodhiates argues that this phrase from the inspired and preserved Scripture speaks of two equals facing each other. Neither is above the other for Both are, with the Holy Spirit, The unified essence of The Trinity of the Godhead.

The fact that Jesus is pictured as sitting on the right hand is a phrase easily understood in early first century society. It is not a picture of a spatial consideration. It is a picture which conveys power, majesty, honor and authority.

This Sacrifice of the human body of Jesus is an act that not only could not, but needed not to ever be repeated. This Self-Sacrifice of Jesus was perfect in all aspects. It cleansed the sins of all, through all the ages of created humanity, who would accept Him as Savior. This was the sacrifice which saves us today, others tomorrow – should Jesus tarry His coming again – and even the Old Testament saints who died before the events of Calvary.

There is, indeed, great "Power in the Blood!"

We must note here that Jesus performed one Sacrifice and sat down to signify the completing of His mission to offer true salvation to all who would come to Him. Those earthly priests of the Old Covenant offered continual sacrifice which could never offer complete salvation from sin and sins power.

Jesus sat from His work of Self-Sacrifice. He stands now to make intercession for us who are His by faith in His Blood.]

10.13 *From henceforth expecting till his enemies be made his footstool.*

[The enemies of Christ will be as His footstool. This is a reference to the eastern custom of putting the foot of the conqueror on the necks of the conquered. (Joshua 10:24; Psalm 110:1)

Since Jesus has completed His great Self-Sacrifice His enemies must realize that their time is short. How short? We cannot know when the time of His final triumph over His enemies will be. It is as His Second appearing. It will be in the fullness, and the perfection, of the time of the choosing of The Father. (Mark 13:32)

Why has the time been so long? No man can answer that question. The best guess is that the grace of God will tarry Jesus coming until the last person to be saved has been saved. God does know the times and the seasons even of the salvation of the saints. We surmise this on II Peter 3:9 where Peter tells us that God is not willing that any should perish. God waits for these to come to Christ for salvation.

We might well wonder just who are the enemies of Jesus. The great archenemy of Jesus is Satan. His doom is assured in Revelation 20:10. Sadly, there will be many of the earth who will join Satan in this bottomless pit. It was not prepared for them. Mankind had a better purpose but refused, far too many refused, to accept the free and offered salvation. They will be "gate crashers," so to speak, joining Satan in the eternal agony of an eternity far from their Creator. (Revelation 20:12-15)

The role of sin is much larger than we might suspect. The disarray we witness in the natural creation is the result of the sin of Adam. When Adam yielded to the blandishments of Satan, and Eve, and took part in the forbidden fruit all nature felt the sting of death in that journey into sin. (Romans 8:22) Even the natural elements of creation must be purged of sin. This will be done. (Micah 1:3-4; Psalm 50:3; II Peter 3:11-13; Revelation 21:1ff)

The final enemy is death. This, too, shall be banished from the restored creation of God. (I Corinthians 15:26)

At the destruction of death, the final enemy, the entire creation will find a rebirth in the love of, and under the righteous rule of, God.]

10.14 *For by one offering he hath perfected for ever them that are sanctified.*

[Jesus has sacrificed Himself in His humanity one time. So powerful is the human blood of the Divine/human man, Jesus, that there is no need for this sacrifice to ever been repeated as were the sacrifices of the animals of creation during the time frame of the Old Covenant.

In the Self-Sacrifice of Jesus at Calvary, He bought for us the potential of perfection. I only use the word "potential" because not all will accept the Lord as Savior. This is choice we must make to reap any benefit of His great Self-Sacrifice for us.

It is interesting to note that He has, in His Self-Sacrifice, granted us an eternal perfection. Now, I know that I am not perfect. If my wife were here she could explain my lack of perfection in verse, chapter and detail. However, because of the power inherent in the Blood of Jesus which was shed for us, we are given a positional perfection. We are not perfect. We are counted as perfect as we are covered in the Blood of He Who is Perfect. In His mediatorial office Jesus pleads this perfection with The Father when our actions are not consistent with our profession.

The perfection is in regards to the remission of our sins. They are under the Blood of Christ and are not *"visible,"* as it were, to God as He has regarded that the Blood of Christ cleanses us from all our sin. (I John 1:7) God has removed our sins from us because of the effectiveness and perfections of the Self-Sacrifice of Jesus. (Psalms 103:12)

This Self-Sacrifice of Jesus has given us an eternal salvation which cannot be either lost or taken away. (Romans 8:1; Ephesians 4:30) Note especially Ephesians 4:30; we do not have the right to act contrary to our profession. The truly redeemed will not so act. There is a "Fatherly punishment" waiting for those who do grieve the Spirit by disobedience. Read it carefully. God has bought us with a price. (I Corinthians 6:20) We are His children. (John 1:12: Ephesians 1:5) With Heaven as our assured destination even what man might consider as the "ultimate punishment" is not severe but loving. (I Corinthians 11:30)

We are, presently, sanctified by the gift of salvation. We may not act very holy; we are considered as holy because of the power of the Blood of Christ. Our "holiness" does not, cannot as we are vessels of clay in the realm and physicality and time, be holy in and of ourselves. What manner of holiness we do exhibit is, as above, not of ourselves. It is a positional holiness based in the work of Jesus at the Cross of Calvary.

This is a holiness which has set us apart from the world at large. We are the saints of God as we are the children of God. We await the full flower of our imparted holiness when we shall be with Him and away from this world. (I Corinthians 15:47-58)

Lest anyone misunderstand, the positional holiness does not mean that we are not to strive to grow in the Lord. "But grow in grace, and in the knowledge of our Lord and Saviour Jesus Christ. To him be glory both now and for ever. Amen." (II Peter 3:18) We will never reach full perfection within this life. I John 2:1 gives us this warning, "My little children, these things write I unto you, that ye sin not. And if any man sin, we have an advocate with the Father, Jesus Christ the righteous..."

When we do fail we need to stand up, confess our shortcoming and sin, and continue to walk as close to the Master as is possible for us to walk. We may even find our walk improved by our experience of His love and advocacy on our part. He is our Mediator; that is the general meaning of advocate in the above verse.]

10.15 *Whereof the Holy Ghost also is a witness to us: for after that he had said before,*

[The Holy Spirit is a witness to us that Jesus has saved us. It is He Who speaks to our hearts in convicting us of sin unto repentance. It is He Who speaks to our hearts that we are the children of God. The Spirit speaks and confirms the Truth of the Gospel.

What we often call "conscience" is often the voice of the Spirit leading into righteousness and away from evil. We must confirm by the Words of the inspired and preserved Words of God just what is ultimate truth. Satan is able to transform himself into an angel of light. (II Corinthians 11:14) If this is true, and the Scripture says that it is, how can we know right from wrong? How do we know the perfect will of God from the pernicious wiles of Satan?

Worry not, dear Christian. "Ye are of God, little children, and have overcome them: because greater is he that is in you, than he that is in the world." (I John 4:4)

Remember that Jesus is our Savior. But, Jesus was also our example of life within this world of man. In Matthew 4:1-11 we have the incident where Satan tried to tempt Jesus in His humanity. Jesus did not invoke His innate Deity in response to Satan. Instead Jesus answered Satan the same way which we should; Jesus spoke Scripture. Satan departed.

It is much easier to speak Scripture if we've spent some time in the Scripture learning the Holy Words which God has inspired and preserved for us. We do need to study the Scripture if we are to be good workmen for God. (II Timothy 2:15) By the way, it would be good to not consider this passage as good advice. It is a direct command from God. So, study to show yourself approved as a workman for God!]

10.16 *This is the covenant that I will make with them after those days, saith the Lord, I will put my laws into their hearts, and in their minds will I write them;*

[Paul is quoting from Jeremiah 31:33. Paul is not quoting exactly; he is expanding the passage from Isaiah. We have a perceived problem with this. Did not Moses say (Deuteronomy 4:2) that the words of the Law – and by extension the words of the prophets which were delivered from the setting of the Mosaic Law – were not to be either added to or diminished from? The same prohibition was given concerning the words of the Gospel of the Age of Grace. (Revelation 22:18-19)

So, why is Paul changing the wording of Jeremiah?

First of all, Paul is writing in Greek whereas the Book of Jeremiah was written in Hebrew. No translation will ever be completely faithful to the original from another tongue. The best it can be is accurate.

Second, Paul is writing the Book but the words are inspired Words from God, not simply the words of Paul. The concept of Divine Inspiration is that God "breathed out" the Words of Scripture. The influence of the Spirit was so strongly upon the penman that the Words so produced were the Words of God rather than the words of any man. Therefore, the Words of this Book of Hebrews are actually the Words of God.

One of the tasks of the Holy Spirit is to lead into all truth. (John 16:13) We understand His Work as we read the Words of the inspired and preserved Scripture.

Passages often seem to leap off the page with a message to our hearts. Often this is an encounter with the Spirit as He illumines a passage to our hearts and understanding.

This is the principle at work in the quotations of Paul in Hebrews. Under the process of inspiration the Spirit illuminated, expanded, the words of Jeremiah to bring the thoughts, intents, and Words of God to bear upon the subject matter being discussed.

Jeremiah 31:33, the verse accessed by Paul at this place says, ""But this shall be the covenant that I will make with the house of Israel; After those days, saith the LORD, I will put my law in their inward parts, and write it in their hearts, and will be their God, and they shall be my people." I include this to highlight the words "shall be" and "I will put." The use of these words obviously refers the actions to a future time.

The Israelite people were already living under the Abrahamic Covenant. It had not yet "blessed all nations" as God had promised. This is not a Covenant to be ended at any point. That particular blessing under the Abrahamic Covenant concerns salvation by the Self-Sacrifice of Messiah. For this Covenant to ever expire it must follow that our very salvation would likewise expire. Since our salvation is eternal this Abrahamic Covenant, which establishes the people of Abraham as the "People of the Covenant" must also be eternal.

But, the people were also living under the Mosaic Covenant of the Law. The purpose of this covenant was two-fold. First, and most obviously to the people who lived under this covenant, there was given a prescribed means to access individual piety. This was tied to the sacrifice and ceremony of the Law.

This, as we have already seen, could never give relief from the burden of personal sin and the burden of the nature of sin inherent in human life. But, the means was given whereby people could express a love of God, devotion to God, faith in God, obedience unto God and a desire for piety before God.

Secondly, and primarily, was the physical illustration of the coming Messiah shown throughout the various acts of this Mosaic Law. Were these to be righteously fulfill by anyone there would be no further purpose served by the shadows and types of the Mosaic Law. The purpose would have been fulfilled. No mere man could ever complete this transaction. Only Messiah could, and did, fulfill every one of the types, shadows, and prophecies of the Law. Thus, fulfilled in its primary function, the Law would pass away as the object of the Law came into view.

Even had it been possible that a mere human would have fully fulfilled the Law and Ceremonies, these ceremonies were prophecies of Messiah and no man would have had the internal capacity to fulfill them, he could not have died for the sins of any other man. Every man born of Adam's blood carries a nature of sin which would preclude the possibility of perfection within every man. Besides this impossibility, we must note that the Offended Party in sin is God. Only God can forgive such violence done toward Him. Only the Pure Perfections of God in the body of a man, Jesus – the Creator from the realm of eternity and pure Spirituality, would have the ability to die in sacrifice for the sins of others.

This has brought us to the New Covenant or New Testament in the Blood of Jesus. The old Law no longer stands except as a moral guide which shows our need of The Savior. Those spiritual principles of the moral Law are still in force as a guide to the Savior. They do not just lead TO Him; they cry out the reality of the great need OF Him in the life of all men.

As has happened so many times in the past two millennia, there will be a time of great national distress for Israel. Yet God will protect His Covenant People from those who seek her annihilation. At the point of seeming great danger for His Covenant People, God will intervene, call them back to Himself, and renew them spiritually and call them to Himself.

"So shall they fear the name of the LORD from the west, and his glory from the rising of the sun. When the enemy shall come in like a flood, the Spirit of the LORD shall lift up a standard against him. And the Redeemer shall come to Zion, and unto them that turn from transgression in Jacob, saith the LORD. As for me, this is my covenant with them, saith the LORD; My spirit that is upon thee, and my words which I have put in thy mouth, shall not depart out of thy mouth, nor out of the mouth of thy seed, nor out of the mouth of thy seed's seed, saith the LORD, from henceforth and for ever." (Isaiah 59:10-21)

The great Abrahamic Covenant has blessed us with the Savior. God still keeps all of His promises.]

10.17 And their sins and iniquities will I remember no more.

[A very interesting miracle was performed by Jesus in the eighth chapter of Matthew, verses 23 to 25: "And he took the blind man by the hand, and led him out of the town; and when he had spit on his eyes, and put his hands upon him, he asked him if he saw ought. And he looked up, and said, I see men as trees, walking. After that he put his hands again upon his eyes, and made him look up: and he was restored, and saw every man clearly."

In Romans, chapter eleven and following, Paul bemoans the fact that most of Israel is seemingly blind to the fact that Messiah has come. There are a few, here and there, who had met Messiah and accepted Him as Savior. But, for the most part the Jew of our day sees only an indistinct and shadowy figure of Jesus. They may agree with their Muslim "cousins" that Jesus was a great prophet. But, few will see Him as He is; He is both their Messiah and can be their eternal Savior.

There is a time promised that the entire nation will be touched by Messiah. Their eyes will be opened to the fact that Jesus is the One Final Sacrifice which will remove sin rather than simply cover sin for another year.

They will understand that Jesus is their Savior. That this opening of the eyes of Israel is a miracle may seem farfetched. To the human eye it may well be. But this is the prophecy of God. All Israel shall be saved by trust in the One they, in their fathers, pierced and crucified. (Romans 11:26) At this point God will no longer remember the sins of Israel. His Covenant People will again covenant to serve Him in purity, peace and pardon.]

10.18 Now when remission of these is, there is no more offering for sin.

[This is the grand theme: Jesus died once to remove our sin. So satisfactory and complete was His death of Self-Sacrifice that there is never any need that it be repeated. It would be good to quote I John 1:7 at this place. "But if we walk in the light, as he is in the light, we have fellowship one with another, and the blood of Jesus Christ his Son cleanseth us from all sin."

Walking in the Light of Jesus, wherein He walked in holiness and perfection, is a thing to which we ought to strive. But, and this is important, there is no saving grace contained even in the best of our efforts. This concept speaks only of fellowship with other believers.

Surely this concept pertains to our fellowship in the Church which Jesus has established. The fellowship of other believers' gives comfort and assistance from each believer in such fellowship and to each believer in such fellowship. It is not given to us to disfellowship from other believers in this manner. We cannot dismiss ourselves from the very organization which Jesus established if we consider ourselves to be true followers of His.

We could move the concept one step further. We have no ability within ourselves to walk in that Light of the Lord. It is only our meeting with Him in Saving grace at the Cross of Calvary which can allow us to walk in this Light of Jesus.

Since our sins are atoned in the one time Self-Sacrifice of Jesus, there is no need for any other sacrifice for sin. It seems the only allowable sacrifices are the sacrifice of praise to the Lord for His great mercy and the offering of ourselves as "living sacrifices" to the service of our great Savior. (Romans 12:1)

An interesting situation is also considered here. The Roman Church has their daily Mass which is considered a sacrifice, according to the Council of Trent, of the Body and Blood of Jesus in the Eucharist since they consider the wafer and wine as such after consecration. Also, their doctrine of purgatory is that there will be sins which are paid for by the faithful in the fires of purgatory before the soul is allowed entrance into Heaven. This verse repudiates those doctrines. I say "interesting" because the Vaticanus, a very old copy of the Scripture which was found in the Vatican library around the time of the Reformation, only carries part of the Book of Hebrews. In this document the Book of Hebrews ends near the beginning of this tenth chapter.

Since this is one of the two "oldest and best," so considered at least, which is often pointed to as a cause to establish the renunciation of the Textus Receptus, there is some irony included in the consideration of this text.

Add this fact to the establishment of the Critical Text, which does rely heavily on Aleph and B, and we begin to see a pattern emerging in the modern English Language translation. Further on this pattern is the inclusion of the Apocryphal books within the text of Scripture makes the pattern even more troubling. I leave it to the reader to consider just what spiritual entity is involved in this pattern.]

10.19 *Having therefore, brethren, boldness to enter into the holiest by the blood of Jesus,*

[Once again Paul does not claim any special position. Those to whom he writes are "brethren" in the same family of God. The terms "laity" and "clergy" are man-made considerations. We are brothers in the family as adopted sons of God.

Paul has already explained the superiority of the New Testament of the Blood of Jesus to the Old Covenant of the Mosaic Law. Whereas the priests of the Old Covenant performed sacrifice of the animals of creation which could never offer any forgiveness of sin. Jesus offered His Own Blood in a Self-Sacrifice of redeeming quality on the Cross of Calvary. The Self-Sacrifice of Jesus would never be repeated. It offered full, complete and unlimited remission of sins from the sprinkling of His perfect blood on the Heavenly Mercy Seat. The sacrifices of those animals of creation by the high priest of humanity needed to be completed over and over as they were the works of fallen man.

Even the high priest of the Levitical Priesthood was a fallen man who must sacrifice for himself before he could presume to sacrifice for others. His term of office always ended at his own death. Jesus did not need a "pre-sacrifice" for His sins before offering up Himself for our salvation. He had no sin which would have required any gift or sacrifice. He lives forever as the Eternal Mediator and Great High Priest of our profession. As Deity, the Offended Party by the sin of Adam, only He had the right to offer forgiveness.

The Old Covenant was never intended to be eternal. In the very essence of the Old Covenant the fact of its demise was evident. The Old Covenant was set up to point toward the coming Messiah. This was the true purpose of the Old Covenant. It never offered remission from sins as its purpose, through its many sacrifice and celebrations, were prophetic pre-figures of Messiah Who was to come.

Yes; those sacrifices and ceremonies of the Old Covenant gave a means for man to worship God. But, those sacrifices and ceremonies never gave a complete removal of sin nor a promise of eternal life within themselves.

With the coming of Messiah, and His complete fulfillment of all the obligations of the law of sacrifice and the figures presented in the ceremonies, the Law could no longer fulfill its primary purpose of pointing to Messiah. The Law had become irrelevant in its purpose even as it was incapable of performing the act of the removal of sin, inherent and observable within sinful humanity. God could not be approached by any except the high priest on the Day of Atonement.

As a religion to bless the world through the line of Abraham the Law was not effective except in showing the way to Messiah. It must decrease even as He increased. (consider John 3:30)

The New Testament of the Blood of Christ succeeded in every area which the Law of the Old Covenant was defective. The Blood of Jesus does cleanse those who accept His Work in faith. Their sin is removed. Through the Blood of the Self-Sacrifice of Jesus on the Cross all Christians are given invitation to boldly come before the Throne of Grace. This is not boldness on any merit within us; it is boldness based on our identification with Jesus who shed His Blood that we might live in righteousness before God.

While the human high priest of the line of Aaron and lineage of Levi only served a short time before his mortal demise, Jesus is The High Priest and Mediator forever unto those who come to God through Him.

We, the humble Christian of the New Birth, have a right superior to that of even the high priest of the Levitical system. We do not wait for any special Day of Ceremony. We are allowed access to the Heavenly Holy of Holies as we daily approach Him in prayer and fellowship.

The Self-Sacrifice of Jesus in the New Testament of His Blood has given the world the blessing which was promised in the Abrahamic Covenant. The entire world has been blessed by the line of Abraham.]

10.20 *By a new and living way, which he hath consecrated for us, through the veil, that is to say, his flesh;*

[We miss the significance of this verse in the English. The Word "new," is "Prosphatos" (4372 in Strong's). It is a compound of two words; the first word is "Pro."

This is 4253 in Strong's and means "In front of, or before.) The last part of the word is "Sphazo" which is 4253 in Strong's. The meaning is to butcher or slaughter an animal for food or sacrifice.

On the Day of Atonement the high priest would enter, through the veil, into the Holy of Holies to sprinkle the blood of the sacrifice upon the mercy seat. This had to be warm blood which was considered to still have the value of life in it. Cold, or coagulated blood could not be used. Thus, we are shown that the Blood of Christ is ever available as effective for the remission of sins. His Blood is "New," Blood that can never lose effectiveness as giving The remission of sins to those who call upon His Name. His Blood is the ever living Way to salvation from our sins and reconciliation with God.

Notice that He has "consecrated" this Way on our behalf. The tabernacle utensils were simple objects made of precious metals and of wood. Even these needed to be ceremonially cleansed in order to be dedicated to their task. This "Way of the Cross" whereby we find salvation through His Blood is a way which has been consecrated as the means of our salvation and sanctification. The ascension of Jesus back into the Heavenlies stands as the proof from God, The Father, that Jesus is the Way to Salvation. The Self-Sacrifice of Jesus on the Cross is testimony that Jesus, Alone, is the Truth of Salvation. The ascension, as Jesus returned to Heaven as our eternal Savior and Mediator, gives evidence to both His Eternal Life and our pledge from Him that we will also enjoy the bliss of eternity with our Savior.

Paul compares the veil to the flesh of Jesus. It is very instructive to note that at the very moment that Jesus died, in His humanity, upon the cross that the veil of the Temple was torn in half from top to bottom. The purpose of that veil was to serve as a barrier between the Holy Place, where only the priests were allowed to minister, and the Holy of Holies, where only the high priest was allowed to enter once a year on the Day of Atonement. The Holy of Holies was considered as the presence of God.

That this veil was torn from top to bottom is a picture that this was of God's doing and not of man's.

Under an ancient rabbinical symbolism, the Tabernacle was said to represent the entire universe of man. The outer court was considered as the domain of all humanity. Going into the Tabernacle within the Tabernacle, the tent which contained the Holy of Holies, the first room would correspond to the righteous of the earth. The second room, the Holy of Holies, was the presence of God. With this symbolism in mind we can easily see that the pious Jew to whom Paul was writing would understand that Jesus was that veil in His humanity.

As the physical veil of the tabernacle was drawn back by the high priest on the Day of Atonement, the high priest entered into the presence of God.

John 1:18 says, "No man hath seen God at any time; the only begotten Son, which is in the bosom of the Father, he hath declared him." By coming to live among men, as a man, Jesus allowed humanity to gaze upon God. In the pages of Scripture we are allowed to see the compassion and love of God as displayed in Jesus. The Veil of the Flesh of Jesus has given us a glimpse inside the Holy of Holies in order that we might see the reality of God.

There is more. The flesh, humanity, of Jesus was given as sacrifice for us that we might enter into that Holy of Holies and fellowship with The very God of Creation. Through the Self-Sacrifice of Jesus on the Cross, we are given the promise of full

HEBREWS: Chapter 10

salvation from our sins and our nature of sin. We are not perfect, of course, but we are allowed to stand in His Perfections as the adopted children of God.

Whereas the Mosaic Law had demanded death of the innocent victim of the animal of creation, the New Testament of the Blood of Jesus has seen the one time Self-Sacrifice of the Savior. He does not lead into death but into life abundant and eternal.

We have the benefit of a New Covenant of life because of His death. We have the benefit of a New Covenant of joy in the Lord as He removes the burden of sin from our lives and conscience. We have the benefit of a New Covenant of purpose as He has called us to walk with, and work for, Him in that newness of life. We have the benefit of a New Covenant of hope and expectation as we look for His Second Appearing. We have the benefit of a New Covenant of eternal anticipation as we are in a journey to the Promised Land of an eternal and blissful life with Him in Heaven. We have the benefit of a New Covenant only because of the Love and Sacrifice of The Savior. We are not worthy of His Love.]

10.21 *And having an high priest over the house of God;*

[It is interesting that Paul uses another word for high priest in this place than he has used previously in the Book of Hebrews. Previously Paul has used "Archiereus" (749 in Strong's). This is another compound word made from "Arche" (746 in Strong's) which means "magistrate, power, principality, principle." When compounded with "Hiereus" (2409 in Strong's), which means "priest," the meaning is "high priest."

Here Paul uses "Megas" (3173 in Strong's) which means "exceedingly, Great(est), high, large, loud, mighty." When combined with Hiereus the concept goes beyond simply a high priest and points to a Great High Priest. Since Paul is speaking of Jesus in this verse I should say "The Great High Priest" rather than simply "a Great High Priest." The point is that Jesus, even when simply considering His Office as High Priest, is exceedingly far above in the dignity and power of His High Priesthood over and above the simple high priest of the Levitical priesthood. Jesus is All; the others are mere shadows of He Who is Messiah, Prophet, Priest and King.

The term "house of God" does not refer to any specific "church" building or assembly; the reference has to do with the Church of the Ages, or all the people of God. With that context we can also argue that, in a specific sense, the meaning would include each individual church – and each truly saved individual of that assembly – each must see Him as the Head of their lives and congregations.

I do know that not every person who has been saved by the Blood of the Lamb has united with a local church. Except in very unusual situations where there is no local assembly available with which to unite, this person has chosen to ignore the headship of Christ in their lives. We cannot claim to be a follower of Jesus and yet refuse to accept the very institution He established.

Make no mistake; Jesus is still the Head over that person. That person stands, in a spiritual sense as a private who has decided to disobey the lawful commands of his general in the army. That particular Christian is derelict in his duty to His Heavenly Commander. At some point, in this life or the next, punishment will fall upon the head of the unruly soldier of the Lord.

As head of the church, I speak here of a local assembly, Jesus presides over the church. We have no license to preach morality, politics, conduct or anything else except in the context of the Message of the inspired and preserved Scripture. Our opinions, and even our convictions, are of no consequence. It is always the Words of God which must be the entire basis of our Message and teaching.

I was going to say "centerpiece of our Message and teaching." I would have been wrong. The concept of "centerpiece" suggests that there is more available. There is nothing available beyond the inspired and preserved Scripture.

I would like to explain why I capitalized the word "Message" above and did not capitalize "teaching." Message pertains to the Words of God. We ought always to strive to preach only that which God has given us. Since that has immediate context with Deity, I capitalized. Teaching would apply to local and time-centric application.

In the eighth chapter of I Corinthians Paul addresses an issue that had specific application to a specific local. His specific teaching at that place may not be applicable to all times and all situations. However, the Spiritual Principles underlying that teaching is always applicable to all Christians in all times and places. We ought to never do anything which would bring discredit upon the Lord and His grace. Some of the worldly "street gangs" will dress is specific colors or manner of wearing their clothing in order to identify with their gang. We ought always to act in such a way and dress in such a way so as to identify as a member of the band of Christ Jesus.

As head of the church Jesus will protect His Church. I see a time coming very soon in my own nation when the fires of persecution of the people of God will burn very hot. Already legal sanctions are being brought against Christian people who do not wish to take part in the sin of others. It seems as though the judicial system in many places has decided that the Constitutional protection of the free exercise of religion does not apply to those who would hold to certain Biblically based convictions. A leading political candidate for the President of the U. S. has declared that she expects us to adjust our belief system to take current politics into account rather than continue in the "old paths" of Biblical realities. Christian beliefs are regularly pilloried in courts, educational establishments, entertainment, public opinion pieces in newspapers and magazines and the general public which is *served* by these elements of our *pluralistic* society. Sadly, this is even happening in many of the churches which purport to name the Name of Christ.

Even our Constitution has been turned on its head. No longer are we to be allowed the free exercise of our religious beliefs; instead those who demand that there be total freedom from all religious expression are highlighted as offended and deserving of protection.

There will be more, and more severe, prosecutions of persecution to follow. The program of God will continue as God will give us ability to withstand assaults and witness to the sublime fact that Jesus Christ died in time so even those that seem to hate Him could live in eternity. "But go ye and learn what that meaneth, I will have mercy, and not sacrifice: for I am not come to call the righteous, but sinners to repentance." (Matthew 9:13)

As head of the church Jesus has promised perpetuity to His Church. The promise of Matthew 16:18 still stands. "And I say also unto thee, That thou art Peter, and upon this rock I will build my church; and the gates of hell shall not prevail against it."

The saints of old worshiped God in the catacombs. There in the catacombs was a place sanctified to the word and worship of God. They continued to preach, a small and persecuted band, until the Words of God were heard throughout the world. Man and his governments of persecution reign for a short time in contrast with the Lord of Glory Who will Reign Forever even as He now reigns within the hearts of the believers.

As head of the church Jesus has promised to populate His Church. Acts 2:47 gives us a picture of the early church. "Praising God, and having favour with all the people. And the Lord added to the church daily such as should be saved."

We see a small and dwindling fellowship in our day. Could it be that we have lost favor with the people because we have lost favor with God. Our churches have all too often become entertainment centers. Folks, we are not to be in competition with the world's amusements. We are to be in contemplation of Heavens abundance.

The size or growth of our congregations is not an issue. The size and growth of our spiritual vitality is an issue. We have a need to heed the Words of the Psalmist. "But it is good for me to draw near to God: I have put my trust in the Lord GOD, that I may declare all thy works." (Psalm 73:28)

Jesus is The High Priest to those who have trusted in Him for salvation. He pleads and mediates for us before The Father. He shows compassion on us as we fall before Him in adoration and praise. He upholds us by His eternal care and Word. He saves us into an eternity of bliss by the power of His Blood.]

10.22 *Let us draw near with a true heart in full assurance of faith, having our hearts sprinkled from an evil conscience, and our bodies washed with pure water.*

[From this is argued by some that either washing or sprinkling is a valid form of baptism. The imagery, however, has to do with a total consecration of our hearts. We are enjoined to both the sprinkling and the washing of our bodies. But, notice the very next verse where we are informed that this is symbolic of faith. This is an appeal to accept all that God has given to us as a gift given to empower and lead.

Having our "hearts sprinkled" is an allusion to Numbers 19:9. In this place there was a command to sacrifice a red heifer. The particular sacrifice was conducted outside the camp. (Numbers 19:3) The cow was to be then burnt completely. The ashes of this sacrifice were to be collected and mixed with water. This water mixed with ashes was called "a water of separation." It was considered as a purification for sin.

Notice that it was not called a sacrifice for sin but was a purification for sin. The purpose was to cleanse the ceremonially unclean so they could enter into the tabernacle worship.

What I see as the application for this day is a confession of, and a departure from, sin in the life of the person who has already experienced salvation. The point being made is that we are not perfect in any way. We have flaws over which we must gain the mastery in order to be useful for God. This is not working *for* but working *within* our salvation.

"For God hath not given us the spirit of fear; but of power, and of love, and of a sound mind." (II Timothy 1:7) The will of the mind being turned toward the things of God, which is settled on prayer and the perusal of His Words, will cast out fear and give us the power to love even the unlovely. This will lead to an increased desire to be faithful to the work which God has given to us. We will begin to depart from sin and direct our steps toward the Lord's will.

God desire is that there be a separation from sin and things sinful. Our worship will be sweeter and even more fruitful as we hold to the things of God and dismiss the things of this world.

The Mosaic Law seemed to always say, "No." It was a Decalogue of "thou shalt not." Grace seems to always say, "Yes." We can approach God in worship. We can serve Him; we are all priests before Him in the service of worship. (I Peter 2:9)

Paul asks that we draw near with a true heart. We have salvation from sin by the Blood of Christ. This should give us full assurance of our ability to approach the Throne of God in prayer and supplication. We are His adopted children. He will not withhold that good thing we need. He may well tarry in the application so that we will consider the greatness of His gifts or to remove us from that allure to the things of the world which so easily enrapture our natural eyes.

Paul also says to draw near in full faith. It is our faith in the Blood of Christ which allows us to come before God. We are not able to come of our own accord but of His salvation which He has given to us.

Paul asked that we come with hearts sprinkled from an evil conscience. We have alluded to the purpose of sprinkling as symbolized by the ashes of the red heifer in Numbers 19:9. It is this separation from the things of the world. (consider I John 2:15-17) We also need to have an ecclesiastical separation from the things of false religious systems. We cannot attempt to take the purposes of false religion and make them seem to be proper. (II Corinthians 6:17)

A word of caution must be given at this point. While we must separate from the uncleanliness of false religious systems, we must do so in love. Those who are bound up in the slavery of false religion have chains about them which are not easily broken. Prevailing prayer is a necessity with these. Indeed, we are asking for a miracle from God when we pray that such as these depart from darkness to come to the Light of the World.

Paul asked that we come to God with bodies which have been washed in pure water. This is not speaking of true Christian baptism. Baptism can never remove sin. True Christian baptism applies only to the one who is already a Blood bought believer in Jesus Christ.

I believe that people need to be baptized soon after conversion. This is Biblical! At the first church I pastored, a teen-age boy accepted Christ. I wanted to take him immediately out to the creek where we did baptisms. The head deacon wouldn't let me do it. He said that the creek was swollen by rain and was running so fast it would not be possible. Both the boy and I would have probably been swept away by the current to our deaths.

I wonder how many people have been baptized with the thought in their minds that this would save them from their sin. No one who has not already become a Christian believer should ever be baptized. The current of that mistake could sweep them into everlasting torment.

The allusion at this place is to those many ceremonial washings of the Law. These were made to make a person ceremonially clean for tabernacle worship. Again, baptism does not make us clean for worship. Trust in Christ does this.

Christian baptism is a testimony that a person has been made clean, already, by the death, burial, and resurrection Jesus. I believe that this makes it easier for one, who has publically stated his faith in Christ, to continue his witness in other areas of his life.]

10.23 *Let us hold fast the profession of our faith without wavering; (for he is faithful that promised;)*

[Let us hold fast to our faith - it is our relationship with the Author of the Universe.

Let us be very clear on this subject. Paul is not talking about losing salvation. His entire argument on this and the next few verses is that God holds our salvation. He made a promise based on the Blood Self-Sacrifice of Jesus on the Cross. Unless we are willing either disbelieve that God is faithful in keeping His promises, or that we are stronger than He and can override His promises, we cannot lose our salvation.

We recently had a new lock put on a door where I live. My grandson lost his key. Does that mean that the lock is no longer functional? Of course not. The lock still works; my grandson cannot access the intended purpose of that lock.

It is the same situation with our salvation. It is there because the Blood of Jesus has the power to install it within our hearts. We may, through sin or the pleasures of the world, not "feel" the power of that salvation but it is still there. What God has applied no mere man may remove on his own volition.

The disciples had a problem in this area. Jesus said that He was leaving and they were afraid that their relationship with Him would no longer exist. Jesus said, "Let not your heart be troubled: ye believe in God, believe also in me. In my Father's house are many mansions: if *it were* not *so,* I would have told you. I go prepare a place for you. And if I go and prepare a place for you, I will come again, and receive you unto myself, that where I am *there* ye may be also." (John 14:1-3)

Read the next few verse in John. You will find that Thomas was worried that Jesus might be mistaken in all this. Did the doubt of Thomas change the outcome of the purposes of Jesus? Of course not! This same spiritual principle is in effect as regards your salvation. Once salvation has been accomplished in the power of Jesus – salvation is never accomplished in our own power – that salvation is eternally secure. It is made so by the power and upon the honor of God.

Since God is so faithful to us, it would behoove us to remain as faithful to Him as much as it is within our ability to do so. It is an understanding of this faithfulness toward us which He displays which will encourage us in all things as regarding our profession of faith.

The word "profession" of our faith means our confession of faith. That is, the fact of our salvation in Christ. I want to use the word in another sense. I do not believe that this does any violence to the meaning.

Profession is often used to describe the type of work a person does. My last "outside" job was as a pizza delivery person. My health problems did not let me do much work outside of the church and my writing. I figured that I could sit down between deliveries and it would make it easier for me to do the work. I had forgotten that some people live on the 2nd and 3rd floor! Since that time my disability from the military has "kicked in" and I no longer even try to work in the work-a-day world. Also, since I am on a military disability I really do not need the money from a secular vocation. With so few jobs available in this day it would be wrong for me to take one and deny another that opportunity.

We need, not just the "church employed" but every single soul saved by the Blood of the Lamb of God, to make this dedication to Christ a profession and treat it as a daily occupation.

Paul has spent much time in explaining that we have better promises with Christ than were available under the Old Covenant. His promises are, indeed, full, complete and wonderful.]

10.24 And let us consider one another to provoke unto love and to good works:

[Let us provoke one another. Did you ever see two kids provoking one another? They are trying to get a reaction. Now, normally it is a bad reaction for which they are searching, one that will get the other child into some sort of trouble. That is the sin nature at work.

Christians should have our grace nature at work! Provoke your preacher next service! Tell him that you appreciate the work that he does for God! You'll be surprised what a better preacher he becomes.

Provoke your Sunday School teacher. Provoke your kids. Provoke your parents. Just be out there provoking one another in the Lord! The other person will feel better for it. I wouldn't be a bit surprised if they even returned the provocation!

Wouldn't that be nice!

Besides, God said to provoke them. You will be doing His Will. Not a bad plan!

The idea is to think well of others. I live right across the street from the "low income" apartments which are, colloquially called, "the projects." In the minds of many, such residence is an indication of people who might not be considered as "good."

As a long time residence near this complex I can say that some of the best people, in the natural, live in "the projects." These are people who have problems of their own. They understand that you might have just a few problems yourself. They are easy to get along with and they are easy to love. That is what Paul has in mind here. Consider the problems of the other people and try to make their day just a little easier. Show them the concept of "love thy neighbor" just as Jesus said to do.

Preaching to people is easy. Loving them is the profession of the Christian who has really chosen to follow Christ.]

10.25 Not forsaking the assembling of ourselves together, as the manner of some is, but exhorting one another: and so much the more as ye see the day approaching:

[I like to use the illustration of my military duty as an example of a church. When I arrived in South Viet Nam in the fall of 1968 I was assigned to a unit of the 4th Infantry Division. In the sense of the etymology of the word, we were a "church." We were a group of men who had been "called out" of the general population of our nation (the Draft was still in force at the time) and assigned a very specific purpose. We were to prosecute a war to the best of our ability.

When Jesus saves our souls, we are called out of this world. We are to unite with a local group of believers for a specific purpose. We are to build one another up in the Lord and to seek the lost that they may also find like salvation.

Many propose that they may gather alone in "The Cathedral of the Pines" and be engaged in Biblical worship. This cannot be done! Besides the meaning of the word "church," which tells us that we are to be part of an "assembly," or a group, this passage specifically tells us not to fail to "assemble together."

No matter how "spiritual" it might seem for one to crawl off by himself, he cannot worship God when he is out of God's will. God's will is for us to assemble together in local churches.

Now, this doesn't preclude that we should get off by ourselves to commune with Him. It does mean that we must return to the assembly to be in true fellowship with Him according to His commandments.

Again, we are commanded to exercise a fellowship one with another. That's church attendance! We also need to note that this is not salvation; the sacrifice of Jesus on Calvary is the basis of our salvation. Our fellowship, one with another, is a response, our love returned to Him, to that great salvation.

Clarke argues that persecution has kept these people from gathering as a full group so they are now meeting in small groups. Persecution will come which may cause us to abandon our large church buildings. Nevertheless, we can worship with just three or four. The important thing is that the Lord be at our meetings together to worship Him. (Matthew 18:20) He will be! Again, He has promised and does not renege on His promises.

In some ways I might agree with Clarke in his assertion. But, considering that this was a letter writing to a larger group of believers, I do have some hesitation. It was, as were so many of the letters of Paul, a circular letter made for being viewed by all the churches rather than just the one to whom it might have been addressed; either view is reasonable.

Why would there be people who did not wish to attend the meetings. One could be, in our time, a disagreement with the pastor. Doctrinal disagreements could mostly be resolved by a meeting with the pastor to discuss them. The pastor could explain his convictions from the Scripture.

Some would say, "I can't do that. After all, he is a trained professional." Folks, if you have a problem you can look into the same text book which that pastor uses. Search out your problem areas and God may even convince you of an error on your own part. Surprisingly, the Living Book of Scripture just might change your own attitude even in disagreement. God can bring His adopted children together – or to the woodshed!

There might also have been people who feared persecution. This was beginning to be a real problem in the Roman Empire. The powers that be did not see the doctrine of the church as a good thing. Persecution comes when society rebels against God. Sin tends to separate people into their own "ghetto" apart from the freedom of Christ.

Also, things were getting rather worrisome in Jerusalem. Less than a decade after this Book of Hebrews was written came the destruction of Jerusalem by the Roman legions. Many Jewish persons were taken prisoner and sold into slavery.

"And we know that all things work together for good to them that love God, to them who are the called according to his purpose." (Romans 8:28) The Church has always flourished in persecution. We cannot always see the purposes of God; He always is able to see us in our need. He supplies what we lack even in tribulation. Paul understood tribulation but used that for the Glory of God. It is an easy thing to say, a hard thing to endure, but if we really have our eyes on Christ we can consider that a few days of persecution in this life is but a microscopically small down payment for the bliss and glory of Heaven for eternity.

My wife used to say that she was really not thrilled with the prospect of her own death. But, she did know that God gave a "dying grace" to those in need. They had no need of this beforehand. Linda was so calm and serene in her final illness that even the doctors were amazed. One of them contacted a newspaper about fifty miles from our home. That newspaper sent a reporter all the way to our home to interview her. The next day Linda's testimony of a lack of fear in the face of certain death covered nearly the entire back page of the first section of that newspaper.

It was not an easy assignment which God gave to her. It was an assignment which she accepted to His glory and her memory among family and friend.

The approaching day could have been the day of the next meeting of the local assembly. It could have been the day of the destruction of Jerusalem. My sense is that this Day was the coming Day of the Lord's second appearing where He would call us out of this world prior to a time of tribulation. It could also have been the Day of the Lord's second coming where the Messianic Kingdom will be set up for the one-thousand-year reign of Jesus on the Throne of David.

Whichever day is meant, we have the assurance that God is in charge. May we meet together to strengthen one another in Him as we give Him the sacrifice of joy in worship.]

10.26 *For if we sin wilfully after that we have received the knowledge of the truth, there remaineth no more sacrifice for sins,*

[There are two ways to consider this verse. I find both are valid and neither does any violence to the words of the apostle. Neither would see a true Christian "sinning himself out of grace." Such a consideration would be anathema to the concept of salvation by the power of Christ. If Jesus is the "Author and Finisher of our faith," (Hebrews 12:2) if our salvation is not in any way of our own works, (Ephesians 2:8-9) if we are kept by the Power of the Holy Spirit, (Ephesians 4:30) then it is not possible that we could renounce – even if we should try – the power of God unto true Salvation. We will certainly find Divine discipline meted out toward us in such a case (Proverbs 3:12; Hebrews 12:6) but we cannot find any abrogation of our salvation.

The lack of chastisement over sin is an indication that one is not an adopted child of God. (Ephesians 1:5; Hebrews 12:8)

The first consideration of this verse is that it be applied to those who are feigning salvation or who are trusting in a cultural Christianity rather than in the true salvation which is in Christ. For the most part these "cultural Christians" are deceiving themselves. They are acting in a way that is consistent with the salvation of those around them in a local church. They may look the part; they may even "talk the part" as they seem to "walk the walk," but they cannot point back to a time when they received the Lord as Savior. There is no true commitment in their past nor is there any time when they have found that "hour of decision" when they trusted Christ as Savior.

The "living sacrifice" of a Christian walk will save no one. There is but One Sacrifice for sin. That is the Self-Sacrifice of Jesus on the Cross of Calvary.

There were those in the congregation to which Paul had written who had learned of Messiah, Jesus, and understood that He was the culmination of the entire Jewish system of sacrifice and ceremony. They were enamored of the thought. But, they were also bound up in the concept of those sacrifices of the animals of creation and the ceremonial displays of their native religion. Sadly, they would be able to find no sacrifice for sin in the Old Covenant. With the coming of the New Testament of His

Blood, those sacrifices and ceremonies of the Old Covenant had lost what power they had once held. The only influence these displays of the Old Covenant held was upon the memories and emotions of people who held to the things of this earth and could not divorce their emotions from the formal display of religion and to the powerful realities of the Spirit. Rejecting the Self-Sacrifice of Jesus there was no other sacrifice which was available.

While all of this is true, I do not believe that this is the meaning of the passage in question. The same general scenario was discussed in Hebrews 6:1-4. At that place Paul has spoken of "those." He did not make an effort to include himself in with this group of non-Christians. Here, however, Paul uses the term "we." He includes himself among the group he is discussing.

Paul says that if "we" – himself included – willfully sin... At this place Paul is describing sin in the life of a Christian. He is not speaking of simple slights and "oops." He is discussing true and willful sin. He is speaking of sins committed which are not casual. These appear as premeditated and purposeful actions of known sin in the life of the Christian.

Some have applied these sins to the great persecutions afflicting Christians in that age. The argument is that persecutions were so severe as to cause Christians to renounce their faith to save their lives. I do see this as possible; but, I see this as too limiting. I do believe that this speaks of sin in the life of a Christian. The general text can support no other context.

This seems to leave us with a problem.

We must always remember that our Salvation has saved our souls even unto the thought and will of the natural man. This would include the eternal existence of the inner man. Our mortal bodies await a further "refining" whereby even our mortal is made fit for our heavenly existence in eternity.

I would quote I Corinthians 15:47-54 – "The first man *is* of the earth; earthly: the second man is the Lord from heaven. And as we have borne the image of the earthly, we shall also bear the image of the heavenly. Now this I say, brethren, that flesh and blood cannot inherit the kingdom of God; neither doth corruption inherit incorruption. Behold, I shew you a mystery; We shall not all sleep, but we shall all be changed, In a moment, in the twinkling of an eye, at the last trump: for the trumpet shall sound, and the dead shall be raised incorruptible, and we shall be changed. For this corruptible must put on incorruption, and this mortal *must* put on immortality. So when this corruptible shall have put on incorruption, and this mortal shall have put on immortality, then shall be brought to pass the saying that is written, Death is swallowed up in victory."

There are two things I would argue from this passage in I Corinthians. First, this Corinthian passage is speaking of the Second Appearing of Christ for His Own in the Rapture of the saints. Second, we are saved body, soul and spirit by the Blood of Jesus Christ. Our soul and spirit immediately go to be with Christ (Philippians 1:21) upon the moment of our earthly demise.

Our bodies, however, are of the clay of the present creation. Although the salvation from the eternal realm has touched that of our eternal soul and spirit – as given humanity in the Breath of Life spoken of in Genesis 2:7 – our bodies are part of the present creation and thus stained by sin (Romans 8:22, II Peter 3:10) and reserved to either judgment or revitalization. Since our sins were all judged at the cross we are not subject to further judgment. The passage in I Corinthians speaks of our revitalization.

With this in mind we look at this verse in relation to the sins of the Christian in his physical body. There are certain "life-style" sins which impact upon our earthly bodies. The Christian is not immune to judgment upon his body in relation to these.

My wife died of brain cancer. God could have chosen to save her temporal life. In His Own wise counsels He chose not to do so. He had other purposes for His child in this life and these included her dying testimony.

Others have died, in the natural, because of things done in the flesh. I have been diagnosed with congenital heart failure and other diseases. Some of these, I am morbidly obese, can be directly traced to sinful life choices. God is not obligated to offer me healing for these.

His Arm is not shortened. He can move where He chooses.

The point is that the Christian is not promised a "free pass" from the results of his sin. If anything, the Christian is more responsible than are others for things which directly fly in the face of the God ordained manner in which we ought to live.

In this regard I would note that this particular verse follows the statement which cautions the Christian not to cease being assembled with other believers in services of worship. To do so is a sin. Jesus has established the organization of the Church. To denigrate this organization by our deliberate avoidance is to denigrate Jesus Who founded the Church. This, obviously, is a command to Christians.

Once again, it follows naturally, that this verse speaks to the born-again Christian.]

10.27 *But a certain fearful looking for of judgment and fiery indignation, which shall devour the adversaries.*

[The Geneva Bible Notes make a wise statement that our current governmental and societal powers should well consider: "For it is another matter to sin through the frailty of man's nature, and another thing to proclaim war on God as on an enemy." We cannot make the Biblical claim that we have ever been a "Christian Nation," although the United States Supreme Court has ruled this in the affirmative. Making this claim, and our general cultural claim for many decades, has given us the responsibility to walk in a Christian manner.

Neither can we reasonably make the claim that we are a Theocratic nation although such an appeal is made in our Declaration of Independence. We are not, as was Israel of old, a special people of the Lord in our civic sense. However, the great blessings which God has bestowed upon this nation should have awakened us to the fact of His protecting Hand which we have brushed aside in anger. "Righteousness exalteth a nation: but sin is a reproach to any people." (Proverbs 14:34)

This isn't primarily what this verse is addressing. The verse is addressing Christians who so sin as to invite the chastening Hand of God upon their lives.

The concept of "a certain fearful looking" considers the very act of an expectation of the correcting rod of God upon His erring children. They are not so far away as they might imagine themselves. It is like the well-known atheist who once said, "There is no God and I hate Him." The sinning Christian has within his conscience the dreadful realization that God will punish.

The sixteenth chapter of Numbers carries the sad story of Korah. He along with many others rebelled against the rule of Moses. There was an attempt to change the religion of "the church in the wilderness" to follow another leader. In verse thirty-five of that sixteenth chapter we see fire come down to cleanse the multitude of the sin of this would-be leader.

Each Christian must consider that he carries with him a witness to the fact of Jesus. He may try to flee this reality but it is not possible. His apostasy carries with it the false establishment of a false religious system. In its attempted repudiation of Jesus there is an unconscious establishment of the religion of man centeredness.

There is no judicial punishment due to the Christian, even the erring and worldly Christian. But, there is the punishment of chastisement from The Heavenly Father. We may respond to this chastisement and find it a restorative punishment which reestablishes that relationship of love with the Lord. Or, as was the case of Ananias and Sapphira, and Korah, which resulted in the sin being removed from the camp by the removal of the sinning one.

Korah was an Israelite when he died. I would not comment upon his having any favor with God at that point because I do not believe that there was any favor. He was an Israelite but, in my estimation, he was a spiritually lost Israelite.

As to Ananias and Sapphira, I honestly believe that they died as Children of God. God removed them from the group to spare the group their example of pride and sin. The same is the outlook for the sinning Christian who refuses to abide as worthy of his faith. (consider I Corinthians 11:29-31) The chastisements of God upon His children are made necessary by the fact of His great love for them and for others of the household of faith.

The sinning Christian is an adversary of God due to his misuse of his own testimony for the truth.]

10.28 *He that despised Moses' law died without mercy under two or three witnesses:*

[Paul was making a comparison at this place. He noted the severity of the punishment upon those who despised and rejected the Mosaic Law. This was considered a capital offense. To those who complain about the harshness of the Old Testament punishments we may note that the reality of a trial is shown in the necessity of at least two witnesses to the violation.

Since the Mosaic Law of the Old Covenant has been repeatedly shown to be inferior to the Law of Grace, this severity in the Old Covenant should be seen as a warning against lightly regarding the New Covenant.

If the punishment was great under the inferior system, how much greater must be the punishment for any disrespect toward the superior system and the Lord of that new and superior Covenant? This question must be asked; the New Covenant is established in the New Testament of the Blood of Jesus. To show a disrespect toward the Law of Grace, by for instance rejecting the concept and demanding that any work of man be added to the finished Work of Christ in salvation, is to show disrespect for the Lord and His Great Self-Sacrifice on the Cross. Is not this evidently true?]

10.29 *Of how much surer punishment, suppose ye, shall he be thought worthy, who hath trodden under foot the Son of God, and hath counted the blood of the covenant, wherewith he was sanctified, an unholy thing, and hath done despite unto the Spirit of grace?*

[The over-riding theme of the Book of Hebrews is apostasy and warning against apostasy. The dictionary definition of apostasy is "To abandon one's religious faith..." There are several other definitions, all approximating this one, but this is the one which Paul uses throughout the Book.

There have been several allusions regarding those who have taken the general teaching of Christianity, and have seemingly internalized the message and doctrine, but have stopped short of actually accepting Christ as Savior. This is a serious thing. From personal experience among such as these I have seen this action to be almost an inoculation against ever accepting Christ as Savior. These seem to have come to the brink of salvation and stepped back never to approach the Savior again. These are not beyond recall but there is a need for fervent prayer for their souls if they are ever to be reached with the Gospel.

This does not seem to be the situation in this entire passage. This passage is speaking of those who have come to the Savior but have renounced their faith. These are still saved. They may argue with the concept but they cannot remove themselves from the power and authority of the Lord.

These remain in a dangerous position.

The danger of their situation lies in the fact that they have not removed themselves from the chastisement of the Lord. In their apostasy they have attempted to "trample under foot" the very Lord they should be serving. Their refusal to acknowledge the Lord means that they have placed themselves in a superior position, in their own minds and lives, to Him. The picture of "under foot" is the picture of a conqueror stepping on the neck of a conquered foe.

A person stopped by a police officer does not have to obey that officer. There are consequences in that refusal. This is analogous to the Christian, not just the apostate but any Christian, who has deemed that he will not concede the Lordship of Jesus in his life.

I have accessed the concept of an erring Christian above. The apostate Christian goes far beyond that simplicity of non-compliance with the duties of our Christian walk. While the erring Christian may be "overtaken in a fault," (Galatians 6:1-3) the apostate Christian is actively antagonistic toward the Lord.

To count the Blood of His Covenant as unholy is to count it as profane and ordinary. It is to count the Blood of Christ as no different from any other blood. In this is the concept that Jesus was rightly condemned to the Cross because He had claimed full divinity when He had no right to do so. This is an attitude of disrespect and a despising of the very grace which will continue to call the apostate back to the Lord.

It is a rebellion against this calling of the Lord which causes, often, such a hatred of the Gospel of Christ. This rebellion finds its home in the sins of the self-willed who despises any belief which would question his complete authority over himself. This will often lead one into even deeper sin.

We may note the chastisement of Annanias and Sepphira in the fifth chapter of Acts. Their sin caused their mortal death. The man who despised the Mosaic Law was in danger of death. But, remembering that the Old Covenant is inferior to the New Covenant, coupled with the concept of the great grace which God wishes to bestow on even His unruly children, we see deeper punishments upon the apostate.

Death of our physical bodies seems the greatest punishment. It is not. For the Christian, even for the unruly Christian, death ends all suffering. There is a better world awaiting us in the Heavenlies. Still, our rewards of obedience come from our life on this world. Death ends any possibility of receiving those heavenly rewards. The grace of God will seek to recall the apostate Christian to his rightful place of service.

The chastisement of God may take many forms in the lives of all Christians. For some these chastisements are intended to teach. For all these chastisements are intended to point to our ineffectiveness in this life so that we might draw close to find the all sufficiency of Jesus.

Paul was buffeted by a "thorn in the flesh." (II Corinthians 12:7) Through this Paul learned that the grace of God was sufficient unto him. The same lesson may be learned by the apostate Christian in his return to the Lord. Corporal punishment of the body may come to the apostate Christian as a means of returning him to the Lord.

There is often a mental anguish in the heart of the apostate Christian. He might even long for the sweet fellowship with the Lord which he had once enjoyed. The lack thereof might cause distress as he reposes in his lack of slumber night after night. Such a one may also long for the lost fellowship of the believers. This could well be the reason for his lack of allowing his faith to rise as he attempts to draw other believers down to share his despair.

There is also the real possibility of the untimely death of that apostate Christian. God may "recall" His erring ambassador. God may remove that apostate Christian from this life and this world in order that the testimony of that person not dishonor the picture of the Grace of God in the lives of other Christians. God may remove that apostate Christian from this life and this world in order that the testimony of other Christians may effectively reach out to the lost.]

10.30 *For we know him that hath said, Vengeance belongeth unto me, I will recompense, saith the Lord. And again, The Lord shall judge his people.*

[This verse says, "...The Lord shall judge his people." This is another indication that this passage does speak of an apostate who remains a Christian even in his hatred and derision. God remains the Sovereign even when we disagree with that fact!

This is an allusion to Deuteronomy 32:35-36.

The apostate Christian is an irritation to the Christian community. God has promised to protect His people. The Christian community will be protected, as they themselves continue to trust in the Lord, from the evil influence of the apostate. The idea of vengeance is often rooted in pride, selfishness and prejudice among humanity. God has asked us to forgo vengeance on our own in order that His vengeance, which is based on the Righteousness of God and His Divine mercies and law, may protect us. In this we can learn to trust Him in all cases.

We can compare this passage with Romans 12:19 where Paul accesses the same passage. "Dearly beloved, avenge not yourselves, but *rather* give place unto wrath: for it is written, Vengeance *is* mine, I will repay, saith the Lord." The phrase "give place unto wrath" obviously does not mean to give wrath a place at the table. Leave wrath out on the curb where the Lord may pick it up and deal with it!

Easy to say and hard to do! Who said that it is always an easy thing to follow the Lord? Everyone should say that it is always a very good and proper – and productive – thing to follow the Lord.

In verse 26, above, we discussed that the Christian is not immune to the Spiritual Principle of sowing and reaping. This also applies to the apostate Christian. God will execute either judgment or chastisement upon any who would defame the Lord Jesus Christ.

I used the terms "judgment and chastisement" above for a simple reason. The Christian, even the apostate Christian, has no judgment awaiting him; he does have chastisement from the Lord for his actions – to include the actions of the imagination! Even an earthly father has the responsibility to chastise his children in order to "bend the twig" toward righteousness and usefulness. But, as an earthly father will chastise none but his own, so will God chastise only His Own; those who are fully outside the household of faith can await a fearful judgment from the God of Glory.

We must remember that God is the Offended Party in all sin. His judgment is righteous even as His mercy is without bounds. His judgments on those outside the household of faith are often judgments for the betterment of His people. We see this principle often in the Old Testament dealings of the nations with the people of Israel.

But, remember that Israel, herself, was judged for their sins by use of God's instruments of judgment, Assyria and Babylon. God will also judge, in the sense of chastisement, His people for their sins and other wrongdoings. This is done so that those wayfaring people may return to the Heavenly Land of their Heavenly Father.]

10.31 *It is a fearful thing to fall into the hands of the living God.*

[But, it is a wonderful and precious thing to be held in the Hands of the Living God as we go about His business! The Hands of God are described several different ways in Scripture. When first we are saved it is the Hand of His Love which we feel upon our soul as we respond to the Gospel Message. As we continue on our Christian walk we often find His Hand of Comfort upon us as we follow His leading. Quite often this is accompanied by His Protecting Hand over us as we are engaged in spiritual warfare.

The erring Christian, even the apostate who is truly born again, will often feel the correcting Hand of God as His chastisement comes upon us in order that we would depart from wickedness and return to the full walk of communion with the Lord.

The unsaved world of man will eventually feel the Hand of the Judgment of the Lord lay heavily upon them. Note again, that the true Christian will not find judgment as his sins have already been judged at the cross. None of our sins were committed before the Cross. I John 1:7b reminds us that, "...the blood of Jesus Christ his Son cleanseth us from all sin." We cannot surprise Him; He knew our every action beforehand when He saved us.

The unsaved will find the fearful Hand of the wrath of God within that rightful judgment with vengeance upon sin and sinful humanity.

The unsaved must understand that the vengeance of God is not abated by time; it is eternal as He is eternal. Sin never stops being sin. Sinners never cease to be sinners. Thus, the concept of a purgatory-like Hell where one can suffer a "term sentence" and then find release is not allowable under the justice of The Holy God. Sin must be punished so long as it remains sin.

The Christian, even the apostate Christian, is not under such a sentence. His sins have been judged at the Cross. Still, he has real reason to stand in a fearful place. God, Who will discipline that straying Christian, has all power. It is a realistic fear of this punishment which may cause real repentance, resulting in restoration, within the heart of the sinning Christian. The justice of God demands the discipline of chastisement upon the wayward Christian.

God will never "get tired and walk away" from His commitment to His people. The Old Testament is filled with stories of those who were disciplined due to their sin against God. We find one such example in the life of David. II Samuel 24:1-25 gives the story of a sin of David and the punishment of God upon David.

It would appear that the sin of David was not as much in the census which was taken as was the purpose of the census as there is not found in the Scripture a specific prohibition to the numbering of the people. Even Moses had numbered the people without incident. It seems that either David was exhibiting pride in the number of people he commanded as king, or was seeing what type of army he could raise against the nations around him. This would have evidenced a lack of faith in, or a disrespect of, the Lord and His provision.

This was an early incident in the reign of King David. This is evidenced by the fact that the prophet Gad confronted David over his sin. Nathan is the prophet most generally associated with David after this point.

Whatever the reason it was a thing which displeased God; even Joab, in II Samuel 24:3, seems to understand that this was not a course of action which should be taken. Nonetheless David persisted.

We might note at this place that while the passage in II Samuel suggests that it was the Lord Who influenced David in this matter, the parallel passage in I Chronicles 21:1 says, "And Satan stood up against Israel, and provoked David to number Israel." When we compare these two verses with the first chapter of Job the meaning becomes clear. Satan desired to tempt David in this manner. Since it was within the eternal counsels of God that David be tried in this manner, Satan was given permission to proceed.

This picture brings to mind the incident where Abraham was told to sacrifice Isaac. The concept of human sacrifice was nowhere within the teaching of God. But, this – especially the sacrifice of a child – was well within the tenets of the pagan people among who Abraham was living. Since Abraham knew that Isaac was the son promised by God, this was a test whereby Abraham could prove that he trusted God even to the point of God raising this son to life if need be.

The purpose was not to test Abraham for the sake of God's knowledge of Abraham. It was for Abraham to have himself tested so that he could find the full faith and assurance which was within himself. Such test would give Abraham the confidence to move forward in a trying time.

The test of David seems more to have been in regards to his fitness to rule over the Covenant people of God. The results of the failure of David bring this out. As the God appointed leader of the people, it was those people who bore the immediate burden of the judgment of God in this matter.

It would be good for every pastor called of God to consider the spiritual principle which is brought out by the incident in the life of David. It would likewise be very good if the political leaders of every nation considered their own actions in light of this very same spiritual principle. Sin and wickedness in the life and policy of a leader will cause shame and wretchedness among the population so governed.

Such is also the expected outcome in the lives of others who are influenced by the rantings of the apostate Christian. Sin never occurs in a vacuum. We can recall that in the sin of David with Bathsheba that he, the king of the land, sent for her and then had her husband slain to cover David's own sin.

David chose to include Bathsheba with him in his sin. Uriah, Bathsheba's lawful husband, became a victim of the sin of David.

As to this incident from II Samuel, the 24th chapter, we see an after-the-fact remorse on David's part in verse ten. David (verse 14) was given a choice of punishment for his sin. I believe that this was a further test. David did not choose famine. Seven years of famine would have had a catastrophic effect on the land. This may have even led to revolt and the overthrow of David's kingship. Since David was the God-ordained king, this would have carried the potential of leading the people into further sin.

David did not choose three months of exile. The resultant war would have also caused political turmoil. More importantly, this would have been an abrogation of the responsibilities which God had given to David. If the lesson were truly learned, if repentance was actually made, this would have been to take David from the place of God's leading. This would have had the potential of leading David into further sin as he exited from God's place of service.

David chose the only alternative offered. There would be three days of pestilence among the people. This object lesson of the effects of sin, death and dissolution of even the physical power of mankind in the disease of sin, would be seen by David even as it was felt within the population of the kingdom.

David did not seek to escape from punishment but accepted the chastening Hand of God as the better place to be. He had a debt to pay for his sin. I think it instructive that others paid the price. No person ever sins without the ripple effects of that sin harming others.

We do see, in verse 17, that David repented of his sin and felt the effects of that sin within himself. His plea was to lighten the horror upon the people even if it meant suffering for himself. The remorse of David was real as his repentance was real. The results were nonetheless still felt in others. This was part of the remorse felt by David; he had caused harm upon others.

We see in verse 22-25 that David was willing to pay a price in order to restore himself to the worship of God.

The illustrations which we find from this sin of David give us a view of the meaning of Paul. It is a thing to be feared to fall into the Hand of God because of our sin. But, that fall into His hands can be that which restores the soul of the apostate Christian who is led to repent due to this.

This verse in Hebrews is a warning to fear consequence of our sinful actions

On the converse side, we ought always to give God the fear of reverence. This is not a call to be frightened, but to be respectful of our Lord.]

10.32 *But call to remembrance the former days, in which, after ye were illuminated, ye endured a great fight of afflictions;*

[Paul asks that those tempted to apostasy, in this case returning to their Jewish religion and roots, to think back to the days after they had first been converted. John wrote these words from Jesus to the people at Ephesus: "Nevertheless I have somewhat against thee, because thou hast left thy first love" (Revelation 2:4)

I am reminded of an old joke. An elderly couple was driving down the street when they passed a car that contained a young couple. The wife looked at the spectacle of the young couple sitting so close together and remarked to her husband, "We used to be like that. What has happened?"

As the husband turned into the supermarket parking lot he said, "I don't know. I'm still sitting where I always did."

Why have we moved away from God since those first heady days of our salvation experience? We have become complacent in our Christianity because it has become a comfortable, "old hat," experience. We seem to no longer feel the thrill of the relationship with the Author of the Universe.

Paul asks his readers to think back to those early days of their salvation. There was persecution then. The stoning of Stephan was soon after Pentecost. I believe that the people to whom Paul was writing had experienced the wonder of those cloven tongues of fire and witness of Pentecost. They had joined with others in the joy of Messiah. That early persecution had not separated them from the group. If anything, that persecution was like a glue which held the early church group together.

Have you ever experienced a leaky faucet while trying to sleep at night? The first drop does not discourage from sleep. The second is only a minor annoyance. The third is a reminder that you will need to tighten the faucet in the morning. The fourth has you putting the pillow over your head to drown out the noise. The fifth causes you to get out of bed so you can try to shut off the water to the sink. When that doesn't work you reason that it is just a small noise which you can ignore. The next drop drives you to prayer! ...or to despair!

Persecution is like that drop of water. At first you gladly back into the ropes so you can fight back. But, eventually you are worn down. The only defense is to hide in the Lord. Prayer over His Word helps. Only that can restore the ability to suffer persecution for the Lord.

There, however, are always those self-made men who maybe have even been saved; they may have never released themselves to the Lord. They have never made the trek to the Master Plumber Who alone can give us peace in the midst of the night of persecution.

It is these that concern Paul. He cares about the rest but these are those who have not the closeness to the Master to shield them in the time of storm – or of leaky pipes of persistent persecution. These are those who will walk away from the banquet table of the love of God and then complain of hunger for fellowship.

The argument of Paul is that all, but especially these, need to return to the faith which they have nearly forgotten. They know where it is they need to be; that is an address underlined in the address book of their soul. Go back to the side of the Savior. Take part in worship with the fellowship. "The LORD is my rock, and my fortress, and my deliverer; my God, my strength, in whom I will trust; my buckler, and the horn of my salvation, and my high tower." (Psalm 18:2)]

10.33 Partly whilst ye were made a gazingstock both by reproaches and afflictions, and partly, whilst ye became companions of them that were so used.

[Clarke has argued that many of the early churches of the Judean area would react to the persecution of one member by standing by that member in proclaiming that they, too, were believers in Messiah. This would put those people in danger, of course; but, it also gave great comfort to all.

That the Christians were reproached is beyond question. The term "gazingstock" means that these Christians were exposed as a theater to the masses. We remember the mention of the crowds around the Cross upon which Jesus was crucified. We remember the crowds through which He was forced to walk on His way to that execution. Criminals, or those considered as criminal, were often treated as public spectacles for the masses. This was a means both of cruelty toward the accused and of warning to others who might think to act likewise.

The Christians were held up to ridicule. Insults, taunts, cruel jokes and physical abuse were a common part of the persecution. What is wonderful is that other Christians would seek to encourage the persecuted believer by taking part with him on such occasion. This companionship of the fellowship was a comfort in an uncomfortable situation. It was Church acting in love one toward another. This was a love centered in Jesus at all times.

The Christian community would offer not only fellowship but also sustenance to those who were imprisoned for their faith.]

10.34 *For ye had compassion of me in my bonds, and took joyfully the spoiling of your good, knowing in yourselves that ye have in heaven a better and an enduring substance.*

[Paul spent some time in bonds in Jerusalem. He spent over two years under ward to a centurion, prison, in Caesarea. There were no prison cooks or laundries. There was no "health" component among the prisons to supply clothing and such. These had to be supplied by the friends of the prisoners. Apparently, it was these people who did so for Paul as he witnessed for Jesus among the inmates and guards.

It is probable that there were more imprisoned for the cause of Christ at this time. These Christians supplied the needs of other Christians.

It was also a fact of life for the Christian that there would be plundering of their own homes because they were Christians. This is suggested in Acts 8:3 concerning Saul before his own conversion and assumption of the name of Paul.

This verse says that the people suffered this "spoiling" of their goods. They suffered it joyfully. This would have given them joy in the obvious illustration that they were the children of God. This sort of persecution gave evidence of their faith among others.

Their joyfulness at such plundering of their possession was assuaged by their understanding of their possession of salvation. Their heavenly possessions were better than any earthly positions; those heavenly possessions were also eternal. No one could steal that which was kept in the Heavenlies.]

10.35 *Cast not away therefore your confidence, which hath great recompence of reward.*

[When an ancient soldier was afraid for his life he might toss away his shield so he could run away faster. In the main this did not save his life because this was a capital offense among the armies. In the Greek Spartan army the "better part of valor" was not to throw the shield away and run; it was to be brought home on the shield if necessary.

Several commentators made that connection with "confidence." They saw the phrase as speaking against renouncing faith and removing salvation from oneself. But, if tossing away the shield placed one under the military condemnation of a death sentence, this particular interpretation must be found lacking. Tossing away the shield would not relieve one of his duties as a soldier; it would only relieve him of his life as even the coward remained a soldier.

The word confidence means confidence. The call is to be strong and brave. We have no need to fear the world. Dr. Kirk DiVietro went to Iraq soon after the war started in the early part of the new millennium. He was attacked by terrorists. When asked if he would return should God call him to so, the reply was, "Of course. You can't scare me with Heaven."

With the probability of real persecution becoming more evident in our nation with each passing year we have the option to be really frightened. We also have the option of continuing to trust in the Lord. That is not only our reasonable service to Him; that is our duty as soldiers of the Cross.]

10.36 *For ye have need of patience that after ye have done the will of God, ye might receive the promise.*

[We have all heard the plaintive cry of modern man: I want patience and I want it NOW! Sorry, folks, this isn't the promise of God. God has promised us that persecution is that which produces patience within the life of the Christian. (Romans 5:3; James 1:3)

We are enjoined to "Thou therefore endure hardness, as a good soldier of Jesus Christ." (II Timothy 3:2) No one should simply decide to live a victorious Christian life. That is the wrong goal. We are called to please the Master. That will result in a victorious Christian life. To attempt to live that life on our own terms is an impossibility. It is true that God furnishes us grace in this life which we are to access and live within. But – this is important – any time we attempt to be "spiritual" without the humility of submission to the Lord, we are working in ourselves.

Still, we do strive to please the Lord by obeying His instructions to us. It would be ludicrous to do otherwise! He has asked that we be patient. We are to be patient in doing well. (Romans 2:7; Galatians 6:9; II Thessalonians 3:13; I Peter 4:19) This should not be hard; this should be the outworking of a holy life yielded unto the Lord.

We are to be patient in trusting God even as we suffer persecution for Him. The fact that we are giving our bodies as a living sacrifice unto Him as we suffer persecution (Romans 12:1) is a reasonable service to Him. This is also a reasonable service to our fellows from the race of humanity. They, as they see our calm acceptance of vile persecution, will be more likely led to consider the claims of Christ. This is a most effective witness.

We are to be patient in doing that which He has called us to do. We might well wish, as pastors, for a larger church. Be patient and do the best job that is possible for those people who God has given you to lead. We might well wish for a larger salary. Be patient and spend your life for the Master. That is an investment which cannot fail! We might well wish for better health and vitality. First, as an obese person I can easily make the point that we fail to gain this often because we have failed to follow the instructions for proper human living in the Book of the Author of humanity. Do you think that it is just possible that He might have our best interest in mind when He gives us those instructions? Exercise passion in the Lord's work and find moderation in all else.

Second, recall that Paul prayed for a "thorn in the flesh" to be removed. It would probably have enhanced his physical comfort. Consider that this physical comfort is an inducement to work a little less. Paul had a great gain in this "thorn in the flesh." He learned that the grace of God really is sufficient. (II Corinthians 12:9)

The will of God for this dispensation is that we would accept Jesus Christ as our Savior. When we have acted upon that promise will He has promised us salvation from our sins. We also have the hope, expectation, reality of that which will come, of the return of the Savior. "He which testifieth these things saith, Surely I come quickly. Amen. Even so, come, Lord Jesus." (Revelation 22:20) May this always be our prayer. May we live our lives so that this prayer is heartfelt (I John 2:28) and honest!]

10.37 For yet a little while, and he that shall come will come, and will not tarry.

[There are several possible explanations offered of this verse. The first reaches back to Habakkuk 2:3 where the Jews of Jerusalem are promised deliverance from Nebuchadnezzar. It is true that there was no deliverance from Babylon until the 70 years of prophesied captivity were completed. After this time the people found themselves back in Jerusalem.

But, He Who was to come did not come at that time unless the leaders of the rebuilding of Jerusalem and the Temple are considered in that office. This seems unlikely since the prophecy seems naturally to apply to Messiah. Still, with the concept of a double fulfillment of much of the Old Testament prophecy this could easily apply to the return of Messiah in a time when Rome was soon to destroy the Temple for the second time.

True, Messiah had come and His Own prophecy was of His soon return. (John 16:16) Still, this is a possible interpretation of the passage. There will be a later time of distress for Israel. Jeremiah 30:7 calls this the time of Jacob's trouble. Since the mention of Jacob will normally mean the entirety of the Israelite people, this concept resonates with me.

The time of Jacob's trouble is the same time frame which the Gentile Christians would call The Great Tribulation. For the Israelite of the New Covenant the time of the trouble is seven years. The last one half of this time, which is often called Great Tribulation, comprises about three and one-half years. Add to this that God has promised to "shorten the days" of this time and we could well argue that the time would be short for the Israelite of that period until He Who will come, does come to set up the expected and promised Messianic Kingdom where Jesus sits on the very throne of David.

In this we see the true hope of the pious Jew of history. He looks for the coming of Messiah to set up the Kingdom of David. It is a time of renewal for Jacob's sons.

Some have applied this, I find scant evidence to support this, to the Habakkuk prophecy as speaking of the Destruction of Jerusalem by the Romans in 70 A.D. It seems that in order for the prophecy to have reference to 70 A.D. the "one who should come" would have to refer to Titus and his legions. They are the ones who came at that point. This seems highly unlikely. This would offer no hope or solace to the Jew who was either killed or taken in slavery at that time.

The final argument, which I do accept, is that the Christian hope of the second appearing of Christ in the Rapture is in view. Jesus did say He would soon return. (John 16:16) The argument could be made as to why such a long time has passed when a soon return is promised.

There are two answers to that charge. The first is that the concept of an imminent return is established in such a way. He said that He is coming back "soon." Thus we must be continually on the lookout for that return. The longer He tarries, the sooner His return will take place.

"And saying, Where is the promise of his coming? for since the fathers fell asleep, all things continue as they were from the beginning of the creation. For this they willingly are ignorant of, that by the word of God the heavens were of old, and the earth standing out of the water and in the water: Whereby the world that then was, being overflowed with water, perished: But the heavens and the earth, which are now, by the same word are kept in store, reserved unto fire against the day of judgment and perdition of ungodly men. But, beloved, be not ignorant of this one thing, that one day is with the Lord as a thousand years, and a thousand years as one day. The Lord is not slack concerning his promise, as some men count slackness; but is longsuffering to us-ward, not willing that any should perish, but that all should come to repentance." (II Peter 3:4-9)

As at the crucifixion of Jesus where the very words of His adversaries were the words they were prophesied to utter, the proof of the reality of the event is shown by the very enemies of the event. (see Psalm 22)

In the light of eternity it is only a short time – a little while – between the prophecy and the fulfillment. The purpose of this seeming delay is the Great Grace and Compassion of God. He is "longsuffering to us-ward, not willing that any should perish..." His seeming delay is His Grace delivered to all those who would come to Him and find salvation and peace from the Savior.

I find both the second appearing of Jesus in which He raptures His Own from this world which is soon to be judged, and the second coming of Jesus in which He established His Kingdom from the Throne of David.]

10.38 *Now the just shall live by faith: but if any man draw back, my soul shall have no pleasure in him.*

[The meaning of the verse seems to hinge on the meaning of "just" in the phrase "the just shall live by faith." The word is "dikaios" (1342) in Strong's where the description is: "equitable (in character or act); by implication, innocent, holy (absolutely or relatively):--just, meet, right(-eous)."

The word is used several times in the writing of Paul. He often uses the word to denote an object or ideal as proper and correct. When he uses it of people the application is to those who give every appearance of being redeemed.

A short scan of the Book of Matthew found the same general consensus. I choose Matthew because this is the gospel which is written from a Jewish perspective to Jewish Christians. Since the Book of Hebrews is also written to Jewish Christians, I thought this most proper. The same general application of the word followed the usage of Paul. The only departure from this general theme occurred in Matthew 23:28 where

Jesus addresses the Scribes and Pharisees. "Even so ye also outwardly appear righteous [the same word as "just" from Hebrews] unto men, but within ye are full of hypocrisy and iniquity."

This one verse in Matthew might be used to consider the "just" in Hebrews as either "cultural Christians," not actually born again, or people who are just following the general life-style of Christianity. However, the verse continues that these "just" will "live by faith." Therefore, I find the only possibility is to consider that these are Christians, true born again Christians, being spoken about in the verse.

It must follow that the *"any man"* of the verse must also apply to the "just" who were mentioned. "Any man" must be drawn from that group or we would have the absurdity of claiming that a rank sinner could perform the same act as would a true child of God in relation to a spiritual consideration of living by faith.

Now we come to the question as to what was withdrawn from. The withdrawal is from a life of faith. The first verse of the very next chapter informs us that, "...faith is the substance of things hoped for, the evidence of things not seen." This is what I would call "walking faith." This is our obligation unto God. This is not the same as "saving faith."

Saving faith is that action whereby God redeems our souls as we respond to the wooing of the convicting Spirit Who calls us to Christ. Ephesians 2:8 says, "For by grace are ye saved through faith; and that not of yourselves: it is the gift of God..." I apply that "gift of God" to be the faith which saves us. Others apply this gift to "saved." Either application would argue that our faith in the Blood of Christ, by which salvation is obtained, comes from the Gracious Will of God. It is His Gift to us and is subject to His Power as the Giver of the Gift. Our reception of that Gift has bound us to Him as His adopted children. There is no court whereby we can bring suit to dissolve our relationship with our Heavenly Father. Neither can we "run away from home." As born again Christian we are His.

Ephesians 2:10 tells us, "For we are his workmanship, created in Christ Jesus unto good works, which God hath before ordained that we should walk in them." Even as our salvation was wholly of the Work of God, so is his provision that we should always walk in good works.

This is "walking faith" in which God expects us to actively and purposefully live within the salvation faith which He has given us as a free gift. I don't believe that any could argue that God will force us to do this. But, we do need to understand that this is what He expects of us.

I would submit that this is the faith from which those apostate Christians have removed themselves. They are not living their possession because they have abandoned their profession. It is likely that the persecution of man has caused them to flee from the provisions of God.

I heard a man being interviewed on the radio yesterday. He was asked about his children. He said that there had been a few "bumps" in the road with them but he was still very proud of the way they had turned out in their adult lives.

God is not pleased with the "bumps" in the road of His adopted children. He is grieved (Ephesians 4:30) any time we are not responding to His love toward us. This does not remove the fact that He has sealed us as His. This does mean that He has no pleasure in us as His adopted children. We are saved. We are unfruitful and contrary when we are unruly children of the King.]

10.39 *But we are not of them who draw back unto perdition; but of them that believe to the saving of the soul.*

[Here Paul again uses the "editorial we." By this he identifies himself with the "just" of the previous verse even as the word "but" separates from them. This "we" is another indication that the word "just" does apply to the born again in verse thirty-eight. However, in this verse Paul disassociates himself from those he speaks of in this verse. The "but" describes a better and stronger people. Paul associates himself with those who do exercise a "walking faith." This is because "we" are not like them described in next phrase of this verse.

I believe that this verse has a two-fold meaning. The one has to do with the person who was a "fellow traveler" with the group of Christians. This one was never saved. His "draw back," whether it is from a refusal to accept to abide the persecution which came upon the believers in the Church, or his "natural man" rebelling against the Spirit of God evidenced among the believers, this man was lost. Any rejection of the Grace of God in the Self-Sacrifice of Jesus Christ, to include never accepting that Grace, is to remain in sin and suffer the eternal consequence of such a decision. (John 3:36) This is an eternity of perdition in the strongest sense!

The other meaning has to do with the Christian who apostatized. He is not lost in the sense of the person above. The meaning of "perdition" has more associated than simple (!?) eternal damnation. There are consequences on earth as well. Perdition is "apoleia" (Strong's 684) with the meaning, "ruin or loss (physical, spiritual or eternal):--damnable(-nation), destruction, die, perdition, X perish, pernicious ways, waste."

We have discussed the concept of the child of God being subject to Divine chastisement. Every step away from fellowship with the Lord is a step toward this chastisement. There is another spiritual principle at work in this place. In Matthew 25:41 we are given a picture of the judgment of God. The unrighteous are cast "into everlasting fire, prepared for the devil and his angels." Luke 12:34 speaks of this same spiritual principle. "For where your treasure is, there will your heart be also."

There were apparently those from the assembly to whom Paul wrote who apostatized. Perhaps the persecutions became more than they could handle. They renounced their Lord in order to escape the persecution. There were probably other excuses. The point is that these people loved their old life in Judaism more than their new life in Christ.

Where their heart was, there their feet took them.

Both Eusebius and Epiphanius wrote of the destruction of Jerusalem in 70 A.D. Both note that not a single Christian lost their life in this invasion. They took to heart the teaching of Jesus in regard to this time of the judgment of God upon the city (24th chapter of Matthew) where Jesus had been wrongfully executed. Those who had departed the assembly for the comfort of the Jewish experience were able to feel that experience as God sent His judgement.

Paul included himself in the group that saw the salvation of both soul and body through the grace of God. This spiritual principle is still at work. Even in death our bodies are reserved for renewal and an eternity of bliss with our Great High Priest and Savior. (I Corinthians 15:50-58)]

HEBREWS - CHAPTER ELEVEN

11.1   Now faith is the substance of things hoped for, the evidence of things not seen.

[I'd like you to notice something important about this chapter in Hebrews. Each of these persons so honored was flawed in some way. Noah was a drunkard at one point in his life. Abraham lied about the status of his wife because of fear of others. Rahab, an ancestor - humanly speaking - of our Lord, was a harlot. On and on goes the litany. Moses was, at the first, afraid to return to Egypt to speak with the Pharaoh.

But, each of these persons had one character trait in common. They each yielded to the will of the Lord. They did not always understand, but they did put aside their unworthiness and accept in faith the Word which He delivered unto them.

We can each do the same. There may be many reasons that we can cull from our life experiences to explain that we are unworthy vessels for the majesty and glory of the message of God. Still, God has committed that message to us. We may understand that we are, indeed, sinners who stand far beneath His contempt as moral beings. Yet we can also understand, because the Bible says that it is so, that He loves each of us. We may not understand how it will be so that we will leave this life, this plane of existence, and remove ourselves to another plane of existence in the spiritual realms. But, we can know - because of His Message to us - that these things are so.

We can understand these through the medium of faith.

Notice, also, that Paul is praising the history of Israel. This may seem strange because he had just been warning the people not to drift back into the Jewish religion. The points up another spiritual principle. While we should always follow the leading of the Word which God has given to us in this dispensation, we should understand that God has given us a spiritual example from that earlier dispensation which we can access when we consider that in light of the present teaching He is giving.

The classical illustration is that God has not told us to build an ark. But, in the incident of the ark God has given us teaching which we can use in our day. The teaching of Scripture can never grow so old as to lose its power to instruct and illumine. The Words of God are eternal in that They <u>are</u> His Words. As such those Words are perfect and timeless. They are all for today in way of instruction about the Glories and Attributes of God. The Bible is One Volume for all people for all time.

Faith gives us the reality of that for which we hope and expect. Faith allows us to see that which is unreality to others but is a precious possession of ours. When fully grasped, faith is the antidote and the protection from the apostasy as described in this Book of Hebrews. The Words of God produce a picture of man as he exists. Mankind is a fallen race unable to meet the just standards of The Holy God. God supplies the answer to the problem His Book has illustrated.

I was substitute teaching in a middle school science class one day. My subject was climate change from season to season. I was using the illustration of the same measure of icing being placed on a small cupcake and large sheet cake. The greater warmth of summer is powered by the more direct sunlight of that season. The less warmth of the winner shows the same energy from the sun spread thinner due to the angle of the earth in relation to that winter sun. Before I had finished my lesson one young lady said something to the effect of, "I am here to learn science. I don't care about your food preferences." I said, "Hang with me. Wait until you see where I am going." Let us allow God to give us the full council of His teaching.

Much error is due to concerning only a small portion of Scripture rather than reading, and studying, the entire record God has given us. A "for instance" is that above paragraph. If that one paragraph were highlighted in a review of this work one might be led to assume that this was a paper on cooking, or teaching, but it is well possible that theology would not be considered as the purpose.

Faith in a discourse such as this is a moral conviction that a religious pattern is correct. Paul asks that we consider the nature of true faith in God. He uses example from the Old Testament Scripture to give credence to his thesis. By doing this Paul is not simply arguing for a history of faith; he is arguing for a present need for faith as illustrated from the past by people who were also under either persecution or duress.

The substance of faith is highlighted. The word is "hupostasis." This is 5287 in Strong's. "a setting under (support), i.e. (figuratively) concretely, essence, or abstractly, assurance (objectively or subjectively):--confidence, confident, person, substance." The first meaning has to do with support. That carries the meaning of "foundation." Our religion is built upon the foundation of faith.

Paul also wrote II Corinthians wherein he used the same word to mean "confident" (II Corinthians 9:4) and "confidence." (II Corinthians 11:17) This consideration would inform us that our faith not only is foundational, that upon which our religion is built, but that Christianity is able to give an assurance of its reliability.

In this Book of Hebrews Paul used the same word in verse three of chapter one. "Who being the brightness of *his* glory, and the express image of his person, and upholding all things by the word of his power, when he had by himself purged our sins, sat down on the right hand of the Majesty on high." The word "person" is the same word as used of "substance" in this first verse of the eleventh chapter of Hebrews.

The verse is speaking of Jesus. This particular reference, however, is to The Father. The verse is pointing out that Jesus is equal to, and of the same essence as, The Father. This understanding of Paul's use of the word points out that our faith, the essence and reality of our faith, is not based in anything we might have done, or be. Even that faith which we call our own flows from the Triune God. Faith is not of ourselves in any manner but is a gift from the Lord of our salvation.

We must also note Romans 10:17, "So then faith *cometh* by hearing, and hearing by the word of God." Any faith which is not founded upon the express Words of God is not, then, a Biblical faith. Let us not forget, however, that our testimony – when based on the Words of God and empowered by the Holy Spirit of God, from Whom we have accessed assistance by prayer – will contain that ingredient of the Words of God as presented by us as we have searched the Scripture to find His Words and Will. Still, it is imperative that our witness be leavened with Scriptural quotations in reliance upon the Words of God rather than simply our human opinions.

Human faith can argue that there is a town in New Jersey called "Collingswood." I have never seen this town. I have seen people who claim to be from this town. These are people I trust; therefore, I believe in Collingswood because I believe in them. We have never seen Heaven. Since we have met the Master in Salvation, and have read of Him in inspired and preserved Scripture, we can believe – have faith – that we have a home in Heaven. It is reasonable!

Sadly, the unsaved of the world are not believers. They have no basis to understand any spiritual truth. Our witness must be saturated in the inspired and preserved Scripture so that we can present that Scripture, that faith may come to the unbeliever, as we pray that the Spirit impart the miracle of understanding to those who are incapable of understanding that Jesus Christ died in time so that they could live in eternity.]

11.2 For by it the elders obtained a good report.

[How was it that these patriarchal men and women received a "good report" from God as evidenced by His inspired Words in His inspired and preserved Book? Could it have been their status as elders in their human community? It is obvious that this was not so because the earliest man, Adam, is not mentioned in this list.

Could this have been because of the long years they lived? It is obvious that this is not so because the man who lived the longest of all in the record of man, Methuselah, is nowhere to be found in this list.

Could it be that these had produced some great works of charity or benevolence? It is obvious that this is not so as the works of not one person is praised. What is praised is the exercise of faith in the life of each from this group.

This is the season of report cards from the local schools. Some of the children went home with their cards in joy and pride. Some of the children tried to forge their parents name and hide the cards. The people listed in this eleventh chapter of Hebrews had a good report card based on their faith. ...and on that alone!

Their faith was a trust in God. This was the same faith which has produced our own salvation. These may have trusted the sacrifice of the animals of creation as demanded by the leading of the Lord at this time. This was faith limited to an understanding of God's requirement. In this sense there was no real faith in those animals of creation. The was real faith in the God Who required that sacrifice of those animals of creation.

These people trusted the Words of God. They trusted the goodness of God to keep all of His promises. They trusted God above all. Their salvation was based, even though they could not have understood this fact, on the Self-Sacrifice of Jesus on the Cross of Calvary. That Cross has always been pardon and salvation throughout the ages of man, and will be the same throughout the ages of eternity. (Revelation 13:8)

These pre-Cross persons were counted of a "good report" of righteousness by faith. Faith is not just, as we sing in our churches, "the victory." Faith is salvation from our sins, peace with God, and an eternity of bliss with Him.]

11.3 Through faith we understand that the worlds were framed by the word of God, so that things which are seen were not made of things which do appear.

John 1:3; Ephesians 3:9; Colossians 1:16

[There is an old joke that several scientists approached God's Throne and said, "We have discovered how to make life. We can make a man from the elements of the earth and impart life to him."

God said, "Go ahead."

The scientists began to take their chemicals and pour them into measuring cups when God said, "Not so fast. Make your own 'dirt' like I did in Genesis." The fact is that God, in the Person of Jesus, made the entire universe from nothing except the power of His majesty and Words.

It is sad that we have preachers in this day, even Fundamentalist preachers, who can see the majesty of the created worlds and wax eloquent about the mighty power of God to create and sustain the entire universe but still doubt the power of God to preserve those Words which He has given to His Church. Why would we suppose that God is powerful enough to sustain His creation but not powerful enough to preserve the Words He has given to His people to learn of Him?

In such a case, we cannot even properly speak of an inspired Word from God. If those Words have been lost the inspiration, which was upon those words, has also been lost.

John 1:3 informs us that the Word of God, Jesus, was the Creative Agent of the very creation of God. Therefore, acknowledging the concept that The Father wills and The Son acts, Jesus could be no created being. Since Jesus is The Creative Agent of the Triune Godhead, He is shown to be eternal, not created, in His being and essence.

All things that may be examined were made from that which cannot be examined. From this we must deduce that there is no eternity of natural matter. The very universe, this verse considers all of creation, was created by fiat by the voice of God. God spoke and the universe came into existence out of nothing.

But, there is a deeper meaning to that verse. This would not have been understood by the human penman of Hebrews. All things that are seen are made from things which are not seen. God gave the concept of molecular biology and sub atomic particle construction of all elements some twenty centuries before humanity caught on to the idea.

The Bible is replete with illustrations such as this. Faith is not blind. God does call us to study His Words and works so we can understand Him. Faith is not of the natural. Consider Jonah; his faith was to trust God despite his own understanding which was at variance with the demands of God. Courage, we may well note, is not being brave. It is acting rightly in spite of our fear. So it is with faith. We trust Him even when we might not understand or even agree.

His ways, works and Words can well stand examination. He is Truth in all His manifestations. But, faith is our God ordained foundation of worship.

The ancient religions argued how the world came into existence. This is a very narrow view which focuses upon man. God tells us how the entire universe came into existence. This is an expansive view which indicates the weakness of man. Psalms 8:4 speaks of this. "What is man, that thou art mindful of him? and the son of man, that thou visitest him?" This is not the view one would expect if man were simply explaining "his place in the cosmos."

Rather than suggesting a mythical beginning of the world from a pre-existent entity, the Bible shows a spiritual beginning of all things. The Bible gives a picture of God; He is not from this physical order of being. He stands outside of our natural universe as the Creator of all. The living creatures which we see of the earth always spring from other living creatures of the earth from that first life which God has ordained. All living things presently on earth spring from existing templates provided in the original creation.

The fact that all these elements, living and non-organic are considered as "framed" in this verse speaks of order we find in all creation. Also, the concept of "framed" is contained in the verse is an indication that there is no "cross-over" within the various elements. A rock can never become a horse. A horse can never become a rabbit. Each "kind" reproduces his own "kind" among the biological creatures. This is not to say there may not be great diversity among the "kinds." We have an American Bulldog and a Terrier Pit mix of dogs. They are of the same "kind" of canine even though they display this diversity.

Water may form either ice or steam and yet remain its own non-organic "kind."]

11.4 *By faith Abel offered unto God a more excellent sacrifice than Cain, by which he obtained witness that he was righteous, God testifying of his gifts and by it he being dead yet speaketh.*

[See note at Hebrews 12:24. The sacrifice was not the means of salvation. It was only a witness to the fact that Abel was already righteous. It was that faith in the revealed Words of God which caused Abel to sacrifice. It was right that Abel sacrifice. This could be called a work of man but it was not. Yes, man carried out the sacrifice but it was the faith of that man that led to the sacrifice. The people of God have always operated in a faith medium.

Another factor in the sacrifice given by Abel is that it looks back to the revealed will of God. In the third chapter of Genesis we see that Adam and Eve tried to hide their sin by hiding themselves from God. The realized that they stood naked in their sin before The Holy God. They tried to hide behind a sort of clothing made from vegetation. God corrected them in the slaying of an animal to provide "coats of skins," to cover the skin of their shame. The obvious understanding was that a blood sacrifice was necessary to cover sin.

From our standpoint of the completion of the inspired and preserved Scripture, we can understand that this pointed to the Ultimate Self-Sacrifice of Jesus to secure salvation **from** our sin.

While Abel followed the known and understood will of God, Cain offered that which was more properly his own work. The sheep had grown from the "mother's milk." This was life created from life originally created by God. This was a returning to God of that which was His by right. It was done by the steward of that life, who owned it only temporarily. His ownership ended when his own life ended. The picture is of Abel giving God the sacrifice of life, the life of the sheep being forfeit because of the life of sin of Abel.

The faith of Abel was founded in the revelation of God. The error of Cain was in not giving consideration to that revelation from God. The "of" of Abel seeks the leading and smile of God; the "from" of Cain seeks the leading and smile of humanity apart from God.

Many of the commentators I consulted came to the conclusion that God voiced His approval of Abel's offering by sending fire down from Heaven to consume it. Scripture is silent on this subject. We may conjecture on this point, possibly by considering the acts with Elijah and the prophets of Baal on Mount Carmel. But, such is speculation. Had it been in the will of God for us to know the manner, He would have told us. To attempt to speculate beyond the inspired and preserved Words of Scripture is to come perilously close to the occult. We have a need to trust the Words of that inspired and preserved Scripture. Speculation is not of faith but of human curiosity. Worse, it is to doubt the goodness of God in the giving of His Message for us.

The crops of Cain may have been an offering but it was an offering devoid of observed life. The crops did grow from seeds given by earlier plants. Once again it was life from life. But, this was not an observed transfer of life as was that of the sheep. The crops grew from seeds hidden in the ground. This was an offering which mirrored the "sin covering" of the parents who tried to hide their sin behind vegetation.

We need not doubt the sincerity of Cain in his offering. But, we must consider that sincerity is an internal act of man. It is not focused on the will of God but on the purpose of man. As such this is not an act of faith in God.

We can easily argue that Cain did not seek an animal of creation to sacrifice. Man was not a carnivore until after the flood. Therefore, it is reasonable to consider that Cain was loath to kill an animal for sacrifice. This view misses the mark of the purpose of sacrifice. Sacrifice of the totality of that sacrifice is the standard. It is the life of the sacrifice which is given for the life of the penitent. In more modern terms, the purpose of sacrifice was not bar-b-que. It was to be totally in the worship of God.

Neither our pleasure nor our comfort is included in the situation. The totality of worship being given to God was the purpose. This is exemplified to the highest degree in the Self-Sacrifice of Jesus. He died that we might live. He has sent The Holy Spirit to show us how to live. He mediates with The Father that we might live holy.

Even the best works done in sin can never approach the Standard of God. Failure to consider His Ways leads away from His presence. No matter how sincere a misdirected sin, or even an attempt at worship, may be it can never be counted as faith in God.

I would make note, here, that baptism is less than this sacrifice of Abel. Abel understood the sacrifice as an expiation of sin. He could not have understood that the sacrifice of an animal of creation was only a symbolic act, albeit one which was sanctioned by God, which was ordained to prefigure the Self-Sacrifice of Jesus on the Cross. In, and on account of, that Self-Sacrifice of Jesus is the actual remedy given by God for the sin of humanity.

Baptism is an act which gives witness to the faith which man already possesses unto salvation. There is no grace to be imparted by the act of baptism. A person is baptized because he is already a believer.

In some manner God, Himself, voiced pleasure at the sacrifice of Abel. Cain certainly understood that God favored the sacrifice of Able while He disdained the offered gift of Cain. The truth of the piety of Abel continues to speak to the hearts of men as they see the object lesson of the sacrifice of Abel accepted by the Holiness of God.

Personally, I would believe that God spoke actual words of affirmation to Abel and words of disapproval to Cain. This was the means by which God spoke to Adam and Eve in the Garden. True, the setting was no longer in the Garden. Also true is the fact that the inspired and preserved Words of the Scripture of God were not available at this time. In the early days of the race of man God would have spoken His word directly. Man was without excuse before his God; God communicated His precepts, with the responsibility falling upon man to continue to recite those words to future generations.

Consider all the names of those who follow Abel just in this chapter. Every man, with the Great Exception of the God/Man Jesus Christ, is expendable. There are no truly great men of God; there are only men of The Great God.]

11.5 *By faith Enoch was translated that he should not see death; and was not found, because God had translated him: for before his translation he had this testimony, that he pleased God.*

[Enoch seems to have been a preacher of righteousness and a prophet. Jude, verses 14-15 records this of him: "And Enoch also, the seventh from Adam, prophesied of these, saying, Behold, the Lord cometh with ten thousands of his saints, To execute judgment upon all, and to convince all that are ungodly among them of all their ungodly deeds which they have ungodly committed, and of all their hard speeches which ungodly sinners have spoken against him."

This passage is quoted from the spurious Book of Enoch. To suppose that a book from before the flood would have survived that destruction is not reasonable. Although all that is in the inspired and preserved Scripture is true, not all that is not included in the inspired and preserved Scripture is always false. The inspiration of the Spirit upon this passage is evidence that this prophecy of Enoch is real. The entire book of Enoch is neither true nor trustworthy; this particular portion is.

We should quickly note that God did not come with ten thousands of his saints at the time of the flood. Therefore we cannot consider these words of Enoch speak of the coming flood. It is more likely that they speak of the final judgments upon this world when the Lord will return with His saints to execute such judgment as described.

Genesis 5:23-24 gives us this from the account of Enoch: "And all the days of Enoch were three hundred sixty and five years: And Enoch walked with God: and he *was* not, for God took him."

The phrase "God took him" could be considered as God taking Enoch in death. Paul informs us that Enoch was "translated." The purpose of such "translation" was that Enoch not see death. Couple this with the fact that only Enoch and Melchizedek, among the "major players," do not have their deaths recorded, and we are led to consider that Enoch did not die.

The writing here will give credence to that truth. We cannot always consider that a thing is true because it seems reasonable. That is a human reasoning and may well be flawed. But, when God says that a thing is true, it is always true. This fact remains even among incidents and things which do not agree with human reasoning. (I Corinthians 2:14)

Melchizedek did suffer death. His death is not recorded only so he can stand as a "type" of the eternal High Priest and King, Jesus. (see notes on the seventh chapter of Hebrews)

It was the faith of Enoch which pleased God.]

11.6 *But without faith it is impossible to please him: for he that cometh to God must believe that he is, and that he is a rewarder of them that diligently seek him.*

[How do we please God? That is the question asked by all the religions of the ages. None of them have ever had the correct answer because they saw a God who needed to be pleased lest He come down and attack. Only true Christianity understands that God is not a celestial ogre who is constantly looking for one excuse to pounce. The True God is The God of Love. He loves to forgive and cleanse His creation. (Luke 15:7)

Faith refers to faith and confidence in the revealed Words of God. For our dispensation it is that we respond to the calling from the Spirit to saving faith in the Lord Jesus Christ. Without this faith of salvation there is no pleasure given to God. We are lost sinners in a wretched condition of sin.

It is the sinner coming to God in faith, seeking the pardon from sin, who is pleasing Him. To know about Him is to place us in the position of realizing our complete sinfulness before Him. In the conviction of this state we are more likely to realize His graciousness in the Self-Sacrifice of Jesus to save us from our sin. We learn of His great grace and love. As we learn more of Him we are convicted of our need to accept Jesus as Savior. When we finally come to the place of accepting Jesus for salvation we will begin to know Him.

In John 6:37 Jesus tells us something very important. "All that the Father giveth me shall come to me; and him that cometh to me I will in no wise cast out."

There is no question of what we must do to inherit eternal life. We must come to Jesus in faith and accept Him as Savior. The firm promise of God is that all who do come to Him will be saved from their sin.

God rewards those who Biblically and diligently seek the Savior. On the basis of the work of Jesus, these – who are responding to the call of the Spirit, though they see only the need of their hearts – will be given an eternal salvation which cannot be taken away.

We seek Him because He has first sought us! (consider Luke 19:10 and I John 4:19) Therein is the truth of the Love of God displayed unto us.]

11.7 *By faith Noah, being warned of God of things not seen as yet, moved with fear, prepared an ark to the saving of his house, by the which he condemned the world, and became heir of the righteousness which is by faith.*

[How was Noah saved from the Great Flood? He was saved from this judgment of God by his faith in God.

How severely must have been the faith of Noah in the Words of God been tested. He began to build his great boat about 120 years before the waters came. I am rather certain that Moses faced taunts and threats by his neighbors. "Hey, Noah, that monstrosity you are building is ruining my property values!" That would have been a mild taunt.

The mental health of Noah would have been called into question. After all, many argue that there had been no rain before the great flood came. There were certainly no floods such as the one Noah described as he preached warning to his neighbors for over one hundred years. The natural understanding of Noah would have been derided.

And then there were all those animals going to visit over at "old crack-pot Noah's house." I would guess that the people simply said, "Of course all those animals are gathering over at Noah's place. Look at all that food he has stockpiled. It just seems wrong that he would stockpile food for all those animals when there are so many hungry people in the world that he ought to be helping out. If that is his religion I am not interested!"

The faith of Noah must be contrasted with the folly of those who refused to trust God.

The people just couldn't see any reason to listen to the preaching of Noah about any flood. The Godly fear of Noah kept him at his task.

We might note that Noah is the first person in the Bible with whom God made any covenant. The first covenant (Genesis 6:17) was that this flood would come. Noah didn't accept this word because it was reasonable or obvious. Noah just trusted that God said what He meant and meant what He said.

I can just hear the sermon from the First Church of Anyone But Noah. "I know what Noah says. He just doesn't understand that God was speaking in parable. We know that God has created a reasonable and static world. Floods do not happen. It is possible that Noah got hold of some bad texts. My translation does not say that God is going to send a flood to destroy the world. The proper text says, "God is going to send us food to delight the world. Noah must have gotten a few letters mixed up. That's all."

The surprise to all the doubters was that the flood came. The entrance door to the ark was closed and men perished – just as God had said.

Noah became the heir of righteousness. This doesn't mean that he inherited anything from the old world before the flood. He didn't want anything of that world of sin. His faith took him to a higher purpose. He saw his inheritance from God to be peace, safety, provision.

This was the second covenant Noah found with God. The rainbow symbolized this. (Genesis 9:8-17) God promised several things to this preacher of righteousness. (II Peter 2:5) God promised that the world would never again be destroyed by water. God also promised that the seasons would each follow their logical and systematic course.

While seeing his family saved, Noah condemned the pre-flood world. He did not judge that world. He testified against it by his piety and trust in the Lord. The life and faith of Noah was a counterbalance to the violent and sinful world of his day. He displayed righteousness while they displayed the rebellion and wretchedness of sin.

I think it also pertinent to remember that Noah was not saved out of the flood of judgment; he was saved by being in the ark of God above that judgment. Noah escaped judgment by his relationship of faith, fidelity and his reverential fear of the Lord.

There is an interesting "sidelight" concerning Noah and his children. Several have noted that the generations of Genesis, chapter five, are highlighted by the phrase repeated that "so and so" lived a set amount of years and begat a child. Then they lived so many more years and begat a child. But of Noah this is written: "And Noah was five hundred years old: and Noah begat Shem, Ham, and Japheth." (Genesis 5:32) It is possible that we have here recorded the first instance of triplets mentioned in the Biblical record.

That, of course, is just a "maybe." But, it is interesting to consider.]

11.8 *By faith Abraham, when he was called to go out into a place which he should after receive for an inheritance, obeyed, and he went out, not knowing whither he went.*

[Abram was called before going to Haran. (see Acts 7:2-4 and note Genesis 12:1 where the LORD "had said unto Abram...")

Now Paul had the attention of the audience to whom he was writing. His readers were a group of Jewish Christians. There was a worry that some of them might apostate from the faith and return to their Jewish "roots." That has been the thrust of the Book of Hebrews. Paul was beginning to explain that even their most illustrious ancestors in the family of Abraham had given the example of living by faith in the Lord.

The obedience of Abram to begin his journey because God had said, "Go" was a particular exercise in faith. This is especially so since God said "Go" in giving a general direction to begin but had not said to where the "go" would lead!

I am sure that at some point during the trip Sarai said, "Just like a man. No map and no idea where he's going!" O. K. Not really!

I would point out that Paul uses the name Abraham even though he is speaking of Abram at this point. Abram would not become Abraham until Genesis 17:5. Abram means "high father." God changed that descriptive name to Abraham – Father of Many Nations.

The first thought upon hearing this name change is to argue. Abraham did not become the father of many nations. He is only the father of the Israelite nation. First, "Israel" was a name given by God to Jacob. Jacob was a grandson of Abraham. It was the sons of Jacob, Israel, who established the twelve tribes of Israel. But, they were all still of one nation which flowed from Abraham.

Paul wrote something very interesting in Romans 4:11. "And he received the sign of circumcision, a seal of the righteousness of the faith which he had yet being uncircumcised: that he might be the father of all them that believe, though they be not circumcised; that righteousness might be imputed unto them also..." In all nations where there are believers there are spiritual children of Abraham. Abraham is, in his faith, truly a father of many nations.

Also, we cannot forget the seed of Abraham produced by the life of Ishmael, Esau, and Keturah. It is true that these are not "children of the Promise." But, in the natural, these are the children of Abraham. Keturah, whom Abraham took to be his wife after the death of Sarah, also gave children to Abraham. Seeing these other children of Abraham, we see that in the natural Abraham was truly a father of many nations.]

11.9 *By faith he sojourned in the land of promise, as in a strange country, dwelling in tabernacles with Isaac and Jacob the heirs with him of the same promise:*

[Abraham lived by faith in the Land of Promise. He lived there as though he were a foreigner, not trying to take that which God had promised. His faith seemed to say, "If it is the will of God that we live here to own the land, He will make it so. It is not for me to try to do that which is the providence and promise of God."

Abraham did not try to impose his own time-line upon God. Instead Abraham calmly accepted the promise as a future thing to be grasped when the perfect time of God was come.

Abraham also had the promise of his posterities sojourn in Egypt. (Genesis 15:12-18) Abraham trusted God to work in His Own time. In the meantime Abraham lived as a stranger in tents in the land to which he possessed title deed from God. He was willing to live the part of a stranger, in a tent, until such time as God would move. The same could be said of his son Isaac and his son's son Jacob.

It was the policy of Abraham to live in peace with his neighbors. The only land he owned, in the land promised to him, was a burial place bought near the end of his earthly life. Father, son and grandson all lived in peace with the people of the land even though the promise of God was that they would, in their children, some day own this entire land.

The "tabernacle" in which each in turn dwelt was a tent which could be easily removed when it was necessary to travel from place to place in their sojourn. Abraham lived as a stranger in his tent even as his eyes of faith looked toward a city which God would prepare.]

11.10 *For he looked for a city which hath foundations, whose builder and maker is God.*

[The city which Abraham sought was not any metropolis of man. It was the structure of life which God would build and supply. Abraham looked for the habitation prepared for him by God. The city of foundations is contrasted with the moveable tabernacle of tents in which Abraham dwelt as a sojourner in the land of promise. He was looking for a sure and steady abode in which to dwell during the storms of life.

Abraham found this dwelling place within his faith in God.

Abraham had been drawn out of the ancient city of Ur. This was a population center and a trading center. In Ur were the best the ancient world had to offer. There were large libraries and, I would suppose, other cultural advantages of life within Ur. It was also a land of pagan idol worship.

Abraham separated himself from this pagan worship to sojourn in the land where God was leading him. Leading a nomadic life-style, Abraham came into contact with many other cities – large and small. One is tempted to say that none of these cities could compare with the grandeur of Ur. But, the land which would be promised to Abraham was on the natural trade routes between Egypt and the rest of the then civilized world.

The great Arabian Desert would have guided the natural route of trade toward the Mediterranean Sea and into the Land of Promise. All the goods and treasures of the ancient world would be found somewhere along these trade routes. This included the same sort of idolatry which Abraham had been called from.

It was not that there was no knowledge of the true God. In Melchizedek Abraham found a priest of the Most High God. There was scant knowledge of God, however.

It was wandering in an area such as this that Abraham was tasked with being true to his faith and his God. The Promise kept Abraham's eyes and desires upon the Lord.

The tents of the nomads were very steady during most storms. It took a large and severe storm to cause any leaks; but it did happen infrequently. Abraham kept his eye of faith upon the Lord. Those Nomadic Tents had no foundation. They were kept steady by the "flying buttress" tension of stakes and ropes.

Abraham looked to an afterlife. He did not intermingle excessively although he did keep friendly relations with the local people as he wandered among them. His "eye of faith" looked to a future life. I would assume that Abraham had an imperfect knowledge of the afterlife. But, Abraham did understand the fact of a better life which followed the death of the body in this life.

Many of the commentators I accessed gave reference to the "New Jerusalem" in allusion to the city built without hands. I disagree. Abraham would have had no concept of such a thing. This is not to say that Abraham's view was not heavenly. It was.

Abraham had seen cities, both in Canaan and in Ur, which were centers of pagan worship. He looked for a city whose God was the Lord. The concept of a city to a nomad living in a tent was a concept of security and rest. Those foundations of the city gave a security during the storms of life. The rest was a rest from constantly building pens for the flocks, setting up tents for the people, and repeating the process in just a few days.

There was the rest of permanence given to the wandering soul in the city built without hands. This view looks past even The Promise given concerning the earthly land. This view looks to an eternal life of peace and rest with the Lord.]

11.11 *Through faith also Sara herself received strength to conceive seed, and was delivered of a child when she was past age, because she judged him faithful who had promised.*

[We look at Genesis 18:10-15 and marvel that Sarah is here listed as one of the heroines of faith. When she first heard the prophecy that she would have a child, she laughed. In the prime of her earthly life Sarah had been barren. Now someone was saying that she would give birth to a child when she was over 90 years old?

Sarah gave a rueful laugh when she heard that being said.

It appears that when Sarah learned Who it was that has said this, Sarah was heartened in her faith and in her body. God gave her a renewal of her body so that she could perform that which He had said would come to pass.

Not only in her body, but also in her faith Sarah judged the Lord as being faithful to keep His Words and His Prophecy. The faith in God which Sarah evidenced was not necessary for the process of pregnancy and child birth to take place. That would be a display of the power of miracle which God would display. God wills and works in His Own good pleasure and purpose. But this faith which Sarah evidenced was that which gave her joy.

Note that there is no mention of Sarah's laughter and doubt. When sin is forgiven it is no longer remembered. (Jeremiah 31:34; Hebrews 8:12; 10:17)]

11.12 *Therefore sprang there even of one, and him as good as dead, so many as the stars of the sky in multitude, and as the sand which is by the sea shore innumerable.*

[Here is a couple, he ninety-nine years old and she ninety. She was counted as barren during her child bearing years. He is now too old to father any children. However, the promise of God was, "...I will certainly return unto thee according to the time of life; and, lo, Sarah thy wife shall have a son..." (Genesis 18:10)

From Abraham and Sarah sprang the great Israelite nation. For nearly three thousand years the world's nations have attempted to exterminate this race. For nearly three thousand years the world has found they cannot undo what God has deemed to do.

Moving even beyond the "children of the Promise," Isaac and Jacob, Abraham also fathered the great Ishmaelite people. Abraham is the father of the Edomite via his grandson Esau. And, lest we forget, after the death of Sarah Abraham took Keturah as a wife. She bore him several children.

At nearly one-hundred years of age the world would have said that Abraham was as good as dead insofar as having any offspring. The promises of God are not dependent upon our view of history. The promises of God are only limited in our minds, not in God's ability!]

11.13 *These all died in faith, not having received the promises, but having seen them afar off, and were persuaded of them, and embraced them, and confessed that they were strangers and pilgrims on the earth.*

["These all" applies to Abraham, Sarah, Isaac, and Jacob. These are the ones to whom the promises were given. The promises given directly to Abraham, and Sarah to an extent, were transferred to Isaac and Jacob as direct offspring of Abraham. These died in faith concerning the coming of the promises. They never actually possessed the fruits of the promise but they never lost track of the future of the promise. They carried faith in the goodness of God to keep His Words and His Promises.

If we expand the promise back to Genesis 3:15, where the promise of The Coming Redeemer is given, we can include Abel and Noah as joining those above in "dying in faith concerning the promise." We cannot include Enoch as he did not die. He did keep faith in the promise of The Redeemer coming into the world.

But, such expansion is not warranted by the verse. The sense of the verse is limited to the promises as given to Abraham. These promises, of land, kings, progeny and the blessing of all nations are the property of the sons, and daughters, of Abraham. These had never possessed the results of the promises. Still, they were able to see themselves as holding these promises in their hands so great was there faith therein. They carried a certainty within their souls that God's promises are given upon the honor of God. As is true with all of His prophecies, the promises of God are certain and without recall.

The certain outcome of these promises was embraced as a precious commodity. The promises were as real to them as was the young baby of a new generation as they held him in their arms and hands.

The holders of these promises of God were strangers upon the earth. They were not part of the general population of unbelievers. They were the people of the covenant of God. They were believers in The True God of Creation; the idols of man were not part of their component of reality.

They were also pilgrims upon this earth. The song says, "This world is not my home." Even though the promises were of the land of the earth, and in their further propagation of the earth, their destination was Heavenly. They knew themselves to be a people of the Lord.]

11.14 *For they that say such things declare plainly that they seek a country.*

[By the actions and considerations of these patriarchs we can see that they are declaring that they have not found their country. They may exist upon this earth but they are not bound by the earth. Heaven awaits!

Christians can say the same. We are citizens of Heaven. (John 8:23) Neither the disappointments of this world nor the joys of this world are to be considered as overly important since these have scant bearing upon our existence in the eternity of

HEBREWS: Chapter 11

Heaven. Our joy should be in doing His Will and our disappointment felt most keenly when we fail Him.

We wait with joy for our "promotion to Glory" wherein we shall see our Savior face to face.]

11.15 *And truly, if they had been mindful of that country from whence they came out, they might have had opportunity to have returned.*

[The old saying is "Home is where the heart is." These people were strangers and wanderers in the land of Canaan. It would have been natural to have longed for "the old home" and "the old friends." But, Abraham – and by extension Isaac and Jacob – had been called out of that place. To have returned would have been to willingly place themselves out of the known will of God. The promises of God were too precious to even consider such a thing.

Although it would have been very easy to go back to old home, I only find this happening three times among the descendants of Abraham. Twice, Isaac and Jacob, returned to some of the family who had departed only as far as Haran. These went to take wives from their old family stock. Why?

First of all, they did not want to marry among the people of Canaan. These, of Canaan, were a people which were going to be displaced when the land was finally transferred to Abraham's seed. The purpose of the transfer was generally to judge the wickedness within the idolatry of those Canaanite people.

Second, it was to keep as the line of promise as pure as was possible among the human descendants of Abraham.

The third return to this general area came when Judah was punished for her national sins by the Babylonian's exile of Judah out of her land.]

11.16 *But now they desire a better country, that is, an heavenly wherefore God is not ashamed to be called their God: for he hath prepared for them a city.*

[The conversation is still concerning Abraham, Sarah, Isaac and Jacob. These were all strangers and wayfarers in the land of Canaan. It would seem that they would look longingly back at the land around Ur.

Being a major trading center close to the Persian Gulf from which even the smaller vessels of the day would take goods into eastern Africa and toward the Indian sub-continent. Goods from these areas would also have found their way to Ur. Exotic and precious articles were readily available in the bazaars and markets.

Ur was also an educational center. Large libraries have been found in the ruins of the city. All in all it would have been, humanly speaking, as fine and exciting a place to reside as the ancient world had to offer.

These people, Abraham and his extended family, had no desire to return to Ur. It was from Ur that God had called them out to be nomads in the area of Canaan. Canaan did not offer the same level of artifacts as did Ur. Canaan was a land on the trade routes so it, too, had much to offer. Abraham, Sarah, Isaac and Jacob could access little of this; considering their nomadic life-style they had only fleeting contact with the population centers. What these sojourning people did have was a relationship with God. In this they possessed a peace and joy that none other could give.

They did want better, still. They understood that the promise of the land was not to soon come upon them. They looked, instead, for Heaven. These people did understand the concept of an "after life." They may not have understood it perfectly. What they did understand was that God had a prepared place, a Heavenly, for His prepared and faithful people.

These people, in their faith and fidelity to Him, were a people whom God would not be ashamed to call by His Name. Their faith and piety had assured them of this position.]

11.17 *By faith Abraham, when he was tried, offered up Isaac: and he that had received the promises offered up his only begotten son,*

[Here is a place where the mind might balk. Abraham is tested by being told to offer his only son as a sacrifice. We first look and see that Isaac was the only son of Abraham. Ishmael is not slighted in this context. Isaac is the only son of Abraham and Sarah. Isaac is the only son of the promise. It was through Isaac, Abraham understood this, that the promises God had given to Abraham would be fulfilled.

Could Abraham have actually believed that God intended for him to sacrifice his son? God had never broached the subject of human sacrifice with Abraham from all we can glean from Scripture. But, the people among whom Abraham was sojourning were in the habit of sacrificing their children.

Abraham must have believed that this was of God because he prepared to do so.

This was a crisis moment for Abraham. The only offspring with the wife of his youth was going to be put to death. It was the hand of Abraham, himself, which would prepare and prosecute the deed.

The word "WHY!" comes quickly to mind. Didn't God already understand the character of Abraham? Didn't God already know the character of the faith of Abraham?

Yes; God knew all about Abraham. But, Abraham didn't know all about Abraham.

The test was not of Abraham. It was a test which was for Abraham.

There are times when the manager of a prize fighter will pick an opponent which had "heavy hands." The manager wants to see how his fighter will respond to this adversity. Sometimes the young fighter will pass the test and move on up the ladder of title contention. Sometimes the young fighter will fail the test and retire from the sport and find a job in other endeavors. He will learn whether he is ready for this sport, or not!

Isaac was being tried as well. He also passed his test. There is no hint of his arguing or trying to get away. He simply submitted to his father and his, supposed, religious duty.

Abraham also passed the test and in doing so learned that he could always put aside his personal feelings and doubts as he submitted to the will of God. Abraham was ready to kill the boy when he was stopped. God provided a substitute.

This is symbolic of our salvation from sin. Isaac was as good as dead. He was ready to be sacrificed. God gave a substitute which saved Isaac from his own death.]

11.18 *Of whom it was said, That in Isaac shall thy seed be called:*

[Here was a real problem. God had said that Isaac was the child of the Promise. It would be through Isaac that the line of Abraham would possess the promises and bring blessing to the entire world. (Genesis 17:19; 17:21; 21:12; Romans 9:7)

There was no doubt in this place. There was no room to find another understanding. Ishmael was not the child of promise. The sons of Keturah, not yet having been born, would not be the child of promise. It was Isaac that was the guarantee of the promises of God which would come through his lineage.

Abraham believed God as to Isaac being the conduit to the establishment of the promises. Abraham also believed God as to the sacrifice of Isaac. Abraham could not understand the process. He could understand that he should always do the will of God.

Abraham prepared to kill his son, Isaac, in obedience to the words of God.

Abraham must have been fearful of the outcome of his actions. Still, to obey God in faith is righteousness.

In the very next verse we see Abraham's faith in God and in the leading of God. The one could not override the other. Abraham believed both to be the will of God. The Scripture was not yet completed; Abraham could not understand that God does not require or accept human sacrifice except where it refers to the Divine Self-Sacrifice of Jesus Christ upon the Cross of Calvary.]

11.19 *Accounting that God was able to raise him up, even from the dead; from whence also he received him in a figure.*

[The only rationalization which Abraham could reach was that God would raise Isaac from the dead. The faith of Abraham believed that God was able to do anything to keep His Words and His promises. "For the which cause I also suffer these things: nevertheless I am not ashamed: for I know whom I have believed, and am persuaded that he is able to keep that which I have committed unto him against that day." (II Timothy 1:12)

The belief of Abraham, when no person had ever been resuscitated before, gives us an understanding of the faith of the patriarch. The resurrection of the dead, be it for a short span in time of for the duration of eternity in Heaven, was part of the belief system of Abraham.

Abraham had received Isaac through miracle. Both mother and father were well beyond the age of, humanly speaking, producing children. It was no small thing for God to perform another miracle and raise Isaac from the ashes of the sacrificial death. So Abraham's faith believed and in this faith of Abraham he proceeded.

Abraham had already sacrificed Isaac in his mind. Therefore this was a resurrection from the dead in parable when the sacrifice was suspended and a substitute was given to Abraham. "In figure" Isaac had been returned from the dead and restored to his father.]

11.20 *By faith Isaac blessed Jacob and Esau concerning things to come.*

[This was a time before any of the written Scripture had been transmitted to man. As God had spoken with Abraham so God seemed to have put the Spirit of Prophecy upon Isaac. Isaac spoke of things to his children, Esau and Jacob, which he could not have known about their futures from the natural standpoint.

The concept of the elder serving the younger would have been laughable to anyone who knew the two boys. Esau, the elder, was a mighty hunter. He was an "outdoorsman" who was acquainted with the rigors of "living off the land." Jacob seems more to have been a "homebody." He might have been at home among the domesticated sheep but he wasn't likely to have been found fighting a lion or bear in defense of the flock.

His time spent among those flocks at home were a real training ground for a man who had to tend sheep for fourteen years to earn a dowry to obtain his wife.

Neither Isaac nor Rebeckah could properly be called completely honorable in the giving of these blessings. Isaac played favorites. He loved Esau more than he cared for Jacob. Isaac decided to give the "family blessing" to Esau even though the prophecy had been that this honor should go to Jacob. (Genesis 26:5)

Meanwhile Rebeckah gave her best "Lucy Ricardo" imitation in her scheme to trick "Ricky" into giving that blessing to her favorite, Jacob. Although it was through this scheme that the prophecy of God came to pass, this was not her purpose. Rebeckah just wanted what she wanted and if it meant tricking her blind husband, well all is fair in love, war and domestic chicanery.

There are times when God will allow us our little "victories" in order to further His Own purposes. Many leaders of the nations of the end times will realize this to their dismay at the day of the Lord's return in Glory.

Even these "victories" become a porridge pot of ashes in the mouth of the schemers. "Be not deceived; God is not mocked: for whatsoever a man soweth, that shall he also reap." (Galatians 6:7) Within a short time the plot was uncovered. Jacob was sent into near exile, never to be seen again by his mother, to save him from the murderous wrath of his brother. Esau, meanwhile to his father's dismay, intermarried into the nations around their little band. "Then when lust hath conceived, it bringeth forth sin: and sin, when it is finished, bringeth forth death." (James 1:15)

Although both of the twins, Esau and Jacob, were blessed as the "sons of Abraham," it was Jacob who continued the line of the promise. God did not forget his promise of favor with Abraham. Jacob carried the Promise of blessing even as Esau was blessed in his physical situation.]

11.21 *By faith Jacob, when he was a dying, blessed both the sons of Joseph; and worshipped, leaning upon the top of his staff.*

[At birth we are a clay tablet. Anything could be written in this moist clay. At the end of our life we are as a fired pottery. Life has written many things upon us as we have been adorned with the dyes and paints of others with whom we have come in contact. All have become part of the vessel of which we are.

At the time of death the clay has dried. No longer are we written upon. We have solidified into that which we are. The testimony of a dying man carries with it much more weight in a court room than that of a man who sees years in his future. It is considered that the dying man has no cause to impress; he merely wishes to state that which is.

It was at this point that Jacob gave a demonstration of His faith in God. He said that some things would happen. He prophesied of the power and prerogative of God. The two sons of Joseph were given the family blessing and adopted into the family of Jacob. Jacob then worshipped God upon his staff.

Jacob was very old at this point. As I age I find more and more that I use a cane when I walk very far. At this stage of his life this was part of the reality for Jacob.

But, that staff also carried a symbolism of the primacy of Jacob among his family, his clan. He used this metaphor in his prophecy of Messiah when he spoke of the Scepter. (Genesis 49:10)

Note that Jacob did not worship his staff. He worshiped the Lord with Whom he had walked the journey of his life. That same Heavenly Companion of his youth would carry Jacob through the valley of the shadow and undo the Light of the World.]

11.22 *By faith Joseph, when he died, made mention of the departing of the children of Israel; and gave commandment concerning his bones.*

[Though not mentioned, this is a great testimony to the piety of Jacob, the father of Joseph. How did Joseph know that the children of Israel would return to their ancestral home in Canaan? Why would Joseph assume that anyone would want to depart from Egypt, the richest and most comfortable nation on earth at the time, to return to a land where the family had been nomadic shepherds? Joseph knew and assumed because he had been taught from his earliest days by his father, Jacob. When a child has been trained the way he should go, that is the way in which he will finally return. (Proverbs 22:6)

The case of Joseph is another where a younger sibling has leaped over his elders to become the principle child through whom the Abrahamic promises were transmitted. There is a difference in Joseph and earlier "offspring" of Abraham. Though his brothers had sold him into slavery, Joseph saved his brothers from starvation in a drought by bringing them into his adopted land. He also lived to see them included, as founders of the tribes of Israel, in the line of fulfillment of the promises given to Abraham.

Joseph remembered the words recited to him concerning his father Abraham about a sojourn in a land which was not the land of promise. (Genesis 15:13-14) He knew that his people would be returning to the land which God had chosen for them. He made the people pledge that his body would accompany them so his final burial would take place in the land of the promise of God. In Exodus 13:14 we see this pledge faithfully carried out.

Jacob's faith in the Words of the Lord was a family trait carried forth in the life of his son, Joseph.

Joseph was a member of the ruling class in Egypt. It is always heartening to see a leader who gives testimony to the leading and power of God. It is actually more important that those who are "under" this leader are willing to follow God even when the leader speaks otherwise. This is a trust that sees God as supreme. While both are heartening it somehow seems it takes more faith to trust God when the "powers that be" account such a course as anathema to their leading.

Meanwhile, of course, the ruling class is much more unlikely to follow God. These have supreme faith in themselves and see no real reason to trust God. What utter fools they are! (Psalm 14:1)]

11.23 *By faith Moses, when he was born, was hid three months of his parents, because they saw he was a proper child; and they were not afraid of the king's commandment.*

[Although not mentioned by name at this place, Amran and Jochebed (the father and mother of Moses), are honored by inclusion in this "hall of hero's" of Scripture. We have but small need of "name recognition" in this world. God knows and see that which is in our hearts. The accolades of earth die with us; the smile of God will warm our hearts throughout eternity.

Notice another thing which has been left out of this verse. There is no mention of the killing of the Egyptian taskmaster by Moses. Repentance of sins will be followed by forgiveness of sins. In forgiveness of our sins God will count them no more against us.

Pharaoh had first asked that the Hebrew midwives kill all the male children at birth. When the births of the male Hebrews continued, Pharaoh asked why this was so. The midwives replied that the Hebrew women were not as the Egyptian women. They gave birth before the midwives arrived.

Like many in our day, Pharaoh demanded dead babies. These male children of the Hebrews were not wanted children. They must be killed. It was the "right" thing to do. Failing this with one strategy, Pharaoh embarked upon another. He opted for a very "late term abortion." "Bring the male babies to the river and drown them," was his decree.

When Moses was born his parents feared God more than they feared man. They did not commit infanticide. They saw Moses as a beautiful child. He seemed very alert as he learned things well during the three months he was hid inside Amran and Jochebed's home. I would imagine that his older sister, Miriam, and brother, Aaron, also loved the child.

When the child, Moses, could no longer be safely hid by his family Miriam helped to put the child into a "basket" which had been given a water-proofing with slime and pitch. Miriam watched as Pharaoh's daughter found Moses and adopted him. Miriam arranged for Jochebed to become the wet-nurse for the child. Moses was allowed to stay at his home until he was weaned. He then took up residence in the palace as the son of Pharaoh's daughter.

Moses, as the son of Pharaoh's daughter, was considered as royalty among the very people who had demanded his death upon his birth. God always protects His servants until such time as they can step into their time of service. He continues to protect His faithful servants until their time of departure arrives.

Many of the commentaries I consulted argued that Amran and Jochebed were waiting for a deliverer for Israel and considered that this son would be that deliverer. I wouldn't agree. They were a pious family; of this I am fairly certain. All three children, Moses, Miriam, and Aaron, were heavily involved in the faith of the exodus. It is possible that the parents prayed that Moses would be that deliverer. I would choose not to speculate upon this.]

11.24 By faith Moses, when he was come to years, refused to be called the son of Pharaoh's daughter:

[The Jamieson/Fausset/Brown Commentary carries this notation: "Thermutis, Pharaoh's daughter, according to the tradition, which Paul under the Spirit sanctions, adopted him, as JOSEPHUS says, with the consent of the king. JOSEPHUS states that when a child, he threw on the ground the diadem put on him in jest, a presage of his subsequent formal rejection of Thermutis' adoption of him." Though this comes from Josephus, an historian of renown in the ancient world, it concerns a situation of about fifteen hundred years before his birth. Thus, any "facts" he presented in such a case were likely colored with much tradition and folklore. The Egyptians were not known to generally promote their monarchs through the line of daughters; it is unlikely that Moses would have been in line for the crown.

It seems more than likely that Moses' rejection of the royal family, of which he would have been a member through his adopted mother, came at the time in which he took his place as a Hebrew and renounced his Egyptian heritage. He would have retained the knowledge he had gained in his education as a member of the royal household.

God gives great gifts to those He calls to do great things. God, knowing history even while it is yet future, would have known of the acts of Moses. The preparation of the royal palace gave Moses and education in the arts and sciences of the Egyptian. He also knew the palace and its protocols. These gave him entrance to the Pharaoh's courts.

It is likely that two things gave Moses the understanding of his Hebrew heritage. First, he would have been circumcised. This was a Hebrew initiation rite. Second, we cannot believe that his mother completely abandoned him when he was turned over to Pharaoh's daughter as her adopted son. Moses was certainly "trained up" in the paths of true religion and faith as to his true heritage as a son of Abraham. (Proverbs 22:6)

At about forty years of age, no youthful indiscretion, Moses chose his place with his people and renounced his Egyptian heritage and the palace of Pharaoh. His choice to be one with the Hebrews was his time of decision to be one of God's people. God continued to teach Moses His ways.]

11.25 *Choosing rather to suffer affliction with the people of God, than to enjoy the pleasures of sin for a season;*

[Remember the experience of Adam and Eve in The Garden. We can argue that Eve was cajoled. We cannot argue this of Adam. Adam was simply presented with the forbidden fruit. He made a cold, calculated choice to abide with the sin of Eve and forsake the favor of God. Moses did the inverse. He made calculated (Not so "cold" as the warmth of family was upon him.) decision to abide with the children of the covenant. In this he found the blessing of God.

It would seem that one of the first acts of Moses after this decision was done in the natural rather than in the spiritual leading of God. He killed and Egyptian taskmaster who was mistreating some of the Hebrew workers.

It is never "good" to do evil in the name of piety. This act forced Moses to choose to flee from his people. For years thereafter Moses was separated from the people with whom he had chosen to identify. God used these years of seeming exile to train Moses beyond the training which the Egyptians had given him. Moses learned the business of shepherding sheep; this would stand him well during the time of exodus when Moses was the leader, humanly speaking, of the flock of God.

We must note that there were true pleasures which were given up by Moses. There are real pleasures in sin. But, these pleasures are only for a season. The pleasures of abiding in God are eternal. We may have our "internship" in the desert as God prepares us for the march into the promised land of His provision. That training is joyful, especially when we consider the journey upon which we are to embark.

The pleasure of sin is never equal to the happiness of the Lord!]

11.26 *Esteeming the reproach of Christ greater riches than the treasures in Egypt, for he had respect unto the recompence of the reward.*

[We cannot properly consider that Moses saw either the reproach or the exaltation of Christ. We can properly consider that Moses saw "Him Who is invisible" in his worship of the True God.

We have often accessed Revelation 13:8. "And all that dwell upon the earth shall worship him, whose names are not written in the book of life of the Lamb slain from the foundation of the world." This is a verse in two parts. The first part speaks of the emptiness of the lives and religion of those during the Tribulation Era who have engaged in the false worship of the beast. They are not of the redeemed; their names are not recorded as followers of Jesus in salvation.

The second part of the verse speaks of Jesus. He is the Lamb of God which Self-Sacrificed His Own mortality as the atonement for the redeemed of all the ages of humanity. The only salvation offered to humanity is that salvation purchased by Jesus on the Cross of Calvary. Therefore, even those who sacrificed the animals of creation in the Old Testament tabernacle sacrifices were not saved by these; they were ultimately saved by that Self-Sacrifice of Jesus.

With this spiritual principle in mind we can see that the righteousness of Moses, and his piety within that Old Testament economy, was in the reality of eternity a relationship with Christ. He did, not understanding but it was accounted to him due to his faith in God, esteem the riches of Christ. The recompense, payment or reward, for this is an eternal inheritance based on the grace of God. Moses did not earn these riches; even Moses received grace from the Throne of Grace.

We cannot lose sight of the fact that Moses did understand the concept of the coming Messiah. Genesis 3:15 assures us of this. But, his understanding was incomplete. He would not have understood all that Jesus means to the believer.

Moses was a type of Christ in many ways. His birth was miraculous in that he was not supposed to be born. The king had demanded that all male children of the Hebrews were to die. This is analogous of King Herod and the "slaughter of the innocents" during the young childhood of Jesus.

Also, we see the Kenosis of Jesus in the fact that Moses gave up his royal linage, although it was not physically his, to identify with the earthly people of the sons of Abraham. In this Moses sought and found the release of his people from bondage and led those who followed him into the land which was of the promise of God.

Moses gave the people a new set of laws. These laws were of God, not of Moses. Jesus gave the new Law of Grace to those who would follow Him.

The "treasures of Egypt" were real to Moses. Although it is doubtful that he could ever ascend to become Pharaoh, he was still the adopted son of Pharaoh's daughter. There was real treasure in his future had he not identified with the people of God rather than the throne of Egypt.

In this idea of "reproach" we see the general attitude of sinful humanity toward the people of God. Read the newspapers, magazines, political flyers, listen to the radio and T.V. commentators and even the late-night comic's; the Christian is reproached for his belief and his Lord. That should be but a small thing for us to endure in order to live within His Heavenly Glory.

It was His faith in the God of his father's which gave Moses the wherewithal to stand, and having done all, to stand (Ephesians 6:13) for God in a hostile nation and against a hostile Pharaoh.]

11.27 *By faith he forsook Egypt, not fearing the wrath of the king: for he endured, as seeing him who is invisible.*

[The first time Moses fled Egypt he did fear the wrath of the king. Moses had acted in his own power and had killed an Egyptian taskmaster over the Hebrew slaves. "Now when Pharaoh heard this thing, he sought to slay Moses. But Moses fled from the face of Pharaoh, and dwelt in the land of Midian: and he sat down by a well." (Exodus 2:15)

Whether it was the same Pharaoh as the flight into Midian or another is not important. This time Moses was on a mission; he was acting under the commission of God as His representative and agent. There was no fear as Moses stood before Pharaoh and demanded that the Hebrew slaves be released, first to worship their God and then just released.

Pharaoh sputtered and stood his ground of denial. Moses simply answered with "Thus saith the Lord," as his petition and power over the Pharaoh.

Pharaoh was incensed that the Hebrews wanted to worship their God. Were not the gods of Egypt sufficient for them? The gods of Egypt were idols of stone and wood. Everyone could see them, touch them, and talk directly to them. The invisible God of Moses brought plague after plague which gave evidence of the weakness and inability of these Egyptian gods.

Moses trusted the invisible God Who was the Creator of the Universe. Moses saw He Who was invisible. He had no fear of Pharaoh because he feared the Lord God of Heaven.

This was not the Moses who had fled in fear to Midian. (Exodus 2:15) This was the Moses who feared only the Lord and came in His Name. His faith was in the Lord.]

11.28 *Through faith he kept the passover, and the sprinkling of blood, lest he that destroyed the firstborn should touch them.*

[It did take faith for Moses to institute and demand the Hebrews to follow in the symbolic acts of the Passover celebration. The plagues which had already come to pass gave the terrorism of reality in the faith to believe that God would send the plague of the death of the first born. Everyone had seen enough demonstration of the power of God to know that what God said He would do should be considered as certainty.

The idea of a blood sacrifice was not a surprising development. This was a very familiar concept to the ancient religions. These religions saw this sacrificial consideration as an attempt to placate an angry deity so that he wouldn't send his fiery judgments upon the people. But, the concept of hiding behind the blood of that sacrifice as a place of safety was not the general idea of the sacrifice among the pagans. Blood to show that one was willing to kill for his god was one thing; this concept that the blood was an evidence of both the piety of the people and the mercy of their God was a new thing which was probably not completely understood.

The blood of the Passover Lamb was put on the door frame of the homes of the devout so that the angel which killed the first born of all Egypt would pass over those homes and spare the lives of those within.

Another "twist" in this instance was that the people then ate the entire lamb which was used in this sacrifice. This was not new. There were always feasts and celebrations associated with the pagan religions. But, there was also – generally speaking – a food offering of some sort made to the pagan idol gods. In this case there was nothing offered to God except faith and a willingness to do His will. There was no idol to please. He who is invisible (verse 27, above) needs no food from man; He delights in obedience and trust.

The blood of the paschal lamb saved the Hebrew from death. He then was to eat the entire lamb as part of the service. This is a picture of salvation. We are saved by the Blood of The Lamb of God. We are then to walk in the newness of life in Him. We are to incorporate His Life into our walk in this life. That the bread of the Passover was to be unleavened gives us the picture that we need nothing but the Savior. Any mixture of the world's goods or intentions is not to be part of our devotion to Him.

As to the applying of the blood of the sacrificial lamb, Exodus 12:22 gives the following instruction: "And ye shall take a bunch of hyssop, and dip it in the blood, that *is* in the bason, and strike the lintel and the two side posts with the blood that *is* in the bason; and none of you shall go out at the door of his house until the morning."

The thing that seems to jump out to me is that this plant is used to "strike" the blood on to the door. Paul uses the term of "sprinkling" in this verse; this is an equivalent phrase for blood so "struck" would be "sprinkled" thereunto. To those Jewish people to whom Paul was writing, this phrase "sprinkled" would immediately bring to mind the high priest on the Day of Atonement who sprinkled the blood of sacrifice on the Mercy Seat in the Holy of Holies.

The fact that the blood was "struck" is also a prophecy of the Savior Who was so horribly mistreated by those who took part in His crucifixion. "But he was wounded for our transgressions, he was bruised for our iniquities: the chastisement of our peace was upon him; and with his stripes we are healed." (Isaiah 53:5)

Even the picture of the people being warned to stay in their house until the next morning when the exodus was to begin, gives us a picture of the separation from the worldly and the religions of the world which is commanded for the Blood Bought Believer.]

11.29 *By faith they passed through the Red sea as by dry land: which the Egyptians assaying to do were drowned.*

[Of just what did the army following Israel out of Egypt consist? On 6 June 1944 the combined armies of the allies invaded Hitler's Europe in the "D-Day" invasion. That is the way we read the story. It isn't completely true. Parts of those "Allied Forces" were involved in the Pacific Theater against the forces of Japan. Parts of those "Allied Forces" were involved in attacking various parts of the southern entrances into Europe. There were even parts of those allied forces who stayed behind in support of the forces of the invasion.

Not all of the forces of Egypt were used in following Israel as she began her exodus from Egypt. There were Egyptian military outposts far away who were tasked with defending the borders. Those immediately under Pharaoh were what we would today call, "his Palace Guard." There were enough highly trained and weaponized troops from Egypt to easily rout the rag-tag group of slaves who made up the bulk of the Israelites. But, it wasn't the entirety of the Egyptian military. The bulk of these

HEBREWS: Chapter 11

were just too far away to arrive in time to chase Israel!

This was specifically "the Pharaoh's army." This was the "palace guard."

Note here that the people of Israel passed over the Red Sea on dry ground. That seems as great a miracle as was the parting of the waters. As to the parting of the waters, take a look at Exodus 14:22 – "And the children of Israel went into the midst of the sea upon the dry ground: and the waters were a wall unto them on their right hand, and on their left."

We have probably all seen some of the documentaries which seek to establish natural explanations for the events of the plagues of Egypt and the parting of the sea. The picture given in the above verse (Exodus 14:22) is not the picture of an Israeli crossing during a tidal wave. The water was welled up into "walls" on both the left and the right hand. A tidal wave would not build up "walls" of water on both sides. Neither would the argument of many theologians that the crossing was at the "Reed Sea" where the water was "only about six inches deep."

Folks, the miracles of God are miraculous. We limit God's power and our faith when we try to make the miraculous appear mundane!

Also, consider the actions of the Egyptian military as they attempted to cross in the same manner as had Israel. There was a "victory song" of Israel which contained this verse from Exodus15:12. "Thou stretchedst out thy right hand, the earth swallowed them." That would be the Egyptian army which the earth swallowed.

"And the Egyptians pursued, and went in after them to the midst of the sea, *even* all Pharaoh's horses, his chariots, and his horsemen. And it came to pass, that in the morning watch the LORD looked unto the host of the Egyptians through the pillar of fire and of the cloud, and troubled the host of the Egyptians, And took off their chariot wheels, that they drave them heavily: so that the Egyptians said, Let us flee from the face of Israel; for the LORD fighteth for them against the Egyptians." (Exodus 14:23-25)

The Scriptural record says that the Israelites crossed through the Red Sea on day land. Nothing of this sort is said of the Egyptians. I submit that the waters were held back for the Egyptians to begin their march through the sea. But the sea bed returned to its natural state of mud. The wheels of the chariots bogged down in the mud. Some, maybe many, of those wheels were removed from the chariots due to the mud.

The Egyptians were drowned by the waters even as the mud of the earth immobilized them; the earth swallowed them up.

The Israelites, probably with much fear and trepidation, followed Moses in faith through the dry land between the walls of water. The Egyptians came into the sea because they saw the Israelis go through. The Egyptians came through physical sight. Faith was not part of their equation. They drowned in their attempt to thwart the will of God.

The Israelites came in faith to the water's edge. They simply followed their leader, Moses, who spoke to them the Words of God as he displayed an example of faith in God. The people moved one small foot step after another on dry land as God prepared for them everything which they needed for their travel.]

11.30 *By faith the walls of Jericho fell down, after they were compassed about seven days.*

[Try to imagine yourself in Jericho at this point. The people have heard what happened to the Egyptians. They were just a little concerned. Since they had already found spies within their walls the people knew that they were at the wrong end of the gun sights. Rahab (Joshua 2:9-12) asked for mercy. She had mentioned just how dire the situation was in her city. If the might of Egypt could not slow down this group, they all understood that one city-state was not going to be able to stand for long.

The people of Jericho brought all the food into the city which they possibly could. They shut up the gates of their large walls and prepared for a long siege. No one could come in and no one could go out. To paraphrase and old gospel song: "Hold the fort! For they are coming!"

For a few days nothing happened. Then, here came the forces of Israel. The call went out for the men to take up their positions on the wall. Then, after just going around the city, the armies of Israel just walked away.

I'd like to have been in the "Jericho War Room" that night. I can imagine the words, "I don't know" were repeated over and over. It was the weirdest thing any of these Jerichoites had ever seen!

Next day, same story. "These guys from Israel aren't even talking. I'd at least expect them to taunt us in some way."

Third day, more of the same. The defenders were probably a little slower getting to their posts. "I'll be right along. I have one more chapter in this "Defenders of Caanan" comic book.

By the fourth day people would bring their small children up to the top of the wall so they could watch the "parade." The kids were probably happy to be there; this was an area where children would be sacrificed to bring good fortune in battle. This was just one of the many sins of the people of this area for which God was using Israel as a rod of His judgment.

On the fifth day a couple of guys showed up on the walls with popcorn and ice tea to sell to the bored defenders.

On the sixth day the defenders brought chairs and radios with them. The University of Southern Philistia was playing for the title. One man grumbled, "I wish television had already been invented. I'd really like to see a replay of that last penalty."

And then day seven arrived. "Hey, they are going to go around again. And again." This was different but not terribly entertaining.

Then, after circling the city seven times, some of the Israelites took out horns. The horns were blown. The Israelites shouted. The walls crumbled beneath the defenders. Only one small section of the wall stood. There was a scarlet thread hanging out from a window. Rahab was saved along with her family. The rest of the city felt the searing judgment of God upon them due to the immorality and irreligion which had been their way of life.

The judgments of God come slowly. But, the judgments of God always arrive on His appointed schedule. It is not necessary that such judgment will fall on anyone. God offers escape and pardon. Faith is the key that will unlock the prison door of sin and allow any to escape to the loving arms of The Father.]

11.31 By faith the harlot Rahab perished not with them that believed not, when she had received the spies with peace.

[And now we come to the harlot Rahab. I am reminded of a story about a man who was writing a history of his family. This family had been one of the founding families of a small Western community. Imagine the horror when this proud writer found that one of his great-grandfathers had been hung as a horse thief. The writer was a direct descendant of this man. He could not leave this name out of the story. Neither did he want to admit such a scoundrel as one of his ancestors.

The writer finally solved his dilemma with the following sentence: "I can't spend too much time writing about my Great Grandfather. Suffice it to say that his death came about when the scaffolding gave way at a public celebration held in his honor."

Many words have been used to describe Rahab as an "innkeeper" rather than a "harlot." However, the word "porne," translated in our text as "harlot" is 4204 in Strong's. "a strumpet; figuratively, an idolater:--harlot, whore." The Old Testament word, "Zanah," is translated as "harlot" in Joshua 6:25. This word is number 2181 in Strong's and is translated as. "a primitive root (highly-fed and therefore wanton); to commit adultery (usually of the female, and less often of simple fornication, rarely of involuntary ravishment); figuratively, to commit idolatry (the Jewish people being regarded as the spouse of Jehovah):--(cause to) commit fornication, X continually, X great, (be an, play the) harlot, (cause to be, play the) whore, (commit, fall to) whoredom, (cause to) go a-whoring, whorish."

Rahab may well have been an "innkeeper" who owned a boarding house. She was also a harlot as our text informs us.

William Burkitt uses a beautiful illustration. "God pardoned it, and the apostle here makes no mention of it; the Holy Ghost lays, as it were, the finger upon the scar, and covers it out of sight, contrary to the practice of the malignant world, who overlook all the good, and reflect only upon the evil of an action; whereas God takes notice of the good, but passes by the evil."

Burkitt was speaking of the lie of Rahab. However, one sin is as malicious as another sin. Rahab is an Old Testament example of a sinner saved by Grace. Even the harlotry of Rahab was covered by the grace of God.

The lie of Rahab was wrong. But, God looked beyond her misconduct and applied His mercy. Rahab had heard the stories of Israel and Israel's God. She had faith that the promises of God were certain. Therein lay her righteousness. She accepted the spies in her faith in God. In doing so, Rahab put herself at great risk from her own countrymen. However, she, as Abraham before her, sought a great land of promise. (Hebrews 11:8)

The sentence used by Paul does not condemn Rahab as a harlot; he simply states that she had been so. The wonderful grace of God is such that there is no sin which cannot be forgiven and forgotten. A story is told of a cowboy in the old West who found a man buried up to his neck in "quick sand." A rope was tossed to the man in the quick sand. But, no manner of pulling, even with the horse of the would-be rescuer joining in the effort could bring the doomed man out of the quick sand. Finally, the man in the sand said, "Do you reckon I ought to take my feet out of the stirrups?"

Take your feet out of the stirrups of your own lack of power and preparation. Trust the rope of God's forgiveness and empowerment. God can still do great things through a man who has faith in Him – and who acts upon that faith. If the greatest faith one is capable of attaining remains "holstered," that person will not even shoot "blanks" at the adversary.

Joshua 6:23 says this of Rahab. "And the young men that were spies went in, and brought out Rahab, and her father, and her mother, and her brethren, and all that she had, and they brought out all her kindred, and left them without the camp of Israel." It seems that they were probably left outside the camp in order to perform some purification rites such as those of Leviticus, the nineteenth chapter.

Rahab was to become a grandmother of King David. Past this she was also an ancestor, humanly speaking, of our Lord Jesus Christ. The forgiveness of God is a wonderful thing to behold!]

11.32 *And what shall I more say? for the time would fail me to tell of Gedeon, and of Barak, and of Samson, and of Jephthae, of David also, and Samuel, and of the prophets:*

[There is an amazing conciseness within the inspired and preserved Scripture of God. The subject matter is of the entire scope of human emotions and aspirations yet the entire library of volumes fits easily into a single volume. Many editions of the sacred Book of Books are so small as to easily fit within a man's shirt pocket.

God has not hidden His precious volume of wisdom, devotion, and power in the "wordiness" of a human author who writes only a story of a few years duration. There is a lesson in that consideration for pastors. We may love our command of the language. We may love exhibiting our knowledge and wit. We may love to show our great ability to find all that is within the Bible. We may love to stand before the people of God and display our command of the great doctrines of the church. And, while we are doing this great work of building confidence in ourselves as the under shepherd of the flock of God, the sheep may wander off into the pasture of day dream and slumber.

Preacher, limit you discourse to fit into a small sack which can be easily carried home by the average man in the pew. We are not performers. We are simply a tool by which God imparts His Truth to those who may consent to sit within our congregation. May we never become an impediment to His purposes. God has been very concise in His inspired and preserved Words to man. May we learn to follow God!

Paul found many examples, too many to place in a short letter to these Hebrew people in the church of God, from the time of the Old Covenant of the Law. How sad it seems that we can find so few examples of Godly faith in this age of grace. We do not tend to stand in the time of trail because we do not lean upon God. An untrusting, and unused, faith is an oxymoron in terminology.

Gideon is first mentioned in this list. His story is found in the sixth through the eighth chapters of Judges. His adversaries are the Midianites and the Amalekites. We are all familiar with Gideon's great victory. His small group, armed with faith in God and little else against the thousands of the enemy, routed the enemy with the shout of, "The Sword of the Lord and of Gideon." (see Judges 7:20)

Considering how puny was the sword of Gideon, and how Powerful and Necessary was the Sword of the Lord, it seems amazing that Gideon's sword is even mentioned. God exalts those who exalt Him. While we may not notice this in this life; we may be certain that God takes notice and pleasure in the person who stands for Him.

Before Gideon was able to "go to war" as God's conscript, Gideon had a moment of faithful service back at the "family farm." Gideon destroyed a grove and altar which were raised to the honor of Baal. This was Gideon's father's grove and altar. Gideon trusted God in this work of opposing false religion. Gideon was then ready to lead the people of God against their oppressors.

Destroy those false gods first. They are not to be feared.

Next Barak is mentioned. This seems somewhat strange since the Prophet and Judge of Israel at this time was a woman by the name of Deborah. Deborah had recruited Barak to fight against the armies of Jabin who were persecuting Israel. The incident is related in Judges, the fourth chapter.

The faith of Barak was that he trusted the Words of God even though they were relayed to him through the instrument of a woman. In a very paternalistic society this would not be expected. Nonetheless, the power of God was upon Deborah. Barak, though his own cultural upbringing would have rebelled at this situation, trusted what were the powerful Words of God even as those Words came from an unexpected source.

The faith of Barak was distinguished in that he disregarded his own preconceptions and comfort of culture as he submitted to the Words of God.

Now we come to Samson. His story is recorded in chapters 13 – 16 of Judges. Samson was called to be a judge in Israel even before his birth. I am tempted to say that we are certainly lucky that Samson's mother decided to allow him life rather than choosing abortion. But, I won't.

In Samson we find a man who was used of God in many ways. Being an example to the youth of our day is probably not one of the ways that God uses him. Samson was a man of extreme passions and appetites of a sensual nature. He seems almost ill fitted to the task of a judge of Israel.

The underlying faith of Samson is shown in the fact that his exploits are always directed against those who would harm his people. Samson was a man known for standing on his feet against the enemies of the Lord.

Though this trait of Samson was often overshadowed by more disquieting factors, we find the inner faith of Samson at the time of his death. He may have not been a perfect man but he was perfectly committed to battle against the forces which were arrayed against the people of God.

God's power reaches even past the natural power of Samson to produce an example of faith while Samson was standing in the entrance to the Valley of the Shadow. The grace of God looks beyond the life experience of the penitent and finds the commitment to faith. God honors faith.

If we had a problem with Samson, consider Jepthah. His story is recalled in Judges, chapters eleven and twelve.

Jephthah was born of a prostitute. He was forced out of his family because of the sins of his mother. But, one day the very people who had forced him into exile came to beg his assistance against the Ammonites.

His faith seemed to center around the promises of the land which God had made with Abraham. This seems amazing in light of the fact that the reason Japhthah was exiled was so that he could not inherit any of the land. (Judges 11:2)

God was gracious to Japhthah in battle. One day Japhthah made a rash vow to sacrifice the first thing that came to greet him upon his return home from battle. The first thing was his daughter, his only child. From the reading of the incident I must conclude that this "offering" was carried out. Even the daughter agreed that to make a promise, a vow, to God was a thing which must be done.

I see no way that this could be justified. It is more than apparent that God did "find a way" to justify Japhthah. The grace of God reaches to the depths of the depravity of man and finds a soul for which Jesus died. God is greater than we could ever imagine!

David, the King, is the next on Paul's short list. There is so much about the life of David that displays the attitude of faith; we cannot begin to plumb the depths of his faith. One often cited example of the faith of David concerns the giant Goliath which is recorded in chapter seventeen of First Samuel

When the term "giant" is used, "giant" is meant. If David were an average sized man of the time he would have been staring directly into Goliath's navel.

David was more than a little upset at Goliath. David was taking some food to his brothers who were in Saul's army when he first saw Goliath. Goliath was standing between the armies of the Philistines and the armies of Israel. He had made a rather simple bid to avoid the bloodshed of a full scale was. "You send out your best fighter against me. If he beats me my people will be your slaves. If I beat him you will become our slaves."

David asked who was going to fight Goliath. Not a single person answered. We might wonder why Saul allowed David to meet Goliath on the field of battle. Well, no one else would stand up against Goliath. The next question is, "Why send anyone?"

This was actually a custom of war at the time. In order to avoid the massive bloodshed of the battle these "champions" of each side would fight as representative of the entire armies. The winner was the winner for his entire army. The loser was the loser for his entire army. Goliath's offer was real. Remember these were not "career soldiers;" these were mostly farmers who needed to get back to their fields so that nation could be fed.

David was allowed to be the "champion" for the Israeli army. He refused armor because it was too large for him. This appeared a mismatch. It was. The faith of David was that he allowed God to empower him. The power of God energized the arm of David who quickly won the battle.

Samuel, himself, is the final individual mentioned. Samuel was the last of the judges of Israel. He was also the first of the prophetic line. It was Samuel who anointed both Saul and David to be king in Israel. He did this in both his status as judge and his authority as prophet.

The first king, Saul, was anointed in Samuel's office as judge. A judge in ancient Israel was a human who was invested with the power of God to fulfill a specific purpose. He was a human person. He did not "rule" in the sense of a "ruler." His rule was more in the line of a military commander. His purpose seems to have been more a matter of leading the defense of the nation than to be any sort of ruler over them.

This was the role of Saul as king. It seemed as though he was a perfect physical specimen. His purpose was to rule, as king; he was also to protect Israel from the forces which oppressed her.

Samuel anointed David from his status as a prophet. A prophet is tasked to be a religious leader in giving the message of God to the people of God. He may also be used of God to foretell certain events. That would have been in his office of giving the message of God to the people of God; that giving of the message of God was the primary function of the prophet.

Anointed as king by the prophet Samuel, David accepted the responsibility to do

HEBREWS: Chapter 11

more than protect the people from oppression by foreign elements, he also bore the responsibility – Israel was a theocratic nation – to lead the people in the ways of God. As we read the Books of the Kings and the Chronicles we find this concept very often.

Make no mistake; the kings did not serve in the capacity of priests. They were, however, responsible for setting the moral tone of civil life in a Godly manner.

As we read the names of these various persons we see that they are not in chronological order. Neither are they "rated" as better or worse. The purpose is to show that the grace of God is extended to many as they exercise faith in God.

Samuel, as a prophet and listed last in this verse, is a bridge to the next verse which describes some of the instance of faith in the lives of His people. The prophet's faith enabled them to speak the Words of God without regard to the repercussions from anyone.]

11.33 Who through faith subdued kingdoms, wrought righteousness, obtained promises, stopped he mouths of lions,

[Hammering through the roadblocks to true faith which the traditions of ceremony had erected in the minds of the recipients of this letter, Paul begins a jackhammer like recitation of some of the great acts of faith illustrated in the Old Testament Scriptures. There was no need for Paul to start a "roll call" and mention each person by name. The background of his listeners would supply the names to associate with the incidents. Indeed, the hearers would supply even more names as Paul reminded them of these great acts of faith. Paul's emphasis was on the results of faith as victories of which ceremony was merely a commentary.

Abraham might have never subdued a kingdom in his own hand, but the hand of his children subdued many kingdoms in answer to The Promise given Abraham. Joshua and Caleb led the children of the exodus journey into this land of promise and subdued the kingdoms of the land in gaining the inheritance which God had promised.

We must note that this conquest was incomplete. The people did not access all of the land which God had given to them. This incomplete obedience resulted in the various judges which God raised up among His people, being forced to re-conquer the same land and kingdoms over and over.

This is a picture reshot by the camera of the Christian's life all too often. We reach a plateau of victory and quickly slide into a mode of rest rather than marching on to victory. We realize that this victory is not of our power or making. We also realize that in the pursuit of this victory we need to remain in constant fellowship with the Lord of the spiritual victory. We tend, however, to replace the Gospel chorus of "I'm Marching On The Upward Way" with the Country/Western turn of "Down In The Valley."

In the pursuit of righteousness these Old Testament people gave us a picture of personal piety which holds to faith as the conduit to the blessings of God. Faith should be a motivating position for our personal and professional lives. Beyond this, we see the administration of civic law in the career of both Samuel, the prophet, and David, the king. The one leads in the paths of righteousness from a religious perspective. The other leads from, not away from but leading from righteousness as a base from which all else flows, in the leading of the civic and legal platforms; these are also to be pleasing to God as giving personal piety a secure ground of practice.

The final fulfillment of the Abrahamic promise was yet in the future. We have seen the coming of the Redeemer. The final promises of the restored Davidic Kingdom with Messiah on the throne is still future. The fact that God kept such subsidiary promises as in battles carried forth by the judges and kings, should give us a security that all of His Promises, to include the great promise of eternal salvation which has been given to the Christian, will certainly be kept by the honor and power of God.

We quickly think of Daniel in the lion's den when we see that the mouths of lions were stopped. We do not as quickly consider the same happened concerning Samson (Judges 14:6) and David (I Samuel 17:34-36). In each of these instances the same power is evident. God will provide the means to do what we cannot do when we approach His service in faith. It is the power of God which subdues the lions of our fear. This is so even today!]

11.34 *Quenched the violence of fire, escaped the edge of the sword, out of weakness were made strong, waxed valiant in fight, turned to flight the armies of the aliens.*

[Paul seems almost caught up in his emotions as he continues a rapid-fire rendition of the wonders of God's protection of His covenant people which are shown in the pages of Scripture and history.

Look at what God has done for us. Look at what God has done for us! LOOK AT WHAT GOD HAS DONE FOR US! LOOK WHAT GOD HAS DONE FOR US! The voice of the writing seems to raise in wonder and fervor with each example.

Could there be any story more inspiring that that of Shadrach, Meshach, and Abednego whose clothes were not even singed with the smell of fire after they had taken a leisurely afternoon stroll through the furnace of Nebuchadnezzar. The fire was so hot that the guards which forced the three Hebrew youths into the inferno died from the heat. But, when Nebuchadnezzar peered into the flames he saw the three walking around with, Nebuchadnezzar said this, "The Son of God."

Isn't it wonderful that God allows us to bring Him glory even as He saves us from our adversaries?

There are almost too many instances where the sword of the enemy could not find its mark when raised against God people. Moses had killed an Egyptian taskmaster. He had to flee the sword of Pharaoh. (Exodus 18:14) Elijah was doubled up; both Jezebel and Ahab wanted to "pin cushion" him with their swords. God said, "No." Saul chased David all over the land but could not find a place to kill a man under the protecting hand of God. After the debacle of the Philistine army sending Goliath to fight David, Saul should have known better. Look at the king of Syria as he seeks to kill Elisha. Once again, the mercy of God overrides the mayhem of an earthly king.

Oh, lest we forget Haman. All of the Jews of the empire escaped his sword due to the faith of Esther, the Queen.

Has any man in history suffered more than Job? His faith while under the severest of trials was rewarded with even more than he had previously lost. His faith was rewarded even past this measure. (Job 19:26) Poor Samson, betrayed in love, blinded by enemies, brought low by demeaning work and taunting he overcame all in the power of his faith in God. He died in faith and favor as he did the work of the Lord. (Judges 16:26-30) Hezekiah had no strength; he was on his death bed. The scene sees Hezekiah taken from his death bed and given an added fifteen years of the strength of physical life to reward the faith of Hezekiah. (Isaiah 38:5)

David was a very stout young boy. But, he stood no chance at all against the Philistine giant, Goliath. Faith once again proved to be the victory as David did his best while realizing that God would do the rest. What a "rock head" was Goliath for taunting the Lord's power and people!

Valiant men? Why even start the list? The Books of Joshua, Judges, I and II Samuel, I and II Kings, and I and II Chronicles give illustration after illustration of men and women who stood because of their faith in the power and promise of God. Even referencing those few Books fail to scratch the surface of all the heroism which faith wrought within the Hebrew community. Several commentaries also referenced the Maccabees as examples of men who were valiant in battle because of faith in the God of The Promises.

If we move to extra-Biblical sources, and I honestly do not feel that entirely warranted as Paul speaks of Biblical examples, we would have to come down to 1948 and the years since. It seems that the Children of the Covenant always fight under the protecting Hand of the Lord of the Universe.

Over and over the fuel of faith caused the engine of war to turn to flight the armies which assailed the people of God in the Land of Promise.]

11.35 Women received their dead raised to life again: and others were tortured, not accepting deliverance; that they might obtain a better resurrection.

[Many suggested that all occurring after the citation of the women receiving their dead raised to life are related to the Maccabean period. Although these might be true events which the originally intended recipients of this letter would have well understood, I have a problem with this interpretation.

Even though it is true that the translators, and many of those who received the translation in its early days, would have also understood the books of the Maccabees, I would still disagree. Paul has been accessing Biblical examples. There is no reason to assume that he would depart from the inspired and preserved Scriptural record and move on to historical events. The Jew of his day did not accept the apocryphal books as part of the inspired record. The first record of the acceptance of these books follows the Protestant Reformation. This was intended to buttress the authority of the Roman Church by giving "scriptural" reference to the doctrine of purgatory.

Since the Roman Church elevates tradition even above Scripture, and for that matter only allows even true Scripture to be doctrinally interpreted by their church. The Popes are granted an assumption of infallibility while the Scripture is not, in practice and functionality, assumed to be infallible.

Even with the above in mind, there was a need to contradict the teaching of the Protestants, whose firm stand was on "Scripture alone," in matters of faith and practice. Thus, the Scriptural record was "expanded" to include "Scripture" which would agree with that seminal doctrine, purgatory, of the Roman Church.

To quickly answer another objection which could be raised: Yes; the King James Bible originally included the apocryphal books. But, they were placed between the Testaments and identified as not part of the inspired record. They were only included for historical and devotional reading in a day when books were few and expensive. In later editions of the King James Bible, the apocrypha was excised; it was never considered as inspired by the translators or the people.

The widows whose sons were raised from the dead were two in the record of Scripture. The first was the widow of Zarephath (I Kings 17:19-32) whose son was raised by Elijah. The second was the Shumammite (II Kings 4:18-37) whose son was raised by Elisha.

The word "tortured" is "Tumpanizo" (# 5178 in Strong's). It is defined as, "from a derivative of 5180 (meaning a drum, "tympanum"); to stretch on an instrument of torture resembling a drum, and thus beat to death:--torture." The meaning seems to concern one who is beaten to death with repeated blows. By stretching a person the blows would cause more damage and pain upon the victim. Such is the hate of the world of man for those who are the children of Heaven through salvation.

The pious would not accept deliverance from this torture. The terms would have been sinful, such as renouncing the Savior. The terms would also have been sinful in regards to the testimony of the person who was released from torture. This would give an appearance of mercy to the merciless!

The concept of a "better resurrection" was also two-fold. First, and I believe primarily in this passage, the resurrection to life eternal which is promised to the child of God is much better than the resurrection to temporal life as alluded to above of the children of the widows. Also, the "resurrection" from certain death at the hands of the torturer was also temporal. A better resurrection is offered by Jesus than this present world has any possibility of offering.]

11.36 *And others had trial of cruel mockings and scourgings, yea, moreover of bonds and imprisonments:*

[A trail is a testing of one's faith. Certainly, these prophets of the Old Covenant endured many trials for their faith. "Now all these things happened unto them for ensamples: and they are written for our admonition, upon whom the ends of the world are come." (I Corinthians 10:11)

To consider cruel mocking we need consider no further than Samson. Samson, the mighty, had terrorized the Philistines for years. He was invincible. Then one day he met a beautiful young lady and fell in love. She enticed him to explain why he was so strong and unbeatable. He was a Nazarite; those Nazarite vows were what set him apart from other men. Under that vow he was an instrument of God to the protection of Israel and the prosecution of judgment to Israel's enemies.

That night Deliah shaved off his hair, an emblem of his Nazarite vows. In effect, his vows were rejected by himself. He might not have known what had been done; but, he had given his assent to the act of rejection by his own lips in the company of an enemy of Israel. Away from the people of God, out of the will of God, Samson was out from the protection of God. "And she said, The Philistines *be* upon thee, Samson. And he awoke out of his sleep, and said, I will go out as at other times before, and shake myself. And he wist not that the LORD was departed from him." (Judges 16:20)

One of the spiritual lessons for us in this debacle of this judge of Israel is that it is a dangerous place to be when we forsake Godly companionship and consort with the enemies of the Lord. (Hebrews 10:25)

Outside of the Lord's will and protection Samson was captured and blinded. When our own emotions and thoughts reside outside the will of the Lord we tend to be captivated by the sin which so easily besets us and blinded to the Glory of obedience to the Lord. (Hebrews 12:1)

Grinding grain like an ox, Samson was easy "sport" to the Philistines. They mocked this "mighty man" who had terrorized them. A great assembly came out to honor their idol god for the great victory over this judge of Israel. By extension they were also arguing that their idol was stronger than the Lord. Samson was brought out as a side show exhibit to show the superiority of the idol above the Lord of Israel.

As had his hair during his imprisonment, the heart of Samson returned to its rightful place. He called upon God. "And Samson called upon the LORD, and said, O Lord GOD, remember me, I pray thee, and strengthen me, I pray thee, only this once, O God, that I may be at once avenged of the Philistines for my two eyes. And Samson took hold of the two middle pillars upon which the house stood, and on which it was born up, of the one with his right hand, and of the other with his left. And Samson said, Let me die with the Philistines. And he bowed himself with *all his* might; and the house fell upon the lords, and upon all the people that *were* therein. So that the dead which he slew at his death were more than *they* which he slew in his life." (Judges 16:28-30)

When God forgives the sin from which we have repented He restores fellowship.

As to scourgings we need look no further than the events surrounding our Lord's crucifixion. "But he was wounded for our transgressions, he was bruised for our iniquities: the chastisement of our peace was upon him; and with his stripes we are healed." (Isaiah 53:5)

Jeremiah was also beaten for his testimony of the Lord. (Jeremiah 20:2) He was placed in bondage for this witness. (Jeremiah 37:15)

Joseph was falsely imprisoned in Egypt. God used the faith of Joseph, even during this false imprisonment, to bring glory to His Name. Jeremiah was held in a filthy pit because he spoke the truth. (Jeremiah 38:6) Micaiah and Hanani were both imprisoned by Ahab due to their testimony for the Lord. (I Kings 22:27; II Chronicles 16:7-10) In all cases the ones who were imprisoned were free in their spirits while those who were free in their natural state were imprisoned within the walls of false religion wherein the end is death.

We must remember that the testimony of God is generally rejected by the wisdom of man. (I Corinthians 2:14) The world of man is at variance with the Truth of God. (Romans 8:7) The spiritual principle is that we, as Christian who live in the Age of Grace, are not immune to the hate and trial of the world. "Blessed are ye, when *men* shall revile you, and persecute *you*, and shall say all manner of evil against you falsely, for my sake. Rejoice, and be exceeding glad for great *is* your reward in heaven: for so persecuted they the prophets which were before you. (Matthew 5:11-12)

This is not a simple possibility for the Christians listed above. We, in my nation, have lived in a land which may have laughed at our naiveté. This is a warning from our Lord that such oppression is a probability. The time is on the horizon when the Christian will face real persecution; it is already happening in some forms even in our nation. More will come. The world of hate will not live in peace with the God of pure love. The persecution of those who name the Name of Jesus which we already see around the world will not fail to "book passage" to our shores.

Our only defense lies with a faith which cannot be moved. Our victory is secure in the Hands of our Lord.]

11.37 *They were stoned, they were sawn asunder, were tempted, were slain with the sword: they wandered about in sheepskins and goatskins, being destitute, afflicted, tormented,*

[In the words of Casey Kasem, "The hits just keep on coming." Indeed they do! Remember that this is case after case revealed of the people of God feeling the affliction and displeasure of man.

How could this be? Didn't Jesus say, "Come unto me, all ye that labour and are heavy laden, and I will give you rest?" (Matthew 11:28) Yes. He did! The "rest" which these servants of God felt was in their souls as they realized the glory of being allowed to suffer for Christ. Paul relates this of Jesus just a few verses past this place. "Looking unto Jesus the author and finisher of our faith; who for the joy that was set before him endured the cross, despising the shame, and is set down at the right hand of the throne of God." (Hebrews 12:2) Paul explains that Jesus looked past the pain and suffering and unto the completion of His mission to offer full and complete salvation to a world in bondage to sin. He did that with joy!

I see a little boy going to a dentist. His pain is real. As he looks at all the instruments of the dentist's trade, the little boy's fear is also real. The dentist sits down next to the little boy in the dental chair. He calmly explains to the boy that the fear he feels is normal. He asks the little boy if he had been "hurting" for the past couple of days. The boy said, "Awfully. But, I think it has stopped now."

The dentist explained that the pain hadn't left forever. It would be back. But, if the little boy would just endure this little procedure that pain would never come back. It would be gone forever. Still apprehensive, but emboldened by the dentist words, the little boy submitted to the procedure. The pain never did return; it was just as the dentist said. Within just a few minutes the little boy was pain free and also glad he had come to this place.

There will be persecutions. Jesus has also promised this. The sin in the world always hates the joy in our hearts. Philippians 1:29 gives the Christian this truth. "For unto you it is given in the behalf of Christ, not only to believe on him, but also to suffer for his sake..." II Timothy 2:12a reminds us, "If we suffer, we shall also reign with him..." Even a long time on earth is but a speck of dust on the mountain top of eternity. There is a joy which cannot be described by words; it must be experienced in the soul. Even the persecution of the world cannot dim this joy. The joy is expanded in our knowledge that our testimony in persecution can be the means of a saving testimony to others. "But the fruit of the Spirit is love, joy, peace, longsuffering, gentleness, goodness, faith..." (Galatians 5:22)

I am rather certain that Stephen, the first recorded martyr of the New Testament Church, did not physically enjoy the stoning which led to his death. But, as he died Stephen said, "...Behold, I see the heavens opened, and the Son of man standing on the right hand of God." (Acts 7:56)

If that is not the best "welcoming party" imaginable I do not know the meaning of "best." But, wait, there is more. Consider the place where these people stoning Stephen laid their coats while attending to the task. "And cast *him* out of the city, and stoned *him*: and the witnesses laid down their clothes at a young man's feet, whose name was Saul." You might know "Saul" by the name he accepted when he became a Christian. He became the great apostle Paul. It would appear that the martyrdom of Stephen, and his acceptance of this death, was a testimony which led directly to the conviction upon the heart of "Saul." Many believe that it was Saul's witness to the death of Stephen which led to the conversion of "Paul."

There were other notable stoning's in Scripture. This seems a "favorite" means of capital punishment used by the ancient Israelites. Jezebel "set up" Naboth to be stoned so Ahab could take his vineyard. Naboth had refused to sell the land, even to the king, because it was part of the inheritance land as parceled out by Joshua. It was his family's inheritance. He was stoned because of his dedication to the tradition of the Promise.

Zechariah was a prophet who preached against the idolatry of his day. (II Chronicles 24:20-21) His earthly reward was to be stoned in the court yard of the Temple. Jesus mentions this as part of His denunciation of the hypocrisy of the Pharisee's. (Matthew 23:35) In this way Jesus gives praise to Zechariah and includes that name among those so honored in the New Testament Scripture. More than just mentioning Zechariah, Jesus also describes him as "righteous." That isn't just an epitaph; that is a description given by the Lord, Himself.

There is Talmudic tradition that Manasseh ordered the execution of Isaiah by sawing him in half. Although this form of punishment was known in ancient Israel, it seems rarely used. Stoning was much more normal. The ancient Romans also, though also rarely, used this form of execution.

Temptation seems almost out of place among these other tortures. But, consider a man told that if he merely converts to another religion, and in so doing renounces his real religion publically, he may continue to wear his head above his shoulders. Of, consider a man being beaten who is told that the beatings will stop if he simply recants his conversion. That is real temptation. It seems so small. "If I just say that Christianity is wrong, I can go?' That is a serious temptation – to deny God His rightful glory.

Once again, there were many who were slain by the sword for the testimony of the Lord. Elijah alludes to this while he was in his cave "hid out." "And he said, I have been very jealous for the LORD God of hosts: for the children of Israel have forsaken thy covenant, thrown down thine altars, and slain thy prophets with the sword; and I, even I only, am left; and they seek my life, to take it away." (I Kings 19:10)

God corrects this misconception of Elijah. "Yet I have left *me* seven thousand in Israel, all the knees which have not bowed unto Baal, and every mouth which hath not kissed him." (I Kings 19:18) The church may seemingly shrink and appear to die. God keeps His remnant, the faithful through the temptation and persecution of the world.

In I Samuel 22:18 we read of one of the results of king Saul's hatred for David. We see that this resulted in 85 being killed by the sword by Doeg, the Edomite. It has been suggested that these were all killed by decapitation. I mention this because of Revelation 20:4 – "And I saw thrones, and they sat upon them, and judgement was given unto them: and *I saw* the souls of them that were beheaded for the witness of Jesus, and for the word of God, and which had not worshiped the beast, neither his image, neither had received *his* mark upon their foreheads, or in their hands; and they lived and reigned with Christ a thousand years."

It would seem that beheading will become a means of stilling the voice of the believers of the Tribulation Era. Beware as we see the props being brought to the stage for this particular act of fury against the Lord and His people.

Sheepskin is a type of clothing which was among the cheapest available. The poorest prophet could array himself in this. Note that this is not "wool,' but rather sheepskin. There is conjecture that this was the construction of the mantle of Elijah. Some have conjectured that this was a near "uniform" for the prophets of old. (II Kings 1:8; Zechariah 13:4 where the description is of sheepskin)

With the word "destitute" I can think of no one more destitute than the prophet Elijah at the brook Cherith where he drank from the brook and counted on the ravens which God sent to bring him food. To that I could only add the apostle Peter who told the beggar in Acts 3:6, "silver and gold have I none." Even in our most destitute situation we can grasp the promise of God, "But my God shall supply all your need according to his riches in glory by Christ Jesus." (Philippians 4:19)

Considering all the afflictions listed, and all the torments listed, Paul would argue for the Christian, "Not that I speak in respect of want: for I have learned, in whatsoever state I am, therewith to be content." (Philippians 4:18) We may fail Him. In truth, we often fail Him and in so doing fail to avail ourselves of the power of His peace. May we exercise the faith of trust in Him. He will never fail us!]

11.38 *(Of whom the world was not worthy:) they wandered in deserts, and in mountains, and in dens and caves of the earth.*

[It has often been conjectured how the world will react to the rapture of the saints. There will have to be some sort of explanation offered in the name of man for this act of God. One of the most intriguing possibilities seems that the blame will fall upon "space aliens" who have observed the great hate and violence upon the earth and have removed those whose philosophy of life is one of hate. They will argue that it is the Christian people who are the biggest perpetrators of hate; thus, they were removed.

Arguing that the Christians are not "fully evolved" this argument could be expanded to explain the removal of children as well.

This is just one theory; it has no validity. The purpose of the Christian is not to theorize what might happen after the Second Appearing of our Lord. The purpose of the Christian of this dispensation is to follow the example of the Lord to seek and to (allow Him) save those that are lost. (Luke 19:10) We can and should exposit upon the inspired and preserved Scripture. But, even within this our primary purpose is to win souls for the kingdom.

The world has never understood that those of God whom they attempt to marginalize are not the "unworthy." In the true spiritual sense, the world is not worthy of us. Neither was the world worthy of the prophets and the righteous that were forced from worldly society. David, anointed to become the king of Israel by Samuel the prophet, fled into the deserts of the wilderness in order to escape the king whom God had rejected from being king, Saul. David hid in caves as he hid from the murderous wrath of Saul.

Obadiah hid prophets in the caves of Israel. (I Kings 18:4) Jezebel had already killed many of the prophets' number. Elijah also found refuge in a cave. (I Kings 19:13) In this manner was the physical life of the prophet saved from the sword of the world. More importantly, in this way was the spiritual life of the prophet enhanced by his removal – for a time – from the corrupting influence of society. It is good to get away and commune with God so that our souls may be strengthened to return with the Message of God to the community of man.

We often do not realize the strategic importance which even the reviled Christian has for the security of lost humanity. In Genesis 18:23 Abraham asks a question of God. "And Abraham drew near, and said, Wilt thou also destroy the righteous with the wicked." This was in reference to the destruction of Sodom and Gomorrah. In the following verses God uses the concern of Abraham to show an important spiritual principle: The graciousness of God to His people will often give at least a temporary shield to the unrighteous.

In the Second Epistle to the Thessalonians Paul speaks of the Antichrist of Revelation. "Let no man deceive you by any means, for *that day shall not come*, except there come a falling away first, and that man of sin be revealed, the son of perdition; Who opposeth and exalteth himself above all that is called God, or that is worshipped, so that he as God sitteth in the temple of God, shewing himself that he is God. Remember ye not that, when I was yet with you, I told you these things? And now ye know what withholdeth that he might be revealed in his time. For the mystery of iniquity doeth already work: only he who now letteth *will let*, until he be taken out of the way. And then shall that wicked be revealed..." (II Thessalonians 2:3-8a – The underline for emphasis was added by this writer.)

The Defined King James Bible identifies the word "let" as "hinder, prevent, obstruct." That word is "katecho" (number 1722 in Strong's); it is defined as, "to hold down (fast), in various applications (literally or figuratively):--have, hold (fast), keep (in memory), let, X make toward, possess, retain, seize on, stay, take, withhold."

The meaning is that extreme evil is already at work in this world. Satan desires to release his full fury upon humanity. It is not that Satan specifically has hatred for humanity; although as the antithesis of the God of Love, Satan is the devil of hatred. Satan specifically has hatred for God. As humanity is the zenith of the creation of God, Satan desires to harm that creation in order to bring "hurt" to God. In the first chapter of Job we see that Satan must obtain the permission from God to afflict Job.

Only when God has a purpose – testing, trial, teaching, etc. – will that permission by given by the permissive will of God. Faith in God is our refuge when this sort of thing seems to assail our lives. That faith in Him will mitigate the trial; we will gain spiritual strength for our walk from such testing and trial. When the purpose is teaching we are given the wonderful opportunity to be conduits of the Message of God to someone or some group. This is a glory which God allows upon His saints from time to time.

God, The Holy Spirit, resides within the heart of the Christian. We are, as was the Tabernacle in the wilderness, the special abode of the omnipresent God of the Universe. The Holy Spirit restrains Satan's darkest desires for humanity. When the Christian is removed at the rapture of the saints, Satan is loosed to visit his full fury upon mankind.

Indeed, the world is not worthy of those whom are loathed by man and the religions of man.]

11.39 And these all, having obtained a good report through faith, received not the promise:

[All of these listed above may have had faults. Each of them had faults; of this there is no question. These were not perfect men. Each of them had one trait in common – they had faith in God. Faith is the victory over all our faults and failures. Note that in II Peter 2:7 Lot is called "just." It must be that the faith of Lot kept him pure from the sin of Sodom. Even the fact that the angels rescued Lot from the condemned city speaks of at least a modicum of righteous behavior within the life of Lot.

As we consider the actions of Lot in the cave after the destruction of Sodom and Gomorrah, we must also consider that he had before this acted strongly to protect the two angels from the perversions of the men of the city. Faith, true faith, in the Words of God and the God who issued those Words is essential. Faith is always expressed by a faithful reaction to the Words of God for any particular dispensation. How glorious it is that we are allowed to reside in the Age of Grace whereby God calls us to the Cross that we might receive salvation despite our own unworthiness.

It was faith in God which supported every one of those mentioned, and a myriad of others not mentioned. The smile of God will always, and only, come upon those who have faith in Him alone.

This verse says that these did not receive the promise. What could these righteous persons have not received? Hebrews 11:15-16 argues that they sought a Heavenly Country. They did not receive this during their sojourn on earth. Neither did they receive the recompense of reward in this life. (Hebrews 11:26) Some of these men were very well-to-do by the standards of their day. But, they never received the Heavenly riches of forgiven sins. The Cross of Jesus is the means of salvation; the sacrifice of the animals of creation was never intended to give spiritual salvation. (Hebrews 10:4) Once again, it was that faith which was placed upon the promises and Words of God which would apply the True Blood of salvation. (Revelation 13:8) This was not a concept which was understood by these persons. It was their faith in God which allowed this Self-Sacrifice of Jesus to be applied to their account.

These Old Testament saints also never received the "better resurrection." (Hebrews 11:35) They believed in the resurrection of the body unto the Heavenly realms. More importantly, and this they could not have understood, the "Best Resurrection" was that of Jesus on the third day. That resurrection was yet in the future for these men. (Consider my notes on Luke 19:16)

Romans 4:3 tells us that these persons did receive and imputed righteousness based on their faith in the Words of God. It is this faith which gave them a good report. Consider that Abel was given a good report of his sacrificial offering while Cain was not. Abel acted in the known will of God. Cain offered the best he could produce without any real reliance upon God.]

11.40 *God having provided some better thing for us, that they without us should not be made perfect.*

[God has given to us the blessing of allowing our physical existence to come during the time of the Gospel dispensation. As with all the graces which God has given to humanity, this has nothing to do with any merit within us. We are pleased to live in the fullness of God's Own time. We can look with faith to the Cross. Others before us had looked at the sacrifice of the animals of creation. We look at the Self-Sacrifice of the very Creator, Himself.

The faith of the Old Testament saints was based in an incomplete understanding of Genesis 3:15. Our faith is based in the God revealed Words of John 3:16. The faith of both us and them is based in the understanding of the love and provision of God; our faith is given the reality of which their faith saw only the shadow.

Theirs was a mighty faith which could not be completed, or perfected, until the Cross of Calvary became a fact of time. The basis of salvation via that cross is from the reality of eternity into the reality of time. But, the action of that cross is of time. It has happened just as God said it would.

This perfection to which they could have faith was in the reality, but not to experience that reality until the time of the Self-Sacrifice of Jesus. "For this we say unto you by the word of the Lord, that we which are alive and remain unto the coming of the Lord shall not prevent them which are asleep. For the Lord himself shall descend from heaven with a shout, with the voice of the archangel, and with the trump of God: and the dead in Christ shall rise first: Then we which are alive and remain shall be caught up together with them in the clouds, to meet the Lord in the air: and so shall we ever be with the Lord." (I Thessalonians 4:15-17) We both, the Old Testament saints and us of the New Testament of His Blood, have faith in the resurrection of the dead. To us, after the Cross, is given the understanding of the beauty of the rapture wherein we need not die in time in order to have our bodies changed so that all, both of us, can enter into the eternal state of Heaven. Consider I Corinthians 15:42-57. The completion of all the Old Covenant promises was not possible until that Old Covenant had been fulfilled and completed by Jesus.

The completion of the promises of their faith must wait past their time and come to the fullness of the time of this Gospel dispensation. It isn't so much that they waited for us as it is that we are privileged to welcome those Old Testament saints into the fullness of the Lord in which we both are allowed to have faith.

We are brought again to understand that everything contained in the inspired and preserved Scripture is always Truth. Not everything which is not contained within the inspired and preserved Scripture is always false. There was a Rabbinical teaching about the state of the dead. In this the abode of the dead was divided into two compartments. One, Hell, was the abode of the unjust. The other, Paradise, was the abode of the righteous. In the sixteenth chapter of Luke, in the relating of the story of Lazarus and the rich man, Jesus gave credence to this tradition. The tradition was elevated from the musing of man to its rightful status of revelation from God.

It is <u>only</u> in this relationship to the inspired and preserved Words of Scripture, by which the previously extra-Biblical teaching can be considered as part of the Message of God to the people of God. If the Bible says a thing is so, it is shown to be Divine Revelation given to us. If the Bible is silent on a thing, that thing has no spiritual validity.

Paradise has no reference to the false doctrine of Purgatory. The concept of Purgatory is a deception whereby the pure love of God is considered as not complete without the work of man. The purpose given for purgatory is to purge sin which was not cleansed during the physical life of a person while on earth. Since we know that, "...the blood of Jesus Christ his Son cleanseth us from all sin," (I John 1:7b) we also know that such a teaching as purgatory is not extra-Biblical it is anti-Biblical.

It is nonetheless true that the concept of Paradise does have to do with sin. God is completely Holy in all His ways. (Psalm 145:17) Sin can have no place with God as sin is anathema to His Holy Nature. Since sin was not taken away by the sacrifice of the animals of humanity, (Hebrews 10:4) the righteous dead of the pre-Cross era were not given their full promise of their "Heavenly country" of Hebrews 11:15-16.

Still, these were ones whose faith had been counted as righteousness. (Romans 4:3)

In Ephesians 4:8-10 we are told that, "Wherefore he saith, When he ascended up on high, he led captivity captive, and gave gifts unto men. (Now that he ascended, what is it but that he also descended first into the lower parts of the earth? He that descended is the same also that ascended up far above all heavens, that he might fill all things.)"

We compare the passage from Ephesians with I Peter 3:19 - 20. "By which also he went and preached unto the spirits in prison; Which sometime were disobedient, when once the longsuffering of God waited in the days of Noah, while the ark was a preparing, wherein few, that is, eight souls were saved by water." The reference to Noah has led some to mistakenly argue that Jesus, during His physical time in the Tomb, went into Sheol to preach to the lost of the era of the great flood.

Note that the waters were not the means of salvation for Noah except that it was the water of the judgment of God which separated Noah from the sinners who perished.

Under the Revelation of Revelation 22:11, "He that is unjust, let him be unjust still: and he which is filthy, let him be filthy still: and he that is righteous, let him be righteous still: and he that is holy, let him be holy still," we see that such a "second opportunity" for salvation after physical death is not spiritually possible.. At the time of physical death the die is cast as to the eternal abode of the human. "And as it is appointed unto men once to die, but after this the judgment..." (Hebrews 9:27)

Comparing the two passages we do, I believe, see some of the actions of Jesus during those three days His physical body reposed in the tomb. Jesus preached righteousness to the righteous of the pre-Cross era. It was here that He supplied His Sacrifice, considered as done before the very creation of man, by which He gave the full gift of eternal salvation to these faithful and, by imputation, righteous of the pre-Cross time of human history. He then led the souls of these people into their Heavenly rest to await the resurrection of the body.

As to those in Hell, they remain in anticipation of another day. "And death and hell were cast into the lake of fire. This is the second death." (Revelation 20:14)

We must also note that it was during these three days, my sense is that this was His first act after Calvary, Jesus approached the Mercy Seat of the Tabernacle of Heaven, made without hands, and presented His Blood of Atonement.

See my note at Luke 16:19.]

HEBREWS - CHAPTER TWELVE

12.1 *Wherefore seeing we also are compassed about with so great a cloud of witnesses, let us lay aside every weight, and the sin which doth so easily beset us, and let us run with patience the race that is set before us,*

[The previous chapter has been called the "Hall of Fame of Scripture." That seems to be true. But, in reality we must understand that there are no great men of God. There are only men who have had the privilege to serve The Great God. Nevertheless, we see these people from our flawed position as weak humans who seek to give what honor and glory we may to the Lord of the Universe. We see them as the greatest examples of true humanity in that they strived to persevere in the power of faith, a gift from God, as they struggled in this world of persecution and tribulation.

Paul says that they are a "great cloud of witnesses." For the most those mentioned are a witness that man can overcome the tendencies to live in the love of the world as these have loved the Lord more than these other things. Theirs is a faith directed life which counts the glory waiting for those that truly love the Lord more than they strive for any transitory glory from men on this earth.

Beyond this there are heavenly witnesses to our struggles and the triumphs which the Lord gives. I don't believe that those who have gone on to their heavenly reward view all our actions on this earth. I could be wrong; that is my belief from studying the inspired and preserved Scripture. I do know that the angels of heaven have an eye upon this earth. Jesus said, "I say unto you, that likewise joy shall be in heaven over one sinner that repenteth, more than over ninety and nine just persons, which need no repentance." (Luke 15:7) It is given us to understand that the angels are attuned to earth to such a respect as to understand and applaud the salvation of a sinner. Likewise, they must be disappointed at the response of one who decides that he does not need the Lord's salvation and thus make an appointment to retain an eternal lodging in perdition.

The allusion Paul has made as regards these witnesses is generally argued as considering the crowd in a great amphitheater where the Olympic style games were performed. These competitors would remove any weight which might cause them to run below their optimum capacity. Often this would include laying aside their robes of clothing. This clothing could have been girded up into a belt so that it would not impede the motion of running; but, the weight would remain.

Our application in regards to these nude athletes, is that we should never be too embarrassed, among those of this world, to give forth the sublime message that Jesus Christ died in time so that we could live in eternity. This is not a plea to forego holy decorum among others. It is a plea to consider the needs of other to be saved as above our own frail inhibitions. Godly decorum is good; and, it is a good witness to the world. Personal fear and pride is an impediment to our commission to be witnesses of Christ throughout the world of men. Let us never fear to witness for, and of, our blessed Lord.

Clothing is a rather necessary item in the world. Even in our day of relaxed moral standards there are still signs in many retain establishments which proclaim, "No Shoes, No Shirts, No Service." There are times the Christian may need to "lay aside" some things which the world views as important. He does this so that his witness for Christ into the world will not be hampered.

Wealth and the things associated with it are not bad. But, they are not always blessings from God. The blessings of God will always enhance our spiritual service to Him. The "blessings" of the unholy spirit will serve as "sand in the gears" to the engine of our spiritual lives.

Sin, and inducements to sin which are often seen as very benign and useful, can easily beset our souls. A tire is very heavy when it is full of air. It may seem as though a car should run better without all that "good air" in those four tires. It doesn't. Neither does our spiritual life move forward in a situation which the world might call "unencumbered."

We are asked to run with patience. Back in 1968 I received a letter from the local "Draft Board." They, in the parlance of an old movie, made me an offer I could not refuse. The offer of their employment was accepted. At the time my first thought was, "Now everyone else will get a two-year head start on me." It seemed as though my life would be on "hold" until this period of enlistment was over.

"Patience," God seemed to say. "Patience. I've got a reason for this." Now, nearly fifty years later, I am beginning to understand. Due to the Veteran's Administration I do not have to worry about medical bills. Due to a V.A. pension because of problems associated with Agent Orange contamination, I am able to be a "full time" pastor. I do not need "outside" employment. It seems that God knew what He was doing all those years ago.

"Running" speaks of moving forward for God. "Patience" means always realizing the need to stay in His will. Many pastors are anxious to find the next bigger church as they rise on their "career ladders." It is sad that so few are nearly as anxious to go to a small church simply because God has a job for them in that place.

Run the race to the best of your ability but make certain that the shoes which carry your feet in the race are from God.]

12.2 *Looking unto Jesus the author and finisher of our faith, who for the joy that was set before him endured the cross, despising the shame, and is set down at the right hand of the throne of God.*

["The joy?" Jesus was not surprised by the events of Good Friday. It was for this purpose that He had come into the world. He came to set people free from their sins. He came to offer a way for people to have fellowship with God. He came to offer eternal life to people who were creeping toward eternal death.

His joy lay in the fact that He was completing His mission. He was not just "staying the course." He was steadying the course of countless millions who would look unto Him as their Savior. He came to offer us a salvation we couldn't earn and a pardon we did not deserve.

He died the death of a substitute for us. He rose as the Conquering Christ. He had defeated Satan, sin and death.

From our standpoint the most important authority of Jesus is as the Author of our faith. Our salvation is entirely of His will. This verse was read from another translation at a church meeting I was at several months ago. That translation said that Jesus was the "beginning" of our faith.

I suppose that this rendition may be correct. But, it is not accurate.

Let me explain the difference. I have a book coming out in the Spring. It is called, "Outline Studies on the Divinity of Christ." I will be listed as the "author" of the work. But, the bibliography runs for six pages. This was used as a study guide for the churches' T.V. program a few years ago. Now, I was there when this particular written work was started. I did do the work in assembling the information and presenting it in a logical formation. But, to say that I was the "author" of this work is to stretch the meaning of that word a little. I am the "compiler" of this work.

(This book did not come out. Instead it was published as a completed work rather than an "Outline Study." The entire outline was kept as an appendix in the book, "The Deity of Jesus, The Christ.")

Correct: I am the author. Accurate: I am the compiler.

Do you notice the difference?

Jesus did all the work associated with our salvation. He has sustained our salvation - one of the reasons that I preach the doctrine of eternal security is based on His power vs. our ability. He will continue this to the completion of our salvation when we reach the hallowed halls of Heaven to be with Him eternally.

But, beyond this, He is the creative force behind our salvation. It was His plan to offer this salvation to sinful mankind.

In the previous chapter Paul had bidden us to look at those who have carried faith in a day prior to the historical cross. Their very salvation was due to that cross although they could not understand that as a fact. In the abstract there was a Messiah to come. Even the earliest, although even they might not have used the term "Messiah," understood the fact that God would send a Deliverer to confront the sin issue among humanity. The understanding may have been dim but the faith was great in the goodness and promise of God was strong. It was based in the very Words of God as delivered to our first parents after The Fall in the Garden. (Genesis 3:15)

Paul now asks that we look to Jesus. We look beyond the secular choices that promise, and fail, to bring a utopia to this world. We look beyond the rulers who are charged with keeping peace and assuring opportunity. We even look beyond our best intentions and plans. We look to Jesus.

We look to Jesus. He has begun a good work within us and He will carry out that work to its completion. (Philippians 1:6) Salvation is not a thing to be grasped by our hands; salvation is a thing that is kept in the Hand of the Lord. Salvation is not of our striving but of His sufferings. We cannot lose that which has been committed to the Hands of the Savior; it is as though our salvation were placed in a Bank in Heaven. Jesus, alone, has the key and His honor demands that the vault of His Love protect our soul's salvation through all time and eternity.

There was a real joy seen by Jesus as He looked forward to the end of the time of the Cross.

In the time of the Roman Empire the death of the cross was the most ignominious sentence reserved only for the lowest of the low. Even to the Jew this was considered as a shameful death. (Deuteronomy 21:22-23) Jesus looked at the shame of this death and despised that shame as beneath His dignity of will and action. There may have been shame in the eyes of others but Jesus saw only glory.

To Jesus the joy of His Self-Sacrifice was a consummation of His entire sojourn into the human race. He was joyous in the fulfilling of The Father's will. He was joyous in fulfilling His prophesied purpose. He was joyous in fulfilling His Own promise made even before the fall of Adam that He would suffer and die to redeem that which sin had tried to purloin. He was joyous in that this was an expression of the Creator's love for His creature. He was also joyous that He would soon redeem that Glory, which was His as God, the Son, which He had laid aside in His identification with humanity.

The rightful place of Power would soon see the Son in His Rightful Glory. ".. . (He) is set down at the right hand of the throne of God" is not a consideration of a simple location. That is the position of power and glory. That is the sense that the "right hand" means. The people to whom Paul was writing would have quickly understood this as a cultural reference to power rather than to a locational reference.]

12.3   *For consider him that endured such contradiction on sinners against himself, lest ye be wearied and faint in your minds.*

[Continuing to look at Jesus will keep us from becoming weary from the assaults of man against the Gospel message we are to carry into the world. Jesus was contradicted, opposed and challenged, by the religious leaders of the day. Their opposition was stronger than any we might face. The opposition which we do face is faced on account of our dedication to our Lord. Jesus warned us of this in John 7:7. "The world cannot hate you; but me it hateth, because I testify of it, that the works thereof are evil."

When we consider the great suffering He endured for us, can we not be expected – indeed, happy! – that we are allowed to suffer for He Who has done so great things for us. Our tribulation is a light and fleeting thing when compared with the reviling He suffered in His ministry to the world even before the events of Calvary. "He came unto his own, and his own received him not." (John 1:11)

We may not be accepted by "our own." But, we will never be rejected by the very people of our own creation, and family, as was Jesus. Jesus was rejected by the Jewish people who had over a thousand years of prophecy which pointed to Him as The promised Messiah. We'll never suffer that rejection.

We need to keep our eyes, and our thoughts and love, on our Lord. If we keep our minds upon ourselves and our tribulations, we will soon weary of the "race" of the Christian life and long for a "pit stop" where we can walk away from the "vehicle" of our convictions and avoid the jeers of the crowd of the world.

Only a consideration of the Lord, and a daily walk with Him, will give us the fuel to continue and the tread to do so unswervingly.]

12.4   *Ye have not yet resisted unto blood, striving against sin.*

[It was the nature of sin within those who opposed Him which caused those of the days of His earthly ministry to be in conflict with Him. The natural human is violently opposed to the true things of God. We are not called to resist with violence. We are called to resist with the grace of Jesus who even willingly went to the cross in order to fulfill The Father's will and to complete His Own mission at the Cross of Calvary.

Paul is telling these people to rejoice in that they have not resisted, themselves, unto blood. It would seem that this applies to the death of martyrdom. Others have applied the phrase to the pugilists of the Olympic games of Greece. Those boxers would cover their fists with leather in order to make their hands harder for punching. Sometimes they would even "load" this leather with sharp objects to inflict further damage. Even today it is often said that no boxer has been fully tested in the ring until he has tasted his own blood. It is a sign that one has "steeled" himself to the fray to continue on in the face of seeing his own blood in that combat.

I would apply the meaning of this verse to martyrdom because the many beatings of the Christians as a means of trying to cause them to deny their Christ would have already produced much blood. Paul was an example of this reality in his own body. (II Corinthians 11:25)

When the prospect is death for a cause only the person fully dedicated to the cause will accept the decree and honor his Lord with his testimony.]

12.5 *And ye have forgotten the exhortation which speaketh unto you as unto children, My son, despise not thou the chastening of the Lord, nor faint when thou art rebuked of him:*

[Remembering that much of this Book of Hebrews was written to Jewish men who were sorely tempted to return to their Jewish roots and disregard the dispensation of Grace. Here Paul asks these people, "Have you forgotten what the Scripture says?" This was a mild rebuke to their failure to submit to the chastisement of the Lord in regards to their stand for the faith. The reference is from Proverbs 3:11-12: "My Son, despise not the chastening of the LORD; neither be weary of his correction: For whom the LORD loveth he correcteth; even as a father the son in whom he delighteth."

This may have been a case of Solomon speaking with one of his sons, as suggested by many commentators. Since God chose to place this verse in His inspired and preserved Words, this is a case of God speaking with us as His adopted children.

There is a difference between tribulation caused by those enemies of the cross and chastisement which is allowed to come to us through the reasoning of God. I would argue that these often describe the same instance. In Romans 8:28 tells us, "And we know that all things work together for good to them that love God, to them who are the called according to *his* purpose."

What Satan intends to us as evil will be turned into good by the Lord of our souls. The politician of the Tribulation Era will see the will of God towards His people, Israel, brought out of base purposes intended by Satan. Likewise, the politician and religious leader of this day who is setting the stage for the work of God in that era will not understand that the purposes of God will always override the pernicious plans of man.

Paul is arguing that there is a comparative lightness to the present afflictions of his readers when compared to the sufferings of our Lord. Even in these, and worse yet to come, the designs of God for His children is always glory. It may not be evident at the time but God looks from an eternal perspective.

The "afflictions" of God upon His children are always and only for correction. I hated all the "rote number afflictions" of my grade school math teacher. Now I can appreciate why she treated us so "poorly." It was not a mean thing on her part; it was a method so that we would learn what we might otherwise have ignored.

The "afflictions" of God upon His children serve a purpose. We are being given a part in the program of God for this present age. The Teacher's Commentary gives this report: "Nor do men to-day face death, as Christ did, for the sake of truth. Conditions have changed. The usual results of truth-speaking and of action in conformity to unwelcome truth are now ridicule, unpopularity, loss of reputation, business, wealth, social standing."

These things as above which we have counted as trial and tribulation have been working to steel our testimony for that which is soon coming. I'll be honest. I am hoping for the rapture to take me out of this world before the natural course of history begins to again see even more martyrdom among the Christian. Martyrdom of the Christian is rampant around the world already. Can it be long in approaching our shores? The "tea leaf's," if I may borrow a profane phrase, of current history certainly suggest it cannot be long in coming to our own land.

Paul cautions that we not weary and faint under affliction from the enemy but submit to the chastening of God that we may stand. "Wherefore take unto you the whole armour of God, that ye may be able to withstand in the evil day, and having done all, to stand." (Ephesians 6:13)

The alterative to standing is to be weary. To be weary in trial is to fail; in such we would deny our Lord. This is an end to our testimony among the true believer. I believe it is an end to proffered grace to the "cultural Christian" who has never received the Lord and only suffers persecution due to his seeming alliance with the believers.

To faint is to become senseless to the chiding of the Lord. It is to refuse His leading and protecting hand. The final end of this is, I honestly believe, "For this cause many are weak and sickly among you, and many sleep." (I Corinthians 11:30) A worldly ambassador is often "recalled" from his assignment if he is found unsuitable for his position. Many will be "recalled" from this earth to their Heavenly home because they have fainted at the call of the chastisement of the Lord.]

12.6 *For whom the Lord loveth he chasteneth, and scourgeth every son whom he receiveth.*

[The chastening of the Lord is hard for us to understand while we are experiencing it. They are above our understanding. Hence, we only see in the "rear view mirror" of our experiences that the love of God was tenderly manifest to us in His chastisement of us.

The scourging is the harshest of punishment we encounter from God. A small child will rarely understand the purpose of his punishment. He may rebel against a certain punishment. In such a case another form of punishment may become necessary in order for that child to understand the error of his ways. Eventually the proper child will learn that improper conduct will elicit unpleasant punishment while proper conduct will bring praise and joy to his day.

In relation to our understanding of the ways of God we are not different from that small child with his imperfect understanding of the expectations of his parents and proper society. We have a large plant in the vestibule of our church. Currently the plant is reaching out the windows to the east of it. Unfortunately, this is a winter month. As the branches of the plant come in contact with the window they also come into contact with the harshest of the winter cold. The plant is unable to understand that its natural inclination to face itself toward the sun will cause it pain, in the form of withered leaves, as it touches the window. We can move the plant but it will continue to repeat its "wrong" behavior.

Sadly, this same thing will often happen in the life of the Christian. He sees what he thinks is pleasant. God chastens His child. The child recoils from the chastening and then returns to the proscribed behavior. Ultimately, and all too often it seems, the child of God will find the scourging touch of God which will finally remove the impetus to evil which was the base desire of the actions of that child of God. He will eventually find the path which God has shown. In this the child will find the true path of joy in The Father's favor.

The plant at church, meanwhile, is an unfeeling brute beast which seems to never realize the error of its reaching. May we never be such spiritually brute beasts as to cause The Loving Father to scourge us a wayward child.

In this verse Paul is quoting from Proverbs 3:12 – "For whom the LORD loveth he correcteth; even as a father the son in whom he delighteth." In the writing of this verse the Spirit has led Paul to write – "For whom the Lord loveth he chasteneth, and scourgeth every son whom he receiveth." As will often happen, the Spirit has expanded His Words to further explain to the saint of this age of grace a concept which is contained within the earlier revelation. This is the spiritual process of both illumination and unfolding teaching.

The general concept remains concerning the fact that the Lord will work to spiritually correct those whom He loves and receives as His Own. The idea of the conditioning work of tribulation is further enhanced for these New Testament times in accordance with the duty of each Christian to be Christ like. John 7:7 will explain the fact of the opposition of the world of men and the need for the Christian to be further trained for this reality of antagonism.]

12.7   If ye endure chastening, God dealeth with you as with sons, for what son is he whom the father chasteneth not?

[The "ye" referenced in this verse as enduring chastening are believers who are the adopted sons of God. This stands in opposition to the general worldly troubles, or even the judgments of God visited upon the unrepentant. This sort of judgment is never visited upon the Blood bought believer. To us, the believer, are given chastisements when we fail God through sin or disobedience (Which is a sin!) to His leading. Rather than a harsh judgment upon us, these are the stripes visited upon a child of His Own.

To the Christian such chastisement can be a joyous occasion, once endured, as it is a proof of the love of God toward us as His adopted children. We are not cast off in our sin; instead, we are called closer in our chastening. The purpose is to "bend the twig" of our attitudes and actions that we may become profitable for Him. In such He puts us in line for even greater rewards than those we might otherwise fail to obtain.

The world has no real consolation within their trials and pain. These may come to them under the judgments of God as their Sovereign. But, to the believer, as the child of God, will come correction in love.

Many of us have said to our children, "This is going to hurt me more than it hurts you." Our children never really believe that old adage. The chastisement of the believer flows only from the Love and tender correction of God for His adopted children under the Cross.]

12.8 *But if ye be without chastisement, whereof all are partakers, then are ye bastards, and not sons.*

[The word chastisement here is "paideia." It is number 3809 in Strong's and is defined as, "tutorage, i.e. education or training; by implication, disciplinary correction:--chastening, chastisement, instruction, nurture." It is to be considered as training in an educational manner as in training for all of life.

Chastisement could be considered as mediatorial in that the intent is not to harm or be vindictive in any way. The purpose is to prepare the believer for standing in the trials which the world will send our way. It is a means for the Word and spiritual wealth of God to be distributed to His Own adopted children. It is so much more than we could ever hope or expect were it not for the suffering of Christ at the Cross of His love for us!

Is our age any less licentious than the age of which Paul wrote? The illegitimate child of that age would not be acknowledged by his father. His mother would bear the shame of raising the child without the benefit of entitlements to the father's resources. She would generally live in poverty along with her child.

Is this not a picture of the person who has not acknowledged God in his own life? The popular phrase, "We are all the children of God," is not true. We are all the creation of God, however. Each of us does owe an allegiance to God; most will never admit to this as they deny Him any space within their lives. These may inhabit a mansion on this earth but they are spiritual paupers.

The love of God is spread upon those who have become believers. As such they have been adopted into the family of God. The redeemed are no longer simply subjects of the Sovereign God. They are now heirs of the Heavenly Father. "And if children, then heirs; heirs of God, and joint-heirs with Christ; if so be that we suffer with him, that we may be also glorified together." (Romans 8:17) We may suffer on this earth; Christ suffered much more. We shall be glorified with Him in the Heavenlies. This is His glory which He allows us to partake of in relation to Him. We have no glory. His glory shines so brightly as to impart a "Son tan" to our souls. His glory has changed each of the redeemed from sinner to saint.

If the above were not glory enough, the chastisement of God given His children is a means to prepare them to live victoriously even on this earth. How sad it is to contemplate the despair of the unconverted who have no such blessings to consider as they languish in the pain and degradation of the often-perverse human condition of the unsaved.]

12.9 *Furthermore we have had fathers of our flesh which corrected us, and we gave them reverence, shall we not much rather be in subjection unto the Father of spirits, and live?*

[Paul asks that we consider a comparison at this place. Our earthly fathers gave us the inheritance of the gift of life which God had originally given Adam. This we received through normal human passion. Upon our adult understanding we can accept that the chastisement which they gave us as children was for our learning and maturing in our human lives. We may give them reverence for this.

When this natural order is contrasted with the spiritual order whereby we were given life to our souls only through the grace of God through the Self-Sacrifice of Jesus at the Cross, we should stand in total awe and subjection to our Heavenly Father. We are but spiritual children, without full comprehension while in this body of clay. Yet, even now we can understand that the chastisement of God is for our betterment. It is a preparation not just for life on this plane but also for an eternal Heavenly life in the Heavenlies.

God is truly The Father of our spirits as it is He Who has quickened us to life eternal though the death of His Son. "And you hath he quickened, who were dead in trespasses and sins..." (Ephesians 2:1)

The phrase "and live" may hearken back to Deuteronomy 21:18-21. In this passage an unruly child was in danger of being stoned. I would note that this passage, in verse 20, strongly suggests that this was not a child but an adult when the sentence was carried out. The purpose was to protect the orderliness of the civil society of ancient Israel as a theocratic nation.

The same sentence may be handed down in the case of an unruly child of God. We are reminded of this in I Corinthians 11:30. In this case from I Corinthians, the punishment is carried out on one who has willfully disregarded his spiritual place. It is by this that grace is shown to both the unruly – he is removed to Heaven – and to the assembly of the church in that a disrupter is removed from their midst.

This is a hard thing for our minds to grasp during this dispensation of Grace. But, it is a very graphic indication of the seriousness of the sin of rebellion toward God. It seems that this is a doubly true concept for the Christian. The sinner, the unrepentant, has no check except his own natural senses against the onslaught of sinful desires. We, the redeemed of the Lord, have the indwelling of the Holy Spirit to guard and guide us. It is a willful carnality within us which is the cause of such rebellion against the holiness of God.

This very realization should cause us to stand in even further awe of the love and grace of God. He does not disown His children. He chastises us to bend our will toward true holiness. The harshest punishment is to call us "home" to Glory so that our malicious will is finally conformed to His perfect will. The most amazing thing, to me, is that by this great transformation we are given full joy and contentment.

How great are the mercies and love of God toward us!]

12.10 *For they verily for a few days chastened us after their own pleasure; but he for our profit, that we might be partakers of his holiness.*

[The time of our subjection to our parents was short indeed. It lasted for only a few years; we eventually learned subjection to their rules and were the better for it. But, sometimes the punishment from them was of caprice. It was not due to righteous leading but to our being a nuisance to them. It was sometimes due to anger or even from things outside of our control as children.

The chastisement of God is always for our profit. It is to prepare us to live in this world as truly blessed servants of God. It is to prepare us to live in Heaven. It is to prepare us to be more fully conformed to His image of holiness. (Romans 8:29)]

12.11 *Now no chastening for the present seemeth to be joyous, but grievous: nevertheless afterward it yieldeth the peaceable fruit of righteousness unto them which are exercised thereby.*

[Chastisement is not an enjoyable thing. It is a training exercise to make us more useful for the kingdom. Every spring the baseball players go to a "Spring Training" exercise. I can imagine that many of them complain that they are just doing things they have already done a thousand times. The training seems tedious and unfruitful. But, that same training causes one to naturally react as he must react in the heat of the "game." He has no need to consider his reactions as his body has been trained to react in a certain manner in a certain situation.

It is the same in any endeavor. Much training is monotonous but it is that monotony which enables the highest degree of attention to the needed details of the endeavor. Rote memorization enables the mind to quickly find the key to a problem in any discipline. This is a consideration when it comes to the memorization of Scripture. Jesus gave us the example of quoting Scripture in the face of temptations. One who has not spent the time to memorize will have scant "ammunition" on the field of spiritual combat.

The very lack of joy at chastisement will also cause a person to flee those things, unspiritual pursuits and a lack of communion with The Father, which cause chastisement to come. This will naturally increase that needed communion. It is true that sorrow will bring the child of God closer to The Heavenly Father.

The chastisement of God will increase the Christians ability to endure under the pressure of opposition from the world. The Book of James reminds us, "My brethren, count it all joy when ye fall into divers temptations; Knowing this, that the trying of your faith worketh patience. But let patience have her perfect work, that ye may be perfect and entire, wanting nothing." (James 1:2-4) In this light we can see that chastisement is actually a gift from the loving God of our Salvation.

Consider that the end result of such chastisement is the gift of peace and righteousness which comes from God.]

12.12 *Wherefore lift up the hands which hang down, and the feeble knees;*

[I recently watched an MMA fight. It was quickly clear that one of the combatants had no concept of how to approach one who was schooled in the art of boxing. One cannot continue to block all the punches of the other with their face. Discouragement will soon set in and defeat is the expected outcome. One must keep their hands up in a defensive posture against the assaults of the enemy. God allows trials that we may be strengthened to stand in an adverse situation.

Paul may be alluding to Isaiah 35:4-5 in this verse. "Strengthen ye the weak hands, and confirm the feeble knees. Say to them that are of a fearful heart, Be strong, fear not: behold, your God will come with vengeance, even God with a recompence; he will come and save you." We may always be certain that even in the strongest of trials, God will remain our strength. We can learn this through the trials of chastisement which God allows. Once that lesson has been learned we may be strengthened in the Lord. His hand will cause us to stand in the day of trial and our hands will be raised in spiritual victory as we trust Him.

In our own power we will weaken and fail. In His power we will find the victory which overcomes the world. (I John 5:4)

The concept of feeble knees is one of illness even more than of fatigue. The meaning seems that even in our weakest we must reach out to the Great Physician to heal the sickness of heart and fear which causes us to "lose heart" and succumb to the siren call of defeat.

The "rest" of defeat is simply loss. The gain of victory is much more reward than is the temporary "gain" of the rest of defeat. Defeat lingers and disposes of further victory. We need to long for the victory which comes from standing for Christ. He is our victory when we have reached the end of our ability.

Our understanding that holy affliction is a gift of love from God. We must allow that gift of His love its work to strengthen us in the truth that God sends His abundant love upon those that love Him.

For a fighter to lift his hands is not only to assume a defensive posture; it is a preparation for fighting back at the opponent. God reminds us of the need to strengthen our resolve by considering His Words to us. "My hands also will I lift up unto thy commandments, which I have loved; and I will meditate in thy statutes." (Psalm 119:48) Our real spiritual strength comes from our understanding and internalizing of His marvelous Words of inspired and preserved Scripture.

Lest we forget, God has given us the good understanding of His love toward us. But, we are encouraged to steady our failing legs and lift our hands into the fray. We are never encouraged to be idle. God call's us to stand for Him and the engage the adversary in Holy Combat based on the Words of Scripture and our faith in the God Who has shown His love to us.]

12.13 And make straight paths for your feet, lest that which is lame be turned out of the way; but let it rather be healed.

[I spent some time in an "Artic Infantry" unit in the Army Reserve. Our "Area of Operation," should we have been activated, was to protect the Alaskan oil pipe line. Our reserve "Summer Camp" was in Northern Minnesota in early February. We set up for the night, during a near "white out" snow storm, in tents. My first day in the unit we were put into a company formation and told that we were going on something like a twenty mile cross country ski course.

Somewhat apprehensive I approached the Lieutenant in charge of our company. I said, "Sir, I am new to this unit. I have never been skiing." Apparently, this office had seen far too many "B" movies. His answer was, "Don't worry, soldier. By the time we get back you will have learned."

Surprisingly, he was right. Cross country skiing is a fairly easy task. It is much easier than using skates down at the local skating rink. One man takes the lead and "cuts the trail" for the rest of us to follow. That is the hard part. Following is really easy.

During our "walk" the leader would drop out and be replaced by another to cut the trail. Each of us took our turn in leading and then following in the trail which had already been cut by others. In this manner we completed our mission without anyone feeling as though we had gone nearly as far as we had gone.

That is somewhat the picture which is given here. If each of us do our part the straight path of doctrinal purity is much easier to follow.

One of the easiest, and most fruitful, "feeding grounds" for the cults is the independent churches. The people from these churches have a zeal for the things of the Lord but are too often not trained in just what those "things" are. A novel idea that sounds really "spiritual" advanced by one of the cultists may well seem a reasonable road for the weak Christian who desires to please his Lord but has not been trained in the manner of walk to which he has been called.

Paul calls us to make "straight paths" which may become the pathway for others in the service of the Lord. Any dalliance with the things of the world may cause one to deviate from the leading of the Lord because our eyes cease to follow Him as we see new and seemingly reasonable things. The devices of Satan are not unreasonable. They do not seem so. They are snares that lead us to ruin.

A man out hunting ducks will often employ a "duck call" and "decoy ducks" on the water. Such subterfuge may well entice a real duck to his doom. It is the true leading of God, and by extension the leadership which points toward Him, which is a hedge against deviation.

Be often in the Scripture and in prayer. Such exercise is the only way in which one may understand the true path from the "deer run" which might send another path to run through our vision.

Call back to fellowship those who have become lame in their spiritual walk through the "rocks and ditches" of false disciples who would lead them astray. This is not the time for a superior attitude but for personal humility and a dependence upon the Lord and the Word.

It is those who have stumbled over the impediments which Satan has strewn into our path which has caused some to become lame in their attempt to cover the course of the Lord. Prayer to The Great Physician may well heal the lame to complete their progress.]

12.14 *Follow peace with all men, and holiness, without which no man shall see the Lord:*

[The concept of "following peace" is in the sense of a hunter who pursues his game in the field. He looks for the game. He looks to find a place where he and the game may come into close proximity. He follows the game even as the game attempts to hide from, or escape from, him.

To live in peace with all is not an easy thing to do. If it were always an easy thing it would not need to be pursued. This was an era of intense persecution of the Christian. The concept of a Christian life was misunderstood and misapplied. It, as was Jesus, hated of men. (John 7:7)

There is an interesting verse at Acts 8:3 concerning the persecution of the early church as carried out by Saul of Tarsus, later the apostle Paul. "As for Saul, he made havock of the church, entering into every house, and haling men and women committing *them* to prison." The Defined King James Bible lists that work "haling" as "*Arc* drawing, pulling with force/violence"

The picture is of an authority figure, Saul was commissioned by the Sanhedrin; we note that he needed to get "letters" – or license – from them when he traveled to Damascus. This authority figure would essentially break into the house of suspected Christians and drag them away, without regard to age or sex, to prison. There was no court of appeal for the Christian.

This is the situation in which the readers of this letter were told to live peaceably among all. This was obviously not an easy task. It was part of their testimony toward their persecutors that they did so. By the way, we see the same sort of persecution being carried out in this day around the world for the "crime" of being a Christian!

Often, especially in this day, that persecution is unto death.

The concepts of "peace with all men" and "holiness" are linked by the word "pursue." We are called to a holy life style. Part of this is a peaceable life style. I can't do it. Can you? We can only pray that in the day of trial we will find the grace of God in our hearts to allow our hearts to be Christ like and stronger in the faith than we are in the world of emotions.

The verse also adds the phrase, "without which no man can see the Lord."

That little phrase is tied in with the first two. God does expect us to be peaceable even while retaining a holy outlook derived from an inward piety. This is only possible with the assistance of the Spirit. Our own spirits are not attuned to such strength of character. It is only with the help of the Lord that we can stand in the day of temptation and trial.]

12.15 Looking diligently lest any man fall of the grace of God, lest any root of bitterness springing up trouble you, and thereby many be defiled;

[This verse is obviously to be considered with the previous verse. Lacking the grace of God will cause bitterness. To the ancients a bitter root was the sign of a poisonous plant. To partake of it was to invite disaster. Envy, strife, hatred – do you see the progression! – are themselves indications of a soul which is not living peaceably among others. This is true whether those "others" be brothers in the faith or those outside the household of faith.

When the "others" are inside the assembly we find a fractured and wounded assembly which cannot fully fulfill the need of the Great Commission into the world. I believe that this is primarily what Paul had in mind at this place. The further reference to Esau is an indication that the reference is to a "family matter."

I have seen the concept of "church politics" from both sides. It is an abhorrent consideration. The church is divided. The people are either taken in a spirit of pride or despondency. Usually both rear their unchristian heads. It is from a spirit such as this that we see "church splits" occurring. Such damage to a church will curtail their message of Christ into the world. People jeer at the mangled message of "Christian love," and Satan cheers at his temporary victory.

When the "others" are outside the household of faith the church is still damaged in its outreach into the world. All Christians are judges as partakers of the spirit of enmity whether they take part or not. Once again, the message of salvation is devalued in the eyes of those who most stand in need.

Those who "fail of the grace of God" can actually be of three considerations. The weaker Christian may walk away from any identification with the things of God. His salvation is of the work of Christ. That is not in any danger. His fellowship with Jesus is certainly in danger. His heart may yearn for the fellowship which he once understood but he begins to salve that hurt with the "joys" of the world. He will have no influence for Christ. He will have a miserable existence as he tries to project joy out of his own hearts bitterness.

The person who, as so often earlier in this Book, has felt the need to accept the grace of God but has not yet done so, will likewise be nauseated by the display of the "Christian brethren." He may find his solace in the doctrines of false religion – as may the weak and abused Christian above. This may give a certain peace of altruism but it will never allow the peace of God!

Finally, the stronger Christian may be effected either in drawing closer to God as he finds the false doctrine anathema to His Lord. Or, worse, he may begin to feel a superior attitude. "I am not like those others..." This is the plea of one who has departed from the place of usefulness for God. He begins to "look down" at those weaker people who "cannot stand strong doctrine."

Many a preacher has used this explanation to relieve himself of the pain of seeing people unwilling to follow him. Perhaps it would have been better had he followed Christ and not attempted to become the perfection of antagonism rather than the shepherd of the hurting.

The simple fact is that the unholy attitude of strife will harm many churches and many individuals. Let us constantly be on guard against the false even as we uphold the only Truth available. Jesus is the way, the truth, and the only real life we can ever experience.

In the final analysis, we must watch to warn those that we love of a deviant doctrine or social stance which would harm the cause of Christ. We pray the power and love of Christ upon the situation. Then we live that same love. That is a march toward holiness wherein we will see the Lord and His work in this world.]

12.16 *Let there be any fornicator, or profane person, as Esau, who for one morsel of meat sold his birthright.*

[Paul is still warning against apostatizing against the Christian faith. Remember, as we mentioned much earlier, one cannot be in a state of apostasy except from that which he has already experienced. An easy example is that a Muslim cannot apostatize from Christianity. He has never experienced, in general terms, Christianity. This is an imperfect example but will give the general sense of the situation. One apostatizes "from" something.

There was a real temptation, especially so considering the persecution of the believers, for those who chose to fellowship with the church to turn back to the Judaism of their youth. To suggest that one could fall from the faith – to lose his salvation – is to suggest a lack of trust in the power of Christ to do that which He has promised. It is to misread verse two of this chapter and call Jesus the Author and... And what? He could not in such a situation be the "Finisher" of our faith if we were to hold the power to abrogate His salvation. He could not even be the "Sustainer" of our faith if salvation were held solely in the palm of our own hands.

Still, I do believe that this passage is concerned with real Christians who have been born again by the Blood and Passion of the Lord. These do not "fall from grace" in the sense of loving relationship with Jesus. These see a "fall from grace" only in the sense that they fall into the chastisement of the Lord. That has been the theme of Paul in this chapter. As listed above, those chastised of the Lord are His adopted children. They are saved. They remain saved. They are given Fatherly discipline because of the error of their ways.

Esau remained a son of Isaac. There can be no real discussion of that fact. He was an erring son; that much is certain. He lost much of the blessing which was occasioned by his lineage as a grandson of Abraham; that much is certain. But, he did remain a son of Isaac and a grandson of Abraham. That much also remains certain.

At this point we look at the word "fornicator." One of the primary meanings here is "male prostitute." Removing the monetary consideration, which is allowable as we have moved from a culture where this was practiced to a culture where this is not so actively practiced, this would apply to one of intemperate sexual appetites. This brings up the question of "spiritual principles" addressed in the situation.

Many have fallen from places of usefulness through sexual sins. I am not going to argue that God cannot forgive any sin. One only has to access King David to see this as also a spiritual principle. David was not removed from the throne whereby he was to serve God as leader of God's people. David was greatly chastised for his sin with Bathsheba. I believe that parts of that chastisement were played out in the life of Solomon, the son of David and Bathsheba. It may even be that God allowed Solomon to succeed David as king when he was not the next in the royal line of succession as a picture of the teaching of God toward His people regarding sin.

The concept of fornicator is that of a sinner who has a propensity to "sell" the pure for a price of base consideration. Esau sold the blessing of the first-born. God had prophesied the concept of this transfer before Esau and Jacob's birth. (Genesis 25:23)

The right of the first born concerned several things. The right of the first born concerned the right of being the family priest, or the family religious leader. The right of the first born considered that he would receive a double portion of the estate of his father. This was tied in with the concept of family religious leader in that the "extra" would allow for sacrifice to be made for the dead father. The right of the first born made him the "head" of the family. We see this concept often in cultures where a "chief" is the ruler of the "clan." As a son of Abraham the first born was to be in the line of Messiah. As the first born it was the duty of this son to give blessing and privilege to his own eldest near the time that the first born would pass from this earth.

These spiritual rights and earthly privileges were counted so little by Esau that he sold all for the base price of one meal. Esau was a profane person in that his interests were on the base things of this earth rather than the higher things of the spiritual. Contained within the "restaurant price" of his meal Esau was shown to prefer the earthly over the spiritual.

We are asked to consider Esau and not undervalue the joy of fellowship with The Father contained within the salvation offered by The Son.]

12.17 *For ye know how that afterward, when he would have inherited the blessing, he was rejected: for he found no place of repentance, though he sought it carefully with tears.*

[The "place of repentance' which Esau could not find is not that of a sinner seeking salvation from the Lord. This repentance had to do with his sorrow at his lost birthright blessing as eldest son. He had counted that so lightly that he sold it. This was in the providence of God as God had chosen the younger, Jacob, rather than the elder, Esau, as was the custom of men of that time. (Genesis 25;21-23; Romans 9:10-12)

Esau sought repentance. The repentance he sought would have been in the mind and will of Isaac. Esau could not repent from a decision which he had made and consummated possibly years before. He had sold the birthright and accepted his requested price. Esau sought the change of Isaac's mind. Esau wanted his father to disavow the promise of blessing he had made over Jacob and transfer them to Esau. This sounds suspiciously like the theology of "Replacement Theology" whereby some advocate that all the promises which God gave to His Covenant People have been removed from them and bestowed upon the Church. Isaac did not renege on his words of blessing; neither will God forsake His Own Words of honor and promise. The promises of God to Abraham and David are still in effect for the people of Abraham and David.

In another sense, this same circumstance would argue against the concept of anyone "losing" their salvation. What God has determined and promised will certainly come to pass. We may be greatly chastised as the adopted sons of God; we will never be disowned by our Heavenly Father.

Even though Jacob and his mother used deception in order to undermine the will of Jacob, they were rewarded in the accomplishment of their goals. This was not a reward for deceit. This was the already declared will of God being carried out. God brought about His Own determinative will because it was His will. The deception of Jacob and his mother was an evil of man which God used to bring about His Own purpose.

This would have been the outcome even had not Jacob and his mother set out on a course of deception. Note that there was a punishment for their sin. Jacob was sent away from the wrath of his brother. Mother and son, as near as we can tell, never saw one another again in this life.

This is a picture of the temporary setting aside of Israel. "For I would not, brethren, that ye should be ignorant of this mystery, lest ye should be wise in your own conceits; that blindness in part is happened to Israel, until the fullness of the Gentiles be come in. And so all Israel shall be saved: as it is written, There shall come out of Sion the Deliverer, and shall turn away ungodliness from Jacob: For this *is* my covenant unto them, when I shall take away their sins. As concerning the gospel, they *are* enemies for your sakes: but as touching the election, *they* are beloved for the fathers' sakes. For the gifts and calling of God are without repentance. For as ye in times past have not believed God, yet have now obtained mercy through their unbelief: Even so have these also now not believed, that through your mercy they also may obtain mercy. For God hath concluded them all in unbelief, that he might have mercy upon all." (Romans 11:25-32)

It is a mistake to take this temporary setting aside of Israel and conclude that it is an eternal removal of the very Words and Promises of God. Israel remains the Covenant People of God. For a time they have disregarded their Messiah. But, we see it is only for a time.

We also see that the Jew of this dispensation remains a Jew; on that there can be no disagreement. Likewise, Paul warns us not of a loss of salvation but a loss of the present glory of our salvation. We may forego the fellowship and power of God upon our temporal lives. Many may look at that and reckon it a small thing. Oh, the fools that count the blessing of God, even the temporal blessing of God, as a small thing. They discount the reality of joy for the temporary pleasure of sin. The loving chastisement of God will wipe away all of the pleasure even as we forfeit the joy of a clear conscious with which to serve Him!]

12.18 *For ye are not come unto the mount that might be touched, and that burned with fire, nor unto blackness, and darkness, and tempest,*

[Paul has already contrasted the weakness of the Levitical priesthood when compared to the eternal priesthood of Christ, the impossibility of sins removal via the sacrifice of the animals of creation when compared to the Blood of Jesus which cleanses our sin, the impermanence of man's religion when compared to the eternal salvation given by the Self-Sacrifice of Jesus, and the strength of the faith of those who did not receive the Promise of Messiah when compared with our blessing of seeing the actual Day of Salvation.

The writer now begins a comparison of the general tenor of the religion of Israel as given through Moses and the religion of Jesus as purchased at the Cross of Calvary. One, that of Moses, is seen as carnal while the other, that of Jesus, is shown to be spiritual. One, that of Moses, is seen as threatening and burdensome while the other, that of Jesus, is shown to be liberating and loving. One, that of Moses, is shown to be based in the precincts of earth while the other, that of Jesus, is shown to flow from the Love of God in Heaven.Going back to the beginning of the religion as revealed by Moses we approach Mount Sinai. It is real. We could walk over to the mountain and touch it with our hand. But, if we did do so we would be stoned. This touching is not allowed. (Exodus 19:12) At its inception the religion revealed to Moses is not universal. It applies only to the Hebrew. Even at this, not all of Israel is allowed to fully partake of the worship described. They must worship through the mediation of the priestly caste.

Even the worship of the pious is not allowed unless it is "filtered" through others.

As the Hebrew looks at the mountain from which the instructions for worship are given he sees a burning fire. Fire in the Scripture is a sign of the judgment of God. This is a worship concerned with punishment and judgment. Even the most pious and just may approach God only through the death of a substitute. In this they are constantly reminded of their own mortality and fragility as humans who seek to worship The God of Eternity and Power.

Their weakness and His Sovereign strength are at all times a counter balance negating any real relationship beyond Sovereign and serf. Such is not a bad thing. It is reality. But, our New Testament relationship of Heavenly Father and adopted children is a much more comforting and glorious consideration.

Looking at the mountain one would see the blackness of smoke billowing above the conversation of Moses and the Lord. Smoke seems to speak of destruction. I have watched a few homes and businesses burn. I recall watching our local library burn back in the 1950s. We sat a mile or more from that library as it burned. We saw the smoke from our yard. Smoke always seems to suggest loss.

The fire on this mountain was not of loss. It was of gain. But, it must have been a terrifying gain to those who observed. In bringing such a situation to the remembrance of these people Paul must have been suggesting the soothing truth of John 14:27. "Peace I leave with you, my peace I give unto you: not as the world giveth, give I unto you. Let not your heart be troubled, neither let it be afraid."

There was also a darkness on that mountain. The darkness was probably caused by the smoke of the great glory of God. But, darkness is gone from this New Testament religion of Jesus. (John 1:9) Darkness seems to speak of the pits of Hell. (Matthew 25:30) Darkness speaks of a time prior to that in which God had prepared the earth for mankind. (Genesis 1:2)

It was through much darkness, the darkness of type and shadow, that we were able to gaze upon the reality which has come into the world through our Lord Jesus Christ. The plan of God for His creation was always the gospel of the good news that Jesus Christ would die in time so that others could live in eternity. (I Peter 1:19-20)

There was also tempest upon the mountain. The Defined King James Bible reports the meaning of "tempest" as "violent storm." We can easily contrast this with the Words of Our Savior, "And he arose, and rebuked the wind, and said unto the sea, Peace, be still. And the wind ceased, and there was a great calm." (Mark 4:39)

None of this is to suggest any sort of imperfection within the events of Sinai. Far from that. This was part of the unfolding plan of God for the people of His creation. It is to suggest that He has greatly blessed us of this dispensation for all that we have learned from past times as given us in His inspired and preserved Scripture. All was, indeed, written for our admonition and blessing. (I Corinthians 10:11)]

12.19 *And the sound of a trumpet, and the voice of words, which voice they that heard intreated that the word should not be spoken to them any more:*

[The word "salpigx" (4536 in Strong's) is always translated as "trumpet" except in I Corinthians 15:52 and I Thessalonians 4:16 where the shortened form of "trump" is used. The purpose is always to call attention to an event. Generally, this event is to call one to attention or assembly. In Revelation 8:2; 6; 13; 9:14 the meaning has to do with loosing, and by extension announcing to the people of the earth, certain judgments of God.

This instance referenced by Paul comes from Exodus 19:19ff in which the entire company of the people of the exodus is called to give attention to the words of God. It would appear from Deuteronomy 5:22 that the words spoken by God were the Ten Commandments.

Whatever the words of God were, they were understandable to the people. God spoke from eternity to the people of time in a manner that His Words could be understood. The people, however, were not able to bear the Words spoken by God. They pleaded that God would speak to Moses. Moses could then speak to the people. (Exodus 20:19)

Here we are given the "genesis" of the first Bible Translation. It is the MLV; it is the Moses Literal Version. In order for the "translation" to be of any real use to the people it was necessary that the Moses rendition be faithful to the True Spoken Words of God. For this reason, as we see by Deuteronomy 5:22, above, that the Words of God were written Words.

It might be instructive to note that these written Words of God were placed in the Ark of the Covenant and resided therein for hundreds of years. The Words of God were not only "written on stone," they were also preserved in the location where they would expect to be found.

So, it has always been with the written Words of God. They have never been lost, as those who rely upon the Critical Text would argue. Those Words have always been available in the place where one would expect they would be. Those Words have always been available among the churches of the faithful wherein a people who are led by the very Spirit of Truth reside.

That Ark stayed mainly in the Tabernacle, and then the Temple – the Temple patterned after the Tabernacle – within the Holy of Holies, understood by the pious as the special place of the presence of God, until the time of the Babylonian Captivity. After that point we no longer hear of the Ark of the Covenant. The people of the Covenant of God had fallen into the hands of the people of the world.

Likewise, in our day there are too many churches which name the Name of Christ that have been captured by the world. Their music is a "Christian adaption" of the music of the world. Their worship is a "Christian adaption" of the culture of the world. The "Words of God" they profess to teach are a "Christian adaption" of the message of man which has supplanted the Message *TO* man of the truly inspired and preserved Words of God.

The average man in the pew has been taught to accept the words of Professor Moses, or Rev. Aaron, or anyone who has the "credentials" to decide what God really said upon the mountain of inspiration.

We are no longer permitted to trust God; we must trust what "ordained and credentialed" men have supposed that which God *might have said* based upon their own scholarship and understanding. We live in a *post Christian age* because we live in a *post Biblical age*.

The NASV might say one thing while the NIV might argue another. The ESV may say the same as either but it does so in different words. Words really do have meaning. We are not searching to find what the meaning of is is. We are searching, or should be, to find what the meaning of the Words of God are. That is the Words of God rather than the Words which men have allowed God to say. Consider the simple argument of Paul in Galatians 3:16 the next time you argue the new doctrine of concept inspiration.

There is a reason that the saints of an earlier day accepted that inspiration was verbal – upon the very Words – and plenary – upon all the Words which God had given. God is not in the habit of blessing error – as the modern scholars suggest to be the words of the Received Text which gave birth to the Reformation and every revival in the past four hundred years – and not blessing truth as those same scholars would suggest the critical text of man to be.

Has the world improved and the church gotten stronger since we, as a church and a people who claim to be of God, jettisoned the preserved Words of God to accept the variable words of man's Critical Text and the myriad of "versions" which have been birthed in the delivery rooms of man's intellect?

We might also consider that this group which could not stand to hear the Words of God would shortly approach the boarders of the Land of Promise. None of them would enter into the rest of the promise as they refused to trust God for the victory. Did they cease to be the sons of Abraham? Of course not. Did they cease to move forward unto victory as God had assured was theirs? Of course.

Their error was not based in who they were but in what they believed of God.]

12.20 (For they could not endure that which was commanded, And if so much as a beast touch the mountain, it shall be stoned, or thrust through with a dart:

[That neither they nor anyone else could bear the commands of God has been proven through history. "For all have sinned, and come short of the glory of God..."

(Romans 3:23) That is **a** meaning of the verse. The primary meaning, however, is that the people could not bear the voice of God. We, as a race of humanity, are indeed short of the glory of God.

This may have been a prefigure of the Tabernacle worship whereby no man except the lawful high priest could enter into the Holy of Holies which was considered to be the special presence of God in that dispensation of time. Even that entrance was only allowed one day a year on the Day of Atonement.

Only Moses was permitted to come upon the mountain as God spoke to Him.

There had been a fence of some sort around the mountain to keep the people from idle human curiosity. (Exodus 19:12) They were not to be allowed to look upon God as He spoke the Words of the Law with Moses.

This event of the giving of the Law is a picture of the awe and power of God. The Christian is called to fully reverence God. But, unlike the limited ability of the people to come near God as shown in this verse and later in the Tabernacle, we are not simply the Covenant People of God. We are the adopted children of God through the Blood of Jesus. (Romans 8:15) Within this relationship we are called to the Throne of the Grace of God; we are not kept away from His Divine Presence. (Hebrews 4:16)

The Grace of God, given us under the Blood of Jesus, calls us to a relationship which is beyond even that enjoyed by the people of the previous chapter even though their faith is celebrated. Even they did not experience the depth of the Love of God which has been shed upon our unworthy hearts and lives.]

12.21 *And so terrible was the sight, that Moses said I exceedingly fear and quake:)*

[Moses was the great law-giver. But, he was only so as an intermediary of God. God gave the Law while Moses only relayed that to the people. James says this of Elijah, "Elias was a man subject to like passions as we are, and he prayed earnestly that it might not rain: and it rained not on the earth by the space of three years and six months." (James 5:17)

We do not have the right to weigh any one man's spirituality against another. I would only note that Elijah was translated into Paradise without having tasted death. Moses died before he was allowed to enter into the land of rest. Does this make one above the other? Of course not. What is shown is that each had a differing purpose in the economy of God as witnesses of His grace.

Moses was a very special man in many respects. He was a man. No man is so close to God as to find a familiarity with Him that would discount the great glory and majesty of the Lord. I can only find one place in Scripture, Deuteronomy 9:19, where Moses admitted to being afraid before God. That was returning to the mountain after he had broken the original tablets upon which God had written His commandments for the people.

That fear seems to have been for the people of the exodus. This was especially so after the "golden calf incident" which was overseen by Aaron. Neither was Aaron perfect in all his ways before God. We find later that none of that group ever entered into the land. Their sin kept them from God's blessing.

But, this verse says that the sight was what brought fear. The sight is that about which the passage has been speaking. The sight of the mountain, the thunder, the fire, the voice, the trumpet and most importantly the Holiness of the Lord of the

HEBREWS: Chapter 12

Universe were, I believe, what brought a fear to Moses.

Moses was a great man as men count greatness. Even he is an example of our utter unworthiness to stand before the Lord of Glory without the passion of Jesus and His Cross of Redemption. How far down that "totem pole," if I may use such a profane phrase, of spirituality are we? I still argue that Paul was only able to call Himself the "chief of sinners" because he had never met me! (I Timothy 1:15)

As Isaiah said, "Woe *is* me! for I am undone; because I *am* a man of unclean lips, and I dwell in the midst of a people of unclean lips: for mine eyes have seen the King, the LORD of Hosts." (Isaiah 6:5)

My only argument is that I met the Lord at the cross of His grace. His very Blood has been applied to my account. He has promised me, "And he said unto me, My grace is sufficient for thee: for my strength is made perfect in weakness..." (II Corinthians 12:9a)

"I am weak.
But, He is strong."
Savior, I acknowledge all my wrong.
May Your love be my only song.
I must trust Him when I would fail.
His blood has carried beyond the veil.
I plead only His power and grace.
I have nothing of merit beyond His face.

12.22 *But ye are come unto mount Sion, and unto the city of the living God, the heavenly Jerusalem, and to an innumerable company of angels,*

["But." The Old Covenant, to which some of the church to which Paul addressed this letter, was based as a reaction to the carnality of humanity. There was a great display of fire and smoke, sound and tremble, display and emotional response.

The New Covenant of the Blood of Christ seeks the inner, spiritual man to be renewed from his carnal state and walk in a newness of life. The targeted action of the New Birth is inward in its restoration of a fellowship of love with God. Where the Old Covenant could only see darkly the concept of love through the harshness of judgment of sins, the New Covenant sees sins purged at the Cross.

"We" are the "ye" of this verse. We are the redeemed of the second birth. We have not come to carnal Sinai; we have come to spiritual (New) Jerusalem. We are not called to stand outside the Tabernacle and observe others as they take part in worship. We are called to take part in the worship of the Lord as adopted children of The Heavenly Father.

Sinai was based on earth as it only pointed to Heaven. The Heavenly Zion is based in Heaven as it reaches out in love to a sin-battered earth and offers salvation, restoration and fellowship with The Lord.

On the earth Zion was a hill within the confines of the city of Jerusalem. In military terms it was the "Strong Point." David saw it as such. He and Solomon built both palace and Temple on Zion. Zion thus became both the seat of government and the seat of Worship within the city and nation.

Because of Christ we have obtained citizenship in this Heavenly Jerusalem. We are the adopted children of the King of Kings and Lord of Lords. We are of the Royal

Family of the entire universe of creation. We are given the privilege to worship the King which was possible only by, or through, the priestly caste of the Old Covenant.

In the Book of Esther, the queen took a real chance when she approached the king. In that culture and time, a person who approached the king without being summoned into his presence risked death should the sovereign not accept the intrusion. We have been invited into the presence of the very Throne of Grace. This is a privilege obtained by the Cross. Those of the Old Covenant could not have dreamed of the possibility of such access. Even the high priest was allowed presence in the Holy of Holies, on that one Day of Atonement each year, and then only to perform his duties as described under the Law. (Leviticus 16:2; Romans 8:15-16; Ephesians 2:18; 3:12; Hebrews 4:16)

We may seem an inferior race in relation to the angels. By our special creation, restored from sin by the events of Calvary, we are elevated to adoption as sons of God. We are called to be ministering spirits, to be sure. We are called to obey Him in all points. But, that special relationship of sinners restored by the Love of God is something which only we of humanity have been called to experience within that depth of grace and love from our God.]

12.23 To the general assembly and church of the firstborn, which are written in heaven, and to God the Judge of all, and to the spirits of just men made perfect,

[The word translated church will generally apply to a local body of believers. The meaning is that of a group called out of the world for specific purpose. I have often argued that my old unit in the 4th Infantry Division during the war in Viet Nam was a "church" in that sense. It was called out of the general population of both the draft age men of the nation and further of those who were in the army at the time. Not all of the army was of the 4th. There were other divisions and groups even in just the army.

But, this spoken of in this verse is especially called "the general assembly." It was a greater group than just one church at one location. It would speak of all the saved of all the earth in all the time of man's sojourn upon this earth. We could probably limit this group just to those who were already in Heaven at the time of this writing except for that phrase "which are written in heaven."

You may recall the events surrounding the human birth of our eternal Lord. His mother and step-father had to travel to the town in which they were "enrolled" for the taxation. The custom of the time was that people would be listed as to which town they were considered to be citizens. Since we are citizens of Heaven, by the grace of our Lord, that enrollment would of necessity include our names.

Some would limit the group of the general assembly to either the Old Testament saints who had died before the Cross. Some would limit the group of the general assembly to the saints of the early church who had died before this epistle was written. Many would combine these two groups as forming the general assembly.

Each of these views seems faulted on one point. God speaks from the perspective of eternity when He speaks of the enrollment of the saints in the eternal general assembly. Therefore these "enrolled" names would include the entirety of the Blood bought saints. This would also, of necessity, include us of this generation as we await our own entry into the Heavenly realms.

We stand as a people who have, as our eternal salvation argues, the rights of eternity. Therefore, we are included in the enumerated "residents" of the eternal "city" of God within that "general assembly." We *are*, present tense included in the sense of eternity, residents of eternity. We see this as prospective. Jesus, as the "Author" of our faith, sees this as a completed reality in the consistent "NOW" of the timeless "age," I use the term only because it is intelligible to us of this time-centric world, of eternity.

This is another argument for the Biblical doctrine and truth of the eternal security of our souls within the power of Jesus. He is the "Author" and the "Completer," Finisher, of our salvation. His promises can never fail. It is a spiritual conceit to argue that we retain the right to nullify that which God has pronounced as finished.

This verse speaks of this group as the church of the firstborn. My first inclination is to apply this to Jesus. I think this does not damage the verse but it would not be completely accurate. We are given a great privilege as adopted children of God in that we are considered as "joint-heirs" with our Lord. (Romans 8:17)

We are the first born from the earth in regard to our position as believer's in the salvation offered by Jesus.

This concept does not mean that we are equal with Jesus in any sense! He is The Firstborn. His station is above our station even as we share in the blessing which He has bestowed upon us. An executor of a will has no real authority; he does have a grave responsibility.

His sole purpose is to see that the purpose of the will of the deceased is carried out in accordance with the stated desires of the deceased.

We, the born again believers, are given the duty to be executors, as it were, of the "will," or New Testament, of the Lord into this world which we inhabit. "And said unto them, Thus it is written, and thus it behoved Christ to suffer, and to rise from the dead the third day: And that repentance and remission of sins should be preached in his name among all nations, beginning at Jerusalem. And ye are witnesses of these things." (Luke 24;46-48)

Not only are we charged with this responsibility, we are also given the assistance of the One Who died and now lives forever. The Spirit is given us as a guide into the Words of that New Testament. He also gives us understanding of the "Old" as this is the groundwork for the "New." The "Old" remains the eternal Words of God. If this were not true we would have no excuse to expect the "New" to be eternal.

The Old Testament gives shadows and pictures of prophecy of Messiah to Whom we are introduced in the New Testament. The entirety of the message of the New Testament is not complete without an understanding of the Old Testament. The full doctrine of the Virgin Birth, as a "for instance," could not be understood without the events of Eden.

God had promised Abraham, and by extension all those of like faith, some enumerated in chapter eleven of this Book, a new city of righteousness. I can understand that some will question this statement. "Show me where God promised that to Abraham." I would reference Hebrews 11:16 in that regard. We have the call of Abraham to leave the city of Ur and journey to the land which God would show him. We do not have any reference that would indicate that God said, "O. K. Abraham. You can stop now. Here it is."

"But now they desire a better country, that is, an heavenly: wherefore God is not ashamed to be called their God: for he hath prepared for them a city." (Hebrews

11:16) Once again, I submit that they never found that city. "And these all, having obtained a good report through faith, received not the promise: God having provided some better thing for us, that they without us should not be made perfect." (Hebrews 11:38-39)

The perfection, or "completion" of all their blessing from God waited for the historical time of the Cross. The Cross, as the only redemption from sin, was promised for the creature even before God had created Adam. (Revelation 13:8) The eternal purposes of God are based in eternity. However, He has placed humanity, as a created being, under the constraints of time and physicality. Thus, the application of the eternal salvation provided by the Cross of Jesus, would not be applied until the historical event of that Self-Sacrifice of Jesus for the atonement of sin.

The saints of the pre-cross days were not completed in their attainment of the promise of righteousness until the day in which we, as a body of believers under the Cross, should live. To them was given the promise awaited. To us is given the promise completed. We await the time of the Day of the Lord's purpose to attain our portion of that promise. We can consider Paul, himself, in this regard according to his words of Philippians 3:12,

I would again refer to my notes on Luke 16:19 in relation to this consideration.

God is called the Judge of all. John 5:22 argues, "For the Father judgeth no man, but hath committed all judgment unto the Son..." This is no contradiction. The Divinity of Jesus is a well-established fact of Scripture. God, The Son, is personally the judgment concerning salvation. (John 3:36) The Cross of Jesus is a judgment seat. Those who come to the Cross and call upon The Son for forgiveness of their sins will see their sins judged at the Cross. Jesus, having taken their sin upon Himself in The Atonement, will pronounce them clean and righteous. Those who fail to avail themselves of this free salvation will find that Cross as a witness against them that they denied The Son in refusing His grace. Those remain lost in their sins awaiting the day of eternal judgment.]

12.24 *And to Jesus the mediator of the new covenant, and to the blood of sprinkling, that speaketh better things than that of Abel.*

Exodus 24:8; Matthew 26:28

[Just a chapter earlier Abel is mentioned as offering a "more excellent sacrifice..." (By faith Abel offered unto God a more excellent sacrifice than Cain, by which he obtained witness that he was righteous, God testifying of his gifts: and by it he being dead yet speaketh." (Hebrews 11:4)

By comparing Scripture with Scripture, these two verses specifically, we see that the Old Testament sacrificial system was able to give witness to the righteous heart. But, it was the sacrifice of Jesus which gave access to the New Birth experience and true salvation.

Paul is still contrasting the power of the New Covenant of Jesus and the Old Covenant as described by Moses. While Moses only conveyed the Words of God to the people, Jesus is the God Who established the very Words of those laws. Moses died after seeing the land he was unable to enter. Jesus died to become the entryway into the Land of Salvation. Jesus is the very Door to eternal life. (John 10:9) Moses came on to the scene and finally turned the keys of leadership over to Joshua. Jesus lives forever to intercede on our behalf. (Hebrews 7:25) Moses gave voice to a temporary and ultimately ineffectual system of religion. The New Testament of the Blood of Jesus has ushered in that to which the entire Old Covenant system had merely pointed. Jesus gives us the means to find an eternal salvation which offers the forgiveness of sins and a relationship with The Father and The Son.

The Old Covenant had offered vengeance, death and judgment. The New Covenant has given love, life and pardon of sins. The Old Covenant had offered no access to God. The New Covenant bids us to say, "Abba, Father," to our loving parent, God. (Galatians 4:6) The Old Covenant passed away as it was fulfilled in and superseded by the New Covenant.

The blood of the Old Covenant animals of creation had to be renewed often. It seemed without power. (Hebrews 10:4) The Blood of the New Covenant is eternal as Jesus continually stands before the Presence of The Father. The Blood of the Self-Sacrifice of Jesus is able to save to the uttermost. (Hebrews 7:25) The Blood of the Old Covenant was the blood of the animals of creation. The Blood of the New Covenant is the Blood of Messiah, God, the son."

The blood sprinkled on the mercy seat of the Old Covenant needed to have a blessing pronounced upon it by carnal priests of humanity. The Blood of the humanity of Jesus, sprinkled upon the Heavenly Mercy Seat needed no further blessing. It was already the Blood of God, The Son. The blood of the Old Covenant needed to be sprinkled often. The Blood of the New Testament of Jesus is powerful throughout time and eternity.

The blood of Abel shouted from the ground for vengeance. The Blood of Jesus showered from the Cross for mercy and pardon. The blood of the sacrifice of Abel was shed in accordance with the Words and purpose of God for that time. It was shed in faith. The Blood of the Self-Sacrifice of Jesus was shed in accordance with the eternal purpose of God. (I Peter 1:19-20) That Blood of Jesus was shed for the faithful of all generations.]

12.25 See that ye refuse not him that speaketh. For if they escaped not who refused him that spake on earth, much more shall not we escape, if we turn away from him that speaketh from heaven.

[There was a severe penalty upon those who disregarded the words of Moses who was only a representative of God. They were condemned under the civil law of the Theocracy of ancient Israel. Moreover, they were condemned as standing in unrighteousness before the God of Creation as they counted His Words as not worthy of their acceptance.

There was a penalty suffered by those who rejected Messiah as He, God clothed in human flesh, spoke His Message to them on this earth. One of those penalties was visited upon the Jewish nation with their dispersion into the world following the destruction of the Temple. This was not a situation where the Temple was any more central in the true worship of God. The veil, rent in twain, no longer kept the individual from the presence of God. In their carnality the Jewish leaders still longed for the worship of the Temple; in this they bypassed the worship of The Son as the entryway into favor with God. This refusal leads to an eternity of regret and judgment.

Those of this dispensation of time refuse the leading of God, the Spirit, as He leads us into the Scriptures which speak of Jesus. (John 5:39) This refusal has led to a weakened church, a message lacking in power and a people who are not followers of Him though this is their claim. We of the church which claims the Name of Christ have become Laodicean as we claim to display the power of God even while we claim the culture of the world above a fidelity to Him. (Revelation 3:14-22)

There is no way that our vision and outreach can be Heavenly when our "church culture" and activity is acclimated to display the world. To what can we possibly call people? We have accepted them and their ways without giving a purpose in repentance. Repentance from what? Repentance to what?

Our music is of the world's style rather than reaching for the Heavenly tremor. Our preaching is muted so as not to displease any who might be enthralled within the "Sanctuary of Satanic Desire." Our Bible's assurance is that God could not preserve His Words so man has had to help Him out by seeking to recover what God had let slip through His fingers. Even our doctrine is settled on the shifting sands of the cultural dance of man's evolutionary journey into perdition. If this is all we have to offer we are just another "brand" on the grocery shelf of man's philosophies.

That last sentence may not be accurate. We have actually placed ourselves in the "discount bin" of discarded produce. The judgment of God must come to the Church of God which has moved from the "provincialism" of Biblical Christianity into the "progressivism" of society's sordidness.]

12.26 *Whose voice then shook the earth: but now he hath promised, saying, Yet once more I shake not the earth only, but also heaven.*

[Many argued that it was God, The Son, Who spoke to Moses in the exodus. I would not argue as it seems that it is the Son Who interacts with lost humanity. It is He Who gives Himself in Sacrifice for the remission of the sins of humanity.

At Sinai the voice of God was accompanied by earthquake, fire, smoke and storm. There were earthquakes associated with the giving of the Law which literally shook the earth. It was an amazing display of the power and majesty of God which those of the exodus witnessed. We would assume that such a display would so overawe the people that the generation which saw these things that they would naturally be disposed to place their complete faith and reliance upon the Lord.

Shortly after these events, possibly even while the events were in progress on Sinai, the people approached Aaron and demanded that an idol be fashioned which they could worship as their "god." Surely Aaron, the brother of Moses and the "founding father" of the Levitical priesthood as the first of their line, would never go along with such sacrilege. After all, Aaron had even gone toward the mountain with Moses.

After Aaron had fashioned a golden calf, interestingly enough this was a replica of one of the Egyptian gods, he led the people in idol worship. Moses came from the mountain with the two tablets, written by the very "finger of God," on which were the Ten Commandments. Meek and mild Moses was so upset that he smashed those tablets. He had to go back to the mountain to get a copy.

As imperfect as were the people in the face of the Words of God, this event of the giving of the Law was a thing which also "shook the world." This wasn't the shaking of the earthquake. This was the shaking of the religious sensitivities of the people. They were instructed that the "golden calf denomination" was not the proper "church" for them to attend.

Priests, and even high priests, were not unknown among the various people of the day. This was in the plan of God. He took what the people knew and understood. He then corrected some of their misconceptions. The plan of God was to set up a religious system of sacrifice and ceremony which would point to The True Messiah. The worship of the people was proper as it was planned and instituted by the Will and Word of God. But, it was temporary. The people didn't fully understand this, of course. But, the purpose of God was that this "religious instruction" would only stand until the reality of the Messiah was culminated at the Cross of Calvary.

There were also some "shakings" in the earth at the time of the Cross. There were earthquakes. The sun was darkened. Some of the graves of the righteous were opened and the occupants walked out to once more be among men for a time.

There was yet another earthquake three days later as the crucified and buried Jesus returned from the dead. He dealt with teaching His church for a few weeks and then returned to Heaven as He once again received His Rightful Glory which He had laid aside as He took upon Himself the robes of humanity that He might identify with us in the atonement. The religion of the Jews was shaken. The Temple "divider" between the people and the presence of God was removed by being torn from the top, the direction of Heaven, and to the bottom, the residence of the people.

Not long after this the Spirit descended upon the small church at Jerusalem. Men began to speak in human languages which they had never learned. Their speech was of the need to trust Messiah. The bulk of the Jewish nation never accepted Jesus as Messiah. But, some did and so did many Gentiles. This was a new thing, a thing which "shook up" the Jewish notion of "separation." Jews and Gentiles gathered together to worship Jesus.

It had been wrong, religiously wrong, for the Jews to join in worship with the Gentile people. Part of that separation was to preserve a "pure line" into which Messiah would come. He had now come. And, unlike the picture presented at Sinai, all nations were invited to come to worship The Son. This was a shocking thing to many Jewish people.

Many of the Jewish people still clung to the "old ways." God sent Titus and his Roman legions to destroy the Temple in Jerusalem. There was another "shake up." The time of the Temple Sacrifice was over. The Self-Sacrifice of Jesus had been that to which the old Temple Sacrifices pointed. The Temple Sacrificial System no longer had any purpose in the plan of God.

Paul also accessed Haggai 2:6-7. "For thus saith the LORD of hosts; Yet once, it *is* a little while, and I will shake the heavens, and the earth, and the sea, and the dry *land*; And I will shake all nations, and the desire of all nations shall come: and I will fill this house with glory, saith the LORD of hosts."

This is the time of the promised return of Israel's Messiah. He will return in the clouds seven years before this to call His Own to be with Him in the Rapture. He will then return to the earth in order to again set up the Throne of David in the city of Jerusalem where He will reign as Lord and King.

Between the time of His return in the clouds and His return to earth will be a seven year period of tribulation upon the earth. The earth will shake; the powers of nature will shake. This is the time of Jacob's trial. (Jeremiah 30:7) We, the church, have been translated out of the world before this time.

The Second Coming of Jesus to the earth at the end of that Tribulation period will see Him not as the humble servant of His first advent. He will come in power and glory to judge the nations and establish the long promised revival of the Davidic Kingdom in Jerusalem. From the throne of David Jesus will rule the world. Satan is bound during this time and does not cause problems among the inhabitants of the earth.

After one thousand years of righteous rule by Jesus, Satan will be loosed for a season. Amazingly enough Satan will find some still willing to revolt against the King of Kings and Lord of Lords. Satan, and his followers, will be defeated and judged.

Then there will be more shaking of the earth and the universe as the sin of Adam is completely eradicated from creation. No more will the creation groan under a load of sin. (Romans 8:22) The present creation will be judged and purged by fire. There will be a new creation, without sin, prepared to replace the present sin cursed creation. (II Peter 3:10-13)]

12.27 And this word, Yet once more, signifieth the removing of those things that are shaken, as of things that are made, that those things which cannot be shaken may remain.

[Haggai 2:6 says, "For thus saith the LORD of hosts; Yet once, it is a little while, and I will shake the heavens, and the earth, and the sea, and the dry land." Much was made of the fact that Paul says "Yet once more," rather that adding "it is a little while" as did Haggai. Once again we are treated to the assertion that Paul chose the Septuagint reading over the Hebrew. I would again caution that there is no extant version of a complete rendering of the Old Testament Scripture in the Greek until the Hexpala of Origen in the third century A.D. It is as likely that the Septuagint follows Paul rather than vice versa.

Theologically, it is perfectly acceptable for the Spirit to refine His Own Words of inspiration from the Old Testament prophecy to the New Testament prophecy. This is especially so considering that Haggai was written before the First Advent of our Lord. The "in a little while" may have not be retained since the shaking, "in a little while," may well have had reference to that First Advent wherein the entire system of Jewish religion under the Mosaic Covenant was shaken by the life, death and resurrection of Jesus during that First Advent.

Or, it may have been that the Spirit wanted the readers of this letter to look forward to the final shaking which will occur at the end of history.

The very next verse does move us from current history to the reception of the kingdom which cannot be moved. We have not, even now, received that kingdom. We have received the promise, as did the saints of the eleventh chapter of Hebrews. But, as they did not receive all which was promised, neither have we.

The things which can be moved are the things of this created world which have been tarnished by the sin of Adam upon the human race. As we have seen earlier, even the religious system of Judaism must be shaken and changed as all of its types and shadows of sacrifice and ceremony have been fulfilled and are no longer tenable as the reality of Jesus has replaced the prophecy of Mosaic religion.

Those spiritual principles of God will remain even as the social and political orders of man falter and fail.

Even the things we would describe as the pillars of creation must fade and fall under the judgment of God. The sin of Adam reached into the very structure of the created world. (Romans 8:22) Sin is a cancer which eats away at the body of physical creation. Sin produces a "countdown clock" which has given us a dying universe. Sin is a blight on the seed of the civilization of mankind. Sin brings death where God had ordained life. Sin brings disarray where God had created harmony. Sin has brought disease into the health of God's creation.

Sin must be finally defeated and eradicated from all of Creation. This is that final shaking where sin is removed and the righteousness, holiness, purity and glory of God's plan for His creation is restored with the final judgment upon sin. (Isaiah 66:22; II Peter 3:10-12; Revelation 21:1)]

12.28 Wherefore we receiving a kingdom which cannot be moved, let us have grace whereby we may serve God acceptably with reverence and godly fear:

[This verse begins with "because." "Wherefore" is because. Why should we do those things asked of us? Simple:

Because of all that Christ has done for us. We are privileged to live in the Age of Grace. We have no need to continually offer an animal of creation as a sacrifice to appease the God of Judgment. Jesus has offered Himself as our sacrifice to pay for the sins which we have committed.

We have a "religion," I am loath to speak of Christianity as a religion as religion is an act of man approaching God – in truth He has approached us with His wonderful salvation, which will never change. The Truths of Christ are all "yea and verily." He never changes and has not left us to fear He will change. His Words to us are eternal and secure.

Even the religion of Moses was not secure from change. Change was "built into" the religion of the Mosaic Covenant. The rites, ceremonies, sacrifices and priests of the Mosaic Covenant were all pictures pointing to Jesus. When He came and fulfilled all the Law became superfluous except as a picture of Jesus and a picture of the eternal spiritual principles of God.

The Cross has been the plan of Jesus for the full redemption of humanity since before the world was completed and humanity was created. (Revelation 13:8) The Age of Grace is the age of eternities blessing. It is not transitory but eternal.

Within this grace, freely given by Jesus although He paid a fearsome price on our behalf, there are things we are asked to do. These do not establish, or confirm us in grace. These are some small little things we are allowed to do in order to show our love of Jesus. Even being allowed these things is a grace given us from God.

We have received the promise of the glorious kingdom of God as our eternal abode. We will live forever with our Savior. It is asked of us that we be in grace – that is our salvation. It is asked that we hold to grace – that is our devotion to our Lord. It is asked that we be gracious – that is our fellowship with the local assembly of the redeemed and it is our duty in spreading the Words and Person of Jesus into the world at large. We witness of Him by being Christian, i.e. Christlike!

We serve Him acceptably when we serve Him in that grace and in the leading of the Holy Spirit of God. We serve Him in reverence by looking at Him in veneration and awe. We are not "special." Our glory is that we are allowed to serve the Great God and Savior, Jesus Christ. He is not "special;" He is more than that in that He is singularly glorious, powerful, and wonderful. True reverence is keeping this distinction ever before us. He is All; we are not worthy expect as He has called us.

The concept of "Godly fear" should not be seen as denoting being afraid. He is love to us. We have nothing to fear from our Heavenly Father. We do need to view Him with the Awe due His majesty and holiness.]

12.29 *For our God is a consuming fire.*

[One of the main concerns I have with the Charismatic, and too many modern Christians, is the easy familiarity with the things of God. I understand that God is a loving parent to His adopted children. I understand that the love of Jesus as shown forth from the Cross is deep and pure. I understand that the Spirit lovingly guides us through the pits falls of our human experiences.

When we lose sight of the responsibility of serving Christ we have replaced Him with the idol fashioned upon that man we see in the mirror as we shave.

May we never overlook the justice of God as we glory in the love of God. May we always consider the holiness of God. God is love. I read I John 4:8. "He that loveth not knoweth not God; for God is love."

I have also read this verse. "For our God is a consuming fire." Reread the commentary on verse 27, above. The great love of God carries a Holy hatred of sin which considered the devastation which sin has shed abroad in this world. Wars, sickness, famine, wickedness and more are the result of sin's intrusion into the perfection which God had created.

Several times God looked upon His creation and said, "It is good." This never happens again in Scripture after the sin of Adam and Eve. It was no more "good" because sin had corrupted the happiness and safety of humanity.

The quotation in this verse is from Deuteronomy 4:24. Sin was banned under the Old Covenant. Sin is still warned against, and banned, under the New Covenant of Grace. II Peter 3:10-12 reminds us that our God is a Consuming Fire because His great love cannot abide the horrors which sin has visited upon His perfect creation.]

HEBREWS - CHAPTER THIRTEEN

13.1   *Let brotherly love continue.*

[This was not a problem among the believers at this assembly. The problem was the incipient signs that the love which was held, one for another, was in danger of growing cold and somewhat formal. Considering I Thessalonians 4:9, the concept of brotherly love was seen as a doctrine of the church. "But as touching brotherly love ye need not that I write unto you: for ye yourselves are taught of God to love one another."

The problem with seeing love of the brethren as a doctrine to be followed was that this would tend to "formalize" what should have been an emotional attachment. It is true that we often will love another only by the utilization of our will. Loving the unlovely is a duty of our Christian spirits. Even the vilest of sinners we are called to love, despite their sin, so that we might reach them with the message of salvation in Christ.

There should be no such situation among the fellowship within the assembly. Our love one for another should be true and unfeigned. This is a display of family love. We are the children of God within the Body of Christ which is the church. This love should not be forced. It is to be a fruit of the Spirit. Therefore, as regards those of the fellowship, a lack in this area becomes a spiritual malady which must be addressed at the Cross.

Even the fact of persecution, as was coming upon the church, can be a motivating force to bring us together. Shared misery can unite. Shared joy, in the worship of Christ even in the face of persecution, will tend to bind our hearts together as our attention becomes focused on the Person of Christ.

Even at the most imperfect of our affections we may consider our sincere allegiance to Jesus as a "stake" to hold the "tent" of our affection toward those of the body of the assembly. In this, if no other conveyance may be found, we are holding true to our Lord, our local assembly, our larger "Church" out into the world, and the population which considers our witness to Christ in light of the love we hold for the brethren. "By this shall all men know that ye are my disciples, if ye have love one to another." (John 13:35)]

13.2   *Be not forgetful to entertain strangers: for thereby some have entertained angels unawares.*

[The phrase "be not forgetful," suggests that this was an always expected thing. In the culture of the Middle East at this time there were few inns. We remember the situation of Mary and Joseph as they came to Bethlehem. Bethlehem was extremely crowded at this time. Even this "guest homes" which people were willing to share with strangers visiting were well filled with "guests."

The hospitality of the Christians was a well-known aspect. The Savior had suggested this as a special way to serve Him by showing Christian love among even those possibly outside the faith. (Matthew 25:35-44) Peter also spoke of the Christian being known for his hospitality. (I Peter 4:9) Paul spoke of this as a Christian virtue in both Romans 12:13 and I Timothy 3:2.

Would there be "clinkers" amongst those served? Of course. That is the nature of the human element. The Christian would have been encouraged to see any such as this as evidence of the world's animosity toward the Lord. Even the unkind would be praised as evidences of being persecuted for the Lord.

There would also be those who would give the valuable gift of their own testimony to the family as they sojourned with them for a night or two. Further, this would be a means of witness out into the broader world of the Love of Christ. Perhaps a stranger would be converted to Christ due to his stay with the Christian family.

A friendly reminder is added. Some people had actually been visited by angels in the guise of strangers who shared the home or tent for a short time. Abraham and Lot come quickly to mind as those who were visited by angelic beings. Abraham, I believe, was honored by being visited by the Lord, Himself, in His pre-incarnate form.

Other Old Testament examples of angles speaking with men and women of creation are Gideon, the soon-to-be parents of Samson, and Joshua also saw the Angel of the Lord, the pre-incarnate Jesus, before the campaign against Jericho.

Let us never forget that angels also attend to us as the people of God in this dispensation. "The angel of the LORD encampeth round about them that fear him, and delivereth them." (Psalm 34:7)

Christians are always to, as the Lord gives us the means to do so, give the proverbial "cup of cold water" into a thirsty world. A caution must be given. At no time may we consider our participation in "alms," whatever form this may take, to stand as a testimony for the Lord by itself. Salvation is of eternity and much superior to a ham sandwich to a hungry man on a Tuesday afternoon. Share what you may as tokens of Christian love and charity. Share the message of salvation as the duty of a Christian to his fellow human.]

13.3 *Remember them that are in bonds, as bound with them; and them which suffer adversity, as being yourselves also in the body.*

["Remember." I am reminded of an old joke. It was at the reading of a rich uncle's will. The will began, "I promised my nephew that I would remember him in my will. Hi, Jim. I hope that all is well with you. And now I begin to speak of those to whom I am leaving tangible goods rather than just remembering them..."

The "remembrance" of which Paul spoke at this place was remembrance of compassion. The previous verse had spoken of hospitality to wayfarers; this verse speaks of the same consideration, compassion, upon those in adversity. James had this to say on the subject: "If a brother or sister be naked, and destitute of daily food, And one of you say unto them, Depart in peace, be ye warmed and filled; notwithstanding ye give them not those things which are needful to the body; what *doth it* profit?" (James 2:15-16)

Wishes rarely show Christian compassion. Actions are concrete examples of the care of a Christian for the needs of another. There were few charitable organizations available at the time of Paul's writing. So powerful was the Christian compulsion to give to the needy that most of the modern philanthropic organizations were begun either by Christians or by those influenced by the Christians.

Let us never forget that the individual obligation still exists. We should have sympathy for those in need. Sympathy without attendant compassion is meaningless.

We offer prayer, to be sure. With those prayers, as examples of the love of God, should come tangible aid where it is possible for us to so give. Past this aid we should also seek to encourage those to whom such troubles may have come.

It is likely that the first thought was that this was to be those of the household of faith. Persecution was a daily fact of life in the early church. This may be the reason that Paul emphasized that those to whom he wrote were also members of the body of the assemblies.

With the above in mind we ought to show love to Christians for Christ's sake. They are His children. But, to those outside of the household of faith we ought also to show this same compassion and consideration for the sake of Christ. In this case it is to send His Message of care and love even to those of this world as He calls them to consider the realities of the next world.

This verse speaks of those in bonds. Bonds and iron bars do not exhaust the context of prisons. These ought to be addressed in our Christian mission into the world. But, there are those who are bound by poverty, illness, pain, loss... Jesus offers solace in all of life for all of humanity who turn to Him. May we never overlook the need to reach out with the hand of faith into the world of hopelessness.

Hospitality and compassion should be natural outreaches which should be utilized to spread the Christian Message that Jesus Christ died in time so that others could live in eternity.]

13.4 *Marriage is honorable in all, and the bed undefiled: but whoremongers and adulterers God will judge.*

[Some have argued that the phrase "honorable in all" refers to all places, times, and situations. However, the conjunctive word "but" compares the people who are whoremongers and adulterers with that phrase. Therefor the phrase "honorable" must apply to people as well. Thus we are told that marriage is honorable to all classes of people. The Roman consideration of a "celibate" clergy cannot stand in reference to this verse.

Early in the history of humanity God noted that "it is not good for man to be alone." (Genesis 2:18) Therefore God fashioned woman from the man. This is an early indication of the Biblical standard that the two would be one in the joining of their bodies. This covers a more expansive consideration than simple procreation. This is a spiritual/bodily union whereby the two are become more complete as the creation of God within the institution of marriage as He intended. This is shown in the prophecy of Adam (Genesis 2:24, I Corinthians 6:16; Ephesians 5:31) as well as in the plan of God for the population of His creation. (Genesis 1:28)

I would also note that this must be a union of one man and one woman as this was the template of the original creation of Adam, and the fashioning of Eve to be his consort.

With this template, it is an obvious continuation that such union, the marriage bed mentioned, must be honorable as it is manifestly the plan and institution of God. For any to disparage this as sinful is to deny that God is wise in all His ways and intents.

When Paul was speaking in the seventh chapter of I Corinthians, his primary consideration was that marriage was good thing. He was not opposed to the institution. His short reference in verse seven that "I would that all men were even as I myself" was speaking as one who was completely dedicated to God. Even at this, the rest of the chapter argues against the idea that he was charging this celibacy for all.

In Philippians 3:5 Paul says that he was a Pharisee. In order for a man to be a Pharisee at this time, he must have been a married man. Did the wife of Paul die? Did the wife of Paul leave him upon his conversion? We have no light on this subject. The point is that Paul never remarried. Even Paul, however, had been married.

Sin is always a perversion, an alteration or distortion, of the purpose and plan of God. Therefore, the whoremonger and fornicator are those who have distorted the pure plan of God and instituted a man centered plan which argues that man's plan is more desirable than is God's perfection.

Beyond the general impurity of humanity, this was an age where temple prostitution was an established fact among many of the heathen religions. Immorality was used in vile religious practices. Most of these were centered in some sort of fertility rite. Some were fashioned to glorify homosexual gratification. All of these will be judged by the Holy Standard of God, Who is the Holy Judge of mankind. Whether in a homosexual venue or heterosexual couplings, these distortions of the institution of marriage as given by God will result in the judgment of God upon the practitioners of such irreligious actions.]

13.5 *Let your conversation be without covetousness; and be content with such things as ye have: for he hath said, I will never leave thee, nor forsake thee.*

["Conversation" is the manner in which one lives his life. We are told to live our lives without covetousness. It is the "want" of something which causes most of us to fail to fully live in the "now" of our present conditions. We want, and plan, and sometimes scheme, with an eye to a "better tomorrow." The bills we run up today are the things which will cause us to live at a lower standard tomorrow.

This is true in the spiritual as it is in the physical. A newly converted man decides that he wants to be something special so he sets out to become without preparing for that becoming. He will become, generally speaking, "ripe pickings" for the purveyors of perverted religious practice. Unless we are willing to spend time in the inspired and preserved Scripture it will not be possible for us to learn what the Bible actually has to say.

In everything we do as humans in this world, the time spent in preparation is time well spent for perfecting ourselves. If we desire to be all we can possibly be for the Lord we must spend those hours with Him in the prayer closet and in the faithful study of His Words to us which He has faithfully preserved for this day.

This "faithfulness" of His preserved Words is part of this promise given in this verse. He has promised to never leave nor forsake us. This was His promise to Jacob (Genesis 28:15), Israel (Deuteronomy 31:6-8), Joshua (Joshua 1:15), Solomon (I Chronicles 28:20), and is now given through inspiration to us in this day.

There is nothing which the world can offer that can come close to this promise of Jesus.

I was watching a television show a few months ago. It was a replay of an old time quiz show. There was excitement on the faces of the contestants as they learned that they had won a "brand new 1956 automobile!" I would guess that by this time all

HEBREWS: Chapter 13

the excitement over winning that car has faded from everyone's memory.

I could be wrong on the year of that car. It was a long time ago. I used that year because it was my 10th year. I can remember very few things from that important year in my life. I can remember one day I sat out in the front yard and read Scripture. Yes, I was hoping that someone would see me.

I remember that because I finally realized that this was pride rather than devotion. There is a vast difference between setting ourselves up to appear "religious" and allowing the Lord to direct our paths. Pride goeth before a fall (Proverbs 16:18) but the Lord is always ready to pick us up, dust us off and lead us rightly into His paths. That is real contentment. (I Timothy 6:6)

It is never a "good" situation when we covet things. It is always good that the Lord is our Constant Contemporary. In that knowledge is real peace in this world.]

13.6 *So that we may boldly say, The Lord is my helper, and I will not fear what man shall do unto me.*

[Paul quotes from Psalm 118:6 at this point. Remembering that this was a time of persecution, Stephen and James – among others, had been put to death simply because they were Christians. The same thing is happening around the world in our day. My conviction is that the same thing will shortly happen within this present citadel of religious "freedom." We increasingly see governmental suggestions which are coupled with societal animosity toward the message, and those who carry the message, of Biblical truths in our day. History suggests that true persecution cannot be far behind these harbingers.

The truth of Jesus is our refuge in the storms of life. Jesus, Himself, as our constant contemporary, will stand with us. His enablement will give us a strength we do not possess. We can stand in the same spirit as did Daniel, Shadrach, Meshach, and Abednego, Stephen, Peter, James, John, the rest of the apostles, even the great theologian Paul, who suffered for the faith once delivered. The tyrants of the world can harm our bodies but Jesus Christ has already saved our souls. What can man do? The power of man ends but the omnipotent power of God is limitless and full. His power is dedicated to His Words of comfort for His adopted children.

"And fear not them which kill the body, but are not able to kill the soul: but rather fear him which is able to destroy both soul and body in hell." (Matthew 10:28)]

13.7 *Remember them which have the rule over you, who have spoken unto you the word of God: whose faith follow, considering the end of their conversation.*

[This verse is somewhat speaking in the past tense. It is asking that the Christian give heed to the teaching of those who have gone before and spoken the Words of God unto the congregation.

In this light the phrase "the rule over you" is not of civic rulers but of Christian leaders who have pointed the way to follow Christ. This is not concerning the leadership of ruling by fiat or compulsion. A more apt illustration may be a military leader who not only commands action but also takes part in that action. One of the biggest compliments an old soldier can give another is, "I would follow you into combat."

The concept of history seems important in this day. We in the churches seem to have lost our bearing. We are not content with following "the old paths;" we seem disposed to find broad new highways of concept in regards to worship. It is one thing to reach out to a new generation. Sadly, we see a tendency reach out from a new paradigm of religious base. They very next verse would remind us that while the world may change around us, we are followers of He Who is changeless.

In this verse we are asked to consider those who have gone before us on this Christian journey. Their lives were consistently dedicated to His Words and His faith. They may have ended their Christian journey on a hospital "death bed," or in an execution carried for by enemies of the Gospel. The manner in which they were able to meet their exit from this world should remain a testimony for the faith. This should be a testimony which we can follow considering that this life is short. Also, we consider the excellency and eternal duration of the life to come!

Follow the "old paths" of faith. Only therein is there a safe harbor for the ship of our soul. Only Christ, who does not change, is the port of our redemption.]

13.8   *Jesus Christ the same yesterday, and to day, and for ever.*

[Jesus is still the same great Creator God which He was in the beginning. That is only a rational conclusion in the light of eternity. The concept of time, as a creation of God, does not denote a parenthesis in eternity. Time is an event during eternity. Therefore, Jesus is Who He was because He remains Who He is.

This verse is not simply a mention that Jesus existed long before Bethlehem. It is more. The term "Yesterday" speaks to His pre-existence from our human standpoint and as it predates even creation. (John 1:3) The term "Today" speaks to His present existence. I might make note here that this passage was written after the crucifixion but still speaks of Jesus in the present tense. The term "Forever" speaks of His permanent existence throughout all of eternity.

This is a clear statement of the Deity of Jesus.

He was Holy before all creation. He is Holy as He fulfills the Office of High Priest for the Christian. He will be Holy for all eternity. There is none about whom this could be said except God. Jesus is God!

This verse informs us of the eternality of Jesus. The word "yesterday" reaches back. The word "today" touches upon the very day of the writing as well as the very day of our reading. The word "forever" touches upon all the succeeding days; it stretches from eternity and into eternity.

This verse speaks of Jesus in the present tense even as it describes Him in the past tense and future tense. Since the Book of Hebrews was written approximately thirty years after the physical death of Jesus it speaks of His immortality as it speaks of Him as a present entity in that time frame. In truth, this verse speaks of Jesus in the eternal sense. Jesus came into time but He is not of time. He, as God, is of eternity where there is no "today, tomorrow, or yesterday."

Thus, this verse attests to the fact that Jesus is eternal. This means that He is God. So often we speak of "Jesus was." I fall into this trap myself. It is wrong. Jesus IS!

We too, as born again believers, are promised an eternal existence with God. That this eternality of Jesus is also stretched back to "eternity past" places Him as The Creator rather than as a Created Being. Thus, once again, Jesus is God.

The Book of Hebrews has been called the "most Jewish Book in the New Testament." Most of the subject matter in the Book has to do with the Temple order and the sacrificial elements of that worship. Surely the human penman of Hebrews was familiar with the Old Testament Book of Malachi when He ascribed the eternality of Jesus in the same terms as was the eternality of God in the Old Testament.

While it is true, I believe, that it was a Jewish audience Paul had in mind when he put pen to the parchment of this Book, we must always consider that Hebrews, as are all the Books of Scripture, is inspired and preserved for all the Christian's throughout history. Jesus is clearly equated with God.

Because Jesus never changes we have a faith which is changeless. Any concept of "new doctrine," "new teaching," or "new Scripture" is a demonstrably false since such concept is a tacit denial of the immutability of Christ. He is the culmination of the Old Covenant, displaying what truth lay within that covenant, even as He is the Author of the New Covenant. In Him the old resides even as over the New He, Alone, presides.]

13.9 *Be not carried about with divers and strange doctrines. For it is a good thing that the heart be established with grace; not with meats, which have not profited them that have been occupied therein.*

[To be carried about with strange doctrine is to be departed from the doctrines of Christ. These are called "diverse" with regard to the strange multiplication of false doctrine among those who depart from the simple grace of the Cross. There are literally hundreds, or more, false cults trolling the world in our day. These all have their beginning in the sin of pride. There is a pride in man that seeks to disavow the rule of God. I once likened the Bible as the warranty book, as in an automobile, which God gave to show man the most efficient manner of life.

There are those who refuse this "owner's manual" for the ultimate life of humanity upon this earth. These want to use their own judgment rather than the judgment of God for all decisions in life. When will humanity learn that the God of Creation understands us even beyond our own understanding of ourselves!

In the pride of establishing a false religion many will still claim some form of "Christianity." "The problem is," they assure us, "Is that the Bible is so unreliable that there is a need to re-establish first century Christianity." This is a denial of the wisdom of Jesus who prophesied that Satan would never be able to close down His churches. (Matthew 16:18) Many churches have been harmed by Satanic attack. Some churches have apostatized from the faith as they have followed "divers and strange" doctrine. God has always kept a remnant of His people true within His Church.

We live in a day in which even the so-called "Fundamentalist Church" has given up on any real trust in the Scripture. In order to defend their practice of "rethinking and rewriting" the Scripture even the fundamentalist has jettisoned the doctrine of the plenary and verbal inspiration of Scripture and replaced it with a new doctrine of "concept inspiration" which allows them to claim a preserved bible even while denying that very preservation.

With no real authoritative Bible, the fundamentalist movement is beginning the slow slide into error and apostasy.

Hebrews is concerned with such apostasy. The prevalent form of such apostasy in the day of the penning of this Book was a return to Judaism. This verse reminds the readers that the true foundation of the New Covenant of Grace is just that: Grace. To have undue speculation concerning the dietary consideration of the Mosaic Law was a divisive argument that had no bearing upon the Church.

The concept of the dietary laws of Moses was of the Old Covenant which Jesus had perfectly fulfilled. With that fulfillment of the Law, Jesus had instituted the New Covenant of the Blood of His Self-Sacrifice. The old types and shadows of Himself, which He had satisfied and finished in His Own body, were no longer in effect. Jesus was now the Great High Priest and all other sacrifices, beyond His Own at Calvary, were simply the works of man.

These things of the Law carried no grace within them. Worse, they were things which tended to obscure the Real Grace of Jesus in that they would inhibit full trust in Him for salvation – the only salvation which had ever been available.]

13.10 *We have an altar, whereof they have no right to eat which serve the tabernacle.*

[The Levites, as "employed" in carrying out the sacrifices of the people unto God, were allowed to eat from the sacrificial offerings of the people. Leviticus 7:5 and Deuteronomy 12:6-7 spelled out this right.

This was not an absolute right, however. On the Day of Atonement, one day a year, there were special offerings where the blood of those offerings was to be sprinkled on the Mercy Seat in the Holy of Holies. Leviticus 16:27 specified that the bodies of these sacrificial animals would be carried outside the camp and burned. These were not given to be eaten.

The Self-Sacrifice of Jesus was such an offering. He offered up Himself as The Atonement for sin. (I Peter 1:19-20; Revelation 13:8) This Self-Sacrifice of Jesus was such a Solemn Sacrifice. As the sacrifice on the Day of Atonement was carried outside the camp to be consumed by the flames of judgment, so was Jesus sacrificed for us outside the city. (Hebrews 13:12) He had no sins of His Own for which He was judged. But, He took upon Himself the judgment for our sins. (Galatians 1:4; Hebrews 1:3; I Peter 2:24; Revelation 1:5)

Those who attend the Jewish alter have no part with Jesus for their faith is not in Him. We who have had our sins forgiven by the Blood of Jesus have the right through His Blood to enter unto His alter. Further, at the Lord's Table, as oft as we celebrate His death, we symbolically eat of His flesh and drink of His Blood. In this we are blessed even above the Levitical priests of the Old Covenant.

We, the Christian, are considered a royal priesthood of a holy nation. (I Peter 2:9) The Levitical priests were not from the royal family. We, as adopted sons of God, are from the royal family of the entire creation even as we are called to be priests unto God. The duty of the priest is to take the needs of man before the throne of God. We do this in our prayers for others even as we take the holy message that Jesus Christ died in time so that others could live in eternity out into the world as ambassadors of the Grace of Jesus. (II Corinthians 5:20)]

13.11 *For the bodies of those beasts, whose blood is brought into the sanctuary by the high priest for sin, are burned without the camp.*

[This is in reference to the Day of Atonement as discussed in verse ten, above. Some argued that this burning of the animals of creation which were sacrificed

HEBREWS: Chapter 13

according to the Day of Atonement were burned outside the city to show that the sins of the people were not forgiven in this sacrifice.

Others, and to this I agree, that the animals were burned as a picture of judgment. That this was outside the camp pointed to the true nature of salvation which would be available to all rather than just to the Israelite.

That the blood of these sacrificial animals of the Day of Atonement was sprinkled upon the Mercy Seat in the Holy of Holies, which was considered as the special place of the residence of God in that dispensation, was a picture that only the One and True God could be seen as The Solution for the sin in humanity.]

13.12 Wherefore Jesus also, that he might sanctify the people with his own blood, suffered without the gate.

[The word "also" gives us a reference to the Tabernacle sacrifices. The sacrifices on the Day of Atonement were burned outside the camp. This was unusual for the bodies of other sacrificial animals were eaten by the Levite as a sort of "pay" for performing their priestly duties.

But, the sacrifices of this special holy day were burned without the camp. The difference was that these were specially sin offerings in that the blood of these animals would be sprinkled on the Mercy Seat in the presence of God.

This brings out attention to the cry of Jesus from the cross, "And at the ninth hour Jesus cried with a loud voice, saying, Eloi, Eloi, lama sabachthani? which is, being interpreted, My God, my God, why hast thou forsaken me?" (Mark 15:34) The Father, God, cannot look upon the evil of sin. It is anathema to Him. The Son, God, was at that point bearing the sins of the entire race of man, from creation forward, who would come to Him in faith. This was the Great Day of Atonement as The Sinless Lamb of God poured out His Own Blood to redeem a world which contained Gentile as well as Jew.

The Blood of that Self-Sacrifice of Jesus would be applied to each person who would accept Him, by faith in His Blood, as Savior. By this act of Jesus each of these persons who accept Him as Savior, are sanctified, or set apart from the world as the people of God.

Jesus suffered this crucifixion outside the city walls of Jerusalem. Jerusalem was the city of the great Temple. The city walls served the same purpose as did the camp of the people of the exodus. As those animals of creation, specially sacrificed on the Day of Atonement, were burned completely outside the camp of Israel, so was Jesus sacrificed outside the "camp."

This was a symbol of the Jewish rejection of their Messiah.

This was a symbol of the Church which Jesus would build outside the camp, to include both Jew and Gentile within her membership.]

13.13 Let us go forth therefore unto him without the camp, bearing his reproach.

[After the sin with the golden calf among the group of the exodus, Moses removed the Tabernacle itself outside the camp. (Exodus 33:7) Those who wished to worship the LORD at that point removed themselves from the camp to come to the Tabernacle.

Likewise, Paul was telling these people that they needed to remove themselves from the Jewish people. They needed to come to Christ outside the city. Meeting Jesus would not happen at the Temple. The need is to meet Jesus at Calvary. The Jewish ceremony and sacrifice were completed in Jesus; it was now time to remove oneself from the Temple and meet the Lord at the Cross upon which He had died in His humanity in order that sinners might find spiritual life from His Blood.]

13.14 *For here have we no continuing city, but we seek one to come.*

[We leave the city to cleave unto Christ. We are called to follow our father, Abraham in the faith of a called out journey. (Hebrews 11:10-16) We are going to a Heavenly land as was Abraham. We might not understand the way. We do understand that Jesus is the Way. (John 14:6)

The readers of Paul's words probably didn't understand, it is entirely possible that Paul didn't completely understand that which inspiration lay on his pen. Jerusalem, with its Temple, history, and prophecy was soon to be downtrodden of the Roman legions. As Jesus had foretold, there would not be one stone left upon another. Jerusalem, the city of David, would be destroyed; the Jews would be driven from her. (Matthew 24:2; Mark 13:2; Luke 19:44; 21:6)

The histories of Josephus tell us that the Christians, heeding the warning of Jesus in regard to the city, did not suffer a single casualty. The Jews lost many dead and sold into slavery.

In Matthew 28:19 Jesus had charged the Christian witness to spread into the world. This did not happen fully until Jerusalem was destroyed and the Christians were forced to flee. It would have been much better for those early Christians to disengage from the Jewish roots of the Church, which held them to a physical path, and follow the Words with which the Lord had charged them.

It must be noted that simply "going forth" is nothing. Going forth unto Jesus is everything.]

13.15 *By him therefore let us offer the sacrifices of praise to God continually, that is, the fruit of our lips giving thanks to his name.*

[There was a rabbinical teaching that during the time of Messiah the only sacrifice offered would be the sacrifice of praise. Paul uses the very teaching of the Jew's to proclaim that Jesus is the promised Messiah of God.

In verse ten, above, Paul had answered an objection of those who would have attempted to Judaize the Christian religion. These argued that to completely do away with the Mosaic system would leave no means by which sacrifice could be offered to God. Their argument went that to destroy the Temple services was to destroy the altar. Should the altar be abolished within the Temple, the access to worship God would also be removed.

Paul reminded these that Jesus is our Altar of Worship. We are told to bring our sacrifice of praise to our Lord. This may have reference to Hosea 14:2. "Take with you words, and turn to the LORD: say unto him, Take away all iniquity, and receive us graciously: so will we render the calves of our lips." Since calves were to be offered in sacrifice upon the altar, we are shown that our lips, praising God with our voices and vocalizations, has always been a means of sacrifice unto the Lord.

The peace offerings were described in Leviticus 3:1-17; 7:11-21; and 29-34. Note that these were not offerings as a result of sin; these were offerings of praise for the relationship of grace which God has seen fit to bestow upon sinful humanity. They do not invoke that grace; they celebrate the fact of that grace.

The peace offerings gave thanksgiving for received blessings. They were used to fulfill a vow, thanks for benefits received, and in freely given spontaneous devotion to God. This is our charge in this dispensation as we worship the Lord Who has saved our souls at such a great cost to himself.

It should be noted that we are only able to offer this praise because of the grace already bestowed upon us by the largess of God's love.]

13.16 *But to do good and to communicate forget not: for with such sacrifice God is well pleased.*

[Paul argues that simply "saying" is not always the same as "doing." This is somewhat a presage to James epistle. Simply talking a good fight will never bring victory in the ring of life. If we are to speak of God's love it seems fitting that we display His love toward others.

My first thought at "to do good and to communicate" is that the best "good" we can do for others is contained within our witness that Jesus died in time so that others could live in eternity. This verse goes beyond even that, although that is foundational. There is nothing more important to a man than the eternal destiny of his immortal soul! We need to never forget that foundational truth.

We can never disparage the concept that the world sees talk as cheap. We must approach them with more. Again, there is a "bed rock" of "more." Prayer by name whenever possible for the sinner is a necessity. No one will ever be converted by our argument – or by our act of "Christian charity." It is the conviction brought by the Spirit which will call a man from the danger of sin and to the safety of salvation.

But, this word "communicate" goes beyond the exercise of our vocal chords. That is a very good and pious thing when it is combined with a heart of love toward God. But, a heart which is truly a heart of love toward God will display Him into the world of man.

We called this a sacrifice. It is. Let us consider, however, that the Old Testament saint who brought his sacrifice to the Tabernacle was about to give up something as an indication of his dedication to God.

Our sacrifice of praise toward God is not of something we have given up but of that which we are willing to share with others. In that it becomes something which, as the parables of Jesus or the "object lessons" of Ezekiel, allows the world to see in things they might understand those things they might otherwise have not understand. Sin does abound into the world; we serve The God Who is both able and willing to overcome the world.

Only when backed with prayer and submission to God does the "social gospel" bring men and women to the Master. It is true that a cup of cold water given a man on a hot day will not relieve the tongue of a rich man in torment. (Luke 16:24) But, given the work of the Spirit upon that man's soul while he is yet in his body of clay may cause him to join Abraham and Lazarus in the true worship of the Lord.

The fishermen at the Sea of Galilee may have used hooks or nets in their pursuit of fish. Christianity is an expansive religion which will use whatever means the Lord shows to us in order to "fish" for the souls of men. These must always be His means. As such any means used must be grounded in the inspired and preserved Scripture.

God is pleased when our praise continues even as our service toward Him abounds into the world.]

13.17 *Obey them that have the rule over you, and submit yourselves: for they watch for your souls, as they that must give account, that they may do it with joy, and not with grief: for that is unprofitable for you.*

[The first part of this chapter had been dealing with temporal situations. This verse talks about spiritual overseers. We have a need to be in subjection to our earthly brothers in the Lord. This will serve as a brake on our natural tendency to puff ourselves up.

The ministry is a heady experience. We, who have taken it upon ourselves to stand before the congregation of the Lord, are in the position of giving forth the message of God to those who sit before us. It is an easy thing, too easy!, to become prideful of our status. Being in subjection to others is a means which will tend to remind us of our place as ministers of the Lord.

Our ultimate fidelity, however, is to God. There may come a time when we must loose the bonds of that subjection in order to rightly follow God.

"Be ye not unequally yoked together with unbelievers: for what fellowship hath righteousness with unrighteousness? and what communion hath light with darkness? And what concord hath Christ with Belial? or what part hath he that believeth with an infidel? And what agreement hath the temple of God with idols? for ye are the temple of the living God; as God hath said, I will dwell in them, and walk in them; and I will be their God, and they shall be my people. Wherefore come out from among them, and be ye separate, saith the Lord, and touch not the unclean thing; and I will receive you." (II Corinthians 6:14-17)

This, spiritual fidelity toward God overriding that of fidelity toward men, is the purpose of one leaving his spiritual "parents" and going off into the wilderness.

Personal pride, petty partisan squabbles, and personality conflicts are NOT a Biblical reason to disfellowship with a church or church group. A good rule of thumb is that if no one who is spiritually discerned agrees with you, you are in the wrong.

Think on that!

God doesn't have any "Lone Rangers." He does have some small scouting parties!

The primary focus of this verse is towards the pastors. The pastor has no authority except to preach and teach the Words of God. The pastor has a heavy responsibility even beyond that to be an example of Christ before the people and before the world. The pastor who would emphasize his leadership is steering the boat rather than following the course of the God Who owns the boat of the church.

Paul was writing to the Church in Jerusalem. He naturally assumes that the leadership of this church, James and the other apostles, are men of God. They are to be watching the souls of the people of that congregation. They are expected to be monitoring the direction, manner, growth and fellowship of the lives within the group.

It is possible, and this is only personal speculation, that Paul did not begin this epistle with his name, as was customary, because he did not want to emphasize his own self or ministry. This would be a case of not wanting that there be any dissention caused by himself among the church at Jerusalem. In such a case we can argue that

Paul gave Godly advice (This is part of the inspired and preserved Scripture, after all!) without any intention of lifting himself up as is the habit of far too many "servants of the Lord."

There is a good reason for this oversight. Those "leaders" are going to give an account of their stewardship. The fact that this stewardship is said to be "unprofitable" in certain situations is an important consideration.

The only pastors who have the "rule" over the church are those who have their own lives ruled by the Master. This entire conversation is grounded in the Words of God. Following the doctrine of one grounded in the Words of God is sound.

The onus here is fully upon the one who has accepted the leadership position in a local assembly. He remains one of that congregation and must give watch over his own soul that he follows the leading of God so as not to mislead others. He must give account!

Beware, and remove yourself from, those who purport to be ministers of the Gospel of Jesus Christ but are ministers of Satan in disguise. Their "good" words and "good" conduct are no guarantee of fidelity to the Lord. (Jude 4) From all such we must turn away for the safety and conduct of our own soul before The Living God. (II Corinthians 6:14-17)]

13.18 Pray for us: for we trust we have a good conscience, in all things willing to live honestly.

[The first thing Paul asks in this verse is for prayer. Even in this he does not set himself as important. He asks the prayer for "us." This includes Timothy, as we shall see later in this chapter. This request would also refer to those of Rome among the church in that location.

Paul includes that he has a "good conscience." Since this epistle had been written to the church where the apostles labored it may have been that some would argue that he was "meddling" in the affairs of others. In asking for the prayers of those who read this letter, Paul was actually placing himself as below them. He was asking for their assistance.

It could also be, in mentioning a good conscience and living honestly, that Paul was making a reference to the fact that he had been arrested while in Jerusalem at one point. He was expressing his intention to suffer, if need be, for the cause of Christ rather than find peace by any compromise with those outside the church. His motives were pure in all things.]

13.19 But I beseech you the rather to do this, that I may be restored to you the sooner.

[Paul asked again for the prayers of the assembly. Although he had written some things that might have "ruffled a few feathers," his desire was to return to the fellowship of the brethren in Jerusalem. It is likely that Paul was still in "prison chains" in Rome at this time. He knew that the prayer of the faithful could open those chains and allow him to return to Jerusalem.]

13.20 Now the God of peace, that brought again from the dead our Lord Jesus, that great shepherd of the sheep, through the blood of the everlasting covenant,

[What we see in Hebrews 13:20 are two statements as to the Deity of Jesus. First, Jesus is called a shepherd. Since this is a title of God, from the 23rd Psalm we must consider that Jesus is God. Second, this verse says that God brought Jesus from the dead. In John 10:18 Jesus said that He, Himself, would take His life back up. Putting those two concepts together we must see that Jesus is God.

Paul had asked for prayer from the assembly. He now offers a prayer for them.

God is called the "God of peace." To the Hebrew mind this spoke of blessing from God. The meaning goes much deeper. At one time we were at enmity with God. Through the everlasting grace of Jesus Christ, we are now brought to peace with The Father through the Self-Sacrifice of The Son.

In this and the following verse we see a picture of the three-fold ministry of Jesus. As the Shepherd, Jesus is shown as a prophet. He is shown to be our priest in the Resurrection as the Covenant of His Blood is shown to be ratified by the Father in accepting us as pardoned. He is also shown to be King by His title as the Lord Jesus Christ.

We must note that Jesus is not just called "a Shepherd." He is called "That Great Shepherd." This is specifically The Shepherd of the church of the redeemed. He is our Great Shepherd and Leader in our Christian walk even while we reside on this earth.

The resurrection of Jesus was His Own Work by the efficiency of His power. That resurrection is considered, also, as the Work of The Father as it is illustrative that The Father had accepted the Blood of The Son as the antidote for the sin of those who would come in faith to the cross to accept the salvation which Jesus purchased for us.

Note the phrase "everlasting covenant." This stands in juxtaposition to the Mosaic Law which was only a "temporary covenant" until the events of the Cross, considered as completed by Divine fiat from eternity (Revelation 13:8) but completed in time as part of the creation of God's design.]

13.21 *Make you perfect in every good work to do his will, working in you that which is wellpleasing in his sight, through Jesus Christ; to whom be glory for ever and ever. Amen.*

[Paul does not suggest that we will reach a state of perfection, complete holiness, within this world. The meaning is that we will be thoroughly furnished (II Timothy 3:17) unto all good works. We are saved that we will walk, continue, within Good Works. (Ephesians 2:10) Indeed, we can do nothing "good" until we have become saved by the Blood of the Lamb.

May we always abound in the Work of God as the Spirit gives unto us the ability to do so. It is this which is pleasing to our Lord.

Note the "doxology" after the Name of Jesus. This is a further statement of the Deity of Jesus as it was the custom of the devout to so speak after uttering the Name of Deity. To have done this after the name of a mere man would have been blasphemous speech.]

13.22 *And I beseech you brethren, suffer the word of exhortation: for I have written a letter unto you in few words.*

[Paul had been tasked by God as an apostle to the Gentiles. Nonetheless, Paul had taken it upon himself to write concerning the superiority of Christ over the Jewish patriarchs and religion.

Here he nearly apologizes to these Hebrew believers. He asks that they consider the doctrinal importance which is addressed. It is a weighty subject and Paul is very careful to "step lightly" so as not to seem disregarding of the apostles who led this particular church. He shows that a Christian must not overstep his bounds but must earnestly contend for the faith. (Jude 3) To have done otherwise would have been a disservice to his Lord and his Lord's people.

Considering the weightiness of the subject Paul may have written a much long treatise than this but considered his audience and held back from writing more. Paul stayed within the bounds of inspiration. He wrote the Words of God and held back from his own words.]

13.23 *Know ye that our brother Timothy is set at liberty; with whom, if he come shortly, I will see you.*

[Obviously Paul expected soon to be, if not already, released from prison. The fact that he called Timothy his "brother" is also indicative that Paul wrote this epistle to the Hebrews.

Timothy being set "at liberty" seems to suggest that he also had been imprisoned. Since this is the only suggestion of an imprisonment of Timothy we look for other possibilities to explain the phrase. We do know that Paul had sent Timothy to Macedonia (Philippians 2:19-24) as his emissary. A more reasonable, to me at least, explanation is that Timothy had completed his assigned duties. Thus, being released from those duties, and was now returning to Paul with his report.

Timothy was often with Paul during Paul's imprisonment. (Colossians 1:1; Philippians 1:1) This could suggest that Timothy was a prisoner as well except that Philemon 1:1 makes reference to Paul being a prisoner while no such reference is made to Timothy even though he is mentioned in that same verse.

It seems that Paul was waiting for Timothy to return so that they could both make the trip to Jerusalem.]

13.24 *Salute all them that have the rule over you, and all the saints. They of Italy salute you.*

[Paul asks that the people who read this epistle will "salute," give good wishes, to those who have the rule over them. This seems to be a reference to the leaders of the church in this context. The word "rule" is "Hegeomia" (2233 in Strong's) which can mean civil officials but also would mean "guides." I think that this would stamp the greeting to the apostles and other leaders, and all the saints (Christians) of the churches.

It would be my guess that Paul was either lately released from prison or expected to be released soon. Those who also saluted the Jerusalem church may have been of the assembly at Rome or those who were attendant upon Paul. Again, my guess is that it includes both groups. The fact that Paul speaks of "Italy" rather than "Rome" would suggest that there were those of other areas of Italy who came to visit Paul from time to time while he was in prison.]

13.25 *Grace be with you all. Amen.*

[Paul ends this epistle with his customary salutation of "Grace." Grace is the great gift of Jesus to the Christian. We deserve judgment; He gives us grace through His Own Blood.

Paul, knowing that some were not of the household of faith though they were of the assembly, desires that the saving grace of Jesus Christ be found among all. With that he ends, "Amen." "May it be so."

The added ending of this epistle is that it was written by Timothy from Rome. Additions to the Words of God carry no authority. Man has tried to "edit" the inspired and preserved Words of God to fit his own scheme. This is always a failure! The actual text argues against this perversion of the true Words of God. Timothy was not even in Rome when Paul penned this epistle according to the inspired and preserved Words of God.

We see this same spirit of "addition" in the many new English versions on the market today. Almost exclusively these are not based on the text of history but are based on the critical text which begins in doubt, that belief is that God could not have preserved His Words, and ends in a single unavoidable false doctrine.

By the human and ecclesiastical history attached to these versions we are asked to conclude that God blessed a false text in regards to the Protestant Reformation and missionary activity of the past 400+ years while He has not blessed the, supposed, "true text" of the scholar who has corrected what God, they would believe and teach by their method of "Bible Translation," could not keep pure.]

JAMES

JAMES - CHAPTER ONE

1.1 *James, a servant of God and of the Lord Jesus Christ, to the twelve tribes which are scattered abroad, greeting.*

[The Book of James was written by James who identifies himself as only a "servant of God and the Lord Jesus Christ."

I would argue that this was the same James who was the pastor, or the presiding officer of the Jerusalem Church. Several notations establish this as fact. That James led the council at Jerusalem in Acts 15:12-30 should be obvious. We also note that Peter, upon being released from prison, sent a report to James of this action. (Acts 12:17) In Galatians 2:9 we find the name of James as first among the "pillars of the church" as noted by Paul. Clarke argues that these facts would argue that James was an apostle.

Paul mentions that James was a brother of Jesus. (Galatians 1:19) Matthew 13:55-56 plainly states that there was a "James" who was a brother of Jesus. With a nod to the unscriptural Roman view of the perpetual virginity of Mary, there were some seriously articulated arguments to explain why this plainly spoken fact was not as it seems among several commentators. Even though the culture of the day would allow for cousins to be called "brethren" and the fact that the fellowship called themselves "brothers and sisters," there is no need for these verbal gymnastics to disallow the simple statement of "brother." The fact that Matthew 1:25 says, "And knew her not till she had brought forth her firstborn son: and he called his name JESUS" argues that Joseph and Mary had normal human relations as man and wife AFTER the birth of Jesus. There is no reason to suggest that James was not a son of Mary and Joseph as the Scripture simply states.

James does not boast of this fact. He merely calls himself a servant. As a leader of the early church, disputing the Roman argument that Peter was the leader of the early church, James would be well-known to the Jewish Christians to whom this Book was written. He would also have been well-known to the Gentile Christians to whom the Spirit sent this inspired and preserved Scripture as well.

The Book is addressed to the twelve tribes "scattered abroad." We speak of the "ten lost tribes;" God knows who they are. They are not lost to the Spirit of inspiration. When Jesus was presented at the Temple soon after His earthly birth, a prophetess named Anna was one who greeted His coming as Messiah. She was said to be of the tribe of Asher. This was a tribe from the Kingdom of Israel which was conquered by the Assyrians and sent from their land to be scattered among the nations of the world. These are the "ten lost tribes." From this "lost tribe" was Anna identified.

There were great genealogical records kept among the Jews. The genealogies of Jesus, given in Matthew and Luke, attest to the reality of these records. The Hebrew of the day would have known from which tribe he had descended. It is assumed that these records were destroyed by the Roman legions in the 70 A.D. destruction of Jerusalem. The designation of "Jew" is a shorthand we have all adopted to speak of the children of Abraham as a race of man since that time.

When we consider the diaspora we must realize that not all Jews decided to return to the land when they were given the chance. Many had established homes and businesses throughout the empires of the world and did not return. Esther 3:8 lets us understand that these Jewish people kept a semblance of their identity in their practices even while among the heathen nations.

Not all, obviously, but many of these diaspora Jews were virtual "missionaries" to the glory and story of God in the world in which they lived. God would have ordained this as a witness to Himself and a preparation to the world at large of the Age of Grace when it should arrive. In this vein we consider that the "three wise men" of the nativity were not Jewish but were very obviously influenced by the tenets and truths of Judaism.

Although this particular Book was written early in the Church era, persecution – as evidenced by Stephen in the Book of Acts – was also an early event in the Church era. Among those scattered into the world. These would have been the focal point in the mind of James, from this opening to the Book, as recipients of the writing.

James seems more interested in the duties of the Christian than in any doctrinal discussion. We need doctrine in order that we might fully understand our duties. It is good that God had allowed us the considerations of James as a path, illuminated by the Spirit, for us to walk as believers in the world.

James speaks as a servant of God and of Jesus Christ. Considering the intended audience which James saw, this is an indication that James considers his personal responsibilities to Jesus as part of his own service to "The God of the Fathers." This very phrase becomes a testimony to the Deity of Jesus as the service to Him is considered as a service to The Father. In this light we look at Jesus being identified as "Christ." "Christ," as we all know, is the Greek form of the Hebrews "Messiah." Jesus is thus identified as the One Who was promised by The Father as far back as Genesis 3:15. The concept of Messiah, the Son of God and God the Son, was not a new idea. It was a doctrine which predates the creation of humanity (Revelation 13:8) even as it is presented as a prepared antidote for the sin of humanity in the Garden.

The "greeting" offered is a Greek consideration of the "Shalom" of the Hebrews. It speaks of a wish for peace and all happiness for the recipient thereof.]

1.2 My brethren, count it all joy when ye fall into divers temptations;

[James starts off this verse very reasonably. He says, "My brethren." I would assume that the intent of James was to state a brotherhood under Abraham. If that were the intent of James it has been over-ridden by the Spirit. "My brethren in Christ" is the real meaning as all of Scripture is written to all of the Lord's people.

Then James seems to fall into whirlpool of pious platitude. He asks that we count it a joyful thing to fall into many temptations. Actually, that is pretty much what he meant. The idea expressed is to into fall into so much trial that we are covered with it.

Note that "fall into" and "run into" are not the same thing. To "fall into" is to be engulfed by the situation as it comes upon us. We are not told to run outside and jump into a mud puddle so we can complain about being wet!

The "temptations" about which James writes are not necessarily designed to induce us to sin. These should be considered as trials which will help to define our relationship with faith in Christ. If I lose my car keys and have to walk ten blocks so I can some groceries, what will be my reaction?

This is not an inducement to sin. Well, unless calling a taxi is a sin! This is something which can try how our Christianity affects our manner of life. We can simply do what we have to do. We can put on our shoes and begin the trek to the store. Or, we can rant and rave. We can complain that God is being unfair and unjust. We can claim demonic activity is harming us. We can do all manner of things which do not allow Christian joy to permeate our lives. Or, we can put on our shoes and begin the trek to the store.

I do not think that James is saying we have to enjoy. But, he is saying that we cannot let the circumstances of life rob us of our joy in the Lord. This type of trial is suited to develop and help define our character as the saved of the earth. Matthew Henry says this, "Philosophy may instruct men to be calm under their troubles; but Christianity teaches them to be joyful..." I guess we could say that the "slings and arrows of outrageous fortune" are things which will show to us whether we have a philosophy of life or live as those who have found the Lord of Life.

It might be good that we consider that we are not asked to be stoic about problems. Stoicism practiced faithfully will simply learn to endure the problems and trials. Christianity will do that, of course, but Christianity will look past the problem and find triumph over the trial because of our faith in the Lord. These trials then are seen as an opportunity to gain spiritual maturity and grace through the overcoming of the problem. Joy is the understood reality that the harm the world might name is actually a molding of our spiritual lives which the world could never understand. It is an enablement to help us become more like Christ. Understanding this, trials are become an evidence of the grace of God into our lives.

Humanly speaking, Jesus was crucified because the religious world of the day could not abide His teaching and love. As much as the world hated Him, that much the world will hate those who follow Him. We might not be killed for our faith. Many around the world, even in our day, are being killed because of faith in Him.

The world will find various forms of "discomfort and ploy" to hurl at us in an attempt to cause us to lose the joy of salvation. They want us as they are – unheeding of the ways of God. Even as the early opponents of the Church sought any means possible to stamp out the faith, so will the same thing happen in our day because the entire world system is violently opposed to the things of God.

Does the world champion a value which the Christian can never accept as he is true to the Lord? We are become known as "intolerant" if we stay true to Christ. The world will never admit their intolerance of us. Instead laws will be passed whose purpose is to disallow our freedom to follow Christ. If we persist in following the will of the Lord we will be called "lawbreakers" and "criminals."

We can never expect any sort of tolerance from the world system. What we can glory in is the fact that God allows such trial in order that our faith may develop into the strength of the character of our testimony for Christ. What the world sees as an attack is actually a victory for the saved!

"Divers" temptations are many faceted and diverse trials which are hurled at those who love the Lord.]

1.3   Knowing this, that the trying of your faith worketh patience.

[This is a spiritual principle we would do well to learn. Understanding the purpose of trials in our life will serve to strengthen our faith and allow us a closer walk with the Lord as He draws us closer to the template of His love for the world and His holiness of walk.

This verse shows that James saw faith as the foundation of true Christianity. He speaks of this faith being tried; were it not foundational there would be no purpose is such trial. One purpose of the trial of our faith is to expose to our own selves the depth of that faith. Abraham was given a trial. He was asked to sacrifice Isaac, his son. It would have been a heart-wrenching trial. The concept of child sacrifice was established among the heathens he dwelt among. God now asked him to follow their example even though he'd been told to worship only the True God of Creation rather than the idols of man among whom this was an established devotional practice.

Not knowing anything else but to follow the Words of God, Abraham prepared to sacrifice his son. As Abraham prepared to do just that, God stopped him.

God had tried the faith of Abraham. God always knew how Abraham would react. Abraham did not know how Abraham would react. This trial gave to Abraham a knowledge of himself and strengthened his faith to follow God.

Patience in the trial of our faith will give us an added opportunity for witness as we are seen to be calm in the face of adversity. The word "patience" suggests a continuing cheerful consistency. This can be self-perpetuating. The patience gained from one trial will allow us to face another trial with the same patience. The pattern can continue in the life of the saint of God.

The trial does not necessarily bring patience. We can rebel against God in the midst of that trial. But, as we submit to the chastening of the Lord, and to the trial of our faith, we can begin to see the purposes of God in the situation. This is faith carrying out the action of bolstering, or building up, faith within us. The most important point is that God be acknowledged as our refuge and strength. We trust Him through the trial. We endure as He gives us the endurance to continue in faith.]

1.4   But let patience have her perfect work, that ye may be perfect and entire, wanting nothing.

[Allow patience to complete the work of making us into the vessel which Christ can use. I keep a bottle of water near my work station. Last night I noticed that there was water on the table where I had put the bottle. I had to throw that bottle into the trash; it was not useful to me for its intended purpose. I had to get another container to hold my water. May we never allow ourselves to become "leaky bottles" when tasked by the Lord to carry the "water of life" to a thirsty world.

A potter will prepare vessels for use. He will mold and "fire" the bottles. He will put design on the vessel. Only when that vessel is complete and finished, with no imperfections, will the potter place that vessel on display as a useful object of his construction. When we feel buffeted and heated with fiery trials may we understand that the Master Potter is preparing us to be beautiful objects to carry the picture of His Love into the world.

Even among the Old Covenant sacrificial system only those animals which were perfect in their physical make up were allowed to become proper sacrifices to the Lord.

We are told to offer our bodies as living sacrifices unto the Lord. (Romans 12:1) It should become joyful for us to feel the Hand of the Lord as He prepares us through the trials and temptations of life to become useful in His service.

We are to seek the patience that will allow us to endure and prosper in the chastening and trial which prepares us to be that object in which the Lord delights to send forth His saving message of sin and salvation to our friends and neighbors as we labor in the Lord's vineyard.

As that patience continues its inexorable path to the Savior's use, even those who would style themselves to be our enemies can be won to the Lord. God will use our quiet patience to convict the hearts of our attackers. We are never the ultimate object of their scorn. It is our love of and for Jesus which will bring them to Him, or will drive them further from Him.

Our purpose is to draw them. The final decision will remain theirs for all will not accept the love of God into their lives.

When patience has given way to acceptance, and acceptance to an even deeper love for Christ we come closer to the Heavenly Template of our Master's love and concern for the lost of the world. We lack nothing as we seek the smile of the Lord upon our lives and testimony for Him. We have only gain!]

1.5 *If any of you lack wisdom, let him ask of God, that giveth to all men liberally, and upbraideth not, and it shall be given him.*

[It has been rightly noted that one is not necessarily educated by knowing facts. One is educated when he is able to find that which he needs to know.

"If" is such an interesting and striking word. "If" we do not understand the trials we endure is the condition which almost all of us find ourselves in most instances. We seek the wisdom of why quite often. With this thought we must consider not to ask, "Why are You doing this to me?" Rather we should consider asking, "What is it that You would have me to learn?"

True religion is to understand the Holiness, Grace, Perfections and Power of God. True wisdom is to learn what we lack. We need to ask of God in general and in specific details what it is which He would have us to understand and become in order for us to be useful in the tasks assigned to us.

It is good for us to ask these things. We can never really count the blessings of God so shallowly as to neglect to ask for them – and about them.

When we ask God for wisdom He gives that wisdom bountifully. He does not reproach us for asking. He doesn't say that we are unworthy – though we certainly are. He treats us as we are, His adopted children. Since wisdom is always for our own good, and necessary in that to which we are tasked in this world, it will be given us.

That wisdom may come through the Words of inspired and preserved Scripture. We should be often in study of His Words to us. Often the answers to the deepest longings of our hearts are simply lying on the page ready to jump out into our minds! Often the Spirit will illumine a truth we've overlooked in answer to our prayer of faith. Sometimes the Lord will use our natural inclinations to lead us to the proper path. Caution: Make certain, with prayer and use of the Scripture that these natural inclinations are of Him. Our hearts are fully capable of leading us astray into our own lusts and desires.

He does not "upbraid" us for asking His leading. He does not complain that we are often "whining" about things. He gives us true and liberal leading when we ask and when we listen to His leading. He is, after all, the Only True Fount of Understanding.]

1.6 *But let him ask in faith, nothing wavering. For he that wavereth is like a wave of the sea driven with the wind and tossed.*

[There is never a need to lack faith when asking for blessing from God. From the span of the sky to the beauty of the sea, from the grandeur of the mountain to the splendor of a valley of wild flower, God is shown to be good and gracious in His manifold gifts to His created world. He will always supply the needs of His Children. He only asks that we ask in acknowledging His Wonder and Power. It has been rightly said that no one can believe too much about the goodness of God.

A wavering person who is not fully persuaded of the goodness of God will see his own hopes rise to great heights only to flounder and sink in despair under the weight of doubt.

Faith is the medium in which we approach the worship of God. As a fish must live in water so must the Christian live constantly in faith. Did you ever stop to realize that fish also breathe oxygen even as do we? It is true. The fish use their gills to separate the oxygen from the water so they can survive. We live in a sea of doubting humanity. The "gills" of our faith allow us to breathe in the good blessings of God while others of humanity flail about with only the "water" of natural reason and human interaction. They cannot access the true blessings of the goodness of God.

The person who is of an unsettled mind, though he might be a true Christian, allows his thoughts to be driven about by the daily news, the whimsies of the daydreams of human reason, the constant shifting of cultural considerations, and more. A lack of complete faith and trust in the goodness and leadership of God will cause one to find his mind restless and apprehensive concerning the future. Even the "escapism" of the entertainment world cannot give any real peace.

God asks faith of us. Faith is the bedrock upon which the superstructure of our lives must be settled. Without faith we are like a rudderless ship on an unstable ocean of fear.

"Driven of the wind" suggests a life that is controlled by outside forces of evil intent. "Tossed" suggests a life that has refused to attach oneself to the Rock which is Christ.]

1.7 *For let not that man think that he shall receive any thing of the Lord.*

[The man who is described in verse six is denied in verse seven. No one who approaches the Lord outside the structure of faith will receive, or can expect to receive, from the Lord any answers to his prayers. He is an unstable man whose divided mind can fathom neither his own needs nor God's provision of power to provide. Where there is no faith a person may pray but cannot expect the favor of an answer from God.

The mere uttering of words does not avail for this is not an exercise of faith. For a time, we had a preacher at church who read his prayers from a "Prayer Book." Such prayers are not of the heart of faith. It matters not how soaring are the words of such a prayer, those beautiful words stay on the paper rather than flying to The Father's ear. They are not true verbalizations of the heart of the reader.]

JAMES: Chapter 1

1.8   A double minded man is unstable in all his ways.

[As Paul in Hebrews, James seems to consider the Jewish Christian who is still enamored with the pageantry of Temple worship. He is fully fixed on neither the grace of Jesus nor the symbolism of the Temple. He is distracted by the earth of the sensual and favorable. In this he fails to fully latch on to the Spiritual realities of Heaven.

Such a one may well be born again but he will never feel the true joy of his salvation as he remains estranged from the leadings of the Savior.

We are often told that being able to hold two conflicting views at the same time is a mark of intelligence. James argues that this is not intellectualism or spirituality. This is a "double minded man" without true convictions or full faith.

The prayers of such an unstable man will not be offered from the position of faith and will not be answered. Even in true salvation such a one will fluctuate between faith and lack of trust in the Lord's provisions.

He is not seen as duplicitous but as indecisive. He seems to have no concept of which way to turn or how to walk forward. He may run his race toward the mark and then quickly return to the starting line before again running toward the finish. He will then retrace his steps. Since this man has no concept of "right," he will often be "wrong" in his spiritual decisions. His own inconsistencies will tend to perplex and torment him rather than lead to true guidance and success in his Christian life.

More often, such a one has never really made his full decision to accept Christ as his Savior due to these fluctuating moral views. It is, however, possible that such a decision was earnestly made. In such a case salvation is real since that is based on the work of Jesus at the Cross. But, such a one will never find the true gumption to actively follow the Lord. He may for a time but will sink back under the waters of the world rather than soaring with the wonder of the heavenly.]

1.9   Let the brother of low degree rejoice in that he is exalted:

[This brother is considered as in low degree by the world at large. He may be living in abject poverty of the world's goods but is rich in the promises of God. Let us consider that this man is a "brother" among the saints of the Lord. Those of the world who are in a similar social or financial situation do not have those heavenly promises.

The term "brother" identifies this person as a member of the fellowship of the assembly. More importantly, this brother is a called servant of God through a salvation relationship with the Lord of Glory. When this man considers the walk of Jesus during His earthly ministry he will rejoice that he is allowed to feel an identification, in his want, with his Lord.

This brother may feel not only the reality of poverty, he may also feel persecution. The persecution of being a societal outcast will be enlarged with the persecution for his faith in Jesus.

Thus, the one of low degree may be doubly rejected. He can consider the rejection of man as a small matter since he has been accepted by God through the grace and love of God.

The brother may even discover that his poverty is a spiritual blessing as his poverty will serve to protect him from many temptations which haunt the lives of the rich.

The exaltations are found in the favor which this man may have from God.

More, the exaltations are found in the favor which this man may have with God in fellowship, prayer, protection from the evil one, and the provision God makes for the service of this man in the cause of Christ. Even the trials of this man's faith are shown to be marks of the favor of God.

The exaltation is found in the blessing of salvation, the sheer human dignity of being a child of God among the sons of man and the honor of suffering for His glory. His freedom from the distractions of human possessions which allows him to discharge his obligations to his Lord is found to be yet another blessing given to the poor.]

1.10 *But the rich, in that he is made low: because as the flower of the grass he shall pass away.*

[The rich man is blessed in that he is allowed to be humbled from his seeming perch above the huddled masses. He can avert his eyes from himself and use them to glory in the spiritual sight of his risen Lord. He may never be able to identify with the poverty which Jesus experienced in His humanity upon this earth. He may well find identification with the sufferings of Christ in some manner of persecution for his faith in the risen Lord.

This rich man may certainly find humiliation as he stands at the foot of the cross and considers the unmerited favor which he has found in faith in the Lord. This spiritual reality will induce some sort of awe that Jesus could love even him. The world may lionize the rich. Jesus will offer salvation from sin, peace with God, and an eternity within a realm where the values of the riches of the world fade into insignificance.

It is possible that the rich could lose all. It does happen. Thieves may break in and steal the accumulations of wealth. A reversal of the world's monetary markets may cause one to lose the wealth that had accumulated on paper holdings. A fire, often seen as a judgement of God in Scripture, may destroy all that one holds dear. The rich may be reduced to poverty in "the twinkling of an eye." The only real wealth of even the wealthy is within the salvation which Jesus supplies to those that accept Him.

Any change in earthly status, from rich to poor and even from poor to rich, is a trial of our faith. Our reactions to such change will show our true commitment to Christ or that our true "faith" resides only in our own manipulations and schemes.

A rich man is described in Luke 12:19 and 20 – "And I will say to my soul, Soul, thou hast much goods laid up for many years; take thine ease, eat, drink, and be merry. But God said unto him, Thou fool, this night thy soul shall be required of thee: then whose shall those things be, which thou hast provided?"

This man was worried about how to control his great wealth. What could he do to hold on to his holdings? God said, "Don't worry about that. You will die tonight and someone else will dispose of your wealth." All wealth is transitory. To worry about wealth is pointless. We cannot actually control "our" wealth. It isn't really ours for we are transitory. Earthly wealth is not important to a man who is dying. The only real importance in this life is the preparation for the next life.

Another rich man was surprised to find himself devoid of his wealth. He couldn't even buy a drop of cold water. "And in hell he lift up his eyes, being in torments, and seeth Abraham afar off, and Lazarus in his bosom. And he cried and said, Father Abraham, have mercy on me, and send Lazarus, that he may dip the tip of his finger in water, and cool my tongue; for I am tormented in this flame." (Luke 16:23-24)

Wealth is a temporary tool which does not survive past our demise. We may enjoy a much longer time of life than does a flower of the grass. But, the time of our life will eventually find the end of our time. It is far better to have the riches of Christ for all eternity than the riches of man for a few years.]

1.11 *For the sun is no sooner risen with a burning heat, but it withereth the grass, and the flower thereof falleth, and the grace of the fashion of it perisheth: so also shall the rich man fade away in his ways.*

[The glory of the earthly, even the beauty thereof, is a transitory element. It carries no permanence within itself. Understanding this truth will help the poor to not covet the "goods" of this earth even as it will help the rich not to depend upon their riches but to desire the things of God. The same outcome of a vision of the Glory of God from different human perspectives should help all to understand the God of Creation is God of All. His works are wondrous to contemplate.

The hot sun may burn away the moisture of the plants during a drought. At this point the grass of the field is useful as hay for the animals. In the deepest of our trials we may find some way to be of service to our God. By the way, isn't it an awe-inspiring concept that we are able to speak of The Great God of Creation as "our God" due to the Blood of the Lamb at the Cross of Calvary!

The sun of the fall, still hot but not the summer sun, will also cause the flower of the field to wither. A life may be long or short. It does not matter how long one lives in the world. His gathered possessions do not survive longer than the length of a man's life. Oh, we can argue that the possessions continue. They do. But, they are no longer the possessions of the man who has died.

Those possessions are either passed on to another or simply taken by another. We may well write our "last will and testament," but we have no real power to enforce it beyond our occupation of the grave.

An important concept here is that it is natural for the sun to be hot in the summer. It is natural for the flower to bloom in the spring. Man may even observe that the very elements of the earth conspire to relieve man of his choicest possessions. It is not of infamy that the rich are deprived of their possession; it is the very living of their lives until the end of those lives that deprives them of those possessions.

Only the very death of the humanity of the Savior has given man the ability to obtain that which he can never lose. The resurrection of the Savior stands as testimony to His absolute power over the elements of time and earth. He alone can give us this salvation which will be ours for all eternity.

The rich man without Christ will fade from the memory of the earth. So, too, shall the man who has found salvation fade from the memory of the earth. The difference between the two is that the man who has found the salvation offered by Christ will live in an eternity of bliss with the Savior. The unconverted will exist for an eternity of torment and regret without the Savior.]

1.12 *Blessed is the man that endureth temptation: for when he is tried, he shall receive the crown of life, which the Lord hath promised to them that love him.*

[Temptation is considered as a blessing from God. Through it, if we be faithful and endure as good soldiers of the Lord, we will receive the reward of a crown. Note that this is not salvation. Salvation can never be of any work which we may accomplish. It is always the work of Jesus. Consider that His cross was considered even before the foundation of the world of man – or of even the first sin of the first man and woman. Salvation was a prepared remedy for sin even before sin had entered the race of man. (consider Revelation 13:8)

II John 8 says, "Look to yourselves, that we lose not those things which we have wrought, but that we receive a full reward." Read the verse very carefully. There is no suggestion that salvation, a gift from God, may be withdrawn by Him or lost by us. This verse speaks to the rewards to be gathered in Heaven.

If these in the above paragraph have suffered loss of reward in Heaven, it stands self-evident that they have not been faithful in their salvation. Following our verse from James at this place, we would argue, in this case at least, that they have not been faithful in enduring temptation. Yet, these are still in Heaven. The Crown of Life is a reward; it cannot be considered as salvation although only those individuals who have experienced salvation through the Blood of the Lamb are in a position to earn this crown.

We must consider that James is a very practical Book of Christian life. He looks for evidence which proves the fact of our faith to others, and often even to ourselves as the trials of life and the temptation of Satan will often cause us to doubt the power and preservation of God.

In view at this place is the evidence of our enduring during trial as an evidence of our trust in Jesus.

The discussion has primarily been of the trials of our faith. Such trials as affliction from the world, sickness, persecution, and such like, are readily used by the enemy of our souls as of convenient tools to tempt us to sin. It is evident that all trials are used as refining tools in the crucible of God for our training and molding into the image of the Lord. This is part of our salvation experience as we are trained by God to become more than we could ever possibly be without Him!

But, this does not discount that Satan can use those very elements in an ungodly fashion upon those who rebel against those very trials which God intended to us for good. Our lack of fidelity to God will place us in danger of spiritual damage by the acts of the enemy. Nonetheless, our salvation remains secure as it is by the work of Jesus and, once settled as we become one of His, may not be removed from us. The promises of God are eternally secure as they are based upon His honor rather than our weakness.

The temptations to evil, when they are from the enemy of our souls, are true illustrations of the fact of sin. Sin is a perversion of the perfections of God. Such temptation, though aimed at our weakness, utilize the favor of the trials which come from God. These are perverted by the enemy into his own nefarious usage.

Those trials from God in which we do accept suffering as to His glory and as a sacrifice of yieldedness to Him, gives an opportunity to give evidence, both to themselves and to others, of the love which one has for the Lord.

See also Genesis 17:2 and Isaiah 28:13.]

JAMES: Chapter 1

1.13 *Let no man say, when he is tempted, I am tempted of God: for God cannot be tempted with evil, neither tempteth he any man.*

[God cannot be tempted. Still in the fourth chapter of Matthew we see that Jesus is tempted. This is a temptation of the humanity of Jesus. Satan attempted to gain control of the mission of Christ by several devious temptations.

The reaction of Jesus to the temptations of Satan was on a human plane. Jesus resorted to Scripture. So should we. Scripture defeated Satan. This was an example of the humanity of Jesus teaching the human of this world how to withstand the power and provocation of Satan.

Satan is knowledgeable. Satan is devious. Satan will use lie and deception to overcome the human. Satan is a powerful being. Satan is more powerful than are any of us. Satan even knows the Scripture better than any of us; he will twist the Scripture to fulfill his own purposes. This all being true the Christian is often at an intellectual loss as to how to defend against the adversary.

God has given us the Scripture as a bulwark of defense against the wiles of Satan.

Satan can never defeat God. Since the Scripture is inspired by God, this means that the Scripture is the very Words of God; when Satan is confronted with Scripture he is confronted by the very Voice of God. Thus, the Scripture is both a defense against Satan and an offensive strategy for the Christian witness in the world at large.

The word "temptation" can have two meanings. One of them is a providential trial such as Abraham was tried in the situation where he was tempted to offer up his son Isaac as a sacrifice to God. Since God never intended that Isaac be thus offered, and God watched over the situation to such an extent as to disallow that from ever happening, this was a trial in which Abraham was tested in order that he would find the place of his dedication to the Words of God.

The other meaning of temptation is as a solicitation to evil. Since God is eminently holy in all of His ways this is a thing completely outside His Divine Character. It is a thing that He would never do.

Consequently, any solicitation to evil is not from God. It cannot be. Such solicitation must always come from either one of two sources. The one is a solicitation to evil from a demonic outside source such as of Eve in the Garden. The other source of temptation is discussed in the following verse.

There is nothing in creation, or in the creation of man, which would be disposed to sin were it not for the sin nature which has been passed down throughout humanity by the male of the species. This, of course, is why God stated – and the Virgin Birth proves – that the promised Deliverer would be from the seed of the woman. (Genesis 3:15)]

1.14 *But every man is tempted, when he is drawn away of his own lust, and enticed.*

[We note that the sin of Adam was not induced. We may argue that Eve was enticed into her sin. But we must argue that the reason which Eve accepted the fruit of the Tree of the Knowledge of Good and Evil was that she wanted something. It may well be that Eve wanted to understand more of God than she could in her present state. While this seems a good and noble purpose, it was in direct contradiction of the known will of God.

It is only by driving around a block that we can make three right turns and go to the left. Even in this consideration is the truth that we must first go away from our objective at the first instance. God is completely holy. We can never approach Him when we have already turned out backs on Him.

We see no such attitude or defense as regards Adam. He was not tempted in the sense of any inducement being offered. He just made the choice to disobey God. The purpose of Adam was not to draw closer to an understanding of God. The purpose of Adam was to depart from Gods presence as he pursued the presence of the woman.

The history of idolatry is always that man seeks to find solace in the creatures of creation rather than in the God of Creation. Even today man despises holiness. He retreats from the ultimate holiness of God and seeks and seeks the comfort of creatures who are sinful as is he, himself.

Adam did try to blame God for his fall. He tried to argue that the fault was of "the woman who thou gave to me." It is both sad and ludicrous to blame the goodness of God, even when that goodness is expressed in a trail for our betterment, as the purpose of our sin. God does not induce men to sin!

The fountain from which all sin flows is located in the desires, ungodly desires, of our own hearts. If a man desires gluttony he will not be able to hide the fact. The same is true of illicit sexual desires, unholy personal habits, even an excess of any area wherein the desire is to find the fulfillment of desires rather than a devotion to the pure things of God.]

1.15 *Then when lust hath conceived, it bringeth forth sin: and sin, when it is finished, bringeth forth death.*

[The desires of the heart will find fulfillment. When these are lustful, even simply to an excess beyond reasonableness, these will cause our devotion to God to wane. Our spiritual desires will fade as the carnal desires of lust will result in the flower of sin to overrun the "garden" of piety and any professed desire to live unto God. This is one entrance of sin which flows from our own desires and wants. These seek gratification. This will prevail unless we have stood in our trials and find the resoluteness to stand firm in the Lord.

The fact of sin, as it was in the Garden, is a rebellion against the reasonable and righteous leadership of God. Since the leadership of God is from the Heart of His Love, such rebellion will always be injurious to the man trapped in the quagmire of sin. The corrupt principle of lust is sin. We are warned that it will mature into habitual manners of sin. As the drug addict seeks further drugs to feed a growing "habit" so will sin not stand idly; it will grow and continue to feed upon the soul who has sold himself to it through repetition and lack of Godly restraint or fellowship with the Lord. He is our only defense against the growing monster of our own lust and the sin birthed thereby.

In the creation of Adam God breathed the "breath of life" into Adam's nostrils. One result of that breath of life was to impart an eternality of existence into Adam's physical body. Sin broke that thread only so much. The eternality of existence stayed. The death of the physical body was a resultant fact of the sin. Now sin will cause a person to eternally exist in the eternal torment of perdition where God is not available. Since humanity was created to have a life in fellowship with God, this lack of fellowship will be a part of the torment. The most basic need of humanity is to worship the Lord.

This denied is part of the torment of the eternal hell.

Lust begets sin. Sin begets punishment. Part of this punishment is an eternity of death. This is not an unconscious eternity. It is truly a conscious eternity of regret and torment away from God. Since all good flows from God, and sin is an evil which warps the blessings of God into evil, this is real and eternal torment within the sin. Lust can no longer be fulfilled but it will not abate the reality of the lust.]

1.16   Do not err, my beloved brethren:

[We have all heard the old canard, "If God is so powerful why does He not stop..." Fill in the blank with the cause of the day. The fact is that God is all powerful. Part of His power is contained within His purposes and decrees. God has given to man the ability to decide the course to live his own earthly life.

We can easily understand that the sin nature, which invaded the race of man with the sin of Adam and has become part of the very nature of man, has caused the desires of humanity to flow in courses which are not of the channel of the original sinless creation of humanity. Sin perverts and distorts to the point of a caricature the paths in which humanity will walk. These ways will cause evil as they are not the holy ways of God but the disfigured ways of man.

But, we also need to understand that the sin of Adam has affected the nature in which man lives his life. Romans 8:22 speaks of the "groaning" of the very creation due to that sin of Adam. Adam had been delegated as the head, under God of course, of the creation of God. Adam was the "capstone" of the creation. (Genesis 1:26-30) With this position of authority and pre-eminence, the sin of Adam caused repercussions in all that was under him in his authority. Thus the natural elements also took on the unruly perverse nature of sin. These unruly weather and situational patterns of the created world were further influenced by the judgment of the Flood which buffeted those natural elements of the earth.

When we consider that sin was eradicated from the earth by the judgment of the flood, this being shown by the events surrounding the drunkenness of Noah, the natural forces did not depart from the "ways of rebellion" as evidence by Sin.

The final judgment of sin will result in the cataclysmic events of II Peter 3:10-11 when the sin encased within nature is finally purged.

We were created with the need to worship God and live in communion with Him. We, as a race of humanity, have decided that we will discard this worship as too restrictive for our purposes. Because of our own lusts we have not been willing to accept the plan of God for our lives. We lust and we want. It is a truism of our sinful condition that we do not want God. He gives us freedom to go our own way. The fact that His Message to us has told us that our own way leads to degradation and death, is not a message we have accepted.

We do not love Him although He has offered His love to us through the Cross of Calvary!

James warns us, as beloved brethren in the faith, that we should not err. Sin is never of God. Never! The source of sin, and the attendant evils of the present world system, is our own lusts and refusal to fully worship the Lord. Certainly, Satan tempts us to sin. But, he finds ready material with which to tempt us from our own lusts and wants.

We can never avoid, or break the bonds of, sin in our own power. We are not gifted in our natures with spiritual powers. The fact of sin is a spiritual malady which is borne within our own bodies and psyche. Without accessing the power of God we are overmatched by the allure and power of the sin which besets and controls us.

We need God in order to fully live our human lives in this world and to prepare to live spiritual lives in the next world.]

1.17 *Every good gift and every perfect gift is from above, and cometh down from the Father of lights, with whom is no variableness, neither shadow of turning.*

[Here the gifts of God are contrasted with the incipient sin which resides within the body and mind of the human. While sin starts small the gifts of God are good, benevolent, even in their beginnings. Sin grows unto death. The gifts of God grow unto perfection, or completeness, within the lives of those so blessed.

So far is God from being the Author of sin, we find that all truly good gifts come from Him. These good gifts are treasures from Heaven. God is called the "Father of Lights." Lights speak of knowledge. He is the Only True source of knowledge. This is especially so in the spiritual and eternal realms.

Man seems disposed to argue that he must "correct" the Scripture. This is not a possibility. No man has ever had, except Jesus, any experience in the realms of eternity and spirit. If the Scripture had ever been lost it would not be possible that man could correct any portion of those Words of God. Man can have no knowledge of the truths of the eternal and spiritual except they are given from those inspired and preserved Words of God.

It is a prideful fool's errand to attempt to correct Scripture. We do not have the knowledge to correct anything of the spiritual world except as the pure Scripture has already given us the knowledge. Man cannot correct that which he cannot understand.

If we consider God as all-powerful, and we must, then any "lost" Scripture must be of His will. To attempt to correct in such a situation is to attempt to thwart the decree of God! It is good that God has preserved His Message to humanity.

God is the "Father of Lights" in that He is the Creator of all which we see, and all we cannot see, in His created universe.

He is also compared with the sun. The ancients understood the concept of the seasons. They knew that the sun would "rise" in the east, reach its zenith, and then continue on to set in the west. God is not like that. He is immutable and continues to stand in His place without any variation of His goodness and power. There is no variation, or change of understanding, in Him as He has self-identified in His inspired and preserved Scripture.

An object will cast a shadow when the sun shines upon it. In effect, that object has blocked the sun in that area. Nothing can block the Eye of God as He sends His blessings and observes His creation.

Note that there is no suggestion of any gifts from Satan. He has no gifts to offer expect death and destruction. Those gifts which God gives of His bounty are always good for His created beings. Sun, rain, air, etc. – these are gifts which God gives even to the wicked. His love is beyond measure and stands without regard to any partiality to man. Though, His best gifts are for His children.]

***1.18** Of his own will begat he us with the word of truth, that we should be a kind of firstfruits of his creation.*

[We can easily harken back to the concept of sin growing from the lusts that war against man's own soul. The works of God are the antithesis of this concept. God has ordained that His love will grow in the production of the redemption of humanity.

We owe our salvation completely to God. It is His purpose, His plan, and His production which brings us to a saving knowledge of Jesus. This begins with His Word of Truth; this is the inspired and preserved Scripture. The preaching of this Word imparts the Message of the fullness of the glory of God into the hearts of those who are enlightened by that Word. All the while the prayer of faith, by the faithful, helps to prepare the heart of the convert to accept the wooing of the Spirit.

While enticing the sinner the Spirit is also convicting that sinner of his need for the reforming power of God within his life. The Spirit offers the gift of faith (Ephesians 2:8-9) so that the sinner, separated from God by indwelt sin, may turn to God to accept that faith and the salvation which is thereby available.

This conversion process allows one born in sin to be reborn into a fit vessel to walk in newness of life with the Savior. Then, and only then, can the convert begin to perform those good works which are the fruit of the Spirit. (Ephesians 2:10)

In Leviticus 23:10 we see the concept of the "first fruits" offering to God. The Jew, to whom James' writing was directed, was the first fruits of salvation in that salvation came first to the Jew before spreading into the entire world of both Jew and Gentile. James sees this as a great privilege of worship as given to the Jew.

At this point we must consider that the true privilege of salvation is not given to groups of people. It is a gracious gift of God given to individuals. In this sense each of us can consider that we, our lives, service and devotion, should also be presented to God as offerings of love to Him. There was a popular saying many years ago – "Today is the first day of the rest of your life."

May each of our "first days" be offered in the spirit of the worship of sacrifice to our Lord and Savior, Jesus Christ. We could call this our duty. We should consider this our delight!]

***1.19** Wherefore, my beloved brethren, let every man be swift to hear, slow to speak, slow to wrath:*

[James has looked at sin as a manifestation of the lusts and failings of men. James has looked at the goodness which God has spread upon those that love Him. Now James has some advice for the brethren. He calls them "beloved brethren." He does not belittle them but accepts them as reasonable people who need to understand how even they can improve. A little of the "jam" of human kindness can help make the "pill" of suggested reform a little easier to swallow!

The primary focus of James is on hearing the Words of God from the Message of God. The more we are willing to listen to the leading of the Spirit and the Word, the more likely we are to conform ourselves to the things of God.

Our interests tend to color or speech and manner of living. If we tend to spend time with God in prayer over His Word we will be more likely to live a life, and speak with words, which is pleasing to Him and spiritually helpful to others.

James asks that we speak less. This is a reasonable request. The more words we employ the more words will tend to be frivolous and hurtful. That is simply human nature. When we are slow to speak we will tend to keep social, and religious, "repair work" to a minimum. If I don't say anything I can't say the wrong thing!

If I don't say anything I will never witness of my Lord. James does not ask that we never speak. He asks that our speech be temperate and reasoned. Generally speaking, to coin a phrase, one who speaks rashly has allowed his words to overrun the thoughts of his mind. He speaks without reasoned consideration. Let us never fail to speak for our Lord. Let us never fail to speak as our Lord would have us to so speak!

Many of us are enamored of an "attack religion." Our example, Jesus, from the Scripture operated on a pattern of "attract religion." He was kind and gracious in His dealings with sinners. He never suggested that sin was reasonable but He pointed to reformation and repentance through faith as better than the sin of a present human situation. His only ire seemed held for those who would seek to use religion to keep sinners from salvation.

We are normally quite anxious to give our opinions even when those opinions are not of the oracles of God. Remembering that the lusts within our hearts are the seeds of sin, we should give the Words of God rather than our opinion. Also, as we give and defend our opinions we tend to become bellicose. That is the next part of James equation. We are to be slow to wrath. That considered speaking part will lend itself to solving this problem.

There are even times when we become upset with God. "God, why did you allow that rain to fall on my head rather than on the field?" Isn't that a failure of our human nature? We calmly accept blessings as though they were our due while the least trial is a cause to accuse our Heavenly Father. The trials of God do not tempt us to evil. Those trials, properly considered, will train us to good.

We should not be angry with a brother in the Lord. This causes dissention in the body and impedes the mission of the church as an organism of the message of grace out into the world.

Neither should we be angry with those outside the household of faith. Slapping someone in the face will never cause them to love the Lord we proclaim. Be careful. Be gentile. Be wise.

Be compassionate, rather than contradictory and contentious.]

1.20   For the wrath of man worketh not the righteousness of God.

[It is the love of God which is displayed by the Cross of Christ. The wrath of man is nowhere in the equation except as in opposition to God's love. God does not call us to hate the sinner. We are to hate the sin. But, even in this it should not be to the extent that we would display anything less than the love of God toward the one bound by that sin. The lifeguard at the beach does not hate the drowning man. Neither does he hate the water. He hates only the thought that the man might die in the water. His entire purpose is to preserve that breath of life within the man in peril.

The wrathful mind will not be set on the grace of God. We are not called to debate the fact of God. We are not even called to defend the grace of God. We are called to spread the grace of God, by bringing man's attention to that fact and the power of the Spirit; so that we can be a witness of the truth of salvation to that man who stands in need.

There is a place for debate over spiritual realities. The is a place for defense of the Words and work of God. But, the place of calling a sinner to salvation in Christ is a time for the love of God and the prayer of the saints. We seek a response of faith among the lost.

It is among the brethren that we are to teach. Note, that the word is "teach" rather than "harangue." Even here wrath is neither a response nor a strategy. We do not beat our brother; we beckon him to find the truth. We can discuss the doctrines of the faith. We are not to fight over them!]

1.21 *Wherefore lay apart all filthiness and superfluity of naughtiness, and receive with meekness the engrafted word, which is able to save your souls.*

[The word "meekness" does not mean spineless. It means a spirit that is not boastful and filled with pride. Moses is said to be a meek man. He was a strong leader for the Lord but he did understand his place of subjection to God.

Because God has called us both to salvation and to service we are to project ourselves as useful servants of the Lord. Part of this is to jettison that from our lives all which is impure and not suitable as tools in the hands of the craftsmen for God which we are called to be.

We are called to lay, not aside but apart from us, every bit of filthiness with which our souls are spotted. We are to consider such as completely loathsome and useless to our lives – both spiritual and physical.

The "superfluity of naughtiness" is an excess of such filthiness which abounds in the hearts of the human species. It is an abiding "wrongness" which must be discarded in its every vestige if we are to be true to our Lord, and to ourselves! We can argue about the spiritual harm of such but we must also consider the "human cost" to ourselves as we fail to follow the prescription of the Great Physician. Jesus understands our humanity better than we do. He is The Creator. He understands that which makes us happy and fulfilled and that which inhibits that fulfillment and joy in our lives.

We are to meekly accept the Word of Truth which has been engrafted into our lives. We do not simply "put on," as with a new shirt, the Gospel. It should become a living part of our lives in every instance of those lives. This is true Christian service and commitment.]

1.22 *But be ye doers of the word, and not hearers only, deceiving your own selves.*

[If a starving man were led to a restaurant and offered a meal, what would he do? In all probability he would eat the meal. He could look at the meal until the steak was cold and the salad was hot; this would not serve his condition.

James asks that we be active in the faith – "doers of the word." Simply hearing of the grace of God can never save a person. Accepting the Lord will bring salvation.

This was one of the problems with the sect of the Gnostics. They believed in much understanding or learning. They sought after the "mysteries of the faith." They ignored the Man of the Cross. A parrot can be taught to "say" to words of a written prayer. That is not praying. That is simply mouthing – or "beaking" – that which is probably not even understood.

In the last verse the concept of engrafting was brought forward. I am not a horticulturalist by any means. But, I do understand that certain plants can be "engrafted" onto another plant and thereby grow. That engrafted plan is cut and attached to the "host" plant is such a way as to give nourishment from the host plant and to the engrafted so that it will live and produce fruit.

Suppose that I was to take some duct tape and simply tape a plant on to another. There would be no growth because the "juices" of life were not coursing through the seemingly engrafted plant. James says that this is the situation of one who only hears the Words of God but does not act upon them. True faith in the heart will produce the fruit of the Spirit in the life of the one who has acted upon, in faith believing, the Gospel message. The work of grace is not a system of laws and ceremonies; it is a pattern of life.

If the life does not grow the fruit there is a real question about the fact of life.]

1.23 *For if any be a hearer of the word, and not a doer, he is like a man beholding his natural face in a glass:*

[The "glass" this person is looking into is the mirror of our souls, the Scripture. In that mirror a person will see his own reflection with all of its imperfections and faults. He will also see the image of Christ whereby he knows he should conform.

Not everyone had a Scripture portion in the day of this writing. Most, however, were familiar with the Words of Scripture. They had been taught, these Jewish men, from their youth the precious inspired and preserved Words of God. Each Sabbath they would gather at the Temple or Synagogue and hear those words pronounced.

The man who shaves every day will gaze intently at his face as he guides the razor over himself. He will see natural things which need correcting. Some of these he can do and some he cannot. The bottom line is that he will see himself as he really is. He does not look at another but at himself.

When he has taken just two steps away from the mirror he will forget the appearance of his natural face and consider himself to be who he fancies himself to be rather than who he has just seen that he is.

It is the same within the religious man as regards his spiritual image from the Scripture. He will see his imperfection plainly evident and may even vow to make the proper changes in his life. However, two steps away from the "worship service" he will forget what manner of man he is and see himself as he views himself to be rather than as who he actually is.

He hears and he understands. But, he quickly loses sight of the image as shown in the Scripture. He heard but he does nothing to correct his correctable spiritual faults. He no longer sees these faults because of the rose-colored glasses of his imagination.]

1.24 *For he beholdeth himself, and goeth his way, and straightway forgetteth what manner of man he was.*

[This man sins by omission. He knew to do what he needed to do when he compared himself in the mirror of the Words. He could have combed his hair but he completely forgot about it when he left the mirror of the Word.

It is as when we are driving down the street. We may forget to put on our seatbelt. After all, we drove for years before that law was passed! But, the mere sight of a police car will remind us of our omission.

As soon as we remove ourselves from the "squad car" of the revealed Words of God we continue on in our own power and prerogatives. We fail to remember the need to live as Christians in the world because we are people of the world in our hearts. "May my own will be done," is all too often the prayer of our hearts.]

1.25 *But whoso looketh into the perfect law of liberty, and continueth therein, he being not a forgetful hearer, but a doer of the work, this man shall be blessed in his deed.*

[Why would we consider it a "perfect law of liberty" if it is the manner in which Scripture tells us we should live rather than the leading of the lusts of our hearts? The real truth of the matter is, and we tend to often forget this, we are in real bondage to the sin which so easily besets us. It is only the pure ways of the pure religion of God which can free us from the lust which wars in our members. It is only this freedom that allows us to live without the chains of lust and sin. This allows us to fulfill our potential as creatures who will acknowledge our Creator and the wisdom He allows us to understand.

The Law of Liberty is a real law in that it imposes actual manners of living which we are shown through the Gospel. There are judgments and chastisements when we fail to live in the constraints of this law. However, this law and its constraints, allows us to live more freely than it would be possible to live otherwise.

Some might consider it a burden to drive on the right side of the road in this nation. If we did not all follow this simple rule driving the roads would be an impossible task. In the rule of the Law of God there is true freedom.

Clarke quotes the following with regard to the man who submits to the Law of God. "There are four kinds of men who visit the synagogues, 1. He who enters but does not work; 2. He who works but does not enter. 3. He who enters and works. 4. He who neither enters nor works. The first two are indifferent characters; the third is the righteous man; the fourth is wholly evil." True freedom is enjoyed by the person who lives under the law given by He Who created us and understands all of our needs. Only therein is true soul safety and happiness.

The word "looketh" implies the man who closely examines that perfect and complete law. It is he who will continue therein for it is he who is honestly enamored of the prospect of faith and fellowship with the Lord.

The law of grace is a law of freedom in that it allows us to have our sins forgiven and cleansed. The Law of Moses was a law of bondage in that it made demands which, even in the keeping, were not able to give freedom from the sin of our human condition. (Hebrews 10:4)]

1.26 *If any man among you seem to be religious, and bridleth not his tongue, but deceiveth his own heart, this man's religion is vain.*

[Jesus was speaking to the religious leaders when He said, "O generation of vipers, how can ye, being evil, speak good things? for out of the abundance of the heart the mouth speaketh." The point being that much can be said and done that appear to be from God. But, the babbling speech of a man who lacks control will give evidence of what lies within his heart.

This lack of self-restraint will give evidence of a man who is not in mature control of his emotions and life. The lustful sins of the heart will "bubble up" in the speech of a man who does not control his tongue. This man cannot glorify God in his witness and conduct. Indeed, such a man has an empty religion which is devoid of the fruits of the Spirit. It is a witness against him among the brethren.

I would caution that we must not consider that this "vain religion" is "empty" – the meaning of vain – of any possibility of salvation. Salvation is always the work – completely the work – of Jesus and not of us! Our reactions therein are often carnal. But, the truth remains that salvation is of Christ and His Work at Calvary! We may not be all that we should be. This is obvious by the need of the trials of God to refine our Christian character as spoken above.

We are actually considering gradations within the Christian life and the appearance of those gradations among those who would examine our supposed religion under their own microscope of consideration. Not all children, even in human families, are equally respectful of the leading of their parents.

The "bottom line" always remains that salvation has nothing to do with our response and everything to do with the redemption which is in Christ. An empty witness before the world is not a proof of no religion but a picture of a lack of mature Christianity. Trial and chastisement will soon find that weak Christian. (See the 11th chapter of Hebrews!)

The unbridled speech is an evidence of an unbridled life. A simple "for instance" is that a tongue which slanders and "back bites" cannot be evidence of a humility of heart. It is a sign of an empty religious profession.

Men bridle horses, as we shall see later, in order to make them useful to the needs of their riders and drivers. An unbridled horse is useless in transportation and business. Thus, an unbridled tongue cannot be properly used in the service of God.

This is analogous to the above consideration of the mirror of the Word. This is a fault which we must find in ourselves and must control. The deceit has nothing to do with salvation and everything to do with service. A man is grossly deceived if he thinks he can serve God without the self-control of his own speech. A loose temper will always produce a lost opportunity for witness and power.]

1.27 Pure religion and undefiled before God and the Father is this, To visit the fatherless and widows in their affliction, and to keep himself unspotted from the world.

[True religious devotion toward God is not shown in knowledge or even understanding. God already possesses these gifts and stands ready to impart them to those who are engaged in His service.

True religious devotion will always consider the purposes of God in spreading the love of God into the world about us. True religion is not cloistered but finds the free range of action among the creation of God. A witness not heard is a witness for God that is not used!

True religion will show love to those who are in need and comfort for those in pain. True religion will not slide into the seat of the scornful and earthly but will ride the wagon of the peace which is offered only through Jesus.

Standing pure before God will lead to such acts of love as are described in this verse. This is not a complete listing. It is a sample of the things that ought to be in the life of the Christian witness. Such acts, while standing pure before God, will serve to keep one unspotted by the defects and unholy desires of the world of man. James is not describing the acts of religion, which is the worship of God, but the effects which the pure worship of religion will elicit from a man.

Pure religion is a religion which had no mixture of conceit, pride, or duty because it is "religious duty," within it. It is a two-sided response to God. One is to spread the love of God into the world – this is our beneficent opportunities which we find in the course of our daily lives and to which we respond in our daily witness of the Love of the Lord among the people of the earth. The other side is to live pure lives which are not encumbered in the lusts of the world. Within this latter consideration is the self-control which allows us to bridle our tongues so as not to speak rashly. This is a major part of living purely as this is the evidence of that pure life. To speak otherwise is to exhibit a rash and lustful heart which has not been brought under subjection to the Lord.

All of this is before, and listed under our worship of the Lord, our God, Savior, and Heavenly Father. It cannot be as an homage to man for man is not our object of worship but of witness. It cannot be for our own selves for it would then be shortly prideful self-indulgence. It must be, and is in truth, an offering of praise and service. It is not so much that we offer these to God as it is that they flow from His Holy influence upon our lives.]

JAMES - CHAPTER TWO

2.1   *My brethren, have not the faith of our Lord Jesus Christ, the Lord of glory, with respect of persons.*

[Once upon a time I was young. I use the standard "fairy tale beginning" because it was so long ago that I can't believe it true even though I know that it must have been.

Anyway, one of the things I remember is playing "sandlot" football in the two vacant lots next to my parents' home.

There were six of us children. I had a sister eight years my elder and another six years older than me. World War II intervened; I was born among the first of the "baby boom" generation. It must have been a shock because the next child, a brother, didn't show up for six more years. After two years another brother came to the family. Last, ten years after me, a sister was born. Because of this stretched out family my wife was able to say that I had all the phobia's and distractions of the oldest, youngest and middle child!

What has this to do with football? Well, with six kids at home, money must have been very tight for my parents. They, of the depression era generation didn't seem to notice it all that much. I know that I never considered it. During one of these impromptu sandlot football games my shirt was literally torn completely from my body. My mother was less than pleased. I vividly remember that!

Considering the financial constraints, even during "fabulous fifties," I realize now that my actions had hurt the family. Money would need to be shifted from one area to another in order to purchase a new shirt. It was an unnecessary expense.

James is considering the content of the Christian life. He argues that a show of partiality among the "brethren" would hurt the cause of Christ. It would be a situation where all of the talk of love and concern would be overshadowed in the life of many by the obvious example of one who was partial to the rich.

It would become very hard to preach that our ultimate resource was the "riches of Christ" when there was an equally obvious respect given for the rich who would have the resources to help others. With this there was a seeming total lack of respect for the poor who could offer probably nothing but encouragement in the Lord.

Oops! Our carnal prejudice was showing! How can we preach unquestioned love when we act with partiality? To be brutally honest, we probably can preach it but it would become very hard for anyone to actually believe our preaching. Would those outside "the household of faith" be inclined to believe our spiritual preaching when they observed our physical bias against those to whom we preached?

James is much more interested in the content of our character rather than the mouthing of the platitudes we proclaim. The old phrase of "either walk the walk or stop the talk" comes to mind. This is important for such partiality gives a false picture of Christ into the world. This would impact, humanly speaking, our witness for Christ.

We call Jesus "The Lord of Glory." He is. There is no question about that fact. Since it is true, and since it is also true that we claim to be followers of Him, we must not present Him into the world as One Who gives respect to the wealthy and only leftovers to the poor.

The Book of James asks that we be what we claim. The Book of James asks that we live what we preach. The Book of James asks that we live out our faith into the world. We do not serve a dead Lord. Our faith, religion, must be an energized religion which is not perceived as dead words and beliefs but as it is a faith which is living and energized to show the spiritual realities into the physical world.]

2.2 *For if there come unto your assembly a man with a gold ring, in goodly apparel, and there come in also a poor man in vile raiment,*

[James addresses his letter to the Jewish believers. With this in mind we consider that the word translated as assembly is the word for synagogue. It is natural that the early church, especially since that early church was dominated by Jewish believers, would meet there. They were, after all, worshipping Messiah. This would be a natural place to congregate for worship and to evangelize those who would understand the concept of Messiah.

This is the only place in the New Testament where the word synagogue is used to represent a place of Christian worship.

This also marks James as a very early letter among the canon of the New Testament. Those synagogues never became expressly populated by the Christians, of course, but they were early places of meeting for many Messianic Jews of the time. The Gentile Christians would never have been allowed entrance therein. It was in the ministries of Paul and Peter that the concept of "house churches" grew to meet the needs of the Gentiles.

Retaining their Jewish identity, the Jews would also frequent the synagogues in order to hear the reading of the Law and the Prophets. These remained very important even among the converted. This understanding may help to give us some insight into the problems which Paul addressed in the Book of Hebrews as he warned against "apostatizing" back into Judaism among the early Christians. This would not have been a problem for the Gentile Christians but would have exerted a tremendous pull upon the hearts of the Jewish Christians.

A little further down in this chapter and we come to the consideration of courts of judgment. These were also often held in the synagogues in legal matters pertaining to the Jew. Under the Roman law the various conquered people would have been allowed great latitude in the administration of their cultural proceedings. This is shown in the events surrounding the "trial" and crucifixion of Jesus. The right of the Sanhedrin to scourge and try Jesus would have been understood. In order to have Him executed it would be necessary to invoke the power of Rome. However, even here where impartiality under the law was a basic understanding, there would often be preference giving to a rich man at the expense of the poor.

One of the ways in which the rich sought to distinguish themselves from the rest was in their outward adornment. Their fine, and often colorful, clothing with the added wearing of jewelry would mark them as rich. They would often wear many rings, even unto several on just one finger, as marks of their opulence.

The figure of the poor man here is of one in very shabby clothing. It may not have even been clean. This reminds me of a church service I attended back in 1967, or thereabout. It was the height of "hippie flower power." A large fundamentalist church where I was in attendance was "graced" by the sight of a long haired young man with the beginnings of a fine beard. My guess is that he was from the local college. He sat in the back by himself. No one moved to go back and sit with him.

I might add that I made no move to go back and sit with him either.

His clothing, while clean and neat, was not the standard "church uniform" of jacket and tie which was expected during this time in our church services. The "hippies" had their uniform and we of the church had ours.

The pastor saw him and began his sermon with an impromptu poem. "I think that I shall never see a thing as ugly as a hippie." The assembled good Christian folk, I among them, looked back to see our guest.

It appeared that the young man was not in the service as a lark. He appeared to have a soul need. He had come for solace. He visibly "deflated" at the attack. He stayed quietly and respectfully and left at the end of the service. Not a single person, I included, dealt with this young man's soul.

Fifty years later I wonder if this young man ever found spiritual solace. Or, did he simply "write off" fundamentalist Christianity as a "show pony" with no use other than to sit prettily on a shelf while the world went to Hell about them.

Did he ever find Christ or did he spend his days fighting Christians as false and opinioned bigots? This was how our version of Christianity was displayed.

Folks, our bias and "righteous indignation" have ramifications in the real world of humanity. We must never accept sin. Neither must we ever accost the sinner with scorn and obvious hatred. To love the world is our noble goal. To love an individual... Well, that may be our charge but it is only rarely within our actions. Is our hypocrisy shown in our actions? James asks that the Lord be shown in both our attitudes and our actions!]

2.3 *And ye have respect to him that weareth the gay clothing, and say unto him, Sit thou here in a good place, and say to the poor, Stand thou there, or sit here under my footstool:*

[We are expected to give "military respect" to those of superior rank and station. We respect no man as above us except the Lord. Neither should we consider any person as below us. We do accept that there are offices to which we owe a manner of respect. We respect a ruler even when we do not agree with their rulings. We respect the judgment of a judge even if we believe that judge is flawed in his reasoning. We respect the policeman even though he may occasionally abuse his power.

This does not mean that in a democracy we fail to take what means we may legally take to rectify those things we find unrighteous. We keep in constant consideration that we have a higher duty to our Lord than to earthly magistrates. But, remembering that we are under scrutiny as followers of the Lord, we still give due respect to the leaders under whom God has seen fit to place us in subjection. This is giving due respect, and righteous honor, to our Lord.

We are under subjection to our Lord. To those who have not accepted Him as Savior we have a duty to treat with equal respect without regard to their station in life. The rich can give us nothing equal to the salvation which Christ has given us. The poor can take nothing from us except that which the Lord allows – the privilege of speaking the oracles of God as we pray for the salvation of souls. Both rich and poor are equal in their need for the grace of God. We are the voices which they will hear as we speak of the Lord. We are the voices which they will ignore when we display anything other than the love of God toward them.

In the Temple there were rooms which were reserved for teaching. The chairs were for the elders or teachers. There were benches for those who were under them. Lastly there were the novices who were consigned to the floor.

For a stranger to come in and be assigned one of the chairs simply because he gave the appearance of being rich was an insult to all the others. Likewise, to be summarily assigned a seat on the floor "over there" was a demeaning situation.

The chairs often had foot stools for the use of those sitting in them. To sit under one's footstool carried a distinct cultural consideration. The victor in a military situation would often place his feet upon the neck of the vanquished. To sit under a footstool was to be asked to consider oneself as less than the one in the chair. It was a demeaning situation though it did allow one to be positioned near the front. In a day prior to microphones it was "good" to sit near the front.

This was preferable to standing in the "mosh pit" of the crowd without the possibility of taking one's ease and resting. But, it was to display ones lower status before all the room.

It is also necessary that we consider that the synagogue was also a place where justice would be considered. It was here that issues of law could be settled among the Jews.

For the judge to consider the rich man as superior to the poor was a sign that the poor man was not going to find justice. He would be more likely to find that he had no real "standing" in the court in comparison with the rich man.

It was customary for both the plaintiff and the accused to both be either seated or standing. Thus, to offer a seat to the one and only the floor to another was an indication of prior favoritism toward the one seated.

As a practical matter in our assemblies, James is arguing that the Christian should not be interested in what he can gain from a rich person. Our view should be centered on the need of both rich and poor for the spiritual riches of Christ. Nothing should obscure that view. Our faith is to be partial only to Christ.]

2.4 *Are ye not then partial in yourselves, and are become judges of evil thoughts?*

[As I read this verse, "partial in yourselves," I am drawn to the fourteenth verse of the first chapter of James. "But every man is tempted, when he is drawn away of his own lust, and enticed." The partiality is a lust which comes from our own hearts.

I can easily show this concept of partiality. My grandson and a neighbor boy would often get into arguments. My son figured that the neighbor was at fault every time. The neighbor boy's grandfather felt that my grandson was a fault every time. We tend to exalt those which are closest to us.

The propensity to judge on the basis of wealth is something that is also within ourselves. It is a lust which births the sin of partiality. The rich man is pleasing to our eyes as a symbol of that to which we aspire. The poor man is vile to our eyes as a warning of what we could easily become. To the rich we are inclined to defer. To the poor we are inclined to patronize. Thus, is our partiality influenced by that which is within us rather than that which is in the character of either the rich or the poor.

Put more simply: It is evil thoughts which produce evil judgments. An earthly judge will, or should, recuse himself from a case when he has a fixed opinion of the facts, or a familiarity with the accused, which may cause him to become prejudicial in his rulings. He realizes that such may inhibit the administration of justice.

Romans 14:13 admonishes us, "Let us not therefore judge one another any more: but judge this rather, that no man put a stumblingblock or an occasion to fall in his brother's way." In this we are shown that we must lay aside our personal judgments of a person. This isn't necessarily for that person's benefit. But it is for the benefit of our testimony before the world.

Note that this does not mean that we simply accept every "prophet" by his proclamation.

The principle has to do with our acceptance of a person. It has nothing to do with our acceptance of a person's ministry or actions. Our first duty is to Christ. Our second duty is to be true to Christ in the promotion of His Kingdom and the spreading of the Word of His Grace. There are many cults and false teachers. To these people we can show due respect. To their teaching we can show no respect without being untrue to our Lord!

Jesus gave a teaching in the sixth chapter of Luke. Verse forty-four says, "For every tree is known by his own fruit. For of thorns men do not gather figs, nor of a bramble bush gather they grapes." The fruit which a ministry, minister, teacher etc., sows will be shown as it grows into a tree of doctrine. When that doctrine is not centered on Scriptural realities and when it denies those Scriptural realities we have an obligation to oppose such teaching. We can love and pray for the teacher but we cannot promote either him or his teachings as this would cause others to be led astray. (Jude 3)

That isn't what James was speaking about. James was speaking of the ill of judging one person as superior to another. Such cannot be exhibited by us. That is the responsibility and work of God. It is He Who judges the hearts. (Psalm 58:11)]

2.5   Hearken, my beloved brethren, hath not God chosen the poor of this world rich in faith, and heirs of the kingdom which he hath promised to them that love him?

[James asks that special attention be paid his argument. "Hearken." He softens his harshness by counting those to whom he speaks as "beloved brethren." Even as he takes them to task due to their mistake of partiality, he identifies with them.

We can easily see a lesson in this. The vilest sinner is a "brother in the flesh" with us. The drug addict, the drunkard, the lowest of society remains one with us as to the humanity of the flesh. We are all the creation of the same God. We are all from the family of Adam. It is only the unmerited favor of the Grace of Jesus Christ which separates us from such a state as they.

This is not the basis of the argument of James. It is the ground under which the reasoning is considered. The love of Christ reaches to the poorest among us. The "old saw" is that "God must have loved the poor; He made so many of them." James asks that we consider that there are more of the poor among the saints of God than rich among that number. It seems that our standard operating procedure of favoring the rich is in counter distinction to the moving of God upon humanity.

When John the Baptist was in prison he sent messengers to Jesus asking if Jesus really was the Messiah which Israel had for so long hoped and anticipated. One of the factors that Jesus considered as validating His Messiahship was that He was preaching the Gospel Message to the poor. (Matthew 11:5)

There is nothing wrong with possessions. The disciples were tradesmen, mostly fishermen with boats, nets, and such when Jesus called them to follow Him. Paul had the trade of tentmaker to fall back upon in an hour of financial need. Matthew was a civic official, tax gatherer, when he was called to follow Jesus. The common thread among all of these is that they counted their physical comfort as so unimportant as to forego their occupational security to follow the Lord even when this following would forge a path to a lower "standard of living."

The twelve gave up personal funding to live a communal life with Judas, the betrayer, as the one holding the office of treasurer for the group. Paul became a prisoner of Rome. He accepted this as an opportunity to live for Christ and worked for the Lord even during that imprisonment.

The poor might have had little of the world's treasure but this did not argue that they were less than the rich. Often it argued that they were more than the rich in the eyes of God.

The "bottom line" of any relationship with God is based completely upon the medium of faith. It is faith, which itself is a gift from God, which is basis of our salvation. (Ephesians 2:8-9) It is obvious that our very salvation is not an earned thing. It is not something for which we can labor. Works follow *from* rather than *toward* salvation. (Ephesians 2:10) Biblical salvation is based upon the work which Jesus has already done. Our only relation to salvation is based on our faith in what He had done at the Cross of Calvary.

The poor understand the need of faith in Christ for they know that they can have no reason to boast of themselves. Personal experience and society have well taught this lesson. The rich, however, have no such advantage. The rich have learned to trust in their own abilities and resources. Paul knew this when he said, "...I have learned, in whatsoever state I am, *therewith* to be content. I know both how to be abased, and I know how to abound: every where and in all things I am instructed both to be full and to be hungry, both to abound and to suffer need." In all of these reversals of riches and acceptance of affluence, Paul had learned one seminal lesson, "I can do all things through Christ which strengtheneth me." (Philippians 4:11b-13)

The poor have been blessed not with the pain of want but with the lesson that Jesus is all that is needed in this world. The poor have been taught the truth of faith. The riches of Heaven await those of this world who have gained faith in this life. Rich or poor is not a spiritual distinction. The distinction of abundance of faith is that to which our spiritual eyes may look upon.]

2.6 *But ye have despised the poor: Do not rich men oppress you, and draw you before the judgment seats?*

[James makes the obvious leap from the partiality shown to the rich to the resultant despicable manner in which the poor are treated. A "level playing field" is a good thing but this is not the manner in which the people of the church were treating the differing classes of the attendees. One side, the rich, was given favor and preference. The other side, the poor, were held in disfavor and treated poorly or even harshly.

James sees this biased behavior as foolish in that the favored rich are more likely to be the persecutor of the church. The smallest slight, perceived slight, or even simply an opportunity to be a persecutor may cause the rich to exercise the power which they have in the courts to bring the Christian, roughly if need be, to the judgment bar of inequity. Acts 9:2 is an example of such "bills of indictment" being drawn up to charge the Christian with defaming the religion of the Jew. Acts 8:3 is an example of the houses of the Christian being "spoiled" by the legal process of the Jewish courts.

There were various reasons that the Christian could be dragged into the court proceedings at the local synagogue. The Roman government gave wide latitude of power for these religious courts to rule in the provinces. We see that in the treatment of Jesus before His crucifixion. The religious courts lacked only the power to condemn to death. This was the reason for the appeal to Herod.

It is interesting that the Christian were being persecuted for worshipping Jesus. This was considered as a blasphemy against the religious life of the Jew under the Law of Moses. Yet, there were those who were brought before the court over financial matters. Though the Law forbade usury, (Exodus 22:25; Leviticus 25:36; Deuteronomy 23:19) there were debtors courts which were used to punish those who had run a higher total debt than they could pay. I would refer you to the Lord's parable in Matthew 18:23-34.

There is, of course, also the consideration of the publicans. The newer English versions translate word this as "tax gatherer." This is a correct translation but it is hardly accurate. Even given the revulsion many feel for the IRS, there is nowhere near the loathing for the IRS to compare with the publican of the New Testament times. Not only were these publicans notorious for their dishonestly, anything they managed to extract above that required would be theirs, they were known as agents of a foreign and occupying power. The common man saw these publicans as traitors as well as crooks. These did, however, tend to become very rich men.

Once brought into the court system, the accused would often find his accuser setting on the panel of the judges of his case.

James asks, "With all of these abuses from the rich, why would you give them any favorable treatment?!"]

2.7   *Do not they blaspheme that worthy name by the which ye are called?*

[This could be an indictment of the Christian who showed partiality to the rich. James is very interested in the outward appearance of the Christian into the world of man. This could apply to the Christian giving an ill connotation to Christ by their unequal treatment among the fellowship. It would call into question the love which Christians are to hold one for another. (John 13:35)

Whether the fact that they were called by the name of Christ, as is the apparent meaning, because the appellation of "Christian" had already been extended to them, or because of Baptism whereby they were baptized in the Name of the Father, the Son and the Holy Ghost, is not known. What is obvious is that their actions were such as to bring either credit or discredit upon the Holy Name of Jesus.

Since this verse appears to be a continuation of verse six, we must conclude that this is an action of some of the rich men. If these were Christian men of the church we would argue the same as in the first paragraph of this commentary. If these were men from outside the fellowship, this would be properly termed as a persecution of the Church since this was directed at the Name of Christ. The Christian involved as the persecuted would simply be the tool to extract damage by the persecutor.]

2.8 *If ye fulfil the royal law according to the scripture; Thou shalt love thy neighbor as thyself, ye do well:*

[James calls the law of impartiality a royal law. This term stamps this law as a general law which is suitable and necessary for all. This is a law of human conduct among all. It is especially so among the Christian in that they are called to love all humanity. Those in the household of faith are brothers and sisters in that faith. With this understanding all are equal in subjection and honor unto the Heavenly Father.

Those outside of the household of faith are virtual brothers and sisters in the common creation of God. There is to be a deep and abiding love for these so that they might see the love of the Creator as shining forth from us for them. (Matthew 5:14-16) As a moth to the flame so should our reflected light of the Light of the Son draw the sinner to see his need and accept the Lord's Grace.

Jesus said that the entire teaching of the Mosaic Law is hinged on two things. The one is the love of God and the returned Love which the creature should have for the Creator. The other is to love our neighbor as ourselves. (Matthew 22:37-40) As a law of Royal Authorship this is seen as a law which we are duty bound to obey. But, more than simply this, we are the adopted children of the Royal Author of this Law. We are doubly bound by the law as subjects and as witnesses to the Truth of this Law.

Our witness to the Truth is that which may be used by our Lord as an example to draw others to the Cross in Salvation. As such we are privileged to be used of the Master and to be used for the Master in His Own Work within the world of man. This is a royal privilege which is given to us as "a royal priesthood." "But ye are a chosen generation, a royal priesthood, an holy nation, a peculiar people; that ye should shew forth the praises of him who hath called you out of darkness into his marvellous light..." (I Peter 2:9)

In fulfilling this law we are told that we do well.]

2.9 *But if ye have respect to persons, ye commit sin, and are convinced of the law as transgressors.*

[Respect, or partiality, toward persons of one class as opposed to those of another class – be it rich considered over poor or poor considered over rich – is a sin against the known teaching of God on the subject of neighborly love. Each class, or person, must be considered impartially in respect to our acceptance of them.

This respect to value, or to treat, one above the other is sin. It is a violation of the Law of God. As such the person so found in this sin is rightly called a sinner. Any breaking of the Law of God, no matter how lightly we might account that particular law, is sin. As such it causes one to be judged as a sinner.

If I am called to court to stand before a judge because I was speeding, I will be in that court room the same as the man called to stand before the judge as a murderer. I understand that there is a break-down in my analogy as to the severity of the cases. But, the fact remains that both the speeder and the murderer will stand before the court as accused criminals.

Our conviction as a sinner is of equal severity before God. As a sinner our actual crime is to stand in opposition to God as we argue with our lives by our actions that we consider His Will to be of no consideration in our minds and hearts. We do not *lose* our salvation in this, but we do set ourselves up for judicial and Parental punishment as children of our Heavenly Father.

Thus sin, whether it is considered as great or small in the eyes of man, is soul-damning in the sight of the judicial system of God. Sin stands as an example of insurrection against the lawful Ruler of the universe. His Words denied are His Words derided. Sin stands as a personal affront to God. We have no recourse to do more "good" to offset our "bad" when all our works are outside of His justice by dint of our rebellion against Him. All for which we can hope is to obtain mercy from Him. Justice from God will surely damn our souls to perdition.

This final paragraph, of course, speaks of those who have not been adopted into sonship by God as a result of accepting Jesus Christ as Lord and Savior. If we do claim Him as Lord, we owe Him obedience as our Lawful Sovereign.]

2.10 *For whosoever shall keep the whole law, and yet offend in one point, he is guilty of all.*

[Returning to the above analogy, I was driving through a construction zone a few weeks ago when I saw a sign that said, "Speed Limits are photographically enforced." That simply means that if I am driving seventy miles-per-hour in a zone marked at no more than forty-five miles-per-hour there is a real chance that an unmanned radar will trigger a picture of my car exceeding the speed limit by twenty-five miles-per-hour.

My argument might be that I wasn't driving that fast all of the time. It was just for that mile that I sped up. The judge might say, "We are not fining you for the entire twenty-five mile construction zone. We are only responding to that one mile when you were speeding." The entire case would not hinge on how "good" I had been for twenty-four miles. The judgment against me would be for speeding, even though it may have been for only 4% of the trip, through the construction zone.

Proverbs 21:4 reminds us that, "An high look, and a proud heart, and the plowing of the wicked, is sin." Plowing is not a sin. It is an extremely important human activity. The point being made in this sin is that no act of man is a good work. The concept of doing good works is only applicable to a person who is already a Christian. Ephesians 2:10 says, "For we are his workmanship, created in Christ Jesus unto good works, which God hath before ordained that we should walk in them." Only the Christian can walk in "good works." He is only allowed this privilege because of his status as born-again by the Blood of Christ.

The sin of a sinner is compounded by that fact that he is a sinner. The Christian who stands before men in the garb of a sinner via sinful acts such as partiality, is rightly judged as a sinner by the world at large. This is from the view of the world, of course. A person judged as cleansed of sin by the Blood of the Lamb is no longer in a state of sin in the eye of God.

This is the thrust of the Book of James. We are to let our light so shine (Matthew 5:16) before men that they may see the Glory of the Father in our actions. A faith which is not disposed to this is worthless as a testimony to the power of God before humanity.

To the unsaved the power of God to transform a life is downgraded or denied. They stand accused as sinners because they are sinners who deny the righteous authority of God to lead into righteousness.]

2.11 *For he that said, Do not commit adultery, said also, Do not Kill. Now if thou commit no adultery, yet if thou kill, thou art become a transgressor of the law.*

[Clarke has noted that, "It was a maxim also among the Jewish doctors that, if a man kept any one commandment carefully, though he broke all the rest, he might assure himself of the favour of God; for while they taught that 'He who transgresses all the precepts of the law has broken the yoke, dissolved the covenant, and exposed the law to contempt, and so has he done who has broken even one precept,' (Mechilta, fol. 5, Yalcut Simeoni, part 1, fol. 59,) they also taught, 'that he who observed any principal command was equal to him who kept the whole law;' (Kiddushin, fol. 39;) and they give for example, 'If a man abandon idolatry, it is the same as if he had fulfilled the whole law,' (Ibid., fol. 40.) To correct this false doctrine James lays down inspired teaching in this 11th verse."

What Clarke is exposing is that the "Jewish Doctors of the Law" on the one hand taught that any breaking of the law in one area was the breaking of the entire structure of the Law. Meanwhile, on the other hand they seemed to argue that some Laws were more important than were other Laws. The major Law was able, in this view, to sanctify one who had broken another supposed lessor law. James argues against the latter view as inconsistent with the nature of the Lord. God is immutable, or unchangeable. So to, since it was He Who gave and administered the Law, must be the nature of the Law. To break the Law in any area was to sully the entirety of the Law and offend the God of that Law.

It was the purpose of the Law to show man his sin. To argue that some of that Law could actually atone for sin was to place the entire concept of the Law in jeopardy of being completely misunderstood. Such a view would cause the Law to lose its primary focus as teaching the sinfulness of sin. Consider Galatians 3:24 under this light.

To break the Law in any instance is to expose one as a Lawbreaker. Once that principle is established in the actions of one's life the lawbreaker is potentially a lawbreaker in every instance. He has shown a disregard for the Law of God and The God of the Law.

The two cases examined by James constitute two of the most heinous violations of duty towards a neighbor.]

2.12 *So speak ye, and so do, as they that shall be judged by the law of liberty.*

[By the mercy of God we have been freed from the burden of the Law of Moses. Therefore, we should act within this liberty by paying heed to the religious and societal principles of this Law. Those principles are spiritual principles of conduct as shown us by the very tenets of that Law. Our liberty has given us salvation from the penalty of consequence; it has not freed us from our spiritual responsibilities, as taught by that Law, toward God and man.

Any faith which argues for license is not the faith which God has given us. Our faith is to follow Jesus Who fulfilled the Law. We are not called to fulfill the Law in that manner. That was the work of Messiah. Neither are we called to ignore those spiritual principles which the Law has taught. We walk in a newness of life in liberty. We do not walk in license as this is made to imply, by some false teachers, that grace has freed us to sin.

Romans 3:31 says, "Do we then make void the law through faith? God forbid: yea, we establish the law." The Law of the Old Covenant has been done away in regards to it being a Law which only established penalty and death. Viewing that Law as a living principle of our spiritual lives established it now as a way of life, or a way for us to live unto God.

This concept of spiritual principles is a powerful and righteous aid to allow us to live up to the potential which God has given us in His mercy. We were not saved to sin. We were saved to live righteously before God and man. We are on this earth to live as a testimony to the unsaved that God has given us a new life, a new liberty, and a new way to walk among men. We are allowed to walk in a manner befitting our station as adopted sons of God.

We display our witness to the Love and Mercy of God among men by showing deference and love toward His commandments. A heart filled with the love of, and towards, God will make every effort to live a life pleasing to Him. This is our duty to both man and God.

Romans 8:15 reminds us, "For ye have not received the spirit of bondage again to fear; but ye have received the Spirit of adoption, whereby we cry, Abba, Father." We are not bound by the Law of sin and death. (Romans 8:2) Rather, we are bound by cords of love to our Heavenly Father. He has made us free from the sins which so often overpower the intents and plans of the children of the world. We are made to be better than that. There is no need for the Christian to be fettered since Christ has made us free!

We are free to drive on the right side of the road. That is the freedom of our liberty. James argues throughout this Book that we are not to scorn the principles of God. We are to embrace them for what they are. They are principles which free us to travel this world in safety and usefulness. We are free to be pliable to the dictates of God as He shows us the Truth of His leadership into the paths which are to our own benefit!]

2.13 *For he shall have judgment without mercy, that hath shewed no mercy, and mercy rejoiceth against judgment.*

[Two things stand out in this verse. The first is that we will be treated in the manner with which we have treated others. Matthew 7:1-2 gives a warning that we do not judge others. If we do judge other harshly we can expect to be judged harshly of others. Psalm 18:25 gives the same sense. We can also figure Matthew 5:7 as an illustration of the fact of this spiritual principle.

The second point would be that mercy will triumph over judgment. This verse puts mercy in a virtual competition against judgment and declares that mercy will win the contest and find joy in victory.

One other thing is obvious. Scripture is of One Author. It cannot be made to argue against itself. Since salvation is presented as the work of Jesus, man has no part in salvation, this passage and its corollaries cannot have any reference to obtaining salvation.

These do have reference to obtaining the heavenly rewards of eternity. I Corinthians 3:10-11 says, "According to the grace of God which is given unto me, as a wise masterbuilder, I have laid the foundation, and another buildeth thereon. But let every man take heed how he buildeth thereupon. For other foundation can no man lay than that is laid, which is Jesus Christ."

When verses 13-15 of that same passage are considered we will see that this concept of judgment, as it refers to the Christian, concerns a judgment of gain in rewards in heaven. One who shows mercy to others, Christian love for the brethren and for the lost, will be rewarded for those works. Conversely, those who fail to display this Christian love will suffer loss.

On earth such a one will also suffer loss in his relationship with his fellow man. A person who shows love toward others will feel the receipt of that love in the good will of his fellow man. One who does not show that love will be apt to find he is scorned and hated. Even the "lionized" rich will feel the sting of this scorn.

In the spiritual side, there will be loss even on earth to the unruly Christian who refuses to display the love of God into the world of man. The passage in I Corinthians 11:29-30 considers a person who dishonors the Lord's Table. Much greater is this unto one who dishonors the Lord, Himself, in the testimony of his life before the unsaved.

James encourages the believers to live a consistent Christian life before the world. While the Law demands judgment; the mercy of God allows grace through His mercy. A truly merciful person will thank God for an opportunity to show mercy into the world as a means of testimony to this free grace of God.

Mercy is the basis of our salvation and should also reign in our lives.]

2.14 What doth it profit, my brethren, though a man say he hath faith, and have not works? can faith save him?

[Actually there are three verses in this same chapter that all reinforce the same general argument; verse 17 and verse 20 could be included here. At first blush these verses seem to buttress an argument that we must work for salvation. This is not the case although many have taken these verses, by themselves, and made that a doctrine of man.

If we are to understand these verses, we must look in their immediate context.

"Be ye does of the word, and not hearers only, deceiving your own selves. For if any be a hearer of the word, and not a doer, he is like unto a man beholding his natural face in a glass: For he beholdeth himself, and goeth his way, and straightway forgetteth what manner of man he was. But whoso looketh into the perfect law of liberty, and continueth therein, he being not a forgetful hearer, but a doer of the work, this man shall be blessed in his deed." (James 1:22-25)

James (Who, by the way, seems to have been the leader of the early church which gathered at Jerusalem, rather than Peter as some allege.) then begins to build his case that true Christianity will change a person.

He follows with several examples, some from the Old Testament and some from general observations, which continue his theme. His thesis is that an encounter with

Christ will change a person. We witness the same argument in the well-known salvation verses of Ephesians 2:8-9 when we include the tenth verse which immediately comes after.

"For by grace are ye saved, through faith: and that not of yourselves; it is the gift of God: Not of works, lest any man should boast. For we are his workmanship, created in Christ Jesus unto good works, which God hath before ordained that we should walk in them."

The question in James is not of salvation via faith; the question is the power of salvation to invoke works within the Christian.

Abraham is referenced, in relation to his willingness to offer Isaac as a sacrifice. So, also, is the harlot Rahab in consideration of her actions towards the two spies from the camp of Israel. It must be noted that each had already been given the promise of grace (Abraham with the blessings of a great nation and Rahab with salvation from the destruction of Jericho) before they acted. Their blessings were each contingent upon the promise of God. In response to this blessing they acted in the faith. Their works were a response to the grace of God rather than a payment made to elicit that grace.

The argument of James is that works are a visible response to the grace of God. Can a faith which does not change lives be an effective faith in relation to salvation? James argues that such a faith is no more than a head knowledge; it is not a heart response to the offerings of God's great gift of salvation.

James argues that this sort of faith is dead. Paul wrote a corollary passage in Ephesians.

"And you hath he quickened, who were dead in trespasses and sins: Wherein in times past ye walked according to the course of this world, according to the prince of the power of the air, the spirit that now worketh in the children of disobedience." (Ephesians 2:1-2)

The word "quickened" means to be made alive. From what state would one be made alive? Obviously, the answer would be "from death." Those who are not of the household of faith, are not Christians, are dead in their sin, as the above verse states. A faith which has not the power to "quicken" one unto good works is a dead faith because it leaves the bearer of that faith to continue in that same situation.

The passage in James is not a call for anyone to work for salvation. Such cannot be done. The Bible is a testimony to the fact that Jesus died in time so that we could live in eternity. It is His work, on the cross, which saves us. Any work we could perform would be meaningless when compared to His Work. Further, to deny His Work is to evidence that we have not placed our faith in Him. It is, in a "bottom line" consideration, a faith in ourselves. Such a faith is, indeed, a dead faith stand taken by spiritually dead persons.

The passage in James is a call for the Christian to examine his standing with God. Again, Paul argues the same thing. "Examine yourselves, whether ye be in the faith..." (II Corinthians 13:5a) Paul goes on in that verse to say that if Christ is not in us we are reprobate, which simply means "ones rejected, condemned, unapproved (after failing the test)." (From The Defined King James Bible)

Our works can never save us. But our works are a gift to the God Who has already saved us. Paul addresses the same issue as James in the sixth chapter of Romans. The question is not of the liberty of the Christian as derived from the mercy of God. The question is, as put forth by Francis Shaffer so many years ago in his book,

"How Then Should We Live?" Our Christian liberty is not to be considered a freedom to live contrary to the standards of the Law among humanity. Neither are we under the Law as to our spiritual lives. We are given the freedom to live *within* the Law as true servants of God and witnesses to man of His grace and mercy.

There is also, of course, the consideration of those who were merely "hangers on" with the Christian community. These, never actually saved by the Blood of Christ, were trying to act the part with the understanding that this would "work out their salvation." The resultant lack of any change within their life stood as a testimony that they had been with the Christian life-style but not with the Christian's Life Giver!

None-the-less, it must be admitted that some of this latter group would lead lives which would seemingly put the true Christians to shame in their fervency.

It would also be good to consider that James says, "If a man **say** he have faith." The argument goes to the proofs that true saving faith actually exists rather than just something which is self-proclaimed. The seeming disagreements between Paul and James come from the sight at which works are seen. Paul argues that works have no saving faith; in this he speaks of works being mistaken as a pattern to *obtain* grace. James speaks of works as flowing from faith; in this he speaks of works as an *evidence* of grace.

We must note that James does not disparage faith. Indeed, he sees is as foundational for the performance of any "good works." Paul speaks of our justification before God. James speaks of the justification of our faith as being evidenced before man.]

2.15   If a brother or sister be naked, and destitute of daily food,

[I was substitute teaching at a high school near my home a few years ago. I noticed that one boy did not go to the cafeteria during the lunch break. I said, "You'd better hurry down to lunch or you'll be late for your next class."

He said, "I don't need to go. I didn't bring any lunch and I don't have any money to buy it today." That was an obvious need that could be met by Christian compassion. Or, it could be met simply by the common sense of spending under two dollars in order to show actual compassion for a young man. James is setting that kind of prospect before us.

To go further, there is a clothing drive late every fall to ensure that every student has a warm coat for the winter months. Suppose we see someone walking down the street to the grocery store with a blanket wrapped around their shoulders. What do we suppose? We would normally consider that this is a person without a coat. What are we, as Christian witnesses, to do?

We also need to consider that everything we do as Christian is either a witness to man on behalf of our Lord or a dereliction of our duty as Christians toward our Lord and the witness of Him before men. "Therefore to him that knoweth to do good, and doeth it not, to him it is sin." (James 4:17) It should be obvious that we either do good in witness or we sin.]

2.16   And one of you say unto them, Depart in peace, be ye warmed and filled, nothwithstanding ye give them not those things which are needful to the body; what shall it profit?

[Just saying something without doing what we can do is a cruel form of hypocrisy! These words are worthless in the life of them to whom we utter our platitude of emptiness. These words are also useless to us as they gain no reward unto us either in Heaven or on earth.

These words may give us a "warm feeling" of our Christian compassion. These words give no reality of Christian concern. Compassion which energizes concern will generate an actual act of tangible witness into the world.

At this point I offer a caution. There are also those outside the household of faith who will consider that we of the church "owe" them something. I think back to a man I was sitting with many years ago. We were in a waiting room of a temporary work office in hopes of being called out to work that day. A man setting across from me let everyone know that he hadn't eaten in a couple of days; he hoped he'd be sent out that morning and get his "daily draw" so he could buy lunch for himself.

This same man reached into his pocket and pulled out a pack of cigarettes. He hadn't eaten but he had found the money to buy his drug of choice. Not all who claim poverty are actually afflicted. We help when, where and how we can. We do not do this out of necessity. We do this out of concern, love and witness to the power of Christ.

A little girl used to come to our house every couple of days to get money because, "Mom says she needs to get milk for the baby." We gave her a few dollars every time. One time she came and we had no money ourselves. We took milk from our refrigerator and food from our pantry and sent the little girl back home. In a few minutes she came back with the larder. "Mom said she wants the money instead of the food."

I related this story to the head of the local mission. He said, "You do realize that you've been buying drugs for the woman." He explained that Christian compassion must be tempered with Christian wisdom. Not all help is actually help. Pray the wisdom of God guide so that you do not give the impression that our Savior is simply another "mark."

Charity? Yes! Love? Yes! Compassion? Yes! Foolishness which gives a false impression that Christianity is to be a "freeload" even for those who will not make the attempt to help themselves? Pray for the wisdom of God!]

2.17 *Even so faith, if it hath not works, is dead, being alone.*

[There is a parallel passage in II Peter 1:3-10. " According as his divine power hath given unto us all things that pertain unto life and godliness, through the knowledge of him that hath called us to glory and virtue: Whereby are given unto us exceeding great and precious promises: that by these ye might be partakers of the divine nature, having escaped the corruption that is in the world through lust. And beside this, giving all diligence, add to your faith virtue; and to virtue knowledge; And to knowledge temperance; and to temperance patience; and to patience godliness; And to godliness brotherly kindness; and to brotherly kindness charity. For if these things be in you, and abound, they make you that ye shall neither be barren nor unfruitful in the knowledge of our Lord Jesus Christ. But he that lacketh these things is blind, and cannot see afar off, and hath forgotten that he was purged from his old sins. Wherefore the rather, brethren, give diligence to make your calling and election sure:

for if ye do these things, ye shall never fall..."

The picture in II Peter is how one ought to progress in his Christian life in reference to the gifts of the Spirit as given us in salvation. The tenth verse warns that the professed Christian compare himself against this list. Since these gifts are given with salvation, the lack of these evidenced within the life of the person may indicate either a stagnant Christian life, as alluded in the commentary on the above verse from James, or to being a mere professor and not a possessor of salvation.

James is making the same point. A body which has had the spirit severed from it is no longer a living body; it is a carcass. A supposed faith which has not seen the energizing power of the Spirit of God is a dead faith in that it is alone, without the power of the new birth evident within it.

Once again, this has no reference to working *for* salvation but has every indication of those works which ought to flow *from* salvation.

A living faith is energized by love. We have a love for God because we have experienced the Love of God within our hearts. (I John 4:19) With this Love of God experienced within our souls we begin to see the Love which God has for others. This realization will cause us to spread our representation of the Love of God through our acts of witness and concern, out into the world of man. This is a living and operative faith in relationship with our Savior and Lord.]

2.18 *Yea, a man may say, Thou hast faith, and I have works: shew me thy faith without thy works, and I will shew thee my faith by my works.*

[The argument at this place is not that one man is saved and the other is not. The argument concerns those evidences which point to the reality of the Christian experience. One may well argue that the body of the Church is made up of people with differing gifts. So, may one not argue that his gifts do not include that of love for his fellow man?

After all, the argument might run, is a tree alive before it produces fruit? Is the flower in seed form alive or does it only become alive as it blooms? Such arguments are spurious when considered within the argument of evidence. If either the flower or the tree is to demonstrate its living vitality it must progress to the display of its fruit.

The one who evidences no fruit of the Spirit has no proof to show relative to his faith. It is the man with works who can point to an exhibited fruit to prove to others in witness to the reality of his salvation.

Again, this does not speak of working *for* salvation but the evidence of salvation into the world of men *by* the works of that salvation being played forth. The ground of salvation is not at issue; the demonstration of that salvation faith among men is the issue.

This is a matter of testimony before men. God already knows the hearts of man.]

2.19 *Thou believest that there is one God, thou doest well: the devils also believe, and tremble.*

[Simple faith is not sufficient. Even the grand faith of the Jew that there was but One God, as opposed to the heathen who had multiple idols, was not of itself an example of a saving faith. Though this was a true and proper faith, this was not a faith unto salvation as is proven by the illustration of the demons spirits which James uses.

This verse does not have in view Satan. He is singular and obviously understands that there is but One Holy God. This particular verse has in mind the demonic world as a whole. My believe is that it was these demons which inhabited the "magicians" of Egypt and allowed them to duplicate some of the plagues which Moses saw inflicted by God upon the Egyptians.

The demons do have some spiritual power. Consider that in Revelation 16:14 they are said to perform miracles. The power of the demons is a limited power to subvert the creation in error. Was not this the case of the serpent being powered by Satan in The Garden? Never is the power of the demonic used to the benefit of the creation of God. (John 10:10, 21)

These demons understand God and His ultimate power. They quake as they consider their end. It was such as these who opposed Jesus and argued that He was acting too early in regards to the time of their end. (Matthew 8:29) These went so far as to confess Jesus was the Messiah of God. Consider that this was a faith of knowledge but it was not a faith unto salvation.

This was a true belief, of course, but by it the demonic world is not granted salvation but it is actually more tormented by this knowledge than if they had not this "faith" in the existence and Unity of God. This is a "know so" faith which carries a "no go" view of eternal rewards.

The faith of the professors of whom James speaks is a dead faith in that it produces none of the Fruit of the Spirit. The evidence is in the lack of fruit.

I recently received a check which is purported to be part of a "class action" lawsuit. I think is probably a false "fishing expedition" by someone seeking to steal. I know that the check exists. I have seen it. I have handled it. I am not going to cash it because I do not trust its veracity.

A saving faith is a faith that has accepted Jesus as Savior. That is more than just knowing about Him. That is an acceptance that He, Alone, is the answer to my soul's need of salvation. (consider Acts 4:12) This is a faith that will produce the Fruit of the Spirit. Should that fruit not be forthcoming one must be led to doubt either the power of the Spirit or the acceptance of Jesus, in full faith, by the penitent.

James answer is that the Holy Spirit will not fail. Any lack in the professor must be on the account of his view of faith.]

2.20 *But wilt thou know, O vain man, that faith without works is dead?*

[James is speaking of a man who was vain in his obstinacy toward being taught and in his lack of understanding of the subject matter of the product of faith. James is not saying that there is no effect from vain faith. He could point to the demons and destroy that argument. Their works, however, were not the fruits of the Spirit, but the fruits of spiritual deception. But, he was saying that faith which did not produce the works which were of the fruits of the Spirit was a vain, or an empty, faith as regards salvation.

The use of the Scripture in a teaching manner would show the argument James wished to make. The argument of James, as is the argument of Paul in Ephesians 2:10, is that true faith will quicken, or make alive, the one who possesses such faith. The walk in the Spirit is not toward but in that Spirit of God. That walk will be a walk which is a walk in obedience unto, and with, good works.

The argument is not that faith is dead for faith is the medium of fellowship with God. James said that faith *without works* shows no evidence of being quickened by the Spirit. A faith which has no evidence of the empowering of the Spirit is dead. "And you hath he quickened, who were dead in trespasses and sins..." (Ephesians 2:1) Paul's argument from Ephesians as to the reality of a living faith is essentially the same as the argument of James in this place.

Garner used the illustration of a man with two oars. One oar was named "faith." The other oar was named "work." When the man used just the oar named "faith" he went in circles and never moved toward his destination. Conversely, when he used only the oar named "work," he did not progress but simply circled in another direction. When both oars were used the man was sent on his way to his intended destination.

We could argue that saving faith puts both the oar of faith and the oar of works into the water in order to direct us in the will of God. "It takes both faith and works to get anywhere in the Christian life. Doing is evidence that one believes."]

2.21 *Was not Abraham our father justified by works, when he had offered Isaac his son upon the altar?*

[This offering of Abraham does not speak of the justification of Abraham. It speaks of the evidence of that justification. God understood the character of Abraham before this test. Abraham did not know this much of his character until such time as he prepared to offer Isaac as a sacrifice unto God.

In effect Abraham did offer Isaac as a burnt offering to God. God provided another sacrifice but Abraham was disposed to complete the deed simply because of his actions being justified from the base rock of his faith in God. This evidence of justification by the work of Abraham flowed from the faith of Abraham. Thus, it was faith and the work which grew out of that faith that James speaks of justification. The justification was already present due to faith. The evidence to others came through the work which was part of the experience of faith.

The point often missed in the surface perusal of the Book of James is that he is not speaking of faith from the standpoint of the believer's heart but of the believer's actions so that others may view those actions and understand the dynamic of faith in the life of that believer.

Abraham is called "our father" as James is writing to the Jewish Christian. The power of inspiration has also applied that very term to be used by the Gentile Christians. (Galatians 3:9) All of Scripture is for all of God's children. Our faith is also strengthened in the reading of the Scripture with our eyes and minds and by the application of that Scripture by the power of the Holy Spirit.]

2.22 *Seest thou how faith wrought with his works, and by works was faith made perfect?*

[Through this act of Abraham God declared to all the world, and all the subsequent history of the world, that the faith of Abraham was a righteous and sustaining faith. The Jew obviously accepts the faith of Abraham as a righteous faith. So, too, does the Christian accept the faith of Abraham as a righteous faith. Even the Muslim, who is an unbeliever outside the covenant of grace, understands the concept of the righteousness of Abraham's faith.

This last understanding points to the purpose of faith into the world. The work *of* faith has saved our souls according to the Gospel of Jesus. The work *in* faith can be an example to others – even to those not saved – of the reality of real faith in Jesus as the basis for true salvation. Even those who would stumble over the "Corner Stone" of the Lord cannot claim that God has been unrighteous towards them. (I Peter 2:8) Truth rejected does not negate the reality of Truth supplied. (Romans 1:28)

The true witness of the Christian is a holy thing even when the "wisdom" of man rejects that witness.

The faith of Abraham was made perfect in the sacrifice of Isaac. The idea of "making perfect" is to complete, or bring to fruition, the faith of Abraham. Once again James gives us the picture of a faith which is energized into action which is a witness unto the power of God beyond the life of the man of faith and out into the world of doubt.

Neither could Abraham have understood the power of his faith until this sacrifice. In this manner we see that the exercise of the faith of Abraham was even a witness unto Abraham, himself.

Faith precedes works. Works proceed from faith. A child is born to woman. That child is helpless. He cannot walk. He cannot talk. He cannot do anything except receive his basic needs from others. The child grows, matures and gains the skills needed to exist within the world. The time will come when the parents of that young baby will look to him for their own needs.

So is faith. It grows from infancy toward adulthood. The Spirit energizes this faith with the power to work the works of the Lord into the world. Finally that faith is ready to reproduce itself in the lives of others. The cycle of the Christian Church continues as faith matures and acts into the world.

The faith of Abraham was not idle but was acting in concert with the works. Which came first, the bullet or the hole in the board through which the bullet traveled? Faith and works are two sides of the same coin of consecration unto Righteousness already, as it is tied unto faith, had existed. This was proven by the works.]

2.23 *And the scripture was fulfilled which saith, Abraham believed God and it was imputed unto him for righteousness: and he was called the Friend of God.*

[James quotes from Genesis 15:6. "And he believed in the LORD; and he counted it to him for righteousness." This was many years before the sacrifice of Isaac. It was many years before the birth of Isaac. It was many years even before the birth of Ishmael. This was at the point that God was explaining to Abram about the Covenant Blessings. Even at this early point the faith of Abram was operative. It was this faith which was counted unto him as righteousness.

However, as we look down the years of time Abraham continued to trust God. He trusted God even in the sacrifice of the covenant child. This act is said by James to be the "perfection" of the faith of Abraham. It was. It was in this ordeal that Abraham himself was able to understand this faith in his God. This was a "high point" in the spiritual life of Abraham. It was a confirmation to himself of the power of that faith.

The last half of this verse is a quotation from II Chronicles 20:7 where Abraham is called a friend of God. In this instance James gives an illustration of the interconnectedness of the Word of God. There may have been forty human penman.

There may be sixty-six Books. The writing of the inspired and preserved Scripture may have taken fifteen hundred years on three continents with the penmen ranging from shepherd to prophet to high government official during differing empires. Still, the inspired and preserved Words of God are ONE VOLUME. The Bible is the, singularly and spectacularly, miracle Book given from the Words of God to the paths of men.

It is interesting that James, who primary focus was on the observed works of man as these proceeded from their faith, argues here for the supremacy of faith. The Book of James has been derided by many as "extra Biblical" in his emphasis on works. Not so! James approaches faith from an observable platform. God proves that of which God approves. James sees this and glories in the fact!]

2.24 *Ye see then how that by works a man is justified, and not by faith only.*

[With this example of the sacrifice of Isaac, James argues that faith which does not give practical demonstration of its veracity, is not a saving faith for it is a faith that has produced no change within a person. Such faith is called a "dead faith" in that it bears no evidence of being "quickened" by the Spirit.

This seems at variance with Paul in Romans 3:28. "Therefore we conclude that a man is justified by faith without the deeds of the law." We must note that James does not demand a keeping of the Law of Moses as necessary for salvation. Neither does Paul argue that a man will not be changed by an encounter with the Lord. Paul argues, in II Corinthians 5:17 that the saved man is a "new creature." This very term presupposes a change in life-style and purpose. As such the saved man, saved by faith, will begin to act as a Christian man under the influence of the Spirit of God. As such his new nature will work itself out into the world. This is works from salvation as argued by James and confirmed by Paul.

Paul does not discount the Law within the life of the Christian. "To them that are without law, as without law, (being not without law to God, but under the law to Christ,) that I might gain them that are without law." (I Corinthians 9:21) While Paul was speaking of living faith which reorders the life of man, James was speaking of dead faith which is simply so many words with no actual heart change of reconciliation unto God.

The argument of James is that a faith which does not show the evidence of itself in action, as Abraham with the sacrifice of Isaac, is not an energized faith and does nothing to display the glory and grace of Christ into the world. As such it is a faith which ignores the "standing order" of the Great Commission. This, the evidence that one has no compulsion to see others born into the Kingdom, is an evidence that the Kingdom of God is considered lightly if at all. The saving faith of one in this state must be open to question.]

2.25 *Likewise also was not Rahab the harlot justified by works, when she had received the messengers, and had sent them out another way?*

[This woman was not a saint. She was a sinner. Neither was she rewarded for her lie. It was her faith, as displayed in her work of hiding the men and dropping them safely from her window, upon which her justification was predicated.

Be careful here. She had expressed her faith already. (Joshua 2:9-13) The "scarlet thread" from her window was evidence of a heart change. Her work at this place proved her already existent faith in God and the Abrahamic Covenants beyond her belief in her native country. The acts of Rahab flowed from that faith. They did not establish a faith that was already active.

But, those acts of Rahab proved to others, specifically the spies who repeated the story to Joshua, that she had faith in the God of Israel. The works of Rahab did justify her in the eyes of the children of Israel.

Rahab also worked to spread her new-found faith. She brought her family to the Lord's people. Have any of us done as much?

We might compare the work of Abraham in the sacrifice of Isaac and the work of Rahab in the sheltering and escape of the spies of Israel. Abraham's faith was shown in a situation where he was never in any danger. Rahab put herself in jeopardy when she hid the spies and left a scarlet thread out her window as a sign for when the forces of Israel should return. That cord could have been seen by the military of the city. This would have resulted in some injurious questions of Rahab.

The faith of Rahab, which was declared before these acts, is seen in her acts. The works of Rahab came from her spirit of faith rather than vice-versa. Still, it was the works of Rahab which led to the victory of Israel.

Works which flowed from faith produced a great victory and salvation for Rahab. Still, we must realize that it was the faith of Rahab which was the spring which gave forth the stream of her works. No faith in Rahab would have meant that there would have been no works by Rahab. No works by Rahab in her faith would have meant that she might not have survived the resulting attack upon her city.

That ground of faith was the starting point for the entire story of Rahab. We must never forget that salient point! It is not the point of James to dwell on that. The consideration of James is only that the works of Rahab gave evidence of a saving faith. It is that evidence upon which James majors.]

2.26 *For as the body without the spirit is dead, so faith without works is dead also.*

[The argument of James is that faith which does not exhibit works is dead and useless.

James does not argue against altruism. There are good works among men done by those who have no contact to either faith or to God. These are seeming good works which are not good works. They do not glorify God. The purpose of such works is to glorify and uplift the created world rather than to bring honor to the Creator.

This is man helping man for the glory of man.

The works engendered by the Spirit, which are of true faith, are in the place of helping humanity. But, their overriding purpose is to bring glory to God and, with the assistance of prayer and the Spirit, to bring people to a saving knowledge of the Lord. The works which flow from true faith have eternity in their sights.

The uniting of body and soul constitutes human life. The uniting of true faith and true works, which flow from this, constitute the role of the Love of God into humanity. In the final analysis we find James and Paul on the same page with different perspectives. They both reach the same conclusion that it is true faith which is the basis of true salvation. Paul emphasizes this reality while James emphasis the reality that true faith is a life changing affirmation of the need to live the reality of a Christian life into the world. Good works flow from the faith of a man who honestly intends to be an ambassador for Christ into the world of man.

James and Paul both affirm that faith saves the soul. James sees the results of this faith in the lives of those who possess it. Paul sees those who attempt to make their "good works" the basis of their salvation and opposes that distortion of true faith. The commonality is that both agree that faith is the basis of salvation. Paul majors on true faith without the examination of James that such faith must be centered in works of the Spirit.

Paul does not downgrade that argument. He sees the problem of people who believe that their works are more important than honest faith and reacts against that misrepresentation. To Paul the old song that "Faith Is The Victory" is the solution to "Works Bring the Victory." James argues the same from the perspective that works are the proof of faith when they are cradled in the "bed" of honest faith.

James meanwhile reacts against those who say that faith the entirety of the Christian walk. He lobbies for the professed Christian to prove his faith by showing the outward proof of his inward conversion. "Let the world see Jesus" is not the plea of James. His plea is "Let the world see Jesus in action." This is the rational in good works. This is the proof of the person who claims convictions as evidenced in his conversion.

The theology of Paul majors on the grace of God. James' majors on "Let the World see Jesus in me." One is centered on Truth. So is the other. James wants a truth that the world, and the other Christians can examine.

The argument of James is mirrored in the words of Paul. "Having a form of godliness, but denying the power thereof: from such turn away." (II Timothy 3:5) James is from Missouri. "If you really are a Christian, show me!"

More importantly, if you really are a Christian you will show others by your works. If not your lack of works point up your own need to find true, life changing faith. "Examine yourselves, whether ye be in the faith; prove your own selves. Know ye not your own selves, how that Jesus Christ is in you, except ye be reprobates?" (II Corinthians 13:5) This is an important point that must be considered. Our response to life will either show the evidence to true conversion – or the lack thereof!

A well-constructed mannequin may appear real but it is not. The faith of a man may give every appearance of reality except if it lacks the power of God to transform a life it is only a "clay dummy." Without the energizing life of the Spirit, false "faith" is a toboggan sledding down the course of a cold world only speeding toward perdition.

Bodies without life within it will still, for a time at least, appear to be a living body. However, it will take neither food nor notice of anything. It is dead. A professed faith which has no notice of change within the soul will give every evidence of being spiritually dead. A faith of action, such as Abraham or Rahab, will contend for the faith. Such work indicates life.]

JAMES - CHAPTER THREE

3.1   My brethren, be not many masters, knowing that we shall receive the greater condemnation.

[James warns against the very human aspiration to stand on the stage before the adoring crowd. Well, that's not exactly what he says. He warns that we should not simply desire the office of a teacher of religion. We should accept that office only when the Lord thrusts it upon us. The assumption of the office of preacher, teacher, leader, etc. within the Christian community carries with it a strong responsibility.

Notice that I did not say that we are strong as we take part in these offices. We must always keep in mind our weakness and spiritual unsuitability. This attitude, actually "this realization," may serve to keep us humble so that all eyes will look past ourselves and find the Savior we all must serve.

Much was made of the word "master." The word thus translated could well have been rendered as "teacher." Since in time of which James was writing the teacher would have been deferentially referred to as "Master," this is not a mistranslation. It is an accurate rendering of the sense of the situation wherein James was writing.

In the context of the verse this word "master" is more accurate than would have been simply "teacher." The context sees those who would usurp the office of teacher in order to use this authority to judge and to censure those who were beneath them in knowledge. Within this consideration we may see that these men were attempting to become "master" of the flock of God.

This also sounds suspiciously akin to my understanding of the Gnostics which sought to change the truth of God into a lie. (Romans 1:25)

There are many masters within the churches. Some of these do not understand the Truth, themselves. These will lead others astray. At one time I would teach that God would not have preserved His Words to man. I would teach that it was only the providence of man that our combined intellect had "reconstituted" that message which had become so muddled.

In this I am certain that I led some astray from finding true faith in the inspired and preserved Words of God. It is only a short walk from that neighborhood to the cathedral where the worship of God is unnecessary. An easy reasoning is that if God could not protect and preserve His Own message to man, it is obvious that He less than powerful. This reasoning has led to a situation where we have so many "versions" of what God might have said, each version differing from the others in order to sanctify their individual copyrights, that we have been left with no Bible we can fully trust unless we shift our doctrine from the "verbal and plenary" inspiration of an earlier time to the "concept" inspiration of today's expert.

Don't worry about the use of Galatians 3:16 where the argument of Paul is centered upon the tense of a single word. After all, we can just change that doctrine when we find a human need to do so in the eyes of the experts. The rest of the "sheep" will follow compliantly. Sadly, this is the poor state of so many churches in this "post-Christian" age. I might add the obvious connection to the concept of a "post-Christian" age and the reality of a "post-Bible" age of competing "versions." We have been bombarded with so many "bibles" that we have no "Bible."

There are also many who have appointed themselves to be "masters." They expect to be followed simply because they are endowed with the "title" of Rev., or Dr., for a first name. From such have come many soul-damning cults of the spiritually doomed.

Some have been appointed by others. My son had a school teacher who was convinced that he should become a pastor because his father was one. There is a long and sad history of people who have "gotten into the family business" and done horrible harm to the cause of Christ. We need go no further than Abimelech, a son of Gideon. Gideon was a judge of Israel. His son "improved" upon that; he reigned as a king in Israel for three years. (Judges 9:22)

This was not of God. It was Abimelech's self-imposed "destiny." He died "in office" but brought great harm into Israel during his time of usurpation.

This is the outcome of these "false masters." They bring harm to the churches and people with their (self) service. Condemnation is the course of this river of deceit. The need of the churches is not necessarily to have a form of sound doctrine but a sanctified leadership, approved and provided by the Hand of God, to lead them into this sound doctrine.

I like cinnamon rolls. When I was young at one time I lived very near a bakery. Every morning I would walk into the bakery and get a cup of coffee and two fresh, warm, cinnamon rolls. The total cost was a quarter for all. It was quite a few days ago!

A friend told me that I could control my "blood sugar" with cinnamon. I have been eating two of these rolls with every meal. It doesn't seem to be helping.

The point of the story? Good things, such as good doctrine, really are good. When someone has appropriated those good things and added to the "cinnamon" his own wants and needs the finished product may not be at its optimum strength. Even "good doctrine" may not be a proper medicine for the spiritual life of the people of God when the prescription has been altered by one who is not the truly called of God to dispense that truth.

Bad doctrine, of course, is worse. But there is a leaven of bad doctrine when the good doctrine is brought by a man who is not authorized of God to stand before God's people as an under-shepherd. It is the leaven of pride and disrespect for the calling of God.

James puts himself in the class of "master." But, he lumps the false in with the true under the heading of "responsibility." Properly considered the place of ministry is not a place of power or performance. It is a place of awesome responsibility.

All of us will fail to be, and to do, all that we should be and do. We remain fallible human beings; we are simple sinners who have been saved by grace. But, those whose only reason for being called "master" is their own "professional choice," will unfailingly lead others astray in their pride and prejudice of personal glory. Human desire, even when coupled with devotion, is not the entire formula for leadership. This does not produce unction. True unction is a gift from God bestowed only upon the work of those whom He has called for their task.

We will all be judged by the Lord. The heavier judgment comes to the one who has led others, even into the paths of righteousness. Being led into those paths of righteousness is only Scriptural when it is for "his name's sake." (Psalm 23:3) God searches the thoughts and intents of the heart. (Hebrews 4:12)

Leading into the paths of righteousness for **MY** names sake is not exactly the same. Pride not only goeth before a fall (Proverbs 16:18), it also goeth before as a press agent to explain how great I am. This is not the attitude of one honestly called of God. The heaviest judgment will come to the one who has held the call of God to the office of teacher outside the known will of God. James makes it a warning. God makes it a promise.

For myself, I know that I would refuse to stand in any pulpit unless God gave me no other choice. I have resisted that position until the irresistible call of God made that choice the only one He would allow. I wanted to set sail for Tarshish. He gave me a ticket for Nineveh. His sovereignty far outweighs my fear of responsibility. If one is to find the chastisement of the Lord it is much preferable that this chastisement lead to obedience.]

3.2 *For in many things we offend all. If any man offend not in word, the same is a perfect man, and able also to bridle the whole body.*

[This could be argued as a statement that if we offend in many things we are guilty of offending in all things. This would be true under the assumption of James 1:10-11, where the entire Law is seen as one Law. To offend in even one point is to have broken the "bottle" of the Law in its entirety.

I won't argue against that consideration. It is a true consideration but a poor exegesis. The meaning is that we all "stumble," or fail to walk circumspectly, from time to time.

Then we come to the argument that if any man is able to not offend, stumble, in word he is perfect. We tie this in, obviously, with the verse immediately preceding, "...be not many masters..." As we have already seen these "masters" were teachers of the flock. Therefore the "words spoken" of verse two would primarily be doctrinal in manner. Considering that the word "perfect" carries with it the meaning of completeness or maturity, we can see that this does not speak of any perfection within the man, but a maturity of doctrine in that he would lead none astray.

But, there is another consideration at work. That last phrase, "able also to bridle the whole body," gives an indication that this "perfection" goes far beyond simple ministerial speech and joins into discussion of the general life-style of that person. It is also obvious that this should be the practice of every "teacher" who takes it upon himself to stand before others and expound on the things of God.

Knowing myself, this is one of those "do as I say and not as I do" moments! To be brutally honest, if words could kill there would be a "vast multitude" of bodies littering my path through life. I do not say this as boast; I only say it as sad truth! It ought not to be!

Jesus said something in Matthew 15:18. The disciples had been walking through a field where they took of the grain and ate. The Pharisees argued that the disciples had broken the Law by not washing before eating. After some small discussion Jesus said, "But those things which proceed out of the mouth come forth from the heart; and they defile the man."

That which is within our hearts will color the content of our speech. We may try to regulate our speech but our true character will betray us with our own words. In the final result that which is within our heart will be that which, in an unguarded moment, will betray our true character before man.

One who has the strength of self-control to such an extent as to be able to control the content of his speech will be able to control the content of his actions. One who can control his tongue will also be able to control his hands, feet, eyes and ears, so that he does not sin in these manners. He is a mature and complete man.]

3.3 *Behold, we put bits in the horses' mouths, that they may obey us, and we turn about their whole body.*

[James does concede that the tongue is a small thing. But even small things can exert great influence. Sometimes these are good things; sometimes these are evil things. The Spurgeon Devotional Commentary compares the tongue to fire. "If it be fire from heaven it brings a Pentecost; if fire from hell it makes a Pandemonium."
The tongue left free can become a wild beast which flies about with uncontrollable fury and rage. The horse is a powerful and spirited animal. Men put small bridles within the horse's mouth. These small bridles will control the horse and unleash his unbridled fury into useful work as the beast follows the bidding of man.
William Burkitt speaks of God using both the spur and the bridle on the beast of humanity. "The grace of God is both spur and bridle to the tongue of man: Grace, like a spur, provokes to speak for God, and for the good of others; and grace, like a bridle, stops us from speaking what may grieve the Spirit of God, and justly offends others." With the spur God will cause us to speak and act according to His Will. With the bridle God will inhibit useless and harmful speech as He gives direction to our daily path.]

3.4 *Behold also the ships, which though they be so great, and are driven of fierce winds, yet are they turned about with a very small helm, whithersoever the governor listeth.*

[Here James moves from the consideration of the natural forces of nature to the devices of man. The comparison of the horse gives way to the comparison of the ship of the sea.

It took a small bridle to harness the energy and power of the horse so that it could be useful to man. The ship is much larger than the horse. The ship has the intelligence of a human designer to prepare it for useful endeavor. Still, the winds of God can cause the sails of the ship to take it into other than useful directions.

Those fierce winds can even drive the ship into an untimely destruction. The bottom of lakes and ocean are littered with the best devices of man. The power of God overcame the pretension of man and drove the ships to the bottom of the water.

Ah, but God has given man the rudder of free will. The power of the wind can often be overturned by the skillful use of the rudder. Ports of safety can be found and entered. There may be an anchor – again a comparatively small thing – which allows the ships to "ride out" a storm even when they cannot reach the port.

None of these are part of the consideration of James. All of our naturalistic boasts and considerations are not in view at this point. They are overridden by the simple understanding of the basic intents and purposes of God. Man plans and schemes; God either allows or disallows according to His Own good favor.

The illustration of James is based in the consideration of the tongue as a small member which can cause great commotion as it finds its own path. It may even seek passage in direct opposition to the winds of the Spirit.

James asks that we seek to control our tongues, that small rudder, with the helm of faith. The power which God has available for our lives is far more than the power of the storms of life which seek to sink our self-constructed ships. May we use our tongue, that great and powerful small instrument, as tool sanctified to God. May we find the port of Heavenly direction.]

3.5 *Even so the tongue is a little member, and boasteth great things. Behold, how great a matter a little fire kindleth!*

[The tongue is quite small when compared with the rest of the body. But, as the bridle in the mouth of a horse or the rudder when compared to the ship, are small it is these which cause the entire "body" of beast or boat to follow its will rather than their own. So is the tongue among men. Though small it is a controlling instrument.

"Give me liberty or give me death," when uttered by Patrick Henry was not a request for a prize but a spark that helped to give birth to the fire of rebellion. The simple rhetoric of "sunshine soldier and summer patriot" was not a call to consider the weather but to pledge oneself to a cause. Benjamin Franklin's use of "We must all hang together or we shall all hang separately," was not a short simile but a solemn warning to those signing the Declaration of Independence.

The tongue has the ability to either inspire to a great cause or to demean to an ungodly path.

Is it any wonder that God sent "tongues of fire" upon the infant Church in order to light a flame of witness which is not quenched unto this day. In many places this fire has grown cold as it has not been properly tended. In many places this fire has faded to a few embers as it awaits a refilling. In many places this fire has continued to burn with the blood of martyrs. But, this fire continues its advance of flame and fuel into the dark and cold nights of a world which longs for the warmth of the Son of God in their hearts.

My son has a "fire pit." He often cooks over this pit in the summer. I have seen that he will put dry brush and small twigs into this pit. He lights these small things. When these begin to "flame up" he will add larger logs to obtain a hotter and longer lasting fire.

The tongue is that kindling. It sends forth a spark of emotion into the forest of man. Sometimes this leads to a noble reaction among the hearers. Sometimes the fire so kindled is destructive. Testimonies and even homes and churches are burned out by the force of the heat of the fire of the tongues of boastful men.]

3.6 *And the tongue is a fire, a world of iniquity: so is the tongue among our members, that it defileth the whole body, and setteth on fire the course of nature; and it is set on fire of hell.*

[The tongue is compared to a fire. That is an interesting phrase because fire often stands for the righteous judgment of God. Could we argue that the tongue will often judge others, as James argues especially in the first chapter of this epistle, with the judgment of man? In such a case should we not argue that the man doing that judgment has usurped the position of God, Who Alone is the Judge of men?

I must admit that I find that situation to be in the verse. But, that is a secondary consideration. Primarily James seems to be talking about how the tongue can cause great destruction in its misuse.

I take this concept back a few years. I received a telephone call from the local Mormon Church. They asked that the church I was pastoring take part with them in some sort of civic venture. I refused. They asked my reason for refusal as this was a reasonable civic venue. My answer was, if I recall the words exactly – and I do! "We cannot join with you in anything at all. We worship the God of Heaven and you worship demons from Hell."

Folks, I stand by the reasoning of what I said but I greatly regret that I said it in such an unchristian manner. Here was an opportunity for witness and I allowed my tongue to turn it into an attack. My witness will never, unless the Lord intercede, again be useful with any local Mormon. Worse, my words gave them fuel to "bunker" into their misguided theology of multiple gods and rejection of the historic Words of God.

This is the type, and there are many more examples, of the havoc wreaked upon others by the unbridled tongue.

That is just in the religious sense. Many more examples could be culled from the political and social realms. Unsanctified speech can cause ripples to roll across the river of life until it floods the towns and villages of humanity with sorrow and hurt. Wars may even result from the unbridled speech of even otherwise good men.

This is not only so in respect to the world of man. Unthoughtful and unrestrained speech can even cause harm in the world of the churches which name the Name of Jesus Christ. I have found it true that most "church splits" are not over doctrinal matters. If they were I could applaud most of them. Those splits are often accompanied by the sad use of unkind words between two people who draw factions about themselves.

The tongue is a small member among our bodies but it causes our entire bodies to be drawn into areas of actions that are most certainly not honoring to the Christ we claim to love and follow.

By oratory, the use of the tongue, and editorial, the use of the word processor as a surrogate tongue, great upheavals of society are effected. Death and destruction occur in the cities of the world by people who are influenced by words. I have heard that Abraham Lincoln, upon meeting Harriet Beecher Stowe, the author of "Uncle Tom's Cabin," said, "So, you are the lady whose little book started this great big war."

Again, many more examples could be cited. Hitler wrote "Mien Kompf." In that book the soon-to-be dictator outlines his plan for purging German society. Others, either swayed by his words or frightened by his words, allowed his plan to be exactly carried out.

Words may be either good or evil. They are not always "just words," as they spread the germ of their seed into society and find the flower of fruition to grow. Their plant may give the shade of refreshment to some. Their plant may just as often block the sun of reason from others.

A misspoken word may color the future opportunities of our lives. These words may become an obstruction in the road of our lives; they may necessitate changes we had not anticipated. They may block paths. They may cause us to rise above the challenges we have set to ourselves and allow us to rise above our limitations. They will only rarely be seen as neutral in our lives paths.

It has been said that the devil is the "gift giver" of the use of a bad tongue. We

JAMES: Chapter 3

ought never to allow Satan to become master of any organ of our lives. As Christians these organs ought to be dedicated the Lord Who has loved us and shown us grace. "Neither yield ye your members as instruments of unrighteousness unto sin: but yield yourselves unto God, as those that are alive from the dead, and your members as instruments of righteousness unto God." (Romans 6:13)]

3.7   *For every kind of beasts, and of birds, and of serpents, and of things in the sea, is tamed, and hath been tamed of mankind:*

[James is drawing attention to the fact that man has, by ingenuity or strength, subdued the animals of creation. This is in answer to the ancient prophecy which God gave upon the creation of Adam. "And God blessed them, and God said unto them, Be fruitful and multiply, and replenish the earth, and subdue it: and have dominion over the fish of the sea, and over the fowl of the air, and over every living that moveth upon the earth." (Genesis 1:28)

Indeed, every "kind," genus, of living being has been subdued by man. The fierce lion will be seen to perform under the direction of man. The dolphin of the sea thrills thousands with his exploits at sea shows. At one time my son had an "ant farm." This may not seem fully as a "subjection;" but, what else could it be as the ants tunnel and feed for the amusement of a child. Even the free-flying bird has been tamed. Consider the ariel displays of the hawks were once used to hunt "game." The canine, the bear, the great cats, these all have their place to play among the families of man.

Those which man has not subdued in training have been subdued as they have become food for man. Many of those subdued, cow, pig, sheep, etc. are also used as food for mankind.

Only the tongue has man not subdued or taken control over. It remains an unruly thing in our lives. It also remains a danger to the man who "owns" it as his lack of control will often cause deep regret and sorrow.

As a person who has just taken two kittens into the house, I might add that I am not certain that we can claim these as trained of man. They don't admit to being trained. They figure that they will train us! Even within their seeming independence, cats are useful for keeping our homes free of vermin. Their "cuddly" nature will also bring joy and peace to an old person's heart on a cold winter night.]

3.8   *But the tongue can no man tame; it is an unruly evil, full of deadly poison.*

[Hidden in the mouth behind rows of teeth and the skin of the cheeks, the tongue lies in wait to attack its prey. James appears to be considering the serpent of the former verse as he gives evidence to the attack of the tongue. The tongue of the serpent, darting in and out in search of a target, is noticed until the poison of the teeth find the mark.

The serpents tongue can argue, "I didn't do anything. It was the teeth that did the damage." Adam said, "It was this woman you gave me." In effect Adam blamed God for his own sin. "It was the serpent that beguiled me," Eve whined. So down through the ages men and woman have used their tongues, the very instruments of so much evil, to give excuse for their own sins.

The animals of creation have either been subdued or domesticated, or they have been used for food. The tongue? Not so much! No one has ever been completely successful at subduing his own tongue. The vile in his heart will surface from time to time. How often have we heard these words from a politician's mouth, either "I was misquoted" or "I misspoke?"

The tongue is an unruly, restless and prone to strike out on its own agenda, evil which has both begun and ended politician's careers. The tongue has also been moved to an excess of animosity towards the one who should have been the object of witness; it has, from the human standpoint, pushed the souls of humanity into the horror of an eternal Hell.

James urges us to bridle our tongues that we may speak no evil. Both Peter and Paul concur with this truth. (Titus 3:2; I Peter 3:10) A good horseman will also have reins by which he may harness an animal so it can perform a task. As our tongues are bridled, may they also be put into the yoke of God that they may be sanctified for His service. This is His Work we are asked to join into. This is our responsibility given us by the Lord of our lives. This is the desperate need of the world as they play follow-the-leader on the broad road to destruction without the witness to salvation given from the tongue of the redeemed.]

3.9 *Therewith bless we God, even the Father; and therewith curse we men, which are made after the similitude of God,*

[The "imperial we" suggests a situation where James includes himself among those who are thus "double-tongued." However, if we consider the "we" to be the "editorial we," the meaning would shift from James as a partner to James as a reporter of the genetic situation where men would act in such a manner. I find both.

The first "we" is to speak well of, or to praise. The second use of "we" is to speak cruelly of someone. I would see the first as "imperial" as it is speaking of Christian men in general, James included. Only the Christian can truly praise God for only the Christian has the new nature which allows him to approach the throne of Grace. (Hebrews 4:16)

The second use of "we" is editorial in that it is speaking of mankind in the general sense. The Christian is included in this; although, this inclusion is to the Christian's shame. All men, generally speaking, will speak ill of others. The carnal Christian will do this out of the evil, unpurged, of his heart even while his spirit will praise God in sincerity.

If we read just John 3:16 we will find the attitude of God toward His creation of humanity. As Christians, those to whom this epistle was written, we ought to love that which God loves, the lost humanity for whom Christ died, and to hate that which God hates, the sin which so easily besets us and separates humanity from God.

When my wife was in high school she took an accounting course where the instructor gave only two grades – "A" or "F." Of course, these averaged out over a semester. But, the argument was that in accounting we are either right or we are wrong. I believe that the classroom of God uses the same rational. Hate for the sinner and his sin merits an "F" concerning our obedience toward God. Love for the sinner and love for his sin merits the same "F." Only a love for the sinner with a concordant hatred for the sin which binds that sinner will merit the favor of the "A" of God upon our lives.

"...which are made after the similitude of God," echoes the words of Genesis

1:26 where God is said to have made man in His Own image. God is spirit while man is primarily physical. Therefore, this cannot be a physical likeness. It is rather our innate creativity in our tasks, our capacity for love, our enjoyment of the beauty of creation – these things and more are given us in the likeness of the God Who created us. To hate humanity who, even within the distorted and mangled manner which sin has left mankind still has the similarity of attributes as does God within the perfections of His Own perfect manner, is to garner a hatred toward God.

The sin of racism and class hatred also exhibits a hatred for God. The argument there is that God was either evil or unthinking when He created certain peoples. The concept of hatred toward others is a sin that ought to be confessed and overcome. Heaven will be peopled, to use the term loosely, with all manner of humanity. The only unifying factor is that each person in Heaven is loved of God. It was the blood of Christ which saved each soul.]

3.10 *Out of the same mouth proceedeth blessing and cursing. My brethren, these things ought not so to be.*

[I Corinthians 5:6 is an interesting verse: "Your glorying is not good. Know ye not that a little leaven leaveneth the whole lump?" Is Paul actually suggesting in that place that there ought not to be glorying in the assembly? Of course not! In the previous few verses he had been addressing the sin of a member in that church. His argument is that this sin was harming the entire church. This is the leaven of sin. It grows and crowds out the rightful praising of God by the people.

The point is that we cannot rightly praise God while cursing another human being who is the creation of God. Remember that the focus in James is what the world will see of the Christian community. The way the Christian acts gives the world their view of what Christianity is all about.

Our understanding of creation is colored by our view of that creation. We see a great symmetry in nature. The stars and planets tend to keep to their orbits. The rivers and seas tend to keep to their bounds. When these bounds are breached it is generally because of some storm. Violent storms are a result of the sin of Adam (consider Romans 8:22) which has distorted the perfections of God's creation.

There is a lack of harmony in the scenario of the same tongue, or multiple tongues of humanity, which both praise and damn. That lack of harmony is itself a violation of the beauty of the creation of God.

"Brethren," so James calls his readers. "This should not be."

It most definitely should not be among the recipients of this epistle. They were supposed to be followers of Christ. It is impossible that one following Christ would follow Him into error!]

3.11 *Doth a fountain send forth at the same place sweet water and bitter?*

[Jesus is the "Living Water." James argues that even natural springs do not give both good and polluted water. We had a well when I was very young. It never occurred to me that we also lived just a few blocks from the city dump. Were we getting good water from our well? Well, it never killed me. Still, I can't really believe that this was the best water possible. Maybe it was; I am no expert in such matters.

James is an expert in the matters of the religion of Jesus. He said, in effect, you can't offer the world the "Living Water" of Jesus when you carry it in a foul and dirty bucket. The world isn't going to accept it!

The city where I am sitting as I write receives its water from the Mississippi River. Along the flow of the river there are many pollutants added to the water from factory, farm and village. We obtain the water from many feet below the bottom of the river. Rocks, sand, earth, etc. all have their part in filtering out these pollutants before the water arrives into our pumping stations. Man-made purifications are provided both there and at the city when the water comes to town.

If this town spends so much time and money in purifying water for cooking, bathing, drinking and so forth, how much more should we guard the polluting effect of our tongues as we disperse the water of life into a thirsty world? If this actually is a question the answer is "to the best of our prayerful efforts!"

Speaking of the incongruity of sweet and bitter water, in consideration of sweet and bitter speech from the Christian, Doddridge has said, "It is not known in the natural, and it ought not to be known in the moral, world."

Of this verse Garner has observed, "The very nature of the question affirms that it is inconsistent for a child of God to spew forth from his mouth a flow of any conversation that would be offensive to God or contradictory to his new nature, which is to have control over his body, Galatians 5:25; 1 John 3:18."]

3.12   Can the fig tree, my brethren, bear olive berries? either a vine, figs? so can no fountain both yield salt water and fresh.

[Barnes returns to James consideration of one who would appoint himself as a "master" over the people of God. He, Barnes, argues that the illustrations of these past few verses expand on the "why" of James assertions. It is obvious that these verses, "show the power of the tongue; they show what a dangerous power it is for a man to wield who has not the proper qualifications; they show that no one should put himself in the position where he may wield this power without such a degree of tried prudence, wisdom, discretion, and piety, that there shall be a moral certainty that he will use it aright."

This Book of James goes far to explain that a novice, one untrained and untested in the faith, should only within the direct and certain leading of God, ever be accepted as a pastor in any church of The True and Living God. (II Timothy 3:6) This same thing must be said of any who has been tried, trained, tested and found lacking in the graces of the fruits of the spirit.

The pulpit or lectern is never the place for a person to glorify themselves. Any lack in the speaker will fail to glorify God. That is not a maxim; that is a bitter and Biblical reality!

At one time Linda and I had an arbor of sweet and delicious grapes. Then our grapes were invaded with "wild" grapes. These were grapes but they were not the ones I wanted to pick off the vine and eat! Our arbor became useless and has been removed. So also, has been the fate of pastors and churches whose dalliance in the world of emotional excess overshadowed their commitment to the Lord. Oh, the buildings and the crowds may remain. But, the honest influence for the salvation of souls and the building up of the saints has suffered to the point of near, and often complete, extinction.

It is true that there have been engrafting's of one type of fruit to another vine. After all, we Christians are an engrafted vine into the pure worship of Jehovah. We are not of the natural stock of Israel. But, any engrafted vine will continue to produce its own fruit. It will not produce two types of fruit from the same vine.

No fountain will give, at least in its natural state untampered by man, both good and salt water. Neither should our discourse which purports to supply the unvarnished truth of the Gospel cover any other. Philosophy is not bad; but it is useless for Christian training unless it can be shown to have Biblical purpose. Culture is a handy "short hand" for Christian teaching; but it is less than useless when it is at variance with the Words of God. The morality of the Scripture of God does not change with generational influence. The Words of God are the only Words of Authority despite the protestations of man.]

3.13 *Who is a wise man and endued with knowledge among you? let him shew out of a good conversation his works with meekness and wisdom.*

[James is looking for a wise man. He isn't looking for just any wise man; he wants a wise man that is endued with knowledge. The wisdom of man would turn this order around. Man would look for a knowledgeable man who happened to be wise.

There is a reason that James inverts the order. Knowledge is a good thing. We can go to school and gain knowledge. We can study and gain knowledge. We can listen intently and gain knowledge. There are too many "we's" in those sentences.

Knowledge is a work of man. A work of man tends to produce pride. Pride in a man tends to lower his trust in God. To put it bluntly, a lack of trust in God is a pretty stupid track to take. Like the rich man trusting in his riches, the knowledgeable man will trust his knowledge. He believes that he has everything all figured out.

From men such as this have come the many "bibles" we have littering the shelves at our campus book stores even in our "fundamentalist" institutions. Our reasoned opinion is that God was not able to preserve the Words of His inspiration, therefore we must, in our knowledge, frame the dialogue to reclaim them.

"Reclaim them?" These are the Words which God gave to humanity. But, they remain the Words of God. How can we revise the perfect Words of God in order to exalt the words of man's choosing?

Wisdom, James tells us a few verses later, comes from God. It is the wisdom to trust God which allows us to seek illumination from the Spirit. We have no need to rewrite the Bible. We do have a desperate need to reaffirm our allegiance to the inspired and preserved Words of God has given to us. This is true wisdom in Scriptural study.

If I didn't know better I would assume that James had watched the old "Dragnet" shows from 1950s television. I can hear the staccato of Jack Webb in the writing of James: "Just the facts." He has already said, "If you have faith, prove it to me with your works." Now he says, "If you have real, Godly, wisdom, prove it to me with your manner of life.

James asks for a life of wisdom and meekness. Sometimes we get the idea that meekness is a synonym for spineless. It isn't. Numbers 12:3 tells us, "(Now the man Moses was very meek, above all the men which were upon the face of the earth.)"

One day this very meek man, Moses, was up on Mt. Sinai. He had just received two tablets written upon by the finger of God. All that was required of Moses was that he read the tablets to the people of Israel. Then Moses heard the sounds of celebration coming from the camp of Israel.

Moses had spent forty days in communion with God on the top of that mountain. When he returned to the camp he found the people had begun to worship a golden calf. It was like the idols of Egypt from which God had just led these people. Worse, the bother of Moses, the priest appointed by God, had fashioned the idol.

Moses smashed those two tablets, written by God, on the ground and broke them into pieces. Moses did discipline the people for their transgression. Aaron was also disciplined for this transgression.

Moses, meanwhile, had to walk back up the mountain. "God, did you keep any carbon copies of those laws you gave me?" Moses had broken every one of those Ten Commandments in one act of anger. He had to prepare two new tablets which God, in His graciousness, gave to Moses.

The point is that meekness is an important part of the personality of any teacher of the people of God. He must continue to understand his place, in humility, as a servant of the Most High. But, when it comes to violations against the Person and Perfections of God, there is a need to "man up," and "stand up," for the doctrine and principles of God. Jude 3 reminds us, "Beloved, when I gave all diligence to write unto you of the common salvation, it was needful for me to write unto you, and exhort you that ye should earnestly contend for the faith which was once delivered unto the saints."

Our meekness and humility extends from a proper view of ourselves as merely clay on the Heavenly Potter's wheel. We are His. We are nothing in comparison to Him. We are merely allowed to impart the Words on those Tablets of His writing.

Our backbone of faith allows us to hear His call to move out in faith. "Every place that the sole of your foot shall tread upon, that have I given unto you, as I said unto Moses." (Joshua 1:3) Our duty as emissaries of The Lord into the world of man demands that we move into that world with the important message that Jesus Christ died in time so that others could live in eternity.

Our works show to others that reality of our faith. Our meekness, humility and love for our fellow man show the reality of wisdom from God within our lives and witness. Simple knowledge without wisdom is useless prattle. Wisdom frees us from our own weakness and allows us to show forth the power of God into a world in need.]

3.14 *But if ye have bitter envying and strife in your hearts, glory not, and lie not against the truth.*

[Do we have envy? Is it a bitter envy? Is there any other kind of envy except that which is so bitter that it keeps us up a night with plans of revenge? I look at the world in which we live and decry the bitterness with which the worldly culture condemns us. Or do I look with envy that our enemies are so lauded in the same culture?

I honestly don't think that the above is the type of envy of which James spoke. I believe that the bile of envy is toast against the muffin of the brethren. We, proudly the "fighting 'fundies,'" we excoriate a brother who wears a blue suit into the pulpit when we believe he ought to wear a red suit. The time is well past when we are to stand with those who stand with us rather than to fight with those who are nigh ready to fight with us.

I am not saying that we give up doctrinal purity. This we cannot do if we are to be true to our Lord.

There is often envy directed toward the pastor of the larger church from the pastor of the small church. You know that this is true; it's just never mentioned. It would be unseemly. Folks, who cares if the field of your labor is sixty souls or six hundred, or six thousand... The point is that if we believe that we are where the Lord has placed us, isn't that all that is important?

Envy, especially bitter envy, is an acid that eats at the soul. We allow this to rob us of the peace which Christ has given us. Envy, especially bitter envy, is a cataract upon the eyes of the soul. We allow this to rob us of the vision which the Lord has for us in the place where He has planted us. We look for the next larger church. Does this mean that we are unhappy with the task given where we are? Do we "short change" the needs of this congregation because we seek to find the next larger? Do we truly do the best we possibly can for the Lord, or do we look only to "professional advancement?"

Bitter envy leads to strife. Do we seek to hold down the emotional cry of our church because we want to be known as "builders" and "conciliators" of the brethren? Are we attempting to fill out our resume, or are we attempting to build up the body in the Lord?

Dangerous questions?

May we never claim to be "Super Christian," when we are "searching Christian." The position of our hearts should never be to give lie to the truth within those hearts. I know that "Mulder and Scully" claim that "The Truth is out there." Folks, the truth is in our hearts. May our hearts always be true to God and His work to which He has called us. ...wherever and whatever that may be!]

3.15 *This wisdom descendeth not from above, but is earthly, sensual, devilish.*

[James says that this sort of wisdom, as described in verse fourteen, is not of God. This is a wisdom that is of the earth. At first glance that may sound reasonable until we realize that the earth is a sin-stained and contaminated entity which is not of God. It is in a spiritual rebellion against God.

It may well be that earth is the creation of God. But, earth was given over to sin when Adam, the "federal head" of the earth gave it unto sin. When the living things of the earth were given into the hand of Adam he became their head in an honest spiritual consideration. When Adam was made in the *image* of God, part of that included the dominion over those living things and the "under shepherd," as it were, of all creation.

God did not give up His ultimate rule and control of creation but He did put Adam, as steward of that creation, in a place of responsibility. Thus, in the sin of Adam, as the old catechism says, "in Adam all men sinned." The deadly "gene" of sin has been passed down from Adam unto his offspring into all of the world down through the years of time.

Not only this, the sin of Adam also infected the entire creation of God with the imperfection and distortion of sin. Romans 8:22 explains the result upon all creation because of the sin of Adam. "For we know that the whole creation groaneth and travaileth in pain together until now." Thus, anything which is earthy, of creation, cannot be spiritual unless sanctified by the Lord.

Since Eve was fashioned from Adam, and yet before the sin of Adam, she has not inherited this male transmitted gene. Eve was not given the same mandate as was Adam in regards to his position in creation. From this basic understanding we are shown that all men, from Adam on, carries the burden of the inherited sin of all humanity. Only the Savior, born of a virgin and not infected with this sin gene, was completely free from both inherited and active sin.

Eve, of course, is guilty of her own sin. But, her position did not allow her to transmit the infection of her sin into future generations. Therefore, the seed of the woman (Genesis 3:15) was a fit candidate to be the entryway for Jesus to become fully human while being fully perfect as God, the Son, and for Him to also be completely free from sin.

That which is earthly, from the earth, has the taint of sin upon it. The "wisdom of man," as shown by verse fourteen is a sin encrusted wisdom which cannot be of Heavenly origin. It is not simply neutral but diametrically opposed to the wisdom of God. The actions born out from the use of earthly wisdom bear out this assessment.

Under this heading we also find that this wisdom of man is sensual. That is, it is opposed to the spiritual constraints and powers of the Heavenly wisdom which comes from God. It is of the spirit of this world, which is sold unto sin and lawlessness.

Such "wisdom," as from verse fourteen, does not glorify God but tends to glorify the creations of God, especially humanity. Since these have been sullied by sin, the result is a genre of results which include pride and self-service. Even the best examples of altruism among men are found to be works of pride encased in the outward show of selfless service on behalf of the creature of creation.

It is an expression of the animal life which has not be sanctified by the breath of life in the nostrils of created humanity.

With this realization we see that such wisdom, although wisdom but not of God, is a wisdom which is "devilish." It is not, and it cannot be, hallowed as a working of, or for, God. As with most of the deceptions of Satan, this wisdom may produce what man would call "good" works but the results of these works would not be to the glory of God or the salvation of man.]

3.16 For where envying and strife is, there is confusion and every evil work.

[James had spoken of the root of envy and strife. The seed had been a wisdom that was earthly – of sin! The plant that grew from the root of this seed was confusion and evil work. Since James had been speaking of teachers in the church I feel it not amiss to consider this in the light of "church politics."

I find most of the "grunt work," to use a military analogy, is done by the smaller churches. Still so many of the larger churches will shout from the rooftops of their great programs for the Christian. All too often these larger churches had taken many of their members from the smaller churches. I have seen this. I have been involved in seeking out "motivated" Christians to increase the flock even at the churches I have pastored.

This is generally, even when I have been involved a wrong thing to do.

Still, I do not think it wrong for a family, especially with children, to move their attendance to a place where the children will be encouraged in the Lord. I do not think it wrong for adults to move their attendance to a church which offers more opportunity to grow in the Lord.

But, this last point is the "sticking point." The larger church will of necessity offer fewer opportunities for the individual to sharpen his own talents for the Lord. To sit in an active assembly is a great benefit. Only so many will be allowed the chance to do actual "work" for the Lord in such a place. There is but one lectern for the teacher. Are the many seats filled with true workers for the Lord? Or, are the many seats filled with "fans" of the teacher?

Now, let's be honest. Could that not be the "sour grapes" of envy speaking on my part? Is the complaint a matter of a lack of humility on my part? To be completely honest, I cannot give an impartial answer to that question. Since I am looking from my perspective, my vision could very well be clouded with the "cataract" of self-pride and hurt feelings.

We must not let the flowers of envy mature into further seeds of strife. We have no reason to react amiss towards those of like faith. We should not attempt to "glean" a field where another is harvesting – even if the harvest is felt to be of "our" field. Our considerations must never fall into arguments with other churches of like faith. While we may consider ourselves to be among those "fighting 'fundies," our "fight," if it be such, is never with the message of the Gospel or with those who are finding the truths of Scripture.

Jude 3 speaks of fighting for the truth of the Gospel. If a cultist has ensnared one of our members in the satanic web of false doctrine, we have a duty to confront and correct. Our only duty to a sister church, of the same Lord, is to pray for their increase. Our pride is not at issue. Our piety is the issue. Our love belongs to our Lord rather than to our attendance board.

I have spoken at Bible conferences where the issue was somewhat contentious. "Stephen Decatur, in 1812, returned from a victorious battle at sea and was feted in New York and Washington. He said, at a dinner party, 'Our country! In her intercourse with foreign nations, may she always be in the right; but our country, right or wrong.'" (Quoted from "Yahoo Answers")

Our contentiousness needs to never be upon anyone else's true Christian witness. Such an attitude, and many of us – I make use of an "imperial 'we'" to my shame – fail in our zeal to hold a position of preference masquerading it as an article of faith. Our Lord is never wrong even though He has chosen many for His kingdom with whom I disagree.

Christian fractionalization is seen as strife. People other than just us have read the Bible. Consider an unsaved person reading John 13:34, 35; 15:12, 17; Romans 12:10; 15:8; Galatians 5:13; Ephesians 4:2; I Thessalonians 3:2; 4:9; Hebrews 10:24; I Peter 1:22; 3:8; I John 3:11; 23; 4:7; 11; 12;   II John 1:5.

Any unsaved person reading these verses and then listening, not even very carefully listening, to some of our sermons, Bible Conferences; writings, and, sadly, even our prayers may just be led to believe that we do not even believe the Bible we preach. Why should he accept our words of witness?

How often is it necessary for the Spirit to say the same thing before we begin to obey?

Think about it. Pray about it. Envy and strife, according to James – and he was putting down the inspired Words of God as he wrote – is the work of Satan. We may spend hours in the study and exegesis of the Scripture. The question must still be asked: "Who are you working for?"

James argues that our walk determines the view others have of our faith. The view which they have determines the validity and value of our witness.]

3.17 *But the wisdom that is from above is first pure, then peaceable, gentle, and easy to be intreated, full of mercy and good fruits, without partiality, and without hypocrisy.*

[At this place James begins to speak of the wisdom that is of God. The anthropomorphism "above" marks this as from the throne of God. This is in counter distinction to the devilish wisdom of humanity as revealed in verse 14 – 16 which is described as "earthly" in verse 15.

The first thing about Godly wisdom is that it is pure. That is the element in which the wisdom of God will operate. Where the mind is pure, the heart will bear out this purity in the manner of living. When the life is purely set upon the things of God there is no room for the pettiness of pride. This leads to a consistent devotion to God. The person thus disposed to live will begin to see others with the love which God has toward them. This, in turn, produces an innocent relationship both toward and with humanity.

Notice how this purity of heart toward others contrasts Heavenly wisdom with the sensual, earthly, attitude toward others of the wisdom of lost humanity.

From the purity established it is a short walk to understand the peaceable relationship with others. Worldly wisdom leads to strife. Strife leads to argumentation. Argumentation leads to an inflexibility of notion among both sides of a question. This inflexibility of notion greatly diminished any witness about the Savior to the sinner.

Worldly wisdom leads to strife while the wisdom of God will lead to the giving of a witness toward Christ. There is a certain rationality within this situation. More important than this rationality is the spiritual production of a convicted heart as given by the Spirit. The wisdom of God allows His children to prepare fallow ground for the seed of the Spirit to plant the crop of salvation among humanity.

We are greatly honored by the God of All when we are given tasks, within His empowerment, in labor for Him.

From this peaceable condition we can advance a gentle nature which is unthreatening toward the object of our witness. With personal pride and agenda not an issue, we are able to be flexible with others of the household of faith. Rather than "defending" our ground, we are able to walk on the pathway which the Savior has given us to walk. If another points out the path, or warns of a snare within the path, we do not need to see this as an attack upon our "authority," as we realize that the Church is the "Body of Christ." We should realize, with Heavenly wisdom that the eye of another might be shown something we have missed. We praise God for His guidance even when it comes from another's reading of the map!

To be "entreated," or compliant to the leading of another in the Lord is to allow the Lord to work His will without our interference. A short caution: We do need to ascertain that the leading is of the Lord. With the wisdom from above we can examine rather than argue the point with a brother.

This attitude excludes envy as it encourages all to seek the Lord's leading. Guidance can be given, of course. But, this guidance must be in the nature of mercy. Mercy suggests compassion. This is a compassion which does not bend the bruised reed of another. A lack of compassion will quench the smoldering of an incipient "fire of zealousness" within another. A compassionate attitude will allow the Great Physician to heal the bruise and fan the flame of another into a burning desire within them and us to be like Jesus. (Matthew 12:20)

The point is that we have the need to stand for the Truth of God. An eye upon another as a rival to our personal authority is an indication that we are not moving in holy wisdom but in sensual wisdom which is not of God.

This is a merciful attitude which comes from the good "fruits" of the Spirit. These can only grow in our souls as we allow our souls to be buried from attitude of pride and watered with the tears of true piety which love the Lord above our own position and person.

James returns for a short sentence, once again, to the idea of impartiality. We never move beyond the basics. Two and two equals four every single time. "God so loved the world," is true every single time. We may move beyond the "milk of the word." It is good and necessary that we do so. But, we must never outgrow our need to consider that "milk" as foundational to our walk with the Lord. (I Peter 2:2)

Finally, we are cautioned against hypocrisy. "Do as I say and not as I do," is not a good attitude for us to cultivate. That is true even though I used that very phrase earlier in commentary in this Book of James. To admit a fault is a very good thing. To correct a fault is a necessary thing.

The importance is that we show to the world a consistent witness. We ought always, for the sake of our witness for the Lord, be what we claim and do what we ask of others. This in the negative is the very reason that many will claim there are too many hypocrites in the church. This does not give us cause to move from the church; this gives us instruction to live the life we preach.

We do not do this for ourselves and our authority. We do this as reasonable workers, as sanctified workers, as honest workers for the Lord. We owe this to Him Who gave everything for us.]

3.18 *And the fruit of righteousness is sown in peace of them that make peace.*

[He who lives consistently in the spiritual principle of divine wisdom will find peace in his heart (John 14:27) even during that time of trial wherein the world would argue panic and fear were desired responses.

A calm person in the midst of any crisis will give courage to others. This is so even in the natural order of men. How much greater can we expect a calm demeanor of the Spirit within a leader of the assembly to encourage and draw others of like faith to the trust of the Savior's promise.

Psalm 126:6 gives a promise from God to the people of God. "He that goeth forth and weepeth, bearing precious seed, shall doubtless come again with rejoicing, bringing his sheaves with him." Although this verse is "pre-cross," I think it not wrong to appropriate the truth to the Christian witness.

The Psalm was written during a time of captivity. There was a promise of joy given to the people even though they were under the captivity of a punishment from

God. As they looked toward Him and recalled His mercy towards them, the people were overcome with the joy of the Lord even during the chastisement of men upon their backs. Though in trial, these people brought with them the fruit of the joy of the Lord.

The tribulation of man can never quench the fire of the love of God among those that love him and have responded to the call to His service. That is the promise we find in the citation in James 3:18. When we walk in the wisdom of the Lord our lives will give witness to this fact. Our soul will find His peace. Our soul will spread the "seeds" of His peace as we give witness to His power and love. The tribulation and persecution of man are but a "moot point" when contrasted with the long, eternal, view of the glory of God and the glories He bestows upon His children.

The thrust of this chapter is that no one who does not give outward evidence of this inward peace can be a fit candidate to give counsel or teaching to the people of God.

The unambiguous impartiality shown to the group, or to individuals, under God will serve to bring peace among the brethren. In this will be established the cry of the angel of "peace on earth" and of goodwill among the men of God. This should start within the household of faith but it should spread, as much as is possible while holding to true doctrine, into the world as a witness of the love of God for the souls of the world. (John 3:16)

This is not "go along, get along." Such is the cry of the world. This is a plea to go along with God, holding pure to His doctrine. We try to "get along" with the world so far as is possible while holding fast to the purity of our witness of Him. Our speech should be Heavenly and distinct. We must be on guard to not speak in the "dialect" of devilish considerations. We need not seek to either harm or subdue. We seek to love others and to draw them to the Master.

Those, James argues, who do not exhibit peace toward others cannot exhibit true righteousness for the wisdom of God is lacking in their witness and life.]

JAMES - CHAPTER FOUR

4.1 *From whence come wars and fightings among you? come they not hence, even of your lusts that war in your members?*

[James asks where these energetic evils of destruction originate. He then answers his own question by noting that they come from inside a person. A couple of the commentaries I consulted argued that it was not necessary to lay all these sins upon the Christians to whom James wrote. The argument was that these things were evident in the world around the church.

I would suppose that the above is possible. After all, those Christians who walked in Godly wisdom would not find such as this among themselves. They, living in the world, would be "among" those who practiced these evils.

Then again, it would be completely unwise to argue that these things never happened among those who named the Name of Christ. Even a cursory examination of religious experience, to include the Christian and the "christian" groups, is to see wars, fightings, lusts and hatred are a staple of mankind's religious journeys.

Our prime example today is that of the Muslim Jihadists. The leaders, those who compel others to "follow" them, will never be so zealous as to sacrifice themselves. Their concept of religion is to kill others in the name of their god. It is interesting to note that, as has been throughout nearly all of history, the religious leadership will extol the glories of martyrdom among others but will shrink from such for themselves.

If we go back only a few decades we find that it was the Pope of Rome who was vilified by the Protestants. Those Protestants were vilified by the Pope. Both sides carried swords which they were not disposed to leave idle.

Our religious views are mirrored by King Richard, III, who is reported by Shakespeare to have said of the young princes that he loved them so much that he sent their souls early to Heaven.

There were wars and insurrections, many of them, against the Roman rule in the Holy Land at the time of James writing. These, too, were fueled by religious zeal among the Jews as they sought to clear the "Promised Land" of the Gentile. The Dome of the Rock stands upon the ruins of the Herodian Temple, which Jesus cleansed twice during His earthy ministry, as a testimony to the effectiveness of these wars of man.

James is showing the counter distinction of the wisdom of man (James 3:15) which is from the earthly. This is not the wisdom of God, which is from above. "But the wisdom that is from above is first pure, then peaceable, gentle, *and* easy to be intreated, full of mercy and good fruits, without partiality, and without hypocrisy." (James 3:17)

Under earthly wisdom, that apart from God, even religious zeal is destructive.

The "bottom line" origin of these enumerated evils is that they grow from the seed of lust. We want others to be in subjection to our determinations of culture. We want others to be in subjection to us as a people. We are benevolent in all this, of course. We are only doing this to "help" the "downtrodden." We love them so much that we would send their souls speedily to Heaven!

We want others to be in subjection to our religious views. I have even seen otherwise good fundamentalist churches, whose doctrine was decidedly Biblical and correct, exhibit extreme hatred toward any of the sheep of their "flock" who did not part their feathers on the correct side of their beak. This is a mixed metaphor that seems well considered among those who would use the good Truths of God not as a way to walk in the world but as a way to ignore the equally good truths of mercy and love.

In the natural we see very few "just wars." We do see many who just war with their neighbors. This is obviously not of God. It is of the spirit of the lusts which lie within the hearts of men. We are again reminded that in the sin of Adam the entire race of humanity fell under the dominion of sin. Thus the natural heart of man is sinful and sinful desires must bloom from that seed.

In Christ we are given a new life which is better than the base life of sin inherited from Adam. Jesus has promised to make us "new creatures" (II Corinthians 5:17) in the restoration of salvation. It is to our shame that so many of us have not walked in the newness of heart which is our right, privilege, and duty to our Lord! (I John 2:1)]

4.2 *Ye lust, and have not: ye kill, and desire to have, and cannot obtain: ye fight and war, yet ye have not, because ye ask not.*

[Once again those who would discourage any study toward the original language of which Scripture was written will find that they have missed part of the message of God. We are reminded that God gave His Words perfectly. Our best English translation of these words, The King James Bible, is nonetheless a translation.

When the word "lust" is used in verse one the meaning is number 2237 in Strong's. The word is "hedone, hay-don-ay' from handano (to please); sensual delight; by implication, desire:--lust, pleasure." The meaning is to desire something for the delight it will bring.

When the word "lust" is used in verse two the meaning is number 1937 from Strong's. The word is "epithumeo, ep-ee-thoo-meh'-o from 1909 and 2372; to set the heart upon, i.e. long for (rightfully or otherwise):--covet, desire, would fain, lust (after)." The sense is more "I must have" than it is "I simply want."

This latter emphasis seems to mirror the warning from James 1:15, "Then when lust hath conceived, it bringeth forth sin: and sin, when it is finished, bringeth forth death." It seems that there is lust and there is an uncontrollable lust which will not rest until it has obtained the object of its desire. It is this escalation of lust which is in mind at this point.

This type of lust can even lead to killing in its search for fulfillment. It is here that we find the concept of the wars of man. It is here that we find the concept of the lust of a single man warring within himself. Since Scripture gives leading for all areas of life but seems most aligned with the individual, I would believe that this latter situation is that to which James is making reference.

In our present "silly season" of presidential politics this is being played out on the airwaves of radio and television. To assassinate the character and reputation of the "opponent" is a "necessary evil," not considered very "evil," if that is the cost of winning the election. That seems the "mega" illustration but there are more.

I just received a call from a man looking for a church. He was relocating to this town. It would be very easy to say of another church, "They are O.K. but..." Pastors do not consider "running down the opposition." Of course not! That is just emphasizing our good points.

That is an everyday occurrence in advertising is it not? Often that is "advertising" for ourselves for one reason or another. We might not actually "kill" the guy standing in our way of a promotion. We just try to "bring him down a little." He is much easier to step over in that case.

When we finally, and we do not always, get to that desire we find that there is a better desire just over the rainbow. So, we put on our red shoes and skip merrily down the yellow brick road of our lusts.

Our eyes find a lusted for "need." But, our short little arms are never able to grasp all we desire.

Then we get out the "Big Guns." We resort to prayer. That has to work, right? William Burkitt has said, "What we ask for amiss we are sure to miss." The problem is that so much of our prayer life is centered on those same lusts. God in His mercy will never hand a supposed blessing to us when it is a certainty that we will consume it on our lusts.

Also, a heart of envy and hatred will never find the grace to pray in the will of God. God understands that to exalt our lusts is to harm our spirit. To harm our spirit is not the purpose of God. He may well give to "all men liberally," (James 1:5) but He will also withhold that which would harm His children.

The glorious promises of God are reserved for those whose hearts are upon the things of the Spirit. A fighting and clawing mindset will always fall far short of the mark of His approval.]

4.3 *Ye ask, and receive not, because ye ask amiss, that ye may consume it upon your lusts.*

[James asks if the readers had prayed for the desires of the hearts. He assumes that many will answer that they have prayed but God has not answered their prayer. Folks, God always answers prayer. Sometimes the answer is "No."

James also has an answer for those who say God did not answer their petition. It was a very simple answer. The answer is in the above verse; when we ask amiss we cannot expect God to violate His Own holy standards to provide us with that which will be "spent" in the "shop" of our own lusts. The word "lust" in this place is the same as it was in verse one. This is a lust which longs for the sensual. It is a lust which stands opposed to the spiritual principles which are of the Cross.

A sensual lust is a lust for the things of the world of the flesh. "Love not the world, neither the things that are in the world. If any man love the world, the love of the Father is not in him. For all that is in the world, the lust of the flesh, and the lust of the eyes, and the pride of life, is not of the Father, but is of the world. And the world passeth away, and the lust thereof: but he that doeth the will of God abideth for ever." (I John 2:15-17)

Even the worldly philosophers have observed, "To thine own self be true." Can we honestly expect God to be untrue to His Own holy standards in order to give us something for our spiritual hurt? Far too often this is exactly the content and expectation of our prayers when they are outside the known will of God.

There are times when the motive of our prayers seems perfectly good, even in relation to spiritual realities. But there are times when the object of those motivations is contrary to the principles of God.

A quick "for instance" of this is contained in an incident related by Charles Simpson, a noted Charismatic author and speaker. He relates that at one time he was praying for revival in the town wherein he preached. The prayer went unanswered. Finally Bro. Simpson said that it was as though God were speaking directly to him – "Charles, there is a great need for revival in this town. Would you mind if I sent it through the church down the street rather than through the church where you preach?"

There are times when we pray "for the glory of God" with our lips and "for the glory of me" with our hearts. This will not be a prayer answered in the affirmative as our motive only sees the object of our own enhancement. We wish to get God to "help us out" only so we can consume the benefit on our own carnal lusts of personal advancement.

Another example of this is very easy for me to see at this particular moment as I write. Our little church is struggling financially. God is taking care of us but in a "month to month," "paycheck to paycheck" manner. We pray to grow. But, why?

Is our prayer for souls and the glory of God? Or, does the object of our prayer consider that more people will mean more money for the churches programs? If that were the reason I would argue that God will never answer us in the affirmative until we gain the spiritual awareness to desire souls for the kingdom and glory rendered unto the God we are to serve.]

4.4 *Ye adulterers and adulteresses, know ye not that the friendship of the world is enmity with God? whosoever therefore will be a friend of the world is the enemy of God.*

[The use of the terms "adulterers and adulteresses" was a very familiar allegory to use in reference to the "twelve tribes" James addresses in the first verse of this letter. The Old Testament Scriptures often spoke of God as the "Husband" of Israel. (Examples: Isaiah 54:5; Jeremiah 3:20; 31:32) The entire Book of Hosea is an object lesson of this reality.

Divorce is a God ordained remedy for this sin. But, divorce, while allowed, is not required. Hosea 2:7 gives a picture of Hosea being instructed to return his adulterous wife to her place beside him. Much of the prophecy from the Old Testament which has not yet been fulfilled has to do with God calling the adulterous people of Abraham back to Himself after they had forsaken Him for idolatry and irreligion. This is a picture of the God of Love calling even those estranged from Him back into fellowship.

That born again Christian who has wandered from his first love for the Master is easily shown in this that God stands anxious to forgive and cleanse. We are never so far from God that we cannot reach out in the prayer of faith and find Him welcoming the wandering prodigal back home. "For this my son was dead, and is alive again; he was lost, and is found. And they began to be merry." (Luke 15:24)

Note well the teaching of this situation. It is possible to be a true child of God via the grace of salvation and yet be so far out of fellowship that we have become enemies of the purposes of God. Consider that God has the right, purpose and love to chastise His erring children!

Since the judgment of the Babylonian captivity national Israel, the people not the kingdom as it was removed by the Assyrians years before Babylon began her march, has never again resorted to idolatry. The judgment and chastisement of God worked its good purpose in His Covenant people. But, the idolatry of irreligion has been often found within their hearts. Irreligion is that attitude which follows the world while ignoring the calling and leading of the way of God.

This spiritual adultery with the world is manifest in seeking the smile of the world more than the smile of God upon our lives. It is not wrong to work toward worldly success when that success may be cast at the feet of the Savior in using that as a means of working for His programs and purposes. It is wrong to call upon the world for blessings of wealth, prestige, power and even comfort while ignoring the God of All in our wants, wishes, duty and manner of life.

We find this corporately in many churches. They have forgotten the Words of God for the words of man even within the choice of scriptural understanding. The Critical Text, which exalts the intellect of man over faith in God and His power, is preferred over the inspired and preserved Words of God. The music of man, which seeks to import the phrases and melodies of the sensual world above that which reaches the spiritual soul of man attuned to the things of the Spirit, is preferred. Worldly wisdom is used to replace the Spiritual wisdom of God. Such things as speak to man in his carnal state are valued above the still, small voice of God. (I Kings 19:12)

I can easily see where a person might find that "a friend of the world is the enemy of God" might be considered as "a little over the top." But, why should we feel that way? Do we disparage the fish because it will not begin to breathe the same good air as do we? Do we get upset with our dogs because they refuse to ask politely to go outside? Do we disciple a three-week-old baby because he can't keep up with us in the grocery store? No! We realize that these are of different species or development with us.

The spirit of the world produces people of the world. They are sinners by nature – and just as often by nurture. They are different from those who are living in the Spirit of God via the new birth. The goals of the two are of opposing purpose. The goal of the spirit of the world is to not follow the things of the Spirit of God. The goal of the Spirit of God is to call to repentance and salvation those men who are bound by the sin nature of the world.

Sports fans, political partisans, even competing brands of bread are all searching for a way to defeat the other side of the aisle. That is in the natural world with the results basically unimportant within a very few years. The spiritual forces are not locked into such a "life and death" issue as are the others. The spiritual forces are locked into an "eternal life and death" struggle. It will matter ten million years from now the outcome upon individuals as to the outcome of these struggles.

The utmost highest stakes demand the utmost highest fervor. A person whose eyes are not upon the prize of the high calling of God is not violently opposed to the siren call of sin upon the lives of others because he is indifferent to such. Such indifference is an attitude of hatred toward others as it refuses to consider the plight of their slavery when the key to the chains which bind is within reach.

Sin is open rebellion against the God of Creation. As such it is a hatred of God. Those entangled in sin may not openly consider this fact. It is, nonetheless, true as evidenced by their opposition to anything that might taste of the pure goodness of God. God, seeing the bitter end of sin, hates the sin that demands judgment so much that

Jesus came to die in time so that others could live in eternity. (see Jude 23)]

4.5 *Do ye think that the scripture saith in vain, The spirit that dwelleth in us lusteth to envy?*

[This verse starts with an appeal to Scripture. Or, does it? The word "Scripture" is "Graphe" (1124 in Strong's). This word is used over fifty times in the New Testament and invariably refers to that Word which the Jews considered as inspired.

There is one time it is not used that way: "As also in all *his* epistles, speaking in them of these things; in which are some things hard to be understood, which they that are unlearned and unstable wrest, as they do also the other scriptures, unto their own destruction." (II Peter 3:16)

The word "scriptures" in this passage from II Peter is the same as used here in James. I said "invariably" in the above paragraph. That is a very exclusionary word. It means, basically, "all the time." The carnal Jew would not consider the epistles of Paul to be the inspired Words of God. That is the difference in the terminology of that one verse. Of course, it is not really a difference because Peter was saying that the same inspiration as was upon the Words of the Old Testament was also upon those Words penned by Paul and the other human penmen of the New Testament.

The Spirit of God very early impressed upon the various churches, and the Christians of their membership, that the Words of the New Testament were the inspired and preserved Words of God. He didn't need to wait for some council to authenticate what He had already pronounced as pure and reliably the Words of God. Those councils did not authenticate anything as Scripture. They only acknowledged what the churches already knew.

But, we do have a seeming problem at this place. Those words "quoted" are not found in any of the Old Testament writings. That, rather than the New Testament writings, would have been the Scripture to which James appealed when speaking to Israel of the Diaspora. It could be argued that the general tenor of those Words was the subject of much of the Old Testament. Although allowable in a general discourse of Scriptural principles, that seems a very unsatisfactory answer.

It seems more likely that James was speaking, especially in light of the allusion to adulterers and adulteresses in the preceding verse, of the well understood concept of Israel being considered as the wife of God in her position as His Covenant People. This concept would need no explanation to Jewish people who were seeped in the religious imagery of the Mosaic Law.

This does bring up another small problem. The word "spirit" is 4151 in Strong's. It could be speaking of either the spirit of man as a natural man. Or, especially as the term "dwelleth in us" would seem to suggest, the Holy Spirit of God. Writing to Messianic Jews, it would not be necessary to use the word "Holy" as a prefix to indicate the Spirit of God when speaking of Him. That would be easily understood.

As we consider the things said of the spirit in this verse we can conclude either of two considerations. The first is to read "The spirit that dwelleth in us lusteth to envy," and realize that this could not be the Spirit of God. God does not lead anyone toward evil. (James 1:13) This view would find the reference to be the spirit of man that dwells within man. While this would be true; (James 1:15) I do not believe it the proper exegesis of the verse.

James had been talking of the wisdom of man as opposed to the pure wisdom of God earlier in this epistle. Consider that this clause ends with a question mark. There is no question that man has lust and evil within his natural heart. James has spent much time dwelling on that fact.

I believe that this is the first clause of the argument of James. He is saying that God does not give us lust to entice us to evil. He is saying that such is not of God. "Would the Holy Spirit of God give us lust to entice us to evil? Of course not!" The second clause follows from the sixth verse. "But He giveth more grace."

The truly inspired and preserved Scripture does not give us "vain," empty and useless, leading. That Scripture gives us grace from God to confront the enemy of our souls and the objects of our witness.]

4.6 *But he giveth more grace. Wherefore he saith, God resisteth the proud, but giveth grace unto the humble.*

[While the world gives more grief and trouble, while the wisdom of the world digs a deeper hole of disfavor among God and man, God gives to His humble servants even more of His grace and love. We serve The amazing God Who values our true piety over the symbols of earthly performance. The people, things, fashions, customs and even the "religions" of the world go away but our Great Lord stays the same. He is our Constant Contemporary as we rest in His Truth rather than floating in the currents of earthy situations.

Nothing of this earth abides for long. I have read many sermons trying to associate the "Big Bang" of science with the Creation Events in Genesis. We may have to excise all those sermons from our data bases. Although the television show is wildly popular, the theory is under attack among some scientist's.

Scofield's venerable "Study Bible" carries notes that attempt to make the Scripture relevant to the scientific heories of the early 1900's. How many of those college science books of that era would be admitted to the science classrooms of today? Some have argued that they cannot accept Christianity because the Bible doesn't "line up" with science. Personally, I'm not surprised by that particular fact. Job 26:7 speaks of the earth being "hung upon nothing." The secular scientist of the day must have laughed at that unenlightened statement. After all, everyone knew that the earth rested upon the back of a turtle – or some such inanity.

If the tenets of Christianity were to "line up" perfectly with the science of the day, the Bible would soon become outmoded as the theories of science are fluid in their pronouncements.

The proud of the world glory in their intellect as they grasp at the shadows of reality while the humble of God are clothed in the substance of His Majesty. The proud of the world will glory that he is able to forge his own path in life. He eventually comes to the "no U-turn and no parking" zone which leads that broad road into the pits of Hell. The humble simply follows the Savior into the glories of an eternal abode in Heaven.

These are, of course, just some observations on pride. The problem with the pride of man is that it is to glory in himself, his possessions and his abilities. So many instances of "his" are in that life. That may be why it is so hard for people to accept the free salvation of God. Salvation is all about the work of Him. His, with the small "h" has no place for the pride of "his" own accomplishment in true, Biblical salvation.

God offers even more of His grace to the humble. Why not? The humble are used to the idea that God is The Giver of Good. The humble are wiser than the proud in that they know they have need of the grace of God. The humble are not trying to "build their own show." They are very happy to accept the gifts and graces of God. They have the personal history of receiving salvation which they did not deserve or earn; of course they understand that "the best things in life are free" when they flow from the God of Salvation.

Some have suggested that James was mirroring the words of Solomon from Proverbs 3:34 in this verse. "Surely he scorneth the scorners: but he giveth grace unto the lowly." Surely Solomon, the wise, understood the situation. Psalm 138:6 also gives the same sense as does this verse. "Though the LORD be high, yet hath he respect unto the lowly: but the proud he knoweth afar off."

The proud really are "afar off" from God. They are wrapped up in the carnality of their own understanding. The spiritual realities are only considered as an opportunity to show their own understanding. In that they have forgotten God's realities. To lift up oneself in this manner is to lower a person's opinion of God. That might not be stated or admitted. That is a reality!

God gives the humble the grace to not glory in his own humility but to glory in the unfathomable Glory of God!]

4.7 *Submit yourselves therefore to God. Resist the devil, and he will flee from you.*

[I have been told, I am far from being a linguist, that the term "Islam" means "submission." There is a spiritual principle in that knowledge. To whom we submit, that is our master. Since there are only two entities in the universe which accept worship, from the spiritual standpoint, God and Satan, we are bound to spiritually follow either one or the other.

All religious, moral and cultural influences which are not of God are of Satan. These may seem quite benevolent and reasonable but they are forces of impulse which will drag the soul of their adherents to the pits of Hell.

This may be a good place and time to note that the cross, as a symbol of Christianity – although not a Biblically mandated symbol, points back to the very real passion of Jesus on Calvary. (I Peter 2:24) It is a reminder that our very salvation is dependent upon the fact of history that the Divine Person of Jesus Christ took a literally human form. It was the Blood of the Humanity of Jesus which has gained our salvation from sin and unto Heaven. Our works are meaningless except as a sacrifice of obedience unto Him.

The symbol of Islam is in the form of a crescent moon. This points back to the fact of history that Allah was an idol dedicated to a moon god when Mohammed chose to jettison the other idols of the kabala and focus on this one. "Who changed the truth of God into a lie, and worshipped and served the creature more than the Creator, who is blessed for ever. Amen." (Romans 1:25)

It might be interesting to note that the famous "writing on the wall" scene in the fifth chapter of Daniel has a small connection, if not in fact then in concept, to Islam. In the sixteenth verse of that chapter we see that Belshazzar offered Daniel the honor of being "third ruler" of Babylon if he could decipher that writing.

Belshazzar was actually the "second ruler" of the realm. His father, Nabonadus, the actual king at the time, had left his throne to his son as he devoted himself to the honor of the idol "Sin" in a temple at the Oasis of Tayma. One of the principle temples of Sin was at Harran. This is important because Harran became a temporary capital of Assyria during the "death throes" of the Assyrian Empire. Sin was a "moon god." This established the practice of such idolatry over one thousand years before Mohammed.

I did find no connection between the two other than the concept of idolatry toward the moon – a part of the creation of the Creator. Consider this in relation to Romans 1:25, above.

Satan has no power to force anyone to sin. James 1:14 comments on this reality. But, Satan is a master psychologist who understands every single thing about each of us. He is able to call upon our own lusts, as James 1:14 reminds us, to extract any result he may desire to our hurt.

The idea of resistance is more than to "just say no." When we look back at the fourth chapter of Matthew we see the temptation of Jesus in His humanity. After a long fast by the Master, Satan tempted him with food and with an easy completion of His mission wherein He could forego the cross.

Had Jesus submitted to this "easy way," mankind would have remained lost in their sin. Had Jesus worshipped Satan, as Satan requested, Jesus would have delivered all who would follow our Lord into the control of Satan.

When we consider the events at Gethsemane we can understand that the humanity of Jesus understood fully the horrors to be visited upon Him during the "trial" and crucifixion. With this knowledge Jesus nonetheless endured the Cross, and the temptations of Satan upon the humanity of Jesus, and offered Himself for our salvation.

From that fourth chapter of Matthew we learn the lesson for standing against Satan. Jesus responded in His humanity as our example of human resistance toward Satan. Jesus resorted to every single temptation with an appeal to the Scripture.

Reading, studying and prayer over the Scripture is our only defense against Satan. We will never win an argument even when that argument is based in the best of our human reasoning. We will lose every time when we plead our own wisdom and power. We are promised victory when we plead the Words of God!

This could be the cause of the sad state of the churches in our day. We have given up the pure Words of God for the pleasing "Reader's Digest" versions of the false Critical Text. Our power to resist and defeat Satan, from our standpoint, lies in a fidelity to the pure Words of God rather than the proffered words of man. History shows this over and over. Germany was a stronghold of faith until they gave up the Words of God for the rationalism of man. England was the greatest missionary force for Christ upon this earth until they took action to "slay the king (James)" and follow after their own rationalistic reasoning that God could not preserve His Own Words.

Our own nation was once a bastion of Christianity. We praised God for military victory and patterned our culture after a Biblical standard. Our "fundamental change" of the past decades has not led to our national glory but to our descent and, I believe, eventual destruction. "Righteousness exalteth a nation: but sin is a reproach to any people." (Proverbs 14:34)

The wisdom of God stands for eternity while the wisdom of man fades into the dust of history.]

4.8 *Draw nigh to God, and he will draw nigh to you. Cleanse your hands, ye sinners; and purify your hearts, ye double minded.*

[The above verse (7) asks us to resist Satan. This verse asks that we draw near to God. In the realities of the Spiritual these are one united object. We must draw near to God in order to be able to resist Satan. This is occasioned by a perusal and an immersion within the Words of God as given in His Word to us. Therein is our path given to spiritual safety in the world of man.

Lest we forget, our understanding of the inspired and preserved Words of God is heightened and enlightened by the Spirit as we pray over those Words of God. In this manner are those words applied to our spirits as well as to our minds.

We are asked to draw near to God with the understanding that He will draw us even nearer to Himself. On the Day of Atonement the high priest would first sacrifice for his own sins before he began to see the sacrifice for the rest of the camp. But, even before this it would be necessary for that high priest to ritually cleanse himself.

The Blood of Jesus has cleansed us from sin. Titus 2:14 reminds us, "Who gave himself for us, that he might redeem us from all iniquity, and purify unto himself a peculiar people, zealous of good works." Jesus has redeemed us from the iniquity of sin. Within that He is working to purify us into a people who will willingly walk in good works. This can only be accomplished in His power and grace.

When we seek to draw nearer to Him we will begin to feel the love and glory which He has spread unto us. This will draw us even closer to His blessed presence. We step forward and like a magnet upon metal, His purity, glory and love draws us even nearer.

The human being is made a tripartite being. We have our physical bodies. Even the plants of the field have physical bodies. We have our soulish desires. Even the animals of the field will search for something to enjoy in their physicality. But, that breath of life which God bestowed upon Adam is an elevating consideration. We have a spiritual component which is fashioned to desire fellowship with the Creator. That is a dignity that is reserved for humanity. That is an emptiness which resides within the spirit of those who do not know Christ in His saving fullness.

We are asked to cleanse our hands. James goes so far as to use the term "sinners" for his readers. He could have been referring to some unconverted among the fellowship to which he addressed his letter. This seems somewhat doubtful. But, the reality is that until the Blood of Christ has made is free of sin we are not redeemed.

When we talk about the "Reformation" of the Churches we are speaking of groups which "came out" of the Roman Church in an effort to cleanse themselves from the errors of Romanism. The purpose was to purify the religious observances of those protestant churches. Most of these "Protestant" churches came out of Rome but they came out with suitcases full of traditions and other baggage. The robes and collars of some give evidence to their journey.

Likewise, we bring many habits and faults into the pure salvation of Christ. James, a very practical writer with an eye to the image we give to the unconverted world, considers that our hands are not yet empty of the world. There are practices and habits which do not honor Christ. In the pure "boat" of salvation we have much unnecessary "baggage" which we need to toss overboard. I'll leave it to the reader to find his own "treasure trove" of activities and desires which are hindrances to his life for Christ.

We Baptist's are wont to call these "besetting sins." The definition of a besetting sin is, "I know I shouldn't do it but I really enjoy it so much!"

If we first cleanse our hands we will be much better prepared to purify our hearts.

James calls such as these "fully but faulty" Christians "double minded." He describes them in verse six of the first chapter. "But let him ask in faith, nothing wavering. For he that wavereth is like a wave of the sea driven with the wind and tossed." Have you ever watched a boat go up and down on the waves of the water? Do you sometimes draw so close to God that you can feel His Hand of Love upon your brow? Five minutes later have you ever wondered where He went?

Double minded. This is a human frailty which James asks that we overcome by drawing near the Lord of our souls.]

4.9 *Be afflicted, and mourn, and weep: let your laughter be turned to mourning, and your joy to heaviness.*

[Scripture is very concise. James does not use many words to give one consideration simply as a literary vehicle. The idea is a repentance that is not simply a fleeting feeling of remorse but a repentance that exhibits a change of walk. It isn't enough to be simply "sorry" for our sins and imperfections. James expects that the character of Christianity will replace our former character of revelry.

True repentance is not the cause of our salvation. The cause of our salvation is the Love of God; we have no part in salvation expect accepting what Jesus has already done.

That being said, true salvation should produce a change in our life. True salvation should work a Godly repentance in our souls. James goes so far as to call this repentance a necessity in our Christian lives as we view our own failures and lament over them. He asks that we exchange carnal joy for Godly sorrow.

We are often told that our witness should hate the sin but love the sinner. Well, we need to hate the sin which so easily besets us to such a degree that we will pass it from our lives. If it is truly good to hate sin, why do we hold so jealousy unto our own? We say "imperfection" when we mean sin. We say "error" when we mean sin. We say "human frailty" when we mean sin.

I have taken to calling myself obese rather than fat. That way it sounds like a medical condition rather than a moral failure. Maybe I ought to erase that sentence. It seems just a little too close to home!

In what way are we spiritually obese?]

4.10 *Humble yourselves in the sight of the Lord, and he shall lift you up.*

[I had some time in a very expensive "hotel" a few years ago. It seems that I had a slight malfunction of my heart. Actually, it was my heart that had the malfunction; I admit to nothing!

I was processed in an Emergency Room for a few hours before I was transported to the Intensive Care Unit. Once the gurney had taken me into the room that was to be my home for the next week we drew up next to a bed. The nurses said, "We are going to lift you from this gurney to the bed."

Knowing how much I weigh (Higher math to get there!), I said, "Don't bother.

I'll just hop from here to there." As I attempted to sit up I realized that, "No. I won't"

There are some things we just cannot do. Worse, there are some things we ought not to ever do. From these we must repent. In light of these we have a need to realize that we are not nearly as great as we had once thought we were.

Verse seven, above asked that we submit to God. Folks, it is a whole lot easier to submit when we are humble. Most of us have very much to be humble about. I once said, "The only reason that Paul said he was chief of sinners is because he never met me." The audience laughed and pretended it was a joke. It is no joke. I know me better than that. God knows me even better than that!

I am a sinner! I am a gross sinner! I have no claim to the favor of God except that Jesus said, "I forgive you." Folks, I ain't proud of my humility. I can say that I've earned it but that would be a boast. I am just a sinner saved by the grace of God.

Sometimes I forget. Sometimes I get the feeling that I am special. We all have a need to seek humility as though it were important. It is! But, humility is of such an ethereal quality that when we reach out to grasp it... Somehow, some way, we need to get a vision of God. That vision should clear our heads of any feelings of importance.

We need to have a true humility before God. We also need to exhibit the traits of humility before man, as well.

He will lift me up. That is important, seriously, only when it concerns being lifted up to see Him face to Face. Oh, that will be glory.

In the meantime, the battle for humility is one we must accept, and expect. Work for it as becoming unto our Lord!]

4.11 *Speak not evil one of another, brethren. He that speaketh evil of his brother, and judgeth his brother, speaketh evil of the law, and judgeth the law: but if thou judge the law, thou art not a doer of the law, but a judge.*

["If ye fulfil the royal law according to the scripture, Thou shalt love thy neighbour as thyself, ye do well..." (James 2:8) James is carrying this law into the Christian community wherein Jesus has said that we ought to love one another. (John 13:34) This also covers the "outside looking in" aspect of our Christian actions being observed by those to whom we witness even when we are not consciously witnessing. (John 13:35)

This latter concern, "outside looking in," is the primary concern of James in this letter. James insists that our walk must be consistent with our talk as Christians so that the world to which we witness will see true Christianity in action and be drawn towards it.

This verse applies both to the conduct of the Christian towards brothers and sisters in the faith and to those outside the faith to whom we must carry the message of the sufficiency of Christ.

James had been speaking of the sin of pride. It is pride in ourselves, our intellect, our piety and our understanding which gives birth to the sin of harshly judging another in their person. "In their person" is an important distinction. We may recall, however that Paul had at one point to oppose Peter over making a difference in the church between Jew and Gentile where God had made none. (Galatians 2:11) Jude reminds us (Jude 3) to "earnestly contend" in matters of faith as touching doctrinal purity.

We are given a level of Christian liberty by the Spirit but this liberty is never an excuse for excess or sin. Nor does our liberty extend to giving offense to a brother who might be weaker in the faith. (I Corinthians 8:13)

One of the problems in the early church was the relationship of the Christian walk with the ceremonies of the Old Covenant. There were many, naturally of Jewish background – those to whom James was addressing his remarks, who had been nurtured in these ceremonies from their earliest youth. To these the concept of worship was tied to these ceremonies. They were very desirous to incorporate such into the rule of faith in Messiah.

Jesus, however, had constituted a New Covenant in His Blood. These old ceremonies were no longer part of worship. They had been sign posts pointing toward Him. When He had fulfilled the substance of which these ceremonies had only hinted, those ceremonies had no more force within the lives of the people of God. The Gentile Christians had never followed these pictures of the Old Covenant. Those who insisted upon them were a cause of dissention within the churches.

Colossians 2:16 says, "Let no man therefore judge you in meat, or in drink, or in respect of an holyday, or of the new moon, or of the Sabbath days." This is not an injunction to follow these things as a part of religious devotion. Rather it is a reminder that "Therefore if any man be in Christ, he is a new creature: old things are passed away; behold, all things are become new." (II Corinthians 5:17) The very next verse after Colossians 2:16 tells us that these things are "...a shadow of things to come..." (Colossians 2:17a) These were fulfilled in Christ. They had no more place as required operations within the New Testament Church.

In the 2008 election campaign Rick Warren, a new evangelical mega church pastor, interviewed Barack Obama. On the subject of abortion Warren asked Obama at what point life began in the unborn child. Obama answered that he could not say. "That question is above my pay grade."

Folks, the judging of another person is above our pay grade. It is to question God for failing to judge that person. When Satan tempted Eve his "winning" argument was that God was being petty by refusing the fruit of the Tree of the Knowledge of Good and Evil. The argument was that God knew the benefits of that fruit and wished it withheld from Adam and Eve.

To set ourselves as judges of God and His Laws is one of the grossest sins which the human mind can conceive. Yet, this is what we do when we set ourselves up as the judge of another person. This is a sin against man and God.]

4.12 *There is one lawgiver, who is able to save and to destroy: who art thou that judgest another?*

["For thou hast said in thine heart, I will ascend into heaven, I will exalt my throne above the stars of God: I will sit also upon the mount of the congregation, in the sides of the north." (Isaiah 14:13) This verse from Isaiah is prophetically speaking of Satan and his great sin of rebellion against God.

Of Himself, God has said, "See now that I, *even* I, *am* he, and *there is* no god with me: I kill, and I make alive; I wound, and I heal; neither is *there any* that can deliver out of my hand." (Deuteronomy 32:29) There is only One Judge in the universe who has the absolute power to save and to destroy. It is He Who has the power to judge among men. Those trivial judges of the earth have only a power which is derived from Him. (Romans 13:1)

Therefore, any who would claim the right to judge others is a usurper of the power and prerogatives of God. This was the original sin of Satan.

Who are we to set ourselves up as judges over the man of God's creation? We are, in such a circumstance, a subject to be ourselves judged harshly. We may judge "in our opinion," or under the law of our own conscience. We do not have the right to set up any law and then to judge others in relation to their consideration of *our* law.

Our own "law" is meaningless in reality except as a token of our rebellion against The God of All.]

4.13 *Go to now ye that say, To day or to morrow we will go into such a city, and continue there a year, and buy and sell, and get gain:*

["Go to now" was an ancient idiom used to call attention to something. It is much like a modern speaker saying, "Listen up!"

The illustration of this verse is not speaking against faithfully planning one's business. Often a merchant would load his "wagon" with items to sell. He would go to a location where the people would be disposed to purchase these items. While in that city he would sell his wares and buy others which he would transport to another location where those items would be in demand.

Continuing this trend over the years, the merchant would amass his fortune. In time he might return to the city of his birth with a fortune to take his ease. It was much more than likely that he would work until his demise.

Therein lay the problem. He could not number his own years. Worse, he had spent his time with his business but had spent only scant time with his Lord.

In this situation the mind goes to Jesus speaking of the coming Day of Judgment in Matthew 24:37-39. "But as the days of Noe were, so shall the coming of the Son of man be. For as in the days that were before the flood they were marrying and giving in marriage, until the day that Noe entered into the ark, And knew not until the flood came, and took them all away; so shall also the coming of the Son of man be."

There is no obvious great wickedness shown in those verses. We know that there was great wickedness in that day but not from these verses. Jesus is just telling His listeners that the people of the day of Noah were simply living their lives day-by-day. But, they gave no thought to the God of their days. They counted Him as less than important to their days and plans.

The man who forgets His God may rest assured that God will never forget him. "And as it is appointed unto men once to die, but after this the judgment:" (Hebrews 9:27)]

4.14 *Whereas ye know not what shall be on the morrow. For what is your life? It is even a vapour, that appeareth for a little time, and then vanisheth away.*

[I am currently near my 70th birthday. It seems absurd when I consider that my mind still flows to what I will do tomorrow and the tomorrow after that. But, such is the considerations of humanity. We scheme and plan as though we had a limitless supply of days upon this earth. We do not, except in the resurrection bodies. "For we are strangers before thee, and sojourners, as were all our fathers: our days on the

earth are as a shadow, and there is none abiding." (II Chronicles 29:15)
    The poet has said:
> Life is a vapor
> Of o're clouding steam.
> The substance of the stuff
> Gives lie to the fact
> Of its transient nature.
> Here today, and
> Not only gone,
> But gone without trace.
> Forgotten,
> Tomorrow.
> It is real.
> But, the slightest breeze,
> The frailest disturbance.
> The short tick of the clock
> Will banish this vapor
> From this earth.
> Such is life.
> Real, but lacking in
> Abiding substance.
> The length of a lifetime is long
> Only in its beginning.
> And that an illusion.
> The truth of its time is,
> Even at advanced age,
> Short.
> It comes in a moment.
> It passes in a minute.
> It is swallowed by eternity.

    We cannot know what the tomorrow of earth holds for us. It is a book which is yet unopened. Our hope of tomorrow is that our times and dreams are in the matchless Hands of the Master for our salvation, peace and happiness!]

4.15   *For that ye ought to say, If the Lord will, we shall live, and do this, or that.*

    [This is not saying that we ought not to plan. What this verse is saying is that we must plan with the realization that our plans are not permanent. Never can anything be certain in this life except the fact that the Savior loves us!

    In acknowledging the power and providence of the Lord we give honor to His Name, Mercy, Grace, Power and Love. It is an act of worship to consider "if the Lord wills" even above "I will."

    This is an attitude which realizes that we are but dust. He is the True Creator and energizer of our mortality as well as the eternal destiny of our spirit.]

4.16   *But now ye rejoice in your boastings all such rejoicing is evil.*

    [An agnostic once declared, "I am a self-made man." One hearer commented,

"I am sure that God appreciates that you take the responsibility for your folly."

Jesus told the story of "...a certain rich man (whose) ground brought forth plentifully. And he thought within himself, saying, What shall I do, because I have no room where to bestow my fruits? And he said, This will I do: I will pull down my barns, and build greater, and there will I bestow all my fruits and my goods. And I will say to my soul, Soul, thou hast much goods laid up for many years; take thine ease, eat, drink, *and* be merry. But God said unto him, *Thou* fool, this night thy soul shall be required of thee: then whose shall those things be, which thou hast provided?" (Luke 12:16b-20)

The boasting is evil in that it is centered upon the man God has created rather than on the Creator of that man. It is to rob God of His rightful glory as Sovereign of all creation.

Our enjoyment of such boasting is that we fancy ourselves as the center of the universe. We forget that it is God Who created not only the universe but also fashioned us from the dust of the ground. Such is our only true glory. We are of the mundane of the creation of God. We have been given great prestige as the zenith of His creation even as we forget that we are simply of that creation of The Creator.

We tend to forget that even the best of our physical and mental strengths are dependent upon His energizing. Without the power of His breath of life in our nostrils we are simply an inert animal visiting the jungle of our habitation without purpose or awareness.]

4.17 *Therefore to him that knoweth to do good, and doeth it not, to him it is sin.*

[One day in the Garden this conversation occurred between God and Adam. "And he said, I heard thy voice in the garden, and I was afraid, because I was naked; and I hid myself. And he said, Who told thee that thou wast naked? Hast thou eaten of the tree, whereof I commanded thee that thou shouldest not eat?" (Genesis 3:10-11)

The serpent had promised Eve that if she partook of the forbidden fruit she would be as God with the knowledge of good and evil. Eve took. Eve gave to Adam and he took. Their eyes were opened and they understood their nakedness before God. There would be no pretense that they did not understand His rule and that they would rue the fact of their sin.

The person who knows what the map of God has to say is more greatly condemned than one who has not known His leading. The neglect of a known duty is a sin. The platoon which knows they are to protect the left flank during a battle are guilty of dereliction of duty if they do not attempt to perform their assigned duty.

The knowledge of God and His ways does not profit our souls unless we perform that knowledge within our hearts and lives. The Great Commission at the conclusion of the Book of Matthew was not a simple suggestion. It was the battle plan given by the Captain of our Souls.

That is a starting place. Our duty is to search the Scripture that we may be ready for Spiritual battle and to march under His banner in whatever capacity He has given us to do so.]

JAMES - CHAPTER FIVE

5.1   Go to now, ye rich men, weep and howl for your miseries that shall come upon you.

[It seems that in this chapter James steps back from considering how the outside world views the Church. He steps back to pick up the mantle of the Old Testament prophet. With this in mind I would argue for a "double fulfillment" of this passage. The "near" meaning has to do with James' pronouncements against the excesses of the rich among the Jews of the day who were defrauding the poor.

We with Fundamentalists backgrounds tend to decry any mention of the term "social justice." But, it is very hard to read the prophetic Books of the Old Testament and not consider that God has much to say about the concept of social justice and His abhorrence of those who abuse their fellow man with fraud and deceit. In order for us to be true to God we must be filled with practical and even human concern for the welfare of the downtrodden.

It is necessary that we do so with an eye to using this care as an entranceway into a discussion of the glories of salvation in Christ. Eternal salvation remains a far superior goal than is a good meal on a Tuesday night! When we forget this fact we are become soulish rather than spiritual in our outlook and religion.

That Tuesday meal remains very important in how others will view our compassion. Upon this view will they understand the realistic concern of the Savior for their soul's eternal residence.

The "near fulfillment" of the prophecy of James was two-fold. In order to understand this we have to understand the "richness" of the Jew. Paul puts it this way: "What advantage then hath the Jew? or what prophet *is there* of circumcision? Much every way; chiefly, because that unto them were committed the oracles of God." (Romans 3:1-2)

The Jew was rich in spirituality. He was, still is, of the Covenant People of God. It was to the Jew that God entrusted the writings of the Old Testament. In this volume we read of the glories of our Lord and we read the teaching of God. Much of this teaching is in the events of time as recorded in this Book of Timelessness. The physical events of the Old Testament show to us in the form of parable those spiritual things which God would have us to learn.

Lest we forget, Jesus was, Himself in His humanity, Jewish. Nearly our entire New Testament record flows, via inspiration of God, from the pen of Jewish men. Thus, in the natural we owe a debt of gratitude to the Jew for our understanding of salvation and of God.

But, this was the time when the Jew had refused, in the main – especially in the main of the leadership, both that Word and the very Word of God, Jesus the Christ.

In 70 A.D., a little less than one generation from the crucifixion of Jesus by the Roman's, and at the instigation of the Jewish religious leaders, the Roman legions destroyed the Jewish Temple and Jerusalem. With the destruction of the Temple there was no legally accepted place for sacrifice.

The Jew did disparage the loss of the Temple. But he did not renounce his Judaism. Instead he eventually transferred the "Oral Law" of the Mishna into a written Law of the Talmud. This change transferred a reliance upon sacrifice to a reliance upon study. No more would the pious Jew travel to Jerusalem's Temple three times a year. Now he would study the writings based upon the Law of the Pentateuch. He would study the realities of his religion and embrace the ceremonies as he had once embraced sacrifice to exhibit his love for God.

The sad fact emerges that this study of Talmud is a "tradition" placed atop the Law and The Prophets. It is nearly the same as the tradition which the Pharisees placed before the Law in the time of the physical sojourn of Jesus. I am not criticizing. This sort of study is not that much different than what I am doing here. "Of the making of commentaries there is no end." (Consider Ecclesiastes 12:12) Still, I am reminded of the man who said, "Study the Scripture of God. It will often shed much light upon the commentaries of man."

In this he replaced his reliance upon that Law with a respect for the writings which explained that law. By this he replaced a religion which was outwardly devoted to the God of sacrifice to an inward religion which was inwardly focused upon the form of the writing.

In 136 A.D., after yet another revolt by a professed Messiah, Simon bar Kochba, the Romans expelled the Jews from Judea. With the newly constructed form of religion, which needed no Temple, the Jew began to wander the world. The extreme hated, unfounded but certainly real, especially of the Christians who should have known better, have buffeted those children of Jacob for two millennia – so far!

I believe that this was part of the prophecy of James at this point. The ancient prophecies remind us that this is not to last. The Jew remains the special Covenant People of God. Eventually, in the good timing of God, He will welcome the Jew back to his place as "the apple of the eye of God." They of the Old Covenant will finally be converted as a people to the New Covenant and become the greatest missionary force ever seen in the world during the Tribulation which we, as the New Testament Church, will have no part. This will be what we call "The Great Tribulation." God calls this "the time of Jacob's trouble." (Jeremiah 30:7)

As has happened so often during the history of this people, the chastening of God will produce the revival of all Israel.

This is a long sustained "near" fulfillment of the prophecy of James. The other portion of the near fulfillment has to do with the evils of the rich when these are shown by their treatments of the poor. This latter fulfillment is that which is primarily considered in the following verses.

The "far" fulfillment concerns that on-going "near" fulfillment of the persecution of Israel during this period of time and culminates in the tribulation era of Jacob's Trouble.]

5.2 *Your riches are corrupted, and your garments are motheaten.*

[The word "corrupted" at this place is 4595 in Strong's. It is "sepo, say'-po ... apparently a primary verb; to putrefy, i.e. (figuratively) perish:--be corrupted." This is an important consideration since the very next verse speaks of the "rust" ("cankered") of their gold and silver. Add in the fact that their fine garments are "motheaten" and the picture is that all of their riches, to include all of their possessions, are failed. All of the accouterments of the riches in which they trust, and because of which they are given "special" preference by some (James 2:3-5) even of the churches, are reduced to no more than the "vile raiment" (James 2:2b) of the poor.

That amassed wealth which could have fed and clothed the poor was to be worthless to the rich men. His worldly riches would be found to have absconded without regard to the station or pride of the formerly rich.

Even the laid up hoard of food which could have fed the starving poor, was not of any use to that rich man as it had become the food of vermin. This would become the reality of the rich of the Diaspora and of the Land. The sacking of Jerusalem and Temple in 70 A.D. created a new class of poor. Many of the formerly rich were taken into slavery at that point as well. As to the future "wandering Jew," poverty would become a constant companion of many.]

5.3   *Your gold and silver is cankered, and the rust of them shall be a witness against you, and shall eat your flesh as it were fire. Ye have heaped treasure together for the last days.*

[The sad point in much of this is that the lost concerned that "heaped treasure" which could have fed and clothed hundreds. That "heaped treasure" was lost to both the poor, who stood in need, and the rich, who stood in pride.

The status of the poor was not changed in all this. They were poor and continued as such. The status of the rich was changed dramatically for the worse. The poor could trust in the God in Whom they had always trusted. The trust of the rich had too often been in his riches. With those riches lost he had no solace.

Silver and gold, properly speaking, do not rust. They will discolor and fade from their brilliance but are not consumed by rust. This discoloration gives the appearance of rust, however. James is interested in how things look to an outsider. In this he properly uses rust at a metaphor of a devalued and lost wealth. In 1931 the phrase "lost millionaires" was used to describe 250 men who had been "paper millionaires" in 1929 but had lost their wealth in the stock market crash. These people still existed, as did the objects of the rich in James thesis, but there were no longer "millionaires" even as the degraded riches of the rich were no longer the actual riches they had in mind to hoard.

So are these "lost rich men" who have seen their riches fade before their eyes. Their careful "oversight" of their riches was the cause of their loss. They had trusted themselves to guard their riches but had not trusted the Lord to hold their souls.

I once bought a used car that was mechanically very sound. But, the body had so rusted that the back bumper literally fell off the automobile. There was not enough solid metal left to even weld a new bumper on the car. That excessive rust was testament to the fact that a previous owner had not kept up any real maintenance on the car even though the motor was still sound.

In like manner the "rust" of the riches of these rich men was a testament to the fact that they had seen an avarice to hoard for themselves as more meaningful than to care for the needs of others. Their look was inward, to their own pleasure, rather than outward, to the social and soul needs of others.

This became as a spiritual cancer which ate at their very life before God and man. They had despised their very soul for the love of riches. The loss which they suffered could not have been alleviated by keeping their riches. The lost which they suffered could not have been alleviated by the giving of their riches. Their cause was not lost because of their riches. Those riches were only a symptom of the poverty of their hearts toward God.

The term "last days" does not refer to the end of the world in this instance. The meaning is that the rich had kept things for the last days of their lives. They amassed riches for their "retirement" when they supposed they could take their ease.

When I was in Vietnam the military did not pay us in dollars and cents. They gave us something called "script." It was a military payment certificate which we could spend as cash in all the post exchanges. It wasn't "real" money but it spent the same on post – and in some "black market" exchanges off post. I knew one man who was sending his entire pay home to his wife. Every payday he would take this "script" and mail it home. He had thoughts of being very rich at the end of his year-long tour of duty.

Then one day the entire post was put on "lock down" as the "script" we had used was converted into another issue of script. The old script was now useless; we were to turn it in and be given the new script in exchange. This was only allowed during this hour of exchange. This soldier finally realized that all of the "money" he had sent home was worthless. He had trusted in a riches he did not understand.

This was the situation of these "rich" men. They set aside the riches of this world for their retirement fund. Only a trust in the Lord is reality for our souls needs. That of the world can be cancelled at any time. The Lord is a Sure Tower in the storms of life. The Lord is the Only Sure Tower in the ends of life. He is our Sword and Shield which is our safety in every circumstance. The riches of this world are fleeting, fluid and failing in the hour of need.]

5.4 *Behold, the hire of the labourers who have reaped down your fields, which is of you kept back by fraud, crieth: and the cries of them which have reaped are entered into the ears of the Lord of sabaoth.*

[During the time between my leaving the first college I attended and entering into the military in early 1968, I often worked for as a "day laborer" for an employment agency. There were two advantages to this. The first was that, being of draft age during the Vietnam Conflict (They say it wasn't a war. No one explained that to the ones who made the bullets and explosives!), I would not be hired by most companies. Since this employment agency was on a day to day employment basis, they didn't really care if I was not to be available after that one day.

The second was the concept of "daily draws." The employment clientele of this company was mostly of transient and homeless men. We would draw each day's pay at the end of that day. The hungry could eat the night after the first day's work rather than seeing their first pay held for two weeks. This was also the concept of pay under the Mosaic Law. (Leviticus 19:13; Deuteronomy 24:15) Jesus speaks of this concept in His parable of the laborers in the twentieth chapter of Matthew.

Apparently, these rich men were not paying "daily draw" to those who labored for them. I can understand this in today's market. It might be necessary for the farmer to sell his crops in order to have cash to pay his harvesters. But, in this time as we have already seen, the rich were hoarding money. It is altogether likely that they could pay the "daily draw" and recoup those wages later when the crops were sold.

This was the custom and this was the expectation of those laborers.

Some of the laborers were "permanent hire" and servant. Those "servants" were not necessarily "slave" but were those who stayed with the master of the fields for extended periods.

But, among those laborers were itinerant workers who would have depended upon the concept of "daily draws" of their wages in order to subsist. To have held back their wages would have worked an extreme hardship upon them. As to the concept of "slave," what could be more egregious to the concept of fair wages than to withhold all pay from a slave?

It is to the spiritual credit of the Scriptures that within a few hundred years of the Protestant Reformation shining the light of Scripture into the world of men that the evil of slavery was abolished from the "Christian nations." It is to their discredit that it took so long for this social evil, called an "institution" to give it some sort of credence, to depart from their borders.

It must also be noted that slavery still exists in the world even unto this day. The Christian cultures have outlawed this relic of evil. Hate and prejudice may remain. That is true. It is a testament to the witness of the cross that even in such a world of bias and hatred this evil has been eradicated.

Consider the list of sins from Malachi 3:5 which include this violation of the Mosaic Law. "And I will come near to you to judgment; and I will be a swift witness against the sorcerers, and against the adulterers, and against false swearers, and against those that oppress the hireling in his wages, the widow, and the fatherless, and that turn aside the stranger from his right, and fear not me, saith the LORD of hosts."

I might note that the phrase "LORD of hosts" and the phrase "Lord of sabaoth" are exactly the same. The one, "hosts," is a Greek rendition of a Hebraism. Number 4519 in Strong's gives the Greek rendition of the Word. Number 6635 in Strong's Hebrew gives the Hebrew rendition of the Word. Both speak of a military commander. Thus, we see the plea of the downtrodden reach the ears of God. This is not an empty consideration for God is powerful to punish the wrongdoer.

Referencing the passages from Leviticus, Deuteronomy and Malachi, Clarke writes: "And on these laws and threatenings is built what we read in Synopsis Sohar, p. 100, l. 45: 'When a poor man does any work in a house, the vapour proceeding from him, through the severity of his work, ascends towards heaven. Woe to his employer if he delay to pay him his wages.' To this James seems particularly to allude, when he says: The cries of them who have reaped are entered into the ears of the Lord of hosts; and the rabbins say, 'The vapour arising from the sweat of the hard-worked labourer ascends up before God.' Both images are sufficiently expressive."

Once again, we have a picture of what we call "the social gospel." Fundamentalists tend to look upon the term and the concept as somewhat alien to the concept of our Christian ministries. It is rather apparent that God does not see it so. James is constantly arguing that if we are not seen as living the Gospel, as Christ taught us to live in His humanity, before men we are amiss in our faith. We show a faulty Gospel, a faulty faith and a faulty relationship of our Lord before men.]

5.5 *Ye have lived in pleasure on the earth, and been wanton, ye have nourished your hearts, as in a day of slaughter:*

[The Geneva Bible Notes tell us that, "The Hebrews call a day that is appointed to solemn banqueting, a day of slaughter or feasting."

There are a couple of things brought to mind in this consideration. First, I recall one time when I was shortly attached to a unit among the indigenous people of the Central Highlands of Vietnam. The village elder died while I was there. A water buffalo was brought down and roasted over a fire. It was a solemn feast in honor of the deceased tribal leader. We of the military unit took part in the feast lest we dishonor the tribe and their elder.

Another consideration is that the pleasure mentioned was a pleasure of excess in many ways. These people lived in luxury and privilege. So did the animals which were to be slaughtered for food. Those were "fattened" for the meal. The animals didn't understand this; all they understood was that they were getting regular, and good, food. They probably enjoyed their life until the time of final judgment came upon them.

The final consideration, and it is this that I believe may be meant, is that these rich people turned even the sacrifice of God and the ceremony of their religion into a celebration rather than the solemn occasion it was meant to be. Paul mentions this attitude among many who partook unworthily of the Lord's Table in the last half of the eleventh chapter of I Corinthians. We must be reminded of the thirtieth verse of that chapter. "For this cause many *are* week and sickly among *you*, and many sleep."

The rich, or any, who go through life seeking only their own cause, with no thought of God, will find the error of their ways eventually. It may be at the Cross in this life. It may be without the Cross in the next existence. "Be not deceived; God is not mocked: for whatsoever a man soweth, that shall he also reap." (Galatians 6:7)

Both Paul, in that eleventh chapter of I Corinthians, and James, especially in the second chapter of this epistle, make note of the rich abusing their position at the expense of the poor. These are guilty; they are blind to the fact of heaping coals of fire upon their own heads in judgment for their actions. Consider the spiritual principle of Romans 12:20. To the unfeeling rich they are guilty of profaning the Lord's purposes even while they induce others to think well of themselves.

This is a concept that should be very easy for us of this time to understand. Every year we have a "Memorial Day" wherein the call is to remember those soldiers who have given the last full measure of their devotion to their native land. In honor of these men and women we attend sporting events and feast on picnic and restaurant food. What has been planned as a somber "civic holy day," has become a day of excess and joy.]

5.6 *Ye have condemned and killed the just, and he doth not resist you.*

[There are a couple of levels here. As to the delivering of Jesus to the Roman Authorities for crucifixion, it was not the poorer classes which took part in this. It was the rich, the influential and especially the highest of the religious class which sought to kill Him. But, He did not resist them even though He well could have. (Matthew 26:53)

I honestly believe that this was a surprise to Judas. I think Judas may have believed that Jesus would simply walk away from His captors at this place. He had done so before. (John 10:39) I would think that this might explain the dramatic reaction of Judas when he realized that Jesus really was going to go to the Cross. This does not lessen the heinous nature of the crime of Judas. I would ask that we consider that Judas may have expressed a modicum of remorse over his act; but, Judas never sought the healing balm of forgiveness from the Savior. Judas committed that great sin and he died, from suicide, with sin upon his lost soul.

The second level was the persecuted believer, Jew and Gentile, who was brought before the councils of the Jews and fed to ravenous beasts by the Romans. These were blameless persons who suffered privation and martyrdom rather than renounce their Savior. In this they showed themselves to be true Christians – followers of Christ – as the willingly suffered for His glory. As their physical lives departed to their Heavenly reward, they let their mute testimonies of praise stand as proof of the love of the Savior.

On yet another level we see that James, called "the just," was also martyred as testimony to his own faith in the Lord he would shortly see in the Heavenlies.

On a much lower level than martyrdom, the rich would often bring legal accusation and punishment upon the poor who had no defender. The rich were powerful accusers while the poor were powerless victims in the courts and judgment halls who found themselves without effective voice in the presence of their accusers.]

5.7 *Be patient therefore, brethren, unto the coming of the Lord. Behold, the husbandman waiteth for the precious fruit of the earth, and hath long patience for it, until he receive the early and latter rain.*

[James had been giving warnings to the rich that they should deal compassionately and with true justice toward the poor. Now he begins to offer consolation to the poor. This is yet another condemnation of the rich of this world. It is an unstated, but obvious, statement that those rich and influential men are of this world and the lusts of this world they will do. (Mark 4:19) But, it is to those who see their poverty among the world to whom He will bestow His most precious blessing.

Thus, has it been among men since Adam and Eve first took of the forbidden fruit. Man, in his sin, will first disregard the clear Words of God and then act in a manner diametrically opposed to those Holy Words. Only the power of the Spirit can soften the heart of man so that a man will allow the will of God to show love to that man. In this manner the man will accept the perfect leading of God; in this the man will show the love and concern of God to his fellow man.

This is the condition of the poor as well as it is the condition of the rich. Both are sinners. The reality is that one has more power to do harm to his fellow man than the other. The heart of both stands as opposed to God when they choose to stand in their earthly "default setting" of the sin which is within their hearts. (Mark 4:19)

As to patience within the trials and tribulations, James reminds the poor of the farmer who must plow, plant, fertilize and wait until the rain to come before he is able to see the fruit of his patient waiting. "...there shall be showers of blessing." (Ezekiel 34:26b) The time of the promised blessing of God shall come in its due season. (II Peter 3:9) He has promised and He will perform.

In the fifteenth chapter of Genesis God is speaking with Abram. The prophecy is made of the long sojourn of the children of Abram in Egypt. The prophecy of the land of promise is confirmed. This will take place after that time of slavery in Egypt. God gives the reason for this seeming delay in verse sixteen. "But in the fourth generation they shall come hither again: for the iniquity of the Amorites is not yet full."

The reason for the delay in the promised blessing for Abram is the grace of God toward the Amorite. Sin must be judged and prosecuted. In this God is both faithful and just. He will give the grace of time for repentance. It is when this time is completed that the judgment will certainly come.

That time may be short. That time may come after some seeming disaster has been visited upon the sinner in order that he may realize he cannot trust his own arm but must lean upon the God of grace. Yes; sometimes the horror of disaster is actually the grace of God shown upon earth. Even that which we do not understand is of the grace of God toward man. The wait of the poor for deliverance from the rich, even this is the grace of God. It is a grace of the time of possible repentance for the rich and the grace of the time of spiritual growth for the poor. Both are a time to praise the Lord for His goodness toward an undeserving mankind.

It is more than possible that James did not see all of these things when he put pen to parchment. The Spirit of Inspiration upon those Words understood fully what was the full intent of the Lord. The Word lives! This is true both of the Incarnate Word of God and the Inspired Word of God. This inspired Word does not change. But, it is living and opens the reality of the true Message of God to those who will prayerfully submit their members to study and listen to that message of Life.

I must add to the above. This is only true of the Words which were originally inspired and preserved by God. The critical text of man, from which nearly every "new" version is produced, has no such promise. As the "modernist" of old said, "The Bible contains the Words of God." Truer words were spoken by the "fundamentalist" of old who said, "The Bible is the Word of God."

The critical text contains the words of God as strained through the intellect and will of "pious" men who have not the faith to accept the preserving power of God. Nor do they have the faith to accept the full inspiration of those Words of God. They, as the modernist of old, trust the "general theme" of the song of the Lord while they cast doubt upon the notes of His Words. How can we have a musical score with no trust in the notes thereof?

The "coming of the Lord" refers to the time of deliverance. That could apply, of course, to the time when we are caught up in the clouds to meet Him. It could apply to the time when the soul is released from this world of sin and degradation to see the Savior face to face. It could apply to the destruction of Jerusalem when the Jewish institutions which were used to subjugate the poor were to be abolished. It could refer to the Second Coming of the Lord in glory when He sets up His Millennial Kingdom to rule in true justice among the men of earth. My presumption on this is that the phrase applies to all of the above. The time of recompense will come. It is not given to us to know the time or the manner of the workings of God. It is given to us to place our full faith and reliance upon the love and grace of The Father.

The "early rain" concerns those first showers of spring in which the earth awakens from its long slumber of winter. It is the time for planting the hope of the harvest. The "latter rain" concerns those showers of early fall in which the promise of the early rain is confirmed by the reality of the time of the latter rain. It is the time for reaping the blessing which God has provided to those that love Him.

Consider a short parenthesis. James speaks of a distinction being made between "rich" and "poor" with the rich as oppressors and the poor as the oppressed. He places both in a spiritual context. The rich are those that trust in the things of this earth as though this were all that mattered in life. I would guess that those riches are all that matter, in a sense, in this life. Even one without goods can trust in the things of this life as though they would continue forever. That person might be considered as "rich" in this world in comparison to his complete poverty in the spiritual.

The poor are those who understand that present riches are worthless in the light of eternity. It is they which give their true trust and allegiance to God by trusting in Him in all things with reference to worldly goods simply as a means to serve the Master. These may even be "men of means." Nicodemus was a well-to-do man. He humbled himself before Jesus in the third chapter of John. After the crucifixion of Jesus he provided myrrh and aloes for the burying of Jesus. (John 19:39) It is probably this which the women brought to the tomb that first Easter morning.

By the way, speaking of that tomb; where did it come from? It came from another rich man. "Joseph of Arimathaea, an honourable counsellor, which also waited for the kingdom of God, came, and went in boldly unto Pilate, and craved the body of Jesus." (Mark 15:43) It was not the normal thing for the bodies of the crucified to be removed. They would often be left hanging on those crosses so that birds and other scavengers would desecrate them. The Romans saw this as a deterrent to other miscreants.

We can say that Pilate was being generous to Jesus because he knew the crucifixion was unjust. We can say that the religious leadership wanted this so that the disciples, a scattered and frightened band at that time, would not steal the body and claim a resurrection. Or we can consider that this was necessary due to the prophecies of God. Psalm 16:10 reads, "For thou wilt not leave my soul in hell; neither wilt thou suffer thine Holy One to see corruption."

About the use of the word "hell" in this place, we note that Hell is not a place of corruption. It is place of conscious suffering which would preclude the idea of the disintegration of corruption of the physical. "The grave" is one of the meanings which Strong's gives to the word "hell." The Treasury of Scriptural Knowledge carries this notation about hell at this verse from Psalm 16:10. "The word hell, from the Saxon hillan or helan, to hide, or from holl,, a cavern, though now used only for the place of torment, anciently denoted the concealed or unseen place of the dead in general; corresponding to the Greek [adev,] i.e., [o aidev topos,] the invisible place and the Hebrew sheol, from shaal, to ask, seek, the place and state of those who are out of the way, and to be sought for."

Understanding these things, we find it necessary for the prophecy of Psalm 16:10 to be fulfilled that the body of Jesus would be placed in a tomb. Acts 2:27 quotes this verse after the Resurrection. That was the reason that Joseph asked for the body and Pilate relinquished it.

Joseph probably didn't understand the coming resurrection. It appears that none of the follows of Jesus really understood the prospect of His resurrection. The offer of the tomb was not a "loan;" it was a permanent offer from a rich man to the Lord.

Even the rich can humble themselves before the Lord. The reality is that so few are disposed to do so as they trust in those riches. Sad.]

5.8   *Be ye also patient; stablish your hearts: for the coming of the Lord draweth nigh.*

[The early Church expected a soon return of the Savior. They did not understand that the "wait" had the purpose of calling into salvation the saints of the ages to come. It is the grace, patience and love of God that has delayed the coming of the Savior. Thousands of souls have heard the story of the love of God as He has continued to call a people for His Name from the expanding population of the world. He allows the history of the world to record both the failure of man and the perfect patience of God. Consider II Peter 3:9 in this light.

What might seem a long time to us, the creatures of physicality and time, is as a second to God Who is of the reality of spirit and eternity. Psalm 143:5 says of David, "I remember the days of old; I meditate on all thy works; I muse on the work of thy hands." If David could consider the Glory of God through the work of His Hands in his day, how much more of the Glory of God can we consider as we view the Work of His Hands in the history of man? God remains in control; His Word of prophecy is simply a newspaper written in full truth before the incidents occurred.

As the early Church waited for that certain coming, so can we. The coming of the Lord in the clouds to call us from this world is imminent. It could happen at any time. The coming of the Lord in the clouds to call us from this world may also be immediate. It could happen NOW! "Even so, come Lord Jesus." These are nearly the last words of the inspired and preserved Scripture. Following these words is the prayer that the Lord be with all Christians. The glory of that verse above (Revelation 22:20b) is that we shall go to be with Him!

In his commentary on this verse Barnes says, "...by scattering them abroad through the world to propagate the new religion." For all the respect that I hold for this particular commentary, I must take issue with this. Christianity is not a "new religion." Though the Old Covenant was preparatory for the New Covenant, it was not a "different" religion.

Verses such as John 17:24; Ephesians 1:4; and I Peter 1:20 all give evidence that the true "religion" of God has always – from before the creation of this world – centered on the work of Jesus. Revelation 13:8 leads us to understand that salvation has always been centered upon the work of Jesus as THE Self-Sacrifice for our sins.

The call and faith of Abraham was confirmed by his encounter with Melchisedec. Even the "religion" of Abraham was not of his vision or invention. There were others who retained the knowledge and religion of The True God before Abraham. Faith, the old song says, is the victory. Faith has always been the medium of true worship. God has given us an inspired and preserved Scripture to point us to the Object of that faith. The object of that faith, even upon those who had no knowledge of the coming cross, has been upon that Cross of Calvary.

The object of that faith could not be idols, made by man of the created elements of earth. Nor could the object of that faith be any man. Man is sinful. He cannot even approach God due to his sin. Nor could the object of that faith be in an ideal of altruism or anything else. Such are of the mind of man. Faith could only find its True Object in God. Faith could only exist within an acceptance of the Self-Revelation of God. As the progressive revelation of God was completed through His Own inspired and preserved Scripture, the use of vision, dream, and direct contact were dissolved as not applicable to true faith. Faith must be centered in the revealed Words of God. The revealed Words of God are only available in His inspired and preserved Scripture. Scripture reveals Jesus. Jesus died for our sins. Any faith which is not founded upon the Work of Jesus cannot be true faith in God.

Founded in the inspired and preserved Scripture are the Words of God for mankind in this day. Scripture does not record a picture of man searching for God and his own place in the cosmos. Scripture speaks of the fact that God has come to find us. (Luke 19:10) This is not a "new religion." This is the revealed faith within which man has to come to God. This has been true even before the sin of Adam. God knew that coming sin of Adam and had prepared the Cross as the antidote for that sin even before Adam had been created.

It is a wonder how great and full is the Love of God toward His creature of creation!

We are instructed to be established in this faith. Even in our greatest temptation and persecution we are instructed to trust the Lord. The feet of our spirit are established on the Strong Rock of the salvation which is in Christ, Jesus. Let us meditate upon that reality and wait patiently upon the Lord.

The precious promise of the soon coming of the Lord is not an exercise in fatalism. It is an exercise in faith and a hope of the reality of the soon coming event. The times are indeed in His Hands. An undeniable truth is that the coming of the Lord is one day closer today than it was yesterday. He is coming. It behooves each of us to wait expectantly and to be so engaged that we will not be ashamed of our conduct when He does appear.]

5.9   *Grudge not one against another, brethren, lest ye be condemned: behold, the judge standeth before the door.*

[It is interesting to note that the judge of all men, Christ, is said to be standing before the door. Compare this with Genesis 4:7 where God is addressing Cain about Cain's unaccepted sacrifice of the fruit of the ground, his labor, as contrasted with Abel's offering and accepted blood sacrifice of a lamb from his flocks. "If thou doest well, shalt thou not be accepted? and if thou doest not well, sin lieth at the door. And unto thee shall be his desire, and thou shalt rule over him."

To Cain it was said that sin "lieth at the door." To the brethren who James addresses came the warning that "behold, the judge standeth before the door." The difference in the two audiences lies in the heart attitudes of both. Cain was upset because God had not accepted his best effort. This displays a heart of pride. This also displays a heart which will not yield to God or His purposes. It is an attitude of superiority. It says, "God needs to change His position and accept MY sacrifice."

Abel, meanwhile, simply said to God, "Thy kingdom come. Thy will be done in earth, as it is in heaven." (Matthew 6:10) The sacrifice of a lamb from the flock of Abel was more than a prophecy of the crucifixion of Jesus. It was that, of course. But, it also gave evidence that in the heart of Abel was a love for the ways of God. Abel had read the third chapter of Genesis and had seen that God sacrificed an animal of the field to make a covering for the sin of Adam and Eve. The attitude of Abel was one of pleasure in the Words and Ways of God. It was an emblem of the love which Abel had for God and of his faith in the promises of God.

O. K.; Abel hadn't read Genesis. But, he had often listened to his parents explain the glories of the Garden and the reason for their expulsion from it. Proverbs 22:6 tells us, "Train up a child in the way he should go: and when he is old, he will not depart from it." It is obvious that Abel took the words about God, given from his parents, to heart.

But, Cain was the proof that sin did lie upon his doorstep. He had the same parents as his brother. He, doubtless, heard the same stories about God and the Garden as had his brother. But that streak of rebellion within the heart of Cain caused him to rebel against the message of God.

We have that same spirit within the churches in our day. I recall a pastor whose wife questioned my use of the King James Bible. She said, "Why do you want to read Shakespeare?"

That little story brings up an interesting situation. Have you ever heard of anyone who wanted to "update" the plays of Shakespeare? I haven't. But, everyone seems to want to "update" the Bible. The only thing that all of these bibles have in common is a copyright and an aversion to the King James Bible. Why is that?

We have all heard of the Textus Receptus. That text has also been called the Constantinoplan, the Syrian, the Text of the Reformation, the Antiochian Text, and by the duo of Hort and Westcott, "that vile text." All of these are wrong, especially that last one which is rooted in sin more than in scholarship. The error is that these terms tend to call this a "localized" text much as the "Western," and "Alexandrian" are localize in the area in which they are likely to appear. The Text of the Textus Receptus, sometimes called the "Traditional Text," is the text of the history of the church. It is found in all areas where the Church existed.

In 1881 a committee headed by Dr's Hort and Westcott, released a new version of scripture. It was called an update of the venerable King James Version. It wasn't. The base line of the text of Scripture had been replaced with another text. Whereas the bulk of the underlying text of the King James was the Greek edition of Beza, the underlying text of that English Revised Version was culled primarily from two sources. Both were ancient. Both were flawed.

The "Vaticanus," a text found under the dust of the Vatican library was one of these. It cuts off in the middle of Hebrews when the text begins to speak of only one sacrifice. Since the daily mass is considered a sacrifice of the body and blood of Jesus, due to the unscriptural doctrine of Transubstantiation, it is obvious – to me at least – why the excised words are missing.

The other was the "Sinaiticus," which was found in its proper location – a burning barrel. This was so corrupt that one is able to find portions erased and corrected by at least seven hands during the centuries. As for it being one of the oldest, I am reminded of a man who was auctioning off an axe that had belonged to George Washington. He said it was the original axe. The head had been changed four times and the handle six, but it was the original axe used by George Washington to chop down his father's cherry tree.

The two, the primary basis for today's "Critical Text," disagree with each other at least 3,000 times just in the New Testament. These are the two "oldest and best" which are listed in the footnotes and margins of our Bibles.

The "upshot" of this is that the modern English bible "versions" are actually not the same Bible. It is a Biblical truth that "...the natural man receiveth not the things of the Spirit of God: for they are foolishness unto him: neither can he know them, because they are spiritually discerned." (I Corinthians 2:14) Therefore, those who like Cain are not disposed to lean towards the Words of God, the modern "versions" allow an escape from God and His purity. They are allowed to "feast" (?) upon a bible which contains a general picture of what God might have said. Indepth study and pious submission are sunk within the sea of pious platitude and professed piety. Not only do our Christian assemblies suffer so, too, does the general culture of man which is not thereby seasoned with the salt of our sanctified testimony.

The story is told of a man who was so weak the only thing he could hold was a grudge. It's a good illustration because it is generally only those who are weak in the Lord who will stoop to hold a grudge against a brother in the Lord. Trust me on this one. Been there. Done that. Sadly, still doing it all too often. No one in this life gets past the place where he needs to fly to the Lord for forgiveness and maybe a little repair (repentance) work.

James is now speaking of persecution which comes primarily from inside the fellowship. The cruelest blows are those that come from the closest associates. Notice that I did not say, "friends." That is a sad but true thing. Friendship seems to fly out the door when we open the latch to grumbling about situations, sighing about perceived slights, and murmuring about those we either dislike or envy.

We look at the term "condemned" and tend to recoil from the thought. We complain that our sins have already been judged at the Cross. Well, maybe "complain" is the wrong word. After all, we do glory in that fact of our contrariness.

Consider I John 2:1 in relation to this. "My little children, these things write I unto you, that ye sin not. And if any man sin, we have an advocate with the Father, Jesus Christ the righteous..." We may honestly be saved. If we've trusted Christ as our Savior we are saved. It is good for us that salvation is all about what He has done for us. We had no part, except acceptance, therein.

It is sort of like taking a bath in one of those Roman Era bathhouses. We are clean. Completely clean! Then we put on our sandals and step out into those unpaved streets that are completely without sidewalks. When we get to our destination someone will surely come to us with water to wash our feet. Such was a custom, a necessary custom, of that day. We may be clean but that daily walk causes us to need a little "touch up."

The groaning of grudgmanship, doesn't just happen. It is a flower whose roots are based in pride. "I'm better than..." Well, fill in the blank and grumble about it. "About them." That is the attitude that says, "I'll put them in their place." The place we see is below us.

This brings the condemnation of judgment upon us. I would really like to say "them." It just seems that "us" is more accurate.

The Judge stands at the door. He is ready to pronounce sentence upon us. He pronounces us as guilty. When we see this we must realize that we have harmed our Savior. We have brought discredit to the Holy Name by which we are called.

Repentance? For the Christian? Yes. It is real. It is cleansing and empowering. It is our duty to Him Who died for us. It is a matter of cleaning our feet after Jesus has cleansed our soul.

It is far better to find Jesus standing to welcome us as He did when Stephen was martyred. (Acts 7:55-56)]

5.10 *Take, my brethren, the prophets, who have spoken in the name of the Lord, for an example of suffering affliction, and of patience.*

[Shakespeare had spoken of opposing the "slings and arrows" of outrageous fortune. God says, "I've got a better idea." Take a look at the reaction of the prophets of old as they encountered persecution.

First, look at the fact that the prophets were persecuted. Natural man would consider the situation and argue that no true prophet of God will be persecuted. "After all, certainly their God will protect those who are doing His work."

Actually, it is the opposite which is true. The condition not taken into consideration is that humanity is a sinful race of people. That sin stands, always, as in an opposition to the Holiness of God. And, when it does not so stand it is only the duplicitous nature of sin which makes it appear so. Satan, we must consider, is not bound by any moral code. His credo is certainly that of the "flapper" from the old song – "Anything goes."

Satan will use two positives in order to make one negative. He transforms his appearance into "...an angel of light" (II Corinthians 11:14) simply to lead into the darkness of the abyss. If he can cause an honest believer to be so deceived as to help him complete his rounds, so much the better. In such a case as this a Christian will have been so corrupted as to lose his own effectiveness in witness. This happens even as that Christian's own soul is out of fellowship with the Eternal Master.

In the appeal to the prophets we do note that this persecution which they suffered was on account of their fidelity to the Lord. We may be attacked because we are either brusque or unloving toward others. This is not an example of Godly persecution. This is an example of another spiritual principle – what one sows he is more than likely to reap. (Galatians 6:7)

In this my mind goes to the group which pickets at the funerals of fallen soldiers. They seem to consider that they are hated because they are doing the work of God. Not so! I have never heard any of them approach anyone as to the salvation of a soul. Matthew 28:18-20 has given to the Church a clear and unequivocal mandate. "Therefore to him that knoweth to do good, and doeth it not, to him it is sin." (James 4:17) Their suffering seems clear from Scripture to be in answer to Galatians 6:7.

One may well fancy himself to be in the mold of an Old Testament prophet. That is not the template which God has given to His New Covenant of the Blood of Jesus, Churches. It seems clear that out mandate is to preach the Good News that Jesus Christ died in time so that others could have their sins forgiven and live in eternity. "And I, if I be lifted up from the earth, will draw all men unto me." (John 12:32) Our call is to lift up the Name of Christ so that sin may be removed from the land – one person at a time. Our call is not to lift up the name of sin that we may exult in our personal persecution.

Even the prophets of doom in the Old Testament held out the hope of personal piety and repentance among the doomed nation.

The prophets of old, and the Christians of the early church were patient in their suffering for the Lord's message. They are not held as examples of antisocial individuals being persecuted for their own doltish behavior. Those engaging in such are, humanly speaking, a great detriment to the cause of Christ.]

5.11 *Behold, we count them happy which endure. Ye have heard of the patience of Job, and have seen the end of the Lord, that the Lord is very pitiful, and of tender mercy.*

[Job has been called a great object lesson of Scripture. As this verse attests, he was more than just that. Job was a real person who lived a real life and suffered real temptations to sin by denying God. He did not. Instead, even in the midst of the agony of his situation he retained his full integrity.

Another reference to Job is contained in Ezekiel 14:14 where Noah and Daniel are mentioned with him as examples of righteousness.

Why was Job so tried by Satan? Why did God allow such trying of Job? The only answer I can give is that the Old Testament will generally teach us of God by using real situations in the life of real people. From the physical events in the Old Testament we are taught spiritual truths which are necessary for us to learn.

This is the explanation of the suffering of Job. From this verse we learn to trust on God in all situations and not to allow ourselves to curse the Lord when He will lead us to ends greater than we can see.

Consider the words of Job while he was still in his distress. "For I know *that* my redeemer liveth, and that he shall stand at the latter *day* upon the earth: And *though* after my skin worms destroy this body, yet in my flesh shall I see God." (Job 19:25-26)

There are times which Job did complain about his lot. He is a human being, after all. I would guess that complaint is better than what he did not do. At no time did Job blame God of unrighteousness. Neither did Job curse God as his wife urged him to do. (Job 2:9)

There are a couple of things worthy of mention in this passage. Not the least of which is that fact that Job understood the concept of an "after life." He expected a resurrection of his body in which he would stand before the God of Creation.

Also, why did Job mention "my skin worms?" The people of his day would not have understood that bacteria, and such, from within our own bodies are responsible for the decomposition of our bodies after death. This was beyond the knowledge of the day. Still Job owned these organisms as being in his possession.

Again, in the midst of his discomfiture, he called God "my redeemer." In regards to this Job also spoke that God was a Living Being rather than a dead idol such as many would have worshipped at this time.

Finally, this passage from Job shows that he understood the concept of a "last days." I would hazard that he didn't understand all about this subject in that time. But, he did understand the concept that God controls the destinies of man and that history is moving toward a climax.

We also find that in the end God blessed Job even above that wherein he had been blessed earlier. God reward Job, even on this earth, for his suffering and patience in that suffering. In this God displayed both pity and mercy upon Job.

We must also note that the people who came to "comfort" Job in his suffering were not really very comforting. We can expect no solace from the world concerning the suffering that the world heaps upon us for the Lord. They will tend to impinge our motives and our God instead of offering real support. They may even give us such support as would tend to draw us further from the Lord!

James has said that the people who endure are counted as happy. This word speaks of blessing. Those who endure hardships and privations for the Lord are blessed even within their persecution.]

5.12 *But above all things, my brethren, swear not, neither by heaven, neither by the earth, neither by any other oath: but let your yea be yea, and your nay, nay, lest ye fall into condemnation.*

Ecclesiastes 5:5; Matthew 5:34-37

[Basically, this is the same message as in Matthew, chapter five. Don't promise what you can't deliver or you will cause yourself problems. Such problems will lower the estimate of the validity of your witness to the lost.

The phrase "above all things" alerts the reader to the fact of the importance of this verse.

Clarke argues that it was common practice to swear with the lips, on anything. His oath would not be considered binding if he annulled the oath in his heart. "Rabbi Akiba taught that "a man might swear with his lips, and annul it in his heart; and then the oath was not binding." Such double speech would not be consistent with the Christian witness. A liar in one area may be a liar in any area – including speaking of spiritual realities. (James 1:8)

James, always vigilant to the stable and trustworthy witness of the Christian asks that they simply say "yes" when the meaning is "yes" and "no" when the meaning is "no." The concept of truthfulness in all things was highly guarded, is still, by men of virtue. Beyond even this is the fact that the Savior required such from His followers. "But let your communication be, Yea, yea; Nay, nay: for whatsoever is more than these cometh of evil." (Matthew 5:37) If we are a people known to the cause of truth there will be no need to swear an oath in everyday conversation.

There are cultish groups which teach that "making a lie for the cause" is a religious duty. It should take very little to convince one that such as these are not to be trusted in any manner. Their "yes" of today may hide a destructive "no" in their representations of their god or religious belief. We can allow no such duplicity among those who worship Jesus. He said of Himself, "...I am the way, the truth, and the life: no man cometh unto the Father, but by me." (John 14:6b) He Who is Truth personified can never be well served by a false oath.

All oaths are not proscribed. But all foolish oaths can cause problems. Consider the foolish oath of Jephthah from Judges 11:30-40.

This prohibition does not extend to swearing an oath before a magistrate or signing a contract when one promises, essentially an oath, to pay the agreed upon amount. These are not the oaths of ordinary conversation but the contracts of legality concerning the ordered society. In these cases, as in killing someone while serving in a military, the fault, if there be any, is laid upon the law of the land which we are also sworn to obey. (Romans 13:1ff) The only time we have the right to disobey the law of the land is when that law contradicts the known law of God. In such a case as this we must say with Peter and the other disciples, "Then Peter and the other apostles answered and said, We ought to obey God rather than men." (Acts 5:29)

The fact that all oaths are not proscribed is shown by the oaths taken by holy men of old. Genesis 21:23; 24:3; 26:28; I Kings 17:1-3; II Corinthians 1:23; and Galatians 1:20. The forbidden oaths are those which might compromise our truthfulness. Although those things of the Spirit should cause us to dwell upon them and hold the honor we give to our Lord as a sacred duty to be honest in all of our dealing with our fellow humans. The other, and the Jews of the time were wont to do this, we cannot swear by our bodies. We are not our own our bodies as Christians; we are bought with the price of the Cross.   (I Corinthians 6:20; and 7:23)

Neither can we swear by our bodies as we have scant control over the physical. "Which of you by taking thought can add one cubit unto his stature?" (Matthew 6:27)

Violation of this rule can put us in danger of chastisement from the Lord. (Consider the spiritual principle of I Corinthians 11:30)]

5.13 *Is any among you afflicted? let him pray. Is any merry? let him sing psalms.*

[The idea of affliction is to be enduring hardships. It may be that persecution has come upon the man or it may the general day-to-day "slings and arrows of outrageous fortune" which befall us all. Either way the remedy is to fly to God in prayer that we may feel His Hand of Comfort. When we are in concrete connection with The God of Eternity the cares of the world will tend to fade into the background.

Prayer is a balm for a weary soul. It is a priceless privilege to lay hold of the throne of grace in bad times and a priceless joy in good times. Unlike the peace the world may offer, there is no cost and no "product" to purchase. The Lord, in His great Self-Sacrifice at Calvary has paid the price of our peace with God and with circumstance when we avail ourselves of His blessed presence

Those afflictions may continue. But, our communion with the Lord will cause a joy that is inexplicable to the world. As Noah rode above the waves of judgment, safe in the ark of salvation, we can endure afflictions with the knowledge that we are safe in the Hands of the Master. The awareness of the eternity of bliss which awaits us in the presence of our Savior will cause the troubles of time to be a small thing to be endured for a short time. Then will come our reward.

The merry may well sing praises to the Lord. He is worthy of our worship.

Note the reference in regards to singing Psalms. This was the practice of the churches for centuries. It is a powerful combination to lift our voices in praise to our God even as we put our thoughts upon the precious inspired and preserved Scripture He has given to us.]

5.14 *Is any sick among you? let him call for the elders of the church; and let them pray over him, anointing him with oil in the name of the Lord:*

[An interesting verse and often misapplied. Far too many will take this verse and hold it up to the Face of God and say, "You have to do this." He has to do nothing that is outside of His Divine Will. There is a sickness unto death. If every prayer healed every afflicted person, none would ever die and go into their reward.

There is also a sickness of chastisement which God will visit upon His erring children. "For this cause many are weak and sickly among you, and many sleep." (I Corinthians 11:30) God will discipline His children out of a heart of love. Our temporary understanding does not make this fact untrue.

There is also a sickness which comes, as with Job, from the tempter. Even here this is often a situation of chastisement from the Lord. Our spiritual weaknesses may be tried and corrected by the crucible of illness wherein we may learn to lean upon the Lord rather than upon our own body of temporal strength. In these situations, the suffering of physical illness is an entry ramp unto the further fellowship with the Lord.

Note the use of anointing with oil. This was a natural medicine – one of the few at this time. It was neither a mystical nor magical cure. In this day of James the "sign gifts" were fully in operation. The united prayers of the elders invoked the Spirit of God into the situation. Had this been an "at all times" miraculous cure the Spirit could have worked just as well without the oil as with it. I can recall of no time that Jesus healed with the assistance of oil.

That the oil had a curative effect is well known. That it is within the power of God to heal at any time He so chooses to act in His directive will is also well known. What we actually see here is the combination of a man sanctioned curative working in harmony with the known grace of God.

In this the healing was not that different from our adherence to the "Great Commission." Our witness will lead to the salvation of no one unless the Spirit puts conviction upon the soul of him to who our witness is gone forth. We are given the great glory of being allowed to work with the God of Creation as we spread the word of His Glory and Salvation. We are not important; we are only allowed to be tools in the Hands of Almighty God.

Prayer is a means of invoking the Divine Graces of the Spirit. Thus, we pray for the sick as they call upon us to do so. Thus, we pray for the lost – by name and fervently! – even as we visit the Name of Christ unto them. Both are to admit that we are powerless but the Spirit is the God of all power.

We might note that the call to pray over the ill is to go out to the elders. This is a plural word. One man in a charismatic service is not a "healer." This is a call to the elders of the church to pray as a united group of believers. Neither is this a "Healing Campaign." There is no "Healing Line" with comment card and spectacle. This is the calling of the elders of the local church to attend to the needs of one of their membership.

Again, this is a call to the elders of the church. This is not a call to the apostles as this is intended, as inspired and preserved Scripture, to be a command to the churches of the ages. This is but one more indication that God has actually preserved His inspired Words to humanity.

Those "sign gifts" were only in effect until the complete record of Scripture was presented to man from the inspiration of God. But, this picture of the care of the Christian by the brothers and sisters in the churches was to continue within all the churches.

I must close this verse with an admonition that is "extra Biblical." I believe that the ill ought to pray for himself. In this communion with God he may find the base cause of his illness. He still should, as James instructs, to call for the elders to unite with him in prayer. There are two reasons for this. The first, obviously, is that this is the command of God. If we fail to follow His dictates we can have little trust in finding His will and favor.

Second, there is something special about a united prayer. We are all, as Christians, invited to come in prayer to the Throne of Grace. (Hebrews 4:16) It is also good to unite with others in prayer. Such a practice will encourage both in their prayers. Such a practice will encourage both to reach unto higher fellowship with the Lord of their petitions.]

5.15 *And the prayer of faith shall save the sick, and the Lord shall raise him up; and if he have committed sins, they shall be forgiven him.*

[Before we get into this verse I would access three references from the New Testament Scripture. The first is II Corinthians 12:7. The second is I Timothy 5:23. The third is II Timothy 4:20.

In that first verse (II Corinthians 12:7) we see that Paul prayed that a "thorn in the flesh" be healed. God said, "No. It's there for a purpose." In the second verse (I Timothy 5:23) we find that Paul advised Timothy to take a little wine for his weak stomach. Don't get excited and vote Paul out of fellowship for this! There were few medicines in that day. Wine, as a sedative of sorts, was one of those few. The third verse (II Timothy 4:20) relates to a man named Trophimus who could not follow with Paul on a missionary journey because he was sick.

Those who would use this verse to argue that God **MUST** heal every time a prayer of faith is offered are left with the sad conclusion that Paul must have not been a man of faith. Just look at all those times he either referred to medicine or gave up on healing.

As we said in the last verse, it is not the will of God to heal in every instance. There are times that healing would work against His purposes in this world. But, every time the prayer of faith is offered it is effective.

What?

The prayer of faith is one which is offered not "in Jesus Name" as a talisman, but "in the Name of Jesus" as a submission to His will. When we pray in faith, which is centered within the will of Jesus, His will will be done and the sick shall be healed. Consider the truth of James 4:3a. "Ye ask, and receive not, because ye ask amiss..."

We can have faith and yet find that our faith is not centered upon the perfect will of God. Consider a man who believes with all of his heart that salvation comes from an idol of a golden calf. Will that faith save him? Of course not! "Neither is there salvation in any other: for there is none other name under heaven given among men, whereby we must be saved." (Acts 4:12)

We can pray to anyone. It really doesn't matter. Only the Jesus of the Bible can save a soul. For even a prayer of faith to be an effective prayer it must be centered upon the directive will and purpose of God.

Notice that even when the answer to a faithful prayer is in the affirmative, "...it is the Lord shall raise him up..." The answer to the prayer is not a formula to follow. It is a faith that God will act. All glory should go to the Lord. Even the elders have no glory in their prayers. Instead they should glory in the Lord Who answers prayer. They should glory that the Lord has allowed them to witness His Glory and wonder working power.

We must be very careful at this point. Our faith is not centered in the prospect of a healing of a man's maladies but in the goodness of God to work His Perfect Will in this man's life. If we have honestly prayed in faith we must give glory and thanks to God whether His answer to our petition is "yea" or "nay."

He fully understands our condition as vessels of clay. His directive will is always for the good of His children. The unsaved have no right to expect anything except the opportunity to fall before the Cross in repentance and acceptance.

It may be that the exercise of faithful prayer may cause the ill person to assess his life and find that the cause of his sickness is sin in his life. In such a case that faithful prayer, becomes just one more good reason for the call for the elders of the church, may be such that the ill will find his sin to be ever before him. He may begin to call upon the Lord for deliverance from sinful habit or action. When his prayer becomes this – and it must be his own prayer as even the elders cannot pray for him in this manner – he may find that Jesus is his advocate and redeemer from his soulish attractions to the things of the world rather than to the God of Salvation.

"...and if he have committed sins, they shall be forgiven him." In such a case the ill man may then rejoice that it was the chastisement of his malady which brought him to the happy fellowship with the Lord. Whether the body is healed or not will be unimportant to the man who has found true solace for his soul.

The Roman doctrine of "extreme unction" is nowhere in this passage. First, the prayer offered by the elders from the church concerned only the wholeness of the mortal body. Second, the prayer which would have caused the forgiveness of sins must have been uttered by the ill person. This would have been only between the penitent and the Lord. Others, such as the elders, may only observe that which is done in such a case.

James does continue to consider the outward signs of the Christian walk. Therefore he notices the "prayer of faith" as a causative agent while obviously stating that the Lord has raised the man from his illness.]

5.16 *Confess your faults one to another, and pray one for another, that ye may be healed. The effectual fervent prayer of a righteous man availeth much.*

[This passage speaks of confessing our sins one to another. James has moved from the elders of the church to the membership of the church. This does not give sanction to the Roman custom of the "Confessional." Confessing one to another has benefit beyond the confessing of our sins to an appointed priest. Confessing one to another is lay our soul bare among those who we know the best and who know us intimately as well.

I do not believe in "confession meetings" where we are required to give a list of our failures. Such has a place but a "forced confession" is not a freely given testimony. At its worst there will be someone in the audience with pen and pad. This could cause great harm to the cause of Christ within the witness of that church.

However, freely confessed failures, sin in our life, to another is a hedge against pride and a strong cord to hold us close to Christ. Among our dearest friends we all seek to find respect and friendship. We will be loath to do wrong, or even to act wrong, among these because we know them best. They are our closest, or should be as members of the church, friends among whom we gather to worship the Lord.

The phrase "that ye may be healed" seems to indicate that the reference is still speaking of the ill person. Also, there is the possibility – especially since "ye" is a plural word speaking of a group of people, that this is intended as a means of healing breaches within the church. I have seen "church splits." The church where I went as a child was formed by splitting from another church. Some fifty years later this church suffered through a "split" of its own. The church where I presently preach was severely harmed from a church split some years ago.

This sort of a spirit of partisanship, pride, and a lack of tolerance is never to be the spirit of the churches which Jesus founded. Indeed, such cannot happen when all the people have their eyes upon the Lord and their hearts attuned to following Him.

Only one of the splits mentioned above was the result of serious spiritual separation. Most church splits happen because of pride in one's own self and intolerance toward another. Be well advised that God does not sanction such as this. These will harm the cause of Christ in the area where they occur.

Generally speaking the confession is from the offender to the offended. Caution must be understood that greater hostility between the two not ensue. A humble spirit of contrition must be evident in the offender while a spirit of love should always be shown by the offended. When we realize the true results of such sin in our life we should acknowledge that we have harmed.

In the fourth verse of the fifty-first Psalm David says, "Against thee, thee only, have I sinned, and done this evil in thy sight: that thou mightest be justified when thou speakest, and be clear when thou judgest." David realizes that the ultimate offense was toward God.

This was in reference to David using his influence as King to entice Bathsheba to his bed. This was also in reference to the virtual murder of Uriah, Bathsheba's husband, in an attempt to cover his sin. David realized that the great harm he had done to Uriah and Bathsheba paled in comparison to his sin against God.

Sin, even when another person is our intended object, is always a sin against God. This ought not to be.

We are also invited to pray one for another. This is probably a very good idea when we consider making confession to another. This may be used to put ourselves into a properly humble frame of mind as we confess our faults. This may also help to put the one we have wronged into a state of mind to accept our apology. The Spirit is able to work wonders beyond any we could hope for or imagine.

Also, the very fact that we are praying for the benefit of another will cause our hearts to open to their health and happiness. This remains a balm to heal our pride as well. We have the "heart-problems" of our conscience healed when we confess our sins and seek the forgiveness of man and God. The cause of much sickness is the guilt of our hearts from the actions of our hands.

The effectual prayer is a fervent prayer. I like the term used by the Holiness people; they speak of "praying through rather than getting through praying." A fervent prayer is one that is heartfelt and nearly anxious in its performance.

Driving through the Rocky Mountains one day when my son was about four years old, I glanced over at him and saw him tighten his seat belt and lock his door. He had no intention of falling out of his seat and tumbling over the cliff. That is a very good picture of prevailing prayer. It is a prayer that is anxious to use all proper means to find the answer. That is a perfect picture of the kind of fervent prayer which is effective to reach the Throne and touch the ear of God.]

5.17 *Elias was a man subject to like passions as we are, and he prayed earnestly that it might not rain: and it rained not on the earth by the space of three years and six months.*

[Clarke, who seems never to have met a variant reading he didn't prefer complains at this point, "This was Elijah, and a consistency between the names of the same persons as expressed in the Old and the New Testaments should be kept up." I guess it would be nice. It'd make things easier at time. So, why are the Names of so many Old Testament persons spelled differently in the New Testament?

Actually, the answer is quite simple. The translators of the King James Bible were acutely aware that they were handling the Word of God. They were very reluctant to make any changes in the wording. The Greek form was not always the same as the Hebrew form of the names. The name of Jesus, for instance, is the same as is Joshua under the Old Testament Hebrew spelling. They simply translated and did not make "correction."

This also explains the use of *italics* in the King James Bible. Any time there was a need to add an English word for clarities sake because of the difference between the languages, the translators would put the added words in *italics* so the reader could easily understand that the words of men had been added, necessary for the sake of understanding, words to the inspired and preserved text in the translation.

Since Elijah was translated, so as not to see death, people might naturally assume that he was not a human such as us. They would not then consider his example as necessary to either study or follow.

James reminds them that Elijah was not a "folk-tale." He was an actual living, breathing man of the Old Testament times. It would be good for us to consider that these are not stories told about men in the Bible. These are historical incidents which God recorded within His inspired and preserved Scripture in order that we could learn spiritual truths from the physical actions of these real people.

The Old Testament (I Kings 28:1) only says that the drought went into the third year. Jesus (Luke 4:25) gave us the information that the drought lasted three years and six months. We must assume Him right. After all, as God, Jesus was literally alive during that time.

It is interesting how often the New Testament gives us further information about the Old Testament Scriptures. When we consider the concept of the progressive revelation of Scripture we can begin to understand this fact.

On this same topic, James notes that Elijah "prayed earnestly." This is not recorded in the Old Testament but is given in this New Testament passage by the inspiration of the Words by the Spirit. It would seem ludicrous to consider that Elijah had stopped the rain from the nation on his own say so. Although the Spirit did empower men of the Old Testament era to perform certain "mighty acts," the stopping of the rain is an obvious act of God in His Power as Creator of the earth.

I Kings 17:1 records Elijah as saying, "As the Lord liveth, there shall not be dew nor rain, but according to my word..." James supplies the information that this word was the words of prayer.

We can understand that the phrase "rained not on the earth" was not speaking the entire earth but of that earth which contained the Land of Promise. This was a plague on Israel for her sins and would not of necessity have spilt over into other lands.]

5.18 *And he prayed again, and the heaven gave rain, and the earth brought forth her fruit.*

[The time of Elijah's second prayer, to renew the rain upon the land was probably in I Kings 18:42b. ",,,And Elijah went up to the top of Carmel; and he cast himself down upon the earth, and put his face between his knee..." This is certainly the physical attitude of prayer for Elijah. This was shortly after his contest with the priests of Baal when God utterly defeated the false idol god, Baal.

It is interesting that the two witnesses of the Tribulation Era are able to shut up the heavens that it rain not for three and one half years. (Revelation 11:6) How often the Bible will show an earlier event to be the precursor of a later event. There is an amazing consistency in the inspired and preserved Scripture. This is an evidence of the Hand of God preserving His Word to man. This is especially so when one considers the length of the time line and the number of penmen – from a myriad of professions – who made up the human instruments who recorded those Divine Words.

Some would argue "Miracle" in these circumstances. James attributes it all to prayer. Therein is a miracle. God condescends to bless the requests of His servants. That is certainly a miracle of grace and love – and the power of God!]

5.19 *Brethren, if any of you do err from the truth, and one convert him,*

[The first thing to notice here is that all rebukes are not condemned. Some are intended to cleanse the fellowship. That this is not speaking of the world of unsaved sinners is shown by the following verse which states to things: 1) "...he which converteth the sinner..." and, 2) "...(he) shall save a soul from death..." Folks, we "gotta know" that we have no ability to convert anyone or to save them from spiritual death. These are both only available under the power of Jesus, the Christ. (Acts 4:12)

The word "convert" in this verse is concerned with changing someone's behavior. It is to cause them to "turn" from a wicked way. There are times when the Christian will act contrary to his "new nature." He will revert to soulish behavior which is unbecoming to a child of The King! Not only will his own testimony be harmed but so will the testimony of the entire church which, as a member or even as an attendee, he automatically represents in the eyes of the community.

The local radio station has been running advertisements for a "stop smoking" seminar. That, causing a change in the behavior of a person, is the sense of the verse. That behavior can be outward. Given the general sense of the epistle of James, that would be my understanding because James seems most interested in the perception of the world as they consider the persons of the Church.

This could be an inward flaw spoken of in this place. It may be the reality of something within a man's private life which stands between him and his full fellowship with the Lord.

"How would James know of a private sin?" This is an honest question. But, it is always true that the heart is betrayed by the outward work, attitude and demeanor of a man. James spent much time earlier in this epistle in arguing that the tongue is a witness of our flaws as it speaks with unbridled clarity to that which is within our hearts.

This could be a doctrinal problem. Many a church has been harmed by the doctrinal confusions of a man in the pew. An example of this is my view of the Antichrist of the Revelation. I believe he will be an Arab and possibly a lapsed, or even a practicing, Muslim. I bring this up because I will always say, when speaking of this, "I am probably wrong because nearly no one agrees with me on this. The Spirit will illumine His Church rather than simply one individual."

In this I have stated my view and the argument that proper interpretation belongs to the Lord and not to me. We must continue to seek His guidance.

Another error of mine came as I administered the Lord's Table. I offered the wine before the bread. This may seem unimportant. It is vitally important! It is the Blood of Christ which cleanseth us from all sin. (I John 1:7) Before His agony on the Cross our Lord walked among men as a man. In this He taught us how to walk in holiness before God. This dual nature, a man of time and The God of Eternity, is a precious thing. To reverse this order of His work would be wrong. He came to earth to live among us and to teach us how to live with Him. He died on the Cross so that our sins might be forgiven in order that we could abide with Him.

It is the Deity of Christ which secures our salvation. Sin is an offense against The God of Holiness. Only the One offended may forgive the offense. But, this Self-Sacrifice from which our salvation flows had to be performed by one of us in order that it be effective for any of us. Hebrews 10:4 makes it clear that the sacrifice of a beast of creation is not eternally sufficient to cleanse the sins of the human. We are not of the same species and that sacrifice can never be associated with our sins.

Besides this, He was cruelly beaten and tormented even before He went to that Cross.

Neither can a man die for another man's sin. Hebrews 9:27 is very clear. "And as it is appointed unto men once to die, but after this the judgment…" Since each human is to be judged for his sin, and he is then found guilty of that sin, it is not possible that any mere human can stand as a substitute for another.

Jesus, however, is one with us in His humanity as the Son of woman. He inherited no original sin nature from His father, Adam, for Adam – nor the son of Adam – was not His Father. Jesus was virgin born into the family of man but the essence of His Being was, and is!, Divine. He is God Who took upon Himself the reality of a human existence while retaining His True Nature as God. Thus Jesus, and only Jesus, is able to stand as our Substitute, our Example, and – gloriously so – as our Savior.

We are not called to live above our brothers and sisters in the Lord. We are called to live with them. In this we are called to guard one another against sin and its tendencies within all of our human hearts.]

5.20 *Let him know, that he which converteth the sinner from the error of his way shall save a soul from death, and shall hide a multitude of sins.*

[James asks that we carefully consider the prospect of our witness. We are doing the work of the Lord's direction when we seek to return a straying sheep to the fold. This verse has nothing to do with salvation. The phrase "converteth the sinner" does not speak of a lost person but of a Christian who has enmeshed himself in carnality and sin. This is made obvious by the fact that "he," the person who deals with this "sinner," is the one which "converts" him.

Once again, we can have no part in the conversion of a lost man except to witness and pray that the conviction of Spirit be laid upon his soul.

If we are to properly assess the epistle of James we must keep in mind that James' primary concern is to examine a person as one outside the faith might examine him. James is concerned that the Christian be a Christian in all walks of his life. He demands that our walk be consistent with the desires of our Lord.

A true Christian may sin. He still lives in a body of clay which will war at times against the new nature of the spirit. James calls to task the Christian who has succumbed to this vileness against his Christian walk. Such chastisement of the Christian by The Heavenly Father may include physical death. (I Corinthians 11:30) Still, the spirit of the man will continue to live within the presence of God. The chastisement of physical death is not judgment as the judgment of the Christian has taken place at the Cross of Christ. This is a chastisement of blessing in light of eternity.

If there were no sin possible for the Christian there would be no need that the Christian ever fall under the chastening Hand of God. Both Proverbs 3:12, under the Old Covenant, and Hebrews 12:6, under the New Covenant, will warn that the Lord will chastise His children in this world. Both verses speak of the correcting purpose of such chastisement. Thus, both speak of children of God which are gone astray but remain His children. It is His love that chastises His own and His purity that judges those outside the household of faith.

Many have argued that the phrase, "shall hide a multitude of sins" would refer to some "special" grace given to the man who led the other from his sins. Nothing could be more further from the truth. God does not deal in indulgences! We do not get a "free pass" to sin in any context.

Consider once again that James is concerned with the perception of the world as they view those of the Church. God forgives sin but, it seems too often, the world – even the "Christian World" – has a long memory for the sins of the past. This includes those forgiven and placed in Divine forgetfulness. Consider Psalm 32:1. "Blessed is he whose transgression is forgiven, whose sin is covered."

The fact that the one "converted" in this place will forego further sin of this sort as he forsakes it and begins to walk anew in the fellowship of the Lord, will mean that these sins in which he had formerly wallowed are no longer evident to the critics of the assembly, or to the assembly for that matter.]

FIRST PETER

FIRST PETER - CHAPTER ONE

1.1   Peter, an apostle of Jesus Christ, to the strangers scattered throughout Pontus, Galatia, Cappadocia, Asia, and Bithynia,

[Peter claims his place as an apostle. The apostles were ones who were specifically chosen and trained by Jesus during His earthly ministry. They were empowered to teach, of course, in all of the churches. Part of this teaching ministry extended to these epistles in which the very words were inspired of God. Our New Testament Scripture is penned either by the apostles or by those who were so closely associated with those apostles as to make their works essentially the words of the apostles.

Even with this caveat it is always the imprint of the Spirit - the inspiration of those words - upon these epistles which marked them as Scripture. That "mark" was impressed upon the Christians of the churches by the Spirit.

Those apostles were also empowered upon special occasion to work miracles, especially those of healing th e physical body. Their "tongues speaking," consider the day of Pentecost, was that they were enabled to speak in human languages which they had never learned in order to give forth the message of God.

These "sign gifts," first evidenced by the 120 at the first Day of Pentecost (See the second chapter of Acts.), were made available to the Christian community in order to authenticate the entrance of the Dispensation of the Gospel Message. (Mark 14:24) With the coming of the entirety of the New Testament Canon, with its inspired and preserved teaching and the work of the Spirit therein, these sign gifts faded from the church. (I Corinthians at:10) The emphasis moved from signs to the reality of faith in the revealed Words of God.

With all of the above, Peter's main claim was that he was under the direction of Jesus, the Christ. It was under the authority of Jesus – and this only! – which Peter was able to do anything.

This particular letter was, as were most of the letters we've retained under the Spirit in the New Testament, was a "circular letter." I often receive "emails." With each of those emails there is a button which allows me to send those emails to another person. That isn't a "circular email." That is a "shared" email. The concept of a circular email would be one that was addressed to several people at the same time.

That was the concept of the circular letter. "I'm sending it to you but share it with others." Most of the letters of the apostles were thus shared. Only those with the imprint of the Holy Spirit upon them were destined to become universal letters with regard to inclusion in the inspired and preserved Scripture.

Many were written but few were inspired.

This particular letter was written to churches within Asia Minor. This was a Roman Province. Many of the recipients within the churches, to which this was addressed, perhaps most, were either native Jews or Jewish proselytes who had further converted to faith in Messiah.

These are here called "strangers" who are scattered throughout the area. This paints them as not among the native inhabitants of the area. Some may well have been of the Diaspora rather than from Judea. They may well have been from Judea, as well, but had met with so much persecution for their faith in Messiah that they were driven to these other lands. In this they were considered as was Abraham, sojourners and strangers in a foreign land.]

1.2 *Elect according to the foreknowledge of God the Father, through sanctification of the Spirit, unto obedience and sprinkling of the blood of Jesus Christ:*

[Election. This is a thorny issue among many in this day. The incursion of the "Reformed Doctrine" of Calvinism has made many inroads into our Baptist churches. The "Five Point" doctrine is, basically that God has chosen some to be saved. These will be saved because of this Sovereign Election of God to the covenant of grace. The obvious corollary to this is that there are those who were not elect. These have no chance of salvation and are predestined for Hell, but only by default as they are not of the elected group.

Obviously this sounds abhorrent to the concept of personal "soul winning" and "seeking that which was lost." If our purpose in our Christian witness is to do the will of God, such is not the case. This doctrine has been argued as an incentive to work harder for the Lord as our labors are based on our love for Him because of His love for us. (I John 4:19) Many good men, and many outstanding soul winners, have been those who held to this doctrine as a rational to work for the Lord.

This has been a quick synopsis of the doctrine. Obviously, there is much more which could be said.

I consider myself a "soft Calvinist." We can not discount the Sovereignty of God when it comes to the matter of either the conviction of the Spirit upon the heart of the sinner or upon the reality that the grace of grace God is entirely of His work. Ephesians 2:10, speaking of salvation, says "For we are his workmanship, created in Christ Jesus unto good works, which God hath before ordained that we should walk in them." Romans 3:11 reminds us that no one will seek God in their natural state.

This verse says, "Elect according to foreknowledge." Therein is the key. Wesley has properly observed that there is, strictly speaking, neither foreknowledge nor post knowledge with God. From His abode in eternity there is only "now knowledge." He sees all of human history in the same instant. Don't ask me to explain that; it is far above my ability to understand the things of God's majesty and power!

This is the basis of the electing power of God. A great power this is! It gives to mortal, sinful man the ability to break the bonds of sin which hold him tightly away from God's eternal love and earth's full personhood. The Spirit sends His conviction upon the lost sinner. The lost sinner responds to this call of love and accepts the Lord as his own Savior.

Does this mean that God does not call any but these He already knows will respond? Of course not. The love of God extends into the humanity of His creation. God is not a respecter of persons. We can see this process in the exodus under Moses. The Land of Promise was a Covenant Promise of God to these people. The task of Moses, along with relating the Law to these people, was to take them to this land of rest. An entire generation refused walk into the Land to which God had led and promised.

These were a called people. These were a chosen people. These were even a separated people. They died in the wilderness because they refused to follow where God had led them. So it is with those who are given the message of Salvation, called into a certain conviction of their need, and still refuse to accept the Savior. Although they are called, they are lost.

This does mean that we have a need to respond to the calling of God to accept His grace. The generation of the exodus which refused to enter the land was given a choice to either follow God or to follow their own way. God knew what their choice, via His omniscient foreknowledge, would be. He still called them. They can never claim that He gave them no choice for it is clear that He did.

It is the same with the sinner. He is given a real choice. If he accepts the grace of God he will be born again and thus show himself to be one of those elect according to the foreknowledge of God. If he refuses he will remain in his sin. But, he has an honest and real choice in the matter. This is not "election by fiat;" this is an election by the fact that God already knows what any sinner will choose. Our duty as Christians is to pray the conviction of the Spirit upon those to whom we witness. Were it not possible that sinners could be saved by grace God would not have called us to offer that witness.

Sadly, and to our shame as "followers of Christ," there are many who never are invited to the feast of salvation because we have never given the invitation. It is my firm belief that we can pray "for the entire world" all we wish. It is more likely that results will be seen when we pray for Tom and Sally and Ted and Sandy. Our prayers need to flow with our outreach.

By the way, it wouldn't hurt if it was our hands reaching out once in a while!

Just before I wrote that last sentence I gave myself a "shot" of insulin. I have to do this every night. It was past time so I just took the needle and medicine and did it almost while I wrote. Why am I telling you this? It is because I hate needles. There is no need for me to worry. The pain is about the same as a leaf falling off a tree and hitting me on the head in the fall.

Still, I dread the fact of doing it. This is true even though I realize that I need to do so. My grandfather died of diabetes in 1956. I have a very good reason to give myself these nightly shots. Still, I dread doing it; but I do it.

Now, how do you feel about witnessing for the Lord? Do you know that it really won't hurt? I'm not saying that you might not have to force yourself sometimes. Still, this is something that we really need to do if we are to call Jesus, "Lord." That title means that He is in charge. We can perform Luke 24:48. It is not just or duty; it is the direction given by He Who died to save our souls.

As an aside, the grace of God extends even to us as we witness. He will assist us as we prayerfully are obedient to Him.

We are called to be sanctified to the Lord by the express will of The Father. His will is based upon His divine foreknowledge, and on His sovereign will; some will reject the message of the Cross but those sanctified will accept that message in faith and be saved.

This sanctification is to be made holy in a practical sense. We are what we are; but we are sanctified holy by the Blood of Christ. This holiness is actual in that it has been accomplished by the work of Jesus in His great Self-Sacrifice at Calvary. We have no real part in this except that we accept it, thus applying the power of His Blood to our own lives in faith. (Ephesians 2:8-9)

The Spirit calls us to this sanctification by His working upon the heart of the sinner in His convicting power. He convicts of sin and the need for salvation. Not all those convicted will respond with the faith needed to accept this sanctified station of salvation.

The sanctification is akin to the vessels used in the Old Testament Tabernacle in that each of those vessels needed to be set aside for the special use of worship within that Tabernacle. Not any "fire," for instance, was "holy fire." Consider the case of Nadab and Abihu who offered "strange fire" which was not consecrated to the holy task. (Leviticus 10:1; Numbers 5:13; 26:11)

The elect are those who are the saved. The Father saw them in His foreknowledge, The Spirit called them due to His foreknowledge. The response of those who accepted the call of The Spirit is evidenced by their faith. That faith is placed on The Son. When placed in any other philosophy or person – to include themselves – this faith is a "strange fire" which is not the required faith of Holiness unto salvation.

The Son, in obedience to the Cross of His Self-Sacrifice, makes possible that the faith of the penitent be accepted as evidence of the true sanctification unto salvation. Our obedience to trust The Son will then give us the sanctification unto God and the salvation unto holiness and redemption which was offered.

The "bottom line" is that all of salvation, at every point, is the work of God. We are the recipients of this salvation as we accept, in faith, Jesus as Savior. Even this acceptance upon our part is not of our own work but stands only in response to the work of The Spirit.

It is the Blood of Jesus which is sprinkled on the Mercy Seat – an Old Testament analogy written to a church peopled, mostly, by Jewish people. This verse does not speak of water baptism. Those who would look for "grace" in the waters of Baptism need to understand that the grace of God is not in any "religious," or other *work* we may do. Grace is all of Christ and nothing of us. Baptism is a sign to the world that we have already been given the grace of God into our hearts. (Ephesians 2:8-9)]

1.3 *Blessed be the God and Father of our Lord Jesus Christ, which according to his abundant mercy hath begotten us again unto a lively hope by the resurrection of Jesus Christ from the dead,*

[This verse begins with, "Blessed be God." That is unusual to our ears. We expect God to bless us. But, we never offer the praise of blessing to Him. Why is that? It is hoped that the reason is our sense of unworthiness. Sadly, the real reason is our sense of spiritual avarice. Our prayers are full of "I wants" and practically devoid of "I love."

That is an attitude which would make for a poor relationship with our spouse, or even our friends, here on earth. It seems as we think more highly of them than we do of God. Him we often fail to praise. This is a sad commentary on the present weakness within our Christian assemblies.

Consider the old Christian hymn. "I serve a risen Savior." Fact. "He's in the world today." Fact. "I know that he is living." Fact. "I see his hand of mercy." Fact. "I hear his voice of cheer." Fact. Now, this is a song I love. But, where is the praise. We have plenty of "fact" within our song but very little "fire."

Facts can comfort us. Facts can educate us. But, it is the fire of praise which will warm our hearts to express love toward our God and Savior. Our weakness often lies in the facts that we know and the fire that has been banked within our souls.

We need a recommitment to our blush of the first love we felt to our Savior when we realized the great love He has showered upon us. We have fallen into the trap of the Ephesian church of the second chapter of Revelation. We have lost the passion of our first love. (Revelation 2:4) We have become Laodicean in our smug understanding. We need to be of Philadelphian, of love. We need love for our fellowman that we would witness. Even more than this we need a burning love for our Lord that we would walk with Him in expectation and excitement.

"Praise Him! Praise Him! Sing of His excellent greatness." The actual words of that song are "Tell of His excellent greatness." To "tell" is to recite. To "sing" is to excite. We have a need to be excited about the glory and majesty of our Lord!

In the phrase "the God and Father of our Lord Jesus Christ" we see an affirmation by Peter of the uniqueness of Jesus. His both God, the Son, and The Son of God. We tend to major on His message to us delivered in His humanity. We tend to major on His great salvation delivered unto us in the Self-sacrifice of His humanity. We tend to major on His mighty works; but, we see them in reference to His humanity.

He is God. He took the step to lay aside for a time all the glory which was rightfully His for the express purpose of purchasing our salvation from sin. This has given us a lively hope. That is a living hope. That is an energetic hope. We have the hope of a better life, despite the real possibility of persecution, because of the death and resurrection of Jesus. We have the hope of the soon return, the imminent return, of the Savior. He is coming back to take us from the sin and sorrow of this world to the reward of the riches of the abode which He has prepared for us. We have the hope of the eternal salvation in His presence.

We have this hope because He has begotten us again. Look at John 3:3 where Jesus assured Nicodemus of a need for the new birth. This is a birth into life eternal whereas our physical births were only unto life decaying. This is more than a hope; it is a pledge from Jesus, the Messiah of God.

This is the reality of the mercy of God.]

1.4 *To an inheritance incorruptible, and undefiled, and that fadeth not away, reserved in heaven for you,*

[What has God set aside for us? It is an inheritance. Consider John 1:12. "But as many as received him, to them gave he power to become the sons of God, even to them that believe on his name." We are considered as adopted sons of our Heavenly Father. Since we are His sons by adoption, He has promised us a certain inheritance of glory. This is an inheritance promised only to His children. The world in general cannot know the glories which await those who love Him and are called to His purposes.

Even we, the saved by His grace, can only partly fathom the greatness of His gifts to us as His children. As His ways are far above our ways so are His blessings to those that truly love Him far above that which we can think or consider.

His gifts to us do not dissolve or decay as do the gifts and riches of the earth. Clothing will go out of style and fade in its brilliance. Food will decay and rot. Riches will devalue through inflation and our expanding wants. The blessing of God will be new and marvelous for the endless eons of eternity.

His gifts are an undefiled inheritance. There is nothing that is impure about His gifts. Neither is there any possibility that any would find an impure use for His gifts. The gifts of God are completely pure and infinitely priceless.

I was not a good husband to my wife. Of that I am certain. One thing I did do was to often, on no schedule and for no reason other than love, bring her fresh flowers from the florist. I would hide them in the kitchen so she would be surprised by the new flowers which spoke to her of the love I could never seem to vocalize properly. But, every few days these beautiful flowers became dried out weeds. The gifts of God are not like this. The gifts of God are always new and precious.

Once on an anniversary Linda and I were met at the door of a small motel restaurant with the unreasonable, to my mind, request, "Do you have a reservation?" Of course, we didn't. This is a small town and this was a small restaurant. We didn't. We had to trek on to *Chez Golden Arches* as we had done for our first anniversary together.

That will never happen in Heaven. God has given us gifts that are reserved for us. They are safe from robbers, rot, and refusal. The gifts of God are assured gifts. Even more, they are free to us. Jesus paid the price for these gifts from God on the Cross of Calvary.]

1.5 *Who are kept by the power of God through faith unto salvation ready to be revealed in the last time.*

[We are kept by the "dunamis" power of God. This word is number 1411 in Strong's and it signifies the miracle working power of God. We are kept in faith. Once again, as Ephesians 2:8 tells us, faith is itself a miracle of God which is wrought upon the hearts of the believers. Faith is a true charismatic gift from God. Even the faith of our salvation is not of our own volition but is imparted by the Spirit into our lives.

We know ourselves only too well. Do we honestly believe that we are worthy of this great salvation? We are only worthy as we are imparted grace from the Throne. This is not our worthiness but the worthiness of Christ which is given to us as a free gift from His passion and resurrection.

Therefore, to argue that we can keep ourselves "saved" is a form of spiritual pride in our own powers. We have not the power to keep that which He has imparted unto us by the miracle of the Spirit upon our hearts. It is His power that holds us. The picture in this verse is of a man kept under guard in a fortress. He is protected from all evil, and the onslaughts of men, by the power of the military garrison of that fort. So is our salvation secured to us by the power of Christ and not by our own will.

The last phrase of this verse deserves comment. "...salvation ready to be revealed in the last time." The first and most obvious meaning to the Christian is that this salvation through faith in Christ is a truth which has only been revealed in these last times. Before the coming and passion of Messiah the old Mosaic Law sufficed for man. In these last days, the Age of Grace we no longer sacrifice the animals of creation to cover our sin. The Lord, Himself, has been sacrificed to do away with our sins. He has redeemed us by His Own Blood. (Revelation 5:9)

A deeper meaning is that the full meaning of our salvation has yet to be seen. Our resurrected bodies are yet to be seen. Our crowns of victory which we will cast at

His feet have yet to be seen. Our glory with Him for all eternity has yet to be seen. Our freedom from the last judgment of the damned is yet to be seen. The glorious face of our Savior, with Whom we will spend eternity, has yet to be seen by mortal eyes!]

1.6 *Wherein ye greatly rejoice, though now for a season, if need be, ye are in heaviness through manifold temptations:*

[Peter acknowledges that we will rightly rejoice in the realization of our salvation. Salvation is a gift from God that brings peace both now and forever. Salvation is a gift from God that brings purpose both now and forever. Salvation is a gift from God that brings joy both now and forever.

Satan is a hater. He hates the peace of God. He hates the gift of salvation from God. He hates the creation of God. And, more to the personal point for us, he hates the redeemed of God.

In this we can find no perverse glory. Satan doesn't care about us, personally, in any way. He sees in us only a tool to grieve the Spirit of God by causing harm to the people of God. While God may send trials to sharpen us as His people, Satan sends dire temptation to rob us of the fellowship which God desires that we have with Him.

Satan sends manifold temptations to the people of God. These can cause us much grief. The temptations at the point of Peter's writing may have been some of the early persecutions of the church. Satan can never send temptation or persecution to the children of God without the permission of God. We see this in the first and second chapter of Job.

We see in the very next verse that the trying of our faith is a precious thing. It will be used of God to strengthen us in our faith.

Why was Job so tempted and tried? We know that it was for his benefit. How? I think that through this trial Job was able to see that he could not fully trust his closest friends and advisors, or even his own wife. Job found that his only true trust was in the Lord. He found this, as did Jonah, even in adversity when he didn't agree with God. The arguments of Job, fully reasonable from the human standpoint of a "veiled view," (I Corinthians 13:12) were out of a heart which believed in the goodness of God but seemed unable to find that goodness.

Job didn't have the New Testament revelation of Romans 8:28. "And we know that all things work together for good to them that love God, to them who are the called according to his purpose." He did have that knowledge which was at the base of his complaints: God is good. Jesus imparted the truth of the goodness of God above all others in Luke 18:19. Despite the complaining of Job, it was that faith in the ultimate goodness of God which kept him from denying God as even his wife urged. (Job 2:9)

I ask again, Why was Job so tempted and tried? I do not have the complete answer to that question. I don't believe that anyone has that full answer. But, I do know this, Job gained a knowledge that his faith could only rest in God. All other seeming venues were untrustworthy. Job did gain more after his affliction that he had lost within it. That, to be honest, seems a sad gain. Job would still be prone to mourn that which he had lost; I do see this. However, even that which Job had lost of sons and daughters would be returned to him in the glory of Heaven. Job did understand this fact. (Job 19:26)

The greatest gain I see in Job is that gain which is given to us because of Job. He was allowed that his own pain and suffering would be a lesson, kept in the inspired and preserved Words of God, for all of history, of the hateful plans of Satan for humanity and the ultimate rescue of humanity by the grace and love of God.

A few weeks ago there was a little excitement in town. It seems that a train didn't really care for the "restriction" of the tracks. From about the middle of the city and on to the south-east city limits a freight train decided to "jump the tracks." It jumped *off* the tracks rather than *on* the tracks. That seems like a small thing. Spatially speaking the train was only about one foot from the tracks. It wasn't a small thing. Once off the tracks, even by that small distance, the train could no longer continue on its journey. On top of that, the tracks would also need some repair so any later train could go on its journey in the same direction.

Transfer that concept to the works of Satan and we can easily see the great damage that Satan can work on an entire church by causing the failure of one person. The entire mission of the church is endangered. These "manifold," that means many and varied, temptations are dangerous to even those outside the church. The mission of the church is evangelism. When that evangelism is hindered there are souls of real men and women, boys and girls, which – from our human standpoint – stand in peril of eternal damnation.

This ought to cause us much heaviness of heart!

It is my belief that Peter was speaking of some persecution in this verse. His voice of experience and comfort at this point was that persecution would only last for a short time. Our lives are short. A ten-year-old might question that statement. By the time that child is seventy he will have learned the truth that life really is short. It comes in a moment and passes in a minute. Eternity is longer than long; it is endless joy and fulfilment.

Temptation and trials pass. Salvation endures.

A child may hate to go to school. Ten years later as that same child reads a letter from a loved one he will not remember the "discomfort" of the long walks to the school. He will not even consider all the time he spent mastering the lessons. All of that is either forgotten or simply ignored as he uses those skills learned in school to read that letter. Trials sent from God are not as temptations hurled at us by Satan. The trials of God are that which prepare us for eternity.

We should take the temptations to the Lord and ask assistance to endure and overcome. We should take the trials to the Lord and thank Him as we seek to learn those lessons which He has for us. As the case of Job proves, God can change the temptations to ruin which Satan brings and change them into trials of blessing to His children

Temptations are lashes of whips of adversity which seek to separate us from fellowship with the Lord. Trails are strokes of love which bring us closer to the Lord.]

1.7 *That the trial of your faith, being much more precious than of gold that perisheth, though it be tried with fire, might be found unto praise and honour and glory at the appearing of Jesus Christ:*

[Why are we tempted as Christians? Part of the answer is the "old man" which lives within us. Far too often we allow ourselves to be tempted because we have our own little "lust buttons" in our minds that we've not fully yielded to the Lord. (James 1:14)

Beyond that temptation is a trial of our faith. Temptations, withstood by fleeing to the Lord will draw us closer to Him. It is so that we will exercise our spiritual "muscles" and become spiritually stronger. It is also a great experience to see the power of God in an escape from the tempter.

That which Satan intends for our harm can become a thing which can be used of God toward our profit. This is only so as we turn the temptation into a trial by taking the problem to the Lord with the plea that we submit to Him rather than to the adversity. At this point I must again access the example of the Master. In the fourth chapter of Matthew we see the temptation of Jesus in His humanity. As we read that passage we must note that for every temptation which Satan hurled at Jesus, Jesus responded with an answer from the inspired and preserved Words of God.

Satan cannot stand against the Words of God. I would add one small consideration. Prayer should always accompany Scripture, whether reading or wielding those precious Words is that which God has inspired and preserved for us. Scripture is one more of the gifts which God has for His children.

Gold is refined with fire. The fire melts the gold so that the dross (impurities) may be removed. Peter reminds us that the trying of our faith is even more precious than the gold. Gold will pass away. (II Peter 3:10) Faith is the reality of a firm and eternal relationship with God.

Peter asks that we stand firm and faithful even in the midst of trail and temptation.

Note that Peter expected the soon return of the Lord in the clouds. His charge to the recipients of this epistle was that they be found faithful at the appearing of the Lord. The imminent, at any moment, return of the Savior in the clouds to receive us unto Himself has been the blessed hope of the Christian down through the ages of this "Church Age."

Even so, come quickly Lord Jesus. May this always be our plea and hope!]

1.8 *Whom having not seen, ye love; in whom, though now ye see him not, yet believing, ye rejoice with joy unspeakable and full of glory:*

[The story is told of Fanny Crosby, the blind hymn writer of earlier days. Someone asked her if she were not sad that she had been sightless since her earliest days. Her reply was, "No. Because the first face I shall see will be that of the Savior."

Probably none of these people to whom Peter wrote had ever seen Jesus during His earthly ministry. Still, they knew Him. They knew of His sinless character. They knew of His teaching and holiness. They knew of His compassion upon the lost and the least. They knew of His searching for sinners. They knew of the great love of His Self-Sacrifice at the Cross of Calvary. They knew of His resurrection. They knew of His ascension into the Heavenlies. They knew of His promise to return for His Own. They knew He was their Savior.

They also knew the words Jesus had spoken to Thomas. "Jesus saith unto him, Thomas, because thou hast seen me, thou hast believed: blessed are they that have not seen, and yet have believed." (John 20:29) Having never seen the humanity of Jesus, these people still exercised faith in Him. "Now faith is the substance of things hoped for, the evidence of things not seen." (Hebrews 11:1)

Their faith in Jesus gave them a realization of the glory of salvation available only through the Heavenly Master. This gave them an unspeakable joy. Compare this passage with Paul speaking of being "caught up" into the "third heaven" in II Corinthians 12:1-4.

These to whom Peter addressed his epistle were also said to be "full of glory." The Spirit, bearing witness to our spirit through His influence in our lives and through the faithful Words of the inspired and preserved Scripture, speaks to us from the realms of Glory. There is so much more available for us in this glorious salvation than we could ever dream or hope.

Praise the Lord! Praise the Lord! Let us hear and heed His voice to us!]

1.9   *Receiving the end of your faith, even the salvation of your souls.*

[This ninth verse is a continuation of verse eight. It speaks of the "end," or "object," of faith in Jesus. This is, of course, salvation.

To the Jew of the day of the earthly sojourn of Jesus, salvation was a physical salvation of his body and nation from a foreign domination. We see that even after the resurrection of Jesus, shortly before His ascension back into Heaven, the disciples were still concerned with the disposition of the nation. "When they therefore were come together, they asked of him saying, Lord, wilt thou at this time restore again the kingdom to Israel?" (Acts 1:7)

It wasn't until the Spirit began to speak to them that the realization came to the apostles that Jesus was not come to restore the kingdom at that point. His purpose was not to remove the yoke of foreign occupation from the people and the land. His purpose was to give salvation from the yoke of Satan and sin upon individuals as they responded in faith to His work on the Cross of Calvary.

The first coming of Jesus was to offer spiritual salvation to those of the entire world who would accept Him as Savior. At the second appearing in the clouds Jesus will call the believers, living and dead, to join Him in glory. Then will come the "Time of Jacob's Trouble." We, the Gentile Christians call this "The Great Tribulation." This time does not concern the Church. We have already been raptured out of this world when this time begins.

This is a time of testing and purging of the Covenant People of God. After this, at the Second Coming to the earth, Jesus will reestablish the Kingdom with Himself on the Throne of David. He will rule over the entire earth from Jerusalem. The people of all Israel, having been converted to their Lord and purified, will once again have their kingdom to be ruled by the line and linage of David.]

1.10   *Of which salvation the prophets have enquired and searched diligently, who prophesied of the grace that should come unto you:*

[After the healing of the man at the pool of Bethesda Jesus was questioned by some of the Jewish religious leaders. They were upset that He had healed on the Sabbath. The answer of Jesus to their inquiries was that these religious leaders should "Search the scriptures; for in them ye think ye have eternal life: and they are they which testify of me." (John 5:39)

This was probably a little upsetting to these leaders. The pious Jew spent much time searching those Old Testament Scriptures which they had. Make no mistake; the study of these men would put almost all of us to shame. They were serious about the study of the Scripture.

I tend to study from a Dispensational perspective. To me this is a logical method to understand the vast writings of the Scripture as the concept of dispensation study demands a literal interpretation whenever that is possible. The old maxim is, "If the plain sense makes sense, seek no other sense." In this way the fantastic flights of fancy of "spiritualizing" passages are done away with and the Scriptures are allowed to speak for themselves.

These ancient men had also systematized their study. The Torah and Mishna which we find today are testament to their scrupulous attention to detail in their study.

They understood all about Messiah. He would come to restore the kingdom to Israel. They did believe that He would give salvation. They also understood that in some way He would bless all nations as was prophesied to Abraham. "...in thee shall all families of the earth be blessed." (Genesis 12:3) But, they never seemed to equate the passages of the "suffering Savior" with the coming Messiah. It was an unfathomable consideration to them.

Ziv Kalishr, a holocaust survivor who fought in the Israeli military, was a Messianic Jew who accepted Messiah Jesus as his Savior. During decades of residence in Israel he dealt with many Jewish souls about salvation. Those with whom he dealt were not familiar with the fifty-third chapter of Isaiah. It seemed that few of the Rabbis who taught these men accessed that portion of their Scripture.

I have had only small contact with Jewish Rabbis. I defer in this instance to Mr. Kalishr for his insight.

Nonetheless, we have an unavoidable picture from current practices and from Biblical references that the Scripture of the Old Covenants was read and studied in general course by many of the Covenant People. Daniel was able to ascertain that the time of the national captivity of Judah was shortly to end as he studied the writing of Jeremiah. (Daniel 9:2-3)

There were things that were mysteries, such as the Church and the fact that Gentile and Jew would both fellowship together in the Lord. (Ephesians 3:3-6)

As we read the Book of Daniel we find places where he did not even understand his own writing. At some points God opened his understanding and at other points Daniel was simply told to write even that he might not have understood. Daniel was told that those things were to be understood at another time.

Peter admitted that even the writings of Paul were often "hard to be understood." (II Peter 3:16) Add to this that there were times when the Spirit of Inspiration was upon the Words of those who were not believer's, although there was always a believer within "earshot" who heard of them, such as Nebuchadnezzar in Daniel 3:25 and Caiaphas in John 11:51. In this we can see some of the difficulty in the full understanding of even the prophets of Israel who put pen to parchment in physically writing the inspired and preserved Words of God.

But, the salient point is that they had such interest in the things of God that they looked with diligence. Should not we as well?

We will never understand all in this life. God has deemed that we are to study His Word so that we can be competent "workmen" for Him. (II Timothy 2:15)

May we praise God that we live during this Age of Grace. It is a blessing beyond compare that we are allowed to have faith in and serve our Lord, the Messiah, Jesus.]

1.11 *Searching what, or what manner of time the Spirit of Christ which was in them did signify, when it testified beforehand the sufferings of Christ, and the glory that should follow.*

[These prophets themselves spent many hours studying their "own" writings and those of others because they had a burning desire to learn more of God. As mentioned in the commentary of the above verse, many did not comprehend the meaning of the Words which had been given them. Being devout men they "searched the Scripture."

There is a fiction brandied about by many that the Old Testament Scripture was not written until after the return of Judah from the captivity of the Babylonians. No. These people left into the captivity with their precious books and returned with them.

Even Daniel, a mere youth at his capture and deportation, had taken copies of the Scripture with him. "In the first year of his reign I Daniel understood by books the number of the years, whereof the word of the LORD came to Jeremiah the prophet, that he would accomplish seventy years in the desolations of Jerusalem." (Daniel 9:2) Please note "books," plural, in this verse.

Even during his duties as a palace official Daniel found time to read and study the sacred scrolls of the Books of Scripture.

"Searching what?" This refers to the "what" of which the prophets wrote. They wrote of Messiah. They wrote prophecies of the people and the relationship of those people to Messiah. A defeated but never humbled people, they understood that the coming of Messiah would lead to the reestablishment of their national kingdom and the glories that this signified. Holding to their understanding that they were the Covenant People of God, they longed for Messiah to sit on the Throne of David and rule them as an independent nation under God.

The study of the priests and the scribes allowed them to explain to the wise men from the east where it was that Messiah should be born. The study of Simeon and Anna allowed them to understand the soon coming of Messiah as they waited at the Temple in the second chapter of Luke. From the prophecies of Daniel there was a general understanding among the population as to the time when Messiah would arrive. This may explain the many who claimed to be the Messiah around the time of Jesus. (Matthew 24:5 Remember, Christ is the Greek form of Messiah of the Hebrew.)

The Old Testament prophets probably looked for Messiah with the same expectations that we search for the Second Appearing of Jesus. They would have searched the inspired and preserved Scripture in an attempt to find that time. As we search the meaning of the times so would they have searched the manner of the times.

The Spirit of inspiration was upon the Words which they prophets of old wrote. Nevertheless, it is obvious that the Spirit was upon them in some manner to write those Divine Words. Possibly we could argue that inspiration lay upon the Words but the Spirit of inspiration worked upon the human penmen in some way so those Words would find their way from the Heavenly template (Psalm 119:89) to the scrolls of the penmen.

This is an interesting concept. In II Timothy 3:16 we are assured that God inspired the Words of Scripture. This verse says that the "Spirit of Christ" was in these men as they wrote. Meanwhile II Peter 1:21 would argue that it was the Holy Ghost

Who moved these men to write the prophecies of God. Meanwhile Hebrews 1:1 argues, especially when compared with the second verse, that it was The Father Who gave these words.

How can we reconcile this seeming discrepancy? Two words explain our lack of understanding where there is no discrepancy: THE TRINITY. The Triune Nature of God inspired the Scripture. We see no overlapping of purpose or performance. There are no contradictions. There is but one Word produced by One God Who acts in the reality of a Triune Nature.

Can I explain this concept of Father, Son, and Holy Ghost as One? I really cannot. My best illustration is a cup of coffee with sugar and cream added. Each element is distinct. Each element is discernable. Each element is combined in such a way as to produce only one beverage. This illustration will break down because it is predicated upon physical understandings of a time centric existence. When we reach the shores of Glory we will see the reality of eternity and the spiritual. For now, I believe what God has said. I believe what the Words of God have said. I believe simply.

This realization that the Spirit of Messiah was upon these writers of prophecy signifies two things. One is, of course, the eternality and Divinity of Jesus. He existed before Bethlehem. The other is the power of prophecy is that of God, Alone. No person of creation can engage in true prophecy. A human may make very informed guesses. During this present "silly season" of presidential polls, we watch this almost daily. But, guesses are guesses and sometimes fail. The prophecy of God is not predictive; it is an actual account of things which have not yet happened. These never fail.

"When it testified" seems a poor choice of words. But, it is an accurate choice of words. The word is number 4303 in Strong's, "promarturomai, prom-ar-too'-rom-ahee... from 4253 and 3143; to be a witness in advance i.e. predict:--testify beforehand." It is used only here. Since it speaks of the action of a witness it is correct. I still prefer the Name of the Spirit in this place but to have used it would have been to editorialize rather than to strictly translate.

The testimony of the Spirit was given beforehand. This is the essence of predictive prophecy and is a prerogative only of God. We can "predict," but strictly speaking we only guess. God does not prognosticate; He states the reality of a situation even before the situation has developed.

That prophecy consisted of two elements. The first, especially seen in Psalm 22 and Isaiah 53, is of the suffering of Messiah. This was not understood by the Jewish people of the time of Jesus. It still seems hard for many to understand. I recently read a book written by a practicing rabbi who used the suffering of Jesus as one reason to reject Him as Messiah.

We can readily understand this when we consider that Messiah is to be the national Savior of all Israel. He is seen in His glorified state in this. This is true. But there is a great valley of the Dispensation of Grace between the suffering and the glorification. It is a natural thing to look past the peak of subjection when our eyes are focused on the peak of glorification.

Jesus, "Christ" is the title – from the Greek – not His last name, is Messiah. He laid aside His glory as God during His earthly sojourn and ministry. He did this for us. His resurrection and His return to Heaven in the clouds, are pictures of His glory being picked back up as a robe laid aside for a time. He is going to return to this earth in His full glory as God and King of kings in this natural and physical time centric world.]

1.12 *Unto whom it was revealed, that not unto themselves, but unto us they did minister the things, which are now reported unto you by them that have preached the gospel unto you with the Holy Ghost sent down from heaven; which things the angels desire to look into.*

[How the prophets of the Old Testament would have been glad to see Revelation 22:10 – "And he said unto me, Seal not the sayings of the prophecy of this book: for the time is at hand." For these Old Testament prophets wrote not of their own time but unto us upon whom the times of the Gospel Age are come.

For those most part those prophets would have seen only the near fulfillment and not considered the far fulfillment. Isaiah would have seen only Rezin and Damascus when he penned Isaiah 7:14. He would not have understood the coming fuller fulfillment of Matthew 1:22-23 which concerned the very Messiah, Jesus.

We are very blessed to live in this age of the Gospel. The stunning Self-Sacrifice of Jesus at Calvary was reported among the prophets but few, it seems, were able to understand that the sacrifices of the Temple were only a preview of Him Who was considered as slain from the foundations of the earth. (Revelation 13:8)

Before Adam had been created or sinned, at the time of the foundation of the earth's creation, Jesus was already considered as slain for the sins of humanity. Before the Mosaic Law decreed the death of those animals of creation, which could not ultimately save anyone from their sins, (Hebrews 10:4) the Lamb of God was considered as slain for the remission of sins.

How glorious and privileged are we to live in this time! The prophecies of Jesus were revealed by the Spirit unto the Old Testament prophets who could not comprehend that which was given to them. Still, they faithfully proclaimed that Message of God that we might learn even more of Him Who died for us.

It is the truth which the Spirit revealed to them that is received of the Spirit by us in this day. This is the message which is faithfully proclaimed from the street corners and Temple of ancient Jerusalem on the Day of Pentecost and from faithful pulpits and witnesses unto our very day. Jesus, the Messiah of God, died in time so that we could live in eternity.

It is a great and glorious salvation. It is beyond that, but words fail mortals to speak of the power, majesty, grace and love of the Lord.

Even the angels desire to study this phenomenon. They see that the Lord of Holiness and Justice has come with mercy, grace and love to redeem the lost of humanity. That grace, itself, is a vindication of His justice and holiness. Consider the cost to Him for our salvation and we can still not fathom the awful depravity of sin. That which we can see, His great eternal love, is even far beyond our ability to learn.

All we can do is accept. Even here it is His Spirit which calls us to repentance and redemption. Salvation seems such a simple word. It is. But, it is an awesome work in which we can rejoice even as we cannot fully comprehend.]

1.13 *Wherefore gird up the loins of your mind, be sober, and hope to the end for the grace that is to be brought unto you at the revelation of Jesus Christ;*

[The first phrase of Peter is to "gird up." This seems to hearken back to the exodus journey. The people kept walking and progressing to the end that they might find their "rest" in the Land of Promise.

It wasn't until the people reached the boarders of this land that they realized the reality that there were already people in that land. These people were to be under the chastening rod of God for their many sins in that land. That was the reason that God had promised the land to the Hebrew. His people were to enter the land and proclaim the power and purity of God in an area which had been sold out to sin and perversion.

Just as the Assyrian concerning the Kingdom of Israel and the Babylonian concerning the Kingdom of Judah, the Hebrews of the exodus were tasked with being that "rod of judgment" unto these sinful people of Canaan. That "land of rest" was to become a land of walking in the paths of the choosing of God. This involved physical warfare under the protecting and leading Hand of God.

That physical warfare of the ancient Hebrews was a type of the spiritual warfare in which the Christian is to progress. Ephesians 6:12 explains our duty as followers of Christ in this age. "For we wrestle not against flesh and blood, but against principalities, against powers, against the rulers of the darkness of this world, against spiritual wickedness in high places."

With this in mind, we are to "gird up the 'loins' of our minds." This was picture of the man of that day who wore a long flowing robe. He would "gird up" his robes into a girdle when he prepared for a vigorous task, warfare, arduous travel or other such activities. That was so the robe would not impede his actions. That we are to gird up our mind suggests an important distinction. Our minds are a battle ground. Whether it be resisting temptation to sin, or the temptation to "nod off" in our study of His Word – or the inclination to forego any evangelistic endeavor – we are to put our mind under subjection to follow the walk with God which He would have us to walk.

In this we are called to be sober. This is the soberness of being vigilant and serious about our task. I like to use humor, whenever possible, as I speak publicly of the Lord. I have been criticized about this by some who would be every sober and somber. That is not the meaning of the verse. We are called to be vigilant and serious about our task. An unfailing somber disposition may not be wrong. But if people observe us to be always gloomy they may decide that if this is our example of "joy in the Lord," they don't want it!

That might be a good time to listen to the words of the preacher in Ecclesiastes 3:4. "A time to weep, and a time to laugh; a time to mourn, and a time to dance." Of course, if you are in a fundamentalist Baptist church you might want to forgo the "dance" part!

We are enjoined to carry hope to the end. That is simply an injunction to not ever give up. We do well if we let the world and the emotion of discouragement pass from us. This is one of the biggest temptations the tempter will throw at us. "It's no use. Look at the world around us. We've already lost." I'll tell you a little secret; we ain't going to lose! I've read the last chapter of The Book and WE WIN!

Seriously, when despondency comes, and it will, that is good time to go into Dr. Psalms for a little "happiness treatment." There is something even better than this, add a dash of prayer to the Lord. Tell Him your troubles. He'll listen. As the old saying goes, "He's going to be up all night anyway."

Peter mentions the grace that is brought to us by the revelation of Christ. I am old and infirm. I no longer say "old and fat." Actually, I never say "fat." I am obese.

That is a medical condition rather than a moral failure. In seriousness, though, in my many maladies I am unable to lose weight because I take so many pills that I am constantly overfed. I am under the Veteran's Administration Medical Care. All of my medications are mailed to me. I never have to go to a pharmacy to pick them up. God is in the habit of mailing blessings and grace to us. It is good to be spiritually active and working for Him. Grace just seems to come along for the walk. This is a great God we serve.

He will be revealed to us. When we are down, He lifts us up. When we read His Word He speaks to us. When we pray to Him, He listens and understands our yearnings! When the time comes for us to walk through the Valley of the Shadow, He will be the Light for our walk.

When He comes for us in the clouds we will not have to go through the "scanners and TSA" obstacles; His flights are reserved for His own and His Personal tarmac. We don't even have to take a cab to the airport; He comes for us.

When we reach the blessed shores of our eternal abode He will be there to welcome us.

What glory and praise!]

1.14 *As obedient children, not fashioning yourselves according to the former lusts in your ignorance:*

[Peter calls the Christian to be obedient children of the Heavenly Father.

Several years ago I showed my granddaughter some pictures of her father when he was the same age as her younger brother. She would not believe that the pictures were not of Eli, her brother. Children do tend to resemble their fathers. This is especially so when they are younger. As the children grow older they do tend to take on their own characteristics. It is still possible to see that image of the parent in the child but the child will tend to grow into his own self. His hair is cut different. He dresses differently. And, he will tend to fill out into the body image of both of his parents. He ceases to be a "copy" of his father and becomes and amalgamation of both of his parents.

The child will grow from that copy of his father to become his own image in other ways. Tastes and choices may change. Sometimes there is a rebellion which will toss a child from a proper path toward a dangerous direction. Choices which would have been anathema to the father may be made. The Godly parent will seek to guide that child back to the ways of God.

In this we claim the promise of Proverbs 22:6. If this training has not been from the cradle the task will be greater. If the training has been from the cradle we still must realize that every person is singly accountable to God. The promise from the verse is that "when the child is old he will not depart." Youthful "wild oats" may be sown. Still prayer, patience and the promises of God may draw him back.

This is all, of course, theoretical and from the natural. But, it is also true in the spiritual. Many Christians were "fire balls" for the Lord shortly after they were saved. Then, after a time, the cares of the world intrude upon the life of that individual. The fire seems to have banked even as the concept of "having a ball" grows. It may not be that they walk away from the Lord. It may be just that they no longer walk with Him.

The cares of the world intrude. Suddenly that time of Scripture reading and prayer is curtailed. "After all, that was a really good football game. I have to get up for work in the morning. I don't really have time to read or pray tonight. I'll make it up tomorrow."

That line from Shakespeare comes to mind: "Tomorrow and tomorrow life creeps its petty pace." Suddenly all of our tomorrows are so filled with the necessities of life that there is no time for God. Some sign, or person, might remind us of what we've lost but we fail to feel the loss.

Peter asks that we act as obedient children of our Heavenly Father. The call is to count the fashions and things of the world as what they are. They are transient. They are of time.

About that football game that was so important: What was the final score? How many yards did the star running back gain? What about the quarterback? What were his stats? Can you even remember five plays from that game?

Who won the World Series three years ago? Who did they beat to gain that victory? Was it really that important?

One hundred years from now will any of those questions have any importance?

Isn't your relationship with the Lord of eternity of more importance? If you are a truly born again in that same one-hundred-year frame you will find yourself in His presence. Isn't it better to be an obedient child of the Heavenly Father today?

He still loves you and invites you Home. Isn't that better than watching thirty-two beer commercials while a meaningless, in the light of eternity, football game blares forth on the television? You could read about it in tomorrow's newspaper.

Think of the real importance when all of our tomorrows are but yesterday.]

1.15   *But as he which hath called you is holy, so be ye holy in all manner of conversation;*

[The thing that just jumps off the page here is that God has called us. Think back to your elementary school days. Do you remember the gym class when the teacher picked two students to be "captains." They were told to choose up sides for a game of dodge ball, basketball, whatever. The first one each picked was their best friend, of course. But, where were you in the line of "picks?" Weren't you proud when they finally called out your name? Hey; they wanted you on their side!

There was always one kid who wasn't picked. One team had to take him because he was the only one left. Was he happy to be "picked" at that point?

Think back to the second verse of this chapter and realize that you are a Christian only because God "picked" you. No person, no one, can be saved without the express convicting call of the Spirit upon his life. God picked you out of all the people in the world who are still standing on the sidelines.

Now that you are on His "team," He asks only one thing of you. Represent! Put on the "Team Colors." God is Holy and asks that we be the same. God is God. We will never reach the standard of perfections which apply to Him. But, we can try.

My Grandson is engaged in martial arts training. Many of the students were brought by their parents. They go through the motions but it is obvious that their hearts are elsewhere. I watched one little girl last night. She wasn't the best. But, she was easily the most enthusiastic. Others were just there; she was committed.

You may never be "Holy Joe from Kokomo." You probably wouldn't want to be. I've got a suspicion that anyone with that nickname is probably full of pride at what he does and doesn't do. He's not really dedicated to the things of God; he's dedicated to others knowing how much better he is than are they.

God didn't ask us to be holy so we could "show off." He asks us to be holy in the sense of following Him as best we can. We do try to become better at forsaking the things of the world but we do this so we can draw closer to God. At our best we may find the single joy of being in His Word, in prayer with Him, knowing that we are living, to the best of our ability, a holy life style. The word "conversation" speaks of our manner of life. still, a little conversation about Him to others might be in order.

Find the enthusiasm of commitment.]

1.16   Because it is written, Be ye holy; for I am holy.

[This verse shows that we are not naturally in a state of holiness. Positionally, because of the redemptive work of Christ, we are considered as holy in Him. This is the basis on which we are admitted to the Throne of Grace in prayer. (Hebrews 4:16) This is the basis on which we are guaranteed a home in Heaven for eternity. Jesus has already paid the debt for our sins. Thus, we are legally pure in our spirits.

This is the picture of a man who has murdered someone but the jury found him "not guilty" at his trial. Although actually guilty of murder the man is granted the status of legal purity because of the results of his trial. The gift of Jesus, based on His passion and resurrection, is a pardon from God for sin. This covers both the weight of the nature of sin which we have inherited from our father Adam and our own sin. Actually this is even more than a simple pardon. In Christ we are admitted as though sin had never touched us. All sin incumbent within us has been eradicated – washed away – in the Blood of the Lamb of God.

The man in the illustration above is free from legal prosecution for murder. He will still be stopped for speeding. He will still be arrested for theft. He is free from one charge but must walk circumspectly before the law because he is not free from later charges against him.

The position of the Blood bought sinner is beyond that of the man in this illustration. We are not only free of sin of Adam, and our own sins, as far as judgment is concerned. Jesus has taken all of our judgment at the cross. We are also adopted as sons of God. We still fail, because of our residence within these bodies of clay, and must seek forgiveness. (I John 2:1) But, we are free from the penalty of the original sin of Adam which caused us, in Adam, to be banished from the Garden of the presence of God.

God has every right, as Creator, Sovereign and Savior, to expect us to walk in holiness before Him. We subject ourselves to chastisement, as His adopted children, when we fail to live up to this standard. He asks us to take on the family trait, as adopted children, of holiness.

Peter was accessing Leviticus 11:45. "For I am the LORD that bringeth you up out of the land of Egypt, to be your God: ye shall therefore be holy, for I am holy." A general spiritual rule is that the physical acts recorded in the Old Testament will give spiritual instruction to those of us living in the New Testament times. As Israel had been miraculously freed from the slavery of Egypt, so have we been miraculously freed from the bondage of sin and Satan. From that point they began a walk to the land of full service to the Lord in Canaan. This was their physical promise and this was their physical goal.

We have been freed from the bondage of sin. We are now begun in our walk toward spiritual goals. These include full service to our Lord while we are on this earth. Heaven, of course, is our eternal reward after our walk on this earth. While on that walk God calls us to be holy. That is to be the manner of our walk. We may, as did the Israelites of old, choose to "camp out" for a time. Our walk is interrupted by the baggage of the sin of carnality. We are called to lay aside these impediments and continue our walk toward the "high calling" of the Lord. (Hebrews 12:1)

The more we are prone to access the Scripture, cross-reference and comparison of the entire counsel of God, the more we are able to access the path of the Lord for our journey. An informed walk for God will assist even the faithful walk for God. I John 5:4 informs us that faith is the victory which overcomes the world. A true faith will be anxious to access the Words which God has inspired and preserved for us. Any faith which walks blindly with no desire to delve into the Words of God is a faith that is weak and prone to stumble. It is the power of God which leads us to the Words of God. Thus the "blindly walking faith" with no desire to search out the Words of God is a suspect faith. It shows no evidence of a walk with the Master.

"Because it is written" is important as it shows the basis of the instruction of God for the child of His even in this day. Those Words of God are endued with His power and His eternality. They are for us in every day. They were for Peter in his day and will be for our grandchildren and beyond should the Lord tarry His coming. He and His Words are our Constant companion and contemporary. To ignore and slight His Words is to ignore and slight Him!]

1.17 *And if ye call on the Father, who without respect of persons judgeth according to every man's work, pass the time of your sojourning here in fear:*

[Moving on from holiness... If that even possible? It is not only possible; it is necessary. If we do indeed begin in holiness there is an undeniable inference that we have a journey to complete. The Israelites of the exodus began their journey. This is obvious evidence that their journey was begun with reference to a completion of that journey. The journey of our Christian life is likewise a journey. God has left us on this earth after our conversion for a divine purpose. We have a walk to take with Him into this world.

In baseball if a man hits a single he becomes a "base runner." He remains a base runner as he progresses through the bases. His base runner status is only removed by three things. First, the inning can end with him still on base. Folks, we serve an eternal God in an eternal purpose. There will be no ending of the inning with us still in service. That leaves only two possibilities.

We could be "picked off" a base, or run into a "force out." That means that we have lost our status of base runner without completing the cycle of the bases. It is here that I Corinthians 11:30 will come into play. There are instances where God will remove a servant from this life. We see this with Ananias and Sapphira in the fifth chapter of Acts. We see this in that eleventh chapter of I Corinthians. There are cases where God will remove a saint from residence upon this earth due to their lack of holiness of life. Sin separates us from God so, it seems, there are certain instances where God will separate the Christian from his sin by calling him "home." This is one, seemingly extreme only to our human view, of the means of the chastisement of God.

From the standpoint of God and the purposes of God upon this earth, this is actually the grace of God in action.

Proverbs 3:12 reminds us, "For whom the LORD loveth he correcteth; even as a father the son in whom he delighteth." Paul reiterates this same concept in Hebrews 12:6. "For whom the Lord loveth he chasteneth, and scourgeth every son whom he receiveth." Paul adds the concept that God receives those who are thus chastised. By definition that chastisement comes upon a disobedient child. Therefore, the concept that any could "lose" their salvation is shown to be a false construct.

There is one more way that a base runner can lose his status as base runner. He could complete the circuit of the bases. There will come a time for each of us to leave this mortal coil of flesh. Either by rapture into the clouds or repose into the earth, each of us is bound to leave this present life. "Henceforth there is laid up for me a crown of righteousness, which the Lord, the righteous judge, shall give me at that day: and not to me only, but unto all them also that love his appearing." (II Timothy 4:8)

What a glorious manner to depart from this world of sin!

Peter is making an argument here that his readers should be serious about their walk with the Lord. He says, "If." If you pray to God... If you claim God as your Heavenly Father... Think about it. A claim without substance is very fragile. If I claim a piece of property at a "lost and found," I may be telling a lie. It might not really be mine. If my name is upon that article the doubt is removed. It is obviously mine.

When we name the Name of Jesus we are claiming that He is our Savior. If He is our Savior, what does that mean? Does it mean that He has done all the work necessary for our salvation? Of course. Does it mean that we owe Him nothing in light of the great price He paid and the great problem of sin He has removed from our account? Of course not!

We may even call Him, Lord. To say that is to acknowledge that He has a claim upon us. What? "I thought that we were just 'set free' by this faith." My son is soon to graduate from his training in college. He will then be free of his studies. His freedom means that he has a need to find a job in his field.

Jesus has both freed us and given us a task in this world. God does not respect persons as one above another. He has called us to a work which He will judge. Note that the word is "work" and not "works." The calling of God is not to one specific task and then to go on our merry way. The call is to live in service and dedication to Him. It is a life of dedication, a profession if you will, to which God calls us to live before men as witnesses to the fact that Jesus died in time so that others could live in eternity.

We can say, "Look at this that I did." Jesus might argue, "Look at all you've left undone." We are called to live for Him Who died for us. He asks that we pass the time of our walk in this life in service to others for Him. We do this by sojourning – living as travelers through this life – in fear of Him. Fear of God does not mean being afraid of Him. Fear means accepting Him and His way of life, holiness, as our standard by which to exist among men. We look to the Lord to set our agenda and do that which we understand to be pleasing to Him.

We should also have a fear of sin as evidenced by the avoiding of this negative aspect which the world will press upon us. This will naturally press us toward the mark of the high calling of Jesus. (Philippians 3:14)]

1.18 *Forasmuch as ye know that ye were not redeemed with corruptible things as silver and gold, from your vain conversation received by tradition from your fathers;*

[Peter praises his readers for their knowledge in that they know they were not redeemed by foreign elements of the creation. It was God, coming to accept the humility of human existence – though not relinquishing His own Divine substance, but setting it aside in some manner the human mind cannot comprehend – has brought salvation from the realms of eternity and the spiritual into the human who lives in the physical and time centric.

Simple silver and gold, a construct of man's desire, could never save us. These are transitory and of time. Our salvation must be everlasting and of eternity. Neither is there any act of contrition which we could consider. These are empty in our life and of no value toward the next. These religious performances are of the tradition of empty religion or culture. Their emptiness contrasts unfavorably with the fullness which is in Christ.

Once again, there is no act centered in the works of creation which can remedy the spiritual disease of sin. There must be a remedy from the eternal and spiritual realms to counteract the ravages of sin. Jesus is that Remedy. Only He can forgive sin for it was against Him that sin was directed as an assault on His holiness.

The redemption spoken of is in the terms of redeeming a man from slavery. We were caught into a slavery to sin when Adam brought the race of man into opposition to the reasoning of God. It is from this slavery that we are redeemed in order than we can freely walk in obedience to God Who created us to so walk.

Neither religion nor culture, both of which arise from the creation which has been sullied with the sin of Adam, (Romans 8:22) can attain a hearing in the perfection of Heaven. It was necessary that God, Himself, come with salvation. Religion accomplishes nothing in the realm of eternity and the spiritual. It is of time and physicality.

Salvation, meanwhile, sent – in the Person and work of Jesus – into time and physicality from its origin point of the spiritual and the eternal is a gift from the Creator to the creature. Only this can effect the salvation of souls. This requires acceptance. Acceptance requires faith. Faith requires the moving of the Spirit upon the heart of man.]

1.19 *But with the precious blood of Christ, as of a lamb without blemish and without spot:*

[Even forging past the fact that Jesus was already in existence before the Creation (John 1:3 reminds us that He created all things and was, therefore, not any part of the Creation except as The Creator.), we see that Jesus was Holy from before the foundation of the world. This means that He has always been Holy.

Always. Never anything but. No other human could make that simple claim. Every single human being born on this planet, with the exception of Adam and Eve, was born with a nature that was profane. We are all born with a sin nature, inherited from Adam.

Adam and Eve began holy; but they sinned and became sinners. In becoming a sinner Adam, as head of the human race, passed this "sin gene" down to every descendant of his. That means every person born of man and woman is born with a nature predisposed toward sin.

Jesus, however, was born via the virgin birth. He had no sin at Bethlehem. He was Holy at the point of His physical birth. This was a different situation from that of any other human ever born. It was not the goodness of His mother; it was the goodness of His Father which produced the physical body which was Holy.

Just above, when I said that Adam and Eve began holy, I did not mean that they were Divine in any sense. They were, however, set apart as a special creation. God breathed life into Adam. This was not done with any of the creatures of the land, air, or sea. God imparted a certain holiness unto them so that they could have fellowship with Him. The two had a holiness but it was not of their own; it was a derived holiness bestowed upon them by God.

The concept of the precious Blood of Jesus is that it is of inestimable value. This is a human phrase which tries to convey a Divine attribute. Simple words fail to speak of the value of the Blood of the Savior. It was holy, pure and – even in His humanity – filled with the perfections of the Divine. The value of the Blood of Jesus has redeemed every soul that has believed and trusted God from the first of creation to the last of the New Heavens and New Earth. Consider the eternal importance of Revelation 13:8b and I Peter 1:20)

Once again we can consider the physical picture from the Old Testament of the Spiritual Truth of the New. In the Old Covenant sacrifices of the Paschal lamb, it was required that there be no spot or blemish on the lamb so sacrificed. That is physical. In Jesus there was no stain of sin, either inherited from Adam or committed by Himself. That is the spiritual truth of the Divine Son of God Who sacrificed Himself for the sins of all who would believe.]

1.20 *Who verily was foreordained before the foundation of the world, but was manifest in these last times for you,*

[Peter reminds his readers that Jesus was considered as slain before the foundation of the world. Revelation 13:8 says that Jesus was considered as slain "from the foundation of the world." This is not a disagreement between the two passages. Revelation only argues that He was considered as the Lamb slain at the foundation; Peter adds the information that this dated from an earlier "time." I put "time" in quotation marks because this refers to an epoch of eternity wherein there, properly speaking, is no time.

The point is made that it was foreordained that Jesus would be sacrificed before the creation. Man had never been created or engaged in sin at this point. Calvary was established as The Cure for sin before sin existed. The fact is that God looked at all of history and saw the sin of man. It was in His determinative counsels that Jesus was called to both his temporary humiliation of the Kenosis and the Cross before the creation of man. Consider the great love and grace in that situation. The Cross was neither afterthought nor correction. It was always within the plan of God to redeem a fallen creation through the passion of Jesus!

Those Old Testament saints did not understand that their sacrifice of the animals of creation was only a sign of He Who should come to effectively wash away their sins. These animals could never remove sin. (Hebrews 10:4) The animals themselves were part of a fallen and sinful creation. God, in His grace, gave this picture to humanity in order that we might understand the great Self-Sacrifice of Jesus for our sins.

FIRST PETER: Chapter 1

We should probably mention that in the 12th chapter of Exodus the great picture of the Passover was given. In this, commemorating the redemption of the people from slavery in Egypt as a picture of the redemption of humanity from the slavery of sin, it should be seen that the Pascal Lamb was set apart from the flock on the tenth day of the month but not sacrificed until the fourteenth day. Even this is a picture of Jesus considered sacrificed before creation but not physically sacrificed unto the Cross.

This reality was not revealed until the time of Peter and the rest. It was hidden under the old Mosaic Law and only manifest at the Crucifixion. It was then explained more fully by the Spirit (John 16:13) Who guided these early apostles, who were to physically write the inspired and preserved Scripture of God. (Psalm 119:89)

Going back to verse two of this chapter, it is so precious to understand that Jesus died for us!

The phrase "last times" speaks of the final times before the return of the Savior ushers in a New Day at His return. This is important. Under the discipline of Dispensational Theology we can see that new revelation, which is not "new" but rather "expanded" in that God never "changes His mind" but only adds further teaching to explain Himself to humanity. (Isaiah 28:10) This, along with the "sign gifts" of the early church, will only occur at the beginning of a Dispensation.

The duty of humanity then is to walk in faith in the revealed teaching of the Words of God. Now, in this fulness of times, we are called to the Cross of Calvary to find full salvation and peace with God. "That in the dispensation of the fulness of times he might gather together in one all things in Christ, both which are in heaven, and which are on earth; even in him…" (Ephesians 1:10).

Therefore, any purported "new" teaching is not allowed. There is no additional testament of Christ beyond that which the apostles and their close associates were penmen of up until the closing of the Canon with the completion of the Revelation of John.

Neither can one claim to be "restoring" the first century teaching of the church. Jesus said that even the "gates of Hell" could not defeat His Church. (Matthew 16:28) There have been times when the lights flickered and the flames were low. Some of the individual churches have seen their candles extinguished. (Revelation 2:5) But, even during these times God always kept a remnant of His Churches true to the doctrine and practice of Christ and the Scripture.

This same truth was shown among Judah during the dark days of the Babylonian Captivity. We see Daniel and Ezekiel as prophets even during that captivity. At the ending of the Captivity we see many who returned to Jerusalem. Many were still known to be Levites and were thus able to return to sanctified Temple worship. There was even a group that could not prove their status as Levites and were refused admittance to the Temple service. (Nehemiah 7:64)]

1.21 *Who by him do believe in God, that raised him up from the dead, and gave him glory, that your faith and hope might be in God.*

[In the Old Testament teaching God if often seen as a stern God of judgment as He shows through physical examples His hatred of sin. In the New Testament Jesus displays the love of God through His Own example as God. "No man hath seen God at any time; the only begotten Son, which is in the bosom of the Father, he hath declared him." (John 1:18)

God is still seen as stern towards sin but loving toward the repentant. Even that sternness is shown to be from His Heart of love in that He desires that the tragedy of sin not provoke any necessary judgment.

While there is still judgment upon sinners, the love of God shines through the Words, Work and Walk of The Son in His humanity. This is a reasonable scenario when we consider that the purpose of The Son has been The Cross since before the worlds were created. It is instructive to consider that The Son, He Who would go to the Cross for the sin of the created beings, was Himself the Agent of that creation. (John 1:3) The Father willed the creation but it was The Son Who was the active Agent of the creation of that which would necessitate His Own passion upon the Cross.

I believe that Peter was writing with a Jewish audience in mind as he said that the belief in God would activate faith in Jesus as Savior. They would have understood the concept of The God. I see The Spirit of God who acts as the Agent of calling men to faith in Christ, Jesus.

This verse says that God raised Jesus from the dead. John 10:18 does not dispute that fact. "No man taketh it from me, but I lay it down of myself. I have power to lay it down, and I have power to take it again. This commandment have I received of my Father." Since John 1:4 tells us that "In him was life; and the life was the light of men" we can easily see that it was God, The Son – that is Jesus – Who was an active Agent also in His resurrection. As the original creative agent this is only reasonable. Nevertheless, I think it evident that The Father and The Spirit were agreed Together in this work of Deity.

The fact that this verse argues that The Father glorified Jesus is perfectly in sync with the words of Jesus in John 17:5. "And now, O Father, glorify thou me with thine own self with the glory which I had with thee before the world was." In the Kenosis Jesus laid aside His outward glory of Deity. Now, close to His crucifixion and resurrection, He calls for The Father, to Whom He always gave deference as our example in His humanity, to restore to Him that glory which was His.

The result of all this was that the people could now worship God in Spirit and in Truth. (John 4:23) This full worship as adopted children of God (John 1:12) was something that had not be possible, or even dreamed of, prior to the coming and Cross of Jesus.

When we consider that Jesus told the woman at the well, "But the hour cometh, and now is, when the true worshippers shall worship the Father in spirit and in truth: for the Father seeketh such to worship him," (John 4:23) we see another intimation of the Trinity. The Father is mentioned as is the Spirit. We also see reference to truth, which, as John 14:6 informs us, is Jesus.

I realize that this is poor exegesis of the passage. Jesus is telling to woman to worship in the attitude of her own spirit and truth. But, I do consider these specific words are, at the very least, an intimation of the three "persons" of the Trinity.]

1.22 Seeing ye have purified your souls in obeying the truth through the Spirit unto unfeigned love of the brethren, see that ye love one another with a pure heart fervently:

[It seems that the Critical Text has left out the phrase "through the Spirit." Despite many claims to the contrary, this is a doctrinal issue. Pilate asked, "What is truth?" To him it may have been a rhetorical question. Jesus gave a definition of truth in John 17:17. "Sanctify them through thy truth: thy word is truth." We must note here that both the calling to salvation (See note at I Peter 1:2) and the sanctification of the soul are accomplished by the Spirit moving upon the elect in respect to the inspired and preserved Words of God.

To have left out this phrase, "through the Spirit," – note especially the capitalization of the words signifying a reference to Deity, i.e. The Holy Spirit – in this reference is a two-fold denial of the work of the Spirit upon the soul of man.

The word "pure" has also been left out with reference to the heart of love one Christian should have toward another. While it may be a "stretch," this omission leaves out, especially with the removal of The Spirit earlier, the real possibility that the "fervent" love would not be pure from either unholy or inordinate desire.

The recipients of Peter's epistle are commended that they have moved forward in holiness (I Peter 1:16-17) under the leading of The Spirit. The proof cited of this was that there was a true and unequivocal love of the brethren among them. This seems to mirror the argument of James that outward works are a proof of inward faith. (James 2:17)

This "work" of brotherly love was not of saving value. It flowed from a heart that was already born-again by the Blood of the Lamb of God, Jesus.]

1.23 *Being born again, not of corruptible seed, but of incorruptible, by the word of God, which liveth and abideth for ever.*

[At first glance this verse seems to be speaking about salvation. That is so. It does speak of salvation. But, the verse is making the point that our salvation is based upon a response to a record that is certain.

In the early years of television there was a program about a man who gave away one million dollars, tax free. It was, of course, a fictional show. Basically, if someone comes by your house and tells you that they are going to give you, tax free, one million dollars, there is only one thing you can take to the bank - it ain't gonna happen!

You've probably gotten the e-mails from a man who claims to be a former government official of an African country. He has thousands of dollars of money that he must find a way to disperse. If you will only send him, say, $1,000.00, he will send you back $500,000.00. I don't have to tell you that this is a scam. Simply put, it is not true.

Some people's word about things is fictional. Other people are dealing in dishonesty and their word cannot be trusted, either. But, the Word of God is certain. That is why we can trust His offer of Salvation. It is backed by His eternal Word.

This verse promises that we are reborn into an incorruptible salvation because of His incorruptible seed. That seed is backed by the Word of God.

"The word of God" is a two-pronged phrase. First, there is Messiah as the Word of God. (John 1:1) This is Jesus. He is our Savior from sin and from the bands of sin which engulf the human species from our birth. This "original sin" has been inherited from Adam. We are all born as fallen creatures. Only faith in the Lord, who died in time that we might live in eternity, can redeem us from that curse.

Then there is the Written Word of God. I was going to say of Messiah, above, that He is the Living Word of God. He is, of course. But the Written Word of God is also the Living Word of God; The inspired and preserved Bible is the "Breath of God." (II Timothy 3:16) As this is inspired of God, the Bible has the attribute of eternality. It can neither change nor fail. In its pages one learns of sin and salvation. In its pages one learns of the need of a relationship with God. In its pages one learns how to approach God and receive His grace into our hearts. (Romans 10:17)

Our salvation is thus seen to not stem from any act or form which we might follow. We, ourselves, are innately corruptible beings. I remember going, years ago, to a monument where the graves of an ancient culture were uncovered. I looked at all the skeletons of the people in that burial mound. Yes, people. That is what they were. I was impressed then with the brevity of live on this earth. Generations fade as another generation takes their place. Eventually all of those people were forgotten – except by their Creator God.

They once walked the earth as we do now. They laughed. They loved. They sorrowed. They perished from this earth. So shall we. After this will come the judgment. (Hebrews 9:27) It is only the incorruptible salvation of God which is of any real importance.]

1.24 *For all flesh is as grass, and all the glory of man as the flower of grass. The grass withereth, and the flower thereof falleth away:*

[I recently read the story of an atheist group which demanded that a picture, it was Salman's "Head of Christ," which had been placed in a school in 1956 as a memorial to a fourteen-year-old student who had collapsed and died in the school, be taken down. The author of the story asked, "If the [atheist group] were required to place a plaque honoring [this deceased student] what would it say?"

I have on my desk a book I just finished about one of the Christian leaders of this past century. It runs about four hundred pages. Folks, none of us need that many pages. The true story of all of our lives upon this earth could be summed up in just seven words. "We were born. We lived. We died." The story is the same whether a person be a president or a peasant. "We were born. We lived. We died." That's it. There really ain't no more!

I am now nearing my seventieth birthday. I can see from this vantage point the brevity of life. What was it Shakespeare said? "Out, out brief candle! Life's but a walking shadow, a poor player that struts and frets his hour upon the stage, and then is heard no more. It is a tale told by an idiot, full of sound and fury, signifying nothing." Life comes. Life goes. The space between the sentences is shortly served and quickly removed.

Paul said, of this short human life: "If in this life only we have hope in Christ, we are of all men most miserable." (I Corinthians 15:19) With the very next verse he shouts the truth from the housetops: "But now is Christ risen from the dead, *and* become the firstfruits of them that slept." This life does not end our existence. One life. One death. One Savior. One eternity of never ending bliss with the Savior!

What a sad and miserable existence befalls the one who does not accept the free grace of Salvation. To paraphrase the song writer: This world was not his own. He was just passing through. And, now he is through.

Sixteen words instead of the seven above. It is still a sad epitaph.]

1.25 *But the word of the Lord endureth for ever. And this is the word which by the gospel is preached unto you.*

Isaiah 40:8

[This would seem to a troublesome concept to those who deny the eternality of the Scriptural record. This verse does not say, "The word of our God shall stand until the faulty copyist makes notations in the margin...", or "until the word of God is changed by church councils...," or "until the sands of time have obscured the real words."

This verse does not say, "The word of our God shall stand until it is lost. But, then some men who do not agree that God has the power to preserve that Word will reconstruct what they believe He might have said."

We have a "know so" religion because we have an "I told you so" God Who has promised that He would preserve His Word for all eternity.

If the Word is not preserved, we can have no reason to hope that its pronouncements are true. I have belabored this point for the past several weeks in my writing and preaching. It remains important. If the Word of God is not secure, we have nothing which can be trusted to tell us anything about God, or salvation, or the spiritual world. We are, if the Word is not secure, in worse shape than the infidel for we trust a lie. Well, maybe not. But, how would we know if the Word of God, and by extension the Person of God, is not trustworthy in preservation?

There are those who would consign the above verses (vv. 24 &25) to only speak of the Gospel message. Their argument is that it is the Gospel message, not the entirety of Scripture, which has been promised preservation.

The Gospel message is vitally important. God has overseen the preservation of this message among humanity. It is by this Gospel that we are saved. But, note that the verse says, "And this is the word by which the gospel is preached unto you."

The Gospel message of sin, salvation and redemption is preached from the preserved Scripture. It is through the preservation of the inspired Scripture that the Gospel message is given to each of the succeeding generations of humanity.

Without the preservation of the Scripture we would have no real knowledge of the Gospel message. Salvation, without the Words of the inspired and preserved Scripture, would be only a vocal message handed down to us from the traditions of the elders.

The "seed" is the Scripture. The "Gospel" is that plant which springs from the seed. Now, I acknowledge that there is much more than simply the gospel message of salvation which is given us from the seed of the Scripture. We learn of God, eternity, the spiritual realities, even the purpose and means of living our earthly lives is contained in Scripture. The Gospel is, of course, foundational to our spiritual lives. Without the faith which comes by the hearing and accepting of the Gospel message we would be unable to access anything which God has for us in His Book.

It is by this inspired and preserved Book that the Gospel of salvation is preached unto the souls of humanity.

It must also be admitted that there is not one of us, scholar or lay person, who has ever resided in the realm of eternity and the spiritual. If the Message of Scripture had ever been lost, for whatever reason, we – as a race of humanity – would not be competent to restore that message. With no experience in the realm of which the

Scripture speaks; no man – scholar or lay person – would be a trusted guide through a territory which was unknown except through the instruction of God in His Book. Any "lost Scripture" must of necessity remain lost.

All talk of, "But, we have the leading of the Spirit," is based upon the message of a Book which would not be considered as trustworthy by those who would claim the Critical Text of man.

In this commentary I have limited the word "Gospel" to refer only to that which is of the Good News of Salvation. That is an arbitrary distinction I have made in order to magnify the entirety of the Scriptural message. In spiritual reality, the entire Scripture is the message of the Gospel. This inspired and preserved volume of God's Authorship is the record of the holiness, purity, grace, love and grandeur of God. Every single paragraph, phrase, word and letter has been given us from the breath of God. The entire record is given to His Church, and the individual Christians of each of those individual churches.

The above cannot be speaking of any translation. Translations of the inspired and preserved Scripture are the works of man. These translations may be accurate in their portrayal of the originally inspired Words. None can be itself inspired. God inspired His Words in the original Hebrew, Greek and Aramaic. The Psalmist tells us, "For ever, O LORD, thy word is settled in heaven." (Psalm 119:89)

Since God does not change, (Malachi 3:6a) He has not decided to "update" His plan for inspiration due to our affinity for a certain translation. A useful translation must be based upon the inspired and preserved Words of God. There is none other than can be considered as true to God.

We can never praise the love of God too highly. We can never esteem His great gift of His Words to us too highly. We can never love Him Who first loved us (I John 4:19) too much. We can never esteem ourselves at all except in reference to the Glory given us by His love! Even at that point we must esteem Him, the Giver, far above ourselves as the ones who are allowed the benefit of His love and gifts.]

FIRST PETER - CHAPTER TWO

2.1 *Wherefore laying aside all malice, and all guile, and hypocrisies, and envies, and all evil speakings,*

[In this verse Peter looks at the undisciplined tongue as had James in the third chapter of his epistle. The real difference between the two lies in the perspective from which they view the problem. James looked from outside in relation to the view that the unsaved would have of the church people concerning problems in this area. Peter looks from the inside and finds a spiritual problem which needs the attention of the people to rest on the Lord.

In light of the blessings of Jesus to as, as recounted for us in the inspired and preserved Scripture, Peter asks that we lay aside certain verbal and behavioral impediments to our Christian walk.

The "laying aside" of these things is not so much removing a shirt and putting it on a hanger for the closet. This picture is more of looking at the shirt and saying, "This thing is gross. I'm tossing it in the trash and setting the whole bag of trash out on the curb so the city sanitation department can get it out of my sight!"

Malice is the impure desire to see harm come to another person. It's as though we heard a brother was being sent to the lions and we felt sorry for the lions. Malice may masquerade as dislike for another. When examined we find that this dislike is actually a hatred.

We can hate sin. We can hate Satan as a defiler of humanity. But, we cannot hate humanity, or any representative of humanity, if we are to call ourselves followers of the Lord. Since Jesus came to this earth as The Substitute for the sinner, He is shown to have a love even for the sinner. Jesus has a love that will call the sinner from that sin and present him a new creature freed of his sin.

If we are to be called followers of Christ, we must love who He loved. He loved the downtrodden, the despicable, the denizens of sins chains. He came to call them from their sin and their spiritual filth. He called them to have their robes washed clean of the stain of sin by the Blood of the Lamb of Calvary.

The other side of this coin is that we are now, as Christians, in the household of faith with other sons and daughters of our Heavenly Father. We may not always "get along with" our brothers and sisters in the Lord. But, we must never wish them ill. It is wrong to do so. We can never walk in harmony with our Lord when we are set against another soul for whom He had died.

I believe that it was Shakespeare's play, "King Richard the Third," where Richard, a usurper to the Throne, has two young children, who were rightful heirs to the throne, killed. He says something to the effect of, "I loved them so much that I sent their souls to heaven early."

It is with great praise that we send some to their, in our estimation, "just rewards." It may not be to their physical death but it might be to a professional death. I went to a Bible Conference when my son was about three or four years old. We had to "room" with another man. He was a pastor who was sent to this conference by some members of the Deacon Board at his church. While he was at this conference, these men "played politics" on the Board and had that pastor fired.

In guile there is only the pretense of compassion used to hide the knife we use to strike a nefarious bargain.

Hypocrisy is likened unto guile. In hypocrisy we see one who plays the part of a lover who is ultimately shown to not care for the heart but for the purse. I think back a few years ago to a church near where I now sit at this keyboard. The pastor hired a man to be an "assistant pastor." That assistant spent his time praising this pastor and his leadership. Meanwhile he was courting the membership to vote out the pastor and hire him. The end result was another "church split" which brought discredit upon the cause of Christ in the city.

Guile will play a part to cause hurt. Hypocrisy will play a part in search of gain at another's expense. Hypocrisy is a "me first" attitude which has neither moral compass nor direction except to the hypocrite's benefit.

Envies play their part in all this. Envies are the garden in which the seeds of discord are planted and watered. "I deserve" is the unspoken guide of the envious spirit.

All of these lead to "evil speaking." This is a tender and alluring plant which is poisonous to spiritual health.]

2.2   *As newborn babes, desire the sincere milk of the word, that ye may grow thereby:*

[Babies tend to get hungry. Generally, this seemed to always happen at 3:00 A.M. when our kids were newborn. At those times the only thing which will satisfy them is feeding them. There may be a diaper change need and there may not. They want nourishment and will complain until they receive it.

We need to earnestly desire the sincere milk of the Word. That is one meaning of the word "sincere" in the verse. To the young Christian, especially, is this verse aimed. But, as the baby never outgrows its need for nourishment, if you don't believe me look at all the old people at *Chez Golden Arches* the next time you are there. But, the young Christian tends to need the "milk" of the Word.

We may instruct him in the doctrines of grace. He desires the discussion of the love of Christ to save the soul. It is a new experience for him. He delights in hearing that expounded. We may preach eschatology. This is a very interesting subject to him. But, even above interesting words, his soul will thrill at the old story of Jesus and His love. He may find reasonable interest in the subject of the transmission of the Scripture. But, to find that stirring of passion within his soul we must speak of the fact that Jesus Christ died in time so this person could live in eternity.

Desire, long for, have passion to learn more of the milk of the Word. We need to read and preach of Jesus. Personal "pet doctrinal issues" may reach into our intellect and excite our spirit of inquiry. Still, we need to read and preach of Jesus. Correcting societal problems through the message of Scripture is part of our duty as pastors. Above all, we need to read and preach of Jesus. Departing from evil and seeking the doctrine of the Lord will become more real only as we read and preach of Jesus.

There is no other place where we can find a pure and unadulterated doctrine and Godly love than in the sincere milk of the Word.

We do need to beware that we are in the Word and not in an adulterated word made not only weaker but misleading by the mixture of the words of man overshadowing the pure words of God. The Jamieson/Fausset/Brown commentary

FIRST PETER: Chapter 2

described one who said that the heretics were mixing chalk with the milk. This is worse than just bad for the baby, this could be fatal.

I have a copy of "The Access Bible." It carries a subtitle of "An ecumenical learning resource for people of faith." (sic) For its text it has chosen the "New Revised Standard Version." This verse is rendered: "Like newborn infants, long for the pure, spiritual milk, so that by it you may grow into salvation." Grow into salvation? Folks, we might grow IN salvation but we cannot grow INTO salvation. We either have it, based on the finished Work of Jesus, or we do not have it.

This is an example of an adulterated milk. It is not the pure milk of the Word of God. It has been spun, as the politicians would argue, to say something completely antithetical to the entire Message of Scripture. It is as an evolutionary ideal that an ape could someday grow into a man. A man born in sin cannot grow into a child of God. He must be changed. There must be a miracle of chromosomal change within his spirit. He must become a new creature by the power and grace of God. (II Corinthians 5:17) Only the miracle of the new birth, based entirely upon the Work and Grace of Jesus, can accomplish this. An ape can live for a thousand years and never morph into a human. A babe in Christ has been instantaneously changed by the miracle of the new birth.

Believe it. Teach it. Preach it. Live as though it has happened if you really are a born-again Christian.

It is this reality which can allow us to grow in grace. (II Peter 3:18)]

2.3 *If so be ye have tasted that the Lord is gracious.*

[The word "if" does not imply doubt in the mind of Peter. It is as though he said. "Because you have tasted..." Things, good things and great things happen when one has tasted of the salvation which is given freely to those who have trusted Christ.

Peter is quoting Psalm 34:8, "O taste and see that the LORD is good: blessed is the man that trusteth in him." The Psalmist says that this man will be blessed – happy. Peter doesn't argue with this but adds the truth of the New Covenant that the man will be happy to an even higher degree. The trusting man will find, to his own happiness, that the Lord is gracious. This word "gracious" is number 5543 in Strong's. The meanings are "good, kind, better, easy." The one who tastes of the Lord finds sublime happiness available to his soul and spirit.

It is interesting that Peter uses the word "tasted." The potato chip company used to say, "Bet you can't eat just one." That is the idea here. The truly born again will taste of the Lord and desire to find even more.

This is not as the man from Hebrews 6:4 who only "tasted" as a fellow traveler. He did not ingest for himself but only, it seems, observed the outward joy of others. (Consider my commentary at that verse.)

This man described by Peter at this place was one who had experienced true salvation by the grace of the Lord. This made a real difference in this man. He had a knowledge of these heavenly things because he had experienced them. The truth of this is the "milk of the word." The song says, "Jesus saves." The experienced knowledge of this man was "Jesus saved." Salvation had come into his heart!]

2.4   *To whom coming, as unto a living stone, disallowed indeed of men, but chosen of God, and precious,*

[John Wesley commenting on this verse: "Rejected indeed by men-Even at this day, not only by Jews, Turks, heathens, infidels; but by all Christians, so called, who live in sin, or who hope to be saved by their own works."

Jesus is called "a living stone." Other places we find Him referred to as "the living bread." Consider John 1:4. "In him was life; and the life was the light of men." Jesus does not "live in the pages of history," as we might say of Abraham Lincoln or George Washington. These men are truly dead. Jesus is alive. He does live in the pages of the Living Word of the inspired and preserved Scripture. He also lives in the hearts of the born again.

But, more glorious than any of this is the fact that Jesus is alive in the reality of all of human experience and in the reality of His mediatorial office as He performs that now. But, even more glorious that any of even that is the fact that Jesus, the Savior, is alive.

The time is soon coming that He will return again in the clouds, just as he left from Jerusalem those many years ago, to call His Own – both the living and the dead – unto Himself. Seven years after that event He will return to this earth, in His Glory as God and in His humanity as Himself, to set up his Kingdom. Kings, presidents, premiers and other potentates will bow their knees in homage to the fact that we, the born again, still serve a risen Savior Who is in the world today!

The phrase "to whom coming" speaks of the Christian who comes to Christ for salvation. We have nothing to offer Him but our love and acceptance. We must approach Him to find His love, mercy and forgiveness.

We come to Him Who is identified as a stone. When we think of Thomas "Stonewall" Jackson, a storied general in the Confederate cause, we think of one who stands his ground against all attacks. Yet, General Jackson was killed, never to rise again in this era of time. Even the cause for which he stood was defeated.

Jesus is called a "living stone." Peter, a devout Jew who had been a disciple of, and who had trusted for salvation, the Lord Jesus would have looked at the great Temple in Jerusalem and seen the stones. Having heard the words of Jesus concerning the destruction of that Temple, he would have felt a certain cultural sadness. But, he also understood that Jesus is the Cornerstone of a greater temple that that of Jerusalem.

My son recently did some work on his house which necessitated the removal of a wall. His main concern was that this not be a "load bearing" wall which he could not take down without seeing the roof fall in about his head. It wasn't.

The cornerstone, especially the Chief cornerstone, is such a "load bearing" stone of construction. From it is built the entire structure. It is the most important stone in the construction. Obviously, many – as Wesley described above – have rejected Him. In doing so, they have rejected the entirety of the salvation offered by God. He is infinitely more precious than the stone of the old Temple which was destroyed in 70 A.D. He is the Ultimate and Only Foundation of the spiritual life of every Christian who ever has, or ever will, come to that spiritual life through the Cross of salvation. We must also see that Jesus is the Ultimate and Only Foundation of His Church.

Peter by admitting that Jesus is that Chief Cornerstone of the Church has agreed that He is not and never has been the head of the church. Therefore no one can claim to "sit in the chair of Peter" as head of the Church of Jesus. That foundation of the Church is the fact that Jesus is The Christ, the Son of God. (Matthew 16:15-18)

This foundation was rejected by the religious leadership of the Jewish nation at the time Jesus offered Himself to them as Messiah. But, this foundation is accepted by God. The resurrection of Jesus and His ascension into Glory are both simple acknowledgments to this acceptance by The Father.

The verse also says that Jesus was "chosen" by The Father. We can compare this with the second verse of the first chapter of this epistle. We were elected to grace, by His grace. He called us to salvation.

In the determinative foreknowledge of God, in the holy counsel of His triune existence, Jesus was foreordained to the task of the Savior of humanity. From eternity past Jesus has held the office of Savior of Humanity. This is important for two reasons. One reason, of course, is that our very salvation is wrapped up in this great love of Jesus.

Another importance of this fact is that it shows the eternal existence of Jesus. He is not a created being. Since "All things were made by him; and without him was not any thing made that was made," this should be an obvious fact not worthy of dispute. (John 1:3)

Jesus is God. We must accept Him as such. He is God Who came into human existence – without denying His actual divinity, and died in His humanity to save our souls. He rose again in His humanity and then, in the sight of hundreds of witnesses, rose from this earth to reenter Heaven and take His place as our mediator of the New Covenant of His Blood and of His great grace.]

2.5 *Ye also, as lively stones, are built up a spiritual house, an holy priesthood, to offer up spiritual sacrifices, acceptable to God by Jesus Christ.*

[Here in this verse we find the meaning of Peter as a rock in Matthew 16:18. "And I say also unto thee, That thou art Peter, and upon this rock I will build my church; and the gates of hell shall not prevail against it." The word "Peter" does signify a rock. But, every instance of the use of Petros, Peter, in the New Testament speaks of Peter, the person. This is number 4074 in Strong's.

Petra, number 4073 in Strong's, also means rock. I could find no reference to this word being used to describe Peter. I found the word describing the rocks of mountains in Revelation 6:15-16. I found it describing the rock that sealed the grave of Jesus in Mark 16:46. I found the word in I Corinthians 10:4 describing the Rock that followed the people of the exodus. There were many other instances of the word. Never was this particular word used to refer to Peter. This is the word used to describe the rock upon which Jesus promised to build His Church. That "Rock" upon which the Church has been built is the statement of Peter that Jesus is the Christ, the Messiah, Who is the Son of God.

We, the Christian – this obviously includes Peter – are described as lively stones. Which is interesting in that Jesus is called The Cornerstone using the same word in stone (number 3037 in Strong's) as was used to describe us. This, of course, points to our identification with Him in His salvation and His identification with us in His incarnation.

We, the called of the ages, are lively, or living, stones which build the structure of a spiritual house. Therein is the church. Jesus is the Cornerstone and we are used to build His edifice. Paul reminds us, in I Corinthians 3:11, "For other foundation can no man lay than that is laid, which is Jesus Christ." This agrees with Peter in the present illustration that Jesus is the Cornerstone of His Church and we, the redeemed of the ages, are that building of which is His Church is constructed.

This is not simply the local church. I am fond of saying "churches" to differentiate true local churches from denominational structures. This word speaks of the Church Universal and Ageless. It is that assembly we will find in Heaven of the redeemed of Christ.

We are, properly speaking, a spiritual Temple. Part of the symbolism of the Tabernacle, and the Temple which followed its plan, was the picture of God dwelling among men. He dwells among us as His children. We dwell among the great mass of humanity as showing to them the presence of God into society. (Matthew 5:16)

In this living Temple of God which we call The Church, we are considered as priests. That is what Peter, writing inspired Words, said. There were many priests who labored within the Temple. They all labored under the High Priest. Jesus is our Great High Priest. (Hebrews 3:1; 4:14; 4:15; 5:5; 5:10; 6:20; 7:26; 8:1; 9:11 – That is just from Hebrews!)

We are called a "spiritual house." This seems to correspond with the Holy of Holies in the Temple scheme. That would put us in the presence of God. We are there as Christians. Adding John 1:3 to the conversation, we are reminded that we are "lively stones" who have received life from Him. This would then be our natural place.

Again, properly speaking, a Temple is a place to offer sacrifice. In Hebrews 9:28 we find that there is only one offering of sacrifice. That one offering would be that of Jesus Christ on the Cross of Calvary. Since the Roman Church, in their unscriptural doctrine of transubsitution, which argues that the wafer and wine of the Eucharist actually become the body and blood of Jesus and is literally offered in the daily mass at each of their churches, the Roman Church is found to be engaging in unbiblical practice at the heart of their religion.

This fact of a bogus *offering* is the reason that the officials of the Roman Church are called "priest" rather than "presbyter."

But, we have identified a problem here. Although there is no more sacrifice to be offered since the Self-Sacrifice of Jesus was the final Blood Sacrifice allowed, or needed, under the dispensation of God, how can we be called "priests?" By definition a priest is one who offers sacrifice. As far back at Exodus 19:6 God had prophesied that His people would become a nation of priests. "And ye shall be unto me a kingdom of priests, and an holy nation. These are the words which thou shalt speak unto the children of Israel." Israel is the Covenant People of God. Surely we are also a type of spiritual covenant people through the great atonement given us by Christ. Consider I Corinthians 10:11. "Now all these things happened unto them for ensamples: and they are written for our admonition, upon whom the ends of the world are come."

As "priests" our task is to offer the fact of the great Self-Sacrifice of Jesus to the world. Now, how do we do that? After all, we have no part in His cross, except that we accept it's Truth. We offer the knowledge, through out witness, of the death of Jesus, to the world at large. We are commissioned to take the witness of the Truth out into the world of men. We preach that Jesus did die, in the theater of time, so that others

FIRST PETER: Chapter 2

can live in the realization of Eternity.

Israel was the physical type of which the Church has become the spiritual reality.

The above cannot mean that Israel has been placed aside permanently. Jeremiah speaks of the Jew in Jeremiah 30:7 when he calls the Tribulation Era the "time of Jacob's trouble." Israel remains the Covenant People of God. They retain possession of all their earthly promises. They have a glorious future in the prophecies of God. They will come to accept Messiah and find salvation in Jesus even as they fulfill their earthly destiny as subjects of the great King Who will set upon the literal Throne of David.

Back, again, to that question about sacrifice. What can we, as priests, do? Romans 12:1 asks that we present our bodies, our earthly lives, as living sacrifices to follow the Lord in all things as pertains to our humanity. Hebrews 13:15, among other places, enjoins us to offer the sacrifice of praise to Him. We find in Revelation 8:3-4 that our prayers are as the censors used by the priests of old to offer service to God.

Paul agrees with Peter in Ephesians 2:20-22 when he argues that we are built upon the Cornerstone of Jesus as we are a "temple to the Lord."]

2.6 *Wherefore also it is contained in the scripture, I lay in Sion a chief corner stone, elect, precious: and he that believeth on him shall not be confounded.*

[I hear Peter holding his scroll aloft and shouting, "The Bible says!" O.K. Maybe he didn't say exactly that. He did say it, though. The proof of our religion is neither the philosophical meanderings of man nor the archeological finds of other men. We have a "know so" religion because we have an "I told you so" God. Outside of this inspired and preserved Book we can have no knowledge of God, Heaven, Hell, salvation, eternity or even of the past of our planet and lives.

With this Book we have everything we ever need to know about sin and salvation. We find the remedy of God for sin and the resuscitation of our souls unto life eternal through our Lord Jesus Christ.

In the passage quoted God promises to set His Cornerstone, more than this – His Chief Cornerstone, on earth to build the edifice of His record and redemption for humanity. He prophecies that this will be done in Jerusalem, Sion (Zion) being within that city of David.

Indeed, this is where Jesus was crucified and rose from the dead. This was where the Church, against which even the gates of Hell cannot lay siege, was begun by our Lord. The church had a beginning at Pentecost. At the time of Peter's great confession of faith, the church was yet future. In Matthew 16:18 Jesus speaks of His church as future. "I will build my church."

Peter adds to his earlier argument that Jesus is the Cornerstone. Quoting from Isaiah 28:16, Peter adds that Jesus is the "Chief Cornerstone" of the plan of salvation and glory. The chief cornerstone will not only uphold the building, it will also unite sections of the building. In this we see the "mystery," as Paul puts it, of the Church into the world of the Gentiles as well as retaining those earlier believers from Judaism. There are two peoples united in the One Messiah, Jesus, into one house of faith.

As to the "election" of Jesus to this office of Redeemer and Savior, we touched on that in the commentary of last verse. Before the worlds were created God looked into the entirety of human history and saw that sin would cast a blight upon His perfect creation. In the determinative counsel of God's Holy Trinity, The Son chose to become the Savior of the as yet uncreated humanity. Looking into the history of this creation, God saw the Cross as the only possible cure for the coming sin of Adam.

We have very small recognition of the great love of God. We blithely read "For God so loved the world..." We very rarely consider how great is that love. The song writer has written, "Grace greater than all my sin." None of us can actually begin to fathom the depth of that love. Even a small glimpse of the great love of God should drive us, weeping, to our knees in sorrowful praise of His great love and in sorrowful regret concerning our great sin!

Words fail when all we can say is that He is precious in His love, grace, power and action of offering Himself in Self-Sacrifice in order to forgive the sin of a rebellious people. We stand in amazement with heads bowed at the realization of the lengths to which He went in order to save our soul.

Isaiah said that he (that's us) that believeth shall not make haste. Peter says that we shall not be confounded. Isaiah speaks of not being hasty to simply enjoy the great excitement and joy of salvation. Why wouldn't they hurry? This was a greater joy than was evident under the Old Covenant. This was a greater joy than they could contemplate. We could add that this full blessing had to also wait for the coming of Messiah.

Even with that, the hesitation was a joyful anticipation and trust that what the Lord had promised He would perform. (Jeremiah 33:14)

We of the Gospel Age will never be confounded, ashamed, of the fact that our trust is in the Lord. (Romans 4:21)]

2.7 *Unto you therefore which believe he is precious: but unto them which be disobedient, the stone which the builders disallowed, the same is made the head of the corner,*

[There is a dichotomy here. The believers find Jesus to be precious. When we stop to consider the fact of our salvation, and the fact of what we would have lost had He not saved us, we find everything about Jesus to be precious.

We find His willingness to come from the realms of Glory, ordained to do so since before the foundation of the world, to be precious in His planning.

As we view Him in Gethsemane, struggling in His humanity with the pain and shame of the coming hours yet steeled to His task, a task which only He could have ever completed, we find Him to precious in His preparation.

As we watch with horror the maltreatment of the soldiers and those who cheered on His death on the Cross of Calvary we find Him to be precious in His passion.

As we see Him defeat death and the tomb on that first Easter morning we marvel at His power and find Him to be precious in His performance of the work of salvation and the calling of souls for the Kingdom.

As we view His return to Glory and the Heavenly Realms at His ascension from this earth we find Him precious in perfections.

As we read of His act of sprinkling His Own Blood on the Heavenly Mercy Seat we find Him precious in the pardoning of our sins and the moral stains of our redeemed souls.

As we realize that He stands as the only Mediator between God and Man we find Him precious in His power to draw us to Himself and to a victorious life we could not have found by ourselves.

As we look forward to either meet Him in the clouds of rapture of the valley of the shadow, we find Him precious as the purchaser of our souls.

Meanwhile the unsaved, those who have rejected His offer of free salvation must one day bow their knees and admit that Jesus is the true Cornerstone of the purpose of God in all of history of the Creation. They will admit this to their shame as their rejection of Him, a foolish and faulty rejection, has doomed them to an eternity without His love. Those who loved not the Lord will find their habitation will be a true Hell for a true eternity.

Their opposition to Jesus has not changed the spiritual truth of Him. Their opposition has only barred them, from the depths of their own souls, from His grace and love.]]

2.8 *And a stone of stumbling, and a rock of offence, even to them which stumble at the word, being disobedient: whereunto also they were appointed.*

Isaiah 8:13-14

[[See note at I Corinthians 10:4. What we have found here is that Isaiah said that the "LORD of hosts" was the Stone of Stumbling. That most definitely refers to God. Meanwhile, Peter claims that Jesus is "a stone of stumbling." Since there can only be One "Stone" of Stumbling, "one" being a limiting factor in that it speaks of a single entity, then Both cannot be this "Stone" unless Jesus is God. Realizing this shows us that both the Old and the New Testament passages speak of the Same One Who is God.

Here is the prophecy of Simeon when he saw the infant Jesus being presented in the Temple by Mary and Joseph. "And Simeon blessed them, and said unto Mary his mother, Behold, this child is set for the fall and rising again of many in Israel; and for a sign which shall be spoken against." (Luke 2:34)

This is a prophecy that, although the Jew was the first and primary recipient of Messiah. Further, it was Jewish men who were the penmen who put the inspired and preserved Words to parchment concerning both Messiah and His Doctrine.

Many of those Jews were saved. Sadly, many more were not saved. Some accepted the Cornerstone of Messiah and rose to salvation. Many more rejected the Cornerstone of Messiah and were crushed beneath that Stone as disobedient sinners.

Now we need to consider Pharaoh at the time of the exodus. "And the LORD said unto Moses, Go in unto Pharaoh: for I have hardened his heart, and the heart of his servants, that I might shew these my signs before him." (Exodus 10:1) Consider that God did not harden the heart of Pharaoh by fiat. Rather, God allowed the natural inclination of Pharaoh to harden his own heart. God used those unholy tendencies of Pharaoh in order to showcase the results of sin and the glory of the grace of God in freeing the Israelites from the bondage of Egyptian slavery.

We also consider Paul's words in relation to the situation here described by Peter. "I say then, Have they stumbled that they should fall? God forbid: but rather through their fall salvation is come unto the Gentiles, for to provoke them to jealousy." (Romans 11:11)

I do not believe that God predestined Israel to fall at this point. But, the foreknowledge of God knew what the result of Israel would be in relation to the mystery of the Church wherein both Jew and Gentile found the equality of Grace.

The pious Jew, conditioned by years of speculation that Messiah would be a political force to free Israel from Roman domination, was not disposed to accept Jesus in His humility of Person – and the seeming defeat of his crucifixion at the hands of those Roman oppressors – as the Glorious Messiah they envisioned. Further, the concept of the Gentiles converts finding grace in the same Covenant God as did they was beyond their understanding. Their natural inclination was to reject this Messiah which had been provided.

In the parable of the wedding feast from Matthew 22:2-10, Jesus describes the situation of the Jewish rejection of Him. Others were bidden to the wedding feast which those originally called had declined. In time the Church which Jesus founded was peopled more by the Gentile than by the Jew.

The "appointment" of the Jewish religious leadership and those that followed them was not to the rejection of Messiah. Although God foreknew that action, the actual act was that of those Jews in their own decision to reject Jesus. The "appointment" was to the just judgment upon them for their sin of that rejection.

Their own disobedience brought the judgment of God upon them. That disobedience also hastened the day of the acceptance of the Gentile into that Church, and the attendant Salvation, which Jesus built.]

2.9 *But ye are a chosen generation, a royal priesthood, an holy nation, a peculiar people; that ye should shew forth the praises of him who hath called you out of darkness into his marvellous light:*

Exodus 19:5-6; Deuteronomy 14:2

[Note the similarities between God's description of the Jewish people of the Old Testament and the Christians of the Church of the New Testament. Some have wrongly assumed that the Church has taken providence of the promises of God to the people of Abraham. Such is not the case. To argue such is to place the very promises of God to the Church, the Bride of Christ, in jeopardy of His whim and caprice. This view postulates a God Who is not unchangeable or eternal as it sees Him vacillating in His very words and promises. There are therefore no certainties in Scripture as God is become a God of time rather than the Master of Eternity.

When we consider the unfolding nature of the revelation of God to the world – He has built His revelations to man from the simple that they might be more easily understood unto the more complex as He reveals more of Himself and His programs, we can easily understand the simple consideration that the Old Testament often reveals in physical form that which the New Testament will unveil as a spiritual truth.

God has given promise and reward to His people. His physical people, Israel, have wonderful and secure promises relating to this physical world. His spiritual people, the Christians of the churches, have wonderful and secure promises relating to the eternal and spiritual entities.

We are informed that we all, those of us who have salvation through the shed blood of Jesus Christ, are priests unto God. It is our duty, and privilege, as overseen by the Spirit, to be faithful in transmitting those Words of Life to the next generation of believers. The next generation of believers is defined as those to whom we share the Gospel unto salvation. This is perpetually continued in the lives of all believers. This is the plan of God.

The purpose of a priest is to take the needs of the people to God and return with the Words of God to the people. That is our job in this day. We pray the convicting power of the Holy Spirit onto the lives of the lost. Then we convey the True Words of God, in witness and in Scripture, to those same people.]

2.10 *Which in times past were not a people, but are now the people of God: which had not obtained mercy, but now have obtained mercy.*

[Peter accesses from Hosea 1:9-10 and 2:23 at this place. This was a prophecy concerning the coming deportations of both the Kingdom of Israel and the Kingdom of Judah due to their unrepented sins. I find three fulfillments considered in this passage from Hosea. The first, the "near" fulfillment has to do with the people judged by the dispersions. God promised to call them back from their time of judgment.

The main controversy which occasioned the dispersion was idolatry. This judgment of God satisfied its purpose. National Israel has never again, despite all the tribulation of even the past 2000 years, fallen into idolatry.

That near fulfillment has to do with the return of the people of Abraham from captivity in order to reestablish their national residence in the Land of Promise. It was the reconstructed Temple – although greatly refurbished – which was in existence at the time of the sojourn of Jesus during His earthly ministry.

The first **far** fulfillment concerned the Gospel being preached to the Gentiles. The word "strangers" in the address of the epistle from verse one of the first chapter, strongly suggests that these churches were strongly peopled by Jews, either of the dispersion or from the persecution of the religious authorities in Jerusalem during the life time of Peter as he wrote. But, this could also refer to those Gentiles who also were found within those churches. The verses from Hosea also a prophecy of the mystery of the Church where Gentiles were also called to worship the God of Abraham through Jesus Christ.

Then there is the **further** fulfillment which will find its expression in the calling back to God of Israel during the time of Jacob's Trouble. (Jeremiah 30:7) There will be a great revival among Israel during the Tribulation Era.

After the time of that tribulation the promises made to Israel of a Land and the Throne of Messiah will be realized. All of the promises to the physical heirs of Abraham will find literal fulfillment on this earth. That is one of the guarantees given us, the "lively stones" of the Church, that all of the promises to the spiritual heirs of Abraham will also find fulfillment. God always keeps His Word! (Numbers 23:19)

This verse explains that the old "proverb" of "The Fatherhood of God and the Brotherhood of Man" is a false construct. We are indeed brothers in the Creation of God. But God is only the Father of those who have come to Christ at the Cross. The people in this verse in First Peter were said to be not of God; and, then they were of God. The natural state of humanity is not piously following God. In his natural state man is opposed to the things of God. (Romans 3:10-11)

It takes the spiritual act of conversion for any person to find grace in the eyes of God. (John 1:12)]

2.11 *Dearly beloved, I beseech you as strangers and pilgrims, abstain from fleshly lusts, which war against the soul;*

[Peter begins this section, a hard one for the person who has one foot in the world and only one toe in the world to come, with the appellation of "Dearly beloved." It is a very tender phrase from the pen of Peter as he begins to caution some hard things.

Before we move blithely away from that phrase let us consider that the words may have been put to parchment by Peter, but the reality of inspiration is upon those words. Those are the Words of God.

This is God saying to me, and you as well, "I've got some hard things to speak of at this place. When the going gets tough I stand alongside you and am ready to assist and help you on this journey. If you find a bridge washed out along this walk, I will help you to ford the stream!"

As Abraham, we seek a Heavenly destination. We are looking beyond the pleasures and problems of this earth. We are walking toward a Heavenly destination. Our Lord is our guide. There is no map to be found at a "travel center." We must seek the Guide of the Spirit and the map of the inspired and preserved Words of God.

This is the "silly season" of political office seeking. I'm looking at candidates for the local offices. I have no interest in the candidates for political office of a very nice city just six miles from where I am now seated. Why? That town is not my home.

Not only is this world not my home, I am a stranger here. That is what this verse says to the Christian. We must remember our citizenship in Heaven. This does not mean that we do not attempt to be good citizens of our local cities and nation. It does mean that even in our interest as concerned citizens, we must still count our enduring citizenship as Heavenly.

Our calling is to change this present world one soul at a time as we impress upon others the facts of sin and salvation. Even this we do not do with the "tools" of the world. We attempt this in the power of the Spirit as we pray His conviction upon those to whom we witness.

We cannot allow the lusts of the flesh, in whichever of the myriad forms this may take, to divorce us from our first passion which should be "And thou shalt love the LORD thy God with all thine heart, and with all thy soul, and with all thy might." (Deuteronomy 6:5)

Our goal should be to depart "fleshy lusts" and instead walk in a kind of spiritual lust, true soul exciting passion, to the Lord. I know; that is a hard task at seven-teen. It isn't markedly easier at seventy! But, if we are to honestly be used of God this is where we must train our minds, our souls, our spirits, and our passions, to turn. I never said, Peter never said, that this was easy. Peter only said it was right and necessary for our spiritual health and happiness.

The true fact is that, even within our fleshy lusts, we are fighting in a spiritual arena. (Ephesians 6:12) Only with constant monitoring of our minds and souls can we even begin to fight effectively. By the way, that which I just said will always lead to defeat. We need to lean upon the Lord, in real prayer, because we cannot begin to function in this fight without His hand upholding us above our own base instincts.

Peter reminded his readers, even in the first verse of this epistle, that they were in fact strangers. We are in fact strangers in this world. We are not citizens of the culture of this world. The culture of this world will never seek to help us become better Christians. That isn't their purpose. Their purpose is to tear down the walls of our hearts. They have already marched around us seven times. Now they are blaring forth the ram's horns of their cause. They want to march into the city of our souls and remove the good things which the Lord has given us. Their goal is to see us defeated and dependent upon their gods of passion for the things of this world.

Not only are we strangers in this world, we are also pilgrims. What do pilgrims do? They keep on moving through the waterless wilderness in search of an oasis to water their flocks. Keep on moving. When you stumble just get back up and start moving again. That oasis of Living Water may be just over the next dune. (I John 2:1) Get up! Get moving! Victory is assured in the Lord!]

2.12 *Having your conversation honest among the Gentiles: that, whereas they speak against you as evildoers, they may by your good works, which they shall behold, glorify God in the day of visitation.*

[This is a call to live honestly, and holy, before all so that glory may be diverted to God.

In the following of this admonition we will be able to defect much of the criticism which is directed against our Lord by defaming us as His Followers. The early church was accused of many evils by those who did not understand this "new" worship. In order for a religion to be legally practiced in the Roman Empire it was necessary that it be a religion stamped as "legal" by the Romans. Judaism was such a protected religion for many years. Christianity was granted a "pass" from Rome because it was considered as a subset of Judaism.

However, it eventually became apparent that the Jew did not accept Christianity as a sect of his religion. The Christian was branded an atheist because he partook of neither all of the Jewish feast days or ceremony. Nor did the Christian partake of heathen festivals and idolatries. Worse, the Christian did not obey the law to bow the knee to the Emperor and accept Him as divine. This was enough to brand the Christian as unpatriotic to Rome as well as atheistic. They didn't even have an idols of their God.

Add to this that many who did not understand the "body and blood of Christ" in the Eucharist, accused the Christians of practicing cannibalism. The Christian was also accused of all manner of other offenses because he was seen as somehow "different" from the rest of society.

Peter argued that the Christian must live a scrupulously honest manner of life among others. The Christian was also enjoined to do good works among others as well as among themselves. This was in keeping with Paul's admonition from Ephesians 2:10 that the born again were called to live in good works. Good works were never a means of salvation but were seen to be an outgrowth of salvation.

Besides being part of personal piety, living in good works was an excellent manner of witness to the power of Christ to those who observed the assembly. Eventually this manner of life did bring some "respectability" to the Church. The downside was that many began to see the church as a social institution for good rather than a religious fellowship calling sinners to repentance and salvation. The many grave errors which crept into the "Imperial Church" after the time of Constantine give evidence to the errors of those who found a social institution of more importance than a spiritual assembly.

There remained true churches and Christians within those churches, which continued to seek and find spiritual solace as accountable only to the Lord. The imperial church, which eventually became the Roman Church organization sought to stamp out what they viewed as "non-conformist churches" within their midst as the age of religious persecution did not pass away. It only became enabled by different masters.

Now we come to the phrase "day of visitation." I found all manner of possible explanations of this term. I do not find the phrase alluding to any great acceptance of the Christian Churches. I do find a phrase which speaks of those who would "glorify God in the day of visitation."

I find two possible situations that seem to fit. One has to do with the day of the visitation of martyrdom among the individual Christians. The way in which the Christians submitted to this, and their sublime refusal to accuse God or renounce Jesus were certainly powerful testimony to those who witnessed them.

But, I do not find any great movement toward piety among the tormenters of the Church. We find individual examples here and there. But, there is no great number of examples of those who gave great glory to God as they martyred the Christian for his faith.

Much more often than not the word "visitation" has to do with a time of the judgment of God upon people. My interpretation of the word is that it refers to the Great Judgment of the lost. "For it is written, As I live, saith the Lord, every knee shall bow to me, and every tongue shall confess to God." (Romans 14:4) Paul sees Isaiah 45:23 in his use of this phrase. Isaiah 4:23 speaks of the renewal of the Israelitish Kingdom of the Millennial Reign of Christ. At this point the world has been judged, Satan has been bound for one thousand years, and there is a time of peace, justice and harmony among the nations of the world as Messiah sits on the literal throne of David in Royal Robes of Power and Rule.]

2.13   Submit yourselves to every ordinance of man for the Lord's sake whether it be to the king, as supreme;

[I recently read a book that described a government plan to remove the Christian influence among the general population by setting up "camps," as in the day of the forced incarceration of those of Japanese descent during World War II. The argument was that the Christians are agents of disharmony among the people. To have them removed would be to insure peace and harmony among the rest of the nation.

To be sure, this seems like the fear of people who fashion aluminum foil hats for protection from television and radio broadcasts. However, there is enough of a germ of truth within this situation to raise some concerns.

Satan, for instance, will rarely lie outright. He will just "shade the truth" enough to send one in the wrong direction. The lie of deception will leaven the entire lump of truth. I do believe that once the initial shock of the rapture has worn away that the world will rejoice that these "fundamentalist troublemakers are gone. It is a good thing."

In this soup of humanity within these camps would be seasoned by preachers preaching a Bible message. It is well known that with a good concordance one can champion almost any cause with "proof passages." This is one of those passages. Peter was not talking about bowing to the government; he was cautioning that we ought to live as under the law of man that we might propagate the Law of Grace into the world of man.

The best defense against such a false teacher, and there are many of these false teachers even in the pulpits of churches across the land in this day, is to become well versed in the "entire counsel of God." (Acts 20:27)

It would be good if all pastors would teach a class on the principles of hermeneutics. That is one of those words that preachers like to throw around to impress people with their knowledge. It simply means finding the truth of the Bible Message. To whom was the passage written? Who spoke and why? What is the situation, worldly and spiritually, of which is written? Above all, prayers to the Spirit of Truth are needed in order to find the Truth of His inspired and preserved Words.

This particular verse was written by an apostle to Christians in the churches. His purpose is to instruct them how to live peaceably among the world so that their testimony would be accepted. It was not a plea to abandon that testimony. Consider Acts 5:29 where Peter is speaking to other evangelists. He is speaking of spreading the Good News that Jesus died in time so others could live in eternity. His argument at that point, and this is the same Peter here and in our text verse, was that the laws of man cannot supersede the Laws of God. When the two collide, we are duty bound to obey the Laws of God.

The two passages are not contradictory. They are complimentary. Both speak in amplification of the other. But, they do describe differing situations.

I can't leave this section without noting the recent Supreme Court legislation concerning homosexual marriage. One of the leading candidates for president (2016) has already stated that our belief system needs to "evolve" to embrace the law of the Land. The laws of man cannot supersede the Laws of God. When the two collide we are duty bound to obey the Laws of God. The king may be supreme ruler of the land but the Lord is Supreme Ruler of the Universe! We give deference to the king concerning the law of the land unless that law comes to the point of disallowing our following the Lord.

The purpose of living a law-abiding life is to give testimony to the world about us of the Truth of God. This is part of our Christian testimony before all men. That testimony is fundamental to our Christian life.]

2.14 Or unto governors, as unto them that are sent by him for the punishment of evildoers, and for the praise of them that do well.

[We could spend time with the terms "governor," "proconsul," and such as Roman institutions which were sent and ordered by the Roman Emperor. Suffice it to say that under the concept of "Spiritual Principles" these still apply to us even though there is no king in our land. Nor do the other offices exist except in type. Also, we might argue that the manner of these "lower" offices being appointed is also different in that we will generally operate under elections rather than "by fiat" appointment. Yet the principle remains.

The command of the Lord, for this is what the Word of the inspired and preserved Scripture is unto us, is to obey and give due reverence not only in the "Macro" sense of national rulers but also in the "Micro" sense of state, county, city and other local "rulers." Rulers in this sense concern both elected and appointed (such a police powers) which are given the task of ensuring public order.

The judiciary is the ultimate enforcement arm of the rulers of an area. They are only to rule on the enforcement of the ordinances under our system of law. The purpose of this enforcement is to punish those who disrupt the public order. The purpose of this enforcement is to afford a manner of praise to those who do not disrupt the public order by giving them the freedom to move about in confidence of the stability of that social order in all of the realms in which government is to exercise power and peace.

Spiritually speaking, these offices stand as the "rods of God," as were the nations of Assyria and Babylon to the ancient Kingdoms of Israel and Judah in reference to divine judgments, to ensure the proper disposition of human order.]

2.15 *For so is the will of God, that with well doing ye may put to silence the ignorance of foolish men:*

[That this, obeying the laws of the land which are not antithetical to the Laws of God, "is the will of God." This has to be a rather troubling sentence to those who would agitate by the breaking of those laws in an attempt to change the tenor of even a, in their estimation, oppressive government. It is a rather damning charge made against those who have the freedom of the ballot box to seek a change of that government but seek violence and unrest as agents of that change.

This is not to say that the Christian may not use all legal means to argue under the law to find protection from that law. Paul did this in Acts 25:11 when he argued that his status as a free-born Roman citizen allowed him to appeal to trial before Caesar rather than journey to Jerusalem where he knew a mob was ready to kill him.

Peter is primarily asking that the Christians in this case live lives of scrupulous honesty in all things before the world. This would not give their enemies any real cause to accuse them of either dishonesty or sedition against the rulers. This would muzzle these enemies in that they could not find any cause to accuse them except one.

When Daniel heard that a law had been signed forbidding anyone from making petition of any but the king for thirty days, Daniel continued to live his devotional life even though this cost him a night in a lion's den. (Daniel 6:10) If only it were so of us that the only charge which could be leveled against us was that we were too scrupulous in our religion!

But, as to any charge of sedition or non-compliance with the laws of man cannot supersede the Laws of God. When the two collide we are duty bound to obey the Laws of God. These could be "brushed aside" by an appeal to a perfectly lawful existence by these Christians.

These enemies of the Christian are called "ignorant." I could properly be argued that most of these accusers were ignorant of the reality of the Christian experience. But, that ignorance was spiritual in nature. (Ephesians 4:18) Their most glaring foolishness lay in their not accepting the salvation offered in Jesus Christ. Instead they chose to fight against Him and the witness of men about Him.]

2.16 *As free, and not using your liberty for a cloke of maliciousness, but as the servants of God.*

[One day Jesus was speaking with the Jewish religious leaders when He said, "And ye shall know the truth, and the truth shall make you free. They answered him, We be Abraham's seed, and were never in bondage to any man: how sayest thou, Ye shall be made free?" (John 8:32-33)

These men told Jesus that they had never been in bondage to any man. Lets see... At the time they said this they were a nation occupied by the Roman legions. They were paying taxes to the Roman treasury. Their religious observance and civil rights were either allowed or disallowed on the authority of Rome. I don't know. It sure looks a little like political bondage to me.

Even when it came to the trial of Jesus it was necessary for the Sanhedrin to get the Roman, Pilate, to condemn Jesus to death because they acknowledged that they did not have the authority to do so. At that time the people of the Sanhedrin proclaimed that, "We have no king but Caesar." (John 19:15) Again, it sure looks a little like political bondage to me!

Much of this attitude of the religious leadership was considered in reference to Deuteronomy 17:5. "Thou shalt in any wise set him king over thee, whom the LORD thy God shall choose: one from among thy brethren shalt thou set king over thee: thou mayest not set a stranger over thee, which is not thy brother." This helps to explain the string of revolts against Roman rule by the Jewish people.

The churches which Peter addresses were well peopled with Jewish Christians who had been brought up from their youth with this verse ringing in their ears. Then they were told that they were free in Christ upon their conversion. For many there was no compulsion to follow the rule of "Gentile Law." Peter has just said, "No. That is not the meaning of your freedom. Do not use this freedom in Christ as a smoke screen to live lawless lives!"

A quick look around them might have allowed them to see that, even after their conversion, they were still living in the world of sin. The "cop on the beat" would still arrest them if they stole. But, their theology, and personal opinion, was based in an extreme and nationalistic libertarianism.

The freedom into which they had come was a spiritual freedom. They were free from the Old Covenant system. They were still expected to remember the Spiritual Principles of that system. Sin may have no longer bound them but it sure seemed to hound them! Even Paul complained, "For the good that I would I do not: but the evil which I would not, that I do." (Romans 7:19) This was a freedom to live above sin but not to wallow within sin. Any sin was to be met with honest repentance and a plea to God for forgiveness. (I John 2:1)

They were no longer bound by chains of threatened judgment to the Law of the Old Covenant. They were bound by chains of love to the Savior and a holy life in His love and power. Indeed it was not a freedom from purity but a freedom to live in purity.

First Corinthians 8:13 set the standard even higher than the people living under the Old Covenant could have imagined. "Wherefore, if meat make my brother to offend, I will eat no flesh while the world standeth, lest I make my brother to offend." Even in spiritual considerations the new Law of Love called us to esteem the need of the other even above our own need.

This is true freedom to live in the pure manner unto which humanity was originally created. This is not license to live for our base desires. Our base desires spring from that sin which nips at our heels as we walk the land of the carnal living.

We are free to be true servants of our Heavenly Father.]

2.17   *Honour all men. Love the brotherhood. Fear God. Honour the king.*

[As I write there is presently a controversy concerning a presidential candidate and the fact that the head of a racist organization has endorsed him. It has brought my mind to the concept of racism. God is the Creator of the entire human race. Although the blood of all men remains the same, (Acts 17:26) it is nonetheless true that the locale of the habitation of men has made certain changes in their outer form. Man remains one creature created by God.

With this reality in mind it is necessary to observe that racism in any form is a sin against the Goodness and Creation of God. It is to call Him flawed for allowing certain of His creation to exist. God is not flawed. While sin has worked its unholy work upon humanity, we must also note that Jesus died in time so that any man who accepts the offered salvation will live in eternity. That is "any man" without regard to race. (I Samuel 16:7)

We are called to honor all men. I'd like to say "honor to whom honor is due." But, that ain't what God has commanded. As the old saying goes, "The Ten Commandments are not suggestions." The same goes at this point. I would argue that we should honor each equally. We find different stations in life among men. We find different ranks in life among men. Now, if that rank is a military rank and you are in the military you might want to amend my suggestions just a bit! But, generally speaking the rank, or station of a man allows one no higher honor than another.

By the way, the verse says to honor all men; it will not hurt anyone to render due honor to women as well. This may seem a "touchy" point considering the wonderful differences God has made within the sexes. But, due honor will keep propriety in view.

Next we are told to love the brethren. The same arguments above are applicable at this point. The difference here lies in the fact that the Brethren, and the Sisteren, are in the Household of Faith. They are the called, as are we, of God unto Salvation. They, as are we, are in the family of God. I honestly believe that we ought to count the Brothers and Sisters in the Lord as a little more precious to us than are those of the world at large.

That concept of equality is even more important within the Household of Faith. I have seen the devastating harm caused to a slighted Christian when they are downgraded in that brotherhood. Such is sin. The only favorite in the sight of God is His beloved Son.

Notice that we are to fear God but only to honor the king. That sequence says two things to me. The first is that only the born again believer is fit to honestly honor the king because he will honor the king even as the king assails him. Let us keep in mind that Emperor Nero was on the throne when Peter wrote these words of instruction to honor the king.

But the fear of God is paramount. This is a holy fear. It is not being frightened of God. It is holding Him in such high esteem that we have a heartfelt fear of letting Him down by our actions. A holy fear is not simply rooted in a full dread of suffering on our part but of doing wrong to the One Who has shown such love into our hearts.

"For God so loved the world, that he gave his only begotten Son, that whosoever believeth in him should not perish, but have everlasting life." (John 3:16) The sentiments of this verse deserve to be shouted out into the world. God loves!]

2.18 *Servants, be subject to your masters with all fear, not only to the good and gentle, but also to the froward.*

[The Bible does not sanction slavery. The Bible does accept that this has been an institution among men. Therefore, the Bible does regulate the sin of the tradition. This, as divorce, seems to come under the heading of a thing allowed by God but not sanctioned as an optimum situation. "He saith unto them, Moses because of the hardness of your hearts suffered you to put away your wives: but from the beginning it was not so." (Matthew 19:8)

It is to the shame of the church that this evil persisted as long as it did after the Reformation called for a return to the Bible as a rule for faith and life. I know that some found the Biblical references to the evil as a cause to continue it. I know that some saw it as a means to evangelize an entire race of humanity. I know that all slave traders were not Western Europeans and there were those who did not want to deny an economy built upon the trade. (This has to be the least compelling reason that it persisted for so long.) I know that some were appalled by the situation. But, it persisted for several hundred years.

It also a credit to the Christian Church that this evil was finally eradicated from the nominally Christian nations. In some it took wars to free men from bondage. In these the guiding cause of the wars was the Christian conviction that slavery was wrong.

In the early days of Christianity, the churches were too small to effect the great economical change necessary to speak against slavery. By the time the Church had grown into a social force, it was too entrenched in the society to make that case.

There are still areas where the reality of slavery abounds. Thankfully, these are not nations which claim a Christian heritage.

After spending that much time on slaves, the word used for servants could be either slave or low level domestic servant. However, the entire epistle of Paul to Philemon concerns Onesimus who was a runaway slave which was being returned to his former, and apparently once again, master. We also note that there were household churches where the "master" sat in the congregation while one of his slaves labored as pastor of the church.]

2.19 *For this is thankworthy, if a man for conscience toward God, endure grief, suffering wrongfully.*

[That there were harsh and unjust masters as well as just and proper masters was a societal fact of that first century. The "froward" of the preceding verse speaks of these harsh and unjust ones. It is generally from these that the grief and wrongful suffering are mentioned in our verse.

Even to these there was an expectation that the Christian servant would give due reverence as he unjustly suffered. The thrust of the preceding verses gives the reason for quietly suffering wrong. It is to give an example of enduring wrongs for the sake of the Lord. There is to be an uncomplaining servant because the Christian finds his sufficiency in the Lord.

The one thus suffering applies this suffering as unto Christ and sees his acceptance as his reasonable service to his ultimate Master, the Lord of Glory.]

2.20 *For what glory is it, if, when ye be buffeted for your faults, ye shall take it patiently? but if, when ye do well, and suffer for it, ye take it patiently, this is acceptable with God.*

[There is suffering and then there is suffering without any cause.

Peter asks if any believe there is any glory in suffering for the things in which they have done wrong. This is a rhetorical question. Of course, there is no glory, even to one who suffers buffeting and accepts it without question or response, if this buffeting has been the fault of the servant for some wrong he has done. There is neither glory nor grace in such a situation. That servant is only reaping what he has sown.

But, the servant who is buffeted when he has done no wrong finds glory in the estimation of God when he accepts this suffering in the silence of his testimony that he is now a Christian. Many servants were saved in their own right. They accepted Christ as Savior even when their master might not have done so. There were times that this caused them problems.

One potential problem was the servant who, since he was now born again, would refuse to join with his master in idol worship. The servant would suffer, not because he had done wrong but because his master was upset with him.

In this situation the servant would suffer for the cause of Christ. Simple suffering was not a cause for glory. Suffering at the hands of man for the testimony of Christ, especially suffering without the response of anger or recrimination, was a cause for glory as suffering for the cause of Christ.]

2.21 *For even hereunto were ye called because Christ also suffered for us, leaving us an example that ye should follow his steps:*

[This verse reminds us that Jesus is to be more than our Savior; He is to be the One after Whom we pattern our lives. Sermons could be written on this simple passage - books of sermons! Distilled to a short description, I would say that Jesus was always secure in His knowledge of right and wrong, sin and salvation, but His outlook, from His humanity, was that He was servant to others.

God would have us to be interested in the souls of those who are not yet saved from their sin. Luke 19:10 would inform us that this is following Jesus! Again, God is Love and He expects us to honestly hate the sin that harms, but to honestly love the sinner who is stricken with this spiritual malady.

From our standpoint as a fallen race of men, we are most thankful that because of the Virgin Birth Jesus was able to become the Perfect Sacrifice for the sin of mankind. The example which He gave, as important as that is to the Christian, is useless to effect salvation from sin. It is only the acceptance of His sacrifice from sin which frees us to begin to strive to follow that example as growing Christians.]

2.22   Who did no sin, neither was guile found in his mouth:

[Jesus was not born as are others of this race of Adam. He is the only begotten Son of God. He was Virgin Born into this world without the inherited trait of sin.

Not only was Jesus born perfect, He never "did...sin." No action of His could ever have been called sin. The fact that there was no "guile found in his mouth," informs us that He also never sinned in word. "Guile" is number 1388 in Strong's. Among the meanings are "craft, deceit, and subtlety."

The politicians are fond of "massaging" words to make them malleable so that words will seem to be exactly what each hearer wants to hear. This is so even if each hearer wants to hear something different. We are reminded of one politician who famously said, "The answer depends on what the meaning of 'is' is." Jesus never used the guile of speech to say anything but honest truth exactly as it was formed in His mind.

Neither was there any sin in the mind or intentions of Jesus. Every facet of His humanity was completely holy. We might consider this as harder to prove except that His words were always stamped upon exactly what He meant. Consider John 8:28, "Then said Jesus unto them, When ye have lifted up the Son of man, then shall ye know that I am he, and that I do nothing of myself; but as my Father hath taught me, I speak these things."

That "lifting up" of the verse speaks of the cruelties attendant with the day of His crucifixion. Even Pilate, the Roman examining official, could find no fault in Jesus. (John 18:38; 19:4; 6) Jesus suffered for our sins but He suffered for no wrong He had ever done to anyone. From the strictly legal standpoint Jesus suffered and died in His humanity without any human cause.]

2.23   Who, when he was reviled, reviled not again; when he suffered, he threatened not; but committed himself to him that judgeth righteously:

[To use a military analogy, Jesus did not "return fire" when reviled and treated in a wicked manner by both His inquisitors and His temporary jailers. He did ask for explanation and incident as to His accusers questions.

Throughout the entire ordeal Jesus reacted with calmness. He displayed no anger and expressed no threat of revenge. Instead He prayed for His tormentors.

Those tormentors included the rich and powerful of society. They attacked Him with both lie and cruel sarcasm even as He was dying on the cross. He was taunted in front of His friends, followers, and family. Again, instead of throwing their hate back into their faces, He calmly accepted the burden of the Office of Savior which He was then fulfilling in the perfect plan of God.

Realizing His purpose in coming into this world, Jesus committed Himself to only two objects. The one, of course, was that fulfilling of His mission. The other was The Father in Heaven. Even this was not a plea for revenge. This was a recognition that God was the Perfect Judge of man and action. He had no personal anger for His antagonists as He willingly died a horrible human death in this time of trial so that others would be able to live in the ageless ages of eternity.

This concept of "committing Himself" is likened to a court official who brings the prisoner to the judge. Jesus willingly went to the Cross in order to become the Savior of all who would accept Him.]

2.24 *Who his own self bare our sins in his own body on the tree, that we, being dead to sins, should live unto righteousness: but whose stripes ye were healed.*

Genesis 2:9; Exodus 15:25; Deuteronomy 21:23; Revelation 22:2

[Peter alludes to Isaiah 53:5-6 in this place. "But he was wounded for our transgressions, he was bruised for our iniquities: the chastisement of our peace was upon him; and with his stripes we are healed. All we like sheep have gone astray; we have turned every one to his own way; and the LORD hath laid on him the iniquity of us all."

Peter said that Jesus was Himself the sin bearer. That is in counter distinction to the Old Covenant where an animal of creation was sacrificed as a representative of the human sinner. Jesus became in His humanity The Actual Representative for us. Hebrews 10:4 reminds us that those Old Testament sacrifices could never defeat sin. Only Jesus, as God having the authority to forgive sins, as man being the actual representative of sinful humanity Who had that identification to impart His salvation to us upon our faith in Him and His Word, could defeat sin for us.

Many of the ancients could not accept that Jesus had actually died on that Cross. They argued that He was too pure to suffer that punishment for us. These died in their sins as they did not accept that soul saving Self-Sacrifice of Jesus which is the only remedy for sin.

Other cultists have argued that there was a substitute for Jesus at the Cross. I have been told that many Muslim's, who see Jesus only as a prophet, believe that Judas was mistaken for Jesus and died in His place. Again, to accept this is to die in one's sins as not having accepted that soul saving Self-Sacrifice of Jesus, the Divine Son of God, in which is the only remedy for sin.

We might note that Jesus bore OUR sins on the Cross. He had no sin of His Own for which He could have died. There is a discussion over who to blame for the crucifixion of Jesus. Should we blame the Jew for his complicity in accusing Jesus or the Romans for actually carrying out the crucifixion? Both answers are wrong. It was our sins which were responsible for the death of Jesus at Calvary. He died in time, on purpose, so that we could live in eternity, in grace!

It was a wooden cross, a Roman Cross, on which Jesus was crucified. Why is the reference in so many places to a tree? One reason is that the Roman Cross was made of the wood of a tree. The other reason harkens back to Deuteronomy 21:22-23. " And if a man have committed a sin worthy of death, and he be to be put to death, and thou hang him on a tree: His body shall not remain all night upon the tree, but thou shalt in any wise bury him that day; (for he that is hanged is accursed of God;) that thy land be not defiled, which the LORD thy God giveth thee for an inheritance."

Jesus was made a curse for us that we might be released from the curse of the Law. (Galatians 1:13) We thus see that this passage from Deuteronomy was a prophecy of the death of Jesus for the sins of humanity unto those who accept Him as Savior. This passage from Deuteromony also adds a little background information as to why the religious leaders were anxious that His body be removed from the cross. They attempted to hasten His death by the breaking of the legs of those on cross' who were executed at the same time and place as was He. They would have broken His legs as well except that He was already dead in His humanity by then. Consider Psalm 34:20 as another prophecy of the death of Jesus.

When Jesus died as our Atonement, we were pronounced dead to sin and to the sin nature. Paul, in Romans 7:1-6 explains the concept by appealing to the status of a widow as regards her marriage to her deceased husband.

Since we are freed from our bondage to the sin of Adam and alive because of the Work of Jesus, we have become alive to the realities of righteousness. (I Corinthians 15:22) While we are still in these bodies of clay we are bound by certain earthy constraints, our spirits, being alive to God, are freed to live in holiness unto Him.

It is those stripes laid upon Jesus by His trial, beatings, and crucifixion which point to His substitutionary death by which His Blood has saved us from the degradation and power of sin. We are healed from the power of sin and from the chains of sin. We are free to live a life in praise unto God.

That word "unto" is important. Our walk as Christians is begun at the point of conversion. We are saved eternally and secure. But, we need to progress within that salvation as good workmen for God. (II Timothy 2:15) This is simply our reasonable service. "I beseech you therefore, brethren, by the mercies of God, that ye present your bodies a living sacrifice, holy, acceptable unto God, which is your reasonable service." (Romans 12:1)]

2.25 *For ye were as sheep going astray, but are now returned unto the Shepherd and bishop of your souls.*

[Peter considers the contrast before his readers were in salvation and now that they are in salvation. Before, they had been as sheep without a shepherd. Without this shepherd there would be no cohesiveness in the unit of the flock. Essentially there would be no flock; instead there would be a mass, ever thinning, of individual sheep going hither and yon with no plan or purpose except the move from the place they were in to any other place.

In this situation of going off by themselves there would be no protection from wild carnivores or from thieves which would steal them only to make a meal. There was no one to either love or care for those semi-wild sheep.

Rather than having a caring shepherd to lead them to good food and still water, sheep do not care for running water, there was only the sinful lusts of carnal desires to lead to sin and desperation.

However, after returning to God by finding that salvation which is in Christ these same sheepish people would find the True Shepherd of their souls. These lost and wandering people would now have the leading of the Heavenly Shepherd to lead them to heal the parched tongue of a thirsty soul. They would now have the Heavenly Shepherd to lead them to rich pasture lands where their souls could find spiritual food for an eternal agenda of life rather than the temporal agenda of death.

This Heavenly Shepherd would protect His sheep from the predatory wolves in sheep's clothing who sought to steal them from the peace of the Heavenly Shepherds watchful eye. Even the "Roaring Lion" of adversity, which sought to devour their souls, would be met by the staff and arm of the protecting shepherd.

This Heavenly Shepherd cares for the sheep of His pasture.

Jesus is even more than the Heavenly Shepherd. He is also the Heavenly Bishop of their souls. The word Bishop means an overseer. He oversees His flock. In the religious sense it is He who keeps His churches both pure and ever expanding in their devotion to Him, their love to Him – as He first loved them, and the strength of their testimony as they draw closer to Him.

When they are attentive to His leading He will warn them of trials and temptations wherein they need to strengthen their stand. He will assist them by giving knowledge of Himself and His doctrine.]

FIRST PETER - CHAPTER THREE

***3.1** Likewise, ye wives, be in subjection to your own husbands; that, if any obey not the word, they also may without the word be won by the conversation of the wives;*

[Peter had discussed the rights of obligations of the Christians in regard to their duties and responsibilities under civil law, their rights and duties as both slave – servant – and masters. He now moves into personal responsibilities in the marriage union.

I would like to caution that some of these are "wifely duties;" for the most part these are a "two-sided" coin. Not only does the wife bear a responsibility to the husband, the husband owes much reverence and responsibility to the husband.

In the Garden, Moses has told us in Genesis, that man was created by fiat of God's voice. Female was made from the rib of Adam. Woman was not "created" in the sense that Adam was created from the dust of the ground.

Our physical bodies are physical; they are made of the "stuff" of the creation of the earth. Somehow this is different from even the creation of the animal and plant life. They are made within the creation. We are made as a part of that creation. Then, within that creation we are given the Breath of God. In this sense we are "of" the world – in our physicality, but we are not "part of" the world – in our spiritual nature. In this we have been given the gift of eternity. We will all either live in bliss for eternity with our Savior or in guilt and regret without that relationship with our Creator.

This fact of salvation takes us from our natural element of the earthly and transforms us into the element consistent with that Breath of God. We take on a newness of life in the salvation of our spiritual.

Now, as to the operation on Adam which produced woman, we find that Adam had a rib removed which was fashioned into woman. (Genesis 2:21) This is the concept of life from life in that woman was not a "new" creation but a creation brought from the already existent life of Adam. Adam recognized this fact and called Eve, "bone of my bone, and flesh of my flesh." (Genesis 2:23)

Adam recognized that this "woman" was not a new creature but actually an extension of his own personhood. At this point Adam became a prophet and prophesized of the marriage of future generations. "Therefore shall a man leave his father and his mother, and shall cleave unto his wife: and they shall be one flesh." (Genesis 1:24)

In a real and spiritual truth, man needs woman to "complete" him. His "rib" is gone and to become fully human there is this necessity that man find woman to complete his own makeup as a created human. The woman also recognizes that she is incomplete without the man and will nurture him as a necessary part of her own spiritual make-up.

This, of course, is not a physical or psychological phenomena; it is a spiritual reality. We cannot but notice that the concept of homosexual relationships is a revolt against the plan of God even as far back as the very creation of man and woman.

The woman is cautioned to continue to give due respect to her husband even if that husband is not a believer. Peter argues that it is possible that a Godly manner of life, as evidenced by the woman may well be used of the Spirit to convict her spouse of his own need for a Savior. The same concept is applicable to the male.

We might note the unspoken in this verse: The husband remains the head of the home as would be the case if both spouses were born again. In no situation is the established civil order to be disrupted by the conversion of one or the other.

We would also note that the wife is said to be in subjection to "her own husband." There are those who would argue for "spiritual marriage" and "spiritual subjection." These are the doctrines of devils. The original template of marriage is that of only one man and only one woman within the bonds of matrimony. These arguments are only used to give a seemingly spiritual purpose behind the devilish plots of seduction.

This is, of course, one of those "two-sided" coins of sinful endeavor.

Any possible interloper is simply one who would pervert the program of God and subject another to join in his own sin. In the natural this was the sin of David accomplished before he and Bathsheba even came together as he called her to the king's bed. In the spiritual this is the position of the serpent in the Garden who sought to entwine Eve into his program of sin.]

3.2 While they behold your chaste conversation coupled with fear.

[Once again the concept is of living one's life, "conversation" being a manner of life, which is pure towards God and all others.

There is real disagreement with the phrase "coupled with fear." Some see "fear of God" as the meaning while others argue for "fear of the husband" with reference to Ephesians 5:33. I see no reason not to accept both in this place. In this view the husband, finding complete acceptance for his headship from his wife, would understand that as part of her reverence toward God.

In either case the word fear would be a Godly fear of respect and reverence. Included would be the concept of loathing even the thought of displeasing either husband or God in respect to the marital relationship.

Once again this admonition would apply to both wife and husband. The husband is giving no license to live as a lout or to not be in reverence to the God of Creation.]

3.3 Whose adorning let it not be that outward adorning of plaiting the hair, and of wearing of gold, or of putting on of apparel,

[The meaning is not that women are not to look the nicest which they possibly can appear. We may note at this place that it seems most men will, as soon as they say, "I do," stop doing that which would make them more attractive to their wives. "I do" stop exercising to keep myself fit. "I do" stop watching what I eat to keep my body in subjection to my lusts. "I do" stop trying to find becoming clothing but will wear what I find utilitarian.

The women generally do the opposite. They try to keep their selves attractive to their husbands. Peter is not arguing against that. Although he may be arguing against the other for the men who let themselves go "to pot."

What he is addressing in this verse is that "tightrope walk" between looking so much like the world that there is no appearance of being Godly.

The "plaiting" of the hair was accomplished with gold combs and such put into the hair. It was a manifestation of slavish detail to worldly style and scant attention to spiritual necessity.

A short walk through a field of wildflowers in the early spring will dispel any notion one might have that God is not interested in beauty. It is our attitudes which are on trial in this verse.

Do we care more about God or more about the fashions of the world? This seems at heart in the discussion of Peter at this place. The conflict is in caring more about our bodies than we do about our souls – and the souls of others.

In many of the cities of the Roman Empire of the time there were temples wherein were employed "temple prostitutes." These women would dress themselves in an excess of jewelry and ostentatious clothing. Peter is simply asking that the women of the churches dress in such a way as to advertise for holiness rather than immorality. They were to be walking advertisements for a Godly way of life.

However, the root problem is when vanity overcomes the impulse to piety. These things are not forbidden if they are not abused by adding pride or an unseemly imitation of the things of the world with them.

Now, to the men with the same spiritual principle we must argue that most of us are poor walking examples of what the Lord has done for our souls. Our bodies advertise sloth, gluttony and lack of care for our bodies as temples of our Lord. Well, mine certainly contains those negative elements. This seems a good place to close for commentary on this verse.

The inspired and preserved Scripture will speak to all of us. How many of us are ready to listen to that message?]

3.4 *But let it be the hidden man of the heart, in that which is not corruptible, even the ornament of a meek and quiet spirit, which is in the sight of God of great price.*

[I know this says the "hidden man of the heart." It is still talking about wives and their daily attire. The word "man" is a generic term for "human being."

The condition does continue to speak of attire. Peter suggests that the people, he is speaking to are women but men would do well to listen, not major on those baubles which are but temporary "show pieces." The $20,000 necklace could easily be stolen. Even when insured the cost of added inflation may not replace the necklace. Or, the necklace would just get old due to the wearing of it.

Like the "old soldier" of the poem, all things physical will eventually fade away. Even the great beauty of the actresses of the silent film era now lies in the grave. Their jewelry is now the possession of another. Isn't it much better to be adorned with the beauty of the ornament of the graces of God?

The quietness of the soul stayed upon God has proceeded from a spirit of the love for the Lord. This quietness is subdued toward those who hate the things and people of God. The meekness of such a person counts the "slings and arrows of outrageous fortune" – and the hated from those who fire those slings and arrows at the children of God, is counted as a great privilege by the one who is thus allowed to bear this burden to the Lord.

God considers such a one as a great treasure. It is the ornamentation of one who loves the Lord with all her heart, soul and spirit. This is one who gives evidence to the fact that she or he, is the adopted child of God. Her testimony is worth more than all the gold in the world. It is a richness which does not fade.]

3.5 For after this manner in the old time the holy women also, who trusted in God, adorned themselves, being in subjection unto their own husbands:

[Peter reminds his readers that this has always been the case. Holy women trusted God. An honest trust in God is the essence of Godly fear and faith. There are holy women in our time as well. Holiness, for woman or for man, is based on trust in God. A fainting, or worried, heart is not stayed upon the things of God. It is a heart which trusts God but finds a "little edge" somewhere "just in case."

A 'just in case" heart is one which ultimately trusts in itself. It is a heart that is in love with itself. This is empty vanity and pride.

The patriarchal women, I guess we should say "matriarchal," are those ancients who did not trust in ornaments of ordaining themselves. They simply were who they were. They radiated a trust in God and this faithful spirit added to their beauty. They subjected themselves to their husbands as their husbands subjected themselves to the Lord.

Once again the phrase "their own husband" is used. The family unit has but one head as there is but One God over all. This does not mean that the wife never reasons with her husband, sometimes this become a necessity, but it does mean that the wife saw her husband, ultimately as the head of that home.

This is a very good physical illustration of the spiritual principle that God is One. The fact of the Trinity does not argue against this spiritual fact. God is the Heavenly Father to the redeemed of the world. We may, should, pray with fervor. But, we realize that His Will is the standard to which we must accede. It is to His Wisdom, His Agenda, His Will to which we understand our greatest good as children of The Heavenly Father.]

3.6 Even as Sara obeyed Abraham, calling him lord: whose daughters ye are, as long as ye do well, and are not afraid with any amazement.

[In the eighteenth chapter of Genesis God declares that Abraham will father a child of the promise of God; Sarah would be the mother of this child. Sarah overheard this promise and laughed. She said, "Therefore Sarah laughed within herself, saying, After I am waxed old shall I have pleasure, my lord being old also?"

Sarah had been barren. This fact seemed to bother her on some level. She seemed unable to produce that "son of promise" whom the Lord had assured Abraham would come from his loins. Sarah was so bothered that she gave her Egyptian maid, Hagar, to her husband so Abraham could raise that son from this liaison.

God had explained to Abraham that the son of promise would not come from a bond woman but would proceed from the union of the free woman, Sarah, who was his lawful wife. Abraham would be the father of that child.

Sarah could not believe this until she did believe it as the promise of the Lord. God can do that which He chooses despite our denials and questions. Faith really is the victory when it is placed in the timeless words of our eternal Savior.

The point which Peter is making is that Sarah was a great woman in her own right. Part of her greatness was her acceptance of her role as the wife of her husband. She called him "lord." To call someone "lord" is to place ourselves in a position of subservience to that person. To call someone "lord" is to agree that we owe to him allegiance and honor.

The Jews accepted Abraham as their father. In like manner the Jewish women counted Sarah as their mother. As Christians who exercise faith in the God of Abraham we are pleased to consider ourselves, also, as children Abraham and Sarah in faith.

As we follow in their example of faith in the Lord of Heaven, we have no fear of what trials the world may bring out way. The Lord of Heaven is our shield against the lies and taunts of Satan and the world of sinful humanity. He is our Bridge over the raging waters which threaten to carry us from His love. (Revelation 12:16)]

3.7 *Likewise, ye husbands, dwell with them according to knowledge, giving honour unto the wife, as unto the weaker vessel, and as being heirs together of the grace of life, that your prayers be not hindered.*

["Likewise, ye husbands..." Peter has a few things to say to the men in the marital relationship. God has not seen fit to provide us with a slave or a servant. He has called us into a union of equality. We are not called into a union of superiority and inferiority. We are, however, called into a union of difference.

That phrase "dwell with them" covers all aspects of marital life. The phrase covers sexual compatibility, intellectual intercourse between the couple, and emotional support in all manner of situations. The concept is to act as a team during this season of life. We are not called to defeat anyone; we are called to uphold one another in whatever triumph or tragedy, joy or sadness, illness or health may come upon us as we, together, journey through life.

That word "knowledge" figures in this as well. It is well that we know the Lord together. A home united in the Lord is united in all.

I think this bond of knowledge also encompasses learning about each other. As we live together we will learn how to please the other with small gifts of encouragement and, sometimes, tolerance. It is not hard to forego some little thing in order to encourage the other. If we would only examine slightly we would probably find that they are already doing that for us.

Knowledge of the weaknesses and strengths of the other will help to dispel hard feelings. Peter says to understand that the woman is the weaker vessel. Now, this is inspired Scripture. I know that it is true in every way. Nonetheless, never even suggest to me that I bear a child.

I understand what Peter was saying, however. Pregnancy and other aspects of child bearing do cause a woman to experience times of weakness to which the man is not subject. During these times the woman may not be physically able to perform all things. There is no need to complain at these times. There is a need to understand and protect especially in these times.

We are both called "heirs together" of the salvation which is in Christ. A family brought together in Christ is a family that can withstand the storms of life as we both will understand the need to anchor our souls in the Haven of Rest.

Lastly in this verse we are called to join together as a family in prayer. That is the meaning of the warning that neglecting the things above will hinder the time of family prayer.

This is an almost offhanded remark from Peter. It is reminiscent of the first verse of the Bible. "In the beginning God..." The fact of God is neither explained nor elaborated upon. It is just a truth which is taken for granted.

So is this reference to family prayer.]

3.8 *Finally, be ye all of one mind, having compassion one of another, love as brethren, be pitiful, be courteous:*

[The Spurgeon Devotional Commentary says, "We cannot wash off dirt with dirt, or cure evil by evil; let us not try to do so. If we are indeed believers, we are blessed, and we are yet to be more blessed, therefore let us bless others."

Peter had touched upon how the Christian ought to live as regarding his relationship with the magistrates of the land. He also spoke of the relationship of slaves/servants and masters. By the way, I would be amiss if I did not reference this as another one of those spiritual principles which govern the relationship of the laborer and "boss."

Peter also spent some time looking at family relationships, especially those of husband and wife. He now begins to speak regarding our relationships with other Christians and, nearly in the same breath, the relationship of Christians and those outside the household of faith.

Peter asks that, as Christians in a church setting, we should all be of one mind. This may mean the Peter wasn't a Baptist. It seems that when you get two Baptists you will find a minimum of three views on most things.

Still, there are certain things where all Biblical Baptists stand in agreement. We immerse people in the Baptismal in the church or in the stream outside the church building. We baptize only believers and never infants. We believe every Word of Scripture as the Words of God. We believe that Messiah Jesus is the son of God and God, the Son. There are a few other things on which we are united. What Peter was speaking about was our need for harmony in the churches.

It has always been my belief that the church must speak with only one voice. That one voice is the Pastor's voice. If we disagree it would behoove us to keep our voices silent until we are alone with the Pastor. When we disagree in a public manner we bring disharmony into the church, disputations among the brethren, and a fractured message into the world.

We are enjoined to have compassion upon others. I believe that this is in consideration both in and outside the fellowship. As to those outside the faith our compassion must never become compromise with unspiritual doctrine, but it is the picture of Godly compassion and love for the creation of God and the lost that need to find salvation.

We should always love one another within the fellowship. I honestly believe that it is within the fellowship that we should find our closest friendships. We do have so much in common in the Lord that this seems like a natural thing.

We ought to display pity upon those who need a hand of pity. We should do this with our eyes to heaven. The idea is not to look down in pity but up in compassion as we consider the Savior's love.

And, we should be courteous. Courtesy is simple the "Golden Rule" in conscious action. I will agree that there are times when this is hard. It just seems to go against our natural inclinations. I was in a military formation one time during the war. A Major stood in front of us and said, "We are going back to 'Hill 29.' We are going to take it. We are going to hold it." We all knew that this was not a pious suggestion. It was a military command. We should consider courtesy as simply an order of our Great Spiritual General. He honestly would not have so ordered if it were not an order which we could carry out with His assistance.]

3.9 *Not rendering evil for evil, or railing for railing: but contrariwise blessing; knowing that ye are thereunto called, that ye should inherit a blessing.*

[I was reminded of an old joke today. A mother was complaining to her son that he was doing too poorly in school. "You just have to learn to try once in a while," the mother said.

"But, I am trying," the little boy said. "As a matter of fact the teacher said that I am the most trying pupil in the entire class."

My problem actually started yesterday. My work-place computer stopped working. Completely. If it had been a horse I would have been forced to shoot it! The computer had been giving me trouble for a few weeks and yesterday it quit giving me trouble. It gave me nothing. I couldn't even turn it on.

I spent a few dollars (!) and bought a new machine so I could continue to write this commentary. My son, and my son-in-law, worked to get the new machine ready for me to use. I happily took the machine over to the office at church, inserted the "flash drive" where I had begun to work, and turned on the machine.

I had inserted my flash drive. I found my work. Then the machine said, "I don't work unless I am on line." This could be a problem since I don't have access to the internet at church. I figured that this was a temporary problem since I wasn't working on anything "on line." It wasn't temporary. The machine would not work if I didn't put it "on line."

I called the place where I had purchased the machine only eighteen hours before. Their "tech person" – apparently the only one they had – told me, "I've never heard of anything like that." He did give me a phone number to call to find someone to help.

After fighting my way through the "phone tree" and "advertising ploys" at the "tech center," I finally was talking to real human being. She was Chinese with a thick accent. I think she may also have been charismatic. There was never a complete sentence in which I was able to understand what she was saying. Well, I did understand one sentence. "My procedure will not allow me to transfer you to technical support unless... Then she went into the ecstasy of "tongues" and there was no interpreter.

I had about an hour and a half before I was slated to pick up my grandson from his school, so I put my new computer and flash drive into my car and went over to the store. I found the entire "tech staff" – one person – at the store. I tried, twice, to tell him that I needed to know how to access the machine for which he had happily taken money from me the day before.

He said that he was busy servicing a woman but would get to me soon. He gave her a complete tour of the store when another person, obviously not a "tech" person, came to help him get something from the back of the store. The woman, meanwhile, had wandered off somewhere.

The two clerks were still too busy to listen to my problem. Fact be known, they scolded me for asking for help while they were still busy with another customer. Both of them.

This is an example of the first phrase of this verse. Don't return evil acts upon those who have committed evil acts toward you. I honestly do not feel that I did. But, by my body language and obvious exasperation, I did convey a little "evil" back at them.

Would you like to know how I figured that out? God kept reminding me what I'd done wrong for the rest of the day. I am trying! And I need not to be. That is what Peter said, with the inspiration of the Spirit upon his written words, in this place.

"Railing" is that speech, sometimes spoken and sometimes acted out, which falls in the same category as above. We are called to be the opposite of what I was and too often am! That is what this word "contrariwise" means. It means to act in a manner which is contrary to our natural human emotional agitation. We are to act as Christians.

By the way, that word "called" would be "ordered" if we were in the military. We are in "The Army of the Redeemed." Jesus is our Leader. We do call Him "Lord," do we not? Consider Matthew 5:44 as in our handbook of military deportment.

The last phrase of the verse gives a very good reason that we should act in this manner. "...that ye should inherit a blessing."

A few weeks ago, I brought my grandson home from school; I stopped at the local grocery store on the way home. He asked for a donut. I said, "Get two." He did.

That night the little boy's mom and dad complained that he wouldn't eat supper. Of course he wouldn't. He had eaten two donuts less than two hours before his evening meal. He was already full of "junk food" so he didn't want real food. We have the blessing of God's recompense upon those who wrong us. This may not happen in our sight. But, God does protect His children. We do not need the "donuts" of our own personal revenge. The empty calories will make us fat and the sugar... Well, I am diabetic.]

3.10 *For he that will love life, and see good days, let him refrain his tongue from evil, and his lips that they speak no guile:*

[We will often not consider that God is our Maker. We own Him as our Sovereign, our Lord, and our Creator. We praise Him as our Friend, our Shelter in a time of life's storms, our Example of how we ought to live. But we tend to forget that as our Creator He has all the "blue-prints" of human existence and understands how to best live our lives in the human plane of that existence.

He, Alone, understands what makes us tic and what makes us toc. He knows our lives and how to live them both to the fullest and to the grandest.

My son recently bought a turtle at a pet store. He was feeding the little amphibian carrots. The turtle loves carrots. Let's face it, it isn't all that often that we find any emotion in a pet turtle. He mentioned this at the pet store. The owner of the store said that carrots were not good for turtles. Now my son swears that the turtle is mad at him for not supplying a daily ration of carrots.

We generally look to the Scripture to explain the things of the next life. That is both true and paramount to our souls good. But, the inspired and preserved Words of God also speak to this present life. As our "Manufacturer," God understands what is best for us as human beings. We can look at this verse and consider Psalm 34:12-16 as the Great Physician's "RX" for this life.

First, the control of our tongues is best in our interpersonal relationships. The Garner-Howes Commentary quotes "W. B. K." as saying, "A dog has many friends because the wag is in his tail, and not in his tongue."

Before I came to this word processor I stopped to pet our dogs. Both dogs wagged their tails furiously. They enjoyed this show of love towards them and reciprocated by expressing love for me.

That same general emotion will exist between humans as well. We are all "sounding boards" in that what we send to others will be returned. The "Golden Rule" in practice will produce a response of the same. The "Leaden Rule" of "do unto others – first!" will find lead returned. Not only will this evil harm our own souls, it will cause hurt in our bodies. Proverbs 17:22 reminds us, "A merry heart doeth good like a medicine: but a broken spirit drieth the bones."

Not only ulcers but other ailments assail us when we allow our bodies to be invaded by vindictive spirits and the acidic fluids which these bring to our digestive tracts.

If we really do love this life we ought to pay heed to what God has said in His inspired and preserved Words to us. An angry man's blood pressure is often an express ticket to the grave.

We haven't even mentioned how contrary spirits will work against the convicting power of the Spirit. A witless and rash person can never properly witness about the Risen Savior!]

3.11 *Let him eschew evil, and do good; let him seek peace, and ensue it.*

[The verse asks that we eschew, avoid, flee from evil. Then, conversely it asks that we do good. Folks these are two separate moves. In football there are two squads with each team. There is an offense squad which is tasked with moving the ball forward toward the goal. There is also a defensive squad which is tasked with making certain that the other team cannot move the ball toward their goal.

That is not a perfect analogy. For instance, there may be a fumble where the defense becomes offense for the remainder of that play. Or, there may be a pass interception where the offense will have to become defensive for the remainder of that play.

Simply not doing evil does not necessarily mean being actively good. It simply means not doing anything evil. For instance, suppose that I find someone's car keys. I am not being evil if I merely lay them back on the ground where I found them. Neither am I being "good" at that point. It is a separate act to find the person who had lost the keys and return them to him.

It might be good, also, to consider James 4:27. "Therefore to him that knoweth to do good, and doeth *it* not, to him it is sin." At some point it is actually evil for one not to do good. It isn't just "sitting out" the situation; it is having the means to rectify a situation and refusing the opportunity to do so.

One of the best means of doing good is to pursue peace. The meaning is to chase down peace when it seems to shrink from your grasp. Chase it down until you have taken hold of it. That is ensuing, seeking, peace in a positive manner.]

3.12 *For the eyes of the Lord are over the righteous, and his ears are open unto their prayers: but the face of the Lord is against them that do evil.*

[In regard to this verse, Wesley's Notes on the Old and New Testament say, "The eyes of the Lord are over the righteous-For good. Anger appears in the whole face; love, chiefly in the eyes."

While I generally agree with Wesley's observation, I do feel this one limited. It speaks of the human attempting to read into another's expression what the heart may feel. The fact that when the eyes of the Lord are said to be over the righteous this implies a protecting situation where God is watching over us much as a parent might watch over a child. It implies a protective stance of constant oversight.

That the face of the Lord is said to be "against them that do evil," seems to invoke the illustration of a military person. Consider Exodus 23:27 where the enemies of Israel are said to turn their backs to Israel – that is to run from Israel in battle, and Joshua 7:8 where the tables are turned and Israel turns their backs on their enemies.

I see in this place a picture of God protecting His people as He holds back and destroys the powers aligned against His people.

The Ears of God at attuned to the prayers of His saints. He will hear when we make prayerful petition to His Throne.]

3.13 *And who is he that will harm you, if ye be followers of that which is good?*

[Matthew Poole answers this question by asserting. "And who is he that will , you?" i.e. None, or few will harm you, as being convinced and overcome by your good deeds..." He then accesses I Samuel 24:16-17 to back up his point. This one instance where the "bad" repented of the evil he had planned for the "good." A reading of the passage down to verse twenty-two will reveal that David and the men with him remained vigilant. It is obvious that they expected further attacks.

Being "nice," even being "Godly," will not guarantee a time of worry free status. Some people will be won over by our demeanor toward them. Others may not. It is rather certain that Satan will never tire of assailing the saints of God. In this world we can expect tribulation. Jesus warned us of such. "If the world hate you, ye know that it hated me before it hated you." (John 15:18)

The closer we come to following the paths of righteousness with our Savior, the more the world will hate us. The present world is dominated by sin. When we honestly display true holiness, we will be anathema to the world.

But, to answer the question put forth by Peter, "who *is* he that will harm you," it is true that the answer is, "no one." Martyrs are still being put to death in our time. This is not a defeat for them; this is a promotion to Glory. Though the world has the power to kill us they do not have the power to harm us. "We are confident, I say, and willing rather to be absent from the body, and to be present with the Lord." (II Corinthians 5:8)

To be completely honest, the world does not even have the power to execute us except it be by the permissive will of God. If this should happen we may be certain that we are released early from this life to find the bliss of eternal life in Heaven. And, physically speaking, this is the greatest act of devotion to our Lord that the mortal man may perform!

Especially in this day it behooves all Christian to be "followers of that which is good," and of He that is perfect. There may come a time when we are asked to give that last full measure of devotion to our Lord.

John, the human penman of the Revelation, would have us to pray, "Even so, come quickly Lord Jesus." If Jesus, in His wisdom and for His eternal purposes, does delay His coming, may we be ready to say, as did our Savior while on the Cross, "Father, into Thy Hands do I commit my spirit."

I fully understand that this comes under the heading of "dying grace granted by the Lord unto His own." I understand that few of us could understand the grace of so dying. If we live daily for the Lord, and if the time would come to us – as it might! – the Lord has promised to give us grace to submit to martyrdom for His testimony and witness.

The Christian never dies as a martyr to a cause or for some temporal purpose. The Christian who dies as a martyr does so only when the Lord deems that testimony as necessary to the cause of salvation. When the first recorded Christian martyr, Stephen, was stoned to death there was a man who held the coats of those who martyred Stephen. That was Saul of Tarsus. This man is better known as Paul the Apostle. Most commentators would argue that the manner of Stephen in his martyrdom led to the conviction upon Paul's heart which led to his conversion.]

3.14 *But and if ye suffer for righteousness' sake, happy are ye: and be not afraid of their terror, neither be troubled;*

[The previous verse had spoken of following good. All truly good proceeds from God. God gives good gifts to His children. The world of men would give us stones for bread. God gives us songs in the night. (Job 35:10)

While Paul and Silas were in the Philippian jail they spent the night in prayer and singing praises to God. (Acts 16:25) What a trust in God can do for a soul in torment at human hands.

As Peter had asked the slaves earlier, we are also asked to be thankful and joyful when we are asked to suffer unjustly for the cause of Christ. That last phrase is very important. If we suffer because we have behaved unseemly, we have no reward. In a sense, when we have wrongly treated others, their recompense upon our heads is a reward for our foolish and unchristian actions and words.

Peter says that we should not fear the terrors of our tormenters. Romans 8:1 reminds us that "There is therefore now no condemnation to them which are in Christ Jesus, who walk not after the flesh, but after the Spirit." The persecutors can threaten all kinds of things. What is the most they can actually do? They can kill the body and release the spirit to the everlasting joys of the Lord. They got nothing! Though their knifes may be sharp, the most their blade can do is separate us from the suffering of this present world and a "homecoming party" in the Heavenlies.

We are also counseled to not fear the coming troubles. We need not fret about what might be because it also might not. Whatever might befall us, we are promised the status of overcomers because Jesus has already overcome.

I know all of this sounds ethereal and of fantasy. However, it is my belief that we have never been, in this society, under the type of persecution we will face in the future. It behooves us to consecrate our lives to the Lord. It is only He Who will allow us to face the persecution of the world. These Bible Words are warnings to prepare.

These Bible Words are promises to overcome in His Power and Might.]

3.15 *But sanctify the Lord God in your hearts: and be ready always to give an answer to every man that asketh you a reason of the hope that is in you with meekness and fear:*

[My wife was brought up in a "Holiness" church. This was a church which taught the doctrine of "entire sanctification" of a believer. The belief is that one could be sanctified so that he would be able to live a sin free life. I really don't want to get into a discussion of that doctrine at this time. Suffice to say that I am living proof that Christians do not live sin free lives. We need to continually, well more often than I'd like to admit, approach the Throne of Grace and ask forgiveness and cleansing. (I John 2:1)

Here, in this verse we are told to "...sanctify the Lord God in your hearts..." From my background with my wife, I look at this verse and ask just how we can sanctify God. He is the Sanctifier, is He not? Of course. He calls us into His salvation and then sets us apart for the task of doing His work in our present world.

That, you see, is the real meaning of the word "Sanctify." It means something which is set apart for a special purpose. Whereas the word from which we get "Church" means an assembly of persons called from the general population to perform a specific task, the word from which we get "Sanctify" means that which is used for a specific task.

My keyboard, on this computer, is not sanctified. I may use this keyboard to prepare sermons and studies for edification. But, I also use this keyboard to play computer games. Now, my Bible, this is sanctified. I use the Scripture for one purpose only: I use the Scripture to approach God and find His will and purpose. I do not use the Scripture for any frivolous purpose.

When we are asked to "sanctify" God in our hearts, I believe that this means that we are to always consider His holiness and His position as Lord of our lives. When we assume to "take charge" of our own lives, after we have claimed that Jesus is Lord, we are demoting Him in our estimation and emotion. We need to consider Him, as He really should be, set aside as the Only Lord of our lives!

Neither should we consider God as a "Santa" figure. First, God is real. He is not a "feel good" balm for our lives. He is the Creator and Sustainer of this universe. Let us always give Him full honor as we recognize His Full Glory.

The point to be made about this, however, has to do with how we approach God. Do we approach Him, always, with our hands out. "Lord, I want." "Lord, I need." "Lord, fetch." Now, God is the Giver of all Good Gifts. That is true. But, we need to understand that He is worthy of all honor and praise. We need to approach Him in an attitude of praise for what He has already done for us. We need to approach Him in an attitude of praise simply for Who He Is and the Greatness Which is His.

That is to sanctify Him in our hearts. We set Him aside as the One Who is due all praise and to Whom we owe our allegiance. As we do this we will be driven, not of force but of love, into His Words. His Word will we hide in our hearts. We will have an answer for any who would ask why we trust Him. The Spirit will provide the ammunition when we are on the firing range of witness.

All of the accouterments of the Tabernacle needed to be sanctified, or set apart as special and holy, before they could be used in the Tabernacle, or Temple, worship.

FIRST PETER: Chapter 3

They were for that purpose and that purpose only.

The idea of "sanctifying" God in our hearts is to realize that He, only He, is The God of the entire Universe of this Creation and of the Spiritual realms. It is only He to Whom we can come in worship and adoration. We are fond of saying that we served a God Who... Fill in the blank with some appropriate paramount feature. We do not serve a God of anything. We serve THE, singular and excusive, GOD OF ALL!

May we be always ready to praise Him and speak of His excellent goodness. It is only by a baptism, by immersion, in His inspired and preserved Word, that we can begin to fulfill this charge. It is only the power of the Spirit that we can expect to stand on His Words in the day of trial.]

3.16 *Having a good conscience; that, whereas they speak evil of you, as of evildoers, they may be ashamed that falsely accuse your good conversation in Christ.*

[See my commentary at I Peter 2:12. The verse at that location is nearly the same as this verse.

Even a "good conscience" is encased within an earthly body of clay which has been sullied by the nature of sin as inherited from Adam. For a conscience to be able to guide our conduct it must be trained and nurtured by the inspired and preserved Words of the Scripture. This conscience must also have residence within a body that has reverenced God so that the Spirit may give His guidance.

As a rule, the concept of a good conversation has little to do with our speech and much to do with that which our entire manner of life has to say about our soul's deportment.

> Words are just words.
> Our walk is a path.
> The prattle of our words
> And the pattern of our path
> Do not always speak
> Of the same Destination

Our walk is to be in Christ. A walk in ourselves may appear quite *religious* and *proper*. But, a walk in self is a vain imitation; it has neither saving grace nor does it garner Heavenly reward.

We must beware when we hear gossip and rumor. Both could be true. But gossip is not gospel and rumor is often the rumination of a fallen mind.]

3.17 *For it is better if the will of God be so, that ye suffer for well doing, than for evil doing.*

[Once again, consider my notes on I Peter 2:19-21 as they cover the same area as does this verse. When God says something once in His inspired and preserved Words, pay heed. When He says the same thing more than once pay special heed. This is a thing He intends for you to understand as a child of the Heavenly Father.

To suffer for wrongs we have done is just judgment. It is right. To suffer for things we have not done is to suffer for the cause of Christ. It is glorious! It is an evidence of the smile of God upon our lives as He has said, "For whom the LORD loveth he correcteth; even as a father the son in whom he delighteth." (Proverbs 3:12) This is such an important concept that it is repeated in the New Testament. "For whom the

Lord loveth he chasteneth, and scourgeth every son whom he receiveth." (Hebrews 12:6)

Are you buffeted without cause in this world? God loves you! The small pains of this world produce the prize of the high calling of God in the next. This may be a temptation from Satan to try your faith. This is a trial from God to make your faith perfect in His will. God can gather the crumbs of Satan's fish and broken loaves and refashion it as a feast in the Bread of Life.

Spurgeon's Devotional Commentary carried this gem. "Yet we hear persons say, 'I would not mind being blamed if I deserved it,' which is very absurd, since it is the deserving of blame which ought to trouble us far more than the rebuke."

One who suffers without cause can be certain that the Lord will hold him guilty who has assailed us falsely.]

3.18 *For Christ also hath once suffered for sins, the just for the unjust, that he might bring us to God, being put to death in the flesh, but quickened by the Spirit:*

[We cannot argue that Jesus suffered for our good. He suffered because of our sin. All of our sin was placed upon Him at the cross. There again we must argue that His foreknowledge of our sin, which gave Him the purpose of the cross, also gave Him a complete knowledge of those who would accept Him as Savior.

In the "macro" sense we could argue that He did die for the sins of the world. In the "micro" sense this is limited to the sins of those who would believe. In theory all souls ever born into the world will find salvation available at the cross; in actuality only those who accept Him are granted this salvation. He thus died for every sin which those He foreknew would ever commit. We cannot surprise Him with our inability. He has graced us in His ultimate ability to save to the uttermost.

He suffered only once as our Advocate and Savior. The animal sacrifice of the Old Testament was ineffectual. The animal could never take away sin. The animal died as a symbol of an innocent life being sacrificed in the place of a guilty life. Jesus is that Actual Innocent in His humanity Who has died for the guilty sinners of the ages who would accept Him as Savior.

He has done this only once. Since His Divine foreknowledge gave Him awareness of every sinner, and every sin, for which He died, it is as though each of us had placed our hand upon the Sacrificial Lamb and transferred all of our guilt to our Advocate. There is, therefore, no need to repeat that which He has already perfectly fulfilled.

Jesus died completely in His humanity. His Spirit, being Divine, could not – and did not, die. At the resurrection the Spirit of Jesus, God the Son, returned life to Jesus as the son of God. His real human body rose from the dead and left the tomb to walk again, for forty days, that first century landscape of men and fields.

After that short time His physical body, a perfect and resurrected human body, returned to Heaven. This return to His glory as God, gave evidence to His completed mission to save the souls of all who would come to Him in faith for eternal salvation.

The fact that Jesus died as the Innocent in place of the guilty, for sins and acts which were never part of His nature or experience, should help us to realize our suffering can be accepted as a sacrifice on our part to Him. We are accepting an amount of "unfairness" which is to our own benefit. When Jesus accepted the Cross, He accepted that which for our benefit. He died in time for the express purpose that we might live in eternity.

This view of His great gift for us should serve to help us endure what suffering we are allowed to withstand as His followers.]

3.19 *By which also he went and preached unto the spirits in prison;*

[The general consensus of those I consulted was that this verse, especially when combined with the following verse, speaks of the eternal and divine Spirit of Jesus preaching through men such as Enoch and Noah to that then current humanity. Peter, meaning this, would have spoken of these men as "spirits in prison" since they had died and were then consigned to Hades in anticipation of their final judgment for the unrighteous of Revelation 20:14-15.

This is the seeming standard argument for this verse's interpretation. I will not disagree with this exegesis. But, I might argue for another view!

Now I will give my argument for an alternate view. A caution here, generally speaking, when I disagree with others it is normally I who am wrong! My major problem here is that I have no real explanation for the following verse (20) under my theologically unsound guess.

I would look first to Ephesians 4:8. "Wherefore he saith, When he ascended up on high, he led captivity captive, and gave gifts unto men."

I would ask that you access my commentary on Luke 16:19 where Abraham and Lazarus speak with the rich man in Hell.

We cannot argue that Jesus, upon the death of His humanity did not go to Paradise. He told the dying thief crucified with Him, that they would meet in Paradise. (Luke 23:43)

Couple that with Hebrews 10:4 which categorically states that the Old Testament sacrificial system could not remove sins. Add in that both I Peter 1:20 and Revelation 13:8b which speak of the fact that the great Self-Sacrifice of Jesus has always, from before the foundation of the earth, been the only means of salvation from sin and we can see that the Old Testament saints were not yet forgiven their sins before the historical fact of the Cross. They were not yet candidates for Heaven as no sin can enter into Heaven. Their sins were not forgiven before the cross as the sacrifices of the animals of creation only "covered" their sin but did not remove their sin.

So, it would follow that Jesus, in the time between the death of His humanity and His resurrection, would have – again this is in taking the full human penalty for our sins as our Representative – gone to Paradise to take these saints to their "heavenly city and reward."

While in Paradise it would be logical that He would have preached a message of judgment upon those of Hades. Note! This does not argue that Jesus went to Hades as part of His assumption of our penalty for sin. Rather, it would seem logical from the Old Testament standard that He would have seen Paradise.

There is nothing in this situation to even suggest that these antediluvian souls were given any chance of escape from their place of judgment. The words of Abraham, "And beside all this, between us and you there is a great gulf fixed: so that they which would pass from hence to you cannot; neither can they pass to us, that *would come* from thence." (Luke 16:26) There is no hint in this incident related by Jesus of either a purgatorial "cleansing" or second chance for salvation after death.

The words of Hebrews 9:27 remain in effect. "And as it is appointed unto men once to die, but after this the judgment..."]

3.20 *Which sometime were disobedient, when once the longsuffering of God waited in the days of Noah, while the ark was a preparing, wherein few, that is, eight souls were saved by water.*

[Billy Graham always spoke of an "Hour of Decision." The people of the flood had many hours of decision. Noah preached righteousness to them for one hundred and twenty years. This verse argues that these antediluvian people were "sometime disobedient." Note that the word is "sometime" rather than "sometimes." This does not speak that they had episodes in which they were disobedient to the call of God. The use of that word suggests that they were constantly disobedient toward God; this was their general manner of deportment.

I have stopped calling myself "fat." I am not fat! I am obese! That is such a nice medical sounding word. It suggests a medical problem rather than a moral failure. The point I am trying to make is that I was obese last year at this time. If something drastic does not happen I will be obese at this time next year. This is just what I is!

These people were disobedient to the callings of God. That is just what they were.

God was very longsuffering of their condition. Noah preached repentance. They did not repent. Noah built the great "object lesson" of the Ark. They did not repent. The people laughed away twenty-four hours of decision each day. The people laughed away 168 hours of decision every week. I'd probably have to take my shoes off to figure out how many hours they laughed away in a month or year. Then the leap year would sneak up on my and I'd lose count again.

The point is that they seemed to just laugh away all those hours of decision God allowed them to have in His patience. Finally, the time came when there was no more laughing away those hours of decision.

Finally, the patience of God's longsuffering ran out. One of the seminal quotes of the justice system is, "Justice delayed is justice denied." All of those hours, minutes, and seconds of decision were over. God gave the people what they really appeared to want. He gave His hour of judgment.

No one can say that God acted rashly. No one can say that the people were not given ample time to repent of their wrongs. No one could say that their hour of judgment was being delayed. The abiding truth of the prophecies of God is that they come to pass. Judgment came!

We could say that only eight people responded to the warnings of God. This isn't true. All of those other millions who died in the flood also responded to the warning of God. They responded with "No."

The amazing fact of the ark of Noah is that it was this, the plan of God, which saved Noah and his family from those waters of judgment. Noah was kept safe, sound and secure by the same water in which the others perished.

The "God of Judgment" which many seem to rail against is the same God Who judged our sins at the Cross and has judged us as "not guilty" due to the Blood of His Son.

How very foolish are those who discount the possibility of salvation because they reject the free gift of forgiveness and eternal salvation!

Clarke has suggested that many were saved by repenting during the falling of the rain. No. The hour of judgment had come and the opportunity was lost. It deserves a bitter wail from anyone to find that they have sinned and sneered past the appointed day of salvation.]

3.21 *The like figure whereunto even baptism doth also now save us (not the putting away of the filth of the flesh, but the answer of a good conscience toward God,) by the resurrection of Jesus Christ:*

[Noah and his family were saved by riding in the Ark of Safety which had been constructed as instructed by God. This passage cannot logically be made to refer to sprinkling, pouring or even proper baptism by immersion. These were waters of judgment, not of salvation. Baptism saves no one. Baptism, properly considered, is a witness that salvation has already arrived. There is no grace in salvation except the witness to the grace of the Savior.

An unsaved person who is baptized is still not saved. He is only lost in his sins and wet.

Some have used the verse to suggest a covenant relationship for Noah to his family and tie their salvation to his salvation. This is unwarranted. If this were so we would expect to find the same situation with Lot. We must note, from reading the 19th chapter of Genesis, that not all of Lot's children would accept his argument unto salvation. We cannot be saved by another. It is the personal choice which each must make for himself to follow, or to deny, the Lord.

Baptism was a rite of initiation into the church membership in the early church. Peter was not saying that anyone could be saved by baptism. His argument was that baptism gave witness to the fact that one was already born again. In case anyone had missed his point, he states plainly that we are not saved by the "washing" of outward "filth." We are only given salvation by faith in the death, burial and resurrection of Jesus Christ. Baptism is a symbol of our acceptance of that fact.

This is the reason that true baptism must come by immersion. This is the only baptism which is true to the word "baptism." This is the only baptism which shows the death, burial and resurrection of Jesus.

Baptism is important as a response by an already Blood bought believer. To others the only meaning is the vain work of man. To them it is a false religious display.]

3.22 *Who is gone into heaven, and is on the right hand of God, angels and authorities and powers being made subject unto him.*

[The human life of Jesus was an example of how we ought to live as human being. He kept Himself, at His volition, in constant subjection to The Father. Thus we, as human beings, do have the choice of living for Him. It is not an impossible project. It is an act of will that we ought to follow Him at all times.

Lazarus was raised from the dead. The son of the widow of Nain was raised from the dead. There were others. It was a great miracle that Jesus rose from the dead. But, that is not the end of the story. Jesus was seen of about 500 people ascending back into Heaven. Angels praised Him and promised His return at that point. This ascension was a proof even beyond that of His resurrection that Jesus is, still today, God, the Son and the son of God. It is a proof beyond contradiction that Jesus is, still today, exactly Who He said He is.

He is, still today, given the seat at the Right Hand of The Father. This not simply a location; this is the honor of power, majesty and glory which belongs to Messiah, the King, Jesus.

Angels, spiritual and temporal authorities and powers, are responsible to His dictates in both their deportment among men and times and are responsible for carrying out those duties He assigns to them. Many of these human authorities fail in these responsibilities; this is the cause of the ills which befall society.

Many of even the religious leaders of the world fail to acknowledge that the Lord is supreme. This is the cause of many failing to find the salvation which is available to all those who believe.

This spirit of rebellion is alive and active in the world as it was in the days of Noah. There will be no flood; God has made that promise. But there will be judgment upon the world which is in rebellion against the rightful Ruler of the Ages.]

FIRST PETER - CHAPTER FOUR

4.1 *Forasmuch then as Christ hath suffered for us in the flesh, arm yourselves likewise with the same mind: for he that hath suffered in the flesh hath ceased from sin,*

[Jesus is our Savior. In His humanity He is also our example as to how we are both to live our lives in the flesh and how we are to relate to God. Jesus suffered in the flesh both from the ravages of a society which hated Him as His entire Being was pure and devoid of any sinful impulse or imperfection, and in His position as The Self-Sacrifice for sin He also suffered the full judgment for sin.

In the former He suffered for well-doing in a world that is sold out to the sin nature of evil-doing. His earthly ministry was of the Personification and Perfection of God walking among a people who were naturally opposed to all things of God. Even the honestly pious among mankind were not disposed to walk in holiness except as to react against their sinful natures in seeking a pardon for their sins which were ever before them.

In the latter Jesus yielded His humanity to the horrors of the Cross. The events in Gethsemane illustrated His knowledge of the dreadfulness which awaited Him on Calvary and His steadfast will which found the path of The Father to be that which was needful for Him to follow.

In His Deity, Jesus had the power to save our souls from sin. In His humanity, Jesus gave us the example of how to walk in this newness of life. (II Corinthians 5:17) It is this spirit of being yielded to the will of The Father to which we are called as followers of Jesus.

James1:13-15 reminds us that it is our own lusts which give a place for the tempter to entice us to sin. The example of Jesus during His mountain temptation in the fourth chapter of Matthew reminds us that having a mind upon the things of God is our best defense against the wiles of the adversary of our souls. (Psalm 119:11; Isaiah 26:3)

Paul expressed this same sentiment in Romans 6:6-7. "Knowing this, that our old man is crucified with him, that the body of sin might be destroyed, that henceforth we should not serve sin. For he that is dead is freed from sin." Jesus died in our place. He crucified our sin – paid the complete penalty for those sins – on the Cross. As such the sin of Adam no longer holds any place in our lives. Positionally we have died to the call of sin in our salvation.

This is not to say that we are perfect. I John 2:1 would remind us of our need to be on guard that we confess our sinful shortcomings to the Lord. But, this does mean that we have a mark to work towards in our human lives. (Philippians 3:12-14)]

4.2 *That he no longer should live the rest of his time in the flesh to the lusts of men, but, to the will of God.*

[Obviously the "he" of this verse is the human who has been saved by the work of Jesus on the Cross of Calvary. The point being that since Jesus has died for us in our place in that He paid the penalty for our sins, His death has freed us from that penalty. Thus our sins are forgiven which frees us to walk in a newness of life without the baggage of the sin nature inherited from our father Adam.

Another illustration from the history of the War Between the States comes to mind. General Robert E. Lee was an officer in the army of the United States. He owed his allegiance to the president of those United States. When he was faced with his duty to that Union as opposed to his duty to his native state, he considered that his higher duty was to Virginia. That consideration led to his renouncing his oath to the United States and accepting an oath to defend his homeland of Virginia. It was not possible, due to events beyond his control, to give fidelity to both. He made a conscious decision which forever removed him from his former commitment and gave his honor of commitment to Virginia and the Confederacy.

In like manner we are called to make a commitment to Christ. We are to renounce our former allegiance to Satan and fully commit ourselves to the Lord. The death of Christ, accepted by us in salvation, gives us the power to live this new life after our conversion experience. Our "old life" before that time is become a thing of the past. Our new reality is that we are indebted to our Savior. This presupposes that we will live in fidelity to Him.

We have become new creatures, (II Corinthians 5:17) with new responsibilities and realities of duty. We are therefore called to remove the "old uniform" of allegiance to the lusts of our carnal flesh as we are dressed in the "new uniform" of faithfulness to our Heavenly Leader.]

4.3 *For the time past of our life may suffer us to have wrought the will of the Gentiles, when we walked in lasciviousness, lusts, excess of wine, revellings, banquetings, and abominable idolatries:*

[Most of these words are fairly easily understood. We might get the idea of an evening "business meeting" at a local restaurant when we see "banqueting." Such is not the case. In this case the word means a "drinking party" when the main course of endeavor is alcohol. Basically, all of these have to do with an excess of carnality. This is an excess unto debauchery.

The thrust of the argument is that the unsaved man will not walk in any understanding of his relationship with God. Since it was the Jew who had been raised in a culture which was seeped in the Scriptural understanding of God, the easy "shorthand" was to say that these people were as Gentiles who had never been appraised of the things of God. When we consider that the early church was nearly all Jewish, this is an easily understood consideration to the readers.

What Peter is saying is that the life of one who was not saved was predicated upon the lusts of his flesh. That should change with the realization that our salvation was from this life and unto a life which would have eschewed the temporary of this physical existence and looked forward to the eternal life of spiritual bliss.]

4.4 *Wherein they think it strange that ye run not with them to the same excess of riot, speaking evil of you:*

[Some argued that the reference to "run with them" had to do with the raucous worship of the god Bacchus. Whether that be so or not, we can readily understand that the unsaved are horrified that their old friends are no longer enamored of their old sinful haunts. As Festus argued of Paul, they think we have left leave of our senses if we find true joy in Christ and not in the passions of worldly lusts. (Acts 26:24)

It is human nature to attack that which we cannot understand. We see this in the silly season of political pontifications. I read of an example of this just a few days ago in the daily newspapers. It seems that an eastern state has considered a law to restore the right to personal religious practice for those business owners who do not feel right in taking part in a homosexual marriage. Some judges have been known to ignore the current "freedom of religion" as guaranteed by the U. S. Constitution. As a reaction to this balancing act of the legislature, the article called such laws as "Hate Laws."

When did it become hate to disagree on the basis of long established religious viewpoints? We have seen this hateful attitude of the world release real hate where none was intended.

Since the world cannot understand the convictions of the Christian, they will attack out of their own ignorance and bias. They will even claim that only they are sane in their ridicule. They will even cross the line from personal vindictive and paint the entirety of religious viewpoint as flawed.

They may not totally disregard religion but they will only accept that religion which agrees with their human reasoning. All other religion will be consigned to the garbage bin of their verbal assault. They will claim that their hate is an expression of their love and tolerance.

Folks, get it in mind and be ready. The world will hate us because we are not of the world. Our standards are not of the world. Our understanding of the realities of the spiritual are not of the world. The world will never accommodate that which they fear and loath. They fear and loath the message of the evangel.

John 15:18 – "If the world hate you, ye know that it hated me before it hated you."]

4.5 *Who shall give account to him that is ready to judge the quick and the dead.*

[We do not need to respond to these in anger. We do need to respond in love lest the message of sin and salvation – the very grace which The God of Love offers to even these – be shouted down without any attempt to fulfill our responsibility to both God and man. We do have a responsibility to speak the truth. In order to do this, we must be seeped in things Biblical – Read your Bible! – and rely upon the Spirit of Truth with fervent prayer!

In another sense we do not need to respond at all. The great Southern Baptist preacher, Robert G. Lee, once preached a very famous sermon: "Pay Day, Some Day." God will judge those who attack His children. Like Martha at the grave of Lazarus, (Jon 11:34) we often consider this only in light of the last judgment.

Such thoughts as these should be beneath us. Jesus has sent us out into the world to call the world to repentance. We should pray, and work and live our religious faith in to the world so that our attackers would come to the Lord. Our charge is not to long for retribution but for regeneration! The true religion of Jesus is not to attack but to attract. We long for souls to come to the Master that they may share in the joy of the Lord.

There are also judgments coming upon the living. The verse says both the quick

– that is the living, and the dead – those are of the final judgments of damnation.

Folks, if we do not see a revival of true Christianity, not religion but Christianity, in this world we will soon see the judgment of God poured out into the world during the time of Jacob's Trouble. The concept of the Tribulation is not a fantasy; it is history that has not yet happened!

We must long to see souls saved by the Master. This is not, as some have charged, to hasten this Tribulation Era. This is to spare friends, family and even enemies, the horrors that await this globe as the righteous judgment of God comes to this unholy generation of humanity living upon this world.

Religion, even secular religion, kills. It is only Jesus Christ that offers true peace and life. (Acts 4:12)]

4.6   *For this cause was the gospel preached also to them that are dead, that they might be judged according to men in the flesh, but live according to God in the spirit.*

[This is a verse of several interpretations. I won't attempt to mention all of them but I will list a few. I believe that all of these few are contained in this verse. The Bible is not a novel; it is the very Message of The Living God. As such the Scripture is a living book as it is infused with the power of the Divine. Again, I am not saying that the Scripture is, itself, divine. I am saying that the power of the Divine has produced this Book and it bears the perfections and eternity of God within its originally inspired and preserved words.

This "layered meaning" could not be so if only the concept, or general story of Scripture, was that which was inspired. A "concept" is rooted in the culture in which it exists. This is not so of the Scripture which is a "Living Book" which speaks the Message of God to people of all ages, cultures and stations.

What is the meaning that the gospel was preached to the dead? Some have accessed Genesis 6:3, several coupling this with I Peter 3:19-20, and argued that there is a chance after death for salvation accorded those who have died. They argue that the meaning here is that the gospel will be preached to departed souls who are then given a "second chance." This view, of course, is in direct contradiction with Hebrews 9:27 which informs us that judgment, not mercy, awaits the unsaved soul.

For the Christian we know that our sins have already been judged at the Cross. We will see the fruits of this judgment when we see the face of our Savior. "Oh, that will be glory," is not just a song. It is a wonderful truth that awaits those who have had their sins washed away in the Blood of the Lamb!

I think the phrase first speaks of those who lived before the Cross. The basic truth of the gospel message is that our hope is in Christ. He was considered as slain before the foundations of the world. (Revelation 13:8b) Salvation has always been in Him.

Those born and died before the Cross came to God in faith, believing His written and spoken Word to them, even as we come to God in faith, believing the Living Word, in these post Cross times. Salvation has always been of faith in the revelation of God's Message to humanity.

This same Gospel has been preached since God provided animal skins, of innocent animals of creation, for the guilty sin of Adam and Eve. The Gospel of God has never changed; in Christ was that Message fulfilled. (Matthew 5:17)

Hebrews 10:4 may tell us that "...the blood of bulls and of goats should never take away sins." But, God did not give a faulty plan to the people of the pre-Cross days. He gave a saving plan as the people responded in faith. These sacrifices of the animals of creation were a prophecy of the coming Savior. It may not have been understood by those earlier people. What was understood was their need to have faith in the Words of God.

This preaching to the dead also shown every time we hand a gospel tract to a stranger, or preach a message of salvation to a crowd, or witness to someone at work or play. The gospel is preached to those who are dead in trespass and sin. (Ephesians 2:1) Some will respond and gain the gift of eternal life, (Romans 6:23) some will not. Either way we have the charge to prayerfully offer that opportunity to the lost.

Peter was also offering consolation. There were many martyrs in the early church. There are many martyrs in the church in this day as well. Christians are still being put to physical death for the crime of loving Christ. The gospel was preached, and received!, by these who are dead to the world but alive forevermore with the Lord.

Salvation is a gift. It is not a right. It is a gift that Jesus wishes us to offer to all. We generally fail in this task. We need to get the vision that Heaven is real! Invite others to join us in this place of eternal bliss. We need to get the vision that Hell is real! Warn others to escape this place of eternal torment.

When people are judged in the flesh, when they have accepted the great Self-Sacrifice of Jesus at the Cross and had their sins judged and cleansed in His Blood, they will live eternally with the Lord.

There is another place where people will stand for judgment. (Revelation 20:12-15) This will not be a judgment unto salvation but will be a judgment unto damnation. We Christians are too polite and pious to tell anyone to go to Hell. Yet, we do this every time we fail to pray and present the Gospel Message that Jesus Christ died in time so others can live in eternity.]

4.7   *But the end of all things is at hand: be ye therefore sober, and watch unto prayer.*

[It would only be a decade, or less, before the destruction of Jerusalem and the Temple. There were both Jews and Gentiles among those to whom Peter wrote this epistle. None of these would feel the immediate impact of the event. The Jews would, of course, have lamented the fact but being somewhat distant even they would not have felt it as greatly as they otherwise might have done.

In Genesis 6:13 Noah was appraised the "the end of all flesh is come." Peter had an even more dire message: "...the end of all things is at hand." He could have been giving a message that the end of their present persecution would soon end. This was true, of course, since the end of these people's lives would end persecution to them as they left this world of woe to enjoy the next world of delight.

Peter could have been speaking of the Second Appearing of Christ to take the saints from this world. He could have looked toward the Second Coming of Christ when the Jewish nation would be restored under the reign of Messiah. Peter understood that the world could not continue in total opposition to God.

Whichever, or all of the above, the call of Peter was for the Christian to remain ever vigilant in prayer. Prayer is that worshipful connection with the Eternal which is given for the Christian to live in victory for his Lord.

Prayer supposes a close relationship with God. A lack of prayer evidences a strained relationship with our Heavenly Father. Prayer is speaking with God. Nearly as important is that prayer helps to build us up in this most holy faith.]

4.8 *And above all things have fervent charity among yourselves: for charity shall cover the multitude of sins,*

["Above all things" gives us a little hint that this might be an important point. It is. This is the base virtue of any society. It is especially so in a close knit society such as a church. Simple respect might be that we would tolerate someone even if they were a real trial to endure. We wouldn't be ready to invite them over to dinner – or to accept their invitation. But we would tolerate them for a while at church.

To respect someone might be fine. But, that might not be a reason to have a real relationship with them. We might listen when they talk or learn from them. Again, this would not be a real relationship. This would be akin to a teacher – student situation where we silently listen; as we wait for the lesson to end so we would be able to meet with our real friends.

But, the concept of "fervent charity" would be more binding. Charity, of course, means love. This is a love which involves sincerely caring for the other person. It is relational in that it means we honestly care what happens to the other. We do not see them as simply another acquaintance but as a real friend. This is someone in whom we have a real interest.

The others we might introduce as "Mr..." This one we introduce as "My good friend..."

The phrase "shall cover a multitude of sins" does not mean that our friendship gains me any special "grace" from God. This isn't even about me.

My friend might say, "You know," after every sentence. With anyone else I would find that an annoying habit. With my friend, I don't care; that just the way he is. That is the concept of covering a multitude of sins. In our love, one for another, we tend to overlook things.

This is not overlooking sins by false flattery or lie. That would not be real friendship. It would be patronization.

Peter makes no suggestions as to any acts. He is not speaking of doing "good works" to gain from God. He is simply speaking of an attitude of caring for the brothers and sisters in Christ beyond that of caring for the acquaintances of the world at large.

We've already been called to prayer in the previous verse. For our friend we pray the blessings of God. For our acquaintance we pray the salvation of his soul.]

4.9 *Use hospitality one to another without grudging.*

[How often do we say, "Oh, it was nothing. Happy to do it," when someone thanks us for something when we've helped out? How often do we mean it? Peter is saying that we ought to help where we can. He is also saying that we ought to thank God for the privilege of being able to do so. That we are able to do so is an indication that we have been blessed of God.

This is even a privilege for us in that we are able to be a blessing, from God, for another individual. No complaining. No grudging. No counting the cost. We are simply blessed that we've been accounted as faithful by the Lord.

We've all heard the phrase, "Paying it forward." Peter uses that concept. "Hospitality one to another" is the concept of "I'll help you as I can," and hearing the recipient say, "If you are ever in need be sure to call me first!"]

4.10 *As every man hath received the gift, even so minister the same one to another, as good stewards of the manifold grace of God.*

[At one time I coached basketball. These were eight and nine-year-old kids. I am not quite qualified to seek a position in the NBA. I did learn something. If there is a youngster who is very good at dribbling the basketball I might want him to be my point guard. If another youngster is tall for his age and excels at jumping I might want him to play under the basket. Different skills lead to different positions.

God has gifted each of His servants with differing skills to be used in His churches. Now, I can't claim to understand each person's God-given gift. However, each individual Christian can be faithful to whatever is the gift which God has given him. By "faithful" I mean to use that gift for the body of Christians.

In the church where I am now ministering we have a young lady who is a school teacher in a town about three hours from our church. Her parents have obviously done a very fine job in raising this young lady. Every summer and every "break" from school she comes back to visit family. While in town she comes to play the piano in our church. She is also possessed of an extraordinary singing voice. She shares her talents and builds up the church in ways that I, as a simple pastor, could never accomplish.

She ministers to us!

We are each steward unto God as to the gifts He has given us. We have a duty to use our gifts as best we can for the Lord. By the way, the phrase "our gifts" is important. If I were to try to sing I would not edify the church. I might empty it!

God asks each of us to do what we can to build up the body of believers in the place wherein He has placed us. In case anyone might have misunderstood that last sentence. God has given each of us a place to exercise our gift. "God don't got no orphans." Each of us has a "home church" to which we owe a fidelity. Any who would argue that they have no "home" church give a strong suggestion that they are out of the will of God. God has placed us there for His purpose!]

4.11 *If any man speak, let him speak as the oracles of God; if any man minister, let him do it as of the ability which God giveth that God in all things may be glorified through Jesus Christ, to whom be praise and dominion for ever and ever. Amen.*

[It is a heady thing to speak before a crowd. Many are drawn to the ministry because they desire sit in a place of authority. They want people to look up to them. Bad reason. The purpose of a preacher is not to have people look up at him; the purpose is to have them look beyond him and find the Lord.

The purpose of ministerial speaking is to be as an oracle of The True God. There were plenty of oracles in the ancient world. Some of these were made to entice the traveler and gain the contents of his purse. Some of these were demonically controlled. We know from the New Testament accounts that demons have the ability to speak. These would speak words of advice which might have seemed reasonable and advantageous to some inquirers. Eventually the words would spell doom to the unwary.

All of these were mere idols.

When the preacher stands in the pulpit his purpose is not to discuss morality or politics. He is not to perform a comedy routine or a fund-raising campaign. His purpose is to give forth the Message of God to the people of God. Even to preach a sociological presentation about the life and times of Messiah is not an accepted discourse. The call is to preach only two things. One is Christ crucified as we call to repentance the sinner. The other is to preach the leading of the Lord for the daily life of the Christian; this is a call to a deeper relationship with the Lord.

The True Oracle of God is the inspired and preserved Word of God. It is this which is the rational for the public proclamation of His Message.

If one is to speak in the church, he must minister God to the people. A "spoonful of sugar" might help the medicine go down in a most delightful way but it is the unction of God upon His Words which can cause the penitent to fall upon his knees at the altar of The Living God.

To minister is not the same as to preach. To minister is to assist someone in some way. A door held open for a person with a walker is an act of ministry. Some bread, a couple pounds of hamburger and a head of lettuce given to a hungry family is an act of ministry. Visiting a family as they grieve at a grave is an act of ministry.

The phrase of "let him do it as of the ability which God giveth" would argue that this is not simply the organized act of a church program. This is the act of a concerned Christian who feels the "fervent charity," love, of verse eight, above.

The purpose of these things is not to make the church grow. That remains the business of God as He leads His faithful servants. The purpose in this is to glorify God through the Christians who name the Name of Jesus as their motivation.

After mentioning The Father and The Son, Peter gives forth a doxology of praise. Only God is worthy of praise and worship. To The Eternal Father, Son, and Holy Ghost belong all praise. The Holy Trinity exercises dominion over time and eternity in glory and power!

We can also see in this that the Deity of Jesus was well understood by the apostles very early on in the Church.]

4.12 *Beloved, think it not strange concerning the fiery trial which is to try you, as though some strange thing happened unto you.*

[Peter uses the personal "beloved" as he introduces a call to endure the trials of persecution. It is interesting to note that these are "trials" and not "temptations." God allows His children to experience trials so that they may be built up in their spirits. They are stronger for having endured, and even while enduring. The strength comes from the fact that trials will cause one to call out to his Savior in faith and supplication.

Temptations, on the other hand, are of Satan and are intended by the adversary of our souls to cause us harm in our spiritual lives. The intent of these is to drive us further from God as we succumb to the siren call of temptations. Unlike the trials which beset us, it is more likely that we will approach the temptation because it is fashioned to enrapture the base lusts which lurk within us. (James 1:14)

Enduring the trials will help us to withstand the temptations. Trials are not strange things to befall the Christian. Trials are expressions of the love of God which drive us to seek to stand closer to the Lord of our salvation.]

4.13 *But rejoice, inasmuch as ye are partakers of Christ's sufferings; that, when his glory shall be revealed, ye may be glad also with exceeding joy.*

[John 15:18 reminds us, "If the world hate you, ye know that it hated me before it hated you." I think back to the time a few years ago when a baptist church (small case intended) visited our city in order to picket at the funeral of a fallen soldier. I am rather certain that they of this church felt that the counter-protesters were there because of their stand for Christ.

I would have disagreed. I felt that the counter-protesters were there because of this churches hubris at claiming a position of moral superiority over the fallen soldier.

Folks, we cannot claim to be partakers of Christ's suffering when we have caused our own problems. When the world hates us because of our identification with Jesus we are suffering because of Him. That is being partakers of Christ's suffering.

Peter reminds us that suffering for Christ in this life will gather "exceeding joy" unto us in the Heavenlies. "Blessed are ye, when *men* shall revile you, and persecute *you*, and shall say all manner of evil against you falsely, for my sake. Rejoice and be exceeding glad: for great *is* your reward in heaven: for so persecuted they the prophets which were before you." (Matthew 5:11-12)]

4.14 *If ye be reproached for the name of Christ, happy are ye, for the spirit of glory and of God resteth upon you: on their part he is evil spoken of, but on your part he is glorified.*

[The same arguments as used in verse thirteen could also be used here.

The point being made is that in our identification with Christ in suffering we are identified with Him in His Glory. This is a picture of the very essence of our salvation. He accepted our sinfulness in order to cleanse us from sin. In this we are seen as standing in His ultimate righteousness. As the Spirit alighted upon Him at His baptism, thereby giving evidence of His righteousness of Office as Savior and Mediator, the Spirit identifies with us as the redeemed of the Lord. This is not an indication of any glory or righteousness we may have obtained; this is in recognition of the redemptive power and Person of the Savior.

While the sinful world speaks evil of the Savior by belittling and cursing His children, that world is giving glory – although unknowingly – to the Lord by thus identifying Him with those He has ransomed by His Blood.

By accepting this revilement from the world, we show the power of Jesus to redeem from the curse of sin.]

4.15 *But let none of you suffer as a murderer, or as a thief, or as an evildoer, or as a busybody in other men's matters.*

[We are reminded that simply suffering for things we have done is justly deserved suffering and of no spiritual benefit. To be truthful, suffering for wrong doing is a blight upon our name as "Christian." It gives ample cause for others to demean the Lord we profess to serve.

Interestingly, we are also warned not to be a "busybody in other men's matters." How many men's lives have been ruined, symbolically murdered, by the tales told by someone whose only purpose was to spread the "dirt" he had either learned, or worse, had overheard by a liar? The same thing has happened countless times by those who *had* to repeat a juicy piece of gossip that may had contained a kernel of truth but was built into an entire fertile field of salacious falsehood.

If we have a need to be about someone else's business, may we suggest that you go about doing the "business" of the Lord in spreading the message that Jesus Christ died in time so that others could live in eternity!]

4.16 *Yet if any man suffer as a Christian; let him not be ashamed; but let him glorify God on this behalf.*

[We recently had a man come into our church who desires to become the next pastor. His wife asked if we would mind changing the name of the church because, "The word 'Baptist' has such a negative connotation in the world today." I have noticed this same attitude in many of the Southern Baptist churches. Why should we be ashamed of the name "Baptist?" If one is ashamed of the name, why would he be part of a Baptist movement? Worse, if we are Baptist but afraid to mention it, are we not operating under false pretense into the world?

Apparently, there were some in the churches to whom Peter wrote who had decided that if there was to be persecution because they identified as "Christian," perhaps there was a need to hide this fact. That is akin to saying that I don't want to get shot at in a war so I'll never wear my military uniform. We are in a spiritual war. We need not to be traitorous to our "side" by denying our Lord. It might be good if we considered Matthew 10:33.

I cannot conceive of a situation where it is proper to deny our Lord. There are countless martyrs down through the ages – and in this day! – who would rather suffer the sword of persecution than to deny their Lord.

Rather than denying our Lord it would be better to stand tall and proud of the fact that we are counted worthy to suffer for His Name. Honestly, I have no desire to face that day of either persecution or martyrdom. But, if and when it comes my Lord has promised to give me the courage to suffer for Him Who died for me.

May I, I pray O Lord, have the courage to not fail thee in any time of trial.]

4.17 *For the time is come that judgment must begin at the house of God: and if it first begin at us, what shall the end be of them that obey not the gospel of God?*

[Ezekiel 9:1-6 - ¹"He cried also in mine ears with a loud voice, saying, Cause them that have charge over the city to draw near, even every man *with* his destroying weapon in his hand. ²And, behold, six men came from the way of the higher gate, which lieth toward the north, and every man a slaughter weapon in his hand; and one man among them *was* clothed in linen, with a writer's inkhorn by his side: and they went in, and stood beside the brasen altar. ³And the glory of the God of Israel was gone up from the cherub, whereupon he was, to the threshold of the house. And he called to the man clothed with linen, which *had* the writer's inkhorn by his side; ⁴And the LORD said unto him, Go through the midst of the city, through the midst of Jerusalem, and set a mark upon the foreheads of the men that sigh and that cry for all the abominations that be done in the midst thereof. ⁵And to the others he said in mine hearing, Go ye after him through the city, and smite: let not your eye spare, neither have ye pity. ⁶Slay utterly old and young, both maids, and little children, and women: but come not near any man upon whom is the mark; and begin at my sanctuary. Then they began at the ancient men which were before the house."

The judgment was set to begin at the "sanctuary" of God. Note the distinction made between the general men of the sanctuary and those who were righteous in that they lamented the sin that was practiced in the city of Jerusalem wherein dwelt that sanctuary. The city was the one which God had chosen to place His name. (I Kings 14:21) The entire city was to be sanctified as the home of the Temple which was recognized as the special residence of God for this dispensation.

This verse in I Peter is aligned with the above from Ezekiel. I would believe that it primarily refers to two times of trial for the Jewish nation. One is near and the other is far. The near has to do with the destruction of Jerusalem and the Temple. That Jewish hatred for Jesus and His followers led the leadership of the Jews into a frenzy of fury against the Lord's anointed. The outworking of this was the judgment of God upon the religion of the Jew which had forsaken the God of the Jew in rejecting their Messiah.

The child's taunt comes quickly to mind, if slightly revised. "I am rubber and you are glue. The persecution you heap on me bounces off me and sticks on you." God judged the Jewish religious leadership with the destruction of their Temple and the enslavement of many of their people.

The persecution of the church by these Jewish leaders, the resultant excesses of Rome in relation to the entire population of the Jewish homeland, became the impetus for the spread of the Message of the early church beyond the borders of Judea and Samaria and into the entire world of Rome – and beyond!

Also, the brutality of the unbiblical and unchristian persecution of the Jew by the emerging Christian movement has heaped two millennia of further persecution upon the Jew. The judgment may be said to have begun at the Temple, "the house of God," but is surely went far beyond those confines.

Realizing that Peter was writing to a Christian group we must consider the judgment beginning at the "house of God" must also consider persecution of the Christian in the world. Much of this was seen in the early church – the "near" fulfillment of this prophecy. Much more will be seen as the Day approaches.

The Church can expect persecution in the coming days. This persecution may be the cause of the falling away as mentioned in II Thessalonians 2:3. I believe that this falling away will be twofold. There will be those who cannot endure the persecution of society, or of anti-Christian entities in society, and will be persuaded to jettison any semblance of a Christian witness or lifestyle. These are probably those described in Hebrews 6:4-6 who were not actual Christians but were close travelers with us. They enjoyed the idea of Christianity until it became a burdensome thing.

The churches will react to this hemorrhaging of favor and popularity by attempting to import the culture of the day into the sanctity of the Church in an attempt to make the church "user friendly" toward those outside the faith. We have already seen this. The churches will often grow under this structure but it is a growth without the root of spirituality. (Mark 4:5-6)

Romans 10:17 reminds us that true spirituality is tied to the true Words of God. A false gospel preached from a false word does not allow the seed of faith to flourish in the depth of the soil of God. We recall that Adam was created from the dust of the ground. All human life has flown from that one man created and energized by God. All spiritual life traces back to the Son of God, God the son, Whose story is repeated in the inspired and preserved pages of the Words of God.

The further persecution will be real rather than social. After the Second Appearing of the Lord has removed His Church from this earth, the earth will enter upon the "Time of Jacob's Trouble." (Ezekiel 30:7)

As the Temple of old was the "special place of residence" of God, so is the Church, true believers, the Temple of God upon this earth. (I Corinthians 6:19) I understand that the Spirit is Omnipresent; this is an attribute of God. But, in some way I do not understand, the Spirit's influence will be removed when the Church is removed. (II Thessalonians 2:4-8) This will allow the "man of sin" free reign to begin the time that we call the Tribulation Era.

There will be people born again during this time. They will be saved the same way we have been saved. It will be a response to the Blood of Christ. But, the persecution of these tribulation age believers will be severe. Martyrdom will even exceed that of any time during the Church age.

Then will come the time of the Second Coming of the Lord to set up His Kingdom on this earth. After this initial Millennial Reign, Satan will be loosed to lead another rebellion against God. The judgment of God will fall upon those who have opposed The King and persecuted His subjects. We read about this in Revelation 20:12-15.

Before the punishment of the wicked God will first judge, or "try" His house in order to prepare us for the coming exercise of His glory and power. We are allowed the great privilege to see our Sovereign defeat the adversary by the Holiness of His Glory and Name.]

4.18 *And if the righteous scarcely be saved, where shall the ungodly and the sinner appear?*

[Clarke argues that the reference is to temporal salvation in the destruction of Jerusalem and Jerusalem in 70 A.D. "...when Cestius Gallus came against Jerusalem, many Christians were shut up in it; when he strangely raised the siege the Christians immediately departed to Pella in Coele-syria, into the dominions of King Agrippa, who was an ally of the Romans, and there they were in safety; and it appears, from the ecclesiastical historians, that they had but barely time to leave the city before the Romans returned under the command of Titus, and never left the place till they had destroyed the temple, razed the city to the ground, slain upwards of a million of those wretched people, and put an end to their civil polity and ecclesiastical state."

It is true that the Christians, recalling the warning of Jesus concerning the destruction of the Temple, did flee the city. (Luke 21:20-21) The Jewish population did not depart and were either killed or sold into slavery. Both of these are historical facts. That both the prophecy and the verse apply here is not contested. But, both the prophecy of Jesus and the verse have other meanings as well.

The prophecy of Jesus relates to both the destruction of the Temple, there have been no sacrificial ceremonies – which were so central to Jewish religious life – since the time of that destruction, but this also refers to the time of Jacob's trouble, which we call the Tribulation.

The destruction of the Temple and the expulsion of the Jew from Judea in 135

A.D. were both times of fundamental change in the Jewish life and religion. With no Temple available to host the great feasts and perform the ritual sacrifices it was necessary that Judaism adapt to a new reality. This they did by stressing the study of the oral Law and the printing of the Mishna and Talmud. This sacrifice of study replaced the sacrifice of the animals of creation as central to the Jewish faith.

Meanwhile the Christian faith which they had persecuted continued into the world. In time and place this Christian faith also morphed into forms never envisioned nor sanctioned by the inspired and preserved Scripture. However, there was always a remnant of the True Church in enclaves as there was always a remnant of the True Scripture available throughout the ages of time.

The religion of Christ, though persecuted and hounded by false religion and false Christianity, survived to carry the torch of the light of truth into the world of darkness even as the "dark ages" swept across the lands of false Christianity.

As to the verse, it is never an easy thing for a person born with a sin nature to renounce that sin and receive the Savior. Indeed, without the conviction wrought within the heart of the sinner by the Holy Spirit of God, such would not be possible. The duty of the Christian is to witness and pray. It is only the Holy Spirit Who brings the increase. We work. It is He Who has wrought salvation within the heart of the object of His convicting power.

Those who do steadfastly refuse the Savior will be found standing before Him as their judge of eternal retribution. (Revelation 20:12-15)]

4.19 *Wherefore let them that suffer according to the will of God commit the keeping of their souls to him in well doing, as unto a faithful Creator.*

[The key here is that the suffering be according to the will of God. Consider the man who has failed to keep his body under subjection. He has been of gluttonous disposition and failed to properly maintain the body given him by the Lord. In old age, should he reach it, he may find many aches and pains which he might consider suffering. These are not of God! These are due to his failure to follow the known will of God from the pages of inspired and preserved Scripture.

Consider the man who has abused alcohol and drugs. His suffering cannot be blamed on God. He knew that his body was designed to be a temple unto the Lord and ignored that truth of spiritual reality. (I Corinthians 6:19) He cannot properly ascribe his suffering to God. He, as the man above, is reaping the *benefits* of an ungodly life.

But, the man who is suffering because of his testimony for Christ can count himself as spiritually blessed. His suffering is from the Lord. He can glory in the fact that the Lord has counted him as worthy to suffer for the sake of Christ. This is the glory of a high calling of God.

It is not an easy thing to accept in our carnality, but the fact that God would send trials of affliction to us is an indication of His love. As we trust Him, and cling to Him, we are blessed to be able to suffer for His sake.

I would caution, it is never for us to seek suffering. To seek suffering is to place ourselves, as did Satan, in the seat of God. We do not have this right. Our duty is to accept suffering by trusting in the Lord and witnessing to the world that His grace is sufficient. (II Corinthians 12:9)

He is always faithful in due time to bless His beloved servant who has faithfully –

and cheerfully before men – borne all burdens to the glory of the Heavenly Master.]

FIRST PETER - CHAPTER FIVE

5.1   The elders which are among you I exhort, who am also an elder, and a witness of the sufferings of Christ, and also a partaker of the glory that shall be revealed.

[To be an elder in the ancient cultures was to be accounted with respect due to the great experience of the aged. Peter was speaking of "elder" in the sense of being worthy of the respect to lead the church. The elder was the leader of the local congregation.

It was not necessary to be an old person to be a pastor. Timothy was noted as a youth, (I Timothy 4:12) yet he was also given the charge to preach the gospel message. (II Timothy 4:2)

This does not mean that a person may just pick up a Bible and begin to be a pastor. Certainly, if God is in it there is no problem. But, generally speaking it is well for a "seasoned" saint to assume a position of responsibility in the churches of the Lord. (I Timothy 3:6) God expects our best for His service. "Our best" is, for the most part, that which we have prepared and labored to become. It is true that the Spirit can use even the least of us; it is equally true that we should seek to give to the Lord the best we can possibly offer from our experience, study and faith. (II Timothy 2:15) A true workman of God will never shirk becoming a true workman for Him.

Peter identifies himself merely as an equal to the elders who have received his epistle. He does not claim a position of authority over them as would be expected were he the "vicar of Christ" upon the earth as claimed by the Roman church. Although the fact was well known, Peter does not even appeal to his status as an apostle. He only claims the equality of an elder addressing other elders.

In this Peter exhorts and urges to action rather than ordering any course of endeavor by the readers of the epistle. In that the Spirit of inspiration lay upon the words of the epistle we may well consider that there is the intent of that Spirit that we do follow the course of the "suggestions" contained within those Words.

Peter does remind his readers that he was with Christ in the sufferings of the Master. Peter was there with Christ in the Garden of Agony. Peter followed Jesus to the judgment hall where He was mistreated and harshly questions. It was at this place that Peter denied his Lord. It is doubtful that Peter followed Christ to the crucifixion. Of all the apostles, it seems that only John actually viewed the events of Golgotha from a first-hand experience. Some may have been, probably were, on the fringes of the crowd but it seems more likely that Peter fled from the scene after his denial. It would be that others gave a report of the events to Peter after the resurrection.

The fact of "partaker" is considered in two lights. The first of these is the privileged view of Peter at the mountain of Transfiguration. Here Peter was allowed a partial glimpse of the True Glory of Jesus.

Peter also speaks in this place of the great rewards which await the faithful when we behold our Master face-to-face in glory. (John 17:21, 24)]

5.2   Feed the flock of God which is among you, taking the oversight thereof not by constraint, but willingly, not for filthy lucre, but of a ready mind;

[A shepherd is expected to do certain things in reference to the flock entrusted to him. First, he is expected to lead the sheep to a secure pasture land. In our day we tend to think of the sheep being driven to a pasture. This is not the New Testament picture. There the sheep were led.

This is an entirely different dynamic. Driven sheep are pushed to a destination by force. The idea of running in fear from whoever, or whatever, is driving the sheep is a reasonable concept. The sheep being led are not fearful. They want to follower their shepherd. They know that he is taking them to a good place. The idea in this case is love, respect and trust in the shepherd rather than fleeing in fear from his herding.

That safe place is one which is protected from all. Ravenous beasts must be defeated when they attempt to feed on the shepherd's flock. Rustlers who would attempt to steal the sheep for their own nefarious purposes must be found and dealt with. Sheep who would attempt to "wander off" from the designated pasture must be found and brought back to the protection of shepherd and flock.

The shepherd who has been hired for the job must keep in mind that the sheep are not his own. This cannot make that shepherd less caring about the sheep. He remains responsible for those entrusted into his care.

The shepherd must also be cognizant of the fact that he is not to shear the sheep except it be by instruction from the owner of the flock. The sheep may need their wool to ward off the cold of a night. The wise shepherd understands and seeks not that which would harm the flock.

Peter asks that the office of oversight, the responsibility of a pastor in the spiritual sense, be willingly assumed. Most pastors in this day work a "secular" job so they can execute the spiritual duties given to them. Most are well trained. Most have incurred the time and expense of college and seminary so they could fulfill their God-called accountabilities as servants of their Lord. They do not look for a "career path," but seek the smile of the Lord upon their endeavors.

Still, there are "ministers" who seek remuneration as their due for "all their training and time." These are the ones who are plying their "trade" even as they search for "career advancement" toward a larger church and salary. It is true that the laborer is worthy of his reward. (I Timothy 5:18) It is at least equally as true that if one's heart is based on financial reward his heart is not dedicated to the people he serves. (Matthew 6:21) Peter does speak of "the flock of God which is among you."

This phrase also seems to preclude the concept of "Church Hierarchy." In the Baptist churches each local assembly is accountable to God, alone. We may join in associations, but we realize that our only Head is the Lord. He is the Head of the Body which is the Church. (Colossians 1:18)

Peter also asks that these pastors accept their positions gladly rather than from expediency. Some would fear to become pastors due to persecution. This was especially true in Peter's day. This is becoming increasingly true in our own day as persecution continues to confront the true churches of Jesus.

The fearful probably shouldn't be accepted anyway. The true pastor must lead from a position of faith in God. The people of God in the pew will never rise above the faith level of their pastor. That is a sad reality. That should also be a somber reality of the responsibility of the pastorate. The pastorate is not a "stage performance;" it is a charge of enormous eternal consequence.]

5.3 *Neither as being lords over God's heritage, but being ensamples to the flock.*

[The word "heritage" is used in the Old Testament (ex. Deuteronomy 32:9; Psalm 33:12; 74:2) speaking of the people of God, the Israelites. Peter, as an observant Jew who had spent three years by the Master's side – Jesus, we recall, came to fulfill the Mosaic Law and would have observed those things a well – would have been familiar with the imagery of the Old Covenant. He would have, as is done here, applied this same term to the Church of The Living God as was used of the "church" of the assembly of the Hebrew people of Old.

The entirety of the Church is the heritage of God. We are His possession. The flock, meanwhile, speaks of those of the congregation to whom the pastor has the responsibility to speak the oracles of God. (I Peter 4:11) The pastor is not of a different order of Christian. He is part of that assembly for which he labors. As are all of the membership of the assembly, he has been gifted by God for a purpose within the assembly. (I Peter 4:10-11) His particular gift is to teach the Word as God leads. He may fulfill other duties under Christ; but this is the particular duty of all who would presume to speak and teach the Scripture.

The pastorate is not a place of lordship. He can, must, guide the church as the Lord leads from His inspired and preserved Scripture. He can not exercise rule over the Church other than by example. This is not ecclesiastical rule. The only Authority under which the churches operate is as under Jesus, the true Head of the Church. (Colossians 1:18)

No person can rightly claim the title of "vicar of Christ" as one who would rule over the Church. The only separation of the clergy is detailed in the sixth chapter of Acts. At this point the apostles gave up the day-to-day administration of the Jerusalem church. Deacons were appointed to service within that church. The apostles, the erstwhile leaders of the infant church as they forwarded the instruction given them by Jesus, took upon themselves only two functions: Prayer and the ministry of the inspired and preserved Words of God. (Acts 6:4)]

5.4 *And when the chief Shepherd shall appear, ye shall receive a crown of glory that fadeth not away.*

[Peter is still speaking to pastors at this point. Jesus is the "Chief Shepherd;" we are only "under shepherds" who are accountable to Him. As way of illustration, consider that Jesus is the Owner of the flock of God. To Him all are accountable. The under shepherd has been hired to oversee the flock while the Master is away. There can be no authority on our part past that which that Owner has delegated to us in the inspired and preserved Scripture.

Therefore, the under shepherd is both honor-, and duty-bound to "Preach the word; be instant in season, out of season; reprove, rebuke, exhort with all longsuffering and doctrine." (II Timothy 4:2) In order to fulfill that Divine mandate the pastor must apply himself to much study in the Word so that he can understand and fulfill the purpose to which he has been called. Indeed, without this "much study," the pastor cannot possibly fulfill the purpose of his calling.

Considering the grave responsibility of the office, Peter reminds those pastor's to whom he writes that there is a reward for their faithful service. Since there is a reward for faithful service it must follow that unfaithful service demands some sort of chastisement from the Lord. We must reflect on the fact that those who choose to undertake the office of pastor have chosen a holy office of grave responsibility.

The man whose "calling" to the pastorate is of either himself or any other has taken upon himself to stand in the place of Satan. Satan's great sin was to desire to ascend to the Throne of God. The uncalled of God man who assumes the pastorate has elevated his private choice above the will of God. He has chosen to speak for God when God did not send him. (Jeremiah 23:21)

Jesus is coming again. First will be His second appearing wherein He comes in the clouds to call His Own out of this world. Second, after the seven year time of Jacob's Trouble (Jeremiah 30:7) He will return in His Glory to this earth to judge the world and establish His Throne in Jerusalem during the Millennial Era.

I believe that the awarding of these crowns will occur at the time of His second appearing as both the dead and the living saints will be given glorified bodies. I understand the awards of reward concerning Church Age saints will occur at that time.

The picture of these crowns seems to be patterned after the understanding of the people as to the victor's crowns at the Greek Olympic Games. These crowns were woven of ivy, parsley, myrtle, olive, or oak. Obviously these faded away as the grass of the fields. The Crown which Jesus bestows will not be as these at is will not fade away. In the spiritual and eternal realm these is no decay as in the created realm of time and physicality which we understand.

This crown is promised to the faithful pastors. As the commercial says, "But Wait! There's More!" Paul speaks of the crowns given in II Timothy 4:7-8. "I have fought a good fight. I have finished my course, I have kept the faith: Henceforth there is laid up for me crown of righteousness, which the Lord, the righteous judge, shall give me at that day: and not to me only, but unto all them also that love his appearing."

The Christian overcomer also sees a crown for his service to the Lord. This is not the kingly crown of authority. We are subjects, adopted sons and daughters but still subjects, of our Lord and God. These are crowns of reward given by the love of God for His Own.

Seeing our unworthiness, we will cast our crowns at the Savior's feet. Only He is worthy! (Revelation 4:10-11)]

5.5 *Likewise, ye younger, submit yourselves unto the elder. Yea, all of you be subject one to another, and be clothed with humility: for God resisteth the proud, and giveth grace to the humble.*

[It is not until the thirty-second chapter of Job that Elihu begins to speak. The reason is that he is the youngest and felt it not his place to speak before the elder, and wiser in experience, men. In the thirtieth chapter Job complains that part of his burden is that younger persons hold him in derision. The point is that in ancient times the experience of the aged was respected as bringing special wisdom to them. Thus, the admonition to respect the elders was simply part of the expected culture; to have gone against this would have been to have not shown their religion in a positive light among men.

Beyond the cultural aspect, the office of pastor within the church was often spoken of as an elder. His duty was to speak with wisdom and authority concerning the tenets of the religion as he gave heed to Scriptural admonition.

This was a matter of keeping proper order in the church. This was in keeping with the concept of "fervent charity" (love) among the household of faith. (I Peter 4:8 – consider commentary at that verse) Those who are disposed to submit to each other will not be inclined to proudly start arguments.

Though there is a time and place, generally private, to discuss differences we might have with others in the church, we may even – as long as it does not concern aberrant doctrine! – bypass this under the heading of being subject one to another. Even under the rubric of wives submitting to their husbands, those husbands are enjoined, "So ought men to love their wives as their own bodies. He that loveth his wife loveth himself." (Ephesians 5:28) This is the concept of mutual respect which is the primary thrust of Peter in this verse. A people who love and respect one another will find a harmonious relationship.

The second chapter of James speaks of men of wealth wearing goodly apparel and a gold ring. That is an ostentatious person who is ready to "show off" his wealth so that everyone will understand that he is an important person.

Peter does not encourage this display any more than did James. To the contrary, Peter encourages people to dress in humiliation. The understanding here is one might even dress in the white robes of a slave; this was the slaves customary dress. Above this would be a tunic which was tied about over that white robe. Some would make the knots of that tying very elaborate with differing colors of thread. Peter argues for simple and humble clothing in all things.

The picture of clothing being used to argue humility is that clothing is the first thing seen in a person. It is that which covers him. The idea is that humility was that for which the person was known in all of his appearance.

I received several small decorations as a soldier. Almost all were of the "I was there and didn't do anything wrong" variety. The decoration of which I was most proud was my Combat Infantry Badge. Normally this was the only "medal" I wore on my uniform. Did you catch the word "pride" in there? It wasn't wrong to wear that medal; I had earned it. It was wrong to wear it as a boast. This is what Peter is warning against.

Do you know why Peter says that "God resisteth the proud?" Almost any sin can be confessed and forsaken. Some are harder than others I will admit. But pride has a way of sneaking up upon us and grabbing us by the throat before we even realize it. A person might say, "I used to smoke; but I gave it up." He can say, "I used to be a drunkard; but I gave it up." He might say, "I used to gamble to excess; but I gave it up." Do you see the problem with that line of argument at a testimony meeting? He isn't giving any glory to God. He is bragging about his accomplishments. These may be good accomplishments but God will not give His glory to another. (Isaiah 42:8)

Pride is a matter of glorying in ourselves. We have nothing of which to glory except that Jesus died for us even though we were rank sinners. Humility realizes this fact. God gives grace to the one who humbles himself before the Lord of the Universe.]

5.6 *Humble yourselves therefore under the mighty hand of God, that he may exalt you in due time.*

[It is a spiritual principle that if we do not humble ourselves before God He will humble us through His chastisements upon us for the sin of pride. It is another spiritual principle that God will not allow us to be exalted even in station within the church before we are ready to give Him the glory for that position.

Don't misunderstand. There are those who are seen as exalted in the eyes of men who God has not exalted. They are not exalted in the eyes of God. They are heaping coals of fire upon their own heads as they sashay down the road of this life in their unseemly pride. Consider the words of Christ to some unsaved persons: "And then will I profess unto them, I never knew you: depart from me, ye that work iniquity." (Matthew 7:23)

Make no mistake. There will be many who will "elbow their way to the front of the line" in Heaven to receive *their* crown only to find that their salvation, while real because of the Cross, is as the life of Job while under severe trial, "My bone cleaveth to my skin and to my flesh, and I am escaped with the skin of my teeth." (Job 19:20)

One of the reasons that "God loveth a cheerful giver," (II Corinthians 9:7) is because the cheerful giver is not seeking to "buy" the favor of God. That person is simply giving what he can out of a heart of gratitude and love for God.]

5.7 *Casting all your care upon him; for he careth for you.*

Psalm 37:5; 55:22; Matthew 6:25; Luke 12:22; Philippians 4:6; Hebrews 13:5

[My natural position in basketball was as a point guard. I was not a good "shot" with the basketball. I only shot the ball often enough to keep the defense "honest." My "game" was passing the ball to those who were better than me so that our team could score. I didn't worry about scoring points. I only "cast" the ball to others so our team could score enough points to win.

That is the meaning of this verse. Oh, we care about our daily trials and tribulations. How could we not? The answer to that question is that we cast our cares to the Lord. He can handle that which we cannot. We can see this in Hebrews 4:16 where we are not invited to prayer. We are told that it is our duty to boldly come before God with our praises and problems.

If we never praise Him we would seem to be as a whiny child who only approaches his parents with incessant requests. Give me, give me, give me. If we never present our problems to Him we seem as lacking in faith that He will bless.

God understands that there are issues in this life which we are not able to handle. He loves us and desires to assist where we are unable to confront the problems of life. The idols and false religions see a god who only demands obedience and service. The Only True and Living God, Who we worship, loves us. Don't misunderstand. He does desire our obedience and service. But, He does not call us to these things through fear or intimidation. He calls us as He has saved us; it is through His demonstrated love for us.

Even when it comes time for us to walk through the valley of the shadow, our God will show forth His love to us. We have a "know so" salvation; this is founded on the inspired and preserved Book in which He has explained His glory, our unworthiness, and His love that looks past our unworthiness and hides us behind the Cross of Calvary. It was the supreme love of God which sent Jesus Christ to die in time so we would have the assurance that we will live in eternity.

He cares for us. O, happy thought!]

5.8 *Be sober, be vigilant; because your adversary the devil, as a roaring lion, walketh about, seeking whom he may devour:*

[Although the concept of not being drunk with wine is encased within this word, I would argue that being sober considers more than just this. The use of the word "vigilant" supports this contention. To be sure, alcoholic drunkenness is also to be avoided. The drunk on alcohol cannot be at the same time "drunk in the Spirit." (consider Ephesians 5:18) Such a person has his faculties of reason impaired. Thus he cannot vigilantly be on moral watch against the adversary.

Satan can neither take, nor induce us to renounce, our salvation. Once the grace of Jesus is accepted, we have "sealed the contract." We have passed from the ownership of Satan via our inherited sin natures, into the adoption as children of God. The Spirit has sealed us into this salvation until we are called home to Heaven. No one, not even ourselves, has the power to overcome Christ and remove from Him that which He has purchased by His Own Blood at the Cross of Calvary.

Still, we do need to be vigilant because of the adversary. Our failures will grieve the Spirit Who has sealed us. (Ephesians 4:30) This seems the primary focus of the attacks of Satan upon the redeemed. Don't let you pride grow; Satan does not care about us in the least. His purpose is to harm the creation of God in order to cause this grief to the Divine. Although Satan will try his best to defeat the purposes of God, he still harbors the hope that he can ascend to a throne above that of God.

He cannot do this, of course. He must realize this. He must realize that his time is short; judgment is certainly coming. He will use what time he does have to inflict this grief upon God. That this harm will also inflict grief upon the redeemed is just "so much gravy" upon Satan's feast of hate. Satan is indeed an adversary to the redeemed of the Lord.

Satan is described as a lion in this passage. That is interesting because in Revelation 5:5 Jesus is described as the "Lion of the Tribe of Judah." Satan is also described in II Corinthians 11:14 as being able to transform himself into an angel of light. This is not surprising as Satan was originally named "Lucifer." The meaning of that name is "morning star." He fell, through sin, from this lofty position and now seeks to destroy whom he may.

In this light Satan attempts to mimic the reality of God so that worship may be diverted to himself. It is very instructive to realize that Satan is described as a destroyer in Revelation 9:11. "And they had a king over them, which is the angel of the bottomless pit, whose name in the Hebrew tongue is Abaddon, but in the Greek tongue hath his name Apollyon." Both Abaddon, in the Hebrew, and Apollyon, in the Greek, translate as "destroyer."

Many Christian apologists for Islam will argue that we both worship the same God. We just use different names. I would point out a very significant difference. When Islam identifies one they call an infidel they are as apt as not to destroy that person or group of persons. When Biblical Christianity sees one who we would call an infidel we are called to pray for them even though they are attacking us. (Matthew 5:44) One comes in love, even seeking to covert by prayer and the witness of the Spirit. The other comes to either convert or destroy.

The Christian will wield a "sword;" the sword of the Christian is the inspired and preserved Word of God. (Hebrews 4:12) The purpose of our "sword" is not to separate the head from the body but to restore the spirit of man to the worship of his Creator.

The devil is called a "roaring lion." The roar of the lion sends terror into the hearts of the beasts of the field. They are warned that the lion is on the prowl. But, the roar is not the time of trouble. The lion will sneak up upon his prey. The game may be diligent but it is unknowing of how close the time of danger is until the lion pounces from his hiding and destroys the victim.

That is why we are to be vigilantly watching. We know the adversary is there. We do not know in what way the attack will come. Satan is active. He is described as "walking about." Satan is looking for his point of attack. He will patiently wait unto the object, us, is sufficiently vulnerable to attack.

That waiting period is a time of terror in that we wait and watch and wait some more. Any relaxation of our guard and he will come. He wants to devour our peace with God. He wants to devour our witness for God. He would have us leave the "ivory palaces" and come to the "congested sewer." He does not seek our good but our ruination.

If our souls cannot be dragged down into the pit of his coming judgment and destruction, he will see to it that our witness to others will bear no fruit of souls for the Master. If he can do just that one thing, he will feel victory. May we reside rightly near our Lord so that others "may see Jesus in me" and come to find the Lord as a result of my witness and prayer to the Spirit.]

5.9 *Whom resist stedfast in the faith, knowing that the same afflictions are accomplished in your brethren that are in the world.*

[Most of us have been told that if we just resist Satan he will flee from us. Did you ever read the entire verse where this is stated? It is James 4:7 – "Submit yourselves therefore to God. Resist the devil, and he will flee from you."

After undefeated boxer Michael Spinks had been knocked out in the first round by Mike Tyson, he said, "I've finally met a man who could beat me." Folks, Satan has never met a man who could defeat him. The only exception to this rule is Jesus Christ, the Son of God and God, the son. We cannot follow the advice of James 4:7, or of this verse – I Peter 5:9, without accessing the power of God through our Lord.

The Spinks/Tyson fight looked like a mismatch. Any of us trying to resist Satan in our own power will not look like a mismatch. It will appear as what it is: a monumentally hopeless venture on our part. It is only as we stand in the Lord, in His power, that we will find Satan to be helpless before the Lord. Scripture will defeat Satan every time unless we are simply accessing our memory. If the Spirit brings to our mind Scripture which we have studies and prayed over, it is still God that gives us the victory.

We must resist Satan in the faith. The flesh will always miserably fail.

We also need to understand that our affliction is not uncommon. It may seem so if we've not experienced it before. But, Satan does not have any "new" ideas. He does have plenty of old ones that are tried and true to his purpose. Unless we are grounded in the Word, both the Living and the Written Word, the plans of Satan will sway us in their assault on our souls.

In the tenth chapter of I Kings, verse 10, Elijah complains that he is the only one who has stayed true to God. In the eighteenth verse of that chapter God informs

Elijah that there are seven thousand who have not worshiped Baal. Remembering I Peter 4:12 we know that our trials and tribulations are not "some strange thing." What has come upon others, who God held up through their suffering, might come also upon us. We are not unique. But, we are saved if we have accepted Christ as Savior; we must always lean upon Him in the time of trial and persecution.

He will deliver us in His Own perfect way. Should that be through martyrdom, the persecution has lost its presence and left our person. We have been delivered to the safety of the Savior. The persecutor can have no real power over the saint of God. It remains eternally true that, "Ye are of God, little children, and have overcome them: because greater is he that is in you, than he that is in the world." (I John 4:4)

We win because Jesus has already secured the victory. The victory is His!]

5.10 *But the God of all grace, who hath called us unto his eternal glory by Christ Jesus, after that ye have suffered a while, make you perfect, stablish, strengthen, settle you.*

[Peter begins his prayer at the conclusion of this epistle by admitting that the only spiritual grace available is from The God of the Bible. From the standpoint of humanity this is nearly tragically true. The false religions of man can offer no grace, though it is purported that they do. They can offer no remission of sins; most would not even claim to do so. They can offer no peace or happiness on this earth. That which they do offer is shallow and transitory in light of the bleak condition of their lack of eternal reward. There is more that could be said. Suffice to use the same phrase as does Peter: "The God of ALL grace."

It is also abundantly true that He has called us unto His eternal glory. It is the Spirit Who calls man by His convicting power. The Spirit convicts us of sin. It is this sin which separates us from God by such a great gulf that we can never bridge our way back to fellowship with God.

The Spirit calls us by His offer of this great salvation made available by the Blood of Jesus Christ on the Cross of Calvary. It is an amazing salvation which, were we left to our own devices without the wooing of the Spirit, we would never consider seeking. (Romans 3:11) We can never accurately say that we have found the Lord. He appeared in our path and invited us to join with Him. (Matthew 11:28; John 6:65)

One of the commentators I accessed said that Jesus gives us part of His Glory. NO! Jesus does give us His glory. His Glory is as God! Such transfer is the fantasy of Satan's temptation of Eve and the promise of many false religions. What gory we do receive is an imparted from Him, not removed from Him, Glory. Strictly speaking it is a glory that gives Him even more glory as the worship of eternity will see the manifestation of His love and mercy to His created creatures.

We may be called upon to suffer from the persecution of others. Not so strangely, this persecution will most often come from people who claim a religious basis for the persecution. Since any religion which is not Biblically based is a false religion, and since only the Triune God and the fallen Satan can be the true recipients of worship, it is a reality that all false religions find a cadre of believers who are, mostly unknowingly so during time and tragically so during eternity, become worshippers of Satan. It is not surprising that such as these would persecution the believer's in The One True God.

The suffering within, and the reality within, true salvation will give gifts to these believers who are tested and tried on this earth. This persecution will be for an infinitesimally short period when compared with the glories and bliss of our Heavenly estate.

But, there is more within this life, even within the persecution of this life. Our faith is perfected in these persecutions. The concept of this word is that we are grown to maturity of faith within this persecution. We are actually made more fit citizens of Heaven by our experience of trust in trial with the Lord.

Persecution will also cause us to be established in the faith. As we fly to the Savior in faith and petition under persecution we are made more secure, in our hearts as our souls are secure because of the Lord's one-time work of Self-Sacrifice, which will cause us to be able to endure even more persecution. As we realize that we are enduring this as unto the Lord, our hearts and souls find blessing, even temporal blessing, as the world attempts their persecution. Instead of persecution, which was the only intent of our enemies, we are allowed to find peace and joy in the Lord. As true followers of Christ we will even attempt to call our tormenters to an encounter with the Lord. Certainly we will pray for them to find Christ.

We are strengthened in the faith as we respond to the persecution by standing even closer to the Lord as we recoil from the human element of our ungodly attackers. We may even take heart as we thank the Lord that we are accounted worthy to suffer for His Name.

We do not need to be promised worldly pleasures in the future. Nor do we need to hate our oppressors. Instead we are called to pray for these souls who live to torture others. We will rejoice if but one, though we pray for all, of our tormenters accepts the Lord's promise of free salvation and becomes, himself, a pilgrim on this earth as he sees the future of a heavenly paradise of bliss with Jesus Who died in time that others might find eternal life in the realms of eternity.

In all of this, even as our physical bodies may be tortured and destroyed, we are pleased to settle in spiritual comfort in the tender arms of our Risen Lord.]

5.11 *To him be glory and dominion for ever and ever. Amen.*

[This is not a prayer of petition. It is a praise of recognition. He is all glorious. He does rule the universe in power and justice just as He will one day rule the entire earth from the Throne of David in Jerusalem. Unlike the earthly potentates and empires, the rule of Jesus will never fade. He will rule throughout the ageless ages of eternity. The light of His power and glory shall never dim. He is the King of kings. He is the Lord of lords. He is my Savior.

He is all this because His glory is that of God. Jesus died, on purpose in His humanity so that He could redeem all those of all the ages of time who would come to Him in faith believing.

What Savior is like unto Him? None! No human person could be. Not even any angelic being could be. Only God, taking upon Himself the mantle of human flesh at His insistence and for His eternal purposes, could be the Savior of the Word.

Amen. So be it! Jesus, the now glorified One, died in my place to redeem me from my sins. Why? "For God so loved the world, that he gave his only begotten Son, that whosoever believeth in him should not perish, but have everlasting life." (John 3:16)

Amen! Hallelujah! This litany of praise could continue forever but I have not the words to describe, or to exalt His praises!]

5.12 *By Silvanus, a faithful brother unto you, as I suppose, I have written briefly, exhorting, and testifying that this is the true grace of God wherein ye stand.*

[The word "Silvanus" is, of course, an early Latin phrase for "Old Television Set." If any of you "got" that terrible pun you must be old like me. The Silvania Television was one of the popular early television sets.

Actually, Silvanus is of Latin derivatization. It is supposed that Silvanus is the same person as Paul's frequent companion Silas. The conjecture of several commentators is that Silas had labored among these churches to whom the epistle was to originally go. The argument goes that Peter sent the letter by the hand of Silas. Seeing the piety of Silvanus, Peter supposed that he had been a faithful brother to those churches.

It is interesting that Peter both begins (v. 1:2) and ends (here) his writing with a mention of the grace of God. He notes that this letter bears the truth of the Gospel. In this Truth, the inspired and preserved Words of God, stand all true followers of Jesus.

It is possible that Silvanus transcribed this letter for Peter. Paul normally used scribes to pen the words he dictated. Consider that Paul made mention to the Galatians that he did personally write to them. (Galatians 6:11) The most articulated reason is that Paul had some disease of the eyes. This would be the "thorn in the flesh" to which he alluded in II Corinthians 12:7. This would also explain why those same Galatians would have plucked out their own eyes for him had it been possible. (Galatians 6:15)

We find no evidence of such a thing concerning Peter. It is more reasonable to consider that Silvanus was a messenger rather than a transcribing secretary for Peter.]

5.13 *The church that is at Babylon, elected together with you, saluteth you, and so doth Marcus my son.*

[Upon reading of the fall of Babylon to the Medes and Persians in the Book of Daniel we are predisposed to consider that Babylon ceased to exist at that time. Such is not the case. After his campaigns in India, and upon the illness which claimed his life, Alexander resided and died in the city of Babylon wherein the Jews had been taken captive. Josephus informs us that there was a large Jewish population in the city during the times of the apostles.

It is altogether reasonable to consider that Peter would go there to preach the Gospel. It is also likely that a large contingent from that city had been present at the Day of Pentecost in Jerusalem. The church in that city may have well been founded through the work of Peter. Whether that is so or not is unimportant. As an apostle Peter would certainly been welcome by whatever church was existent in the city.

This church sent greetings to the sister-churches which were brought to the same faith as that which had brought salvation to themselves.

It is strongly suspected that "Marcus" was John Mark. (consider Acts 12:6-17, esp. v. 12) This would have been the same Mark who penned the Gospel ascribed to him. This Mark is known as a frequent companion of Peter; it was from Peter, in the natural, that the memoir of Mark was culled.

The designation of "son," given by Peter concerning Mark is probably due to the fact that it was Peter who was instrumental in leading Mark to the Lord in salvation. Paul uses the same rational in regards to Timothy and for the same reason. (I Timothy 1:2; 1:18; II Timothy 1:2)]

5.14 *Greet ye one another with a kiss of charity. Peace be with you all that are in Christ Jesus. Amen.*

[This not the kiss of lust but the kiss of sanctified love one for another in the churches of Jesus Christ. Generally speaking, as we observe in many cultures today, this was a kiss directed to the cheek. It was a sign of holy affection for those saints of God. As such it was a sign meant to call the group to fellowship in the Lord.

Many times Jesus wished peace among the apostles. Possibly the most beautiful of these times was when He appeared in the locked upper room. (John 20:26) It was at this time that the Lord addressed Thomas. Thomas had doubted the resurrection but one look at the Savior and all doubts were gone.

Notice that the benediction of "peace" was only directed toward those who were of the fellowship. There is no promise of peace to the wicked. (Isaiah 48:22; 57:21) The blessings of the believer are reserved for those that truly love the Lord and have been called to Him in salvation.

The Book ends with the doxological phrase of "Amen." So be it!]

ADDENDA

LUKE 16:19

Luke 16:19 *There was a certain rich man, which was clothed in purple and fine linen, and fared sumptuously every day:*

Ephesians 4:8; Hebrews 10:4

[vv. 19-31. First, it would be wise for us to consider that this was not a parable. Jesus never mentioned a person by name when He taught by parable. This is a true incident concerning two "certain" people – one named, the other not named.

Even if this passage had been a parable, we must remember that the spiritual facts would still be true as Jesus never taught error.

Jesus was acting as a Gentleman when He named the one but not the other. Lazarus, the man in Paradise was named. His family and friends could take comfort in this. The rich man is not named; rather, Jesus simply described the situation of that man. Two things were accomplished in this. The surviving relatives of this man were not unduly given even more grief at the death of their family member. At the same time that family, and all other families with similar circumstance, were given the warning about their own souls.

We need to compare other passages in relation to this story. The first concerns the rich man, Revelation 20:14-15, "And death and hell were cast into the lake of fire. This is the second death. And whosoever was not found written in the book of life was cast into the lake of fire."

We also need to consider several verses in relation to the beggar, Lazarus. While on the cross Jesus was asked by one of the malefactors who were being crucified alongside Him that He would remember the man when He came into His kingdom. (Luke 23:43) In the very next verse Jesus replied, "...To day shalt thou be with me in paradise."

Strong (3857) refers to paradise as a place of happiness. Since Jesus said that this man would be with Him this may refer to Heaven. I would suggest that this may not be so. The ancient Talmud describes Hades as a place of the dead. It is possible to use the word to describe the grave although such was not the situation, obviously, in this passage. In the Talmudic tradition Hades is divided into two "compartments." One of these is Hell, the place of punishment for the sinner, and the other is Paradise, the place where the righteous go. Jesus gives credence to this teaching in this incident.

To the sinner this was a time prior to the final judgment when they are cast into the Lake of Fire which was originally prepared for the devil and his angels. (Matthew 25:41) These sinned before the creation of humanity. The unregenerate who are consigned to the Lake of Fire will be there as followers of Satan and thus share in his judgments.

To the righteous dead this was a time prior to the sacrifice of Jesus at Calvary. The penman of Hebrews tells us that "For *it is* not possible that the blood of bulls and of goats should take away sins." (Hebrews 10:4) Therefore the Old Testament saints were not yet fully cleansed of their sins. Their sins were covered by their faithful acceptance of the Words of God given during their dispensations. But, the Blood of

Jesus, superior to the blood of those Old Testament sacrifices in that His Blood has the capacity to cleanse sin rather than to cover sin in accordance with the sacrifices which were a shadow of Him to come, had not yet been shed as a full atonement for the sins of the believer.

SECOND PETER

SECOND PETER - CHAPTER ONE

1.1 *Simon Peter, a servant and an apostle of Jesus Christ, to them that have obtained like precious faith with us through the righteousness of God and our Saviour Jesus Christ.*

[In his former epistle he had identified himself only as "Peter." Jesus, Himself, had given that name to Peter after his great affirmation of the Truth that Jesus was the both Messiah of the Jews and Son of God. (Matthew 16:15-18) There is a possibility that some of the readers of the previous epistle may have been miffed with Peter, feeling that he had slighted his family or Jewish heritage, by not using the name which he had been given at his circumcision, Simon Barjona, "Simon, the son of Jona." (Matthew 16:17)

Simon Peter was the name by which Peter was known concerning his mission for his Lord. When the servants of Cornelius came to find Peter to take the knowledge of salvation back to the house of their master, this was they name under which he was sought. (Acts 10:5; 18; 32)

There were more important facts about Peter. He was a servant. That word carried the connotation of "slave" in the mind of Peter. Paul also used this picture of servanthood in Romans 1:1 and Titus 1:1. After describing himself first as a servant, Peter adds that he is also an apostle of Jesus.

In relating the fact that he was an apostle, Peter is claiming that he has the right to teach in the churches of Lord. Peter is reminding his readers that he had spent time with the Master and had been specially commissioned, and taught, by Him. By first claiming that he was a mere servant of the Lord, Peter is reminding his readers that Jesus is All Important. Peter is simply a servant used by the Lord for His purposes.

Peter reminds those readers that salvation came to all, himself included, by the power and calling of God. Salvation was based only on the righteousness of God rather than through any agency of man.

He calls this salvation "precious." It was precious in its price. Salvation comes to each of us who accept it from the actions of The Lord on the Cross of Calvary. Our own work is meaningless. The Work of Jesus is wondrously effective in the salvation of souls and the triumph over sin.

Salvation is precious in its profit to us. We are bought from sin and slavery to that sin, unto the glorious light of that salvation. "For what is a man profited, if he shall gain the whole world, and lose his own soul? or what shall a man give in exchange for his soul?" (Matthew 16:26)

Salvation is precious in its performance of quickening. "And you hath he quickened, who were dead in trespasses and sins..." (Ephesians 2:1) By this we are made alive to the Spiritual and unto God.

Salvation is precious in its placement. "Beloved, now are we the sons of God, and it doth not yet appear what we shall be: but we know that, when he shall appear, we shall be like him; for we shall see him as he is." (I John 3:2)

Salvation is precious in it pardon. "There is therefore now no condemnation to them which are in Christ Jesus, who walk not after the flesh, but after the Spirit." (Romans 8:1)

Salvation is precious in its permanence. "And grieve not the holy Spirit of God, whereby ye are sealed unto the day of redemption." (Ephesians 4:30)

Note carefully that the word "and" used in the final sentence of this verse is a conjunctive word. "...the righteousness of God AND our Saviour Jesus Christ." (Emphasis added to heighten the natural construction of the verse. This speaks of One Divine Entity. It is an affirmation that Jesus is God. In His Divinity Jesus Christ, as God, Is our Savior. Consider Isaiah 12:2, Luke 1:47, and Titus 2:3 in reference with this verse.]

1.2 *Grace and peace be multiplied unto you through the knowledge of God, and of Jesus our Lord,*

[There is a very interesting concept in this verse. We know that salvation is the grace of God shone into the life of man. (Titus 2:11) This is available to all, both Jew and Gentile, who accept Jesus as Savior. We know also that peace is a gift from God to those who have been called into the grace. (Romans 14:17) But, in this place we find Peter mentioning that this grace and peace can be multiplied in the lives of the redeemed.

We can actually grow in the grace which God has given into our hearts and lives. We can become closer to the ideal of being like our Lord. We will never attain; but, we can strive! It is this striving which allows us to more fully access the grace of His love and the peace, beyond understanding, which the Lord sends to our hearts.

An illustration would be the people of the Exodus. The nation had been formally declared and established at Sinai. At that point the Covenant People of Abraham were christened as the Covenant Nation of the sons Jacob. They were still the people of Abraham, the heirs to his promises from God. Beyond this they were also identified by their tribal *States*, as it were, within that national reality.

They gained more training as to their rights and responsibilities under the original covenant of Abraham as they traveled to the land which had been promised to the descendants of Abraham. Their refusal to enter into their land of promise did not disqualify them from the reality of their status as covenant people. But, this did mean that they would not grow into landowners within the Land of Promise. That status was reserved for a future generation.

We can grow in grace or we can stagnate in grace and lose our heritage of peace. In doing so we will remain in grace but we will lose much of the blessing which is gained within our lives lived within that grace.

The people of the exodus were called to go into their land and physically establish their national identity. Our call is to go into the entire world with the message that Jesus Christ has died in time so that others can live in eternity. They were to go in grace with the mandate of God's protecting hand. Our mandate is to grow in grace with the message of God's proffered salvation. That generation of old refused to trust God's direction and suffered temporal loss. Our generations have refused to trust God's provision to evangelize the world and, though still saved, have suffered spiritual loss; our growth is perversely "underdeveloped" in the spiritual and does not produce all of the spiritual victory God desires to supply.

SECOND PETER: Chapter 1

We are able to access the "multiplication of grace and peace" through the knowledge of God. So, how do we find this knowledge of God? We could argue that we find this knowledge in the pages of the inspired and preserved Words of God. We would be right in that claim. But, the sad truth is that the Bible, to the unsaved is an unopened Book. This does not mean that they unsaved cannot open The Book and read the Words therein. It does mean that there are truths which are spiritually discerned which are not "open" to the unsaved. (I Corinthians 2:14) The reality of the sin nature has blinded the unsaved to spiritual truth.

The called of God, the saved, are endowed with the opening of spiritual eyes that we may begin to understand the truths of God's Message. This happens through a knowledge of God. That does not mean something that we have learned in a "Sunday School" class. That means an experiential knowledge through a saving relationship with Jesus Christ.

One day Philip asked Jesus to show the disciples The Father. (John 14:8) Jesus answered that request. "Jesus saith unto him, Have I been so long time with you, and yet hast thou hast not known me, Philip? he that hath seen me hath seen the Father; and how sayest thou *then*, Shew us the Father?" (John 14:9) We should also consider John 1:18 in this same discussion. "No man hath seen God at any time; the only begotten Son, which is in the bosom of the Father, he hath declared him."

Any understanding we may gain of God is through our relationship with Jesus, the Son of God and God, the Son. He is God and declares Himself to us in our Salvation relationship. It is through The Son that we learn more about The Father. There is One God. There is One Divine Essence of God.]

1.3   *According as his divine power hath given unto us all things that pertain unto life and godliness, through the knowledge of him that hath called us to glory and virtue:*

[The previous verse had argued that grace and peace were subject to multiplication through knowledge of God. This verse argues that it is "through the knowledge of him" that this knowledge was divinely appointed unto the Christian.

Bishop Ussher, whose dating of Biblical events and persons become much more reliable as he comes to the New Testament era, has dated this particular epistle at 66 A.D., which puts the Book towards the end of Peter's earthly life. This also places this Book as squarely within that period of time when the Spirit was using His servants to spread the inspired and preserved Words of God, sealed by eternity but sent into time, (John 14:26; II Timothy 3:16; Psalm 119:89) for the edification of the saints.

With the above in mind I would submit that the powerful Words of God were the Divine Spring from which flowed the river of the knowledge of God and Christ. The Word of God is a Divine Book which is not subject to the natural decay of time as are the books of the words of man.

These early Christian's were doubly blessed in this knowledge of the Divine. The had not only the Old Testament Scriptures which speak of Jesus, they also had the emerging New Testament Scriptures supplied by the inspiration of the Spirit as an unfolding of the story of the work of Jesus and our responsibility toward Him. Added to this were the memories of the apostles. These had been singularly taught by the Savior as they walked with Him for three years.

These apostles expected that Jesus would soon return. Nonetheless, they could not possibly visit every church established by the saints of God witnessing to the world of man. They published memoirs of the Savior's words and works during His ministry on this earth. These became the words of the apostles to the entire church. The Gospel of Mark was not written by an apostle. But, it was written by a man who was such a close associate of Peter that the words and recollection are those of the preaching of Peter to the churches. It honestly could be called "The Gospel of Peter" though his pen did not immediately produce the manuscript. That pen used of Mark was guided by the memory of the words of Peter. That pen was also guided by the Spirit in the inspiration and preservation of those Words.

Peter also reminds us that we are a called people. First, and without this we are not His people, we are called to the grace of salvation. Whether one accepts the Calvinistic concept of elected to grace or simply the concept of being called by the conviction of the Spirit, we are called to the grace of God. We do not, can not, approach the Mercy Seat of our Lord in any other manner. All of us, as a race of people who are disposed to sin, have gone astray from The Creator God. (Isaiah 53:6) No one in their natural state as sinners will ever seek God. (Romans 3:11) This is why Isaiah 55:6 implores us to "Seek ye the LORD while he may be found, call ye upon him while he is near..." Salvation is available to the one who seeks the Lord in response to being sought by the Lord.

But, with the above said, the primary focus of this verse is upon the saint who has already experienced salvation. He is told to walk in the way of the Lord. In this is true glory and virtue found for the days of our lives on this earth. This is not so much the concept of "finding Heaven while on this earth," as it is spreading the peace of Heaven to others who share our walk on this earth. As James might have put it, "It is showing the reality of your salvation to others that they might wish to find true religion for themselves."]

1.4 *Whereby are given unto us exceeding great and precious promises: that by these ye might be partakers of the divine nature, having escaped the corruption that is in the world through lust.*

[We have been given great and precious promises even in this world. We have heard much talk about "Pie in the sky, By and by, When I die," and these are great promises. A life of eternal life in bliss with the Lord; folks, that ain't chopped liver. That is a pretty good promise. ...And, it is true!

As to our present companionship with the Lord; that ain't bad, either! There is the promise of prayer to the One Who can make a real difference. That ain't bad! A purpose in this life isn't a shallow thing to a person who cares. The privilege of working with the Master in the propagation of the faith is certainly a present promise.

These are exceeding and great promises which can sustain us even during the darkest hours of the darkest days we may find in this present life. There is, of course, much more blessing given those who love the Lord. Those promises of the future are compelling but God hasn't forgotten that we, created human beings, do live in this world at this time. He shows His care even now!

This verse promises that we will become "partakers of the divine nature." First, it would be good to consider what this does not mean. It not any sort of pantheism whereby our soul is absorbed into the "divine essence." Read Revelation, or Ezekiel, or

Jeremiah, or even Job (Job 19:26) where he is assured he will stand – in his skin, before the Lord. In these, and more, places we are shown the existence of individuality after death. In the Transfiguration we see Jesus and some Old Testament persons standing and conversing as individuals. In Luke 19:23-31 we see the rich man, in his individuality during the torment of Hades, and Abraham, in his bliss in Paradise, talking to one another as individuals.

Besides these Biblical examples we must also consider the perfections of God. If God is perfect, from eternity past even before the creations of our "natural order," what would become of His perfection were He to change by absorbing the creature into the Creator? If He had been somehow "incomplete" before, how was He able to create? How would it be possible that we could praise Him if our individuality were absorbed?

We are instead said to become partakers of His divine natures. That is not the same as being the essence of His Divine nature. In John 10:30 Jesus says, "I and my Father are one." He was not claiming that His purpose was one with The Father; He was claiming equality with God. Since there is but ONE GOD, it becomes obvious that Jesus, in some way that I will confess I do not understand, is of ONE ESSENCE with The Father.

This is what the religious leaders understood Him to have said. "The Jews answered him, saying, For a good work we stone thee not; but for blasphemy; and because that thou, being a man, makest thyself God." (John 10:33)

Jesus did not correct any misconception on their part. He "doubled down" on His assertion. He gave some Old Testament references where people had been called "god" because they stood as administrators of God's Law. "If he called them gods, unto whom the word of God came, and the scripture cannot be broken; Say ye of him, whom the Father hath sanctified, and sent into the word, Thou blasphemest, because I said, I am the Son of God?" (John 10:35-36)

The opinion as to what Jesus had said remained the same. "Therefore they sought again to take him; but he escaped out of their hand." (John 10:39)

We are not promised to be of the essence of God, as Jesus clearly claimed to be. We are promised to share, partake – that is the meaning of the word, in His nature. The apostle John said the same thing concerning our glorified bodies during eternity. "Beloved, now are we the sons of God, and it doth not yet appear what we shall be; but we know that, when he shall appear, we shall be like him, for we shall see him as he is." (I John 3:2)

We will not be Gods. There can be only ONE ALMIGHTY and that position is filled. But, our nature will be like His. Our nature, our view, our feelings, our delights and joys will be as are His. We will be *like Him*. We will not *be* Him.

It is via the salvation of our souls, by the Cross of Calvary, that this eventuality is wrought within us. Since the fall of Adam in the Garden, all humanity – with the exception of the virgin born Lord, have carried this "gene" of sin within their human makeup. We have been freed from this "gene" through salvation. We can live above sin.

When our bodies are glorified at the Second Appearing of Christ we will be changed into that which was the original condition of man before that fall. James reminds us, "But every man is tempted, when he is drawn away of his own lust, and enticed. Then when lust hath conceived, it bringeth forth sin..." (James 1:14-15a)

In essence James was saying that we sin because we want to. We lust for a specific thing and Satan will use our own lusts to draw us away from God. Christian, while we are in this carnal body we are subject to like passions as are others. Satan will seek our hurt as well as, possibly more so than, others. We need to find a place near the Lord, and the Lord's inspired and preserved Words, that we may resist the wiles of the devil.

The glorious reality is that in our glorified bodies all the "wants to" of sin are taken out of our bodies. The "breath of life" from God made us immortal. We are creatures of eternity. The pride of life removed us from the presence of our Creator. We are creatures of sin. Jesus has saved us from sin. Positionally we stand perfect before God in the fact of the great Self-Sacrifice of Jesus on the Cross.

When our bodies are glorified, as our souls have been saved, we will stand as Adam before the fall. Our perfections will be as God originally intended in His Creation. God only creates "Good." The plan of Satan is to sully the perfection of God's creation with the sin of rebellion. God already had the remedy for Satan's chicanery. (Consider Revelation 13:8b) At the Cross we are allowed to apply the remedy of God to the reprobation of our souls. We will stand cleansed and perfect in our resurrected and glorified bodies.

One more thing, we will also stand fully fulfilled and joyous at that time. The creation of God, restored, has no place for regret, pain or sorrow of any kind. We serve The Great God. His mercies are beyond our comprehension!]

1.5 *And beside this, giving all diligence, add to your faith virtue; and to virtue knowledge;*

[Besides all the wonders of grace given to the believer in the previous verse, we are called to add these other things mentioned in this and the following verses. This concept harkens back to verse two where we are informed that grace and peace can be multiplied unto us. We grow in grace that we may go with the message of grace into the world.

My grandson brought some homework from school last night. Rather than immediately beginning this work he called his girlfriend to have a little chat. That call was not a bad thing of itself. What made it wrong was that it preceded, and preempted, his time of study. He first looked for an enjoyment rather than looking to his employment of acquiring knowledge.

Peter is reminding us that we have brought home some "homework" from our salvation. This is not of the nature of grace as far as the initial salvation is considered. It is, however, a part of that salvation. It is our duty due to the great grace of salvation God has given to us.

It might be good to look at Ephesians 2:8-9 in this consideration. "For by grace are ye saved through faith; and that not of yourselves: *it is* the gift of God: Not of works, lest any man should boast." Salvation, even the faith of that salvation, is a gift from God. It has nothing to do with our own efforts.

But, salvation does entail certain presuppositions that we are honor bound to fulfill. Consider verse ten which immediately follows the above passage. "For we are his workmanship, created in Christ Jesus unto good works, which God hath before ordained that we should walk in them." Works flow *from* salvation rather than *to* salvation as most religious systems would suppose. We are not saved by our works and cannot be *kept saved* by any of our own works of piety. Salvation is entirely of God.

Peter is considering several things that we ought to do inside our salvation. None of these are works of grace as far as salvation is concerned. But, they are all works which flow from our response to that Grace whereby God has given us this great salvation. We are enjoined to give due diligence to these works which should flow from salvation as naturally as the intake of oxygen into our lungs presupposes that we will exhale.

As the act of breathing is only possible within the living organism, so is the reality of received grace and works within that grace only possible in one who has felt the living grace of God upon his soul.

That word "diligence" puts the burden of responding upon our persons. We "live out" the life which God has called us to in salvation.

The first thing mentioned is virtue. The word does not mean simply a life of perfect morality, although that meaning is surely included. The word is drawn from number 730 in Strong's. It is to be "manly," or of valor. Courageous in the face of opposition might be an acceptable translation. The meaning is that one is not afraid to stand for God and Godly principles regardless of the temptation to abandon principle, or the cost of such a stand.

When the Roman city of Pompeii was destroyed by the volcano, excavations found that the population had tried to hide, had tried to flee, or had simply "given up" and died where they were. An exception was that of a Roman guard who was found still at his post with his hand on his weapon. He did not flee; he stood his post of responsibility. This is the meaning of virtue in this passage.

To this virtue we are to add knowledge. This is more knowledge of the requirements and duties as soldiers in the Army of the Redeemed. We have this charge. Peter, an apostle of Jesus Christ, was well trained as one who had been with the Lord and had heard His teaching from his own ears.

Wouldn't it be wonderful if Peter and the other apostles were still alive? Think what a great treasure would be their remembrances of the Lord. Those apostles are all gone from this earth. But, we have their words and records. They left behind the memoirs of the Gospels. They left behind the teachings of the epistles. They left behind the prophecies of Revelation. They left behind the history of the early churches in The Acts of the Apostles. They left behind the Old Testament Scriptures which clearly speak of Jesus and our Christian walk.

If one is to seek knowledge, he must begin with a perusal of the inspired and preserved Words of God in the pages of Scripture. Beyond this he need not travel to find the knowledge of the Holy.]

1.6 *And to knowledge temperance; and to temperance patience; and to patience godliness;*

[You will notice in this list that there is neither progression nor "smorgasbord." Progression would suggest a ladder whereby we leave behind one step when we reach another step. The smorgasbord would suggest that we could simply "pick and choose." The argument is not to choose; it is an "all of the above" situation to which we are called. Properly understood this is not a progression; it is a collection. Don't leave any of these precious things behind. The loss will be your own if you do not "collect" all.

Many likened this concept to the Greek dancers who often held their hands one with another, linked in the line, as the danced upon the stage.

"Add to knowledge." As the saved of the earth we do not find the knowledge of our faith from the world. Neither do we find our standards among those of the world at large. I do see this beginning to happen more often in the churches as we have left the Standard of an inspired and preserved Scripture. Too many versions in our English language has left us with no Bible in our hands. I could go one step further and note that most of these "versions" have a base-line text which is culled from the minds of men "editing" which words they prefer rather and accepting the Words which God has given. The "Critical Text" is a text of faith in man and man's judgments with only the hope that they have become "closer" to what God "may have said." This is a sad and dangerous ground on which to base the eternal hope of one's immortal soul.

We find knowledge of the Holy, and for our walk in this present world, only through the Words of the inspired and preserved Scripture. In concert with this we pray to the Holy Spirit to find what is His illumination for our day and time. God's standards and methods do not change. We are called to be holy before men as we exercise faith in the Words and Person of The Eternal.

To this knowledge we add temperance. Temperance could easily be explained as self-control. I could give a very good illustration of this word by adding a picture of myself at this place. I am a few points past the point of obesity. This is a terrible witness to the world and a terrible failure before God. Simply admitting that it is true does not relieve my guilt.

The idea of temperance is to do good things in moderation when this concerns our own benefit. If I have enough food to reach my present proportions, it means that I have not supplied the needs of others even as I have abused my own body with gluttonous excess. That is a picture of Christian indifference and egocentrism.

The next example of temperance may surprise. Our knowledge must be tempered. What? In the time of the early Christian churches there was a group known as Gnostics. Their picture of salvation was tied to their knowledge. They believed themselves to be more knowledgeable and found knowledge to be the ultimate virtue.

There are actually times when the Scripture stands silent on various issues. I don't mean moral issues; the Scripture is very clear about these. But, there are other things where the Bible has not given us light past, "This Is Truth." How, for example, can God be One and yet The Son's subjection in all things to The Father during His earthly ministry is evident. We can explain that through the Kenosis Jesus accepted certain limitations as He laid aside His rightful glory to take upon Him the robes of the flesh of humanity; in this manner He became our example of how to live as human beings even as He gave His human life on the Cross to purchase our eternal salvation.

But, this does not really explain the concept of the Divine Trinity. Our illustrations, such as a cup of coffee with cream and sugar is one beverage although each element is noticeable, fall far short of describing the glory of the Divine Trinity.

How can we reconcile John 3:13, wherein Jesus says that He is in Heaven even as He is talking with Nicodemus in Jerusalem on earth? We cannot fully explain that mystery of Godliness.

Rather than arguing with God or dismissing the Truth as error, we simply trust God to explain our questions when we reach the shores of Glory. We trust the

Perfection of God and count our inability to completely understand as it is, a result of the sin of Adam passed down to all his children. In the arena of faith this is a simple reality we all find.

But, there are also those who consult extra-Biblical sources. The most popular of these is to consider the horoscopes in the daily newspapers. To involve oneself in these endeavors is to seek the answer of an occultist. This is seeking spiritual knowledge. But, it does not concern the Spirit of the Lord for it is as the worship of an idol. This is a knowledge which we don't need if we are trusting the Lord for our provision in this life. To seek this sort of knowledge is to accuse God of unrighteousness in "withholding" information from us. This is to bow down to the "tune of the tempter" as did Eve in the Garden of God's perfect provision.

We add temperance to our knowledge. To that we add patience. The old joke is, "Lord, I want patience. I ain't waiting. I want it NOW!"

The exercise of patience is the exercise of faith in God. To the generation which first received this epistle from Peter, this was probably seen as an injunction to have patience in persecution. But, there is more. There would be much less debt in the membership of the Christian churches if we would wait until we could afford that new car. We could wait until we had the cost needed to purchase. A little down and a little a week often adds up to nothing down and bondage to the broker for many months and years.

Patience displays faith in God. It also displays a responsible attitude to our neighbors as we live our Christian lives before them. Patience means that we keep our "animal instincts" under subjection to our spiritual responsibilities. The spirit is the singular place of happiness.

Add to this "godliness."

To live a "Godly" life is to live a life of piety. This isn't of necessity; it is of a desire to please the Lord Who died for us. In the parlance of the "street," "We owe Him. Big Time!" Godliness says that "We love Him. All the time."

Godliness is a worshipful attitude at all times. It is an adoring and magnifying response to our Lord and Savior. It is exhibited in a reverential fear of the Lord. Outwardly it is a stated regard for His Authority. Inwardly it is a love for the Lord which is evidenced by growing in His Grace.]

1.7   *And to godliness brotherly kindness; and to brotherly kindness charity.*

[Upon true Godliness will come brotherly kindness. This is speaking of love toward the fellowship. There must NEVER be "cliques and clacks" among the churches of our Lord. Cliques are groups that gather together considering them as "elites" among the brethren. A sure corollary of an elitist group is that others are subjugated as "beneath" the others. No Christian in any church is below anyone else.

Clacks are noises as snaps and bangs. There is normally a sound associated with a superior/inferior status. Arguments and weeping from one group and laughing and taunting from the other are heard throughout the churches of the land. This is a sad commentary on the state of too many of our "good fundamentalist churches" in this day.

It has been said that home is where you can go and they have to let you in. Too many "home churches" have to let some in but they really would rather not. When will we Christians realize that the churches are not social clubs.

I recently had a call from a man who was suicidal. Since the church where I presently pastor has been slated for soon closing, I was hesitant to call him to our church; if we do actually close it would be another blow for this man. I called one church in the city which I know to be sound doctrinally to send their bus to pick him up. He had requested to go to church. The pastor at the church I called said, "We can't have a man like that here. We have children that attend!"

What is the mission of a church which excludes the spiritually needy? What is the spiritual health of a church which seeks to exclude the children of God they find personally "offensive?" We have a need to preach the love of God. That, sadly but truthfully, is a place where too many "fundamentalist" churches fail their Lord and their mission.

The bridge from "love for the brethren" to "love (the meaning of "charity," of course) for all humanity," is broken if we forsake the brethren.

Past love for the brethren is love for the entire world. It may be "past" love for the brethren but it is the first order of spirituality. After salvation, we have a commission to find others who also need salvation. All of the above is the support system for John 3:16. We cannot call others to a faith which they cannot see. To what do we call them? From the natural standpoint we call others to the faith which we daily display before them.

We say, "What I have is what you need." What happens when they say, "I've already got much better than I see in you?"

James is a very practical Book. It does not, as many claim, teach any sort of "works salvation." It does teach a very reasonable enticement to Christianity by the lives of those who claim to have been transformed by Christianity.

Sorry to have been so negative. It is a reaction against myself! I often find myself not displaying all the love which God has shown to me. That is a very sad admission. That is a very sorry state of witness. That is a sin against the Holy God Who has given His Son to die for my great sin.]

1.8 *For if these things be in you, and abound, they make you that ye shall neither be barren nor unfruitful in the knowledge of our Lord Jesus Christ.*

[Here we have a promise attached to the exhortation of the previous few verses. If we live in the reality of these things we will be fruitful for God. The one who has followed the Lord will not be as a fallow field. A fallow field is one which has not been plowed or planted. My son is preparing his garden for this summer. Without this preparation he will not reap a harvest. There may be some "volunteer" plants grow up from last year's seed. This does not change the argument. Those volunteer plants are residual blessings from past activity.

The grace of God is not hampered by our inactivity. But, that grace will not be evident in our lives if we are not seriously following the Lord. Grace concerning salvation is not of us. Many have been saved who have refused to become servants. They lose much in the way of the blessings of the Christian life in this world and fail in the rewards they could have earned for the next.

One of the failings of the slothful Christian is that he will be denied, by denying himself, much personal, experimental knowledge of the Lord.]

1.9 *But he that lacketh these things is blind, and cannot see afar off, and hath forgotten that he was purged from his old sins,*

[Here is the argument concerning the Bible doctrine of the eternal security of the believer. The Christian noted here is both blind to the things of God and not walking in the way of the redeemed. He has even forgotten that his sins had been purged. He may have been a "fire brand;" instead he has become a burned out match.

This person is obviously saved. "...he was purged from his old sins." But, he has become carnal due to his refusing to become more spiritual. He is blind to the blessed reality of following Christ. He is perfectly able to see the near things but woefully unable to see the reality of the Heavenly and spiritual.

He is not no longer saved. He is now no longer walking in the faith. His salvation is assured; that is the work of God. His joy in the Lord and reward in the afterlife is missing as he fails to walk in the way of God's sufficiency and fellowship.

He walks as a blind man in the spiritual sense in his inability to see and reside in spiritual truths. The picture is not of a man totally sightless. Such a construct might argue for having "lost" his salvation. Since salvation has nothing to do with man but everything to do with Jesus, this is not a realistic possibility. The meaning of the verse is more of "near sightedness." He can see worldly delights but cannot discern heavenly truths.]

1.10 *Wherefore the rather, brethren, give diligence to make your calling and election sure: for if ye do these things, ye shall never fall:*

[Rather than being the "blind man" of the previous verse, Peter admonishes the believers to examine themselves to see if they really are in the faith. He tells them that this is an important examination. While such examination can never heal the lost soul, such examination may cause one who was not actually saved, to find true salvation.

The first thing to make sure is that the Spirit has ever convicted them of sin and the need for salvation. If this has been done the next thing is to examine their election. We do this by pointing back to a time of commitment to Christ. Have we ever really accepted Him as Savior? If we have really done so we are saved. This proves both the calling of conviction, and election, the result of such calling upon the heart of the penitent.

If these things are done, and we have begun to exhibit the fruits of spiritual life as described in verses five through seven, we will show ourselves to be true children of God. We will be examined and found born again.

Here Peter assures us that we will never fall from grace once we have entered into that grace. The verse does not suggest that we might fall. Rather the verse says that once our true piety is confirmed in Christ we can never fall from grace. A true Christian, confirmed by the Savior and by our own examination can never stumble and fall from that grace. This is the argument of the verse.]

1.11 *For so an entrance shall be ministered unto you abundantly into the everlasting kingdom of our Lord and Saviour Jesus Christ.*

[Today I was offered a seat on one of the "honor flights" whereby former service men and women are offered a trip to see the monuments to them and their service.

About twenty years ago Linda and I visited Washington, D.C. We visited many of these same monuments. We were simple tourists. The concept of the "honor flights" is to offer special honor and dignity to the nations former fighting men.

This is somewhat the distinction given to these "overcomers." We see a special honor given to Stephen, the first recorded martyr of the Christian Church, when Jesus actually stood to welcome him into Heaven. (Acts 7:55) None of us should ever expect such an honor. It will be honor enough, and more, just to hear Him say, "Well done." (Matthew 25:23)

May we each live to hear the voice of our Lord welcome us into His eternal presence.]

1.12 *Wherefore I will not be negligent to put you always in remembrance of these things, though ye know them, and be established in the present truth.*

[In the third chapter of Ecclesiastes there is a list of "times to..." As Paul in the fifth chapter of Hebrews, verse thirteen, laments the fact that he must speak of the "milk of the word," so does Peter nearly glory in that fact. Peter seems to say, "I am going to tell you the rudiments of the faith over and over until you understand them."

Indeed, there is often a need to remind people that Jesus Christ died in time so that others might live in eternity. This is not mere redundancy; this is remarkable reality. Many preachers are so insecure of their own worth that they attempt to come up with "new" things by which to dazzle the congregation. Many preachers and Bible teachers have gone this route. Most of them have become leaders of cultish religion.

Peter says that his duty is to remind people of the rudiments of the faith. He wants to see them established in the Truth of which he now speaks. But, even in this his desire is that the people of God continue in the old, old story of Jesus and His love.

"You have heard this before; it nonetheless bears repeating." Peter, as a teacher of the Gospel understood that redundancy leads to understanding.

We have an old Book. Since it was given to man in time, from God in eternity, it's message may be old but it's teaching is forever now with the fact of eternity upon the Words of God.]

1.13 *Yea, I think it meet, as long as I am in this tabernacle, to stir you up by putting you in remembrance;*

[A tabernacle is a tent wherein a person lives; it is an encampment. By using this idiom Peter was establishing his belief that the body is not the life of a person; instead it is that where the life resides.

Peter says that as long as the breath of his life resides in his body he has the duty to remind the people of the rudiments of the faith in order that they are stirred up, agitated, to consider the things of Christ and His death, resurrection, teaching and love for them. He would see them encouraged to live for Him Who died for them. He wishes for the people to be established in the faith. He wants them excited to witness themselves to the saving Truth of Messiah.]

1.14 *Knowing that shortly I must put off this my tabernacle, even as our Lord Jesus Christ hath shewed me.*

[Whether this from the incident in the twenty-first chapter of John, or by a recent revelation, Peter understood that his physical demise would shortly come to pass. Since he would no longer be able to personally teach these people, his desire was to remind them as often as was possible of those things pertaining to salvation and holy living.

It appears that his understanding was his advancing age, Jesus had said that his demise would come when he was old. (John 21:18) Each of us must sail past time on this river of mortality. Each of us, unless the Lord soon appears to call us to Himself in the air, must soon pass from this tabernacle of earthly existence. May this understanding both be to excite us of our eternal bliss and burden us with the need to work for the Master while there is yet day within this tabernacle of our physical life. (John 9:4)

The night soon comes to each of us when we wake from this dream of physical reality and rise to the day of eternal reward. Will our reward be of seeing our works endure or of seeing our labors as only wood, hay and stubble? (I Corinthians 3:12) May our view of the day of eternity encourage our work in this shadow day of time.

Many continue to prepare for a short human retirement. Few, it seems, prepare for the endless reality of eternity.]

1.15 *Moreover I will endeavor that ye may be able after my decease to have these things always in remembrance.*

[Peter knew that he would soon be leaving his body behind while his soul traveled to the blessed presence of The Master. Thus, the word he used for decease is of a departing not of simply a death. While men to this day still argue about the possibility of an "after-life," the Christian already has the assurance of that truth. Physical death is not the end of existence but the beginning of a wonderful adventure which will carry us throughout the endless "age" of eternity.

It is somehow incredulous that we would carefully pack clothes and provision for a weeklong vacation each year even as we are prone to never consider the preparation for the eternal journey of what we call an "after life." Folks, there is no proper consideration of an "after" life. We fail to realize that this short physical journey is but a "pre-life" when compared to our eternal abode and existence.

Part of the preparation for Peter was to preach the truth, and to write the truth as we see at this place, that eternity is long. To make any search for true happiness must consider this fact. The days of our physical life are but a preparation for the unending day of our eternal existence.

Peter considered this testimony of his Lord so important that he committed it to writing. An "oral tradition" is fine; but it is subject to being born away on the winds of time. The Scripture is the inspired and preserved Words of God for all eternity. To consign this Scripture to decay due to the faultiness of time is an insult to the God Who singularly inspired these truths. We say of a couple being married, "What God hath joined together may no man cut asunder."

Folks, if we can say that of a union of two bodies of temporal clay, can we not understand that this is even more imperative when we consider the eternal Words which God has given to us! The Holy Bible of God's inerrant Words is the Bible for yesterday, today, and for all of the tomorrows of eternity. This Book is the written record of the Words which God has spoken to mankind. In there, alone, we find the truth of our existence and the overriding glory of The God Who has created all.

Had this Scripture actually been tainted by the sands of time we would argue that Peter was mistaken. It would, then, follow that Scripture was not perfectly the eternal Words of God. If Scripture is not eternal and perfect we have nothing on which to base any claim of either God's power or existence.]

1.16 *For we have not followed cunningly devised fables, when we made known unto you the power and coming of our Lord Jesus Christ, but were eyewitnesses of his majesty.*

[Peter assures his readers that this story about Jesus is not one which he had heard from someone else.

We have all heard of "Urban Legends." There were many cults around the time of Jesus, I believe inspired of Satan, where a virgin birth and a resurrection were attributed to some person or other. None of these cultish endeavors had the volume of martyrdom associated with them which accompanied the spread of true Christianity. A prankster, a charlatan, and a true martyr are not made of the same "stuff." The false, when faced with persecution will quickly recant. The true, who had seen these things about Jesus willingly suffered and died for the Truth they had witnessed and experience.

Such was the fervor of the testimony and life of the apostles and early Christians that no one could seriously doubt their message. These were people who staked their very lives on the Truth of the Message, the death, the burial, the resurrection and the ascension of Jesus. He was real and they were transformed by Him. The Spirit gave them both direction and boldness. This was not a "religion;" this was a reality – and they knew it!

Beyond this, Peter – along with James and John, had witnessed the glory of Jesus in the transfiguration. They had heard the voice of The Father speak concerning The Son. The resurrection had convinced a frightened group that their Lord was real and alive. The ascension had been witnessed by about five hundred persons. They had all of this to draw upon, plus the teaching of Jesus and the confirmation of the Holy Spirit, that this same Jesus would appear a second time to rapture the faithful from this earth. This was one of the earliest doctrines of the Church. Jesus is coming back! Maranatha!

This was no fable to the early church; this was blessed reality.]

1.17 *For he received from God the Father honour and glory, when there came such a voice to him from the excellent glory, This is my beloved Son, in whom I am well pleased.*

[Peter is probably referring to the Transfiguration when he says that God honored and glorified Jesus. At that time the voice of the Father spoke of the Son. He said that He was well pleased with Jesus and instructed those apostles present to hear the words of Jesus.

The same thing had also happened at the baptism of Jesus. Only, at this time the Holy Spirit, in the form of a dove, said those words about Jesus. (Matthew 3:17; 17:5; Mark 1:11; 9:7; Luke 3:22; 9:35)

We must also remark that the ascension, accompanied by angels (as had been at his birth) was the stamp of the approval of The Father upon the work of Jesus.

The first of these events was witnessed by John the Baptist and his disciples. The second was witnessed by Peter, James and John. The third was witnessed by "about 500 persons." Peter continued to make the point that this was no fantasy; this was a fact of history authenticated by physical eye witnesses. (I Corinthians 15:6)]

1.18 *And this voice which came from heaven we heard, when we were with him in the holy mount.*

[The mount was sanctified as holy by the presence of the glorified Son of God. It is interesting to note that Sinai was also called a holy mount as it hosted the Glory of God before Moses. The relationship of The Son with the reality of The Father give testimony to the fact that Jesus is God.

Peter, James and John had all confirmed the same incident. At the time of this writing James had been already martyred. We do, however see the same appeal to being eyewitnesses to the glory of Jesus from I John 1:1-3. The apostles do not tell different stories about their experiences with Jesus. They do often give stories which expand the reality of the events as they give more information from one place to another. This information is never contradictory.

The writing by Pilate on the placard which was placed on the Cross with the "crime" committed by the condemned are expansions which fully give the statement when all are considered. I quote from the Scofield Reference Bible, "No one of the Evangelists quotes the entire inscription. All have 'The King of the Jews.' Luke adds to this the further words, 'This is' Matthew quotes the name, 'Jesus' whilst John gives the additional words 'of Nazareth.' The narratives combined give the entire inscription: 'This is [Matthew, Luke] Jesus [Matthew, John] of Nazareth [John] the King of the Jews [all].'"

Thus inspired Scripture is seen not to be simply a "copied memo." It is the actual remembrance of real people who wrote down real memories under the influence of the Holy Spirit to give us the Words of God.]

1.19 *We have also a more sure word of prophecy; whereunto ye do well that ye take heed, as unto a light that shinneth in a dark place, until the day dawn, and the day star arise in your hearts:*

[A more sure word of prophecy? At this time the people had the entire Old Testament Scripture. At this time the apostles had walked with the Lord, absorbing His teaching for more than three years. At this time the miraculous *sign gifts* were in operation within the churches. How could this Scripture even suggest that there is a "more sure" word of prophecy?

Consider that this was said even while all the above was true. Peter wrote to his contemporaries. Although they did not yet possess the entire New Testament it is certain that the bulk of the Word was already in circulation within the churches of the community of the believers.

That "more sure word" was based upon the fact of the Holy Spirit residing within the hearts of the believers. This was not something which would override the prophecies of the Old Testament. This was something, Someone, Who would confirm the truth of those Words of the Hebrew Scriptures.

The story of the events of the earthly ministry, the death, the burial, the resurrection and the ascension of Jesus would serve, as facts were brought to mind, to establish the reality of the Old Testament. Those Words of the Hebrew Scriptures spoke of Jesus in prophecy and type. The experience of the apostles, and even more importantly the work of the Spirit on the hearts of the redeemed, would serve to open those Scriptures of the Old Testament even beyond what the unconverted could possibly have imagined.

Even the "sign gifts" were intended to point the eyes of the people to those inspired and preserved Words of God which were then in existence in this world. The impact of the miraculous was not intended to convert people, although under the power and leading of the Spirit such would occur from time to time. The purpose of those sign gifts was to confirm the Scriptural message of the reality of Christ. (Romans 10:17) The miracles were to show that the power of God rested upon those who trusted the inspired and preserved Words of God.

Peter is, of course, also claiming that his own story, given in pen and ink which testified to Christ, would be available to the churches – and the Christians of those churches – down through the ages of time. It is debatable whether or not Peter was claiming inspiration for his own words. It could well be that the Spirit had impressed this fact upon him.

That is honestly a question which is not important. Whether or not Peter sensed the reality of the inspiring Word of God upon these Words is immaterial. The obvious fact of inspiration has been revealed to the pure churches and blood-bought believers. The intellectual assent of Peter is ultimately not necessary. The Spirit has spoken.

Those early sign gifts have passed into history. They are rarely operative in our day. God can and will revive that reality when it would serve His purpose in this world. But, by and large, those gifts are related only in the histories of Scripture.

However, we still have the completed record of the New Testament, completed by the Revelation of Jesus as given to John on Patmos. We still have the record of the Old Testament which remains a part of the inspired and preserved Words of God. Most importantly, we still have the witness of the Spirit; He illumines His Word and empowers His servants.

Yes; we do still have a more sure word of prophecy! These are illuminated by the Light of the Day of the Lord. Jesus is our Lamp Who leads to truth.]

1.20 *Knowing this first, that no prophecy of the scripture is of any private interpretation.*

[The Roman Church would argue that this verse means that no person may interpret the Scripture. Their argument on this verse is that only The Church - meaning their corporate church, has the right to give meaning to what the Scripture says.

In part they are correct. No person may interpret the Scripture on his own. However, it is not the Roman Church, or any other church body, which has the right to interpret the Scripture.

The Spirit illumines the Scripture to individual Christians. In this way the churches are given the message of God. Along with this concept we must consider this verse in its context. The context, the very next verse, is an allusion to the entirety of Scripture. Many men wrote, as they were moved by the Spirit, but they wrote one volume. The Scripture is not a hodge podge of "sayings;" the Scripture is unified volume which speaks of one unfolding story.

With this spiritual principle in mind we may see that when one man has "found" a new interpretation, one with which no one else has seen in that passage, this person is wrong. If one Spirit illumines the Body of Christ, an aberrant interpretation is a cancer upon that Body. It is not of God. The writer of Ecclesiastes wrote about men when he said, "The thing that hath been, it *is that* which shall be, and that which is done *is* that which shall be done: and *there is* no new *thing* under the sun." (Ecclesiastes 1:9)

This is also true in the matter of interpretation of the Scripture. A "new" thing is an aberration in the discussion of the Old Book. This is not to say that God can not speak from His Word in this day. He can and does. But, if an application is found which has sprung from relating the old principles of Scripture to a new age, that application will be confirmed by the Spirit in illumining many Christians.

A single person with a new "idea" is more likely led by his own pride rather than the leading of the Spirit. Anyone who tries to tell you that he has rediscovered the lost doctrine of primitive Christianity is also in error. He is putting his own understanding above the preserving power of God. Jesus promised to sustain His churches. He has always kept His churches, sometimes a remnant to be sure, in line with His established doctrine and polity.

Another consideration of this verse, especially in light of the appeal to the entirety of the writing of Scripture, is that no one verse may be emphasized above others. "Proof Texting," whereby one seeks verse support of aberrant doctrine, is not allowed. Scripture must be compared with Scripture. We cannot say, "Do not judge others," while ignoring the need to "try the spirits."

Simply put, we cannot build doctrine on one verse. We must search out the entirety of the Scriptural record if we are to understand what God has said. "Study to shew thyself approved unto God, a workman that needeth not to be ashamed, rightly dividing the word of truth." (II Timothy 2:15)]

1.21 *For the prophecy came not in old times by the will of man, but holy men of God spake as they were moved by the Holy Ghost.*

[What was it that made these men holy? It was the power of God displayed through them. Check out these men in Scripture and you will see that they were flawed. It was the power of God displayed on, and in, them that produced the Bible. It was not their own human goodness. The Spirit moved upon these men so that they wrote down the inspired Words of God. It is good, of course, that God in His wisdom did inspire those Words rather than those men. If the inspiration lies upon the Words, then we still have a Message which we can trust today in the faithful transmission of those Words. We have, in reality, the inspired Message in faithful copies of those very words. (see II Peter 1:21) The men who wrote were mere mortal men. But the God, Who inspired their writings, is Supernatural and Powerful in that He could take these men and produce His Book.

Preservation, in a real sense, is no different. The copyists who faithfully made copy upon copy of this Word were mortal men. But the Holy Spirit worked to providentially preserve that which had been inspired.]

SECOND PETER - CHAPTER TWO

2.1   But there were false prophets also among the people, even as there shall be false teachers among you, who privily shall bring in damnable heresies, even denying the Lord that bought them, and bring upon themselves swift destruction.

[This chapter begins with a warning. The previous chapter had ended on a very high note of respect for the inspired and preserved Words of God. The last verse of that first chapter notes that "For the prophecy came not in old time by the will of man: but *holy* men of God spake *as they were* moved by the Holy Ghost."

There is a recurring theme in the Old Testament historical Books toward the end of the Kingdom of Judah. "They say, 'The Lord has said,' when He has not said." It is often the very error of the false which points to the truth of the righteous leading of God. Anyone can claim to speak the Words of the Lord. That is the meaning of the word "prophesy." Prophesy is not necessarily examining the future. True prophecy may, however, include that reality as prophecy is primarily the telling of the Words of God.

Peter is warning his readers that the methods of even religious leaders must be examined to see if they are teaching the Words of God. The standard to which all must be compared is the Words of the inspired and preserved Scripture. A thing may seem good and proper and reasonable. None of that matters. The only true consideration must be whether or not a thing stands in concert with the inerrant Scripture. (Romans 3:4) We are not bound to trust any prophet. We are bound to trust the Scripture. A prophet who speaks contrary to Scripture is Ichabod. (I Samuel 4:21) But, in this case the Ark of God's presence has not departed from Israel but the prophet has separated himself, and his words, from the presence of God.

We must consider that we ought not to "proof text" or "version hop" in hopes of finding some small passage to agree with our view. Rather, we should consider that if we are to be true in our belief and teaching we must agree with the Words of God.

Peter's warning is that there were false prophets among the "people," that is among the Hebrew of old. We have alluded to that above. But, he also warns the people that there will be false prophets among them. Folks, any allusion to "them" is as among us as warning to be considered among us as well. We are still members of the same Church which Jesus founded. We may not be of the Church of Ephesus or Jerusalem but we are members of the Church of the Lord.

Satan hates those churches which stand true to the Words of God and witness of those words to the salvation of souls. Satan desires to "bring the gates of hell" (Matthew 16:18) against the witness and work of those churches and the saints who populate them. Some churches, and some saints, have fallen prey to the pernicious power of the unholy spirit of the age. But, although some, and often many unto a preponderance of professing churches have slid from the "faith once delivered," (Jude 3) God has always reserved to Himself a remnant true to Him and His Word. From time to time the true Church has been wounded but never defeated!

The problem has been that some have brought "damnable heresies" into the purity of the church bodies. Clarke, and a few others, argue that this should be "destructive heresies" as the same word translated as "damnable" in the mid-section of this verse is translated as "destruction" in the last word of the verse.

There is no mistranslation at this point. The word, "apoleia," is number 684 in Strong's. Both "destruction" and "damnation" are acceptable. "from a presumed derivative of 622; ruin or loss (physical, spiritual or eternal):--damnable(-nation), destruction, die, perdition, X perish, pernicious ways, waste."

In the first instance the word is used as an adjective to modify – or explain, the nature of the heresies. In the last instance it is the word which is being modified to explain a sudden destruction. Two different situations explain the need for the translators to use their skills to bring the sense of the Greek into our English ears.

The phrase "denying the Lord" could be considered that someone had been saved and then lost his salvation by renouncing the Lord and His salvation. The argument would be that this act of a Christian had brought "swift destruction" upon himself.

That understanding has no support in this verse. Although the phrase is "denying the Lord that bought them," this does not necessarily refer to one who has been saved. "To be bought" is not identical to having been purchased from sin. It is true that Jesus paid the price of salvation at the Cross. It is not true that every person has been saved because of His Self-Sacrifice. It is obvious that one who denies the Lord Who has paid the price, is not one who has applied the effects of the Cross to themselves. They have denied the Lord in that they have not received Him as Savior.

Part of the dynamic of these "deniers" is that they have brought in "damnable heresy" into the assembly. An obvious "damnable heresy" is to reject, deny, the fact that faith in Jesus – and in Him only – is the only means of salvation. Consider Acts 4:12 in reference to this. Thus this heretical teaching, be it salvation from works or membership in a "religious" organization, automatically disqualifies one from the full faith in Christ which effects true salvation.

The denial of Jesus, The Lord, means that the one described in this verse cannot be a Christian in either the Biblical or Spiritual sense. A "cultural Christian" is devoid of the indwelling of the Spirit. His works, though those works be seen as "good" in the view of the world to include the Spiritual world. But, in such a case the works suggest a "religious lifestyle;" the doctrine which sees no need to fully accept Christ will argue against Godly righteousness and salvation.

The acceptance of a "damnable heresy" is that which brings "swift destruction." That this destruction may come in the existence to come does not mean it is not swift. Time, we must remember, is the short precursor of the reality of eternity.]

2.2 *And many shall follow their pernicious ways, by reason of whom the way of truth shall be evil spoken of.*

[Not only do those who espouse those "damnable heresies" follow those heresies to perdition, they attract followers who follow the same path to the same damnation."

There are several reasons given that some of the people will follow these "leaders into perdition." Verses 14 and 18 of this chapter suggest sexual, or "fleshy," sins which appeal to the soulish desires rather than to the pure Spirit of God. Verse 10 suggests that those who follow are beguiled by pride and the lack of restraint upon their spiritual selves. Verse 19 is likened unto verse 20 in that the exercise of "liberty" – not the freedom from sin which Jesus offers the repentant but the liberty to exercise one's own opinion without regard to any ill influence which may be brought against another.

These inducements to live sinful lives are brought by supposed religious teachers. As the false prophets of the kingdoms of Israel and Judah, these false prophets claim to have a message from God even though their message is clearly one which is not grounded in "the way of Truth" of the true doctrine of God.

It is a good thing to always remember this fractured line from the musical "Porgy and Bess," "The things that your 'preacher' is lauble to teach you, they ain't necessarily true." It is true that false scriptures (so called) and false doctrine (though promulgated in flowery religious sounding words) "ain't necessarily so." The true inspired and preserved Words of God are the "Ways of Truth." All others, even when placed on very real appearing road signs, are false and will lead to the broad road of destruction.

Remember that Satan's argument was very persuasive to Eve in the Garden. Remember, also that Adam took the persona of a lemming and followed Eve from the ground of God's perfections to the drowning in Satan's lie.

These spoken of in the verse also led others into the broad road of destruction. Some did this by displaying a life style so ungodly as to repulse even the worldly people. Some did this by displaying the "best" of the worldly life-style. A "seeker friendly" life, which denies the seminal doctrine and standards of the churches which Christ established, is more often the one seeking a false spiritual life rather than offering a pure spiritual life. (Romans 12:2)]

2.3 *And through covetousness shall they with feigned words make merchandise of you: whose judgment now of a long time, lingereth not, and their damnation slumbereth not.*

[Here is a warning to all those who have been, or are being, duped by false teachers. I think it good at this place to consider that not all false teachers are preaching false doctrine.

What?

There are those who are in the ministry because a friend, a relative, or even a pastor, have "prophesied over" and deemed as called of God even though this "call" seems a surprise to God! This does happen. Sometimes there is one who does preach the pure gospel but has never been gifted with the charismatic gift of being an elder, or pastor. Although preaching only the pure gospel, he will find in his wake harmed churches and people because he has "chosen the ministry" as a position when God's best might have been to teach a Sunday School class and sell insurance.

Though the impact is mainly benign, this person will also harm the churches and people of God as he extends himself beyond the position to which God has honestly called him. To those he has "lost," he will comfort himself with the phrase, "They just could not endure sound doctrine." What are the "ripple effects" of disobedience to God? We may be assured that these ripples will rock many a boat in the river of God's work on earth.

There is also the person who believes that it is his purpose to set the doctrine of humanity on a proper course. Unfortunately, he defines this course by his own agenda. There will be false doctrine, false promise, false reality and the honest reality of a Hellish future for those who follow this doctrine, man and religious system but have

SECOND PETER: Chapter 2

never had the true faith of the True Christ to find True Salvation.

Lest we forget, there is also the truly God-called who has found that to "go along and get along" is easier than standing firm in the faith. He may "preach" the Truth but in practice will "shave the edges" so he can get along with the parishioners. This may be the most pernicious of all. This one must understand that preaching is not the sum total of pastoring. Preaching is a simple activity of oratory. Pastoring is an overwhelming responsibility to God and to those who sit under this preaching. They will never go beyond the level of their leader. When the "leader" is ready for compromise so are the people.

A holy boldness is necessary even when, especially when, it seems very uncomfortable to do so!

Each of these seeks something. Each of these uses the weapon of the pulpit to garner the game of something. For the first it may be to prove that the prophecy of the icon of their early youth was correct. They seek to please their spiritual parent. They may even be trying to please themselves.

For the second it may be to see the world finally understand what they have found. There seems nothing wrong with this, I suppose. The wrong lies in the fact that they are preaching an error and multiplying the sin of another.

The error of the third is much the same as the error of the second. Pride is the problem. He may be preaching truth but in his compromise he is demonstrating error. He probably will not see this fact. But, when he stands before God he must give an account of his leadership. He must give an account for the leading others have taken from his own error.

All of these will used "feigned" words, manufactured words, to cause others to hold to them. Money may not be the biggest goal. A manner of respect may be the goal. Self-fulfillment may be the goal. The sad reality is that the people these men "serve" are but chess pieces on the game board of the pastor's ego.

These will find judgment at the end of the "game." Those chess pieces which played out the goal of the pastors were real people whose relationship with God was underdeveloped because they were led into the world of the "LEADER" rather than into the fellowship of the Lord.

God has not been sleeping while all this has been happening. God has patiently waited for, the Spirit has argued the need for, repentance from error, rejection of the false, repentance from sin. The paycheck will be printed and passed out. This will be a sad day when we find the taxes we still owe to the Kingdom of God because of our military dereliction of duty towards the people we ill-served.

Responsibility, folks, that is the real purpose of standing behind the pulpit of our Lord Jesus Christ as we speak of His Truth, His Leadership, and His Reality as the Real Lord and Object of Worship.]

2.4 *For if God spared not the angels that sinned, but cast them down to hell, and delivered them into chains of darkness, to be reserved unto judgment;*

Jude 6

[Note the progression of this and the following verses. Before this verse there was a short conversation concerning those who would lead others to stray from God through "damnable heresies." The conversation now concerns the fallen angels. There is a connection in that both angels and religious teachers are expected to be ones who carry the message of God to the people of God. There will be a divergence in the following verses as God pours forth the promise of mercy and regeneration, not always accepted but always available, toward the humans.

There is no such mercy suggested concerning these angels. We are reminded that the great Self-Sacrifice of Jesus upon the Cross was intended to offer salvation for the sins of the world. In the Kenosis, the temporary laying aside of His Rightful Glory as God, Jesus identified with humanity. In this He was offered in our place as one of us.

This identification was never made with the angelic hosts. This also renders those theologies false which postulate that Jesus was a created being only *promoted* unto His Seat of Divinity. In point of fact, Jesus was never *created*. He is God, the Son, for all of eternity. I make no claim to understand the mystery of the Triune Existence of God. As someone once said, "God said it. I believe it. That settles it." That's not exactly a true statement. God said it and that settles it. My requirement is to accept what God has said. I cannot meaningfully confirm, nor should I try!, that which I must immediately accept as the Word of Truth.

Clarke seems to look at the immediately following verse and place this event concerning the fallen angels at the time of the Flood. I disagree. I would argue that this happened in eternity past before the creation of this world. Matthew 25:41 speaks of the judgment of these fallen angels. "Then shall he say also unto them on the left hand, Depart from me, ye cursed, into everlasting fire, prepared for the devil and his angels..."

This puts the entire "time frame" of the fall of the angels as synonymous with the fall of Satan. The great sin of Satan, of course, was his great pride which caused him to consider raising his own throne above that of God. Such, of course, would not have been possible. Since these fallen angels are called "his" (meaning Satan's) angels, it would seem obvious that they both joined Satan in his quest and owned him as their leader. Thus, we see that hell is a prepared place for those who refuse the position as subservient to God.

There is also a progression in this act. First, the angels are "cast down." The very word "cast" implies a greater power being inflicted upon a lesser power. Since the Bible almost unfailingly speaks of "up" as a superior position over "down;" up is "good" and down is "bad," we find that Satan – and his cadre of angels – is forcibly removed from a favorable position into an inferior position. This is analogous to our understanding as Heaven being above and earth being below.

Hell would be lower still. This, in fact is the meaning of the word "hell" in this place. Strong's "5020. ...tar-tar-o'-o from Tartaros (the deepest abyss of Hades); to incarcerate in eternal torment:--cast down to hell."

We are thus shown that Hell, the abode of the damned, is the antithesis of the glory and bliss of Heaven. This is a striking thought!

The damned are delivered, themselves, to this pit in chains. The picture of the chains as "chains of darkness" is another counter-point to the glories of Heaven. Revelation 21:23 describes the "New Jerusalem" of the restored creation. "And the city had no need of the sun, neither of the moon, to shine in it: for the glory of God did lighten it, and the Lamb is the light thereof." Beyond this, John 1:8 describes Jesus as "Light." The reality of Hell is that it is a place of utter darkness as it is devoid of God,

SECOND PETER: Chapter 2

and the pleasures of God which He created for the joy of His creation.

The chains of darkness bind one from the "Light of the World, Jesus Christ."

The "reservation" for this judgment does not need a RSVP. The chains assure the arrival of all of the guests.]

2.5 *And spared not the old world, but saved Noah the eighth person, a preacher of righteousness, bringing in the flood upon the world of the ungodly;*

[Now we begin to understand the progression of the fact of grace and mercy into the world of creation.

First, we must realize that there was an "old" world before the flood. The "old" world was of the perfect creation of God. Much of the physicality of that perfection remained. I would believe that the "old" world was of but one large continent. Genesis 1:9 describes the act whereby God separated the water from the dry land. "And God said, Let the waters under the heaven be gathered together unto one place, and let the dry *land* appear: and it was so."

Since "mayim," (4325 in Strong's Hebrew) simple means "water," and "yam" (5220 in Strong's Hebrew) simply means a body of water it could very well be inferred that there was only one large ocean (sea) formed in the original creation of the earth as modified for the presence of man. This is even more strongly to be considered when we read that the waters were gathered together.

This, if there was an absence of modern mountains, would make one large and easily journeyed land mass. Since the animals of creation were to "be fruitful and multiply," and man was to both "replenish" and exercise dominion over the creation of God, (Genesis 1:28) this concept of one land mass with hills but not mountains seems reasonable as to the facts of the situation.

The flood was devastating time for all of the creation. I believe that part of the breaking up of the fountains of the deep (Genesis 7:11) was the time that the tectonic plates were induced to begin their movements which would produce mountains and continental drift.

This picture is a near necessity. Scripture states that the ark landed on the mountains of Ararat. (Genesis 8:4) I would imagine that the "Mountains of Ararat" were mere hills at that time which would grow into the mountain range seen today. All of the animals on the ark would need to disembark to begin their journeys to the ends of the earth. This would explain the different species in some locations. Not all would follow the same "map" to a new homeland.

Many of those animals could not traverse a mountain terrain.

Genesis 10:25 informs us that during the life-time of Peleg the earth began to divide. Most commentators see this as a dispersion due to the language multiplication at the Tower of Babel. That is possible. But, I would see this as the time when the continents and islands of the sea began to depart one from another and begin to "strand" certain people and animals in the locations to which they had traveled. The earth itself dispersed the population.

We thus see a "new" earth, as opposed to the old pre-flood earth.

Noah was not the eighth person from creation. Neither, in all probability, was he the eighth "preacher of righteousness." The meaning is simply that Noah was the eighth person on the ark. There were seven before him. He was the human leader of the group.

We do see that Noah spent time preaching righteousness to the people of his day. Due to his preaching his three sons, their wives, and his own wife were saved from the flood in the same ark of safety which gave him salvation. Our duty is to call others to the same salvation which we enjoy in Jesus Christ!

The rebellious, ungodly, of the earth were punished for their sins of rebellion against the rightful ruler of the universe. But, in the very fact of their judgment we begin to see the mercy of God spreading into the life of Noah, his three sons, and the wives of them all.]

2.6   And turning the cities of Sodom and Gomorrah into ashes condemned them with an overthrow, making them an ensample unto those that after should live ungodly;

[After the mercy shown in the flood, Sodom and Gomorrah are obvious demonstrations that the mercy and forbearance of God is not a license to sin. It is a means of restoring fellowship with God even for those who have been gross sinners in rejecting His leadership.

There are several lessons to be learned from the judgment of God upon these cities. The first, of course, is that God does always judge sin. We may account this judgment as being slow in coming. We need to realize that this is the grace of God being poured out upon the earth. But, eventually sin will find its just punishment from the Just Judge. God would be neither true to His Own Holiness nor to the truly righteous if He was to renounce judgment and condone sin.

In the thirteenth chapter of Genesis we find the incident where Lot and Abraham were to separate their herds because both of them were too richly blessed to continue to allow their herds to graze on the same land. In verse ten and eleven we see that Lot chose the better land.

The destruction of Sodom and Gomorrah is a lesson that what looks good to the world will not always be the best thing spiritually. The sin of Sodom and Gomorrah is a lesson that sin destroys the best man can find.

The ashes of Sodom and Gomorrah are mute testimonies to the fact that the fire of Hell is real. It is to be shunned by seeking the Ark of the Safety of Jesus Christ and His free offer of salvation.]

2.7   And delivered just Lot, vexed with the filthy conversation of the wicked:

[I would ask you to realize that this was written *after* Lot's drunken failure at the cave. (Genesis 19:30-38) This is also a lesson. It is a lesson that the love of God looks far beyond the look of man. We would look at the evidence:

1) Rather than trusting God, Lot sought the best land that man could see. (Genesis 15:9-13)

2) Rather than separating himself from sinners, Lot remained in an unholy situation with unholy men. (II Corinthians 6:27)

3) Rather than living such a witness before men that they would recognize his piety, Lot was simply expected to comply with the request of the ungodly. (Genesis 19:5-9)

4) Lot knew the wickedness of those he dwelt among. (Genesis 19:1-3)

5) Lot allowed his elder daughters to marry outside the faith and into the cesspool of sin!

6) It has been suggested by some that when the forces of Abraham's servants, and a few more, rescued Lot from the five kings in Genesis chapter fourteen, that Lot may have considered his return to Sodom by Abraham to be a tacit approval of his residence in the city. I am certain that Abraham knew of the sin of Sodom; he did not intend to give approval to his nephew of any residence among these sinful people.

However, we have record of neither approval nor disapproval communicated to Lot from Abraham concerning his abode. May we learn that the silence of a pious person as to a matter is to give silent assent to the sin. One must wonder how many we have led *from* following the Lord by selfishly considering that we have no standing to address obvious inducements to sin in the life of another.

The communication of the intent and leading of God will always lead away from sin and toward holiness.

God, however, looked beyond the "evidence" and saw the truth. The heart of Lot was troubled by the sin of the people. His own heart was pure even though his judgment may have failed him. What we might rightly call sin and poor judgment on the part of Lot was covered by the mercy of God and the pure heart of Lot in the land of heinous sin. The entire experience of salvation is based on the mercy of God. We have nothing to offer in the way of righteous. God accepts us as we are, in Lot's case this was Sodom, and moves us from the city of sin by the leading of The Spirit.]

2.8 *(For that righteous man dwelling among them, in seeing and hearing, vexed his righteous soul from day to day with their unlawful deeds,)*

[The truly pious man living in the midst of an unclean people may keep quiet and maintain his own integrity. However, the ramifications of this are to lack and real testimony among the heathen and to see his own family depart from his piousness and consider him as "out of touch with the reality of life as it honestly, in their view, exists." With no history to give credence to his claims, Lot was scoffed at as being himself a mocker rather than a leader to the things of God. (Genesis 19:14)

Lot was well vexed, daily, in his heart and soul by the wickedness of the city. He took no part in the licentious behavior. But, by all appearances he never voiced a disapproval of the vice of the city. The story is told of a young man who went to a godless university. After a year away from home on this ungodly campus he came back to his old church. His pastor asked, "Have you had any trouble because of your Christian faith?"

The young man answered, "No. I have lived so no one can even suspect that I am a Christian."

It is always true that a Christian lifestyle, with no vocalized Christian testimony, is an advertisement that "All is well with the world as it is. There is no need to turn to Christ." It becomes a vocal testimony for a Christless life and a Hellish eternity!]

2.9 *The Lord knoweth how to deliver the godly out of temptations, and to reserve the unjust unto the day of judgment to be punished:*

[As Peter had just illustrated with regard to Noah and Lot, God can easily deliver the godly out of the world's judgments. The temptations to sin and follow the leading of the "spirit of the age" of ungodliness are, and should be, vexing to the true believer. We should never be comfortable with the worldly lusts.

Indeed, these temptations to partake of the sin of this present world may exert an influence upon even the believer. We ought never to succumb to those temptations. That we are prone to do so is testament to the fact that we have not accessed the power given to us from the throne of Grace to resist.

Sometimes our "want to" needs a slight adjustment that we will "want to" flee to the Lord to save us from dire temptations which we cannot resist on our own. Jesus gave us a great example of how to resist temptation in the fourth chapter of Matthew. Jesus was tempted on a mountain after a long fast. His human body was weakened but His Divine Spirit gave us the answer we need to heed.

Jesus answered every one of the temptations of Satan with Scripture. We can, and should!, do the same. But, how can we do so if we ignore the inspired and preserved Written Word of God? Answer: We can't.

We have a need to read for retention. We need to read those precious Words of God in a prayerful spirit. The Spirit will give us spiritual assistance to read and understand the spiritual message if we will only ask.

Simply "reading" is good. That is allowing God to speak concerning His Words to us. True spiritual power demands that we read for effect. To say, "I'm going to 'knock out' the entire Book of Isaiah tonight,' for instance may end up with us being knocked out. A worshipful and prayerful reading, not for mere length – a prideful thing, but for spiritual effect – a worshipful consideration, will more likely turn our hearts and minds toward to Lord.

This is "laying up ammunition," not that we can withstand but that God can use our own worship in defense of our spiritual walk with the Lord. When prayerfully used the Words of God are the best defense against the wiles of the devil.

God fully understands how to deliver His Own from the snares of the tempter. He has done so and will continue to do so for His children.

God also fully understands how to reserve the ungodly. Consider that in regard to the angels who sinned in verse four, above. Their time of final retribution has been hanging over their heads for a long time. Nonetheless, they are reserved, in chains, in darkness with only the just judgment of God on their horizon. While they, and the sinner of time, may understand the concept of the glorious light of salvation in Christ, they will never consider this. The angels have no time of conviction to repentance.

Meanwhile the sinner of humanity has the same route of escape as does the Christian. Any understanding he may have of salvation is a moot point of consideration as he has rejected the Lord and His provision. (John 3:36)]

2.10 *But chiefly them that walk after the flesh in the lust of uncleanness, and despise government. Presumptuous are they, selfwilled, they are not afraid to speak evil of dignities,*

[Peter had been speaking of God bringing punishment to the evil-doers. Some argued those described here would be judged more harshly than others. I would suppose a tenuous case could be made for that view. However, the worst sin imaginable is to reject The Son; this is especially so when one considers the lengths to which He endured the pain and degradation of the Cross in order to provide the possibility of our salvation.

Rather, I think, Peter was following the example of James and pointing out the sinfulness of sin. Those described in this verse are sinners in a most natural state. To watch these people was to see sin defined within their actions.

In that manner I do see these as "chiefly" the object of living as sinners. These walked "after the flesh." In the negative this would argue that they walked as far from the example of the Spirit's leading as was possible. If God was for it, they were against it! Right and wrong was not an object of debate. In their views wrong always trumped right in the lives of these sinners.

Since special mention is made, these people wished to walk in the sins of the flesh. It is an easy walk from that desire to find the most used illustration in the resource material I was able to access. Paul describes such as these in Romans 1:24, "Wherefore God also gave them up uncleanness through the lusts of their own hearts, to dishonor their own bodies between themselves." Continuing through this passage we see the twin sins of idolatry and homosexuality.

Idolatry is a worship of the animals and objects of creation with scant attention paid to the Creator. Homosexuality is a narcissism which finds the worship of one's own self in the mirror image of one's own physical self. Rather than a spiritual union, a homosexual union is a physical glorification of self.

In the Garden we see that God created Adam. It was from the rib of Adam that God fashioned the woman, Eve. Thus, the heterosexual union is of one "completing" the other spiritually by the symbolic restoration of life in the physical union. This is the plan of God. It would not be possible for any other union to fulfill the command to multiply upon the earth.

The concept of a "gay gene" has never been substantiated by scientific inquiry. However, I would not rule out the possibility of such a reality when the doctrine of inherited propensity to sin is considered. The possible "gay gene" may be real as part of the inherited sin nature sent from the original sin in the Garden.

If there is such a construct it would of necessity be among only a miniscule percentage of humanity. Otherwise the "gene" would quickly doom humanity to extinction.

Moving on in the realization that there are many other sins among sinful humanity, these sinners are such as hate all authority. The hatred extends from human governmental authority to ecclesiastical authority within the church. Basically, this is a libertine attitude both in society and in the churches which argues against any "limiting authority." It is the prideful assertion that only I am right. All others must, by definition, be wrong.

We see this in those who contest all displays of religion as too limiting. "Why should I be forced to pay any homage to your definition of God," many an atheist will argue. He only wishes to allow that which is part of his non-theistic philosophical system. He would only allow his system to be heard. All others must quickly move to the back of the bus and exit by the rear door.

He sees himself as the only real authority and demands that others agree with him. His "civil rights" are so strong as to override the lives of all he might wrong. They must be forced to bend to his will. All others will be slandered, fined, imprisoned and silenced to spare him the horror of being "offended" by someone else living their own life.

The only civic order these will accept is that order which is patterned and forced from their own view of culture. Any who would disagree are slandered as "bigots, racist, and 'phobes'" of whatever stripe   is deemed a "protected class."

Before the argument is made, God has the right to dictate certain traits for those He has created. As the "manufacturer," so to speak, only God fully understands that which will allow the organism of Hiscreation to operate at its highest and most fulfilling level.]

2.11 *Whereas angels, which are greater in power and might, bring not railing accusation against them before the Lord.*

[Robertson's Word Pictures considers that the above may be slandering real angels. I was going to write, "I suppose that is possible." But, I would have been wrong to say that. These are humans, "civic officials," religious officials, titans of commerce, entertainment or anything which would disagree with the slanderers.

Even the angels of God, which might be supposed to have the right of moral reality to act in such a manner, do not act in this way. The angels are more mannered and cultured than to engage in such activity. Consider Jude, verse 9, "Yet Michael the archangel, when contending with the devil he disputed about the body of Moses, durst not bring against him a railing accusation, but said, The Lord rebuke thee."

As we consider this great creation from the grandeur of the planets and stars to the magnificence of the lively order within even a clod of dirt, we must be struck with the fact that God is A Being of infinite order and beauty. Sin, and sinners, are the antithesis to all the goodness that is God.]

2.12 *But these, as natural brute beasts, made to be taken and destroyed, speak evil of the things that they understand not, and shall utterly perish in their own corruption;*

[These foolish and profane persons described in verse eleven are shown in this verse as who they are. Having disrespected and refused the spiritual life offered by the "religion" of Christ, they are shown to be no more than the brute animals they resemble in their actions.

It is interesting that they are described as "natural." The world has been captured by the evolutionary mode of thought. Everything is said to be changing for the better even as we see the culture of thousands of years of human interaction falling to the base instincts of the jungle. The concept of right does not belong to the correct but to the strong, or the legally empowered. The concept of force is seemingly the only concept of "crowd control" considered among the contrarian lemmings of our current society.

We have taught several generations that they are simply animals. They differ only in ability to use the weapons of their trade. They are entitled to better than they have because they are the strong. And we sit in huddled groups of singularity behind our walls held up by "burglar alarms," we wonder what has happened to the culture and safety of an earlier generation.

What we see is the reality of revisionist concepts which do not allow the spiritual to be even discussed. The children who shoot each other are only acting as the natural beast we have assured them is their bestial reality.

Our fear of the Truth of Christianity has made the world what it now is! The Western World has succumbed to the siren call of naturalistic thought and now hears the sirens call us from our sleep.

Several commentators argued that the primary purpose of the beast is to be a food upon which the populace subsists. That is partly true. But, this is not the teaching of this verse. This verse teaches that these are to be utterly destroyed because they have torn down that which they do not understand.

We live in an age when the lions have the ammunition and the hunter who would protect the village has become the "trophy" to be displayed on the wall of society's lodge of revulsion.

The world at large does not understand that Jesus has risen from the dead. They continue to attempt to pile stones upon the entrance of the tomb. Folks, the tomb is empty! That which is being unknowingly attacked is the only hope for society. Society, without the truth of Christ is utterly perishing because of its own corruption.

There is a "life line." There is a way of escape from the madness of present day inhumanity. The life line is being hidden behind the television drama and the foolishness of those who would claim it a false hope – even though this is the only hope. The way of escape is papered over with advertisements for "Bread and Circuses."

Had not the truth of the Scripture already given us the reality of the final events of this age of madness we would argue that there was no hope on this globe. There is hope. May we pray and publish the reality that Jesus Christ died in time so that others could live in eternity.]

2.13 And shall receive the reward of unrighteousness, as they that count it pleasure to rise in the day time. Spots they are and blemishes, sporting themselves with their own deceivings while the feast with you;

[Now we come back to the first verse of this chapter and realize to our horror that these beasts are false prophets who have crept into our churches and have seduced the pure doctrine and Word into the licentious fallen woman who leads astray those who profess The Name. They sit in our pews and partake of our communion.

At this point the Old Testament prophet would have intoned that "The wine of your feast is become red with the age of fermentation and the bread has rotted in your mouth." The purity of our religion is become the paramour of the world's delights and deceits.

The spots of the age of Laodicea have spoiled the beauty of pure hands being used for the Lord's Work. Instead our hands dip into the barrel of the excess of sinful access and we find ourselves holding but a memory of the Lord of Glory as we search out the falseness of the lies of gentlemen of earth.

Our riotous living finds the day of easy access. The night is far spent. The evening service is a memory of an earlier, less reasonable time. Our "Worship" is for the day. Folks, unless the rapture returns rapture to our hearts, the day is far spent. The night of television and sport has replaced the faith of the fathers with many faces of the world's famous.

The Old Testament saw the sacrifice of a lamb without spot or blemish. We have deceived ourselves to the point that the church is the blemish upon societies perceived needs and wants. Jesus has promised that the Church shall not fail but we must consider how weakly the church will assist her membership as we toddle unsteadily into that great heavenly gathering.

And, in recognition of the pale visage which is the modern church, who among us will hear the sad words, "Depart from Me. I never knew you." (Matthew 25:41)

As our commitment has weakened so has our doctrine become a mix of the pure water of the Word and the polluted water of culture. How many have we let down – eternally, by our acceptance of the conviviality of comradeship without the consecration of commitment to Christ?]

2.14 *Having eyes full of adultery, and that cannot cease from sin; beguiling unstable souls: an heart they have exercised with covetous practices, cursed children:*

[These sinners are seen looking only upon adulterous manifestations. We know that in the Scripture we find adultery to be more than the simple physical sin. The physical sin, while wrong in its practice, is a type of the spiritual sin which sees the creature divert the creatures worship from the true God, Who only is the proper Recipient of worship, and offer the fruits of religious devotion to idols and other entities. The person does such as this not only diverts worship from the One Proper Object, he also allows his heart to glorify a human, or a spiritual entity such as Satan giving the love and glory of the worship of the creature which is the property of the true Deity.

So enmeshed in this sin are these that they are unable to even see the error of their way. Their mind has become spiritually reprobate in their error. (Romans 1:28) So beguiled in their error are they that they become evangelists to spread their error. They mesmerize others to accept the error of their own ways.

How sad it is that the cultist and atheist, often the most devoted missionaries of the day, will often display a missionary fervor which puts the Christian to shame. We have the Words of Life and seem too ashamed to share them. These have the words of perdition and are anxious to spread the snare of Satan's lie in order to bring to him a harvest of damnation. This leads the children of men to be unable to escape the curse of sins degradation.

The quarry of such is indeed a children *blessed* with the curse of sins snare.]

2.15 *Which have forsaken the right way, and are gone astray, following the way of Balaam the son of Bosor, who loved the wages of unrighteousness;*

[It would appear that Balaam had been a true prophet. Perhaps his early career had been such as Melchizedek. Melchizedek (14th chapter of Genesis) was a true priest of God. Melchizedek was a sort or confirmation of the monotheistic religion of Abraham. With the introduction of Melchizedek we are shown that the concept of religion which Abraham embraced was not new to the Hebrew who sprang from the well of Abraham. The faith of Abraham was an outpouring of Living Water into the desert of the idolatry of Ur.

The ideal of the monotheistic God of Abraham was shown to be not a *new* construct but an important outbreak of a revival of the ancient and true worship of Jehovah. God confirmed the new dispensation of the Abrahamic Covenant by a link to the old dispensation of human government. Melchizedek was a priest/king bearing witness to the truth of which Abraham would walk deeper within.

Balaam began as speaking only the Words of God. This was his testimony. (Numbers 22:18) Within this testimony was a flaw. Within the lure of Balak was the promise of gain if Balaam would but find a way to move beyond the narrow leading of

God. Having already obtained the truth from God, Balaam continued to seek other *versions* which might offer a way to seemingly follow God while obtaining the reward of the world. Even the *faith* of the *testimony* of Balaam's donkey could not dissuade Balaam from the pursuit of the world's goods while claiming a fidelity to the Words of God.

Finally, on Mt. Peor, Balaam hit upon a plan. Since there was no cause for cursing the people of Israel, if they should sin by being seduced to sin by the women of Moab, then God would curse the people. Then Balaam could legally curse the people and fill his own purse with the reward of Balak. Thus we find that the sin of Balaam was his love of money above his love for God. (I Timothy 6:10)

Our next consideration has to do with the fact that Balaam was not of Israel and yet seemed to be a prophet of God. I would have to believe that he was because the Lord gave Him actual prophecies concerning Israel. Once again we would need to consider the status of Melchizedek. He was a true priest of God although he was not in the location where we may have been expected to find such a priest.

This is a reminder to preachers and Christians that we cannot judge on the natural. Our best "guesses" as to the simple salvation of a person has to do with an examination of the spiritual fruit in the life of that person.

Should this be an important consideration in the dispensation? Indeed; it most certainly is because we have an obligation to pray for the salvation of one who has not been born again. With our prayers must come our witness. The best way to examine the spiritual fruit of such a one as this is to compare his works and witness with the leading of the Scripture. Scripture is the inspired and preserved Words of God. The Scripture must be accessed, with prayer to the Spirit, to understand the working of the Spirit in this day. Even a thing which seems not always wrong is always wrong when it goes against the revealed Words of God.

Now, we need to consider if it is possible that Balaam was a righteous man. Did he die *in* his sins or *because of* his sins? (31:8)

Being *saved* is a New Testament phrase. In the Old Testament terminology, we speak of a person being *righteous*. In ALL dispensations true salvation is predicated upon faith in, and obedience to, the Words of God as revealed in that dispensation. True salvation is never based upon the works of anyone. EVER! I Peter 1:19-20 reminds us, "But with the precious blood of Christ, as of a lamb without blemish and without spot: Who verily was foreordained before the foundation of the world, but was manifest in these last times for you." Add Revelation 13:8b into this equation and we find that all salvation, in all ages, was based on the shed blood of Jesus Christ at the Cross of Calvary.

Now, looking at Balaam: He did display a faith in the Words of God. Even his attempted manipulation of the curse of God upon the people of Israel was based in a faith in the righteous Words of God. I would not argue that Balaam was in any way a "poster child" for true Christian conduct. But, neither was Lot. (See verse 7 of this chapter.)

I could find no place where Balaam was called righteous. Neither could I find a place where Balaam was lauded – at all! Nonetheless, I conclude (That's a word for "guess!" Keep that in mind when you read much of worldly philosophy!) that Balaam was "saved," to use our New Testament vocabulary.

Also, to use New Testament consideration, we must conclude that under the provisions of I Corinthians 11:30 – written concerning The Lord's Table but realizing the Spiritual Principle thereof – Balaam was removed from the land of the physically living that his testimony never again could be used to teach error.]

2.16 But was rebuked for his iniquity: the dumb ass speaking with man's voice forbad the madness of the prophet.

[This is one of the first charismatic feats of Tongues Speaking. It happened multiple centuries before the tongues of fire at Pentecost. We find several lessons in this for our own day. One of these is that the power of God is not the power of man. God does not need our permission or participation to work mighty miracles.

Another lesson is that we attempt to limit the power of God when, we out of hand try to explain away, or limit, the power of God into this dispensation of time and physicality. God not only wrote those laws of science we often invoke; He established those laws for His Own Good Pleasure. What we tend to call a miracle is only the Author of the Universe working within His creation.

God did not establish the universe and then go off to "watch a little T.V." so He could come back in a few thousand years and see what had happened. God created and God loves that which He has created. It one is not convinced of this by the events of Calvary, one is living as a brute beast without even the understanding of the beast.

There are times when the "dumb animals" are more cognizant of the power and performance of God than is the apex of the physical creation, mankind. Before the great tidal waves in Indonesia a few years ago we are informed that the animals began to flow to higher ground.

Consider this, the animals understood the working of God in His creation and were saved by the higher ground. Man continued to doubt the power of the working of God and was drowned by the higher water.

There is even a lesson in this story for those who have rejected the inspired and preserved Words of God. Man has sought "easier to read" versions culled from the false readings of the Critical Text. It is good that the text is called "critical" for it is very critical of any who would trust the God of All Power to preserve His Own Words and Message to man.

Why can we trust the power of man to "correct" when we refuse to trust the power of God to protect? Our faith seems misplaced, does it not!

What continues to amaze me in the entire episode from Numbers 23:21-31, is the fact that Balaam showed no surprise at all during his entire conversation with the beast. At the very least I would have been a little chagrined that the "dumb animal" was more attuned to the messenger of God than was I. Too many preachers are ever ready to bray like a beast. They are too often reluctant to show at least the wisdom of a beast and consider the words of the Lord's Message. It does seem that often we are more disposed to exalt our vision without searching for a vision from the Lord.]

2.17 These are wells without water, clouds that are carried with a tempest, to whom the mist of darkness is reserved for ever.

[Many times I have been driving on a highway when the rain became so severe that the "wipers" on my windshield were overworked. It was necessary that I get out of the rain and wait for the storm to abate so I could safely continue.

I have been informed by some even older than I that during the nineteen-thirties the problem was not rain but the lack of rain. During the midst of the droughts a cloud would be seen on the horizon. Hope would rise for the life-giving rain to fill the wells and water the crops so there would be fodder for the herds. Then came the realization that a "dust storm" was upon the land.

Not only would the wells not fill with water, the crops would be buffeted and buried by the dry dust. The cattle would literally be choked to death by dust that rose from the dry fields. There would be no visibility because the good "dirt" of the fields would hide the landscape. One such storm following another removed what moisture was available and scoured off the fields of nutrients. Even had there been water the land denuded of it productivity would not have brought "cash crops" into the area during the long decade of the "crash" of crops and everything else.

Once again, we are reminded that so many of the preachers and Christians who were to be giving forth the Living Water of the Message of Salvation in Christ became spiritual dry wells. We are well able to send the "dust" of human philosophy and the "dirt" of witty illustration but it is showers of blessing that are needed in the land. The life-giving waters of the salvation story of Jesus are needed. We supply the dust of dry knowledge and take the needy past their need as our "Gospel of Good Works" crowds out the wooing of the Spirit under the warbling of man's pride.

We are become dry wells devoid of the Water of Life. We are become boisterous and dry clouds putting on a show of Spirituality but denying the Lord to those who need His Salvation as we preach pride and self instead of preaching with pride about the Savior.

But, praise God, there is still a remnant of those who preach the Good News that Jesus Christ died in time so that others could live in eternity. Praise the God of Glory for the voices of those who still water the earth with the tears of compassion and the voice of salvation.]

2.18 *For when they speak great swelling words of vanity, they allure through the lusts of the flesh, through much wantonness, those that were clean escaped from them who live in error.*

[In the above verse I alluded to Christians who were untrue to their calling to live in harmony with the glorious reality of a walk with Christ. Those who truly are Christians in the Biblical sense have a duty to live as Christians into the world with the full witness and power of the renewed life in Christ.

But, we must realize that all who name the Name of Christ are not true Christians. Many things may have drawn them to the fellowship. Freedom may have been sought under the doctrines allowed by the Roman Empire. Seeing the blessing of communion with God may have caused some to claim the right while refusing the responsibility.

This seems to be the meaning of the verse. An appeal is made to the "freedom which is in Christ" and apply this to things which ought not to be among the people of God. I think at this place to the "beer and pretzel" communion services which are held in taverns where the argument is made that the church must adapt to the people and their haunts.

This is ridiculous, of course. Jesus did not say to the woman taken in adultery,

"Neither do I condemn you if you put a pious purpose upon your former sins." (Compare John 8:11.) The religion of Christianity is one which is to call people *from sin* and *unto Godliness*.

This is the vanity, meaning emptiness, of the words of these false teachers. They take the view that Christian liberty has freed people to sin. It has not. The concept of Christian liberty is that it has freed people *not* to sin.

By using argument which takes the Words of Truth and assigns a meaning not actually associated with the realities of the Spiritual these false teachers appeal to the baser lusts and mentalities of the people. In reality they are teaching a false religion by applying the meaning of sin to the terms of life.

Such as these have even taken those who really have accepted Christ as Savior and perverted the pure religion of Christ into something it is not. But, since they have appealed to base lusts they have found a ready acceptance among those not grounded in the faith. This is harming Christians by stunting their spiritual growth and harming the churches by perverting them *away from* the leading of the Spirit.

Satan gains an undeserved victory as the Words of God are perverted and the power of God is never accessed. This very thing is one of the dangers associated with the modern English versions which have as their base the Critical Texts of man's construction rather than the Received Text of God's direction. Words which sound good to the ears of the unsaved may be so because they do not contain the power of God upon them.

The True Words of God will speak the power of God which, until brought upon the hearts of unregenerate man by the conviction of the Spirit, do not resonate in a heart of sin.]

2.19 *While they promise them liberty, they themselves are the servants of corruption for of whom a man is overcome, of the same is he brought in bondage.*

[Under the ancient rules of war a man who was conquered was considered the property of the man who conquered him. He was slave to the victor. Many, perhaps most of the slaves of the Roman Empire were men captured in war.

The "Christian Liberty" argued by the false teachers was a liberty of licentiousness. They claimed that they were "at liberty" to indulge in the basest of sins. If this were true, I am sure that we would find the severest bondage to be in Heaven! But, it is not so. The concept of Christian Liberty is to be able to overcome sin and live in holiness before the Lord.

A "two-pack-a-day" smoker is not free. He is a slave to his habit. If this is doubted I would suggest a reading of all the advertisements which offer to help one "kick his habit."

Jesus is the Rock of Stability in a weary land of fleshly lusts. One of the best things about our salvation is that we are saved to live the very type of life for which we were originally created. It is a true reality that sin controls. Salvation frees us from that sin which weighs us down with the load of obligation to carnality and lust.]

2.20 *For if after they have escaped the pollutions of the world through the knowledge of the Lord and Saviour Jesus Christ, they are again entangled therein, and overcome, the latter end is worse with them than the beginning.*

[The operative phrase here is "through the knowledge of the Lord and Saviour Jesus Christ." This does not say "through the saving grace, or redemption of the Lord and Savior Jesus Christ." The meaning is not of one who was truly born again. The meaning is of one who has seen the power of Jesus to reform a vile life.

This man has found a way to freedom from the power of his lusts. But, then he sinks back into the old life. Then the false teachers, perhaps even himself, have taught their own meaning of Christian liberty. This man sees that he can have all the best of the "Christian life style" while still dealing with those things which excite.

The man may have been, may still be, enamored of the idea of the Christian religion. But, while holding on to the outward profession he has found an intellectual means to still follow his old carnal lusts. It is no wonder that Peter says the end of this man, entangled and overcome by his favored sins, is worse than the beginning. He will no longer consider a need for repentance. He is less likely, if at all, to ever find true Christianity.

He has found a form of christianity, small case intended, which asks nothing but the enjoyment of carnal lusts.]

2.21 *For it had been better for them not to have known the way of righteousness, than, after they have known it, to turn from the holy commandment delivered unto them.*

[Jesus gave a very illustrative statement. "And thou shalt love the Lord thy God with all thy heart, and with all thy soul, and with all thy mind, and with all thy strength: this is the first commandment." (Mark 12:30) Is it possible for one who truly loves the Lord in such a manner to seek himself first the kingdom of Satan?

Will those who have really known the way of righteousness but have never accepted it because they see it as too narrow and limiting, ever consider actually accepting the Holy Commandment which has been shown to them? They are highly unlikely to ever accept the true liberty of Christ into their lives.]

2.22 *But it is happened unto them according to the true proverb, The dog is turned to his own vomit again, and the sow that was washed to her wallowing in the mire.*

[The "true proverb" is Proverbs 26:11, "As a dog returneth to his vomit, so a fool returneth to his folly." The latter proverb, concerning the sow, is suggested as having been a current Gentile proverb as it concerns a pig.

Whatever is the source, the application remains the same. As we have noted in the above several verses, none of these concern the man who is actually saved. Neither the dog nor the sow has had their essential nature changed. They still act as simple brute beasts.

Several commented that if the sow had become a sheep it would never have considered to again wallow in the mud. That, the change in essential nature, is the promise of the New Birth. A true Christian will not seek to return to his former life of sin. A man who is not a true Christian will long to return to the "mud" of his former haunts. If a "teacher" can assure him that this is consistent with true spirituality, he will quickly remove his Sunday-go-to-meeting suit and slide into the slough of despair.]

SECOND PETER - CHAPTER THREE

3.1   This second epistle, beloved, I now write unto you, in both which I stir up your pure minds by way of remembrance.

[Notice how Paul begins. He says "beloved." This is a term of both respect and affection. It isn't hard for pastors to have affection for the people to whom they impart the Words of life. But, let us never forget to do this in respect. We are not the parent; at our absolute best we can only be a messenger of the Heavenly Father. Rebuke when rebuke is necessary; but, never do so with a stick in our hands. For the pastor rebuke from God upon the people of God is generally necessitated because that pastor has failed in on manner or another.

Love so deeply that rebuke will be a rare occasion. It is faithful teaching of the Words of Life which will produce a people of God who flee to Him in love, in joy, in time of trial and in praise at all times.

The purpose of Peter in this chapter was to warn of false teachers and scoffers who had not faith in the inspired and preserved Words of God. The only way to hold fast to our profession is to hold fast to the preservation of the Words and Message of God. It is those pure Words of God which will give to us the "pure mind" of which Peter speaks. It is only that pure mind meditating on the pure Word which can offer a refuge in a time of trial and temptation.]

3.2   That ye may be mindful of the words which were spoken before by the holy prophets, and of the commandment of us the apostles of the Lord and Saviour.

[Peter is reminding the people to delve into the Scripture. In there they will find the Words and prophecies of God. Others may disagree but the Words of God stand supreme in their truthfulness and inevitability.

Peter also uses the phrase "us the apostles." Some will use this to argue against Peter being the author of this book. Peter is not the author of the book. God is the True Author of this Book via the medium whereby He inspired and preserved these words. Peter is the "penman" who God used in the writing of this Book.

The use of the little word "us" shows us that Peter had grown as a man. He was no longer the proud boastful man of his youth. He was now a mature Christian who understood his frailty as a human being. He seeks no preeminence among the apostles because he has none. Were Peter to be alive today, he would be appalled at the position given him by the Roman Church. Peter was never the "vicar" of Christ. He would only claim the title of "servant" of Christ. And, that he would share with others.

Jesus built His Church. Peter was one of those laboring in the construction and early continuation of what Jesus had established.]

3.3   Knowing this first, that there shall come in the last days scoffers, walking after their own lusts,

II Timothy 3:1; Hebrews 1:2

[There we have that phrase again, "last day." Folks, we are in the last times right now. This present dispensation is to be "book-ended" by the coming of Christ to redeem the world and the coming of Christ to call His Own out of this world. This is the dispensation of the "church age" and the world does not like the concept of a "Church" – a called out assembly of people who are tasked with reproving the world of sin and calling the world to accept Christ.

The sin nature is in opposition to everything of God. It is hateful of everything that is of God. This is the nature which must be eradicated in order to heal the disease of sin. People are comfortable in their sin and will rebel, or should I say "persist in their rebellion," against anything that points up their moral corruption and God's transcendent holiness.

People like these will appear in the last days, as they have throughout the history of these "last days," to argue against the truth of the Gospel. They will not be content with not believing; they will attempt to disallow others from believing. Thus we have the inanity of those who have perverted the first amendment to the U. S. constitution from "free excise of religion" to "freedom from religion." Not content with their own irreligion, they are so "offended" by anyone else simply living a life of religion that they will bring suit to prohibit the rights of others in the name of "freedom."

It would be funny to look at the childishness of these people were it not for the fact that they have found too many judges who would likewise inhibit the freedom of Christians to live their own faith.

The homosexual bigots, not all homosexual people, are so hateful that they seek to demand that no one be allowed to have any religious rights in regard to "gay marriage." Their expectation is that our theologies must change to accept their view of "rights."

The very fact that these things are happening is a proof of the message of the inspired and preserved Scripture is of God.]

***3.4** And saying, Where is the promise of his coming? for since the fathers fell asleep, all things continue as they were from the beginning of the creation.*

[The main thing that has continued as it has always been is that sinful man scoffs at the truths of God. Mankind, in general, does not understand that Jesus is the Controller of History. His prophecies are certain. There is nothing out of His control. We may not understand all that happens. But, we can trust that it remains in His prophetic will!

We will not hear that all things continue as they have been "since the creation" any time soon! But, the fact remains the same. People continue to argue that things have always been as they are today and this is a false construct. Modern science acts from a principle of uniformitarianism. This is the argument that all things remain as they have been. As we peruse the first few chapters of Genesis we find that there have been dramatic changes in the earth since creation.

Peter speaks of the flood. The breaking up of the "fountains of the deep" was probably the impetus of the shift of the tectonic plates. That is a change. The earth was divided in the days of Peleg (Genesis 10:25). This was a change. In Genesis 2:6 we see that the whole earth was watered by a "mist from the ground." This is a change.

There were many changes in the earth. Of these men are willingly ignorant. This is the plight of the scoffers; they look only at what their natural eyes will show them and ignore the great truths which God stands ready to show them in His inspired and preserved Word.

Not content to disbelieve, these scoffers present argument from their inaccurate presumptions and demand that all join in their folly. Beyond simply scoffing, these also lambast and ridicule those who view the entire picture and are rightfully convinced that we must "Be not deceived; God is not mocked," His Words are True and will always come to pass.

Moreover, "for whatsoever a man soweth, that shall he also reap." (Galatians 6:7) The end result of the scoffers of society is witnessed in a society which seems poised to fall apart at any moment.

Such persons as these are positive proofs of the Truth of the Words of God. He said, in His inspired and preserved Word, that these would arrive to attack the Christian. They are here!]

3.5 *For this they willingly are ignorant of, that by the word of God the heavens were of old, and the earth standing out of the water and in the water:*

[A parallel verse here is Romans 1:28 where Paul says, "And even as they did not like to retain God in *their* knowledge, God gave them over to a reprobate mind, to do those things which are not convenient." The word "convenient" in Romans gives the sense of not doing those things which are fit, or proper, to be done.

The meaning of being "willingly ignorant" gives a sense that this is what is chosen as a belief system. This brings up the specter of the innate sin nature within unregenerate humanity as a ruling force within their lives. The old joke is that a man proclaimed loudly that he owed his mettle to no one else because, "I am a self-made man." God then answered, "Thank you for not blaming me for that!"

The spiritual reality is that God does not "make" men to be sinners. They are such because that is their choice; it is this with which they are comfortable.

A man refuses to accept the fact of the Creation of God on "scientific grounds" is a man deluded by his own presuppositions of naturalistic theology wherein the "theos" part of that word does not refer to "God" but to man's reasoning power. Man is become God in his own thought processes.

The truth is that God brought dry land out of wet water by the power of His creative voice. Water, although connected in its natural state, stands in three areas. There is the water of the atmosphere. It is above the earth. There is the water of ocean and lake. It is upon the earth. There is also water in reservoirs under the earth. It is beneath the earth.

This all is of the plan and perfections of God.]

3.6 *Whereby the world that then was being overflowed with water, perished:*

[Man tends to overlook the fact of Genesis 1:1 – "In the beginning God created the heaven and the earth." The meaning here does not concern the Heaven of the abode of God. This is a verse in reference to the creative act of God with allusion to earth. The "heaven" spoken of in Genesis 1:1 is the atmospheric heaven above the earth.

With regard to the argument of Peter at this point we must also consider Genesis 1:2 – "And the earth was without form, and void; and darkness was upon the face of the deep. And the Spirit of God moved upon the face of the waters." The fact of water in relation to the earth was included in the original creation. From these deep waters came the land of the earth.

When we consider the deluge of Noah's time, we are struck with the fact that these waters actually seem to have reclaimed a primordial preeminence upon the earth as all the terrestrial life, with the exception of that which God made specific provision to save, was removed in this flood.

Thus, we see that God had preparation made for the flood to judge society for their sin even before the society had existed. When we couple this fact with Revelation 13:8, wherein we are informed that God had prepared salvation to be available for sinful mankind even before the creation of mankind, we are left to stand in awe of the Great Creator God. He is never surprised by the events of time. His preparation for an event stands in place even before the event has transpired.]

3.7 *But the heavens and the earth, which are now, by the same word are kept in store, reserved unto fire against the day of judgment and perdition of ungodly men.*

[When Peter speaks of the "heavens and the earth, which are now," his meaning is the world in which men resided after the flood. He says that it is the very Word of God which keeps them available at this time.

Consider Colossians 1:17 in concert with this verse. "And he is before all things, and by him all things consist." The verse in Colossians acknowledges that Jesus is the Creator of all. (see John 1:3) Even beyond this the verse in Colossians tells us that "by him all things consist." The meaning of that little phrase is that the Word of God is the "glue" that holds all things together throughout the created universe.

It is, therefore, the forbearance and grace of God which keeps the creation functioning even during these times. The old song says, "Without Him I could do nothing." That song contains more truth than we generally suppose.

I would believe that the flood brought more than just judgment upon the unrighteous men of the age. The earth also began to feel the full horror of sin within her physical communities. From the third chapter of Genesis we know that the earth was cursed in that she no longer gave the fullness of her fruit to mankind. Death, just as God has warned Adam and Eve, had come into the world in the generally declining spiral of the life-times of man and the sacrificial use of innocent animals was a reality because of sin.

After the judgment of the flood, in Genesis 10:9-10, we read that Nimrod was a mighty hunter. Man and many of the formerly benign creatures of the earth became carnivores. Death became a curse of increased proportions upon the earth as sin manifest itself. (Romans 5:12) Romans 8:22 reminds us that the entire creation has been stained by sin.

We tend to think that all things are as they have always been in this earth. This is not so. The physiology of both man and beast was changed to allow those who had been created to be vegan to become carnivore.

Even the physical laws have changed. Before the flood the entire earth was watered by mists of morning dew. (Genesis 2:6) This fact has led many to surmise that the earth was covered by cloud cover which made the entire earth into a "greenhouse" situation whereby the entire earth, at that time one "continent," was able to support abundant greenery for the food of the animals and man.

Genesis 10:25 informs us that the earth was divided at a point not all that long after the flood had subsided. This was the beginning of the movement of the tectonic plates which has given us the continents we know today. Realizing this we can easy see how the animals were able to come to Noah during those long years as he was building the Ark. We can understand how all those animals lived in peace with one another due their universal vegan diet.

Further, considering that the tectonic plates had not yet "built up" the mountain ranges, it is easy to understand how the animals were all able to disembark from the Ark and go to their respective "homes" prior to the beginning of the carnivore diet taking hold among those creatures.

The "mountains of Ararat" (Genesis 8:4) were hills. Considering that four rivers (Genesis 2:10-14) flowed out from Eden, we must realize that Eden occupied a "high ground." Once again, this is a "high ground" rather than a mountain. A hill would have facilitated the work of Adam and Eve in the Garden while giving the beauty of view. A mountain would have obscured their view of their tasks.

We can also look back at Cain as a shepherd and realize that he was not raising mutton; he was raising both wool for clothing, and sacrificial animals for worship.

Along with this came a change in weather patterns. Storms and the fury of the wind and waves now mar the life of both human and animal. Such was not the case prior to the flood. Since rain and storms were unknown in the pre-flood world, no one had ever seen a "rainbow." Perhaps this was even the result of a change in the natural laws of nature due to the sin of Adam.

God used this rainbow (see Genesis 9:8-17) as a token to establish His promise to never again destroy the earth by flood. Instead the natural creation, which has no Savior such as we have in Jesus, is reserved unto the refining fires of the just judgment of God. We must recall that even during the dispensation of the millennium wherein Satan, the tempter of humanity, is chained away from influencing man for one thousand years and the effects of sin upon the elements is held in abeyance for that same time period, man will still fail even this mildest of tests and rebel against the Lord of the Universe.

It is necessary that even the residual sin must be judged and removed for the righteous rule of God to give true peace and full joy to humanity and creation. We must consider that the same faithfulness of God in not destroying the world again by a flood bespeaks of His same faithfulness in carrying out His vengeance as He has promised.

I would further note here that the "baptism of water" in which the ancient sinners perished and the ancient world was burdened, did not "save" anyone. There must still be a judgment of fire to eradicate the sin among the elemental earth. Even this judgment does not save the unrepentant who are ushered into everlasting torment.

Neither does this judgment simply "cleanse" the "old creation." This "old creation" is judged by fire to be reborn as a "new creature." (II Corinthians 5:17) The judgment of God does more than simply judge. The judgment of God cleanses the "computer," removes and purges the "virus" of the infection of sin so it no longer exists, and restores the "new creature" to the original "factory specifications." (consider I Corinthians 15:51-57)]

SECOND PETER: Chapter 3

3.8 *But, beloved, be not ignorant of this one thing, that one day is with the Lord as a thousand years, and a thousand years as one day.*

[The "scoffers" seem to make a large point in the seeming delay of the second coming of Christ. We still get that today. They will make the argument that people have been expecting the end of the world for hundreds of years but here we are. We are not looking for "the end of the world." It is coming but our sight is fixed on looking for the coming Savior!

Peter reminds his hearers of Psalm 90:4. "For a thousand years in thy sight are but as yesterday when it is past, and as a watch in the night." Some have used this verse to elongate the days of creation in Genesis into the ages of evolution in an attempt to make the Bible seem to agree with "modern science." Folks, the Word of God stands secure in the Words of the inspired and preserved Scripture even while the "assured facts of science" become the fables of days gone by.

An overlooked fact is that time and eternity are of two different constructs. I am nearing the fulfillment of my "three score and ten." I no longer look into the future and imagine the things I want to do. Instead I tend to look into the future and lament the things I have not done. Just a couple of weeks ago I spoke to a member of our church and said that I wished I had begun to write commentaries many years ago. That isn't an important consideration, really! There are many commentaries that have been on the market for many years that are far better than anything I might write. It is just a simple illustration of the regrets of old age.

God is of eternity. The constraints of time do not affect Him. The time for any action on His part is not past, as these scoffers seemed to be alleging. As in everything God does, He awaits the perfect time rather than the expedient time. (consider Galatians 4:4)]

3.9 *The Lord is not slack concerning his promise, as some men count slackness, but in longsuffering to us-ward, not willing that any should perish, but that all should come to repentance.*

[The seeming delays of God are the gracious opportunities afforded to man.

We need to have a Biblically based heart's desire. First, we should long for the soon return of our Lord. At the same time, we should have compulsion to see souls won into His Kingdom. We must work for the salvation of souls with the view that Jesus might not come back for a thousand years. We must work for the salvation of souls with the view that Jesus might come back at any second. We need to be expectantly busy about His work,

Consider these two words: Any and all. God does not want "any" of His created race of man to die in their sins. The fact that there is a coming judgment under this situation is just another proof that man has become the master of his own destiny when he declines to accept Jesus Christ as his Savior. (see John 3:16-18)

Meanwhile, Christ delays His coming in order that "all" of the elect may come to repentance and find salvation. (see I Peter 1:2)]

3.10 But the day of the Lord will come as a thief in the night, in the which the heavens shall pass away with great noise, and the elements shall melt with fervent heat, the earth also and the works that are therein shall be burned up.

[See note at Hebrews 1:12] This event comes after the final rebellion is put down at the end of the Millennial Dispensation. The purposes are to end this world system which has been infected by sin, to cleanse the natural creation of sin by judging that sin, to institute a new system which is free from any taint of sin, and to finally judge and sentence the unrepentant.

I am one of the oldest of the "baby boom" generation born after the end of World War II. We were often concerned about "the end of the world" via an atomic conflagration. In my early years I often heard people arguing, "There is water even in the atmosphere. Water is just hydrogen and oxygen mixed together. Remember the Hindenburg Blimp; the hydrogen in that thing blew up. Oxygen can keep a fire burning."

Such adult conversations can make it hard for a young child to find sleep in the night of his terror. Nonetheless, those arguments are true. The final judgment of the earth and the atmospheric heavens around the earth could happen quite easily by a simple manipulation of the elements of the earth by the Creator.

The term "thief in the night" refers to one not expected to come by our home. The general unconverted population scoffs at the idea that Jesus will come again. Folks, it doesn't make any difference what people believe if that belief does not conform to the Truth of Scripture. Jesus is coming again. Man is a rebellious creature. Judgment will overflow this earth.

A thief will remove many precious things we have made and kept. Our greatest treasures of literature, art, science, architecture and so on will be burned in that day. Our only real treasure in this life, which will give us faith in this time is the salvation of our souls by the Savior of our souls.]

3.11 Seeing then that all these things shall be dissolved, what manner of persons ought ye to be in all holy conversation and godliness,

[We find nearly the same admonition in I John 2:15-17. "Love not the world, neither the things *that are* in the world. If any man love the world, the love of the Father is not in him. For all that *is* in the world, the lust of the flesh, and the lust of the eyes, and the pride of life, is not of the Father, but is of the world. And the world passeth away, and the lust thereof: but he that doeth the will of God abideth for ever."

All of these things of the world are transitory. They are going away in the just judgment of God upon sin. Why should we care for them? Our only true treasure is Heavenly with Jesus as our Savior. Considering the fact of the inevitability of these facts, it would seem prudently wise that our minds be fixed on the Savior and our own Heavenly responsibilities.

We live in a world where our greatest treasure is the realization that our real home is with the Savior in Heaven.

Our understanding of these facts should produce in our lives a love of God, a liking of the treasures of opportunity to serve Him here on earth, and a loathing anything which would hinder the salvation of souls in this world. Our understanding of these facts should produce a life which is lived in holiness and imitation of Christ as we strive to be more like Him each day.]

3.12 *Looking for and hasting unto the coming of the day of God, wherein the heavens being on fire shall be dissolved, and elements shall melt with fervent heat?*

[Peter almost sound anxious for this day of destruction to come! I would imagine that he is. So should we be. This is the end of sin and the destruction of the effects of evil upon the perfect creation of God. Have you ever noticed that after each of the creative days God looks upon them and pronounces that, "it is good."

After the entrance of sin into the world in the third chapter of Genesis we never find that phrase again!

I would agree that it is sad, to my human eyes and heart, to consider that the sinner is consigned to perdition. We see in verse nine, above, that the Heart of God is saddened by this fact, as well. Two mitigating facts are to be considered at this point. The first is that sin is an all-encompassing evil which must be removed lest it infect. This is the sad lesson we have learned throughout each of the dispensations. Where given the chance to exist, evil will always infect to draw men away from the perfections of blessing, happiness and fulfillment of humanity.

Second, no person whose soul is infected by the virus of a sin nature could ever be happy in an eternity of praise to the sinless perfections of God. Look about the world today and you will not find a society which is either favorable toward or comfortable with even the witness to the fact that Jesus Christ died in time so that others could live in eternity.

Both the justice and the goodness of God demand this judgment upon sin.

The heavens spoken of in this verse are the created heavens not the Heaven of the abode of God. Romans 8:22 reminds us of the pervasive nature of sin within the created universe.

See verse ten, above, for a short discussion of the fire of judgment even during the flood of Noah. It is this which I believe will usher in the cleansing fire. It is my belief that this crucible of fire will purge the elements of all trace of sin. God will then reconstruct His creation in perfection.

There are many who would suggest that this has already happened at one point. These see Genesis 1:1 as a perfect creation and Genesis 1:2, and all following, as a description of a renewal of that perfection after a judgment upon the sin of Satan and his followers in his attempt to ascend the throne of God in Heaven. I am not decided as to my position on this; I only include this for your own consideration.]

3.13 *Nevertheless we, according to his promise, look for new heavens and a new earth, wherein dwelleth righteousness.*

[In Isaiah 66:22 Isaiah writes, "For as the new heavens and the new earth, which I will make, shall remain before me, saith the LORD, so shall your seed and your name remain." This is a prophecy that the promises which God gave to Abraham and his descendants are eternal promises which will continue to be fulfilled after the destructive fires of judgment have destroyed the present sinful world.

The promises of God will never be violated. The Words of God will never be forsaken.

This will not be another dispensation of trial. This will be a new earth wherein there is a dwelling place for righteousness. As I look out the windows of the study where I am working I see five houses immediately across the street. In each of these houses live a family.

In the "home" of the new earth will dwell the "family" of righteousness. There will be no place found for "unrighteousness" within the dwelling space of the "home" of the new earth. It will be a place free from sin and wholly dedicated to the worship of The God.

I see this not as a *rearrangement* of the present physical world system. I see the results of this judgment as a *renewal* of the creative acts of God. The infection of sin in the elements is eradicated and a new restoration of the perfections of the creation which God said over and over was "good." This happens within the element of creative time as it is a *reestablishment* of the original creative intent. There will be no more need for dispensational testing as man has proved himself to be a creature of less glory than God through his repeated failings in this present world system. This is so even when the external temptations, and the tempter, have been removed during the Millennial Reign of Christ. Man will retain his free will. But, this will be a free will not encumbered by the propensity to either think or act in ways destructive to pure harmony with God. It will be a perfect free will.]

3.14 *Wherefore, beloved, seeing that ye look for such things, be diligent that ye may be found of him in peace, without spot, and blameless.*

[Peter reminds that when we consider the certainty of the prophecies we would do well to so live our physical and spiritual lives in such a way as to be completely blameless before Him.

We would acknowledge that we can never attain to complete holiness of action and thought. This does not mean that we can never strive to find such! This is our duty to attempt.

My son is a big fan of a certain professional football team. His hope is to see that team score each time they have the ball. This does not mean that he expects them to score on each play. Some plays are designed to pick up only few yards. Still, the football player will struggle and attempt to gain every single yard he can. The goal is the goal.

We are not going to attain complete perfection in this life. But, we ought to be struggling and pushing forward at all times to do just that. We may never attain but we can certainly attempt.]

3.15 *And account that the longsuffering of our Lord is salvation; even as our beloved brother Paul also according to the wisdom given unto him hath written unto you;*

[vv. 15-16. The important fact, and it is fact, in this passage is that Peter defended, and used, the words of the epistles of Paul as Scripture. He placed them in the same position as "the other Scriptures."

The fact is that the early New Testament churches were guided by the Holy Spirit to understand that those Epistles and Gospels were Scripture - and to treat them as such.

We, as human beings, are an imperfect people. Although the Holy Spirit guided, not all would accept that guidance. Some churches would dismiss some portions. Other churches would include disputed books. But, in the totality of those first century churches, the Words of God were revered and accepted as Scripture.

Peter addresses the seeming "delay" in the coming of Christ. Please note that while Peter has been speaking of the coming of Christ in judgment, the "coming" expected at any moment was the coming of Christ in the clouds to receive His Own in the rapture.

Peter reminds his readers that this "delay" is for their sake. It isn't that Christ has delayed His coming from sloth or disinterest. The delay of Jesus in His return was a grace in that it gave the Christian more time to evangelize his neighbor and more time for that neighbor to repent and be converted.

Even in this portion of inspired Scripture, Peter will reference another portion of inspired Scripture. A thought to keep in mind is that our reasoning is fallible; it is of time. Our greatest need is to rely upon the Words of inspired and preserved Scripture. Jesus gave us this example in His temptation upon the mountain in the fourth chapter of Matthew. Every time Satan attempted to tempt Jesus, that temptation was met with Scripture.

There is another point to notice in Peter's reference to the letters of Paul. That little phrase "wisdom given unto him" speaks of the inspiration of God upon the Words which were penned by Paul in those circular letters. Several commentators have tried to decide just which letters were in mind as Peter has written. I would argue that there is no need to do so. In these days the canon of Scripture was not complete. Peter was acknowledging a "blanket inspiration" of those letters which the Holy Spirit would reveal to the churches were inspired.

In reference to the above, we must also note that these epistles of Paul, and of Peter for that matter, were copied over and over that each church and Christian might receive the teaching and benefit of those letters. It was in this manner that the Scriptures grew and flourished among those first century churches.

It was the churches, led by the Spirit, which decided upon the canonicity of which were inspired and which were not. Not every church agreed. There were "hold outs" and "heretics" who argued for and against certain inclusions. The Holy Spirit continued His work until the unanimity was reached. No "church council" decided which book was in or which book was out. Those councils only ratified that which the Spirit had ratified among the hearts of the totality of the believers.]

3.16 *As also in all his epistles, speaking in them of these things, in which are some things hard to be understood, which they that are unlearned and unstable wrest, as they do also the other scriptures, unto their own destruction.*

[The purpose of God is not always to make things easy for the Christian. The simple Gospel message is simple enough that anyone can understand. Some of the deeper things of the Scripture are accessible only through diligent work. This work is an indication of our being committed to the Lord. It is not a function of our own intellect; it is a function of our spirit striving to be the best vessel we can be for our Lord. (see II Timothy 2:15 for the command to study the things, and words, of God.)

God will often drop some precious nugget of His truth into our possession as we pan the streams of Scripture. More often He will yield these nuggets to those who take pick and axe and mine the mountains of Scripture.

Notice what Peter was saying in verses sixteen through eighteen. He said that there are passages which are hard to understand. Some people wrestle with them to their own destruction. The purpose of a wrestling match is to find a winner. We do not "win" over The God of the Scripture. We submit to Him. To attempt to take His Good Word and "dumb it down" is a sin. It God made it hard, He did it for a purpose. It is better that we seek the purpose than that we attempt to defeat that purpose. This applies even to a translation committee which might believe that they are handling the Words of God.

Peter also warns us to be wary lest we are led astray by such as these.]

3.17   Ye therefore, beloved, seeing ye know these things before, beware lest ye also, being led away with the error of the wicked, fall from your own stedfastness.

[Peter applauds the knowledge of the people to whom he writes. Nonetheless, he warns them to be on their guard lest they fall from, not salvation which is of Christ alone, but of their steadfastness to the faith. This is the concept of pure doctrine.

Error does not come from one firm push but from many small "adjustments." It may seem that we are being led to a deeper walk when we are being led to another walk. The first error of the Church of Constantine was to replace faith in the protection of the state rather than in full protection of God.

The next major adjustment was a leading to accept everything that was pronounced by the pulpit. Not every word of even a good man is a word of God. Try all things by the Scripture as to whether they be so or whether they be in opposition to the Word.

Small error was laid upon large error until even the Word was abandoned to only the "learned clergy." The leading of the Spirit would come to be accepted only as filtered through man.

Finally, even the Scripture became unnecessary, in the view of the man in the pew, because he believed that he only needed to understand what it was that man had allowed to be viewed as Truth in his own statements.

If we are to know "these things," we must know what the Bible says about "these things." It is not hard to lead a people astray who have no leading unto what is right.]

3.18   But grow in grace, and in the knowledge of our Lord and Saviour Jesus Christ. To him be glory both now and for ever. Amen.

[Honor and glory, not to mention grace and a need to learn more of Him, are to be given to the Person of Jesus. This would be simple sacrilege were it not directed toward the Creator God. Thus, Jesus is shown as God.

Note well the command to "grow in grace." It is a command which can only be fulfilled by an expanding knowledge of Jesus Christ. We grow in Him or not at all.]

FIRST JOHN

FIRST JOHN - CHAPTER ONE

1.1   That which was from the beginning, which we have heard, which we have seen with our eyes, which we have looked upon, and our hands have handled, of the Word of life,

[vv. 1-2. In these verse's John is talking about a man Who had been intently examined. John says that this is an old story which we have investigated in many ways. This isn't a fable that we've heard and accepted. This is something, Someone, with Whom we've traveled and conversed in all manner of ways. We have seen Him in hunger. We have seen Him in fatigue. We have seen Him in danger of the elements. We have seen Him reasoning publicly with experts in His field; and always He has been the more knowledgeable. We have seen Him in betrayal. We have seen Him falsely accused. We have seen Him stand before the court of religion and state. We have seen Him before His executioners. We have seen Him brutally beaten and crucified. And, we have seen Him rise from the dead. We know what we are talking about.

Jesus is from eternity. The life of Jesus is eternal. This is testament to the fact that Jesus is not created. The only conclusion to be reached from the testimony of John is that Jesus is God.

Another verse is referenced to the view of John. Jesus is here the speaker, "I am he that liveth, and was dead, and, behold, I am alive for evermore; Amen, and have the keys of hell and of death." (Revelation 1:18) This verse from Revelation reinforces the concepts of the present passage from I John. John completely accepts Jesus as Divine.

Consider the great dignity which the apostle John could have assumed. It was he to whom the Savior, while in the agony of the cross, commissioned the care of His aging mother. While others fled in fright from the horror of the events of the trial and crucifixion of Jesus, John remained steadfast and gave his physical presence as testimony to his own love for the Lord even during the events surrounding the betrayed Lord.

Yet, John did not begin his own epistle with the writing of his own name. This was the custom of the "letter writers" of the day. John saw the importance of Jesus as paramount and begins this teaching with an account of the majesty of Jesus.

Nonetheless, there is not any question but that John was the penman of this work. The scope of doctrine, the phraseology and the testimony of the Christians from the earliest all confirm that John wrote the Words which bore the mark of the inspiration of God.]

1.2   (For the life was manifested, and we have seen it, and bear witness, and shew unto you that eternal life, which was with the Father, and was manifested unto us;)

I Timothy 3:16

[Compare with John 1:4 where John asserts that life was a possession of The Word. Life was neither conferred upon Him as a son of Adam, nor was a transitory experience with Jesus; life was a possession contained within the essence of the Savior.

Note from I Timothy 3:16 that "God was manifest in the flesh." The unseeable, by the eyes of the physicality of created humanity, made Himself manifest, or seeable, to humanity in the Person of Jesus Christ. This is a simple statement of the deity of Jesus.

God, The Son, chose to manifest Himself before man as a man. Jesus is God. For our sake He became man that He might die as a man and offer us full pardon from our sins.

John claims that he, and the other apostles – and many others for that matter, had seen the physicality of Jesus. In seeing Jesus, they saw God encased in human flesh. Consider John 14:9 where Jesus again asserts the Truth that He is God. Consider John 3:13 where Jesus claims, as He is talking with Nicodemus during a night in Jerusalem, that He is in Heaven at that very instant. This concept of omnipresence is a trait of God, alone. Jesus is very God from eternity unto eternity. He is not a created being. He is the very Agent of Creation. (John 1:3)

John carefully chooses his words. He does not call Jesus "everlasting" at this point. That would leave the possibility of a beginning at some point. John calls Jesus "eternal." Only God is eternal. Therefore, the conclusion must be reached that Jesus is eternal – that is existent throughout the entirety of eternity. This can only be said of God.

Still, John notes that Jesus was *with The Father* in eternity before He was *manifest*, or *revealed* to humanity. This, too is an important phrase used when John says that Jesus was *with The Father*. Jesus often said that He and The Father were One. This phrase speaks of the essential unity of the Triune Godhead. There is but One God. There is one Essene of God. (Hebrews 1:3) Yet the uniqueness of God is revealed via three distinct Persons. *Persons* is not a perfect word to use when describing the Triune God; it may, however, be the best that our human minds can grasp while we are in these bodies of clay. Consider Matthew 28:19 where the baptismal formula is given as "...in the name [SINGULAR] of the Father, and of the Son, and of the Holy Ghost." One Name but three personages.

We are not tasked with understanding the *higher* math of Heaven. The Three, The Father, The Son, and The Holy Ghost **is** one God. Our task is to simply accept that which God has said.

John may have written this down but God inspired and preserved the Words of Truth in His Scripture.]

1.3 *That which we have seen and heard declare we unto you, that ye also may have fellowship with us: and truly our fellowship is with the Father, and with his Son Jesus Christ.*

[We, none of us in the time frame have seen the Lord with our physical eyes. But, we are allowed to look past the ages and see the form and reality of Jesus through the eyes of the apostles. Their memories are opened to us that we may behold the face of the Lord. It is the moving of the Spirit of Inspiration upon these memoirs which enables the "eye of faith" to see the reality of the Lord.

It is within the reality of that eternal Lord that our faith is made complete unto salvation. It is within that salvation that our fellowship is confirmed in the same faith as that of the apostles.

Through the agency of this faith we are allowed fellowship with God through prayer and through the Scripture which He has given us. The Spirit touches our hearts in these acts as well. The fellowship also finds us using those gifts which God has bestowed upon us both in the church to edify other believers and in the world to search out sinners over whom we pray the prayer of faith, as did John at this place, that the Spirit may draw all those who would come to like precious faith.

All of the above is contingent upon saving faith in the Lord. Without this salvation there is no fellowship with the Triune Lord. The Jamieson/Fausett/Brown Commentary notes that this fellowship regarding The Father and The Son emphasizes the unity of the Trinity even as the phrase *with the Father and with the Son* emphasizes the Persons of the Godhead. The Spirit is not mentioned at this point as it is The Spirit Who enables this fellowship. We are privileged to enjoy the fellowship *with* The Spirit in this life as He draws us into fellowship and seals us as the people of God through His ministry. (Ephesians 4:30)]

1.4 *And these things write we unto you, that your joy may be full.*

Psalm 16:11; John 15:11; 16:24; 17:13; I Peter 1:8

[Again we find the same consideration of the people of the exodus. All were sons of Abraham but not all actually entered into the Land. There is a calling to the Name and there is a consecration of the individual to the task. Not all Christians will walk close to the Savior; in the failure to do this they lose joy and rewards which might have been theirs.

John says that this letter is sent to the people so that they might decide to enter fully into the joy of the Lord as they enter fully into their walk as believers. Salvation is based wholly on the Blood of Christ. Far too many Christians have found a "fire escape" from Hell. They will eternally praise God for this. But, they have shirked their duty to fully follow and offer themselves as "living sacrifices" (Romans 12:1) unto God.

For those who would doubt the above, consider that Scripture would not give so much space to appeals for a deeper walk were that deeper walk not available. God saves all who call upon His Name. All who call upon His Name do not always walk in the power available within that salvation experience. We are so often a defeated people because we refuse to reach out and claim the victory God has offered to us even within this world!]

1.5 *This then is the message which we have heard of him, and declare unto you, that God is light, and in him is no darkness at all.*

[I think it important to consider that John has claimed inspiration for this epistle. He disclaims any possibility that the message of this letter is his own. He claims only to be writing what Jesus had declared to him.

It is always a good idea to enter into any religious discussion with the inspired and preserved Words of God. It is only those Words which can defeat Satan. As our example of how we as humans ought to approach temptations, in the fourth chapter of Matthew we find that Jesus answered every temptation with an appeal to Scripture.

Even when Satan attempted to "bend" Scripture to teach an error, Jesus answered with the "straight arrow" of the Written Words of God to defeat the plan of Satan. Even the best of Satan's wiles, and he has a better grasp of the human psyche than do we, can be thwarted every time with an appeal to the true Scripture with true trust in the Lord.

Study the Word in order to become proficient in the use of the Word. No true athlete feels that he has no need to train. Even the professional sports leagues start with a training camp. It the world so cares for that which is transitory, cannot we understand the need to earnestly study the Words of Life. (II Timothy 2:15)

John makes note that God is Light. The same, of course, is also said of God, the Son, in John 1:4. It might be good to consider just what light is. Light is that factor which allows all to see the reality of a situation. In the last couple of chapters of the Book of Revelation, we find that there is no need for the sun or moon in Heaven or the New Jerusalem. It is God that is the light in that situation.

The light which we have in our physical universe is able only to illuminate that which is of creation. It is only within the True Light of God, and the Perfectly inspired and preserved Word of His witness in the Scripture, which allows us to see the Holiness and Power of God as contrasted with the despicable and diabolical works of sin and darkness. Where true light exists, the darkness must flee. Where the power of God exists, sin can never conquer.

It is the power of the light of God which destroys sin even in this world. As God judges the earth for sin, all that will remain of sin is the lesson that sin kills but the Power of God restores and redeems.]

1.6 *If we say that we have fellowship with him, and walk in darkness, we lie, and do not the truth:*

[There is a comedian whose "catchphrase" is "If you knock over a bucket of red paint on to your head you might have a "red neck." O.K. That isn't one of his jokes. His routine is centered on the idea that if you act a certain way it is very likely that you are that way.

Folks, it is a truism that if you continue to walk in sin and have no compulsion to walk in piety of life, you are probably a sinner and not a saint! This is not to say that all Christians will walk a life of "Victory in Jesus." But, a true Christian who is walking contrary to the known will of God will be so convicted by that truth that he will be miserable.

An old sow will be very content to wallow in a mud puddle. A debutant in her high heels and evening gown will work very hard to get out of the mud should she fall into the "pig pen" of the barn yard. If she knew that the pig pen was there she would probably not go near the farm.

A true Christian might fall down and get dirty once in a while. He'll be so miserable that he will struggle to find a shower! I have seen two types of response in a man who was caught in scandal. The unsaved man will be sorry he got caught. The Christian will be devastated that he has let down his Lord.

The man who can walk in sin and feel no compulsion to regret his path gives real evidence that he has never walked with the Master.

My wife organized the local Labor Day Parade for many years before her home going to Glory. The parade organized at Chambers Street, traveled down Main Street, turned south on Cherry Street and traveled to the court house on South Street. If I had a decorated float on the same day, at the same time, and was traveling on Grand Avenue, I might look like I belonged in the parade. I wouldn't be in that parade, however. Just trying to look the part, or even really looking the part, does not make one "of the part." It might, at best, make him a pretender.

John was saying that it made no difference what you looked like, or felt like for that matter. The important thing is to actually be walking the "parade route" with the leading of the Spirit and the fellowship of Jesus.

"Looking" might seem right but only "being" is really being. (II Peter 1:10) Remember that one who lies to himself is still lying.]

1.7 *But if we walk in the light, as he is in the light, we have fellowship one with another, and the blood of Jesus Christ his Son cleanseth us from all sin.*

[See note at Genesis 3:15

It is the Blood of Jesus which cleanses us from sin. The baptism of an infant will only produce a mad and wet infant. The Blood of Jesus is appropriated unto us for salvation when we trust Him in salvation.

Note well the "if." This is a conditional promise. There is a need for certain conditions to be met if the promise is to take effect. It was, and still is, the Blood of Jesus Christ shed on the Cross of Calvary in the great self-sacrifice of Jesus for our sins which is that completed condition. Our acceptance of Jesus as our Savior is an acceptance of these promises. The condition is predicated upon the fact of the atonement of Jesus. We are merely, so to speak, along for the "ride." Even our acceptance is tethered to the fact that the Holy Spirit of God has so convicted our hearts as to call us to this salvation in Jesus.

No one should consider that he had any part at all in salvation. We are not saved by merit; we are granted salvation due to the love of God being expressed upon us in that call from the Spirit of God. Our response is just that, a response. But, what a Heavenly and sweet that response become in our own lives due to the great love of The Father.

Have you ever seen a baby and reached out to see if the child would come to you? Some heartily accept the invitation to be held. They love the comfort of a loving embrace. Others react with fear to the stretched-out hands. They are not comfortable with the "unknown." Some sinners will accept the love of God. Others are only comfortable in their sinful environment; they will not accept even the love of God.

Those who do accept the love of God into their lives will walk in the Light of the Lord. I have a pair of glasses that darken into "sun glasses" when I wear them outside on a sunny day. When I go inside these glasses are so dark that I couldn't find the floor if I tripped over something.

The reality of the building remains reality; it is only my darkened vision that causes me to not see that reality. There are those who are actually born again who have allowed the cares of this present world to nearly blind them to the glories which God has for them. There are times when we need to remove the "glasses" of earthly cares and desires which obscure the spiritual realities. This does not mean that these are not "walking in the Light;" this only means that they are not perceiving the Light which is available.

We need to pray for the erring brother.

There is a problem in this scenario. We need to ascertain whether this is an erring brother or a lost sinner who at one time was smitten with the Light but had never accepted the Lord. Our only reasonable recourse is to pray for guidance. As a general rule of thumb, I would take such a one back to the basics and allow the Spirit to either lead toward reconciliation or repentance in the life of such a one.

Prayer can work wonders when our mind is clouded. It is always a good idea to trust in the leading of the Lord!

Also, notice that it is the Blood of Christ which effects our salvation. I briefly corresponded with the religion editor of a small weekly newspaper. He had found the verse in Leviticus 17:11 wherein it is said that "For the life of the flesh is in the blood..." From this he had extrapolated that salvation by the Blood of Jesus actually meant simply to follow the example of Jesus.

Had this man simply read the rest of the verse, ("...and I have given it to you upon the altar to make an atonement for your souls: for it is the blood that maketh an atonement for the soul") he would have seen that salvation is in the Blood of Jesus. While Jesus did instruct us how we should walk as humans upon this earth, the example of the Life of Jesus has never granted salvation to anyone. It is His Blood, shed at the Self-Sacrifice of Calvary, which has saved every individual who has come to Him in faith and accepted the pardon obtained from this atoning death of Jesus.

It is the Blood of Jesus which has cleansed us from all sin. This, of course, also cleanses us from the penalty of sin. We are saved and secure as Blood bought believers.

Some have used this verse to argue for baptismal regeneration of children. It is the Blood of Jesus which cleanses us from sin. Therefore, the baptism of an infant will only produce a mad and wet infant. The Blood of Jesus is appropriated unto us for salvation when we trust Him in salvation.]

1.8 *If we say that we have no sin, we deceive ourselves, and the truth is not in us.*

[There are those who would use verse seven to argue for the possibility of a type of "sinless perfection." This verse is the antidote to that error.

This verse also argues against the Roman fiction of "supererogation." This is a doctrine that our volume of "good works" can build up an account which will outweigh our "bad works" and give us a type of "reserve fund" with which to approach God. Since we can have not "good works" beyond the "Great Work" of Jesus upon the Cross, we can never have any "merit" with which to stand before God and expect entrance into Heaven.

This verse is not a matter of John using hyperbole as did Paul, "the chief of sinners," in I Timothy 1:15. This is a plain statement of fact brought out by John.

Please note that John is speaking in the present tense. He does not say, "never had sin," but "have (present tense) no sin." It may have been that John was reacting against heresy which was already at work to pervert the pure Gospel. The Gnostics believed that only the physical was sinful; they would argue that they could live such spiritually elite lives as to never be tainted by the physical. Then, they argued, they could have no sin.

The Nicolaitans believed that Christianity meant that nothing was forbidden because the Law was overturned. They sought to use the freedom of Christ as a license to sin. Such, of course, is anathema to true spirituality. We are saved to walk a new life of obedience to the principles of God; these include moral purity before all men.

John corrects these views and adds that one who has such views cannot be walking in the light of Christ. The truth of God cannot be found within the construct of unbridled sin.]

1.9 *If we confess our sins, he is faithful and just to forgive us our sins, and to cleanse us from all unrighteousness.*

[Once again, we find the conditional "if." This time the condition is based upon an acceptance of true doctrine. Since the false doctrine of the Nicolaitans and Gnostics was an unscriptural perversion of true faith in Christ this is rather important condition.

It is possible that a true Christian had been led astray by the false teachers of heresy. In order to restore his fellowship with the church and the Lord it would be necessary for him to renounce error and accept truth into his heart. This was not a search for a rote, "O. K. I'll do it your way." This was a command to accept, honestly and completely, the Truth of God.

Note, please, that this was not a matter of salvation but of fellowship. A Christian who had been led astray was still a Christian. Those God has saved are His. Like the prodigal son they may wander into a far country and live a riotous life. God will bring His Own home. This can be through repentance in this life or by a calling the prodigal from this life and unto his Heavenly home. Consider the Spiritual principle of I Corinthians 11:20 in this light.

What John is saying is that those who had claimed that they could never sin, should confess their sins – this one included!

God had made a promise. He would be counted faithful in the keeping of this promise when He forgave the sin in the life of His child. Notice the word "just" in this light. The purpose is not "justice," as in judging as a magistrate. The sins of the Christian have been judged at the Cross. The promise of God was to be just in the administration of His grace. Those who were truly born again would find the God of Grace to be a welcoming Father even to His erring prodigal.

We might consider this from our understanding of the American Constitution which proscribes the concept of "double jeopardy." A man tried for a crime, murder – for instance, may not be tried a second time for the same crime. Once found "not guilty," the person is – in the eyes of the law of the land, "Not guilty" even if future findings reveal that he did commit that crime.

Our sins have been judged at the Cross of Jesus. We have been found positionally guiltless due the fact that Jesus has pardoned our sin with His blood. Romans 8:1 informs us that, "There is therefore now no condemnation to them which are in Christ Jesus, who walk not after the flesh, but after the Spirit." In salvation we have "walked after" the conviction on our hearts placed by the Spirit; that is the dynamic which allowed us to place our faith upon God. The verse speaks to our place as adopted sons of God.

This idea of confession is important. This allows us to look at ourselves as God looks at us. The confession is a confession of humility that we've done that which is unseemly. We admit that we were wickedly acting within the love of God. We are mistreating the Savior Who died for us. Confess the sin and admit it is as wicked as God knows it to be. Confession is not, "Yeah; I did it." Confession is, "I did this despicable thing and I was wrong!" It is the humbling admission of our insufficiency and error.

The promise of God to such and individual, as are we all in too many instances!, is that He will both forgive our sin and, as we admit and renounce our vileness, He will cleanse that unrighteousness within us which causes such abominations.

The forgiveness of God is not as that of the heathens whereby their "god" withholds a specific punishment due to their groveling before the idol of their construction. The forgiveness of The True God is a forgiveness which considers the sin as though it had never happened because He loves. The forgiveness of God goes beyond even this. The forgiveness of God goes so far as to cleanse the soul of the predisposition to seek out this sin in the future. The cleansing includes the restoration of that walk within the Truth of God whereby we seek His good pleasure because we love Him.

All of this is based upon the salvation which is offered because of the Self-Sacrifice of Jesus at the Cross of Calvary. He shed Blood is the anchor and ground of His offer of salvation and grace.]

1.10   *If we say that we have not sinned, we make him a liar, and his word is not in us.*

[I believe that John was still writing of the false doctrines of the Gnostics and Nicolaitans. This writing was made to Christians who may have been savaged by these heretical doctrines. His words are adaptable to the unsaved, of course, but the primary thrust is to the Christian. He is reminding them of their own propensity to sin. Beyond this he is teaching that any doctrine which teaches the possibility of a sinless perfectionism within the bounds of sinful actions is a "doctrine of devils." (I Timothy 4:1)

The plain fact is that such a doctrine on the shelf of our profession is a proof that the Truth of God, from the Words of God, is not among us or our library of spiritual truths. We are a spiritually defiled person when we doubt the fact that we are sinfully human. We might aspire to the sinless perfection of God but it is a position to which we will never attain in the present life.

When a small boy is with his father he will reach up to hold the hand of his father. The youngster understands that his protector and safety is his dad. So are we with our Heavenly Father. He is our Protector, our Counselor, our Leader and our only Safety within the constraints of time.

It is the height of conceit to claim that we are perfect in any matter. We are not so holy as to be without sin and consequence in this life.

Folks, one thing I would like to warn about as I close commentary for this chapter. It ain't never a wise idea to call God a liar. (Only one negative in there because "ain't" ain't a real word!)

But, this is what we do when we argue that we are completely without sin as we casually prance through this life with complete disregard for spiritual propriety.

It is rather sad to see a person claim not to be a heavy drinker as he crawls from his car and says, "But, officer, I only had only teensy, tiny drink a couple of hours ago." The policeman knows better and will probably issue a ticket.

The person who boasts he does not sin is calling God a liar even as he lies in his assertion. Bad form. God doesn't give tickets but He is still not to be mocked.]

FIRST JOHN - CHAPTER TWO

***2.1**   My little children, these things write I unto you, that ye sin not. And if any man sin, we have an advocate with the Father, Jesus Christ the righteous:*

[Did you notice that verse? "Don't sin; but, when you do..." Jesus understands. He is always ready to accept our honest repentance! Jesus does not expect us to be perfect. He does expect us to try. And, He expects us to be repentant when we fail.

John begins this verse with "My little children." He is therefore writing to Christians. Even the Christian can fail God by committing sin. It is, however, the duty of that Christian to confess and forsake that sin.

That word "advocate" is number 3875 in Strong's. It is defined as "an intercessor, consoler:--advocate, comforter." As our "Lawyer" Jesus pleads the Blood of His Self-Sacrifice in regard to our case. When we have sinned we are notetheless not separated from His great love. Notice that the word means both advocate and comforter. Not only does He plead His Blood *for* us as concerns our salvation, He also pleads His Blood *to* us in respect to the fellowship which is ours with Him. We have been unruly children but we remain children of our Heavenly Father.

The same word is used of the Holy Spirit in His Office of calling to repentance and upholding the saint with His empowering of the believer in the Christian walk, protection of the believer in the purposes and leading of God's program for the believer in this life, and the guiding the progression in holiness of the believer.

The fact that John calls us his "little children" is speaking to his elder age and office. He is addressing us as children in the faith who owe a debt of attention to the counsel of one who has been a close associate of our Lord. John is speaking from his office as an apostle of the Lord. This simple concept is drawn on even deeper water when we consider that these Words are the inspired and preserved Words of the Scripture.

We need to understand the context of which John wrote. As was noted in the commentary on the previous chapter, it seems likely that John was writing to confront the error of both the Gnostics and the Nicolaitans who both approached the same heresy, although from differing angels, that the Christian could live both above and in sin at the same time. The verse is not to encourage a sinful experience but to discourage such with the reminder to repent and renounce sin as not natural within the Christian walk.]

***2.2**   And he is the propitiation for our sins: and not for ours only, but also for the sins of the whole world.*

[The picture here is somewhat that of the Mosaic sacrificial system. The purpose of the priest under the Law was to make sacrifice for the penitent which would atone for the sin of that penitent person. But, Hebrews 10:4 tells us that "For *it is* not possible that the blood of bulls and of goats should take away sin."

While using the imagery of the Mosaic Law, John is speaking of Jesus Who's Self-Sacrifice at Calvary was sufficient to remove the stain of sin. This, the events of the Cross, was the plan of God for the sin of man even before the creation of Adam. The perfect foreknowledge of God saw the devastation of sin in Adam would require the events of Calvary. The perfect Love of God set the course toward Calvary and the redemption of lost humanity. (Consider Revelation 13:8b and I Peter 1:20.)

The question must be asked: If "the blood of bulls and of goats" could not take away sin, why did God institute the Mosaic Law of Sacrifice?

To see the answer to that question we must consider, first, Genesis 15:6. "And he believed in the LORD; and he counted it to him for righteousness." We must disabuse ourselves of the notion that Abraham was the first monotheist. Just one chapter before this, Genesis the 14th chapter, we are introduced to Melchizedek who was a true priest of The True and Living God.

Melchizedek confirms Abraham. Abraham did not have a great "brainstorm" and *invent* worship of Jehovah. Abraham had a conversion experience and accepted Jehovah worship. Since Ur, from where Abraham was called, was a great trading city, it is possible that Abraham would have been introduced to this truth before his call came to enter into a "land which he knew not."

Whatever the chronology or means, since these were pre-Scripture days, it is also easy to accept that God spoke to Abraham about the Truth, it is obvious that Abraham had believed in God and accepted His Words in faith.

As in all ages it is faith that is the operating principle of righteousness. This isn't a nebulous "faith" founded in anything except the Words of God. This is why Samuel was able to tell King Saul, "And Samuel said, Hath the LORD as great delight in burnt offerings and sacrifices, as in obeying the voice of the LORD? Behold, to obey is better than sacrifice, and to hearken than the fat of rams." (I Samuel 15:22)

Even during the times of the prophets, within the Mosaic Covenant, we find that faith in God is the "gold standard" of fellowship with Him.

I do not believe the old saying that the Old Testament saints were saved by looking forward to the Cross. Even though the Old Testament Scriptures teach the Truth of the Suffering Savior, that was a mystery hidden from their eyes. Their righteousness was based on their faith in the revealed Words of God. Though they did not understand, their salvation – as is the salvation of anyone in the history of creation, is predicated on the shed Blood of Jesus Christ at the Cross of Calvary. See my notes at Luke 16:9 for a fuller discussion of these Old Testaments saints.

What we have seen is that there has always been only one basis for the salvation of souls; that is the Self-Sacrifice of Jesus on the Cross of Calvary. Our part in this, and this is only due to the calling of the Spirit upon our lives, is to exercise faith in the Words of God as revealed to us in this Dispensation of Grace.

It can be argued, "But what of the Mosaic Law era saints who trusted in the sacrifice of the animals of creation?" Their faith was rewarded with the designation of "righteousness." Faith is always the means of salvation. The "righteous" were then saved by the Blood of Christ. Once again, please refer to my notes on Luke 16:9 as noted above.

There are not two means of salvation. There is but one which is the grace of God through the Cross. Before the Cross people were saved by faith and trust on the light they had. That is the same in our day. In this dispensation we are called to faith in Christ. Consider Paul's discussion at Mars Hill in Acts 17:26-32.

This brings us to a real difference between the Old Testament Hebrew and the

New Testament Christian. Genesis 12:3 contains the call and promise to Abraham. "And I will bless them that bless thee, and curse him that curseth thee: and in thee shall all families of the earth be blessed."

That verse has been wonderfully fulfilled. Pick any endeavor of humanity, from medicine to education, from sports to entertainment, from science to literature, from economics to politics and you will find the Children of Abraham near the top of the field. This world would be a much darker place physically, religiously and culturally were it not for the contributions of the people who came from Abraham as his extended offspring.

Even the very inspired and preserved Scripture which speaks to us in this day was given to us through the inspiration of God upon Words committed to parchment by the people of Abraham. (Romans 3:1-2)

The greatest blessing to come from Abraham is the Lord, Jesus Christ. In His humanity Jesus is a Grandson of Abraham. The coming of Jesus into the world was not simply a joyous event for His mother. Jesus spoke of His purpose of taking upon Himself the robes of humanity. "Even as the Son of man came not to be ministered unto, but to minister, and to give his life a ransom for many." (Matthew 20:28)

The next time you see a Christmas display consider that Baby in the manger. Consider that the real "reason for the season" is the Cross of Calvary. Jesus came to die in time so that others could live in eternity. This is the reason for all of those Old Testament sacrifices. They were effective in their time and place but they were designed to be done away with when their teaching was culminated by the fulfillment of their prophecy. The Self-Sacrifice of Jesus was THE sacrifice to end all other sacrifices.

A discrepancy has been imagined. The verse in Matthew says "a ransom for many," but the verse in First John says that just died for the sins of the whole world. There is no contradiction; Jesus died potentially for the sins of every person who has ever lived. Only those who actually accept Him as Savior will benefit in His offered gift of eternal salvation.

Moving on from the concept of the Mosaic Law we find that salvation is now open to all members of all the families of the earth.]

2.3   And hereby we do know that we know him, if we keep his commandments.

[As with the second verse "He," the personal pronoun "Him," speaks of "Jesus Christ the righteous" spoken of in verse one. This is another blow to the Gnostic doctrine of the flesh always being evil. As an aside, we are on dangerous ground when we call the creative acts of God as producing evil! (Acts 10:15) This verse hearkens back to the teachings of Jesus while He was in His physical body on this earth. So physical was His body that He offered it on the Cross.

The resurrection of Jesus was of this same physical body. More of His rightful glory was returned to Him after His resurrection. But, His body was the same body. The nail marks in His hands and feet were testimony to this fact. His ability to enter into locked rooms and even to hide His true identity, as with the men on the Emmaus Road, testified to the glorification of His physical body. The meal He shared with His disciples in John 21:15 testifies to the fact

The Gnostic sect boasted of their great knowledge. But, their lives did not show a commitment to the commandments of faith.

This verse does speak of the "good works" of keeping the commandments of Christ. Once again we are informed that "good works" of any kind flow from salvation. Before salvation there can be no truly good works in the spiritual sense. Salvation is not of our earning. Salvation is a gift which Jesus bestows upon His children when they come in faith to Him.]

2.4 *He that saith, I know him, and keepeth not his commandments, is a liar, and the truth is not in him.*

[This speaks of one who protests that he is born again but continually discards the commandments of Christ to live a holy life before man and God. Such a one is either mistaken or deliberately deceptive. The unsaved may claim salvation but when there is no evidence displayed to support this assertion it is likely to be false.
The Lord is the Truth, the Way and the Life. (John 14:6) He does not reside in a saving manner within one who has not accepted Him as Savior. The saddest thing is that this may be a person who believes he is saved because he has adopted some of the cultural "trappings" of salvation but has never received the Lord. This unsaved one may have been persuaded that there was no need to adopt the Savior by others who claimed salvation but did not possess it themselves.
Once again, one who lies to himself is nonetheless a liar.]

2.5 *But whoso keepeth his word, in him verily is the love of God perfected: hereby know we that we are in him.*

["Keepeth his word" is somewhat analogous to the phrase "The Word of God." When we use that phrase we are speaking of the entirety of Scripture. Likewise, keeping "his word" is a phrase which speaks of keeping all of the pure religion of Christ and all that this implies.
The concept is not a sinless perfectionism. It is a consistant walk with Christ. Once again this can be juxtaposed with the doctrine of the Gnostics and Nicolaitans whose habit was to walk outside the revealed religion of Jesus.
I would also report that this is not a fearful consideration where one is afraid of a "God of Wrath" Who waits to pounce on the smallest error. This is in consideration of the Love of God. (I John 4:18) This is a walk which is anxious to please the Lord Who has redeemed us and loved us with an everlasting love. (Jeremiah 31:3)]

2.6 *He that saith he abideth in him ought himself also so to walk, even as he walked.*

[The very etymology of the word "Christian" is "one who is like Christ." The one who abides within the Christian should become the center of our walk, wants, and goals. One can easily claim the indwelling of the Spirit but the proof of the veracity of that statement is shown by a walk consistent with the claim.
Once again this is not a sinless perfectionism. This is the lively habit of living out the life of Christian witness and walk into the world. Luther said, "It is not Christ's walking on the sea, but His ordinary walk, that we are called on to imitate." God does not expect us to do more than we are able; this is why He enables us in so many ways. But, God does expect us to do all that we can for and with Him.
Once again, as John will often emphasize, the entire process is energized both

by the Love of God for us and the reciprocation of our love to Him. As a love of baseball will cause one to spend many lazy afternoons in the company of flys and bats, so will a love of the Lord cause us to spend time in His Word and praying praise to His Name.]

***2.7** Brethren, I write no new commandment unto you, but an old commandment which ye had from the beginning. The old commandment is the word which ye have heard from the beginning.*

[Be very wary of anyone who has discovered a new doctrinal truth. There may be extension and deeper consideration of the old doctrine. But, the very use of the word "new" would presuppose that the thing was not found in the "Old Book."

To be brutally honest, this is the error of those who would claim inspiration for the King James Bible. We can argue that the King James Bible is an accurate representation of the Words originally inspired of God. But, to argue for inspiration is to make a claim that God has either inspired two works, from which we might find a "spiritual smorgasbord," or He has replaced the one with the other. Either way we are left with an unstable Scriptural base.

Let me illustrate this principle. Suppose I went to a store and bought a book of recipes. It is clear that someone has made the cakes in this book before sharing the recipe. My effort to bake a cake according to the recipe would not produce the original cake. It would produce at best a cake *like* that original cake. It would be a cake, like the original, made available to me many years later. Such is a translation. It is not the originally inspired Words of God; it is a replica, at its best, of that originally inspired Word for people who have neither access nor ability to read the original words.

Another illustration is in order since we will all agree that inspiration lay only upon those Words of the original manuscripts. This morning I found myself going 40 mph in a 30 mph zone. I wasn't arrested. But, had I been could I have refused the ticket unless the office had seen for himself the original law establishing that speed zone. I could argue that it is well possible that there have been changes in his "law books" which may not agree with the original law. How could I be arrested under such a fallible situation?

Had I argued such a thing it is likely that I'd have met more personal from this officers "denomination." I probably would have been given a nice set of jewelry for my wrists and escorted to the local "Steel Bar Hotel" for an evening's lodging had I persisted in such a discussion.

Any law written in an officer's handbook which contained the same wording as in the original written law is an official version of that law.. Can we faithfully claim less authority for the inspired and preserved Words of God in over 90% of the available evidence existing today? Our venerable King James Bible is a faithful representation of those Words and can be authoritative to the Christian of this day.

This is not to say that all of the Old Testament was fully understood in the pre-Cross days. The concept of the Suffering Savior seems to have been not grasped by most. Simeon prophesied of this very thing in Luke 2:34-35. It seems doubtful that even he understood the significance of his words.

Jesus is come as Light into the world. (John 1:4-5) In Him the dark things, not before understood, are now revealed.

Looking back from this verse we see the concept of a walk with Jesus. Deuteronomy 6:5 had already expressed the need to love the LORD. Leviticus 20:7 had spoken that we must be holy even as God is Holy. Surely this is the concept of walking in Jesus. He is God, the Son, and fully worthy of our devotion even as He is the son of God and has served as our example in His humanity.

This is not a grievous command. This is not an impossible goal. This is a privilege given us so that our joy may be full. (I John 1:4)]

2.8 *Again, a new commandment I write unto you, which thing is true in him and in you: because the darkness is past, and the true light now shinneth.*

[John concedes that these old doctrines are become new in their application. Jesus, Himself, mentioned this in John 13:34, "A new commandment I give unto you, That ye love one another; as I have loved you, that ye also love one another."

John is preparing to move on to the concept of the love of the brethren. This was a command of Leviticus 19:18. It is still a command. But, the emphasis on the command is now in the light of Jesus Christ and the salvation and brotherhood He has given us with the fellowship of the church. This is more than simply "mutual respect." This is mutual respect in the fellowship of the Lord.

Contained herein is a picture of the concept of progressive revelation. The revelation of God never contradicts an earlier revelation. It will expand and explain that earlier revelation. Much of the Old Testament concerns physical acts which explain, under the teaching of the Holy Spirit, spiritual truths which we need to understand as the adopted children of God.

John is beginning to explain the spiritual ramifications and responsibility of love one for another. This is not a *new* commandment; it is a *newly constructed* commandment. It is as though the motoring law had once said to drive in a manner to keep the vehicle under control but now gave a certain speed limit to achieve that end. Love was to no longer be predicated on a principle of civil order; it was now given a higher attachment, not that the lower was not a principle to consider, of an obligation of response to our Lord and Savior.

The Light of the Word, Jesus, has given to us a more perfect understanding of the reality of God and our relationship with Him. The darkness of some of the mystery is past as the Love of God is revealed by the Light of Jesus. The shadows and types of Moses and the prophets have found their perfect fulfillment in the Person and religion of Jesus, the Christ.

This Light is found reflected in the pages of inspired and preserved Scripture. As we walk in Him we are privileged to find His pure light in a personal manner within our walk and also within our fellowship among the brethren. This properly reflects the concept of "new" within our verse. It is "new" as to its freshness of beauty and purpose.]

2.9 *He that saith he is in the light, and hateth his brother, is in darkness even until now.*

[I was taking a shower a few days ago when soap got into my eyes. Past the pain, not much but still effective in blocking my vision, I found myself blinking and unable to find my towel for a few seconds. If the Love of Christ, salvation, is not truly within our souls we have a compromised ability to see and act properly.

One who has the Light of Jesus Christ in his life will not only see clearly but act clearly in his physical, as well as his spiritual, life. Brotherly love, especially for those within the household of faith is a command of Jesus for our Christian lives. As a lawful command from our Heavenly Commander, this is an expectation of our Lord.

One of the purposes of "Basic Training" in the military is to convert a civilian into a soldier. It is not natural in our society to obey someone's orders simply because they have voiced the order. It is necessary in the military to obey the order of anyone who is our superior in rank. Failure to follow those orders argues for one of two things. The first is that the person refusing is not a member of the military. The second is that the person refusing is derelict in his duty.

John bypasses the second as irrelevant and argues that if one has hatred, rather than love, for his brother, he is not in the military. He is in darkness rather than in the light. I would be disposed to argue that this person was not saved except for the use of the word "brother." That word suggests that there does exist a fellowship, whether or not accepted by both parties, of a familial existence between the two.

In this case it would be an erring brother who was derelict in his duty to his Lord who does not love his brother.

The only other consideration would be that the man who hates is not Christian, despite his protestations otherwise, as he walks in darkness.

Hesitantly, I would opt for the former exegesis. The use of the word "brother" and the exhortation to walk in the light (verse six above) could not be properly given to one outside the faith.

Walking in the light is not the final evidence of conversion. We can only observe what we see. One may well appear to be walking in the things of the light and only be living a lie to himself and others. Walking in seeming darkness could reflect either the evidence of an unsaved person or the evidence of a Christian who lives within an unseemly carnality. We can only observe what we see.

Prayer for either party to find conversion or consecration is deeply needed. Seeking the wisdom of the Spirit in order to pray rightly is essential.]

2.10 *He that loveth his brother abideth in the light, and there is none occasion of stumbling in him.*

[Here is a verse that could have come from James. The thought is there that this man loves his brother to the extent that he will seek to keep from stumbling himself so that others would not see him and fail themselves. Paul uses the same reasoning in I Corinthians 8:13, "Wherefore, if meat make my brother to offend, I will eat no flesh while the world standeth, lest I make my brother to offend."

In walking in the light this person is careful to follow the commands which Jesus gave to His followers and to follow the example which Jesus, in His humanity, gave to His Church.

Jesus (John 12:32) said that He would draw men to himself. By walking in the commandments and example of Jesus we may show Him to the world. Although verbal witness is imperative, this exercise of personal piety in being a true follower of Jesus, must be part of our witness or will not ring true.]

2.11   *But he that hateth his brother is in darkness, and walketh in darkness, and knoweth not whither he goeth, because that darkness hath blinded his eyes.*

[Not only is this man in darkness, the darkness has caused him to be blind. This isn't just not seeing; this extends to not having any idea where he is going.

The picture is more than simply not liking. It is carried on to an actual loathing. Once again there is the use of the word "brother." Since John seems to use "brother" in the sense of the brotherhood of believers, we must carefully consider if this man who is hating is an actual, also woefully unscriptural, Christian. The fact that the man is in darkness even as he walks therein, would not suggest a Christian. Neither should the phrase that this man does not know where he is going suggest a Christian.

Or does it? The sinner should have no illusion about his eternity in Hell. Some, of course, do not fully understand and expect to find Heaven in one manner or another. But, why should a sinner's eyes be blinded to Spiritual truth? It would seem that Satan would more likely banish the concept of the Spiritual realities from the sinner's eyes and minds.

I would argue that we have once again encountered a warning concerning the Gnostic and Nicolatian. These are not Christians, for the most part as a few may be beguiled Christians. They would be disposed to hate the true Christians among the brotherhood since these walk fully in the light and do not cross to the "dark side" of heresy.

Ensnared by the false doctrine, these would not walk in the light for they have found the darkness to be more comfortable in the license and error. Thinking themselves to be wise in their own conceits, they would naturally oppose any who opposed them. They would not realize that their spiritual darkness, which they would deny, was leading them to the precipice of ruin at the gate of Hell.]

2.12   *I write unto you, little children, because your sins are forgiven you for his name's sake.*

[Once again using title of "little children," John is writing specifically to Christians. He is embarked on teaching and uplifting the flock of God. May we especially note that they are this to the Glory of Jesus. It was the plan of God to save humanity from their sin even before man had been created. This is a glorious testimony to the Lord Jesus Christ and His love for His creation.

It is a wondrous thing to consider our salvation. It is even more wonderful to consider the power and purposes of God Who looked down through the years of time and made all possible. The need of man was too daunting to be considered by man. The love, power and grace of God looked down upon a creation which had rebelled against Him and said, "I'll do for you what you cannot do for yourselves." He called us to an unattainable salvation by the strength of His unalterable grace and love.

May we often offer the sacrifice of praise and adoration to Him. We could call this our duty in response to His love. It is more proper in all this vast privilege of salvation that we reflect upon all that God is and does! As the old song says, "Without Him I could do nothing."

Consider that in the next few verses John addressed fathers, young men and children. There is some argument to be made that this corresponds to differing ages as concerns the profession of faith. "Little children" would then refer to the newly saved.

"Young men" would then refer to those who were growing, but not yet grown, in the faith. "Fathers" would then refer to those who were mature teachers within the church.

These distinctions are probably accurate in some cases. But, I find no need to spiritualize the plain words of John.

It is probably true that the term, as it does earlier in the first verse of the chapter, "little children" is a reference to the saints of the church to whom John is an elder and leader. It seems probable that John was the "spiritual father" of many of the church as he led them into salvation, himself.

Nonetheless we consider this from the plain standpoint that John was speaking differing ages of people within the church.

John reminds all true Christians that the Lord has forgiven their sins. This is foundational in the Christian walk. Until our sins are forgiven by the Blood of Jesus Christ, we cannot walk the Christian walk.]

2.13 *I write unto you, fathers, because ye have known him that is from the beginning. I write unto you, young men, because ye have overcome the wicked one. I write unto you, little children, because ye have known the Father.*

[John writes to fathers, young men, and little children. Why are there no old men among this group? There probably are some elderly among the group. But, there will be few. An old mind is generally set in concrete. It hard to find a true conversion among the elderly because they have their minds set in their ways. That may be a subliminal warning given by John at this place.

John says, "I write." This is followed by statements from his own perspective as currently writing as he put pen to parchment. Nonetheless, we realize that while John wrote, the concept of the inspiration of God was upon the words. John wrote, and composed in a sense. But, the True Author of the inspired and preserved Word is God.

The fathers had been in belief the longest of all. They had learned more of the things of God and were now those who would teach the Truth to their sons – adolescent sons and young sons. This is the proper way for the life of a Christian community to flower and grow.

The young men were those who had overcome the temptations of youth. Constantly buffeted by the slings and arrows of outrageous temptation, they had overcome the wiles of the devil by fleeing to the side of the Savior in the hour of temptation.

The little children are reminded that the true faith does not lie in their cunning but in a reliance upon the Savior. They have known their own fathers and followed their spiritual leading. They had also learned of the Heavenly Father and the need to concern themselves in worship of Him.]

2.14 *I have written unto you, fathers, because ye have known him that is from the beginning. I have written unto you, young men, because ye are strong, and the word of God abideth in you, and ye have overcome the wicked one.*

[This is neither duplication nor repetition. The style of John was to repeat things from differing angles to as to make them better understood. God used the personality of the penmen of Scripture even as He led them to use the exact words to repeat the

Scripture which was already settled in Heaven. (Psalm 119:89)

He reminds the father that they have known Him, that is Christ, from the beginning of their salvation experience. That sentence also is an application of eternity to the Person of Jesus. He did not "begin" in Bethlehem. As John notes in John 1:1-2, Jesus is The Very Eternal God.

The young men are reminded of their strength. But, the importance of the inspired and preserved Scripture abides within them as they have studied. This is a reminder that they have overcome the wicked one through the Scripture rather than through their own powers.

This is also a warning that Satan will be back to tempt them. They need to continually be ready for his wiles and fiery darts.

The phrase "I have written" is to be taken from the perspective of the recipients of the epistle. Verse thirteen mentioned "I write" while this verse says "I have written." It is a style of writing that differentiates between "write," John's perspective and "written," the perspective of his readers. To me it seems a willingness to be always ready to live our Christian lives in all times and situations.

I find it interesting that this verse so closely parallels the preceding verse and yet does not include any reference to the little children. First, I would argue that the little children are stronger in their faith than we may realize. They have accepted Jesus as Savior and now cling to that Truth. May we continue to emphasize Jesus to the children. He is Salvation to those that believe.

Second, the little children are of shorter attention spans. To attempt to "cram too much into their little noggins" is a thing which might chase them out of the room. We pay close attention to them. We answer their questions on levels which they may understand. And, we allow the Spirit to speak to them. He's better at it than are we!]

2.15 *Love not the world, neither the things that are in the world. If any man love the world, the love of the Father is not in him.*

[Matthew 6:21 records these words of Jesus: "For where your treasure is, there will your heart be also." That thing which we treasure is the thing nearest to our hearts. This is not a hard concept to understand. Any man who has stayed home on Sunday Night to watch a football game has demonstrated his love for football as above his love for the evening service.

The protest may be made, "But, I went to the morning service." One must wonder if there had been an early game would he have done so.

Suppose that at the end of the month I have $10.00 extra in my pocket. What will I do? Will I respond to a missionary offering appeal or while I keep the "ten spot" and visit *Chez Golden Arches*? Decisions must be made. Those decisions will reflect the issues upon which our heart most heartily resides.

Do the above illustrations indicate that this verse argues such a one is not saved? I don't believe so. I do believe that the responses do show that the love for God is not paramount in the man's heart.

The verse doesn't reference the love of the man for God, however. The statement is that the love *of* God is not in this person. Consider Ephesians 4:30 in this. It is possible that we can grieve God by our actions. This is not good! But, this verse from Ephesians speaks of our grieving God. Ephesians speaks of the Christian, the born-again person. I would add verse twenty of that chapter, "But ye have not so learned Christ," and verse twenty-seven, "Neither give place to the devil," and find that this person is a Christian who has so grieved the Holy Spirit.

I might add that verse thirty does mention that the Spirit has sealed us into the faith all the way to the day of redemption. The passage in Ephesians definitely speaks of a Christian. Reading the preceding verses, especially twelve through fourteen, and we must conclude that John is speaking of a Christian who looks to the world. This does not elicit the love of God but the discipline of God into that Christians life.

This verse would serve as a warning to the Christian concerning his fellowship with the Lord. It would also serve as a warning to the Christian as to his walk among those of the world. A sinful lifestyle will neither grain reward from God nor entice anyone to come to the Savior.

This, then, is a case of loving someone into the eternal fires of Hell. Is it any wonder that God will find a need to wipe away tears in Heaven (Revelation 21:4) as the redeemed realize that their loss of reward includes, from the natural, the loss of Heaven for friends and family?

We are comforted by the image of our tears of joy as we finally see the Savior's Face for all eternity.]

2.16 *For all that is in the world, the lust of the flesh, and the lust of the eyes, and the pride of life, is not of the Father, but is of the world.*

[The world is the creation of God. It is not the abode of God. However, this world was created to be peopled by a creation of intelligent beings that lived in communion with their Creator. All of the beauty of the world, from the vast oceans scenes to the beauty of the animals of creation was created for the enjoyment of man. Even the abundance of plant life was placed within the earth for the physical sustenance and pleasure of the human.

With Eden serving Him man was only given one prohibition. Rather than tempting man to disobey, this prohibition was a gift to man. By observing this one thing the creature was allowed to express his love and thankfulness to his Creator.

Instead of observing this one prohibition out of love for God, Adam displayed his greater love for the creature. He joined Eve in her sin and thus polluted the entire creation of God with the curse of sin. No longer would that fellowship with God be paramount and unbroken. Even the beauty and provision of that creation became a curse to further separate man from God.

The argument can easily be made that Eve was fashioned as a helper and companion for Adam. Therefore, Adam's desire to exalt companionship with Eve above his companionship with God was a departure from God and God's goodness to him.

Anything which any man considers as more important to him than fellowship with God is the creation of an idol. It is not possible to give spiritual worship to an idol. An idol is a construct of creation. As such it is not capable of receiving worship. Satan is, however, a spiritual being as he is from the spiritual realms. It is obvious that he can receive, although unlawfully, worship.

Consider Matthew 4:8-10. "Again, the devil taketh him up into an exceeding high mountain, and sheweth him all the kingdoms of the world, and the glory of them; And saith unto him, All these things will I give thee, if thou wilt bow down and worship me. Then saith Jesus unto him, Get thee hence, Satan: for it is written, Thou shalt worship the Lord thy God, and him only shalt thou serve."

I Samuel 7:3 records this sentiment. Many other passages decry any semblance of idol worship. The fact is that any worship of anything other than The Creator God, is a form of Satan worship.

The lust of the flesh is any appeal to the bestial of our fleshy nature. It was in this that David, despite his many wives and concubines, succumbed with Bathsheba. This sin culminated in the murder of her husband.

This isn't the limit of fleshy lust. Gluttony is known as one of the "seven deadly sins." Joining, as a general rule of reality, with the sin of idleness. God told Adam that he should gain his daily bread by the sweat of his brow. The lust to gamble is a lust of the flesh in that it seeks gain without gainful work.

The lust of the eye is what enjoined the lust of the flesh in David's dalliance with Bathsheba. Advertisers are constantly sending temptations to customers. Wouldn't you like to have this car? Wouldn't you be proud if your house were this clean?

The old joke is that a man is on a "seafood" diet. If he's sees food he eats it. That is the gist of the lust of the eye. A man sees something and wants it. Achan ran into this sin when he saw a stash of tempting goods in Jericho where God had said that no "spoil" was to be taken.

The "pride of life" is somewhat like the "lust of the eye." The difference is that we want others to see us with these things. It is the pride which causes us to want others to know how great we are. Publishing little "press releases" about our writing falls under this category. It is a "look what I did" thing. That isn't necessary all the time unless one is doing this as a profession and needs the advertising.

The difference in the two is illustrated by "The Fiddler on the Roof." He sings, "If I were a rich man." His goal is riches for riches sake. A person who already has riches and wishes others to sing praise about him is ensnared in the sin of the pride of life. The fiddler saw a treasure in his day dreams and fell victim to the lust of his eyes of desire.

The blessing of God is far better than the blessing of this world. He satisfies and gives peace and comfort. The world gives ulcers in trying to fulfill our worldly desires!]

2.17 *And the world passeth away, and the lust thereof: but he that doeth the will of God abideth for ever.*

[Everyone has probably heard the story about a man who had been murdered. He had been stabbed in the heart. No weapon was found. The only evidence available was that someone had apparently thrown water upon him after his death because of the puddle of water on his chest and the flow about him.

Sherlock Holmes arrived on the scene and announced, "It is obvious that the man was killed by an ice sickle." The ice sickle couldn't be found, of course, it was gone.

All of those great things for which man lusts are but ice sickles. They will soon be gone.

My wife and I had the great privilege to meet a sitting president of the United States. After our meeting with President Bill Clinton, Linda and I picked up our son at his school. One lady, who knew why we were slightly late in picking him up, rushed to our car and put her hand out to Linda. "I want to shake the hand that shook the hand."

I have a picture in my office of our meeting. Since we have talked about pride not being a good thing, I'll pass on why it is there.

All things about which we are so proud will pass away. That "brand new 1952 Ford" which a contestant won on a televised game show probably resides in a "junk yard" somewhere.

It is more than likely that the contestant lies in a small plot of land with a marker stating his name and date of birth which does not contain anything about that car of which he was so proud.

The things of this world either pass or we pass from them. Consider the rich farmer of Luke 12:20. He no longer has to worry about new barns and storing his goods.

That is how it is with everything in this world and this physical life. At my age I am considering the "disposition of my worldly goods." That simply means that I realize that I have to leave either in the rapture or in death. Either way, I ain't talking all that with me.

The ~~good~~ great thing about this is that I won't be missing any of my "precious" possessions. I will have the glory of being with Jesus. This won't be a passing thing. This is an eternal fellowship of joy.]

2.18 *Little children, it is the last time: and as ye have heard the antichrist shall come, even now are there many antichrists; whereby we know that it is the last time.*

[This phrase, little children, is used five times in the New Testament epistles to speak of the Christian. Four of these are in the second and third chapters of I John. Although Paul used the phrase once (Galatians 4:19), it seems to be a phrase unique to John, the Apostle.

We can search the Scripture to gain an understanding of the use of the phrase. I think part of the answer is from Matthew 19:14 where Jesus said "...Suffer little children, and forbid them not, to come unto me: for of such is the kingdom of heaven."

The faith of a child is so pure and unquestioning. The faith of the child simply accepts that Jesus is. But, this unquestioning faith has one flaw: it does not seek out the deeper things of the faith. This particular verse which we now examine asks for the deeper faith of one who studies the things of God. Specifically, this verse asks that we prepare ourselves for His soon coming.

A growing Christian, one who has spent time in the study of the Word and conversation with the Author of that Word, is to have moved beyond the mere milk of the Word (Hebrews 5:15). John is speaking to Christians who have complete confidence and faith. But, he is also speaking to those who are growing in the faith.

John could have been harkening back to the words of Jesus. "Little children, yet a little while I am with you. Ye shall seek me: and as I said unto the Jews, Whither I go, ye cannot come; so now I say unto you. A new commandment I give unto you, That ye love one another; as I have loved you, that ye also love one another." (John 13:33-34)

John was there when Jesus said these things. I am certain that the words of Jesus made an impression on John. But, I do not believe that this was the intent of John at this place. John wasn't talking about the brotherhood of the saints. John was talking about personal responsibility.

I believe that John had the same reference in mind as did Paul. "My little children, of whom I travail in birth again until Christ be formed in you." (Galatians 4:19) Paul was speaking of those to whom he had taken the Gospel message. Paul was speaking as a "spiritual father" in that he had led these people to accept Jesus as their Savior. When Paul spoke of Christ being formed in these people he wasn't speaking of the salvation experience. He was speaking of these people growing in grace so that they would more and more be Christlike in their daily walks.

John was an old man when he wrote this First Epistle. This book is believed to have been written about AD 90. This would put the age of John in his mid to late eighties. But, he wasn't speaking to these people as physical children. He was reminding them that they were spiritual children. They were not perfect, to be sure. But, they were already "children of the King."

He was reminding them that they had, even though - especially though - they were Christians that they had much growing to do in the faith.

May we also realize that we will never attain that level of spiritual maturity to which we must strive. May we remember to strive.

Since this verse spoke that the "last time" was then upon the world, and since the culmination of history has not occurred in the interval, we know that we are still in the same "time" (dispensation) as were the New Testament writers. We, therefore, know that the bulk of the New Testament was written not only for us but also to us. There is no further revelation of God's will for us than which He gave us in His Word.

Therefore, we must understand that any "new revelation" which comes down the pike is not of God. Jesus argued that His churches would not fail. We are still in the church age. For anyone to argue that they have restored "first century Christianity" is the same as arguing that Jesus was mistaken.

Further, the principle of God is always that new or further revelation comes at the beginning of a new dispensation. Since we are still in the "last days," there can be no more "new" revelation until the Lord comes again to take His Own to be with Him.

There is a doctrinal distinctive between "antichrists" and "The AntiChrist" of prophecy. But, both hold a certain character trait: They are those which would turn people from the things of Christ and toward their own agenda of evil.

One thing we must consider is that we are still in the last times. This is the final dispensation before the great cleansing of the Great Tribulation. Considering that new revelation, actually expanded revelation, to introduce and explain a new dispensation only occurs at the beginning of the dispensation, any writing which purports to be a "new revelation from God" cannot be within the program of God. It must be a Satanic deception. Since John has given the revelation that this is the "last times," there can be no new revelation past that which John, the last of the remaining apostles of Jesus, lived and wrote.

The canon of Scripture ended with the death of John, God's servant and apostle.]

2.19 *They went out from us, but they were not of us, for if they had been of us, they would no doubt have continued with us: but they went out, that they might be made manifest that they were not all of us.*

[The antichrists of the preceding verse were once in full fellowship with the believers and expressed agreement with the doctrine of the apostles. Nonetheless, they were never truly part of the fellowship despite the "evidence" they once presented.

Had they been part of the true fellowship of the believers they would have continued in that position. This speaks against the possibility of falling from grace as it says those who had been "fellow travelers" with us, and gave all the appearances of being believers, were never true believers. They may have deceived many. They may have even deceived themselves. But, the fact that they did depart from the faith and fellowship is an obvious fact that they were never Christians in the first place.

I find two situations with the phrase "they were not all of us." The first is the obvious. Not all of the church was in a hypocritical state. Simply stated, not all of the church was hypocritical. Those that were proved themselves to be showed the truth of themselves by their departure from faith and fellowship.

Second: It is logical to assume that this "church split," as it were, pulled some of the true Christians into false situations. These true Christians have lost fellowship with the Lord and the fellowship of the true believers. In such a situation they would not be lost but would be subject to the discipline of the Lord. "For whom the Lord loveth he chasteneth, and scourgeth every son whom he receiveth." (Hebrews 12:6)

This is a warning to pastors to, "Preach the word; be instant in season, out of season; reprove, rebuke, exhort with all longsuffering and doctrine." (II Timothy 4:2) Satan is ever trolling in the Garden of God. He cannot pick the fruit; the Spirit has sealed us to Himself. (Ephesians 4:30) But he does delight himself in causing harm to the children so that The Father might be grieved.]

2.20   *But ye have an unction from the Holy One, and ye know all things.*

Luke 24:49; John 12:16; 14:16, 26; 15:26; 16:7; 16:13; I John 2:27

[John tells the Christians that they do not need to fear the false teachers which may have seduced others. Unction is a type of salve or oil used in anointing a person for task. It is as the anointing of kings. We have been anointed by the Holy Spirit (John 16:13) by which He instructs us in all things.

We are told in I Peter 2:9 that we are a "royal priesthood." Consider that the Book of Hebrews constantly reminds us that Jesus is The Great High Priest of this covenant of salvation wherein we are the called of God into free salvation due to the great Self-Sacrifice of Jesus at the Cross. We serve under Him as witnesses of this great salvation. Our purpose is to give the Truth of the gospel to those fellow humans who stand in need. None of us can have any real part in the salvation of others. Our purpose is to preach, by deed and word, the facts of sin and offered salvation from that sin. This witness is coupled with prayer that The Spirit send conviction upon the sinner so that the lost will allow the Great Shepherd of our souls, Jesus, to find the lost and bring salvation to them. (Luke 19:10)

We are protected from the power of the evil one by the Spirit of our anointing. We have been correctly taught by the Spirit and understand the error of seducing spirits. Our only need is to resist as we lean upon the Lord and pray as we look into the inspired and preserved Written Word of the Scripture.

The Spirit instructs us and empowers our spiritual walk as we meet Him in the Word and seek to walk daily with Him.

The final phrase, "ye know all things," is two pronged in its application. The first has to do with the work of The Spirit in bringing spiritual truths to our minds as the need arises. As we study the Scripture we are endowed to know more than we might understand we know. In a time of trial, adversity or witness, the Spirit brings the flower of truth to the furrowed fields of our mind. (Mark 13:11)

The verse also speaks in counter-distinction to the doctrine of the Gnostics. Their core belief that much knowledge is the path of salvation is shown to be false. Our personal knowledge is of a transitory nature. True spiritual knowledge is of The Holy Spirit of God. It is the Spirit who guides the child of God into true knowledge. (John 16:13)

Our search for spiritual knowledge is not a search for salvation but a response to the salvation we already possess due to the Work of Jesus and the leading of The Spirit. Let us never fail to consider that we are, each of us, called to study the Scripture. (II Timothy 2:15) Even as we see our eyes opened to deeper Truth by the work of The Spirit, so are we called to study the Words of God to prepare ourselves to understand that which The Spirit opens to us.]

2.21 *I have not written unto you because ye know not the truth, but because ye know it, and that no lie is of the truth.*

[John says that he has not written to the people to correct them in some error which they may have entered. They know the truth of the Gospel. He has only written to confirm them in the faith and to brush away and semblance of doubt that might have grown in their minds over the corrupting influence of false teachers.

Those false teachers may make many good arguments. They may even seem quite reasonable in their assertions. But, if they teach anything contrary to the pure Gospel which the people to whom the epistle is addressed know so well, they must reject it as error.

A lie cannot be added to truth to make the truth more truthful. That is not a reasonable assumption. Therefore, the people are being cautioned to remain true to the truth which these antichrists of the previous verse are subtly attacking.]

2.22 *Who is a liar but he that denieth that Jesus is the Christ? He is antichrist, that denieth the Father and the Son.*

[Not only does such a one call the Father a liar, one also calls the Son, Jesus, a liar when the Sonship of Jesus is denied. The phrase "the Father and the Son" seems to imply that the attack has been centered upon the Deity of Christ. As the Son of God, Jesus is God within the flesh of a human.

This was a necessity. It was needed so that He could righteously stand in the place of, as a substitute for, humanity. Had Jesus been simply a son of man he would have been burdened with the sin of Adam. He could not have died; no person ever born except Jesus could die for the sins of anyone else.

Also, Jesus is God, the Son. As such Jesus is God from eternity. He is the Creator of all that is. (John 1:3) He is not a created being. As God, since God is the offended Party by the sin of mankind, Jesus has the necessary standing to forgive sin. Only the offended can properly forgive.

Any who would deny these truths are speaking lies as a lie is the antithesis of truth. As such this person would be antichrist.

This would also show the lie incumbent in the *new age* teaching that Jesus is but one of many ascended masters. This makes Him to be no more than another human being who has been indwelt by the "Christ Spirit." Jesus, however, did not possess any "Christ Spirit." In His humanity He literally was "Christ," the Messiah of Whom the prophets foretold and came to this earth from Heaven.

Consider carefully John 3:13 – "And no man hath ascended up to heaven, but he that came down from heaven, even the Son of man which is in heaven." The attribute of omnipresence is an attribute only of God. Therefore, Jesus is shown to be God.

To deny this fact is to deny both The Father and The Son. Such a person can have no true knowledge of either. This is especially so when we consider that such a one is denying the testimony of the Truth of Both.]

2.23 Whosoever denieth the Son, the same hath not the Father: (but he that acknowledgeth the Son hath the Father also.

[The Geneva Bible Notes made the obvious connection. They said (I paraphrase) that we can make no claim that the Muslim and the Christian worship the same God. The Muslim does not accept the divinity of Jesus. Any person who denies that Jesus is the Son of God cannot possibly have fellowship with The Father. John 1:18 says, "No man hath seen God at any time, the only begotten Son, which is in the bosom of the Father, he hath declared *him*."

Only the person who has accepted Jesus as Who He is can possibly have any communion with The Father. Without saving faith in God, the Son, there can be no relationship with God, the Father.]

2.24 Let that therefore abide in you, which ye have heard from the beginning. If that which ye have heard from the beginning shall remain in you, ye also shall continue in the Son, and in the Father.

[I like the words of Spurgeon's Devotional Bible on this verse. "You cannot find a better gospel; persevere, then, in what you already know." That is so true. There is no other gospel message which carries with it the words of passage to Heaven.

At one point many of the early followers of Jesus began to forsake Him. He asked His disciples if they would also depart. "Then Simon Peter answered him, Lord, to whom shall we go? thou hast the words of eternal life." (John 6:68) In Acts 4:12 Luke expands on this by saying that salvation can come only through Jesus.

At this place John asks his readers to remember this. There is no need to follow any other doctrine than that which they had first received when they came to Christ.

We must do the same. There will always be someone who "comes down the pike" with a "new and improved" religious doctrine. Ignore this temptation. The same Jesus Who has saved your souls has never changed and never will. (Hebrews 13:8) Faith in Him is salvation for all eternity.

As we abide in the doctrine of Jesus' death, burial and resurrection we continue to abide in the sure love of God. Christian, stay where you are founded in the Love of God found at the Cross of Christ. You cannot find a better doctrine for this is true. Any other is false.

As you do this you will assuredly remain in the faith once delivered. (Jude 3)]

2.25   *And this is the promise that he hath promised us, even eternal life.*

[Note the repetition of the word promise. That is a promise of the surety of the original promise. The promise is salvation. Who made this promise? Jesus, Himself. Upon what did He base that promise? He based the promise within the original Gospel message which these people had at the first received.

Upon what right had He to make such a promise? He is the Son of God and God, the Son. Thus, he could never fail because God cannot fail.

We might note at this place that the Gospel message is based completely upon the Self-Sacrifice of Jesus on the Cross of Calvary. It is the Gospel of His death, burial and resurrection. Much has been added about this. But, there has never been anything added to it in the Scriptural record or in the Halls of Heaven which are the guarantee of this Scripture. (Psalm 119:89)

The Scripture cannot be defeated by the sands of time. Neither will the culture of man discard the Truth that Jesus Christ died in time so that we could live in eternity.]

2.26   *These things have I written unto you concerning them that seduce you.*

[John says that he was written to these people about the attempts are made to lead them from the pure Gospel of Jesus. He was not writing to reform these people, that would have been counter to his plea that they never leave that pure gospel which they had first received. Neither was he attempting to lead them into deeper truth at this point. That would have also been counter to his plea that they never move beyond the fact of the gospel of saving grace.

The purpose of John was to be a warning sign on the narrow way of life. "Look out! There are those who would cause you to get stuck in the rut of legalism or the soft dirt of the shoulder of false understanding."

John asks that they stay on the solid pavement. It wasn't that this might lose their salvation. It was so that they could avoid those wrecks which cause pain and delay. He wanted them to enjoy their salvation.

The Spirit had already anointed them to understand the things of God. John was sounding the warning that not everyone who says, "Thus saith the Lord," had actually heard anything from the Lord. False prophets had led ancient Judah astray and into captivity. Through it all they remained the children of Abraham. But, there was much which they had to endure because they had forgotten their first love. (Revelation 2:4)]

2.27   *But the anointing which ye have received of him abideth in you, and ye need not that any man teach you: but as the same anointing teacheth you of all things, and is truth, and is no lie, and even as it hath taught you, ye shall abide in him.*

Luke 24:49; John 12:16; 14:16, 26; 15:36; 16:7, 13; I John 2:20

[This was written to all Christians but not specifically to apostles; it cannot therefore give any credence to the introduction of inspired, so called, Scripture in this day. Thus the writings, and the corrections, of modern day "scholars" or "prophets" can neither claim inspiration for new texts of their composure nor for corrections which they may consider to the Text which God has previously inspired.

This does speak of the indwelling of the Spirit which will give illumination of the meaning of the inspired and preserved Scripture to the saint of God.

The anointing of the Spirit would protect them as they walked in the Words of the Lord.

The Holy Spirit is with us. That Word, originally inspired and providentially preserved by The Holy Spirit is still with us. Any teaching which stands at variance with that originally inspired and preserved Scripture is an antichrist teaching. God does not say one thing and then contradict Himself just because someone has had a flash of insight, given to him alone. Jesus works through the churches He has established. Any individual who contradicts the plain teaching of The Spirit through the Words preserved, is an individual in error who ought not be given any credence. (Romans 3:4)]

2.28 *And now, little children, abide in him; that, when he shall appear, we may have confidence, and not be ashamed before him at his coming.*

[John is quite aged at this point. When he uses the phrase "little children" he is speaking as an old man to the younger Christians. This is not suggesting infant baptism as some have alleged.

Note very carefully the phrase "and not be ashamed before him at his coming." The early church clearly expected Jesus to return. The Second Appearing of the Lord is not a new doctrine it is as early as the ascension of Jesus into the clouds. (Acts 1:9-11)

John does not ask the people who received this epistle to abide in Him lest they lose their salvation. His call is to have confidence and not to be ashamed of their behavior when Jesus returned for His Own.

This is not the time referenced when Jesus will return to judge the world. That is the Second Coming to the Earth in power and glory. That spoken of in this place is His return in the clouds to receive His Own unto Him preceding the Seven Year Time of Jacob's Trouble which we know as the Great Tribulation.

These people will not be on the earth at that time. They have been called from the earth seven years earlier. The saved have had their sins judged at the Cross and have no part in the judgment of God upon Israel and the earth in that Tribulation Era.]

2.29 *If ye know that he is righteous, ye know that every one that doeth righteousness is born of him.*

[The Bible very plainly states that, "As it is written, There is none righteous, no, not one." (Romans 3:10) But, this verse speaks of many who do righteousness. Why? The answer is within this verse.

The verse starts with a rhetorical question, actually more of a statement, "Since you know that Jesus is righteous..." This being true, we may extrapolate that anyone who is walking in righteousness is obviously walking with the Savior. They are, therefore, born again – from this world of sin and into the spiritual reality of salvation within Jesus.

Back to the original argument against sinless perfectionism within a sinful lifestyle as some of the early cultist's postulated. If a person is not walking in righteousness, it is necessary to affirm that they are not children of God. They are not,

nor can they be, saved individuals.
   Therefore, their entire doctrine is shown to be false.]

FIRST JOHN - CHAPTER THREE

3.1   Behold, what manner of love the Father hath bestowed upon us, that we should be called the sons of God: therefore the world knoweth us not, because it knew him not.

[The word "behold" means to observe, to witness, to see. More than just meaning these things, "behold" is a call to pay attention to the scene before one. John uses this word to make the following statements of the verse.

John also uses the word in a sense of wonderment at what the wonder means! There is no question as to what the love of the Father is; there is a marveling consideration that this love exists at all. This is especially so when one considers just what this love means.

This love means that within our salvation, which is a glorious consideration simply in that we are saved from the penalty of our sin, there is more. We have actually been adopted by God. (Romans 8:15; 23; Galatians 4:5; Ephesians 1:5) This is even more than is said of the Jewish adoption to the be the Covenant People of God. (Consider John 1:12 and Romans 9:4)

The seed of Abraham had been adopted to fulfill certain covenant rituals and relationships so that the "seed of Abraham," which was also the seed of woman as stated in Genesis 3:15, would bless all the families of the nations of the entire world. (Genesis 12:3)

We, however, are called to be "sons of God." Consider Galatians 4:6, "And because ye are sons, God hath sent forth the Spirit of his Son into your hearts, crying, Abba, Father." Whereas the Hebrews had been called to a national responsibility of purity, each of us who are born again have been called to an individual responsibility of service. (I Corinthians, chapter 12)

We must exercise a certain caution at this point. All of the promises to the seed of Abraham remain theirs. God is faithful in that He has not taken those promises from the people to whom He made those promises. But, we must also realize that God has called His adoptive children, us, to those tasks to which He has bestowed the enablement of the Spirit. We labor as faithful children or we are lazy as unfaithful children.

We must beware, also, at this point that we do not miss the point of adoption. We are "sons of God" by adoption. Only Jesus is The Son of God by His eternal nature. We are not in line to become "gods." This was the lie of Satan in the Garden. This remains the lie of Satan in several of the unbiblical cults of the day.

John considers the great glory given to us in this adoption. The fact of this adoption means we must have great gratitude to God for that which He has called us to become. Out of this gratitude we owe a debt of service to our Lord.

Within this service we will find a manner of persecution from the world. We are called from the world of sin. Sin is the antithesis of the holiness of God. It is this holiness in which He wills that we are to walk. The world of sin will never understand the holiness into which we have been called. Consider the way in which Christ was treated in this world. Many came to hear and see miracles. These people sought healing. But, many of these same people were in the crowds shouting "Crucify Him!"

Go to any "death row" inmate and you may well find one who has "found religion." The world wants what they can get from us but they do not want the holiness of God. They can never understand the full joy which is available to the true Christian. Generally speaking, this is simply an attempt to use The God of Glory for the advancement of the personal agenda of an honestly unrepentant sinner.

The world did not understand the reality of the Messiahship of Jesus. The "messiah" for which they hoped was a military commander to restore the temporal kingdom of Israel by freeing them from the political yoke of Rome. They did not understand His relationship with The Father. Much less could lthey understand His real relationship with the Jewish religion or the people of the world. Neither will they understand that which He has given to those that love Him

The world cannot know us as servants of God. The world doesn't understand the reality of the God Whom we serve.]

3.2 *Beloved, now are we the sons of God, and it doth not yet appear what we shall be: but we know that, when he shall appear, we shall be like him, for we shall see him as he is.*

Psalm 17:15

[Paul gives some background as to the culture of the day concerning sons who have not yet reached their majority years. "Now I say, *That* the heir, as long as he is a child, differeth nothing from a servant, though he be lord of all, But is under tutors and governors until the time appointed of the father. Even so we, when we were children, were in bondage under the elements of the world: But when the fullness of the time was come, God sent forth his Son, made of a woman, made under the law, To redeem them that were under the law, that we might receive the adoption of sons." (Galatians 4:1-5)

It is important to realize that these two passages are not equal. Paul was speaking of our salvation from the curse of the Law. Under Christ we who are born again are free from the Law. We are no longer called to serve the Law in fear of offending. We are called to consider the spiritual principles inherent in the Law and act accordingly in a personal response of love to He Who died for us.

Neither was John speaking any frivolous attitude of disrespect toward the Law. His vision was of our mundane life on this earth and the glory of life in the eternities which is to be ours. Verse six in the passage of Galatians gives us an insight into John's thesis. "And because ye are sons, God hath sent forth the Spirit of his Son into your hearts, crying, Abba, Father."

In this life we continue to grow in grace. We strive for the perfections of our Heavenly estate; we will never fully reach these until we are actually transferred to that Heavenly plane. Although we are no longer under the tutelage of the Mosaic Law. Remember that John was addressing first century Christian's who had been taught this law from their earliest years. Although we are now, present tense intended by John, the adopted sons of God, we remain as yet imperfect within that sonship. The apostolic memories of the teachings of Jesus, (John 14:26) the Scripture, the work of the Spirit, even our prayer life are tutors teaching us to grow closer to Him. Our working *for* Him is also an important part of this maturing process.

I have a pair of glasses which darken in the sunlight. That is good. But, when I come inside I can barely find the floor as my vision is obscured by those darkened lenses. Likewise, when we reach the Heavenlies we will have the "dark glasses" of the humanity of our physical eyes removed. We will finally see Jesus in all of His eternal glory. The limitations of earth are removed and we are allowed to become that which we should have been all along!

At His appearing means in the verse means that John was speaking about the Second Appearing of Christ. John lived in expectancy that Jesus was soon coming back in the clouds to take His Own out of this world. I Corinthians 15:51 informs us that, "Behold, I shew you a mystery; We shall not all sleep, but we shall all be changed." At this Second Appearing we who are alive – I'm not looking for an undertaker; I'm praying for an "Upertaker!" – our mortal bodies will be glorified. We will see Jesus as He is!

The wonderful effect of that sight will transform our natures as we behold His glory. We will drop off the carnality which besets our best intentions to live fully for Him and grasp the true spirituality with which our Creator intended we should possess.

I like to look for restorations in Scripture. The Grand Theme in Scripture is the perfection of God's creation. Man sinned and began an excessive digression from the original intent of God for the man of creation. The progression of man, in his sin, was always to walk further and further from the glorious prospect of his originally created being. The rescue of God is the Cross of Calvary. The restoration is that man is returned, spiritually, to the purpose of God's creation. Due to the contamination of sin within creation, man was only partially restored. The final act of restoration is to see man removed from the sin-stained created realms and fully restored in the Heavenlies. II Peter 3:10 gives us the final act of the restoration of the physical creation when even the elements are judged and purified.

It is important to note that we shall be *like* Him. We shall not *be* Him. He is Eternal God in His very essence. We are to be allowed to share in His perfections. He remains the Glorious *First Born Son*. There is not any suggestion that we may follow to become gods in any sense of the word. We are beneficiaries; we are not beneficent of ourselves. Our purpose to serve the Lord throughout eternity allows us the great dignity of serving the One Who Is Our Master. He stands far above us as The God Who has bestowed His graces upon us.

He is The Great Creator and Sovereign of all!

The world can never understand any of this. It is beyond the comprehension of mortal man to understand the spiritual things of God. Only the Spirit can lift even these veils from the eyes of the unsaved, and that only at the Cross.]

3.3   *And every man that hath this hope in him purifieth himself, even as he is pure.*

Psalm 17:15

[Paul gives some background as to the culture of the day concerning sons who have not yet reached their majority years. "Now I say, *That* the heir, as long as he is a child, differeth nothing from a servant, though he be lord of all, But is under tutors and governors until the time appointed of the father. Even so we, when we were children, were in bondage under the elements of the world: But when the fullness of the time was come, God sent forth his Son, made of a woman, made under the law, To redeem them that were under the law, that we might receive the adoption of sons." (Galatians 4:1-5)

It is important to realize that these two passages are not equal. Paul was speaking of our salvation from the curse of the Law. Under Christ we who are born again are free from the Law. We are no longer called to serve the Law in fear of offending. We are called to consider the spiritual principles inherent in the Law and act accordingly in a personal response of love to He Who died for us.

The world can never understand any of this. It is beyond the comprehension of mortal man to understand the spiritual things of God. Only the Spirit can lift even these veils from the eyes of the unsaved, and that only at the Cross.]

3.4   *Whosoever committeth sin transgresseth also the law: for sin is a transgression of the law.*

[Sin is a transgression of the Law. When we consider this truth we realize that all sin is against God in its formation and act. David even related his sin against both Uriah, murder, and Bathsheba, calling her to the king's chamber, was a sin against God. Consider the entire 51st Psalm of David as he poured out his confession to God. Pay special attention to verse four.

If our sin is an affront to God, and it is!, we have insulted the Very One Who poured out His life Blood on the Cross for the express purpose of rescuing us from the penalty of sin.

On this I must comment that many of us want to be "Lawyers" in the docket of God's justice. We say, "I didn't do *that*." "I only did *this*." Our intent seems to be to outsmart God's judicial system. Consider the fifth chapter of Matthew. In verse 22 Jesus speaks of hate. In verse 28 Jesus speaks of lust. In verse 32 Jesus speaks of divorce. In verse 34 Jesus speaks of swearing an oath. In verse 39 Jesus speaks about violent resistance to persecution. In verse 44 Jesus speaks about love toward enemies. Interesting speaking on all accounts.

Jesus spoke about the *spirit of the law* in each of the above cases. The act blooms in lust and flowers in action. He who offends the spirit of the law has offended the meaning of the Law. It can be rightly argued that we are not in this age of grace under the letter of the Law. But, we stand as responsible to the spirit of the Law. Jesus said this over and over again.

Since sin is known opposition to the revealed Law of God, even in the matter of the spirit of the offense, we must consider any sin as a further disobedience to our Lord. Sin is a Personal affront from us to Jesus.

This situation cannot be divorced from the first chapter when John has mentioned two distinct walks. We remember that he was pointing out the fallacy of the heretic who argued that he could walk in perfection even while walking in sin.

Couple this with James 1:14-15 where we see that sin flows from an enticement to a man's own lusts. The "lust" in that passage does not mean only fleshly lusts. It would easily cover other areas such as pride. The point is that a sinner has been compromised by his own walk. He has given Satan an avenue of which temptation may easily flow to his own heart. This is the walk in darkness rather than a walk in Christ.

There is a need for one who has sinned to confess his sin and seek reconciliation with God. Again, this is the writing of John in the first verse of the second chapter. The last verse in the first chapter had argued that it is the province of all to sin. At that point John was still speaking to Christians. We find in this that Christians can and do sin. They should not! The heretical group had argued they could not sin and thus any action they might take was not possibly a sin.

John argument was that it was possible, but wrong, for a Christian to sin. When the point would come that fact of sin was realized there was an expected repentance. Again, the sinner by nature might hate that he has been found out in his sin. But, the Christian will feel sorrow that he has harmed his Lord by defaming Him in his actions.

Again, and in the following verses, the question is not salvation which has been settled once and for all at the moment of conversion. The Spirit has set His Own seal upon this conversion and it cannot be voided. This discussion must center upon both fellowship with the Lord and discipline from Him. As my daughter once said when she was very young, "It is not a good idea to get God mad at you!"]

3.5 *And ye know that he was manifested to take away our sins, and in him is no sin.*

[We may say that Jesus was a Great Teacher, and He was. We may say that Jesus was a Great Example, and He was. We may say that Jesus was a Great moral force for good in the earth, and He was. But, the primary purpose of the entrance of Jesus into humanity was to effect the cure for sin.

Considering the fact that the reason which Jesus came into this world, was manifest on earth, was to destroy the works of sin in the human life, it is somehow ridiculous to consider that we could serve Him by living a life of sin.

Yet, even Paul argues that he was subject to failings in his Christian walk. (Romans 7:14-25) This was not a thing he admitted with delight. It was a burden to his soul that his fleshly body sometimes took power over his spiritual purposes.

We recall that John was writing, at least partially, to combat those who claimed a sinlessness even though they were living in sin. The doctrine of these persons argued that they were not capable of sin due to their profession of Christianity. John was showing the absurdity and soul danger of such a doctrine.]

3.6 *Whosoever abideth in him sinneth not: whosoever sinneth hath not seen him, neither known him.*

[Compare this verse with the first few verses of chapter two of this epistle where the concept of perfectionism was shown to be false among the heretical groups. Note especially the words "abideth in Him." Couple this with the calls to Christians to walk in the Light of Christ. In this we see the need to walk in fellowship with Jesus in order to resist the urges toward sinfulness.

If we take this verse to teach a doctrine of sinless perfectionism, we must extend this concept to all who are under the Blood. The reference from Romans, chapter seven, above would prove this is not so. Further, if we were to teach an absolute sinless perfection as existing among the people of God we would be forced to excise nearly all of the eleventh chapter of Hebrews. Each of these "hero's" had some sort of fault in their lives.

Both Abraham and Isaac lied in claiming that their wives were their sisters. David committed murder by proxy on the husband of Bathsheba, with whom he had an adulterous relationship. Peter denied the Lord at His trial prior to His crucifixion. The list could continue.

Once again, I would caution to consider the heresy which John was combating in much of this epistle. The argument is that the true Christian will not *walk* in sin *habitually*. This simple explanation gives purpose to the many cautions to the Christian to not continue in sin lest the chastisement of God fall upon him.]

3.7 *Little children, let no man deceive you: he that doeth righteousness is righteous, even as he is righteous.*

[Before we start with this verse I would again refer you to the commentary on verse six, above. This verse does not suggest sinless perfection. Were it to do so we would be forced to view every act and intent to be righteous in the sense of gospel righteousness. Since this is not found in any, either of Scriptural example or the historical example of the Christians of the ages, but is found in Christ, alone, we cannot read into this verse perfection except the perfection of Christ as imparted to the Christian within the salvation experience.

Consider Philippians 3:9 – "And be found in him, not having mine own righteousness, which is of the law, but that which is through the faith of Christ, the righteousness which is of God by faith." Here we see that even the apostle Paul did not claim and righteousness for himself except the imparted Righteousness of Christ via faith in the atonement.

We ought also to include II Corinthians 5:17 in this discussion. "Therefore if any man be in Christ, he is a new creature: old things are passed away; behold, all things are become new."

The "old things" which have departed are the works of the Law. This speaks of righteousness from a legal status. Christ has moved us from this to the new perspective of salvation, and righteousness, wholly by grace. He, not our works even of the Mosaic Law, is our righteousness. We could not perform any good works to secure the favor of God because, without the shedding of the Blood of Christ in His Self-Sacrifice to cleanse our sins, we were not capable of righteousness. Neither are we now capable of righteousness except as we are under His Blood of Redemption.

John warns his readers not to fall prey to the seducing spirit of the antinomian doctrine which recognizes no moral imperative. These see themselves are "free agents" who can sin with impunity. This is a mark that they have not the righteousness of Christ. Therefore, they have no Scriptural claim to salvation. They remain lost sinners and act according to that reality.

The purpose of Jesus coming into this world was to destroy the works of sin, not to make those works more readily available to His, supposed, followers.
What a travesty of heresy it is to claim that His followers are to live in sin!]

3.8 *He that committeth sin is of the devil; for the devil sinneth from the beginning. For the purpose of the Son of God was manifested, that he might destroy the works of the devil.*

[Jesus came to this earth to destroy the works of Satan. I believe the taxation of the early portion of Luke, which led Mary and Joseph to Bethlehem, was instigated by Satan as he attempted to kill Jesus before He could be born into the world. God used that very event to fulfill His Own prophecies.

I believe that Satan really did offer the kingdoms of the world to Jesus during the temptation in the wilderness. Jesus used this as an object lesson that we must only worship God.

I believe that Satan thought that the voice of Jesus could be stilled by the crucifixion. God used this to save people from their sins. At every turn Satan is a defeated foe. Why can't we just accept this and live above our fears and in faith as Jesus has asked.

We see this power most readily observable in the salvation of a soul. That which Satan had controlled is converted into a follower of Jesus.

As to the phrase "He that committeth sin is of the devil," must be considered as walking in sin rather than a single, or even several, instance of disobedience. The examples of so many in Scripture who have fallen short of the mark, sinned, and yet were shown to be Godly persons is an argument against the philosophy of "one sin and you're out of the game." An easily understood example of this is Samson. Hebrews 11:32 includes him as one of the heroes of the faith. We cannot, well I cannot, argue that Samson lived a life as an example to be emulated. That he proved his true faith at the end of his life is undeniable.

It is stated that the devil was a sinner from the beginning. That does not mean at the beginning of his creation for he was an angel of light in his creation. His fall came when he introduced sin into the physical world of the creation of God with the temptation of Eve and Adam. That is the meaning of "beginning" in reference to the career of sin concerning Satan as concerns the human race.

When the Christian does sin, one of the purposes of John's writing is to show that Christians must strive to live a life of walking with the Lord. It is an argument therefore of John that the Christian will sometimes fail his Lord, we find that erring Christian to honestly be fulfilling the will of Satan.

Can it be any wonder that we will grieve the Holy Spirit in this abrogation of our duty to the Lord? (Ephesians 4:30)

The one who persists in this is shown to be a child of Satan rather than a child of God. Even a professed theological argument to the contrary will not take away this fact. Simply put, any who live an ungodly life of sin, this includes those who seem to be morally upright but have never accepted Christ as Savior and do not have the redeeming value of His Righteousness; such a person is shown to be a follower of Satan. This fact may not be either acknowledged or understood by the individual. The fact remains fact! Salvation is only offered in the work of Christ in His Self-Sacrifice at the Cross of Calvary.

This verse begins with that phrase, "...the devil sinneth from the beginning..." The picture is of a continuous career of sin. That is abiding in sin. That is the picture as well of the one who "committeth sin" since he is said to be "of the devil."

Jesus came to break this cycle of sin. Jesus came to defeat Satan and sin. That the individual Christian would fall back, even for a short time since as children of God the purpose of His chastisement is to refine them into His image, is an abomination. It is to mistreat the Lord Who so loved us. Look at John 21:7; Peter cast himself into the sea rather than to joyously greet his Lord.

In verse eleven of that chapter we find Peter finally coming to shore and working with The Master. Peter was not lost and coming to repentance. Peter was ashamed of his conduct and coming back into fellowship as we witness by the conversation between Peter and Jesus later in that same chapter.

Jesus came to destroy the works of Satan. This He did at Calvary. This He does when a sinner repents and receives Him as Savior. This He does when He chastises an erring child and restores them to Himself.]

3.9 *Whosoever is born of God doth not commit sin, for his seed remaineth in him: and he cannot sin, because he is born of God.*

Romans 6:1; 6:15

[Carrying forward the concept of a habitual style of life, the argument must be that the one who is truly born of God will never fall into a sinful lifestyle. However, the meaning here goes much deeper than this.

The meaning cannot be that the person can never sin. This would disagree with John's earlier statements from chapter 1:9 through chapter 2:2.

The seed that remains in this person is of Jesus. "His seed" speaks of the same Person as did the preceding verse when it said that "he might destroy the works of the devil." If, as the verse plainly says, the "seed" of Christ remains in this Christian so that he cannot return to the life of sin, we have a strong argument for the Biblical doctrine of the eternal security of the believer.

This verse is seen not to question the Christian's ability to "hold on to" his salvation, but it is an affirmation that it is Jesus Who holds the Christian's salvation in His Hands. We cannot fall from grace because Jesus has (v. 8) destroyed the works of the devil in our lives. This person is born of God, a child of God, and cannot fall back into habitual sin because he is kept by the grace and power of the Blood of The Son. The chastisement of God will drive the true Christian to his knees and his Lord. Consider Hebrews 12:8 with regard to that straying child of God!

The verse does not argue that one *was* born of God but that this one *is*, present tense continuing forward, born of God. The meaning is to be generated, conceived, born of the will of God and the grace of the Lord.]

3.10 *In this the children of God are manifest, and the children of the devil: whosoever doeth not righteousness is not of God, neither he that loveth not his brother.*

[John sees both the children of God and the children of Satan as manifest in the world. That is, they show their family traits before men. The children of God show the Family traits of walking in faithfulness to God and harmony, as much as is possible in a world which hates the things of God, among all men. This is especially shown among the brotherhood of believers.

The children of Satan follow a life dedicated to sin and in alienation toward God. They walk in the ways of Satan. Wars, rumors of war, backbiting, jealousy, hatred for those of the household of faith, distrust, the list could continue! These give no real evidence, even among the most altruistic, of a walk with the Savior for they do not walk with Him.

This walk of love among the believers is a witness of God to the world. In many cases this is used as an inducement to call the sinner to salvation. In all cases this is an evidence before all, the world and the household of faith, that we are children of our Heavenly Father. This is true even when the world choses to reject the truth of God.]

3.11 *For this is the message that ye heard from the beginning, that we should love one another.*

John 13:34

[John speaks here of filial love of the brethren as a foundational theme among the denizens of the Church of Jesus, the Christ. We are to walk therein and see other fruits of the spirit grown from the branch of this love.

We must note that this is a fruit of righteousness. But, it is a message for us to heed rather than a command, as of the Law, to fear. We are called by the Love of Christ to the love of others. His love flows to, and as His Own, through us to others.

This is a call to discipline. There are those we just cannot bring ourselves to like. They might not be abrasive but they do "rub our fur the wrong way." God says to love them anyway. This is a call to discipline our lives to exhibit the things of God even when It may be hard, in the natural, to do so. That effort will succeed in changing us into a closer walk with Christ.

This concept brings the short Old Testament book of Jonah to mind. Read it. It's only four chapters long. Jonah never, it seems, agree with God. But, after his time in the belly of the specially prepared fish, Jonah did submit to do the will of God. This is so even when Jonah did not agree. He did it anyway!

This is a call to decorum within the church. There is an old poem that everyone has heard:

> To live up above with those that we love,
> Ah, that will be glory!
> To live here below with those that we know,
> That is a completely different story!

Living in love of the brethren will keep order and harmony within the Church. This will be a means by which others will learn of God and the paths He would call them to tread. We must also consider that such love and companionship will give greater solace to those who are going through the pains of persecution for the Lord's sake.

This will even give us the opportunity to show the love of Christ to the persecuted brethren. And, them also toward us in our hour of need.

This is a call to dispense the Gospel Message. The world will see our love for one another and see something that is lacking within the world system. This is a means of drawing others to Christ. Even as we love the brethren we must learn to express love toward those who are not yet of the household of faith.

Our witness needs to be spoken. Without the physical effort to decorate those words with the Example of the Savior our words will ring hollow. May our message always be the same as our meandering in the world. No matter where we go, or how we get there, our most precious cargo of life is the message that Jesus Christ died in time so that others could live in eternity!]

3.12 *Not as Cain, who was of that wicked one, and slew his brother. And wherefore slew he him? Because his own works were evil, and his brother's righteous.*

[Cain manifest himself to be a child of Satan by his wicked act of murder. Some have attempted to make excuse for Cain and say that he did not understand the concept of murder; he had no intention of actually killing Abel.

I disagree. Cain knew exactly what he was doing. He was trying to remove that which reminded him of his lack. He was not righteous. He was not a true worshiper of God. He was not approved for the work of his own hands. Cain was the very first person to persecute a true believer. He was the first tormenter of the followers of God. Abel was the very first martyr for the cause of righteousness.

We might note that Adam was cast from the Garden for his disobedience. Cain was cast even from the fellowship of his family for his sin. Jealousy and hatred, rather than love and acceptance of the brethren, move one to leave the influence of the Godly and wander among the followers of Satan in full vigor.

Adam and Eve, who we believe to be Godly but flawed, were allowed to continue to seek the face of the Lord in worship. Cain, who we know to be murderously sinful was consigned to walk in fellowship within the world of men who were sinful like himself.]

3.13 *Marvel not, my brethren, if the world hate you.*

John 15:18-19; 17:14; II Timothy 3:12

[John asks that his readers consider the sin of Cain. John asks that his readers consider the spirit in which Cain walked was that of Satan. He ties these thoughts together with the profession of the Christian to walk as Christ walked.

It is ever true that the seed of Satan will attack the seed of God. "And I will put enmity between thee and the woman, and between thy seed and her seed; it shall bruise thy head, and thou shalt bruise his heel." (Genesis 3:15) One of the very first prophecies in Scripture had said that this would happen.

The children of Satan are as of Cain. They hate those who are truly the children of God. It is not that they desire the smile of God upon them. It is that they hate the things of God. God has judged them as surly as He judged Belshazzar at the riotous party the night that Babylon fell. They have been weighed in the balances of the justice of God and found wanting.

They ask what right God has to judge them. They are not His subjects for they worship another. They hate God and His people. Consider the reaction of the devils to Jesus in Matthew 9:29.

Martyrdom is only slightly behind the veneer of polite society. It is on the front page of the society of many of the "newspapers" of the society of humanity. That we have not yet been persecuted unto death is only by the grace of God. When His glory is to shine forth from our walk within that valley of shadows, we will be privileged to face the sword of the persecutor.

Folks, be ready and stand in the knowledge that God is The God of Life. We can never lose that which He has promised unto us. An early entrance into Heaven is not a threat; it is an honor and privilege.]

3.14 *We know that we have passed from death unto life, because we love the brethren. He that loveth not his brother abideth in death.*

[We cannot properly read this verse in isolation. Such isolation leads us to the concept of an unholy love of all the world. We must understand this verse in reference to the flow of the idea of which John was referencing.

Neither can this verse be made to say that such love manufactures our salvation. It does not; nor can it. (Acts 4:12) Brotherly love is an outgrowth of that salvation. This love grows from salvation not into salvation.

Cain hated his brother because of his brother's certification by God. Jealousy certainly had it hand in the deed. But, so did the fact that God had not respected the offering of the works of the hands of Cain. Cain was mad at God because God had rejected the best he could offer. As Abel was obviously loved of God, Cain hated his brother as a representative of the fashion of God.

Cain is a representative of the worldly system of Satan which is diametrically opposed to the holiness of God. The world hates us because they hate God and we are representative of The True and Living God of Creation.

The world may love to worship. This need to worship is part of human nature as a creation of God. But, as we read in the first chapter of Romans, the love of the world is centered upon themselves in that they love the created things rather than the Creator.

The ancient world fashioned idols which featured the things of the world. Mankind still does this in his near deification of learning and science which tells him that he is the master of all. His mind is the conqueror of all. His glory is the fashion of the glory of all. Ultimately, to love the world is to love Satan.

When we love the brethren we are loving that, those, who are of the family of God. To hate them is to exhibit a hatred of God.

Lest is be imagined that I am arguing against any love of humanity, I am not. But, our love toward them must be as is the Savior's love toward them. He died the death of the Cross so that He could offer them salvation. True Christian love is not shown in simply being accepting of all despite their sin. True Christian love cannot be divorced from calling sinners from their sin and until the Lord of Salvation.

To remain quiet on this front is to, humanly speaking, allow them unhindered access to the fires of Hell for all eternity. Any *accepting* which does not include *calling* to salvation is not love. It is a coward's way to avoid persecution for the cause of Christ. (Luke 19:10)

We could ask the question: Does our love of the world cover over our love for Christ? Or, does our love for the world long to see them find eternal rest in the worship of God in Christ? Just what really is Christian love for his fellow man?]

3.15 Whosoever hateth his brother is a murderer: and ye know that no murderer hath eternal life abiding in him.

[Considering that John has used this illustration of Cain, we must reflect that those who would hate are serving the same master as did Cain. Therefore, the concept of murder cannot be discounted as fanciful. It is but a further journey across the same stage – with the same "director" of life's performance.

Among the most brutal and amoral of humanity are those that hate others for not following the same "religion," be it theistic or secular, which they favor. The echo the words of Paul before Agrippa. In verse 29 of the 26th chapter of Acts Paul expresses his wish that all might be as him in the faith. Down through the ages of true faith this echo has expressed the wish of Paul twisted by the world's view in the torturing and killing of Christian that they might be dead in the physical even as those tormentors are spiritually dead.

To those who would argue that this verse teaches no one who has committed murder can ever find forgiveness for his sin, this isn't the teaching of the verse. No one verse stands alone. It must be considered in the light of the context around it to determine the meaning.

When we "back track" the concept of murder from John's argument we find that it includes the fact of hate. It includes every person who is not of the household of faith. The fact that Jesus died on the cross to make available salvation for sinners argues against the doctrinal stance that no murderer can be saved.

That idea of any lack of opportunity for salvation of the murderer is not what the verse says. The argument is that a hating person does not (Abiding is present tense. So is the word "is.") presently abide in faith. There is no argument that he can never seek pardon from the Lord.]

3.16 *Hereby perceive we the love of God, because he laid down his life for us and we ought to lay down our lives for the brethren.*

[Again, the magnitude of the love of God shines through the death of the human body of Jesus on the cross. He died in our place. He rose again as proof that death is a conquered foe because of the events of that cross.

As the hate of one is of the same spirit of murder toward another, so is the love of the Christian toward another that we ought to love his soul to the extent that we would do anything, to include the laying aside of our own concern for bodily safety, in order to spread the message that Jesus Christ died in time so that others might live in eternity.

There were many instances of men who threw themselves on hand grenades in order to save the life of their comrades in arms during time of war. For the most part these men had no notion of committing suicide. They didn't consider their own lives. The simply reacted out of love for country and the closeness which a military unit in combat feels for one another. They did not *spend* their lives; the *used* their lives to save others. It was an act of unfeigned love for their fellow soldiers.

John says to think of the great work of Christ upon the cross. He gave His physical life for others. Will we be willing to do the same for our *family* in Christ? I am reminded of an oft repeated phrase used by Linda, my late wife. She often talked of *dying grace*. The concept was that she did not like to consider her own demise. But, she was convinced that when the time of her departure came, the Lord would give her peace as He ushered her into His presence.

When the doctor's pronounced the "death sentence" of cancer upon her, Linda exhibited this grace. So fully did she exhibit this grace that a newspaper in a city fifty miles from our home sent a reporter to examine her Christian testimony. Nearly an entire back page of that newspaper was devoted to this devoted servant of Christ.

I couldn't do what John suggests here. I pray that if the necessity comes that I offer up myself for the glory of God, His grace will be sufficient. (II Corinthians 12:9) It always has been in other times of trial.]

3.17 *But whoso hath this world's good, and seeth his brother have need, and shutteth up his bowels of compassion from him, how dwelleth the love of God in him?*

[Several years ago I received a call from a man who said that he and his wife were traveling evangelists. They were in great need of a meal for the evening, a hotel room for the night and the fare for a bus ticket to St. Louis in the morning.

I told them that they had "hit the jackpot." I was going to speak at the mission later in the day. The mission would give them a meal and had rooms for married couples where they could rest for the night and have some privacy. To top it all off, I was going to St. Louis in the morning and would give them a ride in my vehicle.

They refused my offer. All of my offer had been honest truth. The wanted a restaurant meal, a room in a nice motel and a bus ticket. With that our conversation ended with their refusal of my offered assistance.

I was speaking with the mission director the following morning. He chuckled and then said, "Now I know why Rev. ------ of the ----- Church was with that couple I didn't know last night at the hotel restaurant on the square."

I learned from that brother that day. Sometimes the best assistance is to shun a con job and not reward chicanery.

The world expects the Christian to be an easy mark and treats us as such. This is not an invitation to witness of Christ for the Christian. It is an attempt by the worldly "con man" to defame the Name of Christ by showing the Christians to be thoughtless "rubes" who can be easily manipulated because we are stupid!

Most people who need help are not like this couple. Most of the time we will only hear an offhand comment about a need in someone's life. They are not looking for a handout; to these we need to offer a hand up!

This verse does not speak of rich people. Basically, the verse says, if you have it and someone else is in need, offer help. I would also say not to be boisterous about the gift. Never say, "I am so blessed that I can handle someone's else's problem. How much do you need? My charity shall supply all your need!"

That isn't "alms giving." That is boastful action to massage our own ego!

My answer in giving, and I do give when I can, is that this is just what Christian's do for others. If I have it, I will share it with others in need. When I don't have it, I will offer prayer and encouragement. It is Christ who supplies all of our needs. (Philippians 4:19)

He who refuses the possible is not a witness for God.

I must add that once we have supplied, as God has blessed us, the act is forgotten and never mentioned again. Otherwise we are not supplying as God has blessed; we are merely "showing off" to our own glory!]

3.18 *My little children, let us not love in word, neither in tongue, but in deed and in truth.*

[Jesus does not care for hypocrisy. He will not be fooled by a false show of religiosity by anyone who simply claims to be His follower. Have you ever wondered why in the twenty-first chapter of Matthew, verses 19-20, Jesus cursed a fig tree so that it withered? Was He "ticked off" at the tree? Did the pressure of His soon coming crucifixion put Him on edge?

After the event, in verses 21-22, Jesus used the incident to speak of the necessity of faith for the disciples. This is the primary focus of this particular miracle.

But, there is more. Let's start with verse eighteen. "Now in the morning as he returned into the city, he hungered. And when he saw a fig tree in the way, he came to it, and found nothing thereon, but leaves only, and said unto it, Let no fruit grow on thee henceforward for ever, And presently the tree withered away. and when the disciples saw it, they marvelled, saying, How soon is the fig tree withered away!"

What we see here is that Jesus was hungry. He Who had fed the multitudes with nothing but a few loaves and some small fish was, himself, hungry. Could He not have performed a miracle and turned some of the stones of the ground into bread?

We might recall that Satan had suggested this very thing in Matthew 4:3. Jesus was never disposed to find any suggestion of Satan as a rule to follow. We recall that in Matthew 20:28 Jesus said that He did not come into the world to be ministered unto.

Now it might seem that we have a problem since it seems that Jesus expected this tree to minister to His hunger. No; His hunger set the stage for teaching the disciples. The fig tree had leaves which held out the suggestion of bearing fruit. But, it did not.

Basically we could easily argue that the tree was hypocritical in its appearance. I believe that this was the underlying principle. The call of Jesus in the next few verses is to show real faith not just to talk about how wonderful it is.

That is the same thing John is writing about in this verse. Doctrine is good thing. But, if all we do is talk about our doctrinal positions we have not accomplished anything more than heating up the air around our mouths.

The doctrine of love unperformed is simply a philosophical point rendered useless by not acting upon it. It is no more than "play money" when the guy at the counter of *Chez Golden Arches* wants us to present real money to pay for our burger. It isn't just useless; it is exasperating for the man who thought he had made a real sale.

The tongue can sing the praises of a good hamburger. No one has their hunger sated with a discourse on the flavor of a hamburger.

True love is not a printed page of our churches statement of faith. True love is not the recitation of a doctrinal dissertation. True love is action that alleviates the suffering of another. That is Christianity in reality of action.

Is our life of Christian love filled with leaves of promise or is it the carrying forth of His love into the world of men? We might talk about His example of love. This isn't bad if our performance of Christian love follows those words.]

3.19 *And hereby we know that we are of the truth, and shall assure our hearts before him.*

[God is very gracious to us. It has been said that there are no atheists in a foxhole. Another truth, generally not acknowledged, is that most Christians will have times when they begin to doubt their salvation. It is true, as Romans 8:16 tells us that, "The Spirit itself beareth witness with our spirit, that we are the children of God," but we are still in these bodies of clay.

There are times, there should not be but there are, when we do not "tune in" to God. We begin to lack the closeness with Him that is our right and responsibility. We become as was the father of the child possessed of demons. He went to Jesus in urgency of heart with a petition that his child be healed. Jesus said, "If you believe, the child will be healed." In despair the father cried, "And straightway the father of the child cried out, and said with tears, Lord, I believe; help thou mine unbelief." (Mark 9:24)

This was a Biblical prayer of petition. Jesus granted that petition.

This is no more than confession to God when we ask forgiveness for such a problem. God's answer is to trust the Word. If God said it, it is true. Our love for the brethren is an indication that we are the children of God – that we are saved. A child of the world will not honestly love the brethren of Jesus.

The world may love our acts of charity and dedication to harm no one. The world may love the spirit of humility which should be in each of us. But the world will never fully love us as the children of God. Our love of the brethren is an indication that we are walking with Him.]

3.20 *For if our heart condemn us, God is greater than our heart, and knoweth all things.*

[This verse can be considered from either of two perspectives. On the one hand our hearts may condemn us for known sin in our life. This disrupts the fellowship which God desires that we have with Him.

In this we can consider Peter's reaction to Jesus question, "Do you love me, Peter?" The memory of Peter of his denial of the Lord at the trial before the Jewish inquisitors was still fresh in the mind of Peter. It burned his conscience. He answered, "Lord, you know I love You."

Three times Jesus asked this question of Peter in the twenty-first chapter of John's Gospel. Three times Peter answered, "Lord, you know I love You."

Twice, verses 15 and 16, Jesus asks Peter if he loves Him. Jesus uses the word Agapao which signifies a close bond of love. Peter answer's that he loves Jesus using the word Phileo which signifies a friendship.

In verse 17 Jesus again asks the question but this time uses the same word for "love" as had Peter. Peter again affirms his love for the Master.

In this we see the desire to call Peter closer in fellowship to Himself. Jesus actually goes the route to call Peter back to service, note the "feed my lambs" of Jesus' discourse, by using the same word which Peter had used. Jesus knew the heart of Peter even more than Peter understood his own heart. Jesus saw the bruised heart of Peter and reached out to His broken disciple to restore him to his place of service.

On the other hand, there may be a disciple who has full confidence in his standing with God. This is not presumption in such a case. This is faith reacting to the promises of God. It is saying, "I am nothing but God is all and has called me to be His child. I trust Him because His Word is always true."

This is also a display of faith. God knows the heart of such a one and will honor the faith which trusts Him.

The former is one who has confidence in the love of God which is shining in the heart of repentance for known sin of which has been repented. The latter has confidence in the Words of God from the inspired and preserved Scripture of God which has promised salvation to those which love Him. Both responses and hopes are based on that faith which says that God always honor's those promises He had given to His children.]

3.21 *Beloved, if our heart condemn us not, then have we confidence toward God.*

[It is true that there are those who have apostatized from fellowship. Such were never really saved or the Spirit would have sealed them unto Himself. (Ephesians 4:30) But, such a one as this had seen the things of God, agreed in principle with them, and then departed from the faith without actually committing to that saving relationship with God. (II Timothy 4:1-2)

These had had their conscience seared to such an extent that they feel no real compulsion to come to the Savior. They can look the part of a true Christian so convincingly that they even are able to fool themselves. Compare II Corinthians 13:5

where we are told to examine ourselves to confirm our faith.

Without the realization of a conversion experience, where Jesus has been wholly trusted as the Means, Power, and Production of our salvation, we have *seen* Him but we have not *met* Him in saving grace. It is not Scriptural to simply *realize* that we are a Christian. We must make the decision, under the calling and conviction of the Spirit, to such a point as we *accept* the Savior as our only means of salvation.

This verse is speaking of one who has had that reality of decision to accept Christ. We know that we are changed into His saints because we have begun to love what He loves. We have begun to desire what He desires. We have begun to walk within His Light.

This realization, based on faith that God is God and does not lie, will give us the true confidence that we are in fact born again. We do not see this in any way dependent upon any merit or work of our own. We see this is based completely upon faith in the promise of God.

We might also note that this faith is not based on our understanding of the doctrine of our churches. That is, generally speaking, based on the study of man. It may well be the doctrine of God contained within our doctrinal statements but it is the study by man which produces a written doctrinal statement. John's view at this point is faith based only on the Holiness and Grace of God. We know that God can never lie nor recant of His promises to us. We do revise our church doctrinal statements from time to time.]

3.22 *And whatsoever we ask, we receive of him, because we keep his commandments, and do those things that are pleasing in his sight.*

["So, if I ask God for million dollars, will He give it? Isn't that the promise made here?"

No; that is not the promise made in this place. Once again, this verse is not out on a ledge all by itself. It is part of a larger consideration. That consideration is that we are walking according to the Will and Person of God. This prayer if it is of the will of God will be answered in the affirmative. It the prayer is not in the directive will of God it will be answered in the negative.

The "Fiddler on the Roof" asked if there were some great eternal purpose which kept him poor. The simple truth is that God understands our hearts and often sees no spiritual "upside" to a sudden increase in our wealth. Rather than enhance our ability to serve God such a windfall of wealth might well cause us to live further from God. Our faith would reach for our checkbook balance rather than the spiritual balance of The Bank of Heavenly Rewards.

It we are keeping His commandments the result will be that we are walking in His Will. Our prayers often end "In The Name of Jesus." This is not a "magic phrase." This is an acknowledgement that we seek the will of God in all that we pray and resolve.

The great purpose of our prayers is not to change the will of God. It is that we would be changed to want the will of God in all things. Such a prayer of faith will always be answered by the Lord – just as the verse says.

All prayers in our own wills will also be answered. In these the answer may well be "No" from the Heavenly Father Who gives not earthy goods to divert our eyes from

Him, but spiritual endowments to bring us further into fellowship with Him.]

3.23 *And this is his commandment, That we should believe on the name of his Son Jesus Christ, and love one another, as he gave us commandment.*

[Notice that the command is one. Believe on the Person of Jesus Christ for salvation and walk in love toward others. This is an entirely reasonable consideration. If we honestly have accepted Him as our Lord we must consider that He ranks far above us.

When I was in the army there were many "superiors" who I didn't, in the natural, care all that much for. That all made no difference. It was my shown duty to ask "How high" on the way up when they ordered me to jump. That was the code of the military discipline. That code could, and often did, save one's life in a combat situation. If we had argued the point, or pointed out our own feelings on the subject, we may well have died by the bullet of a less self-involved enemy soldier.

Satan, and all those aligned with him, are enemies of our Lord and all of us who serve under Him. Even if our own spiritual good were not served by obedience to the Lord, and it is!, we owe all to Him and must have no recourse to our own pride.

Besides this, if we honestly love Him we have placed our full faith and trust upon His Words. We want to follow His commandments.

The commandment to love is not counter to the walk of the Christian as it is an agreement with the walk of the Lord. The call of God gives us the promise that we can live above the shallow lives of the unsaved.

Under the concept of love, we find our duty to forgive wrongs done against us. Under the concept of love, we find our need to reconcile to those we have wronged. Under the concept of love, we find our need to spread good will into the world with the message that Jesus Christ died in time so that others could live in eternity.

Most glorious of all is the fact that under the concept of love we find even sweeter communion with our Lord.

His commandments are neither grievous nor unreasonable in light of eternity. His commandments are neither grievous nor unreasonable in light of the fact that we remain the creature who was lovingly created by the Lord Who desired fellowship with us. His commandments are neither grievous nor unreasonable in light of the events surrounding Calvary. That was all for us!]

3.24 *And he that keepeth his commandments dwelleth in him, and he in him. And hereby we know that he abideth in us, by the Spirit which he hath given us.*

[The desire to keep His commandments is an indication that we dwell in Him. The most nonsensical construct in the universe is that any of this sin-cursed race of humanity would desire to keep the holy commandments of The Holy God. Everything about our humanity argues for a propensity to sin. That is one of the demonstrated traits of even an infant.

If we tell a crawling infant that there are things he must not touch he will want to grab that very thing in order to examine why it is so special. In their perfect environment Adam and Eve fatally sought the only thing that God had prohibited to them.

Social physiologists will tell us that a single prohibition was too great of a temptation for a human to resist. That is exactly the point. Sinful urges will cause a person to want what he is not allowed. Why? Any limitation upon a person is viewed as a limitation of his *natural* curiosity. The Christian, with his mind upon the revelation of God in the Scripture will easily understand that the natural things are those of the created world which is sullied by the reality of sin.

The act of Adam and Eve to disobey that one rule, which rule had the noble purpose of allowing mankind to show his love for the Creator in limiting himself from the fruit of only one tree, became the act of man asserting his own dominance over His Creator.

Make no mistake. This departure from the one rule of God in the Garden was more than simple disobedience. It was a complete repudiation of the rule and prerogative of God to be Supreme within His Own created realm.

Sin goes directly to the matter of respect and obedience. By sin, an inherited trait of all men born of man and woman, man is shown total disrespect and denial of God and His Holy Office as Lord of the Universe. The only Human Who ever broke this stream of rebellion was Jesus Christ. In His Virgin Birth Jesus was free of the stain of the sin of Adam.

Eve also sinned, of course. But Adam was designated as the head of the race of man due to his standing as the first human and the directive will of God. (Genesis 1:28-30) Sin always has flowed from the man through the human race. (Consider James 1:13-14)

Eve had no such place of the primacy of the first born of the created race. This lack of "standing" disallow her place of prominence among her offspring in the sense that Adam's sin contaminated all who would follow. Therefore, it was not possible that she would send the result of her sin on to future generations except as the wife of the man.

It was the sin of Adam which produced the fact of sin in humanity, and the resultant curse of sin, throughout the human race. (Romans 5:12)

The Holy Spirit alerts us to the fact that Jesus indwells the believer. (Romans 8:9) One who dwells in a building is not always a "renter." By indwelling us Jesus is able to "redecorate." Our lives are changed by His presence from sin and unto His holiness. This is even further proved by the fact that not only does He dwell in us, we are also allowed to spiritually dwell in Him.

Our vile bodies and minds of sinful infestation are cleansed through the power of His holiness and perfections. We still live in this world of sin. As the first verse of this chapter reminds us, we can have but scant understanding of the glory that awaits in our gloried state as we dwell with the Lord. But, the spiritual reality is that our true residence has been removed from the earth of trail and pain. We are without question on the narrow road that leads to Heaven with our Lord.

The fact that the Spirit enlightens our minds to the Spiritual realities which the world can never understand is an indication of our renewed status in Christ. Our minds are not as the world's minds because our minds have been renewed by the Blood of the Lamb. Even our affections are elevated to see the panorama of Heaven. We no longer look to the world of sin to find our fulfillments.

Even in our most profane moments we are prone to long for that sweet fellowship of The Savior. We have been transformed by the indwelling of the Lord to find ourselves longing for that which is His longings. We are become more human than we were before salvation because the Lord is renewing our minds and hearts to His Glorious Image.

We will never reach this place while we inhabit these bodies of humanity within this sinful land which is infected with the sin of Adam. But, when we finally see Him as He is, in His great glory and majesty, we will be like Him. We will be fully restored to the "original specifications" and find a joy unspeakable in the bright sunlight of His image.

The Spirit relates these truths to us which we could have never imagined without Him.]

FIRST JOHN - CHAPTER FOUR

4.1 *Beloved, believe not every spirit, but try the spirits whether they are of God: because many false prophets are gone out into the world.*

[John was saying that we need to consider just where the throngs are being led. A large crowd is not the indelible mark of God's pleasure on the ministry of a man. Many people followed Jim Jones into suicide. His was not the ministry of the True God.

Many people have followed Joseph Smith into error. Many have gone the way of Mary Baker Eddy. Many have followed the cult of the Jehovah's Witness program into a Christless eternity.

What is the test of a prophet, a ministry, a minister, or a movement? "Beloved, when I gave all diligence to write unto you of the common salvation, it was needful for me to write unto you, and exhort you that ye should earnestly contend for the faith which was once delivered unto the saints." (Jude 3)

God is eternal. His truth is eternal as well. Beware when you find someone trying to say that God has just entrusted a new truth to him. First, that is pride speaking. Second, that is to imply that God has changed His mind about His program for earth. To say that this new doctrine is simply a return to the doctrine of the early church, which had been somehow lost, is to imply that man is stronger than God - that God somehow lost control of His church.

It is to argue that Jesus was either mistaken or not honest when He said that even the gates of Hell could not defeat His Church. (Matthew 16:18)

We tend to see the monolith of the "Western Church" (The Roman Catholic Church) as spreading out into the entire world as the voice of Christianity during the early years of the Middle Ages. First of all, the Roman Church was not always of completely aberrant doctrine. The churches which morphed into the Roman Church began to slowly drift away from the pure doctrine of Christ when they accepted the Roman State as their protector. This political affiliation also caused them to begin to see themselves as protectors of the Roman culture rather than as positioned to draw people from the culture of the world and into real conversion unto Christ. There were many small steps of departing from the Word until that church tradition saw themselves as the arbitrators of the doctrine of faith rather than seeing only the Scripture as having the True Words of Life.

These "small steps" cumulatively became a full retreat from the religion of Christ and the apostles.

Also, we must not forget that the Eastern Church was a rival during this entire period. They also considered only themselves to be the repository of true Christianity. They did not "bow the knee" to the Catholic Church because they believed themselves to be the continuation of the apostle's doctrine.

Even in a combined manner, neither nor both of these covered the entire earth of the faith which claimed the Name of Christ. Here and there, even within these enclaves of error, there were true churches which God held as His remnant people. We first find reference to Apollos in Acts 18:24-28. He taught the baptism of John. Aquila and Priscilla taught him "more perfectly" the facts about Jesus.

I bring up this for a specific purpose. We who are Baptists are fond of tracing our heritage back to John the Baptist. After all, he does have "Baptist" in his title. If we do this however, we are preaching from a very shaky foundation. The baptism of John was an Old Testament baptism of repentance. That is a religion of works not of faith. John saw the coming Messiah but his preaching was preparatory to the coming of Jesus. It was not fully engaged in the Cross. I don't believe that John ever saw the Cross. In Matthew 11:2-3 we find that John sent two of his disciples to Jesus to ask if He were really the coming Messiah.

We see the Church as traced back to the Day of Pentecost when the Church was established with the irrefutable power of God. Though the flame may have flickered from time to time during the days of history, the gates of Hell never did extinguish that flame. Neither has the inspired and preserved Scripture which sings forth the glories of Jesus and His Church ever been corrupted by the assaults of Satan! Satan and his often unknowing allies can never destroy the Words of God or the Church which the eternal Word of God established. (John 1:1-3)

As we scroll down to verse six of this chapter we will see that there is a spirit of truth and a spirit of error. The meaning of John here, in verse one, does not speak specifically of the Holy Spirit. The argument is to determine in which *spirit*, truth or error, a teacher is giving prophecy. The true prophet, spiritual teacher is meant here, is giving forth a message bound by the inspired and preserved Word of God. The false prophet is speaking in the name of the unholy spirit of Satan. We see this reality over and over in the "death throes" of the kingdom of Judah as false prophets led them from the Words of God.

False prophets always seem to "tickle the ears" of the worldly. (II Timothy 4:3) They say what the world wants to hear rather than what The Spirit knows that they need to hear!

I have always heard that we tend to "shrink," or get shorter, as we age. My theory is that we don't really get shorter. It's just that some inches flee from our height and attach themselves to our waist.

I was at the doctor's office a few days ago. One of the nurses checked my current height. She didn't just look and guess; she took a measuring device and used it to see my actual height. That is the demand of John in this place. We are not to see how we consider the teaching of the teacher, prophet, but to compare his doctrine with the Standard of God's Word. If that prophet's words measure up with the Standard we can listen and consider his teaching. If that prophet's words do not measure up with that Standard we are to reject both the teaching and the prophet who has given it.

Any semblance of "reasonableness" is not necessarily the Standard. Only the resemblance to the Standard of the Words of God is the Standard ordained of God for us!

Beware of new doctrine. Trust the preserved Word!]

4.2   Hereby know ye the Spirit of God: Every spirit that confesseth that Jesus Christ is come in the flesh is of God:

[John gives a fairly simple argument at this place to determine the spirit of which a prophet speaks. Does he speak in the Spirit of God or in the spirit of Satan? He who speaks of the fact that actual God inhabited actual human flesh is speaking truth.

This goes far beyond the simple holding of this truth. How do those prophets hold to that truth? It was necessary that the great Self-Sacrifice of Jesus on the Cross of Calvary be an actual human being. Without this truth He could not die on our behalf as one of us. This would not be a death *for us*. Rather, it would be a death to *instruct us* in some manner of the other. Hebrews 10:4 reminds us that even the deaths of the animals of creation under the Mosaic Law could not remove sin from us. Instead, they were teaching elements to explain Messiah Who was to come to die in our place a substitutionary death to remove sin from those who accept Jesus for their salvation. That was the purpose of the entire Mosaic Law and its attendant ceremonies and types.

Also, Jesus must be understood to actually be God within that human flesh or His death would not have had the power necessary to remove sin. A son of Adam could not even die to eradicate his own sin. It is important that II Timothy 3:16 says, "And without controversy great is the mystery of godliness: God was manifest in the flesh, justified in the Spirit, seen of angels, preached unto the Gentiles, believed on in the world, received up into glory."

Many of the modern versions say that "He" was manifest in the flesh. But, who is "he?" We can extrapolate from the verse that "he" is Jesus. But, with this reading it is possible to make the whole episode of the crucifixion seem only an exercise in vanity – or emptiness. It was God Who was manifest in the flesh of Jesus. By this our sins may be forgiven. Only by this!

The Roman Church teaches a doctrine of the "immaculate conception" of Mary, the mother of Jesus. This doctrine is shown to be false as it takes away His literal human body by which He became One of us! In such a case no salvation may be available by His death on the Cross.

The Gnostics, and others, argue that Jesus was not real. He was a mere "phantom" who seemed to be real but was not. In such a case no salvation may be available by His seeming death on the Cross.

The liberal, and others, reject His Deity. In such a case no salvation may be available by His death on the Cross. Following His example does not save. His is the Blood of the Eternal Atonement. That, alone, can save our souls.]

4.3 *And every spirit that confesseth not that Jesus Christ is come in the flesh is not of God: and this is that spirit of antichrist, whereof ye have heard that it should come, and even now already is it in the world.*

[The full Deity of Jesus Christ is such a seminal doctrine of Christianity that I cannot conceive the possibility that a person who would reject the full Deity of Jesus Christ could be considered a Christian in the Biblical sense of the word.

We are called to faith in the Person of Jesus, and of His substitutionary death on the Cross of Calvary, as a condition of our salvation and fellowship. If the view held of the Person of Christ is faulty, then the faith cannot reside in the true Person of Jesus. If Jesus is not accepted as Who He is, the faith so directed is not directed at Jesus.

Lack of faith in the reality of the Person, and Deity, of Jesus Christ is a cancer which will doom a soul to an eternity far from His presence.

Those who accept the Bible must accept the Deity of Jesus Christ because the Bible teaches such is the truth. It is a simple matter of placing trust in the Biblical record as we place trust in the Savior.

We are used to hearing of the Antichrist who shall come in the last days during the Tribulation Period. There are those who have displayed the same spirit of evil and opposition to the things of God throughout this dispensation of grace.

It is an antichrist spirit which denies the truth of the Sonship and Deity of Jesus.

I must add at this point that the modern teaching that both Christianity and Islam have sprung from Judaism and, therefore, we both worship the same God is not true! It cannot be true. Any system which denies that Jesus Christ came in flesh as God, incarnate, is not of the Spirit of God.

The working of, supposed, miracles is not the mark of a true follower of Jesus. The Egyptian court of Pharaoh was able to "copy" some of the miraculous works of Aaron and Moses. Consider Matthew 24:24 where some end times, and especially tribulation era, charlatans will deceive many. Consider Revelation 13:13-15.

Paul reminds us, "For I am not ashamed of the gospel of Christ: for it is the power *of* God unto salvation to every one that believeth; to the Jew first, and also to the Greek." (Romans 1:16) The seeming miraculous is impressive. But, the true power of God leads to the salvation of souls. The spirit of antichrist always works against true salvation!]

4.4 *Ye are of God, little children, and have overcome them: because greater is he that is in you, than he that is in the world.*

[In verses 12-14 of the second chapter of I John differing groups of people are mentioned in reference to their age. Here, in this 4th verse of chapter 4, John returns to the pastoral use of the term "little children." He is speaking as an elder and teacher to the flock of God's Church as he is writing to all of the believers rather than referencing groups.

John is happily ready to announce that the true believers have overcome the inducement of the false prophets mentioned above. Pastors especially notice how the people overcame those false prophets. It was in the power of God rather than in the power of a pastor's Wednesday Night class on the cults.

We tend to make ourselves seem pretty important in our own minds. It is not us that protects the people of God. It is God. We need more preaching from the inspired and preserved Bible and less "teaching" on how to avoid the daily pitfalls of society. When the people have heard the preaching of the Gospel they will feel led to flee to the safety of the God of that Bible. When the people have witnessed the Word in their own daily perusal of the Scripture they will understand the difference between the "fiery darts" of Satan and the soothing fellowship of the Lord.

When the people of God have a daily conversation with Him in the prayer closet, as opposed to the formality of far too many church "prayer services," they will find themselves on speaking terms with the Lord Who will say, "Watch out for that bump in the road!" He will lead them from the false prophets and unto the free grace which is in Jesus.

These "little children" were of God because they were honestly born again. They were not looking for religion because they had found Christ. They were not looking for a way to find peace with a Deity. They already had trusted the Lord Who had given them peace. "And the peace of God, which passeth all understanding, shall keep your hearts and minds through Christ Jesus." (Philippians 4:7)

We often hear of parents, and others, who lament that some cult has stolen a child, or friend, who had been so faithful to the church for years. The misunderstanding is that God does not look for someone who is simply *faithful to the church*. Such faithfulness is not wrong. But, the fact is that it is not even our faithfulness to the Cross which insures the pardon of God. In both of these scenarios the same misunderstanding is voiced. It is not our faithfulness to God that brings the power of God to bear upon our lives. The true conduit of spiritual power is in the faithfulness of God to His Children!

Our best efforts to live a truly spiritual and effective Christian life must be preceded by accepting Christ, well apart from any work on our part, as our Savior. Unless we are saved by the Blood of Christ we are not the adopted children of God.

Linda and I were once driving to a city about fifty miles from here. About thirty miles into the trip Linda said, "I forgot to get gas!" We had already passed the last exit for gas on our way to our destination. About ten miles further up the road the car said, "That's it. I ain't going to go any further until you 'feed' me." We were out of gas.

The vehicle looked ready to go. It wasn't. What was wrong? It had no gas in its tank. Unless Jesus resides in the heart of a person there is no protection from the false prophets who would lead a "religious journey" into the pits of Hell!

The God of Truth is far greater than any "prophet" of error. The Spirit of God is our full protection from the spirit of Satan. God cares for His Own and watches over us. Sign the card of faith at the foot of the Cross. Satan is a defeated foe.]

4.5 *They are of the world: therefore speak they of the world, and the world heareth them.*

[Barnes makes the point that the false prophets are worldly teachers and are not part of the church. At first glance we might consider the ungodly preachers and teachers of some churches of the day and argue against him. But, Barnes is right. Though a man may occupy a pulpit or the professor's chair at a religious institution, if he is not born again by the Blood of Jesus Christ, he is not of the Church which Jesus founded.

There are many in a pew of which the same could be said. Before my father built the house in which I grew up, we all lived in the garage he had first built. Living in a garage did not make us cars. This confession must be made in faith as the Spirit draws a person to salvation. This is not to be considered a "magic" phrase. It is not the phrase, although this must be confessed in the soul as it is the True Christ to whom we come for salvation.

The Gnostic sees Jesus as incorporeal. They would discount His physical, human, body. No! Jesus is truly human while he is also truly God. The Gnostic view of Jesus is a false view with no redeeming power. If Jesus were not fully human, via the virgin birth which discounted the "original sin" of Adam, He could not have died as our Representative.

The theological liberal, and the secularist, will both see Jesus as simply a very good man. This denial of His essential Deity would mean that He had no power to forgive sins.

The practitioners of a *New Age* philosophy would see Jesus as only another "ascended Master." This also discounts His unique status as the Only Begotten Son of

God. (John 3:16) This view sees Jesus as a mere man with certain spiritual endowments. This view seeks to rob Jesus of His essential Deity.

Other "faith traditions" will often see Jesus as a created being rather than the very Creator God of the Bible. (John 1:3)

These false "Jesus'" cannot offer salvation through the atonement because they are not the reality of Who Jesus actually is.

Going to even a Gospel preaching and teaching church does not make one a Christian. "Going forward" at a service does not make one a true Christian. A true Christian is one who has turned his back on the world of sin by asking Jesus to save his soul based on only the Work of Jesus at the Cross.

Salvation is not by osmosis. Salvation is always by accepting the Savior as our Only means of pardon from sin, peace with God, and a home in Heaven. Salvation is of Christ's Blood not of our "profession."

This is a problem I have with those who argue for "a Bible the world will read." The world is not attuned to the things of God. Neither are they looking for God until the Spirit brings true conviction upon them. I am not surprised at the lack of power within the churches since we have begun to jettison the Holy Bible and seek guidance from the world's Bible.

When the "prophet" is from the world he will preach a worldly way of life. He will depart from sacrifice to endorse ease. He will teach a Gospel of accommodation to the things of the world with the argument, "We must be like the world if we are to gain the world." He will find more purpose in the things of the world than in the things of God.

Yesterday I threw out an entire loaf of bread. I didn't even open the wrapper to look at it. The entire bottom of the loaf was green. It was rather easy to see it was not good bread. Even though our dogs really wanted it I refused to give it even to them. Bad bread is only good as trash.

The same can be said of a gospel which reeks more of the world than of the sweet aroma of the Rose of Sharon.]

4.6 *We are of God: he that knoweth God heareth us, he that is not of God heareth not us. Hereby know we the spirit of truth, and the spirit of error.*

[John was an apostle. He was very probable the lone remaining apostle at this time. When he spoke of spiritual things it was natural to assume that his word was actually a word which was approved of God.

Wouldn't it be nice to have an apostle to whom we could go with our spiritual questions in this day? We have the memoirs and teachings of those apostles available in the inspired and preserved Scripture. The Holy Spirit has given the True Word through these apostles and the other writers of Scripture. We can trust that He has kept the Words of Scripture available for us even in this day.

This is certain. Can we actually conceive of God as being so weak that He could not preserve His Words for us in this day? Why not? It is because of the witness of His Spirit with our spirit that the Words of God were given in Love and Perfection. The Spirit witnesses to the fact that we are the children of God.

That which is perfect cannot become "more" perfect unless we redefine the word "perfect." The Words of God, perfectly given, must be perfectly preserved unless somehow the evil spirit has overcome the Holy Spirit.

That which is given in love will not be withdrawn. God considered His Message to man to be so important that He gave it in written form. Unless those Words, faithful copies of them to be sure, are available to us today, we must assume that God loves us less than He did those who originally received them.

Peter wrote, "But the word of the Lord endureth *for* ever. And this *is* the word which by the gospel is preached unto you." (I Peter 1:25) Some have tried to make this verse argue that only the gospel message has been preserved. That is ludicrous. The verse argues that the gospel message is preached *from* the preserved words. God has kept His Words, the original Hebrew, Greek and Aramaic of those originally penned by His servants, throughout the centuries of time by His Own power and grace.

Further, John says that anyone who has fellowship with God, only the born again have this fellowship, will find the Words of God to resonate with them. It is only those from outside the household of faith who will not abide the Truth of the Words of God.]

4.7   *Beloved, let us love one another: for love is of God; and every one that loveth is born of God, and knoweth God.*

[It can be rightly argued that true love has it genesis in the Love of God. The love of God is an unselfish love which led Him to create humanity as an expression of His true love. When we look at Revelation 13:8b we will realize that the Cross was not a "fix up" of a creation gone wrong. God understood that sin would mar the race of man. How could He Who knows all from beginning to end not have known? Yet, knowing that the Cross was the inevitable price to redeem created humanity, Jesus created mankind.

Yes; you read that right. It was the same Jesus Who would occupy the Cross of the Crucifixion Who created humanity. (John 1:3) Jesus, in the Kenosis, would become one of the Created race of man via the virgin birth. He would be hated, mistreated, spoken despitefully of, and killed in the most gruesome manner which the vile race of humanity could devise.

When we consider the glories of the Easter Season may we recall the horror which was visited upon the Person of Jesus in His humanity. As we glory in the fact of His resurrection may we recall that His closest earthy friends deserted Him to bear the Cross alone. Even as we think upon these things, we can never understand the love which He exhibited when He created the race of man. He fully understood the depravity of man and the future of the Cross by which He would restore many to fellowship with Him.

We should not just consider ourselves as unworthy. We should praise Him with every fiber of our being as we contemplate, we can never realize fully, the depth of His love and grace which He has bestowed upon us!

We human beings can display a great affection for others. We can even call it "love." The husband who loves his wife to the point that he would sacrifice himself for her can be used as an example. Even he falls short of the Love of God. The mother who loves her child above her own life can be used as but a poor example of the Great Love of God. Even the soldier who lays down his life to protect his comrade in arms shows but a fraction of the enormity of the Love of God.

"For scarcely for a righteous man will one die: yet peradventure for a good man some would even dare to die. But God commendeth his love toward us, in that, while we were yet sinners Christ died for us." (Romans 5:7-8)

Love is from God to us. In light of Revelation 13:8b we must conclude that even though He understood the vileness of man, the hatred which man would display toward Him, and the desperate need of mankind, Jesus created the race which He knew would cause Him to die the death of Calvary.

Christian's down through the ages, and still today in parts of the world, will suffer martyrdom rather than hide the Gospel message that Jesus Christ died in time so that others could live in eternity.

Our time, even in this nation, will come to make the same choice. The love of God, spread abroad in the hearts of His children, will make the same choice. Dr. Kirk DiVietro said it best, "You can't scare me with Heaven." It is only God Who gives the grace to die out of love. The adherents of Islam are well known for being willing to die for their religion. They kill others as they do so. It is often given to the Christian to die for the message of salvation to be given to others. The Christian will not seek this. He will submit to it only when necessary and then, only in love for his killers and tormenters.]

4.8 *He that loveth not knoweth not God; for God is love.*

[The meaning of not knowing God is not simply to misunderstand the tenets of Christianity or the Scripture. The phrase speaks of not enjoying an experiential knowledge of God. Such a one may know much about God, but has never felt the love of God course through the veins of his heart. He is no child of God but remains a child of Satan.

This verse reminds me of John 14:6 where Jesus said, "...I am the way, the truth, and the life: no man cometh unto the Father, but by me." Jesus did not say that He could show us the way to God. He said that He, Personally, is the Way to God. Jesus did not say that He could teach us truth. He said that He, Personally, is Ultimate Truth. Jesus did not say that He could impart life. He said that He, Personally, is life.

John 1:4 tells us that, "In him was life..." Life is not a "thing" which animates Jesus. Jesus is that Holy Being in Whom the entire concept of "life" resides. Life is His possession to dispense or withhold.

Likewise, this present verse says that God *is* love. It seems that all other aspects of His Divine Being emanates from His Love. His holiness is an expression of His Love. His justice is an expression of His Love. His power, glory and on and on when considering the majesty of His transcendent glory are expressions of His Love.

This is not an argument that Love is God. This would imply a love that does not contain holiness, justice and all the others things considered above. This is simply to argue that God always displays His love. We can argue that God is Light (I John 1:5) without doing violence to that precept. His love is displayed in that light. We can argue that God is Spirit (John 4:24) without doing violence to that precept. His Being of Love is Spirit.

It is not possible for one who has not experienced the true Love of God in their lives by the salvation experience to know God in any real manner. Such a person may well be altruistic; we consider that our creation as a race was in the image of God. Such image was not in form of appearance but in essential human nature of existence.

The entrance of sin into humanity has blunted much of this but the reality remains.

However, even the most altruistic among us can never display the depth of Spiritual love which is in Christ.]

4.9 *In this was manifested the love of God toward us, because that God sent his only begotten Son into the world, that we might live through him.*

[We can read John 3:16 or we can understand John 3:16. That verse simply says that "For God so loved the world..." When we contemplate the meaning "...that he gave his only begotten Son," we can begin to understand just a little better the depth of that love. This was not just another person. This is the Only begotten Son of God. There was no other in all eternity to whom that claim could have been made. God, the Son, came to be our Savior.

This is a picture of the Love of God. This isn't just a picture; from our perspective as sin cursed humanity this is a definitive picture of the Love of God in a form we can understand. He came to earth, set aside in the Kenosis His rightful Glory as God, and took the form of a man – for us! He endured being born in the form of a human baby. He did not come as a king of humanity. He did not come into a rich family. He did not come in an angelic procession to proclaim His rightful importance.

He did come into a nation which was suffering under the strain of a foreign occupation.

He suffered hunger and thirst. He suffered bone gnawing fatigue. He suffered rejection from the very people, the religious professionals, who should have welcomed Him. And, in His hour of extreme humiliation, He suffered being deserted by almost all who claimed to follow Him. His human death was the most gruesome that human ingenuity could fathom. Yet, it was for this He had come.

He came to a world which hated Him. He came to a nation which rejected Him. He came to offer salvation and eternal life to people who were in rebellion against Him.

Many other things had demonstrated the Love of God for His creation. This, the fact that Jesus Christ died in time – and the manner of that death – in order that we might live in eternity still stands as the greatest example and statement of the Love of God for His created race of man.]

4.10 *Herein is love, not that we loved God, but that he loved us, and sent his Son to be the propitiation for our sins.*

[The entire time of the earthly ministry of Jesus upon this earth showed nothing of our love for Him. It did show the depth and quality of His love for us. The same could be said, as we have noted above, about His entire pre-existence. This was no accident. Jesus always intended to come into this world to die for our sins.

Jesus came to become the appeasement for our sins we had committed against Him. The love by which God loved us is far beyond anything we could ever contemplate. Our human words and emotions fall far short of understanding the Love of God. The only thing we can do is to fall to our knees and accept His gift of pure love. Even in this, we know that it is only the Love of God in the conviction of the Spirit upon our hearts that can draw us to that place of repentance and acceptance.

When our human hearts hear this story we are tempted to say, "I can't believe that God would love so deeply." The glory is that the Spirit takes our incredulity and turns it into complete joy as we accept the gift of salvation from the Lord Jesus Christ. It is all of Him. It is all of Him!

It is interesting to note that it was John, along with James, who asked that Jesus should command them to send down fire to consume a Samaritan city because the people of the city had not received Jesus. (Luke 9:54) Even the best of Christians are prone to fail the uniqueness of their Heavenly calling. The love of Jesus never fails.]

4.11 *Beloved, if God so loved us, we ought also to love one another.*

[The word "Christian," which means to be like Christ, had been coined in Antioch. (Acts 11:26) We could ascribe this verse to that fact. But, I do not believe that this is the reason. As Christians we are to be followers of Jesus. Jesus loved us when, especially spiritually speaking, we were completely unlovely. (Consider Romans 5:6)

We have been commissioned to love the brethren often already in this epistle. Here is another time! I would notice this: Jesus so deeply loved us that He died for us while we were yet sinners in rebellion against Him. We cannot claim that any of the brethren are so terrible that we cannot love them. I would caution that the more we love someone we can't seem to stand, the more we will grow to like that person.

We also need to love those that are in the world. Even to those who persecute us we are called to display Christian love. We do this so that we can draw them to ourselves. If that fails, they may even begin to understand that we treat them more properly simply because we are Christians. We do this even when they attack us! This may cause them to consider the facts of Jesus and His love.

Remember that Jesus loved us while we were rank sinners! We can love others if we pray to the Spirit to empower us. We might argue, "It would take a miracle for me to love that person!" Well, Who better to ask about a miracle than the Lord as we pray unto Him.]

4.12 *No man hath seen God at any time. If we love one another, God dwelleth in us, and his love is perfected in us.*

[Back in John 1:18 we read, "No man hath seen God at any time; the only begotten Son, which is in the bosom of the Father, he hath declared *him*." Now in this verse we read that we are asked to become witnesses of Jesus by our lives.

"For whom he did foreknow, he also did predestinate to be conformed to the image of his Son, that he might be the firstborn among many brethren." (Romans 8:29) John has written much against the idea of sinless perfection. Here, in I John, he writes of the Love of Christ being perfected in us. The idea of perfection in this sense is of an action being completed to its intended goal. The goal is that our love becomes as is His love into the world.

This goal will propel us to become more interested in winning souls on the street than on writing commentary in a church study.

Oops! I shouldn't have written that line. The point is that I fail God very often. That "shouldn't oughta be!" The fact is that each of us has a need to "...press toward the mark for the prize of the high calling of God in Christ Jesus." (Philippians 3:14) You may notice that I excised the word "I" from that verse. We all need to learn that all of the inspired and preserved Scripture is written to all of us!]

4.13 *Hereby know we that we dwell in him, and he in us, because he hath given us of his Spirit.*

[Turn back to the last chapter and see the notes on I John 3:24 which covers the same area that we dwell in Jesus even as He dwells in us.

Here we are told that the reality of this is known to us because the Spirit also indwells the believer. The skeptic will argue that this is not possible given that there are so many professing Christians scattered around the world. That really is no problem. First of all, God is of the Spiritual realms without our physical limitations.

Open your King James Bible, and if you do not have one, get one! (I would suggest *The Defined King James Bible* which is published by "The Bible For Today" of Collingswood, New Jersey. The definitions are located on the bottom of the page so those "old and uncommon" words are easily understandable without intruding upon the text of a passage.) In John 3:13 we see that Jesus, even while He is speaking with Nicodemus in first century Jerusalem, is also residing in Heaven.

God, and only God, has the attribute called "Omnipresence" which means that He is everywhere at the same time. This is not moving quickly. This is actually being everywhere at the same time. Read the verses which precede Ephesians 1:23 and then pay special attention to that twenty-third verse. "Which is his body, the fulness of him that filleth all in all." As God, the Son, is not limited by spatial considerations but is able to be all places at all times, so is God, the Father and God, the Holy Spirit.

There is but One God. But, the essence of this One Being is manifest through three distinct Personalities. I can't explain this and will not try. Let it suffice to say that the New Testament teaches this as fact. There is some difference in the Spiritual state of eternity than in the physical state of time. It is enough to say that God understands more than we can possibly fathom!

The Spirit gives to the Christian certain graces. One of these is the witness that we are, indeed, the children of God. (Romans 8:16)]

4.14 *And we have seen and do testify that the Father sent the Son to be the Saviour of the world.*

[The apostles testified to the truth that they had seen and been taught of The Son in His life, through His death and even in His resurrection and ascension. The argument was that this testimony was no fable that had grown over the years but was a fact witnessed by many.

Some have trouble with the phrase "the Father sent the Son." There is no need to misunderstand the phrase. This in no way argues against the reality of the Divinity of Jesus.

What this phrase does show is the essential unity of The Triune God. It was the Love of The Father which commissioned Jesus to become the Savior of mankind.

It was the Love of The Son which led Him to the Cross. The death, real and physical, of the humanity of Jesus consummated that Love of God for His created beings.

It is the Love of The Holy Spirit which now empowers the penitent to walk in a newness of life as a child of God.

When we look at only the dichotomy of Each we look with the eyes of humanity. We see from our perspective of time and the physical. God, from the reality of Heaven and Eternity does not see things as we see them. There is a reality of the essential unity of the Godhead of which John writes.

Rather than a problematic situation to our ears, this phrase is a beautiful affirmation of the Triune Essence of God. There is a complete unity of process and Person within this verse as to the essential Deity of The Father, The Son, and the Holy Spirit. We might consider Matthew 28:19 – "Go ye therefore, and teach all nations, baptizing them in the name of the Father, and of the Son, and of the Holy Ghost."

Note the verse well. Under the singular of "name" there are three distinct Persons referenced. One God Who exists in a tripartite existence far above our human capacity to understand. Yet, the meaning is clear.]

4.15 *Whosoever shall confess that Jesus is the Son of God, God dwelleth in him, and he in God.*

[In these post-Christian days of ecumenical fervor, we often lose sight of the fact that true Christianity is somewhat exclusive. Oh, anyone can become a Christian. But, to gain eternal life and peace with God - forgiveness of sins - one must always accept Jesus as his Savior. There is no other way. While other "religious traditions" might lead one to an exemplary life on this earth; only a relationship with Jesus Christ can not only insure, but guarantee, salvation from sin, peace with God and an eternal home in Heaven.

All other paths are false and will lead to an eternal Hell. This is not a message which the world wants to hear. Still, they do need to hear the eternal truth that Jesus Christ died in time so that they might live in eternity.

This confession must be made in faith as the Spirit draws a person to salvation. This is not to be considered a "magic" phrase. It is not the phrase, although this must be confessed in the soul as it is the True Christ to whom we come for salvation.

The Gnostic sees Jesus as incorporeal. They would discount His physical, human, body. No! Jesus is truly human while he is also truly God. The Gnostic view of Jesus is a false view with no redeeming power. If Jesus were not fully human, via the virgin birth which discounted the "original sin" of Adam, He could not have died as our Representative.

The theological liberal, and the secularist, will both see Jesus as simply a very good man. This denial of His essential Deity would mean that He had no power to forgive sins.

The practitioners of a *New Age* philosophy would see Jesus as only another "Ascended Master." This also discounts His unique status as the Only Begotten Son of God. (John 3:16) This view sees Jesus as a mere man with certain spiritual endowments. This view seeks to rob Jesus of His essential Deity.

Other "faith traditions" will often see Jesus as a created being rather than the very Creator God of the Bible. (John 1:3)

These false "Jesus'" cannot offer salvation through the atonement because they are not the reality of Who Jesus actually is.]

4.16 *And we have known and believed the love that God hath to us. God is love, and he that dwelleth in love dwelleth in God, and God in him.*

[That which we have both known, experientially, and have believed, by faith, of the love of God is a truth of our salvation experience. Even our belief was centered upon the love of God's gracious gifts to us. (Ephesians 2:8-9)

In this we are in Him safe in the Arms of His Love. Likewise, He is in us displaying His Love and teaching us that closer walk which strengthens and emboldens us to overcome the things of the world which seek to conquer us but can never ultimately do so!

The closer we walk with God, the stronger we feel His love radiating to us. The further we slide from that blessed fellowship with Him, the less we feel His hand of love upon us. That hand of love is still active within us though through our own disobedience as children of God although it may be the hand of loving discipline.

The mention was made above of His love radiating to us. The elements of a cake batter can be combined and placed within an oven. The heat radiating from that oven will transform the semi-liquid of the cake batter into a cake fit to celebrate a child's birthday or an elderly couple's fiftieth anniversary. God desires for us to "bake" into a celebration of His glory and message of salvation throughout this world of men who need to respond in like manner as did we at our own salvation.

When we are honestly walking with Him we will feel the fervor of His love to call sinners to salvation. Without this desire in our hearts it is difficult to assume that we have His salvation in our soul. Matthew 20:28 reminds us that, "Even as the Son of man came not to be ministered unto, but to minister, and to give his life a ransom for many."

Conversely, I would believe that as we gain the vision, through prayer and Scripture, of the lostness of lost men and women, we will draw even closer to the Lord. Heaven is real goal for which only true salvation prepares one.

Also, Hell is a real destination which awaits all who have never accepted Jesus as Savior. How many have we warned of this fact? Should I have said, "How few have we warned of this fact?"]

4.17 *Herein is our love made perfect, that we may have boldness in the day of judgment: because as he is, so are we in this world.*

["Our love?" We have no true love of our own to send into the world. But, there is a glorious truth to consider.

In 1955 my father bought me a baseball glove. It was useless to me. I was once told, in a baseball sense, that I couldn't catch flies with a jar of honey spread over my head. I was also considered a fairly good volleyball player in the outfield. I never actually caught the ball but I did swat at it a few times.

The point is that my father picked out that glove. He paid the entire price for that glove from money he had earned at his job. The glove was only mine because my father had given me that which I had not earned and with which I could not well perform.

In that sense our salvation is "ours" only because the Savior bought it at the Cross and gave it to us free of any charge except receiving it by faith. He even gave us the faith to receive that gift! There are times we perform very poorly as recipients of that Great Salvation.

Practice, however, makes perfect. Well, not my baseball practice. I still can't catch a baseball unless it is very carefully handed to me!

Our perfection is to become a promised reality. God does not lie. He said it; He will perform it. This is true in spite of our short comings. Practice the ability that God has placed within the lives of those who have been born again by the Precious Blood of the Lamb.

T The completion of the perfection, the means of "made perfect," will await our coming to our home of Heaven to see the Savior's face of love. In the meantime we can have a boldness to spread the Word of His love into the world.

For the born again, our sins are judged at the Cross when we give our sins to Jesus for forgiveness. This verse speaks of judgment upon the world. We have no need to fear the world's judgment. We've been judged and pardoned by the King. What have we to fear from the underlings of this temporal world?

Jesus was murdered by the people of time. He overcame that as His physical body resurrected from the grave and death. He lives forevermore in eternity. His death was for us.

Our persecution in this present world will come from foes of our God and our Savior. We are promised that we will, as did Jesus, overcome all. The most that the world can do to us is to kill our bodies. Even in that eventuality we have been promised that the Lord will raise our bodies to everlasting life. It is not that "we shall overcome." It is that we have already overcome in the Precious Blood of The Lamb.]

4.18 *There is no fear in love; but perfect love casteth out fear: because fear hath torment. He that feareth is not made perfect in love.*

[I like the words of Spurgeon on this verse from his Devotional Commentary: "Fear dwells upon the punishment deserved, and so has no rest. When perfect love assures the soul of pardoned sin, the heart has joyful rest."

We need have no fear either in this world or in dread of the next. Fear is of the unknown. We know Jesus. Fear is of a punishment for either failure or performance contrary to a right standard. Jesus has abolished the sting of both the Law and death for us. We are not alone in this universe for Jesus holds our hands even as we traverse the Valley of the Shadow.

Fear, for the true Christian, is simply a result of not fully trusting the power, love and grace of our Lord. His Words of the inspired and preserved Scripture and His wonderful love which upholds and establishes us leads us to perfect His love within to that natural destination to which we are called. That is the glory of the perfections He has for us in the Heavenlies.

Worthy of what, may be asked. God is worthy of all adoration, fear, love, obedience, respect, and much more such like. Mere words fail when we attempt to describe the manifold glories of our Majestic Lord and Savior!

Just as darkness must depart when light appears, so must fear depart when we view – even in our mind's eye – the love of God promised and provided to His people. The Love of God, fully understood, will cast out fear because fear is the antithesis of Love.

The fear which raises its ugly head in the life of a Christian is a reminder that we are not fully perfected as saints of our Lord. We retain, as long as we are in this body of clay, the need to rest often in the Words of the inspired and preserved Scripture and prayer with our Lord. We are never to assume that we are perfect in and of our selves.

We stand perfect before God only because of the Work of the Lord at Calvary. "Not by works of righteousness which we have done, but according to his mercy he saved us, by the washing of regeneration, and renewing of the Holy Ghost..." (Titus 3:5)]

4.19 *We love him, because he first loved us.*

[I like the way that Matthew Poole illustrated this concept. "His is the fountain love, ours but the stream..." I think that this illustration gives a good sense of the meaning of the verse. We could not love Him if He did not shed His Love abroad within our hearts by the salvation of our souls. (Romans 3:10-11)

We were sinners who were totally opposed to all things of God. Our very nature was ungodly. When we look at the spectacle of horror which is the Cross and realize that this is the way which sinful mankind expressed their feelings about our Savior, we can just begin to realize the depth of the antagonism of unregenerate man toward the things of God.

A look at nearly any mass media magazine or newspaper opinion pages will reveal that the same hate for the purity of God continues to exist in this day. It is a reflection of the innate process of carnal human thought.

To consider that we, or any truly born again person, have come from that degree of complete hate to a love of God is a miracle of the first order. The Spirit of God worked that miracle upon our hearts in His role of convicting us of sin and drawing us to the Savior. We could never have made that transition without Him.

Another consideration, which I also accept as a secondary interpretation of this verse is that our love of the brethren, and of the world for that matter, is a result of the Love of God which is given into us in Salvation. This Love of His toward us has become that Fountain Spring which leads us to flow into the world of man with the loving message that Jesus Christ died in time so that others could live in eternity.

I would also like to note that both the original ASV and the original RSV had jettisoned the word "Him" in the phrase "We love him." This could be considered simply an unnecessary aberration were it not for the fact that to remove "Him," "God," from the equation is to remove God as the source of our Love both toward Him and toward all men, the brethren and the world. This is to give man an inbred "goodness" which cannot exist within a sinner. In the Christian this would remove the fact of our own response to the Love of God and make it in our goodness rather than in dependence upon His grace.

See also notes at Genesis 26:3.]

4.20 *If a man say, I love God, and hateth his brother, he is a liar: for he that loveth not his brother whom he hath seen, how can he love God whom he hath not seen?*

[John begins this fourth chapter with the admonition in verse one to "...try the spirits whether they are of God..." Now he is asking that we try our own spirit to see if it is God we are following or whether we are following the spirit of the world.

We humans are of carnal stock. This applies in our physical sense even to the born again Christian. Our human bodies are of the natural creation. Even the apostle Paul wrestled against his human nature at times. (Romans 7:15-19) This reality caused him the pain which drove him closer to the Savior so as to flee from human lusts. (II Timothy 2:22)

This being true, how much more likely are we to display love towards one we have seen. We have seen his need and our compassion would alleviate that need if possible. This is a naturally occurring process within the shared community of humanity. Blood banks, food banks, charitable institutions all of these reach out even from the unsaved. It is a natural thing to feel better about ourselves when we are allowed to help others.

As an aside, I honestly believe that much of this altruism among the unsaved is actually gendered by the feeling of superiority which comes from helping one who is "less fortunate than ourselves." That is not Christian love; it is simply humanity acting out his own self worth with others often the objects of our use.

God has commanded us to love others. God has commanded us especially to love others of the household of faith.

John asks how we can claim to love God, Who is of Spirit and not visible to our human eyes, when we fail to show love toward those of humanity who were created in the image of God. His answer is that we really cannot. The reality of any true love of God will drive us to fulfill the commands of God to love one another.

A true walk in the love of God will cause us to love others even as God loves His human creation and for whom Jesus died on the cross.

We must be careful at this point. The love of God for lost humanity gave Jesus to the world to die as a sacrifice for their salvation. This does not extend to salvation being simply poured out on all. Such a construct ignores the warnings of Scripture which so fervently call for true repentance and belief. The Great Love of God allows man to make his choice of Hell if that is a man's real preference. Sadly, many are so blinded by the sin nature of their own that this is their choice. A pastor of mine used to say, "God is a perfect Gentleman. He forces no one to choose to love Him against their will. The Spirit does woo them. He does not force them."]

4.21 *And this commandment have we from him, That he who loveth God love his brother also.*

[This is being written just a few days after a remembrance of "D-Day." Do you believe that the military approached these brave men and said, "Anyone who wants to get into one of these landing crafts and invade Hitler's Europe, climb aboard?" Probably not. It is more likely that the command was, "Let's move out quickly!"

We love the brethren in the full knowledge that Christ loves them. We love the world, the humanity of the world not the world systems which are often antichrist, because each person stands in desperate need of the only salvation which is available for their eternal souls. We love all because God loves us and we partially return that love in full obedience to His commandments. We are not saved by obeying His commandments. We obey His commandments because we are already saved!

To fail to love our brother is to show a disposition which also fails to love the commandments of God. To fail to love the commandments of God is not only a disrespectful dereliction of Christian duty; it is an indication of a lack of love of God on our part.

When we refuse to love our brother, and it is a choice to love in the manner which has been discussed, we fail to display love toward God Who created man in His image.]

FIRST JOHN - CHAPTER FIVE

5.1   Whosoever believeth that Jesus is the Christ is born of God: and every one that loveth him that begat loveth him also that is begotten of him.

[Once again, we go back to consider the purpose of John's writing. He was combatting certain false views of Jesus. An historical assent that a Person by the Name of Jesus Bar Joseph lived and taught in the first century is not enough to engender salvation. The Holy Spirit must be seen as attesting to the fact of the Jesus of our salvation.

This Jesus is shown to be the Christ, the Messiah, of God. Within that affirmation we understand that Jesus was not only sent *of* God, the Father, to assume the Office of Savior of the World. This Jesus also *was* God, the Son. Even in His humanity Jesus is of deity. In His essence of existence Jesus is deity. The full understanding of Jesus is that He was sent of God and as God, The Father, into this world of men to become one of us through the fact of human birth.

Even within this, Jesus retained His essential deity. Much of the glory of this deity was voluntarily set aside. His outward glory as God was set aside so that He could live as an example of how we, humanity, ought to live and relate to God. In this, the Kenosis, Jesus retained His pure essence of deity as God in order to die an effectual death of Sacrifice for our sins.

John is arguing that one who believes in the real Jesus is born of God via salvation into the family of God as adopted sons. This does not mean that we become Gods or take on all the attributes of deity into our own personal existence. The meaning is that we become "like Him" in the perfections He assigns to us as the redeemed of the earth.

We are created beings released from the burden of sin and accepted, through the Blood of Jesus, as the children of God and the Bride of Christ. (Revelation 19:9) We shall forever dwell with Him, praising His Name and His Glory.

Through this we return to the "factory specifications" of our creation as humans in that we love God and fellowship with Him. This is all predicated on His Love which has shown us the Glory of Christ and called us into fellowship with Him in the New Birth.

John argues also that our love for God is shown by us in our love for the brethren upon whom God has also displayed the same love for them as He has for us. They are our brothers and sisters as fellow adopted children of God. A lack of love for them is an evidence of a lack of love for God. This brings into question our very salvation.

Salvation is not founded on the love we have for the brethren. That love of the brethren is a fruit that grows on the branches of our life as we live for Him Who has died, and lives forevermore, for us.]

5.2   By this we know that we love the children of God, when we love God, and keep his commandments.

[This love of the brethren is shown because we love God. These brethren are to be loved as the brethren are repositories of the Love of God on this earth. If we have no real love for the brethren, we have no love for the work of God in redeeming this lost race of humanity. If we have no love for the redeeming of lost humanity we can have no real love for the Savior as He died for that very purpose.

Once again, we must consider the reality of our salvation if we do not love that which God loves. It is possible to be saved in such a case, of course, but it would be a lonely faith which had no joy in salvation. For such a one to pray to the Lord, he would find censure for failing one of the first commandments: that we love one another even as Christ has loved us.

Still, this does remain a litmus test. Can we claim to love God when we disobey His commandments? Our salvation is based upon His Love towards us. Many have honestly accepted His salvation but have refused His leading in many areas.

I must admit that I find it hard to consider salvation as apprehended by such a person. Then I recall that many Biblical examples of truly righteous people who are flawed people at some point in their lives. This is the purpose of the discipline of God upon His unruly Children.

Note: What I have writing about, and what I believe John was addressing is those Christians, truly born again, are in a backslidden condition when they refuse to comply with the leading of the Holy Spirit as to the commandments of God. Such as these remain Christians. John has spent much time regarding the fact that Christians sometimes do sin; they are not capable of true sinless perfection in this world. Their souls have been transformed but their bodies of clay war against that transformation. The weaker will fail.

This failure will set up judicial, not judging of sin for that was accomplished at the Cross, punishment of a Fatherly nature of discipline. Such disciple may even include the calling of the straying Christian home to Heaven. Consider the spiritual principle of I Corinthians 5:5 and 11:30.]

5.3 *For this is the love of God, that we keep his commandments and his commandments are not grievous.*

[It is a reasonable thing to love the brethren in the faith. It is a natural thing. We count them among our closest friends as we meet so often with them. Even those we initially could "just not stand" will tend to "grow on us" as we share the fellowship of the Lord.

It is that fellowship which becomes the foundation of a friendship we might not have sought had we not been of the same family with God as adopted children of The Heavenly Father.

A few minutes ago I moved an old lawn mower in a shed. Apparently there was still some gas in the old machine. Now I am sitting at this keyboard, working at what I needed to accomplish. I simply removed the mower from the shed and propped the door to the shed open so the small spill could be removed by the wind and air of the day. That isn't a hard task. As a matter of fact, any time I can just sit and allow the wind to do my work I am very happy.

The commandments of God are not grievous. Given our new nature as born again saints, those commandments are suddenly become our happiest tasks. "Love the brethren." "Really; You are going to let me find a group of people with the same interests as I have found in salvation. I am supposed to enjoy a fellowship of love instead of harboring ill and competition among a worldly group who are opposed to the things I stand for?"

It's really not too hard to say "thank you, Lord," as we obey His commandments of Love and Strength. Even if we do "bog down" from time to time we will find that The Spirit assists us in completing these joyful tasks for our Savior.

My wife and I used to enjoy taking walks in the gentle rain. The charged air made by the coming storm is so enjoyable. God has "charged" our air with His blessedness. It is a joy to walk with Him. We realize just how great that joy is when we find another path and become so anxious to scurry back to Him and His Hand of Love.]

5.4 *For whatsoever is born of God overcometh the world: and this is the victory that overcometh the world, even our faith.*

[The true Christian will often fail his Lord. This is sad. We should not be as willy-nilly as this. But, we are. This fact is borne out in so many of our lives that it does not bear serious rebuttal.

But, we are better than this! We are given the promise that we have overcome the world which would drag us down to its level. This victory, which we often fail to grasp even though it is a present gift in corollary with our Salvation, is based on faith.

Therein is something we need to understand. The victory is not of our own making. As a matter of plain fact, an attempt to overcome in our own power is the reason so many of us will fail so often! The victory, assured when we access it, lays in faith. Faith lies in Christ. Therefore, to find the promised victory we are to walk with the Lord. More than simply walking with the Lord, we have a need to commune with Him – often! – in the Spirit and prayer. We need to read our *Manual* of the inspired and preserved Scripture. In the mountain of temptation Jesus taught us to use the Scripture to oppose the blandishments of the tempter.

We cannot do this unless we have a "working knowledge" of what that inspired and preserved Scripture has to say. Don't give a "but I'm so stupid I'll never be able to remember what the Bible says to me. (Mark 13:11) The Spirit has promised to help in a time of need. He'll do it! Just trust Him in faith.

While we read the Scripture, we gain a working knowledge of its contents and the Spirit brings spiritual food to our souls.]

5.5 *Who is he that overcometh the world, but he that believeth that Jesus is the Son of God?*

[What is meant by overcoming the world? We could answer this by positing another question. Ephesians 2:2 explains this. "Wherein in time past ye walked according to the course of this world, according to the prince of the power of the air, the spirit that now worketh in the children of disobedience"

The present world system is dominated by sin. As such it is diametrically opposed to God and the things of God. We, with our witness of the Spirit of Christ into the world are also opposed by the world. To overcome the world is to conquer the world by upholding the banner of Christ into the world.

To overcome the world is also a matter of keeping our Christian joy and fellowship with the Master despite the blandishments to evil or despair which would rob us of communion with Jesus.

To believe that Jesus is the Son of God is to accept Him as the Divine. In this we understand His complete humanity even as we accept His essence as God, the Son.]

5.6 *This is he that came by water and blood, even Jesus Christ; not by water only, but by water and blood. And it is the Spirit that beareth witness, because the Spirit is truth.*

[Many commentators made impressive displays of theological gymnastics in order to make the phrase "water" apply to the baptism of Jesus. It does not. The main argument for this seems to be that it was at this time that He received His commission to be Savior of the World. Matthew 20:28 reminds us that this was the reason for which Jesus had come into the world. Both Revelation 13:8b and I Peter 1:20 show that the plan of Salvation has always been in the Cross of Christ. Since He came to earth for this very purpose, sent by The Father (John 3:16) for this task, the concept of an "Investiture Service" seems out of place for One already dedicated to the task.

The idea that Jesus received the "Christ Spirit" at this time is likewise faulty thinking. Jesus knew Who He was even through the seeming "fog" of His Self-imposed Kenosis. We recall Him speaking with the teachers at the Temple when His parents found Him there after they had thought Him lost. He testified to His knowledge of Himself when He called God His Father even as He spoke with Joseph.

Such a view as this would seem to inappropriately elevate baptism beyond its place as an initiation rite into a local assembly of Christians and a witness to the world that one has been brought to salvation through the Cross.

More specifically we must understand "water" as speaking of His natural birth into the community of humanity. Any woman who has given birth, and any husband who has heard his wife shout, "My water burst. Get me to the hospital." will easily understand that this has to do with the natural birth of a human being.

In the nineteenth chapter of Numbers we read of the total sacrifice of a young heifer by burning. Her ashes, all of them, are then mixed with water. (see verse 17) This will produce a water of purification. This is a picture of the dual nature of Jesus. He is both fully human and fully God. His great Self-Sacrifice at Calvary was outside the walls of Jerusalem. Compare this with the third verse of the nineteenth chapter of Numbers and we see the significance of this "coincidence" of man's making.

"Water" speaks of the identification of Jesus with humanity.

The many purification rituals, some Biblical and some not Biblical, of the Jews of the time of Christ's physical sojourn on this earth, also bolster the picture of the water referring to the fact that Jesus identified with us in His humanity.

The "Blood" does speak of Jesus. But in this place it refers specifically to His purchase of our salvation. We, as born-again believers who are Blood Bought by Calvary, are witnesses to the fact of Jesus in this world as Savior. Our salvation is dependent upon the fact that Jesus, as our representative and as God, has given Himself for our salvation. No mere man could have done this; only Jesus, the God-man has the authority to forgive sins. (Mark 2:7-11)

The Spirit speaks of Jesus. (John 15:26) Thus we do find three witnesses to the fact and Divinity of Jesus. All three speak of the reality of the historical Jesus as a virgin born Person upon this earth. He is not simply a phantom. He is actual humanity,

FIRST JOHN: Chapter 5

as He is actual Deity, Who walked this earth and gave Himself to be sacrificed for the sins of the population of created humanity upon this earth.]

5.7   For there are three that bear record in heaven, the Father, the Word, and the Holy Ghost: and these three are one.

[Some will argue against the authenticity of this verse by arguing that no Greek manuscript earlier than the 1600's contains it. The fact is that most of the earlier manuscripts were ritually burned when they became "worn out" in much the same manner as a soiled U.S. flag is ritually burned for the same reason. Many other copies were confiscated during the persecutions and burned. About the only early surviving complete, or nearly complete, copies were those of Gnostic origin which were buried in the sands of Egypt.

In such a cacertain men se as this we will often return to the writings of the "Church Fathers" to get a sense of what was included in the copies of Scripture they quoted. As early as 200 A.D. Tertullian quoted this verse in his *Apology Against Praxas*. Other examples abound.

The Latin Bible of the Waldensians, which was translated from the original Greek in about 157 A.D., contains the verse. It is therefore obvious that the verse was in the template from which the copy was made. This is not the Latin of Jerome but a far earlier copy.

Most favorable to the verse is that it has been accepted by both the Pre- and the Post-Reformation churches which were populated by born again, Biblical, Christians upon whom the Holy Spirit impressed the validity of the verse.

Jesus is called "God" in a unique sense in the Bible. Adam, for instance, is called the son of God by the fact of his creation. The nation of Israel was called God's son by their special election as God's Chosen People. In the New Testament all Christians are children (sons) of God by the regeneration of the New Birth.

However, when one considers Jesus, He is called the Son of God in an entirely differing manner. Only Jesus is described as that "monogenesis," the unique and one of a kind, only begotten Son of God. "For God so loved the world, that he gave his only begotten Son, that whosoever believeth in him should not perish, but have everlasting life." (John 3:16)

There were others in Bible times that were referred to as "gods." This was one of the troubles associated with the infant church and the Roman government. The Caesars were, by imperial law, to be worshiped as deities; the Christians refused to do this.

This is a much maligned verse in today's newer English Language Versions. We are constantly reminded by footnote and margin reference, and sometimes buy deletion and bracket, that much of modern "critical text" study finds this verse as an insertion not originally part of the text.

For now, I would just remind the reader that the verdict of the early church fathers validates the verse. Tertullian quoted the verse in about 200 AD in his "Apology Against Praxeas." The verse is in the original Latin Vulgate which was translated about 157 AD. Both of these point to a still earlier text from which they worked.

This verse is one of the clearest statements in Scripture as to the deity of Jesus. As we look at the extended passage we will see that verses five and six make mention of the Trinity. In verse five Jesus is mentioned as "the Son of God;" this is a mention, albeit by inference, of the Father. Verse six picks up on the point of the miraculous incarnation. This verse also speaks of the "third" member of the Trinity in that it says that the Spirit gives His witness to these facts.

Verse seven, the verse in question, is an outright affirmation of the Trinity.

Verse eight speaks of three witnesses on earth that bear witness to the same Truth, that of the incarnation of Jesus. These three are the Spirit, the water which is an intimation of the physical birth of Jesus, and the blood which is an intimation of the divine pre-existence of Jesus.

This is three instances of mention of the Trinity of the Godhead. This just seems an interesting formula to me. The formula also, as it appears here, is the belief of the churches on earth, as based in the reality in Heaven. We are then, in the final verse, given the fact that the witness of Heaven is even greater than the witness of man on earth.

This is a verse, however, which has been under constant attack in "church" circles. Some of the reasons for the attack are, I would believe, quite valid. Still, I accept this verse as part of the preserved Words of God.

Hills (The King James Version Defended) argues for the verse. There are manuscripts which do not contain this verse. Of them Hills would argue that, if, during the 2nd and 3rd centuries, this phrase was dropped through carelessness, it might be continued to be omitted because of the Sabellian heresy. The Sabellian's held that the members of the Trinity are identical; they are but different views of the One Being, rather than the orthodox view that, while The Members of the Trinity are of the same *essence*, They are individual Personalities. The orthodox would see the copies which contained this phrase as being favorable to the heresy of the Sabellian and would consider those which did not contain it to be the pure text.

We often use the illustration of the Trinity that it is like a man who is a father, husband, and son. He is the same man in whatever place he stands. It is just that he is viewed in different lights by different people. This is not, however, an accurate representation of the Trinity. If it were we would have the absurdity of Jesus praying to Himself in the Gospels. At the stoning of Stephen we would see Jesus sitting at His Own right hand.

Granted, if God said that those things were true in the Spiritual realm, they would be true. But, we understand the Trinity to be three distinct Persons Who are of One Essence. In John 1:1 we read, "In the beginning was the Word, and the Word was with God, and the Word was God." The picture here is of two equals sitting face to face.

When we speak of the Trinity, as it is revealed in the Bible, we are often at a loss to explain a concept of Spirit and Eternity as we work within the confines of the physical and time. There are things we will not understand until we are passed from this existence into our eternal existence. "For *as* the heavens are higher than the earth, so are my ways higher than your ways, and my thoughts than your thoughts." (Isaiah 55:9)

A better illustration of the concept of the Trinity might be sitting near me right now. It is a simple cup of coffee with sugar and cream. The three elements are distinct elements. I can taste them each as I drink the coffee. But, they are joined together to produce just one beverage. They are inseparable even as they are diverse.

This is an admittedly poor illustration. But, it is the best I have to offer for us to consider the Spiritual things of God with our finite minds. Faith remains the medium of the Christian.

Hills also argues that the "Johannine comma" might have actually dropped out of the Greek manuscripts only to be preserved by the Western Church in the Latin Text. "...on the basis of the external evidence it is at least possible that the *Johannine comma* is a reading that somehow dropped out of the Greek New Testament text but was preserved in the Latin Text..."

"It is found in r an Old Latin manuscript of the 5th or 6th century, and in the **Speculum**, a treatise which contains the Old Latin text. It was not included in Jerome's original edition of the Latin Vulgate, but around the year 800 it was taken into the text from the Old Latin manuscripts..."

It is very important to note the above. This verse was not originally in Jerome's Vulgate. It was, however, in a writing which was based on the Old Latin text. The Old Latin Vulgate, the word "Vulgate" simply meaning "common," and was applied to a translation made around 157 A.D., would give the verse the imprimatur of antiquity. Such a translation, obviously a translation of an even older document, would argue for Apostolic authority for the verse.

Hills further argues in the negative for the inclusion of the verse in our Bibles today. "If the comma originated in a trinitarian interpretation of I John 5, why does it not contain the usual trinitarian formula, namely, the Father, the Son, and the Holy Spirit? Why does it exhibit the singular combination never met with elsewhere, the Father, the Word, and the Holy Spirit? According to some critics, the unusual phraseology was due to the efforts of the interpolator who first inserted the Johannine Comma into the New Testament text. In a mistaken attempt to imitate the style of the Apostle John, he changed the term Son into the term Word. But this is to attribute to the interpolation, which was surely to uphold the doctrine of the Trinity, including the eternal generation of the Son. With this as his main concern it is very unlikely that he would abandon the time-honored formula, Father, Son, and Holy Spirit, and devise an altogether new one, Father, Word, and Holy Spirit."

This argument from the negative is that, if a forger had wanted to make this verse only *seem* to be part of the original, he would not have written it as it is written. A forger who wanted his fake money to be accepted would not substitute my picture on a one dollar bill for that of George Washington. Even though my hair is approaching the color of Mr. Washington's powdered wig, it would not be accepted.

Finally, Hills argues that God has worked with man, specifically through the Spirit's influence upon the churches, to preserve the Canon of Scripture. "...the Textus Receptus has both its human aspect and its divine aspect, like the Protestant Reformation itself or any other work of God's providence. And when we consider the manner in which the Johannine Comma entered the Textus Receptus, we see the human element at work. Erasmus omitted the Johannine Comma from his first edition (1516) of his printed Greek New Testament on the ground that it occurred only in the Latin version and not in any Greek manuscript. To quiet the outcry that arose, he agreed to restore it if but one Greek manuscript could be found which contained it. When one such manuscript was discovered soon afterwards, bound by his promise, he included the disputed reading and thus it gained a permanent place in the Textus Receptus. The manuscript which forced Erasmus to reverse his stand was written at

Oxford about 1520 for the special purpose of refuting Erasmus, and this is what Erasmus himself suggested in his notes."

Some have disputed the veracity of the story about the "specially prepared manuscript" above. The story, however, is unimportant. What is important is the great outcry about the lack of one verse. It seems that the Spirit of God moved upon the people of God in the churches of God in defense of the proper reading.

The Words of God have been preserved for us in exactly this manner. The true churches, peopled by the true Blood bought believers, have been gifted to "try the spirits." "Beloved, believe not every spirit, but try the spirits whether they are of God: because many false prophets are gone out into the world." (I John 4:1)

The Words of God had been preserved in many old manuscripts. A fresh supply of them flooded Europe after the fall of Constantinople. Those Words were not being brought into the Protestant Reformation. This was an area where the Latin of Jerome had held sway for hundreds of years. The dominant Roman Church has decreed that the populace could not have Bibles in their own languages. The Roman Church had kept the precious Words of God, the Words meant for all humanity, under the lock and key of Church control and tradition.

Now that a new day had dawned, the people wanted the True, and Pure, Words which God had inspired and preserved. I believe that the Spirit acted strongly upon the people to rescue the Words of this verse from power of Satan as he attempted to "downgrade" Jesus in the eyes of the people. A less than divine Christ would be a false Christ. A false Christ would be a weak Christ in the eyes of the people. This could be used as a wedge to drive the emerging movement back into the error of Catholicism which proclaimed herself as the power of God on earth and her pontiff as the true representative of Christ, through the chair of Peter, on earth.

In conclusion, many of the disputed passages are the result of copyist errors. The most common error was to see a word, or a set of words, on one line and then to look back after copying that passage and seeing same words or set of words at another place on the page. In this manner words, sentences, even paragraphs could be left out (or more uncommonly, copied twice) through fatigue or carelessness of the copyist. I have caught myself doing that very thing as I copy from my note cards onto these pages.

The point, here, is that it would be quite easy for a passage, such as I John 5:7, to be dropped from some manuscripts. It is not anywhere near as easy for a copyist to insert such a passage.

So much space has been used to defend this verse that the meaning has not been addressed. The meaning is quite simple. The Father, The Word – which (Compare John 1:1) is a phrase used by John to describe Jesus, the human/Divine Son of God, as an Active Force of God into the world, and The Spirit are all witnesses from Heaven that Jesus came to earth as a man and in His divinity. These three are One. I cannot explain the Holy Trinity of God. It is a Spiritual and Eternal concept that seems almost foreign to our physical and time-centric ears. Nonetheless, it is true that these three constitute but One God. This is not a "legislative assembly" of Supreme Beings. He, God, is Triune but of one essence.

I would like to note that this revelation has special importance in our day. So effective has the lie of Satan concerning an evolutionary model been that even the inspired and preserved Scripture has been called into question by men who argue that

FIRST JOHN: Chapter 5

the sands of time have obscured the real Scripture to such an extent that only the basic minimum of a "concept" of what God *might* have said is now available. It is considered necessary that sinful humanity must examine the available evidence and decide what God *probably* said.

NO! God is active through history in the defense of His Message to mankind. His Word is guaranteed as it is HIS WORD given to humanity to explain sin, salvation, doctrine and even His Glory into a world which needs the Savior. He did not create and then sit back to see what would happen. He created and controls the destiny of humanity, as a whole, and as individual persons. He is THE great God Who loves His creation. He would not send us to the winds of a sin cursed world. He guides us through the turbulence in the safe vessel of His love.]

5.8 *And there are three that bear witness on earth, the Spirit, and the water, and the blood: and these three agree in one.*

[John notes that there are three that bear witness of the facts of Jesus on the earth. One of these is, of course, The Spirit. The Spirit has spoken on earth at the Baptism of Jesus. We recall that from Matthew 3:16-17. The Spirit also spoke through the ministry of Jesus here on earth. Isaiah 11:2 prophecies of Messiah. "And the spirit of the LORD shall rest upon him, the spirit of wisdom and understanding, the spirit of counsel and might, the spirit of knowledge and the fear of the LORD."

The question can easily be asked as to why God, the Spirit, found it necessary to rest upon Messiah, God, the Son. My answer is simple; I don't know. What I do find from this is a clear indication of the Triune nature of God. Jesus is God, the Son. In the Kenosis He willingly divested Himself of some of His rightful glory as God. We also know that Jesus was fully human, albeit without any trace of a sin nature. Due to the virgin birth He did not inherit the taint of sin from Adam. His Father is God.

What we see in this incarnation of Jesus is that God, the Son, was given empowerments within His humanity by God, the Spirit. Through all of this Jesus did the will of God, the Father. The total explanation is beyond my human mind. The truth of the synthesis is beyond reasonable question taught by the inspired and preserved Scripture.

Jesus, in His physical life, death and resurrection, as well as His ascension back into Heaven, still testifies of Himself as Messiah. He is the Anointed One Who died in time so that we could live in eternity.

Scroll back to our commentary on verse six to see our reasoning that both the water and the Blood speak of Jesus. The water testifying through His sinless human life as to His Messiahship. The Blood is speaking of His essential deity. The water speaks of the Father as He commissioned Jesus to the task of becoming a sacrifice for the sins of man. Jesus was that water but, He was commissioned and sent by the Father. (John 3:16)

Therefore, it is the witness of the Triune God through the events of the sojourn, and death, of Jesus upon this earth which bears witness to the Truth of Jesus as Messiah and Savior.

Note carefully that the verse says that these Three agree **_IN_** one rather than as one. As they are united as the eternal essence of The One God, so is their testimony united to the Salvation which is in Christ alone.]

5.9 *If we receive the witness of men, the witness of God is greater: for this is the witness of God which he hath testified of his Son.*

[Some have suggested that the testimony of men in this place applies to the testimony of those false prophets who argued that Jesus did not come in the flesh. Upon consideration of the context of this verse I would tend to agree with that assessment.

An alternate view, and truthfully a more generally accepted view, would take into account the Old Testament concept of at least two, and often three, witnesses necessary to establish a fact. (Deuteronomy 19:15) Both Jesus (Matthew 18:16) and Paul (II Corinthians 13:1; I Timothy 5:19) alluded to this law in their teaching.

However, the situation seen to in this place concerns the fact of Jesus as the Son of God and as God, the Son. The amalgamation of His human and divine natures is the question at issue. These false prophets had brought questions, actually statements which opposed that belief. The question of John seems to be this. "Are you going to believe these false prophets or are you going to believe God?"

Romans 3:4 carries the answer of John to that question. "God forbid: yea, let God be true, but every man a liar; as it is written, That thou mightest be justified in thy sayings, and mightest overcome when thou art judged."]

5.10 *He that believeth on the Son of God hath the witness in himself: he that believeth not God hath made him a liar, because he believeth not the record that God gave of his Son.*

[The Sonship of Jesus is important to Jesus' ability to save sinners. As mentioned above (see note on I John 5:7), if Jesus had sinned He would not have had the power to save others. Had Jesus sinned He would have been simply another man born of woman in the natural manner. As God the possibility of sin did not reside within Jesus. He was a wholly and righteous Person in that He was God. He still is God! It is not in the divine nature of God to sin. As the eternal Son of God it is not within the Divine nature of Jesus Christ to sin.

Since Jesus did not sin, indeed as God He was not capable of sin, He has standing to impart grace and forgiveness to those who come to Him by faith and accept His substitutionary death on the cross as payment for the sin of the penitent.

Since Jesus declared on many occasions that He was the Son of God, the concept of His Sonship is important to the very truthfulness of the Savior. Since Jesus did not sin, He always told the complete truth. He did not lie. Therefore, by His own testimony, He is the Son of God.

Since the Bible declares on many occasions that Jesus was the Son of God, the concept of His Sonship is important to the very truthfulness of the Scripture. Since the Scripture is the inspired and preserved Words of God, we know that the Scripture is not capable of error. Therefore, by the testimony of Scripture Jesus is the Son of God.

So established is this truth in the world through the testimony of Scripture and by the testimony of the Spirit upon the hearts of Christians, that to not believe the Truth that Jesus is the divine Son of God is to not be in the faith. It is to argue against the Truth of God's witness into the World. Further, it is to accuse God of lying about what He has vigorously affirmed. This sin is very close to the unpardonable sin of blasphemy as it defames the witness of the Holy Ghost. (Luke 12:10)

Any person who does not believe that Jesus died in his place as The Atonement for his sin cannot accept Jesus in faith. Any person who does not accept that Jesus has the righteous ability through His Own deity to be That Atonement for sin cannot accept Jesus in faith for salvation. Any person who denies these two cardinal doctrines of Christianity cannot claim to be a born-again Christian. Any person who resists such a plain truth of Scripture cannot accept the Words of the Scripture in any area. This means that such a one as this can never find the Christ of Salvation. (John 5:39; Acts 4:12)]

5.11 *And this is the record, that God hath given to us eternal life, and this life is in his Son.*

[Once again we see that the concept of salvation is exclusionary in the Scripture. Jesus is the only Savior available to humanity. No work, no worship, no other way is it possible to come to God. Only Jesus can offer salvation from sin, a relationship with God, and a home in Heaven.

We see here that the eternal life is a gift from God. We also see that this gift is encased in Jesus. This fact, from Scripture, attests to the full Divinity of Jesus Christ.

John 1:4 records these words, "In him was life; and the life was the light of men." Folks, life is still in Him and only in Him. He bestows the full life of grace within those who accept Him as Savior. There is no other place where we may go to attain that life. It is the province of the Savior.]

5.12 *He that hath the Son hath life; and he that hath not the Son of God hath not life.*

[It isn't that Christianity is a "narrow" religion, or that God is bigoted. The truth of the matter is that God has provided, through the sacrifice of Jesus on the Cross of Calvary, a means of redemption for mankind. To refuse that gift is to refuse the Giver of that Gift.

John Wesley, in his notes on the Old and New Testaments, said of this verse: "In the former clause, the apostle says simply, the Son; because believers know him: in the latter, the Son of God; that unbelievers may know how great a blessing they fall short of."

The best illustration of this I have heard speaks of a five dollar bill hidden within the pages of a Bible. We cannot search through the pages to find that money until we have that Bible in our hands. Likewise the concept of eternal life is in Christ, Jesus. Until we have Him we cannot have eternal life because in Him is life. So, how do we obtain Him that we might obtain life? Faith is the key. In all ages it is necessary to approach God through the medium of faith. When by faith we accept Him as Savior He will impart this life to us. Life is His free gift to those who have accepted Him.][

5.13 *These things have I written unto you that believe on the name of the Son of God; that ye may know that ye have eternal life, and that ye may believe on the name of the Son of God.*

[This is nearly the same epitaph which John included near the end of his gospel memoirs. (John 20:31) The great passion of John was that unconverted people would find the glory of salvation from their sins.

Preachers preach truth from the Scripture. They are necessary in the church that the people, especially in the age of John when so few actually had even small portions of the Scripture to read, will be helped to understand the great truths of the faith.

Pastors will pastor. That is the exercise of leading the flock of God into safe pastures where they may find sweet fellowship in the Lord. Sometimes this is done by reiterating precious passages which remind the Christian of the rudiments of the faith.

This restatement will help to build up the people of God in this most holy faith. This restatement will comfort the "doubting Thomas'" which know the truth but find it nearly too wonderful to understand. In the final analysis of most Christians, we do not have faith because it is so easy for us to believe. We have faith because the Spirit of God holds us to our profession in His pastoral power.

Preaching is an easy "performance." Pastoring can be easy when the pastor allows the Spirit to lead beside the still waters. Still waters may be teaming with fish just below the surface. The stillness quiets our soul's restlessness while the fish satisfy our spiritual hunger to grow in grace.]

5.14 *And this is the confidence that we have in him, that, if we ask any thing according to his will, he heareth us:*

[We can have full confidence that God will hear our prayers. We can also fully believe that anything we ask according to his will, will be granted.

This brings up an interesting consideration. How do we know that for which we petition Him is according to His will? There are two considerations. First, we must be considering the glory of God in our petition. Will an affirmative answer give full glory to God? Or, do we ask that we might be glorified? One prayer we know is in the will of God; the other prayer may very well not be in His will. It would work to our detriment as it would be an exercise in our own pride. We may find it important. But, it may not be of eternal importance.

Why is the glory of God so important? Jesus said this, "And I, if I be lifted up from the earth, will draw all men unto me." (John 12:32) I know that this verse has to do with the crucifixion where Jesus was lifted up on the Cross. But, I do not think I do any violence to the verse when we consider that Jesus being preached is to lift Him up before men that they may see the offered salvation and the One Who offers that salvation.

Giving glory to God is to set the eyes of men upon the Savior and see their position of absolute need under Him.

The second thing to be considered about a prayer is to understand if it is in the will of God. God has a program for this earth. We may pray at cross purposes to His intended will. This is easy to understand, in a sense, in this day of presidential elections. We may pray for "our" candidate. God may have already seen fit to use the other candidate to further the purposes of His program for the earth. God will not put our enthusiasm above His Own Holy will and purpose for history.]

5.15 *And if we know that he hear us, whatsoever we ask, we know that we have the petitions that we desired of him.*

[This verse was argued to speak of the parent's faith being effective for the baptism of an infant. But, we are reminded that each person is saved by his own

FIRST JOHN: Chapter 5

choice of faith in Jesus.

While we are on that subject I would like to consider that many commentators used the reference above to consider the "grace of baptism." Folks, there is no grace in baptism. Baptism is simply a rite to be used as a testimony that one has already been saved. Baptizing a person who is not already a Christian will only get him wet. It may also hasten, from a human standpoint, his descent into the Hell of a Christless eternity. Many have trusted their Baptism into Hell who should have trusted the Lord into Heaven.

As in the above verse, we will have the petitions asked if they are in the will of God. Sometimes our prayers are in the will of ourselves. These have no guarantee of an affirmative answer. These will be answered. The answer will generally be "no."

Also, there are times when the answers, although granted, are delayed. God may see that we are not yet ready to receive that thing we ask. We need to see His refining work of discipline prepare us for that answer.]

5.16 *If any man see his brother sin a sin which is not unto death, he shall ask, and he shall give him life for them that sin not unto death. There is a sin unto death: I do not say that he shall pray for it.*

[The word "brother" would seem to indicate that this person was a Christian. That is not necessarily so. The "brother" could be one who was a member of the local assembly but was not a Christian. Many would come into the assembly and fellowship with the saints. The time would come, either in persecution or in the seducing spirits of false prophets, when these would finally show their true colors and would apostatize from the light they had found among the preaching of the true Words of God.

This apostasy would draw them from fellowship into false opposition. They may even have begun to attack the true doctrine of the church. They may have even moved beyond mere opposition to attacking the very Spirit of God as a spirit of Satan. God would always lead away from following Satan's lies. This spirit of blasphemy will not be forgiven for it has rejected the work of the True Spirit of God.

John did not say to pray for these. Neither did he forbid such prayer. We cannot know what is in a person's heart. We may well suspect blasphemy when it has not actually occurred. God knows.

There is also the case of the true brother who has backslidden in sin to the extent that a physical death sentence has been passed upon him. This was the case with Ananias and Sapphira in the fifth chapter of Acts. Their sin was unto physical death. The sin was not that the couple held back part of the proceeds of the sale of their land. The sin was that they had told everyone, the Spirit included, that they were giving all.

The consequence of this lie to the Spirit was physical death.

Consider I Corinthians 11:30 in this same light. The sin of disruptive behavior concerning the Lord's Table was sometimes punished with physical death as well.

One overwhelming caution is in order. We cannot pray the prayer of repentance for another. We must, however, pray that the Spirit would convict such a one that he would be driven to prayer for himself.]

5.17 *All unrighteousness is sin: and there is a sin not unto death.*

[John speaks as a theologian when he reminds the people that any breech of the moral and judicial code of God's righteousness is sin. Every time this is sin. Here, also as a theologian, John would argue that the Christian cannot commit the sin of blasphemy. An unpardonable sin to issue from an already pardoned individual is a paradox not admitted among the adopted children of God. Satan may attack in many areas but this one is closed to him. Again, consider the illustration of Job as illustrated in verse eighteen, below.

Then, John speaks as a pastor. He reminds the people that not every sin will negate the love of God. Even the sinning Christian can approach the Throne of Grace and beg forgiveness in the assurance that God will forgive the truly repentant child. Paul reminds us that, "Therefore if any man be in Christ, he is a new creature: old things are passed away; behold, all things are become new. And all things are of God, who hath reconciled us to himself by Jesus Christ, and hath given to us the ministry of reconciliation." (II Corinthians 5:17-18)

We are now the children of God. Our Heavenly Father will chastise and correct us when we err; but, He will not disown His own. He may, as referenced in the notes on the above verse, call us to return home so that we will not sully the "family name" in this world of sin.]

5.18 *We know that whosoever is born of God sinneth not; but he that is begotten of God keepeth himself, and that wicked one toucheth him not.*

[The Geneva Bible Notes sum up the meaning of this verse concerning the fact that the Christian is not consumed by sin. "A reason why not all, or rather why no sin is mortal to some: that is, because they are born of God, that is to say, made the sons of God in Christ, and being ended with his Spirit, they do not serve sin, nor are they mortally wounded by Satan."

If we read this verse to argue that it is impossible for the believer to sin we would do violence to the entire thrust of the epistle. John has been arguing that it is possible, even probable, that the child of God will fail his Lord by acts of sin. That is why the call has been made to confess and repent of known sin.

A preemptive strike is to be made against the tempter by diligently keeping ourselves in the fellowship and love of the Lord. This will help to keep our minds on the mercies of the Lord. (Jude 21) With this reality the tempter will find less "raw material" within our souls by which he may assail us. Consider James 1:14 in this light.

This is an assurance that though we may well fail our Lord, we need have no fear of losing our salvation. We are children of the King. He will not allow His children to be snatched from His Hands. His Blood is the surety of our perseverance.

We are not kept in salvation by our own efforts. Such would ascribe salvation to our works rather than to Christ. Still, as we do these things to hold to our profession of faith we gain the victory over Satan's temptations as we see the reality of the fellowship of the love of God within our souls. Within this reality we are kept from habitual sin which so often ensnares the children of this world.

Thus, we do not continue in sin as adopted sons of God. Such is not of our new nature. Consider my notes on I John 3:9.

We note that the wicked one cannot touch the believer. This does not mean that he cannot, or does not, often attack us. This does mean that even at his best effort Satan can never touch us with a mortal wound. (Job 2:3-6)

Job was greatly buffeted by Satan but he never lost his testimony of the love of God. He did not understand all that befell him but he knew that God had some inscrutable purpose in it all. This is not to say, obviously, that Job did not complain in his hour of tribulation. It does mean that his faith never departed from the goodness of God even when he did not understand it.

Job, with all of his trials and temptations is an example that Satan cannot rupture that relationship which the child of God has with his Heavenly Father. Our possession of eternal life is promised on the Blood of Jesus Christ. It is not Biblically sound to believe that salvation, once given by the passion of Christ on the Cross, can ever depart from our souls.

There is the issue of martyrdom. This may be allowed by the determinative will of God. In this God gives us the grace, and the supreme opportunity, to display His Grace among men in a manner that would not be otherwise possible. Even in this it is a display of His sovereign love for us.]

5.19 *And we know that we are of God, and the whole world lieth in wickedness.*

[Several years before her home going to Glory, my wife and I visited Canada where I was to speak at a Bible Conference. While there we drove around to see the sights. At one point we came upon an area of beautiful – and very large – homes. Relating this to some of the people at the conference we were told that we had been visiting "Embassy Row." Their word, not mine.

Consider that in each nation there are such embassies. They are small, relatively, parcels of land which are considered to be parts of whatever native lands they represent. In this sense we can consider the "sacking" of our embassy in Tehran in the late 1970's to have been an invasion of the United States. We have chosen to not consider it as that. But, technically speaking, that is what it was.

We who are born again, and the true churches of the Lord, are outposts of the Government of God into this world of sin and dominion by Satan. With the witness of the Spirit in our hearts we understand that we are born into the new "nationality" of the adopted sons of God. On those times when we allow Satan to steal our joy, we can still understand this by considering the Truth of the inspired and preserved Scripture which attests to this fact.

We are of God.

Sadly, those not born again are not of God. They may seem to be very good and proper human beings. They are not of God. The great abundance of evil in the world proves this as fact! I am writing this just a few days after a radical Islamist killed nearly fifty people. We can feel quite smug about this until we realize that similar atrocities have been committed by people who claim the Name of Christ.

There is one striking difference. Our Holy Book of Scripture does not sanction any of this. We are only called to witness and pray for those who oppose us. Those who have no grounding in the New Testament of the Blood of Jesus Christ may see that which they consider to be evil and respond. Their response is evil and in the province of the evil one because that is where they live and have their being.

This verse tells us that evil is in the world because the unregenerate world, the people thereof, are in Satan as their guiding force. This may reference itself in a gentle witness that sin is not bad; it is to be enjoyed in friendship and conviviality. The sad realization will come to even these seemingly "good," as well as the obviously "bad," people that sin in any course of conduct leads on a broad road to destruction and an eternal Hell.

Every single religion of man has death within the pot of its pottage. (II Kings 4:40) Only True, Biblical, Christianity offers life eternal. (John 5:24)]

5.20 *And we know that the Son of God is come, and hath given us an understanding, that we may know him that is true, and we are in him that is true, even in his Son Jesus Christ. That is the true God, and eternal life.*

[The phrase "This is the true God, and eternal life" is our focus in this verse. The immediate antecedent of this statement is "Jesus," thus causing one to assume on simple grammatical grounds that Jesus is being called "the True God." Such an assumption would be correct. To have called the Father the True God would have been redundant and unnecessary. Consider that this was, humanly speaking, penned by a Jewish man brought up with the Old Testament Scriptures which constantly remind the reader that ",,,the LORD our God *is* one LORD." (Deuteronomy 6:4b) He, and most of those to whom this epistle was written understood that God was God.

Consider, also that the human penman, John, was also the human author of the Book which bears his name. In John 1:4 John wrote, "In him was life, and the life was the light of men." Therefore, the obvious connection is that the True God, Who was eternal life, would be Jesus. Barnes (Barnes' Notes on the New Testament) states the obvious when he tells us that both the "True God" and "Jesus" here refer to eternal life.

We also need to consider Revelation 1:8. "I am Alpha and Omega, the beginning and the ending, saith the Lord, which is, and which was, and which is to come, the Almighty." Salem Kirban (Salem Kirban Reference Bible) asks us to consider that Jesus is here described as both the beginning and the conclusion. Since this could only be said of the Self-Existent One, God, this is a statement that Jesus is God.

This verse is fully in agreement with John 1:4 which attributes life to be part of the essence of Jesus into this world. When this is fully understood there is no reason to consider any other fact than that Jesus is fully God in Human Form. John has mentioned this often in this epistle and closes with that truth. The Father is God. The Holy Spirit is God. Jesus is God. This is the essential reality of the One True God. He is triune in His nature and attributes. That this is beyond our human understanding is true. That does not make the fact, as presented in the pages of Scripture untrue. Any other understanding does violence to the Words of Inspiration of the very inspired and preserved Scripture.

The arguments of the false prophets had sought to obscure or fully hide this truth. Satan would not oppose any faith in a false concept of Jesus. Saving faith must reside in the Truth of Who Jesus is in reality.

We do know that Jesus has come into the world. We do know that Jesus is True God. This is a strong affirmation of the dual nature of Jesus as is necessary if His death on the Cross is to have the power to redeem us from our sins and present us faultless before The Father. Consider, once again, the twenty-fourth verse of the epistle of Jude.

We might also consider the fact that it was Jesus Who gave us the understanding to know Him. Thus, Jesus has given us heavenly understanding. Consider John 3:11-12 in this light. Jesus could not have given us information concerning the heavenly and eternal if He were a mere man who was generated only in this present earth. This is another testimony to His Heavenly position as God, incarnate.]

5.21 *Little children, keep yourselves from idols. Amen.*

[John had just referenced that Jesus was True God. Since the time of the Babylonian exile the Jewish people had shunned any sort of idolatry. With this light shining from the memory of his people's culture, John has told his readers to keep away from idols even as he has informed them that Jesus is True God. This is another affirmation of the Full Divinity of Jesus.

We must understand that idolatry is placing anything before us which would obscure our view of God. Preachers can become idols if the people seek out them rather than seeking out the Words of the inspired and preserved Scripture. Our prayers belong to God rather than to a man as a representative of God. If we would know the Scripture, we must peruse the Scripture while in prayer to the Spirit as we seek His guidance.

Nothing, not a "bucket list" goal, not a mate, not a child, not a job, nothing must come between us and God. Any loss we might suffer on this earth is meaningless when we consider the majesty of glory of Jesus and His great love for us.

John closes with "amen." This is "so be it." This is also a shout of joy we may consider at the great message of The Great God has given us in the reading of His Words.]

SECOND JOHN

1.1 *The elder unto the elect lady and her children, whom I love in the truth; and not I only, but also all they that have known the truth;*

[There are two distinct schools of thought as to the recipient of this short epistle. One school holds that this was written to a woman who may have hosted a church within her home. This is possible. This was the age of "house churches."

If this was the case, the lady in question was well known for her hospitality to the brothers in the faith. Again, if there were the case, this lady was known for the piousness of her family. Both her children and her sister – and that sister's children – are commended for walking in the truth.

Further, if this lady did host a church within her home, a common occurrence in this time period, we see this epistle as a circular letter sent to the churches at large – the recipient church to share with other churches – rather than a personal letter to simply one person.

The other school of thought holds that the "elect lady" is a church; her "children" then being her membership. Her sister would then speak of other churches with the "children" of membership. In this case we must exercise care not to drift into a "denominational" mindset.

While I hold with the first concept, there is little difference in application of the two. There is difference, as one holds primarily to the concept of the Body of the Church, while the other speaks to a pious home life. For our purposes in this commentary I find the concept that both would ultimately see the fact of the message as for the church. As inspired and preserved Scripture this epistle must be seen as for all believers down through the ages. It is with this realization that I continue.

The Word is for all of us who are the called of the Lord.

Sisters, both married obviously with children, do not necessarily live under the same roof. The illustration would then be of churches of the same doctrine of the Apostles who fellowshipped together in the Lord but did not live in the same "home" of denominational existence. As each sister would have her own husband, so would each church be under the headship of the Lord. The churches would be separate, each sister not cooking meals for the other's husband, but united in the universality of submission to the same Lord.

John speaks of himself as an elder. It is likely that John was the only remaining living member of the apostles of Jesus. He does not claim that title, though it is his, but only claims to be an elder of the fellowship. The love of which he spoke is that love for the brethren and "sisteren" in the Lord.

John admits that the warm feeling which he has for those to whom he writes is shared by others. The concept of Christian love is not of a reciprocal love. It is a love akin to the out flowing of the "tongues of fire" on the Day of Pentecost. It is a love which is shed upon us by the Spirit and permeates the fellowship of believers. Properly speaking this is not a love of one's own, but the love of God as expressed by each of the born again.

John was careful in his first epistle to show that Christian love was a fruit, an evidence, that we have been with the Lord.]

1.2   *For the truth's sake, which dwelleth in us, and shall be with us for ever.*

Matthew 16:18; 23:35; 28:20; Ephesians 3:21

[We must not separate the first verse from the second. The division into verses is a great help to understanding Scripture, but it is of man rather than of God. Adding the first verse along with this second we see that John is saying that we have known the truth for the Truth's sake. That may sound somewhat circular but it is not.

That experiential love we have felt from the Lord cannot be something which is "dammed up," or held within us. It is a love which excites us to spread the love out from ourselves and into the world. This first flows to, and from, the brethren of the local assembly. Then it flows to "sisters and their children" of like faith and practice.

At the same time that these two are at work we have the compulsion from the Lord to love the world to the extent that we long to see others born into the fellowship.

We see the fields "white with harvest" and desire to be laborers together with the Lord to bring in His harvest of souls. Our love extends to others as we understand the glories of salvation and the horrors of a Christless eternity.

It is this emphasis which causes the membership of the churches to preach the message of the Cross out into a dying world. This is the work of the Spirit within us. This continues to be the vision, often dimmed among many but nevertheless consistent, of the church as the Army of the Redeemed until the Lord calls us home.]

1.3   *Grace be with you, mercy, and peace, from God the Father, and from the Lord Jesus Christ, the Son of the Father, in truth and love.*

[John desires that all experience the grace of God in their lives. This grace comes to humanity through the mercy of God. True peace is available only to those who have found the mercy of God within their lives.

Grace is that unmerited favor of God that flows upon all who experience salvation. Grace is imparted upon those that believe. This is the forgiveness of sin. Mercy is that which allows a sinner to respond to God's call to grace. These are they who have found peace with God through the Atonement.

When John speaks of Jesus being the Son of God he is not speaking simply of the fact of the generation of the humanity of Jesus. Included, indeed an evidence of the full deity of Jesus is contained within that phrase. Rather than considering that Jesus took on the nature of divinity as any time, this is the fact that deity took upon Himself the nature of man.

This is not a "downgrade" of deity. Neither is this an "upgrade" of general humanity. By speaking of Jesus as the Son of God, John is attesting to the uniqueness of Jesus as the fact that God, the Son, came to inhabit a real human body. This is a unique, only seen in Jesus in all the history of humanity, situation whereby the perfection of humanity in the Person of Jesus died on the Cross as the full remedy for the sin problem of mankind. Jesus, as one of us in His humanity, died in our place when and whereby He took upon Himself the full penalty for our sins.

To those who accept this gift, Jesus has provided a full pardon from sin as our sins were judged at the Cross. We have freedom from sin through the Self-Sacrifice of Jesus at the hands of His executioners. That He was able to accomplish this abrogating of our sins is based on His dual nature. He died, humanly, as one of us for our sins. His blood was shed as an appeasement for our sins. This appeasement is based on His

SECOND JOHN

divine nature which only would have had the ability to forgive sins.

Sin is an offense against the moral perfections of God. Only God has the "standing" to forgive sin. No man or priest can forgive sin because sin is an offense against God. No one but God clothed in the humanity of mankind could possibly forgive sin. Even the apostles could not forgive another's sin. To them was given the task, as it is also given to us, to point another to Jesus for salvation.

The prayer of John was that this grace would accomplish mercy within the life of his readers so that they could find the peace of God which is available only in Jesus.]

1.4 *I rejoiced greatly that I found of thy children walking in truth, as we have received a commandment from the Father.*

[As I mentioned in the first verse, I feel that this epistle was addressed to a specific woman at whose home there was a "house church." This seems to support that contention as not all of her children were walking in Christian truth. The phrase "of thy children" is an indication that not all, but of them, were walking in the piousness.

Of course, this could also speak to a church where only part of the assembly exhibited the fruits of the Spirit in their lives. Still, I apply this to a certain family.

If only part of her family were walking in the truth, what does this say of the rest? In truth this says nothing of the rest of the family. It is possible that John had only met a few and was heartened by their response to the Gospel. All could have been living a pious life; John only responded to what he knew to be the truth.

In a "family" sense this passage rebukes the concept of "covenant grace" whereby children are said to be saved by the salvation of their parents. Such is not a Biblical consideration. Each person is accountable for himself in his response to the message of the Gospel.

It is possible that John had made contact with some of the family as they journeyed through the world on their own business. It is also possible that John had heard reports from this lady's sister. (verse 13) It is apparent that he had contact with the sister (church?) at some point as he relays good tidings from that precinct.]

1.5 *And now I beseech thee, lady, not as though I wrote a new commandment unto thee, but that which we had from th e beginning, that we love one another.*

[The Jamieson/Fausset/Brown Commentary appeals to this verse to prove that this epistle was written to a church rather than to an individual. Clarke, meanwhile, appeals to this verse to prove that this epistle was written to an individual rather than to a church. This is the manner of the "higher criticism" which breeds a mistrust of the Scripture. The importance of Scripture lies within the words which were inspired and preserved by God. It is the Message of God to His saints of the ages which is communicated which is of importance. The inspiration of that Message is the important thing, not our deconstruction of that Message.

God used this beloved apostle to pen the words of Scripture. We may well study the man who put the words on parchment. But, we submit to those Words as they are new every time we peruse the Scripture. The Author and Speaker of those Words is God. Being from Him, the Words carry the imprint of the eternal. This argues, first of all, that those Words are timeless and will never go out of date. This also argues for the preservation of the text. To argue that the sands of time could ever overcome the

Words of God, given to His people to address His Message to them, is to hold a very low opinion of both the power of God and of His Words to humanity.

Commentaries, such as this, are good in that they tend to give us the understanding of an individual as to a certain passage. The Spirit may even use these commentaries to bring out certain aspects of His Message to man. May we ever consider that a commentary is only the opinion of man. The Words are the edict of God.

As one put it many years ago, "Commentaries are very useful to the preacher. It is well that the Scripture often gives quite a bit of light on what the commentary may have said." The chief purpose of a commentator is to urge his readers to search the Scriptures for themselves.

In his wonderful book, "The Complete Idiot's Guide to Jewish History and Culture," Rabbi Benjamin Blech wrote concerning the Roman destruction of the Temple, "It took four years from start to finish, but eventually (the war) was over (in 70 AD) And when the Jews looked at their calendars, they recoiled with horror at the realization that the Temple went up in flames on the ninth day of Av ... *exactly* the same day on which their first Temple had been destroyed.

"What did this amazing coincidence mean? Clearly it proved that it was no coincidence! God must have been behind these two great tragedies." Rabbi Blech continues with the words of Rabbi Abraham Isaac Kook, former chief rabbi of Israel: "The Temple was destroyed only because of the needless, undeserved hatred between Jews. It will only be rebuilt because of needless undeserved love – when Jews show their concern for others, even when they differ from them in their values, ideas, and levels of observance."

John said that this was no new commandment. Indeed, this concept was as old as the pure religion of Jehovah worship. Cain violated this commandment when he said, "Am I my brother's keeper?"

True love is of God. Godly love is the requirement that we show that love to others both in and out of the household of faith. We love one another as the special creation of God. We love so deeply that we preach the truth that Jesus Christ died in time so others could live in eternity. That is a love given even towards those with whom we might be in violent opposition religiously. Our very desire that these may find the pure grace of God and turn from any error is expressed in that love.]

1.6 *And this is love, that we walk after his commandments. This is the commandment, That as ye have heard from the beginning, ye should walk in it.*

[Spurgeon in his Devotional Commentary said, "Obedience to Christ is love. 'Be ye holy' is the most ancient rubric of the church; all lovers of God obey it." This is true. But, it is not completely accurate.

The first table of the Law gives our responsibilities toward God. The second table gives our responsibilities toward our fellow man. Ture holiness is not an ascetic response toward life. The monk in his cubical cannot fulfill the commandments of God. The love of God within us is not to be shuttered away from all contact with other human beings. True love of God demands that it be shared with the world around us.

We cannot be Christian and retreat from the world. Our call is to not succumb to the blandishments of the world. We are to overcome the world with the love of the

Savior. We can never do this without sharing Him among others.

While doing this sharing, we must consider the words of James in his epistle. We advertise our relationship with God with our lives and love into the world. We spread this love with our consistent witness as backed by our persistent holiness and love.]

1.7 *For many deceivers are entered into the world, who confess not that Jesus Christ is come in the flesh. This is a deceiver and an antichrist.*

[Ronald Reagan is known for his understanding of treaties between nations. His phrase, used often, was "trust and verify." The Christian is told to "love but examine." There is a place, a high place, for Christian love to show itself into the world of men. But, just as certainly there is a place for Christian separation from the things of the world. In II Corinthians 6:17 Paul calls to us, "Wherefore come out from among them, and be ye separate, saith the Lord, and touch not the unclean thing; and I will receive you,"

In the third verse of his epistle Jude calls us, "Beloved, when I gave all diligence to write unto you of the common salvation, it was needful for me to write unto you, and exhort you that ye should earnestly contend for the faith which was once delivered unto the saints."

There does come a time when we must stand for the things of God. At those times our "love" must not be overcome by the deceit of an antichrist spirit. In times such as these the concept of love is in danger of being bastardized. In times such as these we must not allow the concept of "love" to stand for acquiesce with false doctrine which would lead away from the things of God.

Part of the concept of "love not the world, neither the things of the world, neither the things *that are* in the world..." (I John 2:15) is to separate from theological deception. That a Christian is to have no fellowship with idols, all of which are means of false religion, is a spiritual principle which carries over to any spiritual fellowship with false Christianity. Differences in opinion are not proscribed. John makes it quite clear that there can be no basis of fellowship, on a religious level, between true believers and those who deny the full humanity and divinity of our Savior.

Differences of opinion might concern such as who is to be the Antichrist. This is not really a thing given for us to know. (II Thessalonians 2:3) Could I be wrong in my "draft pick" for antichrist, or even in my exegesis of the verse from II Thessalonians? Of course! But, that is my opinion.

But, differences which touch upon the nature of Jesus Christ are disqualifications for Christian fellowship. Christian love, of course, continues. But, the fellowship around the Throne is not possible with either idols or false prophets who do not teach the truth!

In such cases we would see our concept of "love" turned into hate in the destruction of the message of salvation and Christology. A view of a false "Christ" is not a view which leads to salvation. The higher plane of Christian love concerns itself with true salvation.

A deceiver who preaches a false gospel and a false Christ can never show the love of God. He is instead preaching the "gospel" of Satan. He is antichrist. Against such we must stand in order to be true representatives of the salvation of Jesus.

Against such we must stand in order to show the reality of the love of God into the world.

We can never contend for the faith when we carry the false water of the world into the corner of an antichrist.]

1.8 *Look to yourselves, that we lose not those things which we have wrought, but that we receive a full reward.*

[This verse is very reminiscent of II Corinthians 13:5. In that verse Paul asks that the Christian examine himself that he may be certain that he has made the commitment to Christ to secure salvation based on the Blood of Jesus. Many are known to be culturally attached to the community of believers who had never accepted Jesus as Savior. Sadly, this continues to happen.

This is not a matter of examining our basis for faith but of examining our acceptance of that faith. There was no problem that we might "lose" salvation. The question was whether we had actually possessed this salvation.

That which we might lose was our very soul's residence in Heaven for eternity. To believe that this was ours when we had never accepted Jesus as Savior was the tragedy of allowing Satan to cause us to believe that our "work" would secure the Savior's salvation when the only "work" accepted by God is that very Self-Sacrifice of Jesus on the Cross of Calvary.

On a more personal note, John did not want any to be missing from that great "roll call" of the saints in Heaven. He longed for the joy of seeing them in Heaven for eternity.

The word "wrought" is further evidence that some were performing some manner of "religious" actions thinking that their work would secure salvation. John reminds that there is no work which will secure salvation except that blessed work of Jesus on the Cross.]

1.9 *Whosoever transgresseth, and abideth not in the doctrine of Christ, hath not God. He that abideth in the doctrine of Christ, he hath both the Father and the Son.*

[I am going to do something I do not like to do. I'm going to "update" two of these words from the venerable King James Bible. I do not do this lightly. I only do this because the commentaries I consulted argued about the meaning of these words.

Whosoever "violates the command" of the "teaching" of Jesus... Several of those I consulted wanted to change the first word to "going beyond." Personally, I would like that to be true; then I could use this verse to combat those who long for "a new gospel for a new day."

Sorry, folks, that's not the way this works. If you wish for a new gospel for a new day don't try to advance it using a false Bible. Many are doing so in this day! That's like arguing that you can't be tried for an offense because the Law, itself, is too old.

That is the argument of too many judges who legislate from their bench. "Sure, the Constitution says that we can't do this. But, that Constitution is so old it doesn't reflect the changing times and culture."

The problem with this construct, especially so in regards to the Christian religion, is that God and His Words are eternal. They always represent His will. Any

SECOND JOHN

attempt to change the commandments of Christ is to call Him out of date. This is to deny His eternal nature as God.

This is akin to those who argue about the "changes" in the King James Bible. There are no real changes in the various editions. Yes, the old German typeface was changed. Yes, the Apocrypha was removed from between the testaments because too many were reading it as Scripture when it was clearly marked as not authentic Scripture. True, much of the spelling was standardized. But, the King James Bible is only a reflection of the originally inspired and preserved Words of God. That never changed. The only change, if we may call it change, was that those changes made the King James Bible easier to understand in English all of those things originally related from the Hebrew, Greek and Aramaic.

If we attempt to change those eternal Words of God we transgress against them and attempt to void, on our own power, the practice of God speaking to humanity.

Also, this verse refers to the teaching of Christ, which is His doctrinal teaching. The argument as to the doctrine *about* Jesus is definitely an important point as John has often mentioned. But, in this verse the meaning seems to be about the doctrine which Jesus taught. It was this "bedrock" of teaching which some of the heretical teachers were attempting to overcome.

O. K. The rant is over. Now back to commentary.

The Gnostic was a major influence on the early Church. The Gnostic attempted to mold the doctrine of Christ and the Church into his own mold. Within the first few centuries Egypt was nearly overrun, as far as the churches were concerned, with Gnostic Heresy. This could account for the fact that we still continue to unearth Gnostic texts from the arid sands of Egypt.

The Gnostic did not believe that Jesus had come in the flesh. They also denied His full divinity. Their consideration was that Jesus was a type of "phantom" sent from the world of spirit. He only seemed to be human. His purpose was to teach humans the folly of living as flesh any more than was necessary in this world of time. Since their conception of Jesus was faulty, they would discard – or *spiritualize* – His teaching to conform to their beliefs. Left with only a mythical "Jesus," the Gnostic could not offer true salvation.

John argued that those who fully believed in the real Jesus could walk in the teaching of Jesus. Then, in a major affirmation of the Truth of the Divine/human nature of Jesus; John said that anyone who followed the true doctrine was walking with **both The Father and The Son.**]

1.10 *If there come any unto you, and bring not this doctrine, receive him not into your house, neither bid him God speed.*

[It would seem that the lady to whom this epistle was addressed was well known to be hospitable to wayfaring strangers. Also, she seems to have been a proprietor of a local house church. She could be expected to receive such visitors.

The warning seems more of a "when" than an "if." The warning was not to be hostile or impolite. The warning would have been understood to allow regular polite social intercourse and greetings. But, that was it! These strangers, who were known to be "selling" an unauthorized product of unbiblical teaching, were to not be admitted into the home – or, especially the church which met at that home.

In our day there are several of the cults which will "work" a neighborhood. We must be polite. To do otherwise is to fail to display a Christian attitude which may well be used of the Spirit to light the Light of Christ to salvation even within the darkened heart of a cultist. Still, we must be firm in our denial to them of any religious conversation.

Also, we must be ever mindful of who would occupy our religious pulpits. A false message is worse than false. It is soul damning to the unwary.

As for not wishing this person, "God speed," I would only add a few things. This is very friendly salutation. But, it is also a salutation which suggests a note of agreement in that the blessing of God is asked upon the work of this person.

If such a one asks to part with prayer, this may only be granted if the Christian is the one praying and makes it clear that he has no countenance with error. If the heretic begins to pray we must walk away or close the door. We must have no part in any "religious worship" of Satan!

Finally, may we be cognizant that we are witnesses for Christ. To be seen as in covenant with a servant of Satan may harm others. Our testimony for Christ is a very precious commodity. May we guard it closely.]

1.11   *For he that biddeth him God speed is partaker of his evil deeds.*

[Any "aid or comfort" given to such a heretic must be considered as traitorous against the cause of Christ. One seen leaving our residence can logically be considered as a friend. Thus we become emissaries to the enemy of men's souls.

Further, to attend a "series of lectures" by such a one, or even to attend a service considering a political or other "non-church" related issue will give aid just by our presence to the positions of heresy such a one may propagate.

When Satan is able to use us as advertisement for error I would assume he is very happy with us!]

1.12   *Having many things to write unto you, I would not write with paper and ink: but I trust to come unto you, and speak face to face, that our joy may be full.*

[John seems to nearly apologize at the briefness of his letter. This is the shortest epistle in the New Testament. He had other things which he wanted to relate here. This is strongly indicative of the action of inspiration by the Holy Spirit. Some things John wanted to write. Some things John thought it good to relate. Only other things were sent by the inspiration of the Spirit unto all the churches.

It may be interesting to speculate on what other things John had in mind. It isn't necessary that we do so. All things needful for us from John at this point were included in this writing.

Consider also the notes at III John 1:13 where nearly the same thing is mentioned.]

1.13   *The children of thy elect sister greet thee. Amen.*

[As in verse five, above, The Jamieson/Fausset/Brown Commentary argues from this verse that the epistle speaks of another church. This epistle is assumed to have been sent to a church rather than a specific person. This is seen as the reason why no "sister" was named. In this we see the congregation (children) of the other church sending their greetings to this church.

Most of the others consulted, reckoning a physical sister of a specific elect lady, surmised that the sister had graduated to glory. This would account for her not being mentioned. The deceased sister's children would have then sent their own greetings to their aunt.

If a church is intended to be understood we have the faithful fellowship of faithful churches displayed. The idea of love for the brethren is endorsed between the two churches.

If an actual lady, and her sister, is to be considered, it must be understood that familial love is also a command of the Lord to His people.]

THIRD JOHN

1.1   *The elder unto the well beloved Gaius, whom I love in the truth.*

[Once again John describes himself as simply "the elder." This could have been in regards to his age since it is generally accepted that he was around 80 years old at the time of the writing. My personal sense is that John was speaking of his office as a pastor. In this he was identifying with those who, like him, preached the Gospel of Jesus Christ into a world in need of that message.

John gives no hint of the time in which he composed this epistle. There is reference to neither the events of the fall of Jerusalem nor of Patmos. His issue of importance was the truth of the Gospel rather than the events of fleeting time. It is in this vein that he addressed Gaius as one who is loved in the truth. In speaking of the truth, John was speaking of the truth of the Gospel as the remainder of the epistle clearly shows.

"Gaius" is the Greek rendition of the Roman name "Caius." There are at least four men by this name in the New Testament. First, we see Romans 16:23 where Paul is said to have been hosted by, or resided for a time at the home of Gaius. It would appear that this was a house church wherein Paul was lodged for a time.

Second, we see I Corinthians 1:14 where Paul mentioned that he baptized Gaius. This may well be the same person as mentioned in Romans. In any event, it is unlikely that this is the man spoken of by John as the 4th verse of III John strongly suggests that John was the instrument used of God to bring a saving knowledge of Christ to the Gaius in III John. (Consider I Corinthians 4:15.) Given that the New Testament shows baptism to follow closely after a profession of faith, it would be unusual for Paul to baptize a convert of John's ministry. Besides this, baptism is never spoken of as having any relationship to salvation except as a witness to an already possessed salvation based on the shed blood of Jesus Christ.

Third, and fourth, we see mentioned in Acts 19:29 and 20:4 a man of this name who accompanied Paul on some missionary journeys. It does not seem that any of these men "fit the bill" exactly as the Gaius of this greeting. That seems appropriate. This epistle may have been originally written to a particular man and church, but as part of the inspired and preserved Scripture, this epistle speaks universally to the entire fellowship of believers in all ages.

The fact that John speaks of love in the truth of Jesus Christ to this man is a reminder that all true Christian love will be bound in the love of God. It is not the love of the fellow Christian which would lead anyone to teach and speak that which is false and separate from the truth that Jesus Christ is the eternal Son of God, and is very God in His Divine essence and Person.]

1.2   *Beloved, I wish above all things that thou mayest prosper and be in health, even as thy soul prospereth.*

[Note that the wish that Gaius would prosper and be in good physical health was not tied to the standards of "prosperity preachers." All was tied to the prosperity of his soul. Apparently, his soul was fine as it rested in Christ.

There seems to have been some concern for the material and physical health of Gaius, of course. But, this was not so that he could become rich and "live to 120." The concern is more likely that Gaius would be able to continue his work of welcoming the saints and providing a place of rest for them in their labors for the Lord.]

1.3 *For I rejoiced greatly, when the brethren came and testified of the truth that is in thee, even as thou walkest in the truth.*

[It is interesting to consider that this man, Gaius, ministered to John, the apostle, with his fidelity to the Person and Doctrine of Christ. When we walk rightly with the Lord, we become a blessing to the entire local church.

Generally gossip is not a good thing among the brethren. However, a form of "gossip" which praises another believer can be a blessing both to the righteous believer and to those who are encouraged by his faithfulness.

Rather than "gossip" this is a testimony of the power of Christ to enlarge a person beyond that which the world can do. This is an evidence of the reforming of a person from a child of Satan into the likeness of Christ. This is "reformation" on the highest plane for it forges a new creature in Christ as written of in II Corinthians 5:17. This is not a natural change of life direction; this is a supernatural miracle of God in the life of his adopted children. Consider Galatians 4:5.]

1.4 *I have no greater joy than to hear that my children walk in truth.*

[Consider this verse in conjunction with the fourth verse of II John. It has been argued by many that these three epistles of I, II, and III John were penned in the same time frame. "I rejoiced greatly that I found of thy children walking in truth, as we have received a commandment from the Father." Notice that in neither place is the phrase "the truth" used. I am as bad as anyone is using the verbal shorthand of saying, "We serve a God Who..." Folks, we don't serve "a" God! We serve "THE" (singular and imperative) God of creation and glory. There is no other.

Likewise, John was glorying in the fact that the people of this church were walking in the eternal and immutable TRUTH of Jesus Christ. There are many competing life styles in the world. There are many competing versions of what the world claims as truth. But there is only One eternal and spiritual truth. That is the Truth of God as revealed in His Inspired and Preserved Words. It may be argued that the modern English alphabet versions contain parts of the truth as they inject the many words of man in their pages; but, it is the Traditional Text which contains the full truth of God as revealed over the years of His sending His message to man. No version can contain all that God has for us for a version, or translation, must of necessity consider the religious views of those translators in forwarding their vision of God's inspired and preserved Words.

The recipient church of II John was a soul-winning church. As John, in this III John, speaks of Gaius as his child in Christ. The saved of the II John church speaks of their children.

Under the provisions of the tenth verse of Philemon, we see that Paul claims to have "begotten Onesimus...in my bonds." This could not be speaking of a natural birth process. Onesimus was already a fully-grown slave of Philemon when Paul came into contact with him. We look beyond the evil of slavery and consider the birth of

Onesimus into the freedom of Christ at the preaching of Paul. Paul was in a type of slavery, himself. He was a prisoner who was fully controlled in his person by the soldiers and jailers of the Roman empire. Even while in this situation, Paul was able to set others free in the faith of the crucified Savior.

Likewise, we must consider that John was used as the instrument which was used of God to reach Gaius with a saving knowledge of our crucified Savior.

In Wesley's notes on the Old and New Testament we are counseled to consider that this joy is a joy shared by all pastors as they see growth and steadfastness in the faith once delivered among those whom they have labored to impart the Words of Truth.

Wesley continues to expand our understanding of the verse as he argues that this is the joy of a parent to see his child grow into Christian maturity. This understanding is an application of the Christian message to our daily walk with Christ in this world of opportunity to spread the Word of the Savior.]

1.5 *Beloved, thou doest faithfully whatsoever thou doest to the brethren, and the strangers;*

[Generally this verse has been interpreted as brethren, local believers, and strangers - believers who have been forced to either flee persecution or were traveling in evangelistic endeavors such as Paul's missionary journeys. The concept of hospitality toward the community of believer's, even those who not of the local group, was a well-received trait among the early believers.

Those displaced by persecution were generally traveling without much in the way of possessions. Consider that Paul, as Saul, had persecuted the early Christians by obtaining letter from the Sanhedrin which allowed him to legally take them bound to Jerusalem for trial in a religious court. Acts 9:2. Being thus bound, these believers would not be able to protect their possessions from thieves. Further. There was legal precedent whereby the goods of those thus bound could be taken by the authorities. Consider Matthew 5:4 in this light.

The evangelistic travelers were loath to accept any support from the people to whom they carried the message of salvation. This would have made them appear as making merchandise of the Gospel message. Therefore, these were also dependent upon the local Christian community for their necessary support. These is a need for the church members who are gainfully employed in an area to offer support for the work of the ministry, specifically support of those who thus minister, as part of their own dedication to the cause of Christ. He who labors for the Master is due the support of others of the Master's household of faith. If there is an outside means of support it is not required that the laborer accept such support. But, he who is so engaged in a labor for Christ that he is unable to pursue an occupational support of his own, is to be supported by the saints as part of their duty toward the Lord.

Also, I would like to consider another view of this verse. The Christian should give due honor to his brothers and sisters in the Lord. That is simply a "given." But, there is no possibility that such due honor should be withheld simply because a "stranger" is not part of the body of believers. Indeed, such a consideration is a poor testimony to the world. We live in fellowship among the Lord's Own. We live in testimony of the love of Christ among the world's denizens as one means of evangelistic outreach.]

1.6 *Which have borne witness of thy charity before the, who if thou bring forward on their journey after a godly start, thou shalt do well.*

[This verse, and those following, show that my "another view" in the last paragraph above, is another application of the 5th verse but is not the strict meaning of that verse. An application is a device whereby the truth of the verse is carried forth into our walk as Christians among the world.

Several commentaries I consulted argued that John was a pastor in Ephesus. If so, it might be that certain traveling evangelists had come by that church and had praised the hospitality of Gaius. Such hospitality enabled those evangelists to "bring forward" their journey to another place of service for Christ. This help may have been by accompanying them for a certain distance to encourage them with a testimony for the Lord. It may have been by supplying funds and/or food to facilitate those journeys. It almost certainly included a place of rest and repose, and with refreshment for their journey at the home of Gaius.

These same itinerant Christians may have been coming for a return visit. If, as is likely in such a case, they informed John of their intent, he may have been encouraging Gaius to continue his hospitality toward them. These men were "employed" in spreading the Name and religion of Jesus into heathen lands. They would have been loath to accept payment from the unsaved as this would have made it seem that they were only interested in a "job" and not the Jesus of Salvation. Likewise, it is known that the itinerant preachers would often refuse to accept any support from the infant churches. Again, it may have appeared that their interest was in a salary rather than spreading the Word about the Savior. Paul allowed such in I Corinthians, the 9th chapter. But, it might have been interpreted as seeking money rather than as giving a message of The Savior.]

1.7 *Because that for his name's sake they went forth, taking nothing of the Gentiles.*

II Kinga 5:15-16; Matthew 17:25; Luke 10:7; Acts 8:3-4; I Corinthians 9:15; II Corinthians 11:8

[Whether through persecution (Acts 8:3-4) or response to the Lord's Great Commission (Matthew 28:19-20), these evangelists were spreading the Gospel of the Name of Jesus into the entire world of humanity – both Jew and Gentile. Although they had the right to receive remuneration from their hearers, it seems that they chose not to do so. This would have opened them to a charge of spreading the Gospel for riches when they were interested in spreading the riches of Christ and salvation to their hearers.

Instead of requesting, or receiving, any living expenses from those to whom they preached, the accepted support from already established churches and Christians such as Gaius.]

1.8 *We therefore ought to receive such, that we might be fellowhelpers to the truth.*

[Spurgeon's Devotional Commentary summed the first part of this verse as it pertains to Gaius and as it should be considered among the saints: "Gaius could not preach, but he lodged those who did, and so he obtained a prophet's reward." We, through our giving and hospitality to those itinerant preachers become co-labors with those who do preach and, by extension, with the very Spirit of Truth.

The Spirit (John 15:26) and Christ (John 14:6) are The Truth of God. We are called to be fellow-laborers with this Spirit in the spreading of the Gospel of Christ into the world. We do our part in this through assistance of the preachers in their land of endeavor and through our own witness wherever we may be. John, we may notice, called himself a "fellowhelper" in this sense.

Not only do we assist by our giving, but we also give encouragement to those who are working in the fields of the Lord. Notice the two instances of "we" in the verse. All preachers of the Truth are to be involved in spreading that truth. Also, all Christians – whether preacher or parishioner, are to be involved in spreading that truth in any manner they are able to contribute.]

1.9 *I wrote unto the church: but Diotrephes, who loveth to have the preeminence among them, received us not.*

[The meaning of the name Diotrephes is "nourished by Jupiter." This name strongly suggests that this man was not brought up in a pious Jewish home. Rather, it suggests that Diotrephes was a gentile convert to Christianity. We must remember that at this time the churches were largely Jewish enclaves. This, alone, does not disqualify Diotrephes as a pastor in one of God's churches.

However, without the background in the Scripture, at least of what we would term "the Old Testament," that would have been given him as a Jew, he may have been a "novice" in the things of God. Paul had warned young Timothy that a pastor should be grounded in the faith. Consider I Timothy 3:6 where Paul was giving the qualifications of a pastor. "Not a novice, lest being lifted up with pride he fall into the condemnation of the devil." It would appear that Diotrephes had fallen into self-pride as he "withstood" John in the matter of the evangelists. John, we may remember was a disciple, and apostle of, Jesus.

It is possible that Diotrephes was the pastor of the church which Gaius belonged. John had written this same argument to support certain evangelists to Diotrephes, but Diotrephes had disregarded John's authority as an apostle and apparently suppressed the letter. We have no knowledge about this letter beyond this short mention by John. It, obviously, did not bear the mark of inspiration upon its words or it would have survived.

We hear much in this day of "lost" books of the Bible. It is a rather easy thing to determine the canonicity of the Books of Scripture. If they have been available to the churches down through the ages, they are of God. If not, they are not of God.

All of us have seen notations in the margins of our Bibles which claim "the oldest and best do not agree." Who are these oldest and best? One of them was found in the burning barrel of a monastery in the Sinai. The readings of that manuscript, B, are not of the inspired Words of God. Had they been they would have been always available to the churches rather than hidden in one monastery. It might be well to consider that Tischendorf found this while on a journey to discover older manuscripts due to his doubt that God had preserved His Words. The entire journey, and discovery, were begun with a lack of faith in the power and goodness of God.

The other manuscript was found in the Vatican Library near the time of the Reformation. The same arguments as from the previous paragraph pertain here, as well.

It may also be noted that the Roman Catholic edition of an English language Bible was in existence thirty years before the King James Bible was first printed. Therefore, we cannot logically argue that these are manuscripts overlooked by the editors and translators of the King James – the Authorized – Bible. The "readings" are available even in the Catholic edition. The true point is that the translators of the King James Bible rejected much of what the church world today accepts. More to the point of our verse is the person of Diotrephes. His arrogance in rejecting, and even attacking, and apostle of the Lord should be well noted. He may have been a pastor in the church which Gaius resided. He was, it seems, some sort of "church official" if, indeed John had written to him first. Ambition and covetousness are unbecoming evils among a pastor. His first duty is to feed the flock of God in the area of his calling. He feeds the Words of God and teaches the precepts of God. He must remember that He is not a god unto the people. He only stands as a representative of God before them.

To overly worry about his personal position is to ignore his need to proclaim the Words of God. He is not a shepherd. He is only the under shepherd who serves under Christ.

Nevertheless, there is a dignity to the office of pastor which must be accepted until such time as God chooses to remove him from his place if he engage in a dereliction of duty before the Lord.]

1.10 *Wherefore, if I come, I will remember his deed, which he doeth, prating against us with malicious words, and not content therewith, neither doth he himself receive the brethren, and forbiddeth them that would, and casteth them out of the church.*

[Diotrephes is described by Adam Clarke as one who, "He had the complete dog in the manger principle: he would neither do, nor let do; and when good was done that he did not approve, he endeavoured to undo it." Being a convert, quite possibly to Judaism first and then to Christianity, he may have been very interested in "Judaizing the church." This would have mitigated him against the thought of missions to the Gentiles. Even Peter fell into this "Judaizing" error. (Galatians 2:1-16) As such Diotrephes would countenance no Gentile evangelistic efforts, no support of such efforts, and would stand against any who might suggest otherwise. He would even dismiss from the assembly those who did not agree with his stands.

It is good that we have standards and abide by them. It is bad when our standards are at variance with the will of God. That any church might accept such as one as a pastor is not surprising as we are too often seduced by the show of religious pomposity and an "easy tongue" which might "tickle our ears" while leading our souls astray. Paul also advises Timothy that "...the time will come when they will not endure sound doctrine; but after their own lusts shall they heap to themselves teachers, having itching ears..." (II Timothy 4:3)

We normally tend to assign this trait to the end times but it has shown itself throughout the history of the church. From such come, sometimes small and sometimes large, error which leads to apostasy among the churches. From this attitude have sprung many of the cults and the coldness of many of the true churches which have lapsed into error.

The verse also argues that this Diotrephes spoke evil of John and those itinerant

THIRD JOHN

evangelists. Had this man only spoken evil of John, it is doubtful that John would have promised to withstand him. But, the error had to do with John being spoken against it is doubtful that anything further would have happened. But, John also had the responsibilities of the churches as an apostle of Christ. Further, Diotrophes had also undone the good some from the church had attempted by "excommunicating" them from the assembly. More to the point, Diotrophes had undermined the apostolic authority to the church. In this last point, since the full Scripture was not yet available, we could well argue that Diotrophes had undermined the very authority of the Scripture in that the apostles were the penmen of that Scripture. In order to be true to his own calling it was necessary that John withstand Diotrophes as did Paul of Peter in Galatians. This was for the pure order of the churches.

The deacon board should always be filled with men who are grounded in the Scripture for they have the oversight of the Pastor as part of their own duty. Every person needs an accountability or thy will tend to overstep their boundaries. "Absolute power corrupts absolutely" is the best-known quotation of the 19th century British politician Lord Acton. This is a true statement of which even the church must understand. It is the duty of the pastor to lead the church into the Words of God. It is the duty of the membership, especially the deacon board, to keep a spiritual watch over the pastor in order to help keep him true to the Word even as they support him in the teaching of that Word.

The notes of the British Family Bible contains this quotation: : Private offences against ourselves must be forgiven and forgotten: but when the offence is an impediment to the faith, and very prejudicial to the church, it is to be opposed and openly reproved." It is a true and spiritual pronouncement.

Going back to the practice of "Judaizing" the church. The ancient Jews were to remove from their group those who refused circumcision. It may well be that Diotrophes was extreme in his Judaizing views. He would not have been alone in this error as the second chapter of Galatians would remind us. That same chapter of Galatians recounts the results of a church council at Jerusalem which would have also reprimanded Diotrophes. See the 15th chapter of Acts for a description of that council.]

1.11 *Beloved, follow not that which is evil, but that which is good. He that doeth good is of God: but he that doeth evil hath not seen God.*

Exodus 23:2; Psalm 37:27; Proverbs 12:11; Isaiah 1:16-17; John 3:20; 20:27; I Corinthians 11:1; Philippians 3:17; I Thessalonians 2:19; Hebrews 6:12; I Peter 3:11-13; I John 2:29; 3:6-9

[The evil doer has never seen the God of Salvation. John argues that the word of Diotrephes reveal that he has not been born again. He is still in his sin; this explains why his sins are so heinous toward the brotherhood of believers. Diotrephes may have talked the talk of a follower of Jesus, but his actions show that he has never walked with Jesus.

Gaius is warned to not follow evil even when it is enticingly presented by a leader of a local church. Instead, he should follow good as displayed by Jesus and true faith in Him.]

1.12 *Demetrius hath good report of all men, and of the truth itself: yea, and we also bear record, and ye know that out record is true.*

[It is apparent that John knew Demetrius personally for Demetrius has earned the recommendation of the aged apostle. It may be that he was also a member of the assembly to which Gaius was attached. If so the recommendation of John would have been vital since it is obvious that Diotrephes would have opposed him as he opposed those who disagreed with his opinion.

In either his pride, or in his insecurities which caused his possessiveness of his "church position," Deotrephes would have railed against Demetrius as he had railed against John.

Once again we appeal to the letter of Paul in I Timothy 3:2: "A bishop then must be blameless, the husband of one wife, vigilant, sober, of good behaviour, given to hospitality, apt to teach..." It would be obvious that Demetrius was likewise given to hospitality. This would have run counter to the demeanor of Deotrephes, and probably have incurred his wrath. Better to feel the wrath of man so that the smile of God may rest upon one.

Rather than seeking the approval of a church leader, Demetrius was known for his fidelity to the Truth of Christ. Can anything be more of a compliment to any Christian than such a recognition among the brethren?

I would also believe that Deotrephes would be of such tenor as to be an abrasive person to any, in the brotherhood or without, who would disagree in the slightest with him. But, Paul advises Timothy that a pastor should, "Moreover he must have a good report of them which are without; lest he fall into reproach and the snare of the devil." (I Timothy 3:7) This is not to suggest a "go along to get along" personality since it is sometimes necessary to stand for the faith once delivered. But there is but a small separation between standing and smiting. As good pastor, called of God, would understand the difference and apply himself to the task of being a witness for the Truth even to those without the church.

Satan will always seek to attack the church in its weakest link. In this case it may well have been Deotrephes who had gifts of oratory and persuasion but lacked the gifts of the Spirit so necessary in the leadership of a local assembly, and also necessary among those of that local assembly.

Since this epistle is written some thirty years after a silversmith opposed Paul in Acts 19:24, some have argued that this is the same Demetrius. This seems somewhat doubtful. Even if the man from Acts 19:24 had been converted, which we hope is the case, it would seem that his natural personality was too volatile to be the same man as recommended by John.

It is more likely that this Demetrius was either a member of the church from which John was teaching and acted as a courier with John's letter to Gaius. It is probably more likely that John had met him on some missionary Journey, or been informed by those with whom he labored, or was a member of the same assembly as Gaius. I *choose* to accept the latter as correct.]

1.13 *I had many things to write, but I will not with ink and pen write unto thee:*

[I would give two reasons why John did not write the other things he considered. The first may have had to do with his aversion to saying more about Diothrephes. It may well have been that hard words were in order but John would not do so from the anonymity of a letter. It would be better to say those things in private rather than speak ill of a church leader. This would have given those outside the household of faith to doubt the unity of the Church of Jesus. It would bring shame to His name. It was not necessary that such be done. This also presupposes a certain standard of decorum which must be evidenced within the brotherhood. Caution: This does not mean that we should fail to oppose error; this does mean that we must be civil in our conduct of all – even those with whom we must oppose on doctrinal ground. Hate the sin but love the sinner. Also, stand for the truth but do it in Christian love before the world. A "church fight" or a church split only tend to give pause to those whom we would seek to evangelize.

The second reason is that this private meeting, face-to-face, would give Diothrephes the chance to defend himself while not giving him the luxury of calling his opponents into question, themselves as enemies of the Cross. It would keep civility and Christian love within the assembly.

There is a third reason: This is inspired Scripture. That is, it contains the words of God rather than the words of man. As such, John may have been prohibited from speaking beyond that which the Lord had spoken! Consider, also the notes at II John 1:12.

We must, from the natural, also consider that John wished to see these people with his own eyes that he might find joy in the companionship of others of like faith. This is a thing that all Christians should desire. We are all of the "family" when we are Christians. A "family reunion," even among others we might not have before met, is a joyous thing for our spirits as we fellowship in the Lord.]

1.14 *But I trust I shall shortly see thee, and we shall speak face to face. Peace be to thee. Our friends salute thee. Greet the friends by name.*

[John seems to be a very friendly and gregarious person as he ends each of his short epistles with a greeting to his friends. John, as we should all be, is a man who never met a Christian who he did not consider to be a friend.

We note that John asks that the "friends" be greeted by name. We are quickly reminded that those whom Jesus has called will know His voice of leading. "To him the porter openeth; and the sheep hear his voice: and he calleth his own sheep by name, and leadeth them out." (John 10:3)

Further, we are reminded that Jesus laid down His physical life for His friends. "Greater love hath no man than this, that a man lay down his life for his friends." (John 15:13) Consider the glory in that verse. We have also been called in fellowship and salvation by the Savior. He is our friend. It is great pride when we can say that we have met some famous person. It is a greater pride to say that this famous person is our friend. Folks, the King of Glory calls us His friend when we have responded to Him in faith, believing for salvation.

To the apostles, and to us as sharing in the glory of salvation even with them, Jesus said, "Henceforth I call you not servants; for the servant knoweth not what his lord doeth: but I have called you friends; for all things that I have heard of my Father I have made known unto you." (John 15:15) Oh, the absolute glory and thrill to be so called by the Master of the Universe.

One more verse I would cite: "Ye are my friends, if ye do whatsoever I command you." (John 15:14)   What has the Lord commanded us?   He has commanded us to come to Him, and Him alone, for the salvation of our souls. There is no other means of salvation.

After this, in simple homage to our great Friend and Savior, we have need to tell the old, old story of Jesus and His love as we walk out into the world of man. We must not dishonor our Heavenly Friend by disregarding His wishes for us.]

JUDE

***1.1** Jude, the servant of Jesus Christ, and brother of James, to them that are sanctified by God the Father, and preserved in Jesus Christ, and called:*

[Matthew 13:55 makes mention that two of the half-brothers of Jesus, born to Mary and Joseph after the birth of Jesus, carried these names. Luke 6:16 and Acts 1:13 both mention apostles of these names. Which Jude was the author? About this there is much debate. I almost called it "fruitless" debate since the true Author of this little book is the Spirit of God as it was He Who inspired the Words used.

I tend to assign the penmanship of the human instrument used of God as Jude, the apostle. We must note that "Jude" is a shortened version of Judas. Although Iscariot had also been an apostle, it obvious that he was a false apostle, a charlatan rather than a true follower of Christ. James and this Jude were the sons of Alpheus. (Matthew 10:3 – note that Jude was also called "Alphaeus" and "Lebbaeus." These were surnames.)

Jude does not identify himself as an apostle. However, neither did Paul in Philippians, I and II Thessalonians, and Philemon. It was not necessary that he do so since he was well known to the believers as the brother of James, who was the leader of the Jerusalem assembly of believers. (Acts 21:17-18)

More important, even, than who he was is the truth written down in the inspired and preserved Words. Jude simply calls himself the servant of Jesus, the Messiah. He mentioned his brother as also a follower of Jesus. This is both and identifying statement and an homage to the concept of faith within a family. To be a servant, was to be a slave. Further, the concept of "slave" was to admit that one was owned by another. This is a touching tribute to the fact of the Savior. The penman was fully committed to following the Lord.

Mention is made that the believer, to whom this epistle was sent, was one who has been called into the blessed state of salvation by the calling of the Spirit. In this they are "sanctified," or called holy by the will of the Father. Not only are they the called of the Lord, they are also preserved in that salvation. Our salvation is all in, and of, Christ. We are called to accept Him as Lord and Savior. It is He who holds us in His hand and will never fail in holding us in Salvation. Finally, it is He who will deliver us to His side when we leave this earth. Salvation is all of Him; we are simply the unworthy recipients of His Grace and Salvation – for eternity. Jesus will never fail!!!]

***1.2** Mercy unto you, and peace, and love, be multiplied.*

[Spiritual peace comes from the abounding mercy of Jesus Christ to His own. From this peace should grow an abiding love of Jesus for His manifold gifts which stem from the salvation from sin which is given us solely on His account. We accept these by faith even even as we realize that this very faith is a gift from Him. (see Ephesians 2:8-9) Realizing His great love toward us should cause us to love Him even more. (see I John 4:19)

This love should then also flow to those for whom He died. To apply this concept simply to those already saved would be error. We must love the brethren.

This is part of our testimony before the world. (see John 13:35) We must also love the unsaved to the extent that we would share the message that Jesus Christ died in time so that others might live in eternity. Any consideration of the love that sent Jesus to the Cross must yearn for the conversion of the lost; thus, abounding love is a love into all the world which will guide our prayers, our thoughts, and even our interpersonal actions to such an extent that we will speak out, even as we live out, the Love of Christ into the entire world.]

1.3 *Beloved, when I gave all diligence to write unto you of the common salvation, it was needful for me to write unto you, and exhort you that ye should earnestly contend for the faith which was once delivered unto the saints.*

[We contend for the faith "once delivered." If a pastor, evangelist, or even a "theologian" comes with the message that God wasn't powerful enough to preserve His Word, or that it was somehow lost to the faithful for any number of years, we should stand up and say, "No! God gave us a secure Word. He said that Hell and all her forces could not destroy the Message of that Word to the Churches which name His Name!"

We do not look for new doctrinal stances; we look for old Biblical assurances. I just read today that a major denomination was ready to give its approval to "gay," so-called, marriages. Why, if this is proper, did not churchmen of the past champion the issue? It is because they based their doctrinal stance upon the revealed Word of God. Today we have a very sad theology which is based more on cultural leading than on the leading of the Holy Spirit of God as revealed through the Preserved Word of God.

Now, I have nothing against the homosexual. I really don't. Most of those which I have known I have been happy to call "friend." Does that mean that I condone that lifestyle? No. I cannot condone what God has condemned.

In the meantime, I am reminded that I am an old and fat guy! What does the Word say about sloth and gluttony? Now I done quit preaching and started a meddlin'. I had better not begin to feel superior to anyone! The only good thing I can say about myself is that I am a child of the King through the grace of the Father!

We need to contend for the faith. God's doctrine is worth standing for even when we stand against some intellectual theologians. That is especially true when they put more faith in their intellect and theology than they do in God and His Holy Word!

I am not against theologians or learning. I have five college degrees myself. But, I can acknowledge that I will never understand more than the God Who created Heaven and Earth and all that is therein. I'd better just trust Him - even on those few instances when I feel like I want to disagree. Remember Jonah? Read his book; it's only four short chapters. We remember him today not because of his great intellect or social ideals; we remember him because he honored God (finally!) even when he disagreed!

We need to contend for the faith!]

1.4 *For there are certain men crept in unaware, who were before of old ordained to this condemnation, ungodly men, turning the grace of our God into lasciviousness, and denying the only Lord God, and our Lord Jesus Christ.*

[Note well the phrase "certain men." Not all who are in error are nefarious. There are doctrines which we can see as incorrect which are not ones which deny the Lord. My wife took a position of a mid-tribulation rapture. Was she wrong? I believe so. Am I wrong to hold to a pre-tribulation rapture? I believe not. I, as was she, am basing my theology on an understanding of the Words of God. This may be a point of debate; it was for us. But, it in no way brings discredit upon the Lord or the Christians who follow Him. One of us, obviously, is in error. I would teach that the error was hers and now that she is in glory she has found the truth.

There are those who have "crept in" to the church with willful error which causes great harm to the people of God. The Roman doctrine of salvation being gained by being baptized into the church is only one such error. That impacts souls to not trust Jesus, and Him alone, for salvation. Without this exclusive faith in the Lord there can be no salvation. (Acts 4:12)

How does such error creep into the churches? One way is small error, not corrected by Bible truth will grow into great error. The above error of "church salvation" began with an untrue view of baptismal regeneration. There is no grace incumbent within baptism. Baptism is simply and outward ordinance that gives testimony to the faith of an individual. In the beginning of the churches, Baptism soon followed a declaration of faith. It was an outward sign, in going under the water and being brought back out of the water, there was a picture of the death, burial and resurrection of Jesus. Since this was often a "membership rite" wherein one was baptized into the church fellowship. Small errors in judgment saw this as a means of salvation since it brought people into the fellowship of the local assembly. The larger error, baptismal regeneration and salvation vested in the church followed in time.

The small things happened so slowly that the people were unaware of the change from the apostle's doctrine.

In a mirror of the doctrine of Grace, we see that these men were "ordained" to be the carriers of this error into the churches. Actually, the meaning is that the error of these men had been prophesized.

Still, we would be well advised to consider than Satan delights in perverting the pure teaching of God so that his counterfeit claims will seem more reasonable.

Such false teachers will have their eternal reward outside the presence of God. (Proverbs 16:4) God does punish sin, and sinners.

Why would God allow such evil men to flourish, even for a short time, within the brethren of the churches? I find three points in the purposes of God. The first is that the true Christian, by taking part in this Spiritual Warfare, will be strengthened in his own personal walk with Jesus as he flees to the side of the Savior in this time of testing. Second, this will cause the true Christian to search the Scriptures to find the Truth of God. And, third, through this time of testing the Christian will learn to trust Jesus for his own daily walk.

Those false teachers, who seemed so reasonable and spiritual in their inducements to seduce the Christian, will find themselves condemned of the Lord. Many preachers who went into pulpit "service" will not find the "Well done, thou good and faithful servant" from the Lord's lips. These have made a career decision to be "pastors" and will be dismayed when the Lord says, "Depart from me." God is still looking for men who love to serve Him rather than to "work" as a mercenary in the Army of the Lord.

Where do we stand, preacher? Are we servants of the Lord, or are we just looking for the next payday and the trappings of respectability? It is an important question well worthy of consideration!

Such may be "Rev.", or even "Rev. Dr." But are they, we, Godly men or are we simply looking for a payday, a nice house, and the praise of men? We who are allowed to stand before the people in that pride inducing pulpit read II Timothy 4:2-3 as a sad commentary on the state of the general Christian: "For the time will come when they will not endure sound doctrine; but after their own lusts shall they heap to themselves teachers, having itching ears; And they shall turn away their ears from the truth, and shall be turned unto fables."

But, we tend to fail to apply the same verses to ourselves. Are we not also prone to pride and a desire to be "respectable?" Do we not all too often fall for the argument that to get along we must go along. And often go alone without heeding the leading of the Spirit? Is there not the tug to forget about the importance of a fidelity to the Scripture and seek to inflate our own ego with the praise of a false Biblical text that argues against the eternal security of the Words of God? Do we not fail to trust the Spirit to bless, so that we begin to bring in the world to lure the "crowd," in such a manner as to forget to, "Preach the word; be instant in season, out of season; reprove, rebuke, exhort with all longsuffering and doctrine"?

As self-appointed "leaders of the church," have we become guilty of leading others astray?

It is conjectured that the men spoken of in this place were in the house of the Nicolaitans. These taught that we enjoy great freedom in Christ. Such a great freedom as to be unable to actually sin. This is the error of the antinomians. It was a heady and popular doctrine to many. "Salvation is all of the Lord. We have no possibility of sinning while we are in Him." But, it is a doctrine of error. Leviticus 11:45 has never been repealed: "For I am the LORD that bringeth you up out of the land of Egypt, to be your God: ye shall therefore be holy, for I am holy." Salvation was never intended to give us license to sin. Salvation will give us freedom from sin. We are given a freedom to stand holy before the Lord. I Peter 2:9 gives us the picture of what is expected from the redeemed of the Lord: "But ye are a chosen generation, a royal priesthood, an holy nation, a peculiar people; that ye should shew forth the praises of him who hath called you out of darkness into his marvellous light..." We are to be a people who serve the Lord, before the world, in that we show His power to change and make us new creatures.

We are not to deny the power of our Lord and Savior. We are to be witnesses of His power as the God/man Jesus Christ who is the ruler of the universe.]

1.5 *I will therefore put you in remembrance, though ye once knew this, how that the Lord having saved the people out of the land of Egypt, afterward destroyed them that believed not.*

[Preachers sometimes have to repeat themselves. A continual restating of the great truths of Scripture is to evidence a continued reliance upon, and a show of the importance of, the Words of God given in His inspired and preserved Scripture. Here Jude says, you have heard this before and probably understand the importance of this Truths.

JUDE

We must hearken back to the Book of Hebrews. That first generation, with the exception of Joshua and Caleb, of these former slaves were denied entrance into the Land of Promise. We must also remember that the Land is not to be confused as a picture of Heaven. To briefly restate the typology of the Exodus we must first consider that those in bondage in Egypt are to be considered as those who are in bondage to sin. The initial removing of the people from Egypt is a picture of salvation. The path through the Red Sea is, then, seen as a type of Baptism of a people who were already freed from the land of sin. This is followed by the wandering which is clearly a time of learning for the former slaves as they became a great nation in learning to obey and reverence the God Who had saved them.

Entering into the land is not a picture of entering Heaven. There are no battles to be fought upon entering Heaven. There is no *foreign people* to be displaced upon entering Heaven. However, the committed Christian does find these realities as He comes to consecrate Himself in living Holy before God and man. This consecrated man will find the peace of God even during time of trial. He will walk in an evangelistic fervor which will seek to remove the sin-cursed people he finds in this world and repatriate them to become followers of the Lord of Glory. This is the true typology of "*entering the land."*

The belief, or lack thereof, of those denied entry into the land only concerned their trust that the Lord would carry them through. They were still of the House of Jacob even though they did not fully trust the truth of that reality.

We cannot use the historical reality of those who were denied entrance into the Land of Rest as an argument that one may somehow *lose his salvation.* These people who were denied entrance lost nothing except their opportunity to rest in the knowledge of the Lord's provision during battle. They were Jews during the trek and they were still Jews even though they died during the forty years of wilderness wandering. They retained their family realities, which were fixed long before this great sin of inaction on their part. Their lack of faith in this instance did not negate the truth of their familial situation.

By the way, I understand that calling these Israelites, "Jews" is a misnomer. When we consider the diaspora we come upon the term "Jew" as a shorthand to describe those of Abraham's lineage. The Romans destroyed the great genealogical libraries at Jerusalem's Temple. Few can, today, find their place among which tribe they represent. Since the central land was called "Judah," we tend to call the people "Jew" even though this would not apply to all.

An interesting point of history. In about 130 A.D. a man named Simon Bar Kokhba announced himself as Messiah. Rabbi Akivi agreed with him and, for about three years, Israel became a nation free of Rome. This revolt was finally put down in 135 A.D. At that time, tired of the propensity of revolt by the Jews, Rome declared the land of Judea to be kept free of the Jewish element. They were removed. The land was renamed Palestine, in honor of the ancient enemies of the Hebrews, the Philistines. This error still has ramifications even unto this day.]

1.6 *And the angels which kept not their first estate, but left their own habitation, he hath reserved in everlasting chains under darkness unto the judgment of the great day.*

[We have our attention drawn to the angles which followed Lucifer in his rebellion against God. They willfully left their great station as angels of the Lord when they rebelled against Him. Most seem to have been already cast into the darkness of Eternal retribution for their sin. Satan has, apparently, access to the Heavenly realms although his primary abode is earth. He also has some freedom to remove himself from the area of the "air" of the earth, which is his primary abode, (See Ephesians 2:2) in order to accuse the righteous. (See Job 1:6-10)

There seems to be a group of *demons* which are somehow free of the restriction to Hades at this time as they await the awful reality of the Hell of the Second Death of Revelation 20:14. At the beginning of the second half of the Great Tribulation, the time of Jacob's trial, (See Jeremiah 30:7) the full demonic forces seem to be unleashed for a short, a time, times, and half a time eg. 3 and ½ years, to torment the earth.

The full reality of this should strike us. We ain't seen nothing yet. There will be greater temptation during this time of God's wrath showered upon mankind than ever before in history. (Consider James 1:13-15. Most of our sin is not "the devil made me do it." Most of our sin is, "I wanted to do it!" We must never underestimate the demons of Satan. Likewise, we must never underestimate our own propensity to sin!

Then angels were created, I believe, prior to the creation of this earth. They were to be a group dedicated to serving God. It would appear that these angels were given a prohibition period much as was Adam. Fully one-third of those angels failed their time of testing and, under the leadership of Satan, they rebelled against God as did Adam. But, for these fallen angels there was no Genesis 3:15 to offer them the possibility or redemption. Our redemption is predicated upon Jesus becoming one of us so that He might take the full penalty for our sin and, thus, offer us pardon and reconciliation.

There is no such provision made for the rebellious angels. Their fate was sealed by their willful sin against The Holy God. They now stand in chains of darkness, with no access to the light of God, awaiting their time of ultimate doom and imprisonment in the second death. (See Matthew 25:41) Those righteous angels who did not rebel also saw their fate sealed by their faithfulness to God. They would be forever faithful, as would Adam had been had he not sinned in taking part in the forbidden fruit.

The intent of this particular passage, verses 5-8, is to remind that, although God is a God of love and mercy, He is also The God of Righteous Judgment and Vengeance upon sin and sinners, lawbreakers of His standards of purity and those who rebel against His righteous standards of Creation.

By the way, that phrase "eternal fire" should serve as a warning that we have a literal Hell to avoid and a literal Heaven of eternal bliss to gain by trusting Jesus as the full payment for our sins!]

1.7 *Even as Sodom and Gomorrha, and the cities about them in like manner, giving themselves over to fornication, and going after strange flesh, are set forth for an example, suffering the vengeance of eternal fire.*

[These three examples stand as proof that God does judicially punish those who choose to depart from His standards of conduct. His standards are not just rules, they are reasoned actions denoted by the Creator and *Manufacturer* of humanity. His standards are the recommended procedure to enhance even human life on this plane of time and physicality. As the Creator, God knows what is best for us in every situation and will guide us to make proper choices in order to live more fully our lives in the world of His Creation.

Those who depart from His leading are not only judged as sinners, they stand as ignorant of even the basics of a happy and healthy human existence. The people of Sodom and Gomorrha were destroyed by fire and, as now residents of Hell, are still being destroyed by an eternal fire. Likewise, the very cites were destroyed and have never been rebuilt. The devastation of the fire has rendered even the rebuilding of the cities as impossible. The cities sites are now believed to be inundated under the Dead Sea.

Romans 1:27 describe the sin of which the people were guilty. "And likewise also the men, leaving the natural use of the woman, burned in their lust one toward another; men with men working that which is unseemly, and receiving in themselves that recompence of their error which was meet." Homosexuality is not a "life style choice;" it is a choice of sin over the obvious plan of God. (For $5.00, in the U.S., I can send a copy of my short booklet, "Same Sex Marriage – A Biblical Perspective.)

The phrase "going after strange flesh," is another reference to homosexuality. Compare Romans 1:26-27.

It would be well if my countrymen, of my own nation, considered that the very city/state nations of Sodom and Gomorrha were destroyed along with the people who so sinned. Of the natural creation we are told that "For we know that the whole creation groaneth and travaileth in pain together until now." It is a spiritual principle that when a people pervert themselves in the land, even the land suffers.

The vengeance of God stands ready to make righteous judgment upon the sin of any people. He also stands to offer full forgiveness and pardon based on the Cross of Jesus Christ and His sacrifice, thereon.]

1.8 *Likewise also these filthy dreamers defile the flesh, despise dominion, and speak evil of dignities.*

[Jude has shown three classes of rebellion against God in this world. First is shown the individual rebellion of refusing to follow the Words of the Lord in the matter of the conquest of the Land. We must note that this refusal even was seen in those who did enter the land forty years later. There was a "rest" after one part was made pure. The conquest was never completed.

We see this even in our day. The Philistines were the ancient enemy of the Jewish people as they entered the land. In 135 AD the Romans put down yet another rebellion by the Israelite peoples. After this rebellion was quelled, the Romans demanded all Jews to remove themselves from their land. The provinces of Galilee and Samaria were renamed "Palestine" after this ancient, and unconquered enemy of the Jew. The continued fallacy of this misnomer has found its way into the modern news cycles. There is a real reason why we need to fully follow the commands of God for this life. To do otherwise is to invite error to plague our daily walk.

Jude also speaks of those angels who rebelled against God. We still in our day are impacted by the sin of Adam and Eve. The angels who rebelled will find their own doom. But first they will attempt to cause the pollution of so many of God's creation. We, as failed human beings, are part of that great cosmic sin of Satan and his angels in that we grieve the great loving heart of our Heavenly Father as we walk in opposition to

Him and His gracious commandments. Ephesians 4:30 asks that we, "And grieve not the holy Spirit of God, whereby ye are sealed unto the day of redemption."

Even we, the saved by Grace sinner, so often fail our Lord. We grieve Him Who Loved us so much that He sent His Only begotten Son to die for us on that cruel cross. This misbehavior of our personal rejecting of His gentle leading is a direct rebellion of His Lordship in our lives. Yet, He still stands ready to forgive. (I John 1:10-2:1)

The third class of sinner associated with Jude's condemnation is that of Sodom and Gomorrha.

How evil were the people of these cities and area's. God judged them with a little foretaste of the horrors of Hell.

Dr. Sorenson said this in regard to the sin of Sodomy: "History overflows with record of the moral impurity of those who depart from the spiritual truth..." Indeed, the profane among the linotype operators have gleefully set headlines in the newspapers of the day detailing the moral failure of those who were supposed to stand for God. Sin always will lead to a declining slope of fidelity to our Lord.

Dr. Sorenson has also rightly noted that, "The word translated as filthy dreamers (enupniazomai) has the sense to 'dream sensual dreams.'" The pastor at the church I presently attend made mention just last week that Satan seems to attack us in two primary areas. He will attack us in our sensuality and in our theology. That pretty much sums up the three illustrations of Jude in this area.

Those who are weak in their personal lives, and in their theological leadership will have no respect or consideration of the "rules of the road" of daily living. They despise dominion, or constricting rules of any sort, upon their lives. They only wish to follow that which pleases them and others, working from the Bible or even a civil situation, will be shunned and vilified. This is why a pastor who reads his Bible and refuses to, for example, solemnize a "wedding" of two homosexual or lesbian persons – a same sex wedding - is called a bigot or a hater. In reality, especially in a land when "religious freedom" is enshrined in our Constitution, the bigot is one who refuses to allow another to enjoy his own religious freedom to not take part in that with which he sees as abhorrent in the eyes of God.

Biblically, we are enjoined to, "Then Peter and the other apostles answered and said, We ought to obey God rather than men." (Acts 5:29) With our religious freedoms imperiled in this day, to obey God will often put us up to social scorn and judicial ruin.

This is an example of speaking evil of dignities in the church. We also see many in this day who speak evil of dignities – elected officials – in this day of "General Sherman" political discourse. I haven't even spoken of religious discrimination and hate flowing from the denominal structure. We who hold to the inspired and preserved Scripture are often painted with the broad brush of intolerance as we are branded "foolish" and "out of touch" when we seek to hold to the historically preserved text of Scripture rather than accepting the critical text which did not exist before 1881 and the Westcott and Hort jettisoning of the traditional text. It is instructive to note that those who chide us who hold to a perfectly preserved text as the basis for our Scripture are called "unloving" in a most "unloving" manner.]

***1.9** Yet Michael the archangel, when contending with the devil he disputed about the body of Moses, durst not bring against him a railing accusation, but said, The Lord rebuke thee.*

[There was a tradition that Satan wanted the body of Moses in order to tempt the children of Israel to sin by worshipping Moses as a demigod, of sorts. Whether that tradition was true, or not, is not at issue. The truth of the confrontation between Michael and Lucifer is not in question since the Spirit has included this situation in the actual inspired and preserved Scripture of God. In the tenth chapter of Daniel, verses twelve and following we are given a small glimpse into the spiritual realms of angelic warfare. This present verse from Jude alludes to that same spiritual warfare. As in verse 14, below, Jude quotes from a non-canonical source. The entirety of this source is not considered as inspired. This one section is given authority as historically correct. Even that is only considered as inspired because the Spirit chose to bring those few words into the inspired text of inspired and preserved Scripture.

There are many things that are true. Only those things included in the Sacred Text are to be considered as inspired. These are not considered as inspired simply because they are true. When the Truth of an incident is included in the inspired and preserved text it is then shown to be inspired of the Spirit.

The thing to notice at this point is that even Michael, the archangel, did not fight in his own power. He trusted his argument to the sure Words of the Lord. When we go off, halfcocked, our weapon is not ready to be used. Our weapon is the inspired and preserved Scripture. We can trust this because it is the Word, and Power, of God. It is fully ready to defend us and to defeat Satan because truly inspired Scripture is the Words of God. Those Words have never been lost in time because they are of eternal power and performance. Time has no real power upon the inspired and preserved Words of God.

Compare also the notes on verse 14 below.]

1.10 *But these speak evil of those things which they know not: but what they know naturally, as brute beasts, in those things they corrupt themselves.*

[They reject the inspired and preserved Scripture without even knowing what it says. They know that it is considered the "Words of God." That is enough for them to disregard it and to disobey any thought of God having become a ruling reality in their lives. Their naturalistic hate does not let them even want to know anything of the Special Revelation of Scripture.

As a brute beast which has not read the Words of God, they only understand anything of Him via General Revelation. Even this they have corrupted with their sin cursed natural "brute beast-like" lives. (Consider Romans 1:24-32)]

1.11 *Woe unto them! for they have gone in the way of Cain, and ran greedily after the error of Balaam for reward, and perished in the gainsaying of Core.*

[As Cain killed his brother Abel physically, the false religionists have killed their followers spiritually by leading them from the Bible and the God of that Bible. They are "called" from receiving Christ as Savior by the doctrines of man's perversions of true religion.

Balaam sought money, power, and the praise of men as he sought to prophecy woe and foreboding upon the Israelites. That he failed in this was only by the intervention of God. His resultant failure did not mitigate against his willingness to be so used. In effect Balaam mishandled the Words of God and the office of a prophet of

God. In doing this he did violence to the pure worship of God. The principle of Godly separation from evil was violated by his compromise with ungodly elements.

In Numbers, the sixteenth chapter, we read the rebellion of Korah, Dathan and Abiram. They revolted against Moses and Aaron, who were the God-appointed leaders of the Exodus. Moses, at the leading of God, had established the Aaronic priesthood. This was a departure from the norm of family elders leading the family in worship. There is still a place, an important place, for family worship and respect for family elders. But, God was beginning to teach the great truth of the coming sacrifice of Jesus for the sins of the world. This rebellion was a prideful refusal to follow the ways of God as enunciated by His chosen servants. Ultimately is was a rebellion against God.

We can go back in Scripture and see that each of these mentioned persons were judged of God. Sin begs for the just judgment of God upon the sinner. Such is necessary, especially in the Churches of the Living God. This was extremely important in this age before the full cannon of Scripture was available to those churches.

Even in this age there is a need for decorum in the Churches. A church must speak with one voice – that is the voice of the pastor as He faithfully gives forth the Words of God. When a pastor fails in this regard it is time for the church to seek a new spiritual under shepherd.]

1.12 These are spots in your feasts of charity, when they feast with you, feeding themselves without fear: clouds they are without water, carried about of winds; trees whose fruit withereth, without fruit, twice dead, plucked up by the roots;

[In the eleventh chapter of I Corinthians, Paul speaks of those who dishonor the Lord's table. That seems to not be the point of this verse. These were church leaders, I believe, who were charting a course of spiritual death. They were teaching (feeding the flock of God) with poisonous fruit. They were ensnaring the unwary in false doctrine such as the Nicolaitians, an early heretical sect who taught a form of "sinless perfection." Their argument was that, since we have been freed from the bondage to sin, anything we do is not sin. This led to a licentious lifestyle rather than a closer walk with Christ.

It was leading the sheep of Christ to feed in a pasture of poison. They looked very spiritual and taught a popular message for many. But, their spirituality was an empty sham. They were a cloud born on the winds of the sky which could produce no rain for a thirsty crop of Christians seeking to bear the fruit of the Spirit but only found rotten berries on the Tree of Knowledge. The did not feed on the Tree of Life.]

1.13 Raging waves of the sea, foaming out their own shame; wandering stars, to whom is reserved the blackness of darkness for ever.

[James uses this same illustration in James 3:4 – "Behold also the ships, which are so great, and driven by violent winds, are turned about by a very small rudder, wherever the pleasure of the helmsman will." Those who are not taught the true faith of Jesus are in danger. They may believe a lie and thus will sink in the storms of life and miss the safe harbor of salvation.]

1.14 *And Enoch, also, the seventh from Adam, prophesied of these, saying, Behold, the Lord cometh with ten thousands of his saints,*

[Jude quotes here from a non-canonical source. Does this mean that the source is to be considered as Scripture? No! This simply means that this one statement was true. We are actually taught a little about Satan in this verse. Satan will not always come at us with an obvious falsehood. Satan will normally wrap his "gift" of perversion in a pious party paper. My son's wife-to-be has a cat that must be given daily medicine which the cat hates. She wraps the medicine in cheese, which this cat loves, and the cat takes his disgusting (to his way of thinking) medicine quite happily. Don't simply trust something because it "just sounds right." From such have come many of the aberrant cults of our day. Even a counterfeit bill looks like a real one. Be immersed in the totality of the Word by reading and studying from all of its pages with prayer. Remember, if something sounds "just a little wrong," it is probably far off the mark of truth. The reason that a handgun is less accurate than a long gun is that the barrel is too short to easily aim. What starts off as a small error is greatly magnified by time and distance. It is good if we go beyond those well known "proof texts" and favorite passages.

It seems that every week we are assaulted with fresh charges that some "lost book" of the Bible was wrongly omitted. I use a very simple "litmus test" to consider the True Words, and Books, of God's Scripture: "The words of the LORD *are* pure words: *as* silver tried in a furnace of earth, purified seven times. Thou shalt keep them, O LORD, thou shalt preserve them from this generation *for* ever." (Psalm 12:6-7)] Those who would "correct" the preserved Words of God will attempt to make these verses refer to people! Unwarranted. These words refer to the preserving power of God concerning His inspired Words. God ain't foolish. He would not promise inspiration for what was easily lost.

Also, God ain't weak. No one can remove His eternal Words in this time centric universe we inhabit. It is the things of time which bow to the things of eternity.

My test? If God has preserved Words or Books in the Bible's of the faithful of His churches, this is His mark of inspiration and acceptance. If there are "books" or readings which have been "lost," or unavailable, to His faithful of His churches, this is a sign that these works and words are spurious.

Compare also the notes on verse 9, above.]

1.15 *To execute judgment upon all, and to convince all that are ungodly among them of all their ungodly deeds which they have ungodly committed, and all of their hard speeches which ungodly sinners have spoken against him.*

[It would seem that Jude is still quoting from Enoch. Enoch must have preached to the unrighteous generation before the flood. Since his prophecy of coming judgment would have been interpreted as speaking of the flood, we do no damage to his prophecy by invoking the *law of double fulfillment* to his prophecy. That law is the truth that the prophecies of, especially, the Old Testament warnings would speak to a then present fulfillment while also speaking to a much later fulfillment of that prophecy. We see this in Isaiah 7:14 where the prophecy of a virgin is nearly immediately fulfilled in the time of Ahaz. Verse 16 plainly says that when this child is born to a woman who was a virgin when the prophecy was made. Before that child is come to the age of accountability, both Israel and Judah will be delivered. That is the near fulfillment.

But, consider Matthew 1:22-23, "Now all this was done, that it might be fulfilled which was spoken of the Lord by the prophet, saying, Behold, a virgin shall be with child, and shall bring forth a son, and they shall call his name Emmanuel, which being interpreted is, God with us." The Spirit of Inspiration informs us of the *far* fulfillment, long past the time of Ahaz. This verse is also a prophecy of the birth of Jesus. Likewise, the promise of just judgment upon the people of Enoch's time is also speaking of the time of the tribulation period judgment.

Whether near or far, the just judgment of God is certain. The ungodly are to be convinced of their ungodly lives and actions. No one will have any real defense of their actions when they stand before the Lord at the judgment of the nations. At that time, even though they are being judged eternally, the unrighteous will be convinced and convicted of their culpability.

These people are ungodly in their lives and dreams and actions. Their ungodly actions spring from an ungodly person, themselves. Satan had been bound for 1000 years and the people still revolted against God because they were ungodly in themselves. The devil didn't make them do it; they acted on the lusts of their own hearts. (James 1:14-15)

These people will speak profane things out of the wickedness of their own hearts, against the Lord and those who serve Him. This is so even in our own day.]

1.16 *These are murmurers, complainers, walking after their own lusts, and their mouth speaketh great swelling words, having men's persons in admiration because of advantage.*

["Murmurers, complainers, those walking after their own lusts," these were the sins of Korah against Moses, the servant of God. These, and those who were induced to follow them into destruction, were guilty of all this and of calling others to join them in their rebellion against God and God's chosen instruments.]

1.17 *But, beloved, remember ye the words which were spoken before of the apostles of our Lord Jesus Christ;*

[Rather than following those who would pervert the teaching of God's pure religion in Christ, we should pay heed to the words of those apostles. Our spiritual eyes must always be on the Scripture. "Thus sayeth the LORD" is always superior to "Did you hear what that new preacher said?"

We should follow man only as man follows God.]

1.18 *How that they told you there should be mockers in the last time, who should walk after their own ungodly lusts.*

Acts 20:29; I Timothy 4:1-2; II Timothy 3:1-5; 4:3; II Peter 2:1; 3:3

[Consider the verse citations in the line above. It is amazing how fully the Scripture confirms itself. We do not have a "hodge-podge" of sayings in the Scripture. God has given us an amazingly constructed volume which bears the mark of one Mind, one Author, and one God.

We have a Bible we can trust because we have The God Who may always be trusted.

The unbeliever may "believe" something. But the believer has the assurance of He Who can be trusted with our immortal souls. All else is secondary to a man when compared with the eternal abode of his immortal soul!]

1.19 *These be they who separate themselves, sensual, having not the Spirit.*

[The focus here is those mockers of the previous verse who walk after their own ungodly lusts. They are separatists who shun the Godly counsel of the body of the church. They feel they have no need to place themselves under the leadership of the apostles, as Diotrephes in the ninth verse of III John. Feeling superior to the others, either by much learning or leaning upon pagan philosophies, these see themselves as more spiritual than those who are anointed to be spiritual leaders.

The problem with separating themselves is that they have no one to whom they are in subjection. Thus, they are prone to live in their own animal lusts rather than living in the Spirit. Jesus told Nichodemus, "Jesus answered, Verily, verily, I say unto thee, Except a man be born of water and of the Spirit, he cannot enter into the kingdom of God." (John 3:5)

Being born of water is the natural birth of humanity. Being born of the Spirit is the supernatural birth of the believer. This is the root problem about which Jude is speaking. Ones such as this are trusting their own reasoning rather than trusting the Truth of Jesus Christ. Their own salvation must be brought into question since they show no influence of the Spirit upon their lives.]

1.20 *But ye, beloved, building up yourselves on the most holy faith, praying in the Holy Ghost,*

[Jude has spoken of those who give no evidence of the Spirit in their lives and religion. Now he speaks to the true Christians. He calls them "beloved," an affection we ought to have for those who are *family members* with us as heirs, and joint heirs of Christ. (Consider John 1:12 in this light.)

Rather than seeking to divide, or to divide from, the local assembly, we are called to build ourselves up in the most holy faith. A holy faith leads to holy living. A holy faith leads away from dividing ourselves from the assembly and leads us to support that assembly with our presence, prayers and promotion of the assembly. Jesus is often called "the Head of the Church" in the New Testament. That which we do to build up the local assembly in the faith is something we do to show our love to Christ. Conversely, when we fail to do this we fail to give proper reverence to Jesus.

The call to pray in the Holy Ghost is not a call to religious ecstasy. It is a call to a reasoned and fervent prayer which seeks to promote the cause of Christ rather than to build up our own reputation and personal power. It is a call to put ourselves under the Spirit as fully yielded to Him.]

1.21 *Keep yourselves in the love of God, looking for the mercy of our Lord Jesus Christ unto eternal life:*

[This is not telling the people to keep themselves saved. True salvation is all of Christ. We have no part in either obtaining or keeping salvation. It is a finished work of Jesus at the Cross of Calvary. Consider Ephesians 2:8-10 in this regard. Our personal "good works" are a result of salvation not a reason for gaining it. In truth, we have no good works as we are only the recipients of the Good Work of the Lord in cleansing our souls and giving us this great salvation.

The call is to keep the love for God burning in our souls. I John 4:19 reminds us that we only love Him because He first loved us. Meditating upon the mercy of our Lord Jesus Christ Who has given us this eternal life will help us to love others even as does He. This will help create in us a burden to spread the message of His salvation to those who have not yet heard. As we couple this burden with prayer, by name for those to whom we preach, the convicting power of the Holy Spirit will draw men and women to the Cross of Christ. It will serve to lead them to this blessed salvation.

This is the plan of Christ for all His children. We are saved to bring others to the Lord. To fail to do this is to count His sacrifice as only important for us. In this we neglect our duty, and love, to Him and to our fellow human brothers and sisters.]

1.22 *And of some have compassion, making a difference:*

[Our compassion is telling the good news to others is true compassion. It is not compassion to allow a sinner to forsake the Lord and fail to find salvation from sin and a home in Heaven. It is compassion when we honor the Lord and warn the fallen that there is, indeed, a real Hell to shun and a real full redeemed life to gain which will lead to an eternal home in Heaven with full fellowship in the love of Christ.]

1.23 *And others save with fear, pulling them out of the fire, hating even the garment spotted by the flesh.*

[Some are saved because they are warned of the need of salvation in order to avoid the pains of the rejection of Him. Some we approach with fear in our own hearts. It is not always an easy thing to present the claims of Christ. Persecution for His name's sake is always a real possibility.

But, the is another fear. That is the fear of God, full respect of His Person and His call upon our lives, which will cause us to move out in faith to spread the message that Jesus Christ died in time so that others could live in eternity. What a privilege He has given us to work His fields with His assisting Hand of mercy and power. When we realize that great glory which is given us in this endeavor, we can learn to hate the fires of Hell which seek to drown the souls of men in sensual and foolish ways that keep others from responding to the call of the Lord.]

1.24 *Now unto him that is able to keep you from falling, and to present you faultless before the presence of his glory with exceeding joy,*

[Note that it is the power of God which keeps one from falling. It is not our work but the power of the Lord which upholds us in the faith. Not only this, it is His power which allows Him to present us faultless before the throne of God. Salvation is all of Him. We are only the blessed receipents of His great grace and gift of salvation and a relationship with the Son and the Father as we stand in the Spirit.]

1.25 *To the only wise God our Saviour, be glory, and majesty, dominion and power both now and ever. Amen.*

JUDE

[Jude calls Jesus both Savior and God. Further, Jude sees all power throughout eternity to be the domain of Jesus. Jude sees Jesus as God.]

ADDENDA

These are verses, of which the attendant commentary was alluded to in the text of this book's comments but was not available in this volume:

Genesis 3:15

And I will put enmity between thee and the woman, and between thy seed and her seed; it shall bruise thy head, and thou shalt bruise his heel:

[It is well known that this verse is the first verse in the Bible which promises the coming of the Savior. In the popular Scofield Reference Bible, Scofield says that this verse begins the "chain of references" to Jesus, His birth and work of His time on the earth in a human body. It could be added that this verse begins that chain which speaks of His work of salvation. I think it is important to also note that this verse comes even before the curse of sin upon the natural bodies of Adam and Eve are explained.

God's plan of salvation was not an "Oops; something went wrong. What'll I do to fix it?" God had planned for the salvation of humanity, knowing that this meant the Cross of Calvary, even before the creation of the first man. (Revelation 13:8)

The serpent, who at this point was the personification of Satan, was cursed in verse fourteen. Now, in verse fifteen, God tells Satan that he is a defeated foe.

We often overlook the fact that this verse also prophecies the Virgin Birth of Jesus. The statement is made that the seed of woman will defeat Satan. The verse does not mention the seed of an earthy father. Considering the Patriarchal nature of society at the time of Moses writing down this history this should cause us to look closely at this concept.

Satan had tempted, and triumphed over, Eve. Eve was still guilty as a sinner. Her subsequent hiding from God because of her nakedness (vv. 7-13) confirms this fact as God had already prophesied as a warning.

Adam, meanwhile, had been presented with a clear choice. There is no indication that Adam was coerced. As such, he was not the aggrieved party - to the extent as was Eve - in the drama. He was still a sinner, but his sin was of his own volition. Adam actively chose to turn from God. This is a picture of what is needed in the conversion experience. People need to make that active choice to choose God. Salvation does not come by osmosis or simple birth. Salvation comes by accepting the Lord Jesus Christ.

The verse also indicates that the ultimate salvation of humanity from sin would need to come through the agency of a human. Although God gave the symbol of the blood sacrifice when He made coats of skins to cover the nakedness of Adam and Eve, this could not effect their ultimate salvation. The coats could only cover. They would not eradicate that sin which was hidden beneath.

Their nakedness remained under the coats of skins.

It would be necessary for a human to shed his blood to offer an escape from the sin nature. This human could not come from the actions of the male who had willingly given control of himself over to Satan. Neither could this human be a female as Adam was the head of the race. Also, it was the sin of Adam which caused the eyes of them both to be opened. Although a sinner, and thus doomed by her sin, Eve seemed to have no such realization as she offered the fruit to Adam.

We are, therefore, presented with the need that a human male be sacrificed for the sins of humanity. Yet, this male could not come through the effort of man. The birth could not be of the normal human progression. This male could not have the taint of sin in his own nature. Further, it would be necessary that the male would have power over the tempter. Only God could have that power.

This is a prophecy of the Virgin Birth of Jesus Christ, the very Son of God, Who would be human while retaining His Own Deity, is contained within the verse and its context within Scripture.

Into Adam was breathed the breath of life (Genesis 2:7). This "spark of life" is what energizes humanity unto this day. Life from life. The coming Savior, Who must be of the race of humanity in order to fulfill this prophecy of defeating Satan, could not be a recipient of life from Adam. Thus, the agency of the Virgin Birth was a necessity. Jesus did not need to receive a life passed on from Adam because Jesus contained life within His Own Eternal Being (see John 1:4 where the meaning is not that Jesus "carried life," but that life was {is!} a very possession of His.)

Note the consideration of life from life flowing through Adam after God had breathed the breath of life into him. Eve was taken from Adam (life from life) after this but before the sin of Adam. Thus, the curse of sin would flow from Adam through woman to their offspring. But, as Eve was fashioned (again, life from life) from Adam before his sin she would not be the "carrier" of the "sin gene," so to speak. Thus a human born of man would have sin as a consequence of his very life. A human born of woman only (the Virgin Birth) would not have this stain of original sin upon his life. Thus Jesus was born, life from life, of Adam – a true representative of the human race however without sin as He is the physical offspring of woman. Therefore, the Scripture consistently refers to Jesus in His humanity as One who was born of woman. (Galatians 4:4)

In theological jargon, this is called the "Protoevangelium." That's one of those "big" words which so many theologians use to impress people to trust them! Seriously, this is just the first verse of many in the Scripture which promise the coming Savior.

This particular verse is very important to the concept of the Virgin Birth of Jesus. Dr. M. R. DeHaan (Portraits of Christ in Genesis) points out that this is the only place in the Bible where a person is called the "seed of a woman."

This is a very significant point of fact. If the coming Redeemer were to be born in the race of man in the normal manner, this phrasing would not have been used. Throughout the Bible the term "seed," when it is used in connection with the propagation of the human species, is used of man and man alone. The Bible is a very precise Book when it comes to language.

This is one of the reasons why this writer rejects the new idea of "concept inspiration." I believe that God gave the inspired Words exactly as He wished them to be used. This was so that His message would be understood. The concept of literal interpretation goes hand in hand with the concept of literal inspiration. This also implies the need for a literal preservation. This verse is but one more illustration of that fact.

For God to have made this specific distinction, at this particular place, is important. He was making the point that the coming Redeemer would be Virgin Born.

ADDENDA

I do not believe that the human writer, Moses, or even Adam and Eve would have considered the importance of this small distinction. For the human writer, especially in a male dominated culture, to write "her seed" is a strong indication of the full inspiration of the account.

As the story is read here in the third chapter of Genesis we are struck with the fact that there is no mention of anything happening when Eve took part of the fruit. According to the Words of God we must understand that Eve was lost, spiritually dead, at the point of her sin. But, the great upheaval of creation did not happen until Adam partook of the fruit.

I would believe that there are two things at work. Adam was the first of the human creation of God. It was into Adam that God breathed the breath of life. As we read the expanded version of the creation of man as given in chapter two, we see that the Garden was prepared for the man before woman had been created as a "helper" and "companion" for man. It was to man that the command was given to not eat of the Tree of the Knowledge of Good and Evil.

It is obvious that Eve understood this command of God. It is possible that God may have repeated the prohibition to Eve after her creation. It is also possible that Adam may have "witnessed" the fact to her. However the fact was communicated to Eve, she was without excuse before God when she departed from His Words to her.

Man was the head of the race and carried with him the responsibility to oversee, have dominion over, the temporal creation.

It could be argued that Eve was cajoled, or tempted, to partake of the fruit. There is no such temptation related in reference to Adam. It seems that Adam made a cold and calculated decision to disobey God. In this decision, and in his responsibilities, the sin of Adam caused a great upheaval in the perfect creation of God. "For we know that the whole creation groaneth and travaileth in pain together until now." (Romans 8:22)

We read some of the curse upon the earth in the middle of the third chapter of Genesis.

At this point the creation was cursed from the sin of Adam. From that time forth every person born of Adam carried the curse of sin within them as an inheritance from Adam. Eve, who had her own sin for which to account, would not have been a recipient of this "sin nature" as she was taken from Adam before he had sinned.

Thus, for the Savior of humanity to be born as a human – in order to be representative of the race of humanity – it would be necessary that He not be born of Adam. Jesus, the virgin born offspring of humanity in the natural, was therefore free from the stain of the inherited sin of Adam. As God He could not sin; as man He did not sin.

Neither could Jesus sin in his humanity. Without the inheritance of the sin nature from Adam, Jesus would have no "inner compulsion" to sin as would any other human born of man and woman. Further, considering the union of Deity and humanity within Jesus, the possibility that Jesus could sin is disallowed because Deity does not consort with sin. Therefore, to suggest that Jesus could have sinned but did not is to suggest that Deity would be willingly joined to imperfection. Further, this would have disallowed His ability to be our substitute in His sacrifice for sin. Such is to demean both the absolute Deity and absolute humanity of Jesus. Such also removes the possibility of our salvation based on the acts of Calvary.]

Genesis 17:2

And I will make my covenant between me and thee, and will multiply thee exceedingly.

[This may seem a strange conversation. God had already voiced the covenant back in chapter twelve. In the fifteenth chapter God had sealed the covenant with the contract of offering on the part of Abram and God, Himself, passing between the sacrificed meat. At this point God was expanding that covenant by providing more information.

This is the same concept as that by which the Scripture was given. "But the word of the LORD was unto them precept upon precept, precept upon precept; line upon line, line upon line; here a little *and* there a little; that they might go, and fall backward, and be broken and snared, and taken." (Isaiah 28:13)

God taught through His Words of Scripture. First He taught in simple lesion. Man was a creature of time and physicality; God was teaching of the spirit and eternity. Man could not understand because he had no experiential basis on which to place his understanding. God taught a little that man could understand and then continued to build upon this through subsequent revelation until the canon of Scripture was complete with the Revelation to John at Patmos. Still, the Spirit must come to illume even that.

The point is that the message of God never changed down through the centuries. What may look like change to our human eyes is simply an expansion of the teaching of God.

The same is true of the dispensations. God never changed His message. His principles stand forever. He has always wanted mankind to respond in a faith medium with trust and obedience toward the revealed Words of God.

The portion of the passage from Isaiah, "...that they might go, and fall backward, and be broken and snared, and taken," might seem confusing. It may help if we consider James 1:12: "Blessed is the man that endureth temptation: for when he is tried, he shall receive the crown of life, which the Lord hath promised to them that love him." We can see this work out in the life of Abram.

He began to follow God as he moved into the Land of Promise. Then he strayed into Egypt where he should not have been. He must have known that this was outside the will of God. He compounded his sin when he demanded that his wife mislead the Egyptians into believing that she was his sister rather than his wife. We see that he was tried of the Lord through these things. I believe that his heart was broken as he discovered the lack of faith he displayed in his backslidden condition. But, God used the Egyptians, who sent him out of the land of Egypt and back to the Land of Promise, to restore Abram to his proper place of residence. This is a physical picture of a spiritual truth that the true man of God will repent of his sin and seek restoration into the good pleasure of fellowship with God.

Scripture always explains itself. It is all one book from the grace of The Father.]

Genesis 26:3

Sojourn in this land, and I will be with thee, and will bless thee; and unto thee, and unto thy seed, I will give all these countries, and I will perform the oath which I sware unto Abraham the father.

[The cross is the nexus point of all human history. These great Old Testament patriarchs were all preparation for He Who was to come. The promise to Isaac was the same as the promise given to Abraham: "Trust in the LORD with all thine heart, and lean not unto thine own understanding. In all they ways acknowledge him, and he shall direct thy paths." (Proverbs 3:5-6) The promises would all certainly flow.

The principles continue. We, on this side of the Cross still trust in the leading of God. His desire for us is that we live our lives in the Land of His spiritual promises. We are not to cast the tent of our desires and ambitions in the land of sin. Our Land is the promises of God. It is there that we are to "move, and live, and have our being." (Acts 17:28) It is from this land that we must cast our line of witness as we seek to become fishers of men. (Matthew 4:19) The promises will all certainly flow.

It seems that this was a conditional promise as the formula is "abide in the land ... and I will." The Jew has not always abode in the Land but deep within his heart God has placed a longing to reside there. This is akin to the stoney and fleshly heart promise of Ezekiel 11:19 – "And I will give them one heart, and I will put a new spirit within you; and I will take the stony heart out of their flesh, and will give them an heart of flesh…"

Israel remains God's earthly chosen people. The above passage from Ezekiel has to do with God's supernatural, spiritual, reawakening of national Israel to the Truth of her Messiah. That God effects this by His grace, even in the midst of the horrors of the tribulation era, is a picture of our own salvation. We are not saved by either our works or our complete volition. We are saved wholly by the unmerited grace of God. We respond in faith because He has first called us. Consider I John 4:19 with special consideration to verses 9 and 10 of that same chapter.

The point is that we can call this a conditional promise because of the "if you...I will" formula. However, alongside this is the truth that God has so constructed His people as to cause them to long for the Land. God is the motivating force from both sides of the coin. Therefore, in His grace He has assumed the responsibility even for the "if you" part of the equation. Thus, the conditional promise is actually an unconditional promise for God has decreed that this is a thing which will come to pass. The promise is shown to be, ultimately, based upon the Honor of God to His Words. It has become, from our physical standpoint, a spiritually based unconditional promise.]

Isaiah 28:13

But the word of the LORD was unto them precept upon precept, precept upon precept; line upon line, line upon line; her a little, and there a little, that they might go, and fall backward, and be broken, and snared, and taken.

[See also Genesis 17:2 and James 1:12]

Luke 16:19

There was a certain rich man, which was clothed in purple and fine linen, and fared sumptuously every day:

Ephesians 4:8; Hebrews 10:4

[vv. 19-31. First, it would be wise for us to consider that this was not a parable. Jesus never mentioned a person by name when He taught by parable. This is a true incident concerning two "certain" people – one named, the other not named.

Even if this passage had been a parable, we must remember that the spiritual facts would still be true as Jesus never taught error.

Jesus was acting as a Gentleman when He named the one but not the other. Lazarus, the man in Paradise was named. His family and friends could take comfort in this. The rich man is not named; rather, Jesus simply described the situation of that man. Two things were accomplished in this. The surviving relatives of this man were not unduly given even more grief at the death of their family member. At the same time that family, and all other families with similar circumstance, were given the warning about their own souls.

We need to compare other passages in relation to this story. The first concerns the rich man, Revelation 20:14-15, "And death and hell were cast into the lake of fire. This is the second death. And whosoever was not found written in the book of life was cast into the lake of fire."

We also need to consider several verses in relation to the beggar, Lazarus. While on the cross Jesus was asked by one of the malefactors who were being crucified alongside Him that He would remember the man when He came into His kingdom. (Luke 23:43) In the very next verse Jesus replied, "...To day shalt thou be with me in paradise."

Strong's (3857) refers to paradise as a place of happiness. Since Jesus said that this man would be with Him this may refer to Heaven. I would suggest that this may not be so. The ancient Talmud describes Hades as a place of the dead. It is possible to use the word to describe the grave although such was not the situation, obviously, in this passage. In the Talmudic tradition Hades is divided into two "compartments." One of these is Hell, the place of punishment for the sinner, and the other is Paradise, the place where the righteous go. Jesus gives credence to this teaching in this incident.

To the sinner this was a time prior to the final judgment when they are cast into the Lake of Fire which was originally prepared for the devil and his angels. (Matthew 25:41) These sinned before the creation of humanity. The unregenerate who are consigned to the Lake of Fire will be there as followers of Satan and thus share in his judgments.

To the righteous dead this was a time prior to the sacrifice of Jesus at Calvary. The penman of Hebrews tells us that "For *it is* not possible that the blood of bulls and of goats should take away sins." (Hebrews 10:4) Therefore the Old Testament saints were not yet fully cleansed of their sins. Their sins were covered by their faithful acceptance of the Words of God given during their dispensations. But, the Blood of Jesus, superior to the blood of those Old Testament sacrifices in that His Blood has the capacity to cleanse sin rather than to cover sin in accordance with the sacrifices which were a shadow of Him to come, had not yet been shed as a full atonement for the sins

ADDENDA

of the believer. Therefore these saints, made righteous by faith, could not yet be in the full presence of God.

This explains Ephesians 4:8-10. "Wherefore he saith, When he ascended up on high, he led captivity captive, and gave gifts unto men. (Now that he ascended, what is it that he also descended first into the lower parts of the earth? He that descended is the same one that ascended up far above the all heavens, that he might fill all things."

The picture is that Jesus went to Paradise and, as His shed blood was effective to cleanse those Old Testament saints, He led them from Paradise to be ever with Him in Heaven. Now, in this Dispensation of Grace, we depart from this life to be with Him in Heaven. (see Acts 7:56-60; II Corinthians 5:8; Philippians 1:23)]

First Corinthians 10:4

And did all drink the same spiritual drink: for they drank of that spiritual Rock that followed them: and that Rock was Christ.

[We must consider several verses where this term "Rock" was used so we can better understand the Biblical meaning and use of the word.

First we go all the way back to Deuteronomy. "*He is* the Rock, his work *is* perfect: for all his ways *are* judgment: a God of truth and without iniquity, just and right *is* he." (Deuteronomy 32:4) Here, obviously, Moses was speaking of God. We are told here an evident truth: God is without sin. Here God is called "the Rock."

Next we go just a few verses further into this chapter. "But Jeshurun waxed fat, and kicked: thou are waxen fat, thou art grown thick, thou are covered *with fatness*; then he forsook God *which* made him, and lightly esteemed the Rock of his salvation." (Deuteronomy 32:15) This is a story about a man who was, to all appearances, slothful and lazy. Further, he was intemperate as he could not control his gluttony.

It is clear that his slovenly physical life was carried over into his spiritual life. He forsook God Who was the Rock of his salvation.

We move further forward in this chapter. "And he shall say, Where *are* their gods, their rock in whom they trusted." (Deuteronomy 32:37) Even the false gods were called "rocks." In these ancient times rocks were weapons. David slew Goliath with some smooth stones and the power of God. When Saul was pursuing David, David was known to hide in the rocks of caves. Rocks were both offensive and defensive in the art of war. God was the Rock that protected His people and the Rock that could defeat their enemies.

We are now sent to I Samuel 2:2. "*There is* none holy as the LORD for *there is* none beside thee: neither *is there* any rock like our God." The verse asserts that there is no god which is equal to the true God. The other, supposed, gods are but false images of false trust. Only in the true God is there true power and majesty.

Next we move into II Samuel. This is a rather large passage (II Samuel 22:2-23:3ff) which I would ask that you read. I will only comment on three or four representative verses.

This is David speaking in worship of God. "The God of my rock; in him will I trust: *he is* my shield, and the horn of my salvation, my high tower, and my refuge, my saviour; thou savest me from violence." (II Samuel 22:3) Here David revels in the power of God to protect him even in the trying of circumstances.

"For who *is* God, save the LORD? and who *is* a rock, save our God." (II Samuel 22:32) Once again God is set in opposition to the false gods of the world and shown to be not only superior but true as opposed to those false gods of the heathen. Once again God is identified as a "Rock."

"The LORD liveth, and blessed *be* my rock; and exalted be the God of the rock of my salvation." (II Samuel 22:47) Again God is called a "Rock" and is worshipped. Who but God could be the "Rock of my salvation?" It is, of course, Jesus Who is the Rock upon which our salvation rests.

"The God of Israel said, the Rock of Israel spake to me, He that ruleth over men *must be* just, ruling in the fear of God." (II Samuel 23:3) In verse two we see that it was the voice of the LORD who was speaking to David. David was reminded that a just ruler must be attuned to the Voice of God. "The Rock of Israel" is a reference to God.

The background of the following verse concerns the Children of Israel as they journeyed from slavery in Egypt to freedom in the land of promise. "Behold, I [the LORD] shall stand before thee there upon the rock in Horeb, and thou shalt smite the rock, and there shall come water out of it, that the people may drink. And Moses did so in the sight of the elders of Israel." (Exodus 17:6) Here the rock was a river of life giving water for the people.

"Behold, he smote the rock, that the waters gushed out, and the streams overflowed, can he give bread also? can he provide flesh for his people?" (Psalm 78:20) We must be reminded that Jesus fulfilled this prophecy on at least two occasions as He fed the multitudes with an abundance from just a few fish (flesh) and loaves (bread).

We further see of Jesus, "But whosoever drinketh of the water that I shall give him shall never thirst, but the water that I shall give him shall be to him a well of water springing up into everlasting life." (John 4:14)

The New Testament also speaks of this Rock. Romans 9:33 calls Jesus a "Rock of Stumbling" to those who do not believe. "As it is written, Behold, I lay in Sion a stumblingstone and rock of offense and whosoever believeth on him shall not be ashamed."

This verse can be compared with Psalms 118:22. "The stone *which* the builders refused is become the head *stone* of the corner." Jesus was that "Stone" which was rejected by the religious leadership. That same Jesus is now become the Head of the churches of God. Isaiah 8:14 also speaks to this conclusion where He is a sanctuary to those that trust Him but a "rock of offence" to those that do not.

The last verse we will consider in this portion is I Peter 2:8. The verse continues the same thought as does the previous. "And a stone of stumbling, and a rock of offense *even to them* which stumble at the word, being disobedient: whereunto also they were appointed." These religious leaders were appointed to positions of leadership to show the way to God. Instead they refused God and looked away from Him in the Person of Jesus.

What we are seeing here is that Jesus is described as a "Rock" in the New Testament. Since the human penmen of the New Testament were all Jewish men, versed in the Old Testament texts, Jesus was seen as God by the earliest of the early churches and those who were His disciples.]

BIBLIOGRAPHY OF CONSULTED BOOKS

The Power Bible CD; Online Publishing; P.0. Bix 21; Bronson, MI 49028 (PowerBible.com) – containing:
1599 Geneva Bible Notes
Adam Clarke's Commentary
Albert Barnes New Testament Commentary
American Tract Society Dictionary
Annotated Bible Notes
Brethren New Testament Commentary
British Family Bible Notes
Easton's Bible Dictionary
Family Bible Notes
Hall's Explication of Hard Texts
Hitchcock's Bible Names
International Standard Bible Encyclopedia
Jamieson/Fausset/Brown Commentary
John Wesley's Notes on the Old and New Testaments
Macknight on the Epistles
Matthew Henry's Commentary on the Whole Bible
Matthew Henry's Concise Commentary
Matthew Poole's Commentary
Patrick/Lowth/Whitby/Lowman Commentary
Peoples New Testament Commentary
Philip Dandridge New Testament Commentary
Protestant Dictionary, A
Ripley 4 Gospels
Robertson's New Testament Word Pictures
Smith's Bible Dictionary
Spurgeon Devotional Commentary
Spurgeon on Matthew Commentary
Teacher's Commentary
The Fourfold Gospel
The Treasury of Scriptural Knowledge
Thomas Haweis Commentary
Thomas Scott Commentary
The Treasury of David
William Burkitt Commentary
Strong's Hebrew Dictionary
Strong's Greek Dictionary

Baptist Bible Commentary, The; Garner-Howes; Blessed Hope Foundation, The; P.O Box 3505,Lakeland, FL 33802 (email: bhf@bhfbc)Complete Idiot's Guide to Jewish History and Culture, The; Rabbi Benjamin Blech; Alpha Books; New York, New York, 1999

Defined King James Bible, The; Pastor D. A. Waite, Th.D, Ph.D, General Editor, The Bible for Today Press, Collingswood, NJ; 2012

Understanding the Bible (An Independent Baptist Commentary); Sorenson, Dr. David H.; Northstar Ministries (A ministry of Northstar Baptist Church); 1830 W. Morgan St. Duluth, MN 55811; 2008

*Please note that there will be a few places in this book where a source is listed by name but not included in this Bibliography. In the main, these are works which have been read, the citations come to mind from that reading, but I no longer have these books in my Library. I quoted from memory and have given that memory as citation but did not have the physical book to access pertinent information.

ABOUT THE AUTHOR

Dr. DeWitt was born in late 1946, early in the "Baby Boom" generation. He has held memberships in both MENSA and INTERTEL and was a combat infantryman during the Vietnamese Conflict, serving from 1968-1969. Now receiving a military disability payment from Agent Orange Exposure, he retired from the active pastorate after having served for more than forty years in five churches in Louisiana and Illinois.

Married for over thirty years to the former Linda Guenther, until her homegoing to Heaven in May of 2000, he is the father of two children, Amy and Ethan. Twelve days after his marriage Dr. DeWitt left for a year of service to his country during the Vietnamese Conflict. Grandchildren Elijah and Shandi round out his "Genesis, chapter six," generations.

Dr. DeWitt is a thoroughly trained theologian and is the author of seventeen books examining the Christian Religion. For ten years he also hosted a television ministry covering the same area.

During his time in the pulpit ministry, he worked a variety of secular professions from, literally, digging graves to delivering pizza. His writing style is colored by his employment history. He is able to speak to the man of the street in that man's language while using his theological background to effectively speak the things of Christ.

www.ingramcontent.com/pod-product-compliance
Lightning Source LLC
Chambersburg PA
CBHW060501300426
44112CB00017B/2519